*LESTER F. WARD*

Portrait of Lester F. Ward at the Age of 34

# *Lester F. Ward*
# THE AMERICAN ARISTOTLE

☆ ☆ ☆

## A SUMMARY AND INTERPRETATION
## OF HIS SOCIOLOGY

BY

### SAMUEL CHUGERMAN

1965
### OCTAGON BOOKS, INC.
*New York*

*Reprinted 1965*
*by special arrangement with Duke University Press*

## OCTAGON BOOKS, INC.
175 FIFTH AVENUE
NEW YORK, N. Y. 10010

LIBRARY OF CONGRESS CATALOG CARD NUMBER: 65-25883

*Printed in U.S.A. by*
NOBLE OFFSET PRINTERS, INC.
NEW YORK 3, N. Y.

DEDICATED

TO THE MEMORY OF

*LESTER F. WARD*

THE FOUNDER OF SOCIOLOGY

IN AMERICA

# SPONSORS

A_MONG THE ORIGINAL sponsors of this study of Lester F. Ward's sociology were the following: Dr. Harry Elmer Barnes, New School for Social Research; Prof. Raymond Bellamy, Florida State College for Women; Prof. L. L. Bernard, Washington University, St. Louis; Prof. Rudolph M. Binder, New York University; President W. B. Bizzel, University of Oklahoma; Prof. Frank W. Blackmar, (late) University of Kansas; Prof. Morris R. Cohen, University of Chicago; Dr. Jerome Davis, formerly of Yale University; Prof. Edgar Dawson, Hunter College; Dr. Cecil H. Desch, F. R. S., London; Prof. Charles A. Ellwood, Duke University; Dr. W. H. P. Faunce, late President, Brown University; Prof. J. M. Gillette, University of North Dakota; Dr. A. B. Hall, (late) The Brookings Institute, formerly President of the University of Oregon; Dr. John A. Hobson, London; Prof. I. W. Howerth, Colorado State Teachers College, Greeley; Dr. Horace M. Kallen, New School for Social Research; Prof. Harold J. Laski, University of London; Dr. C. C. Little, Director, American Society for Control of Cancer; formerly President of the University of Michigan; Dr. Joseph Mayer, Library of Congress; Rev. A. J. Muste, Director, Labor Temple, New York City; Prof. David S. Muzzey, Columbia University; Dr. Roscoe Pound, formerly Dean, Harvard Law School; Prof. Paul R. Radosavljevich, New York University; Prof. Edward B. Reuter, State University of Iowa; Prof. Woodbridge Riley, (late) Vassar College; Prof. James Harvey Robinson, (late) New School for Social Research; Prof. Edward Alsworth Ross, University of Wisconsin; Prof. Nathaniel Schmidt, Emeritus, Cornell University; Prof. U. G. Weatherly, Indiana University; Devere Allen; Roger N. Baldwin; Harriet Stanton Blatch; John L. Elliott, New York Ethical Culture Society; John Palmer Gavit, Editor, *Survey;* Arthur Garfield Hays; Dr. John Haynes Holmes, Community Church, New York; Dr. Owen R. Lovejoy; Alfred W. Martin (late); Lewis Mumford; Dr. Henry Neumann, Brooklyn Ethical Culture Society; George E. O'Dell, Editor, *The Standard;* Dr. James P. Warbasse.

# CONTENTS

[ x ]

# ILLUSTRATIONS

# TABLES AND CHARTS

*LESTER F. WARD*

# EDITORIAL NOTE

In A LITTLE MORE than two years will occur the hundredth anniversary of the birth of Lester F. Ward, the pioneer of American sociology. The editors of this series believe that a science develops best when the effort of its devotees is directed not so much at producing the novel and the different as at building upon the sound foundations laid by its pioneers. At any rate, whatever their errors and defects, the work of pioneers always deserves careful study, especially in the case of new sciences. For, as Comte said, "A new science must be pursued historically, the only thing to be done being to study in chronological order the different works that have contributed to the progress of the science."

Yet there are many indications that the significance of Ward's work may be lost to sociology, unless some effort is made to point out his enduring contributions. For example, a recent textbook in sociology declares that "Ward's contributions to present-day sociology are almost negligible." Mr. Chugerman vigorously contends otherwise, and the editors of this series agree with him. Three major contributions to sociology were made by Ward which are of enduring importance, not to mention many minor contributions.

The first of these contributions was the emphasis which Ward placed upon psychic factors in interhuman relations. He contended that the significant factors in human relations are human feelings, wishes, and desires, all of which are increasingly capable of being guided and controlled by human intelligence. In other words, Ward found in the more or less intelligent purposes of men the real basis of human society, in opposition to finding that basis in physical factors. Human society, Ward emphasized, is understood only through the human mind and especially through the growth of the human mind. Thus he gave sociology a basis in human teleology.

The second contribution of Ward of major importance for present-day sociologists is his emphasis upon human achievement as the proper subject matter for sociology. He defined human achievement as the "artificial modification of natural phenomena," and he denied that any animal species below man is capable of this. Ward did not come to

[ 3 ]

this view until he published his *Pure Sociology* in 1903. In *Dynamic Sociology* (1883) he gave an almost purely naturalistic view of human society, but in *Pure Sociology* he made a change to an almost completely cultural view. In effect, Ward holds in *Pure Sociology* that sociology is a science of civilization or "culture," which is built up at first accidentally and unconsciously by the desires and purposes of men, but is capable of being transformed by intelligent social purposes.

The third major contribution of Ward is his passionate affirmation of the possibility of intelligent social progress, or of the future improvement of human society, through the development of sociological science. For Ward held to the belief that "the real object of science is to benefit man." Hence he repudiated the laissez-faire policy advocated by Spencer and Sumner. Such a policy, Ward held, is discredited by human experience, and by his own demonstration of the superiority of the artificial over the natural in social evolution. He did not deny that most of the attempts at interference with the natural process of social evolution in the past had been unwise; but he held that the enlightenment, the social education of the masses, would make possible intelligent, planned social progress in the future. The one safe method, he said, is education, not force. We may regret that Ward's conception of education as the diffusion of scientific information was narrow, and that he did not make a large enough place for that education of the emotions which sane religion attempts. We may also regret that his definition of social progress as the increase of the happiness of mankind may appeal to some as inadequate. Still it remains true that Ward's social philosophy laid a firm foundation for a scientific social meliorism.

It is Mr. Chugerman's contention that sociology cannot get its best development as a science unless sociologists remember these contributions of Ward and build upon the foundations he laid; and with this contention the editors cordially agree.

Some readers may wonder why so much space is given to the presentation of Ward's somewhat crude naturalism. The reply is that Ward's thought must be presented as a whole and "without varnish" in order to understand him; and this the author has rightly attempted to do. It must be remembered also that Ward, like Spencer, made his sociology a part of his general cosmic philosophy.

Finally, the suggestion of the author that Ward may be regarded as our American Aristotle is a not unhappy one. The knowledge of both was, for their age, "cosmic." Both made mistakes. But in spite of their mistakes, both laid foundations for the social sciences which we cannot afford to ignore.

CHARLES A. ELLWOOD and
HOWARD E. JENSEN, *Duke University*

# INTRODUCTION

LESTER F. WARD, admittedly the great American pioneer in the field of sociology, lived his quiet yet strenuous life of threescore and ten, and died in 1913 in the city of Washington, where a large part of his life had been spent. His death was almost unnoticed by the press, though deeply regretted by his fellow-workers in sociology and his colleagues at Brown University.

The first half of Ward's life was spent in the midst of poverty on the frontier, as a soldier in the Civil War, and as a participant in the Darwinian controversies of the seventies. The latter half was devoted to the study of science and philosophy and to the formation and elaboration of his system of sociology, with its stress on psychic factors and telic progress. Throughout his life he sought to synthesize knowledge and to emphasize the necessity of its general diffusion among all social classes. He was at once a scientist, a synthetic philosopher, and a prophet of progress among men, through sociocracy. Such thinkers in the long run never die; in later years their teachings become recognized and applied, and their names are added to the roll of the immortals.

Among the intellectuals of Europe he was concededly an equal, as his correspondence plainly shows. In the United States he was a recognized authority in the several fields of science in which he studied and wrote. In labor circles at home and abroad, he was often quoted because of his interest in the larger education and advancement of the workers of the world. Women who sought rights and greater opportunities for their sex, found in him a powerful advocate. He taught of a social progress that was to come, not merely for or through the privileged few, but by the united efforts and for the benefit of the whole people.

Ward's works are written in simple language and clear English, but seem complex to many because of his wealth of scientific illustration and his fondness for expressing an exact meaning in some newly coined word. He failed to realize that the average man is not familiar with the classical languages and the sciences. For this reason there is

[ 7 ]

a demand for an interpretation of his teachings in simple vocabulary, largely free from scientific analogies and allusions, yet conveying the essentials of his system of sociology. This demand the author of the following chapters has met by his exposition and comment on the many-sided aspects of that system.

The author has studied Ward's sociology deeply and earnestly, has faithfully explained it, and then, by his own comment, indicated the viewpoint of a younger generation with its newer interpretations. In Ward's social philosophy, the diffusion of knowledge is seen as the greatest of social needs. Were he living, he would rejoice to see so excellent a commentary on his writings, though he would doubtless have demurred at the subtitle "The American Aristotle." He would, in my opinion, be especially delighted that the author, an alien by birth and descent, caught in his American home the hope of the gospel of opportunity, and found the inspiration to devote his hard-earned leisure to a labor of love. The reader will agree that he has performed his task with efficiency and in strong, terse English, readily understood.

JAMES Q. DEALEY,
*Late Professor Emeritus of Sociology, Brown University.*

# FOREWORD

In THIS AGE of confusion and depression, of economic revolution and social evolution, the ideas of Lester F. Ward are especially relevant and encouraging because they furnish the scientific basis of the popular movement to express the social will.

In this book, the author has produced not only a most comprehensive survey of Ward's system of dynamic sociology, but also a penetrating analysis and sound interpretation of Ward's social philosophy and his general outlook on life. Ward's theses that the only purpose of science is to enrich and ennoble human life; that as social science approaches the level of accuracy and impartiality achieved in the natural sciences, the mind can triumph over the opposition both of nature and habit; that something more than altruism or good moral intent is necessary to make society a civilized and happy order; and that sound government must rest on sound social science, such ideas will never cramp any intelligence, but will inspire all who are capable of serious thought. Because these fundamental doctrines are clearly developed in this book, it is enthusiastically recommended to all sorts and conditions of men.

The report of President Hoover's "Committee on Social Trends," which preceded the social planning outlined by President Roosevelt's "Brain Trust," must have recalled vividly to the minds of all sociologists the life work of Professor Lester F. Ward, the late dean of their profession. In his pioneer works on sociology, the importance of which cannot be overestimated, will be found the scientific roots of the present forward-looking social experiments, investigations, and reports which are the most notable steps thus far taken in the United States to promote government on the basis of precise knowledge. President Roosevelt's attempts to curb the system of ruthless individualism may be weak and ineffectual, but it is the first application of social theory in America by a national government. If it does not point directly to a new turn in social evolution, or if it is not a part of a coming cooperative system, it is at least a novel example of social science guiding the government in our complex urban and industrial civilization.

[ 9 ]

Lester F. Ward and Jeremy Bentham are probably the only thinkers to whom a progressive contemporary mind may do homage as pioneers in sociology, without becoming involved in rigid dogmas or paralyzing stereotypes. The effort to encourage government by intelligence and to develop a science of social progress can boast a long history. Plato's *Republic* and *Laws* were based upon the aspiration to rule through the superior wisdom of philosophers who are kings, and of kings who are philosophers. Aristotle, while less utopian, went about as far as he could to develop in his *Politics* a science of political leadership. But perhaps the first writer to argue comprehensively for a true science of consciously directed human progress was the Abbé de Saint-Pierre, who wrote at the opening of the eighteenth century.

The Abbé had participated in making the treaty of peace which ended the long and disastrous wars of Louis XIV. He felt as so many did after the World War, that an impartial and synthetic body of scientific knowledge could be developed to save humanity from repeating the staggering mistakes involved in a bloody conflict. Yet his fellow-countrymen failed to heed him. France did not move on to higher levels of well-being through scientific planning of her social future, but drifted stupidly into revolution and carnage under the aegis of lesser Bourbons than the "Grand Monarque."

The French Revolution, together with the progress of science and the rise of the new industrialism, stimulated another Frenchman to argue once more for the necessity of a science of social guidance. This was the brilliant and versatile Count Henri de Saint-Simon. He contended that progress will never be assured unless social development is controlled by some science of social change. Good intentions, even of a Voltaire or a Rousseau, would never suffice to direct society safely amidst the perplexities of the modern age.

Saint-Simon's pupil, the prolific French philosopher Auguste Comte, went far beyond his master, and founded the new science of sociology. In his voluminous works, *Positive Philosophy* and *Positive Polity*, he described the nature of a society and a government based upon such a science. But for all his learning and industry, Comte only cleared the ground and built the framework for the new science, and left the task of completing the structure to later thinkers. As for Herbert Spencer, the world champion of individualism, his failure to make his synthetic philosophy the basis of a true social science is well known. It remained for Lester F. Ward, a son of pioneer frontier life in America, to complete the synthesis of sociological knowledge in his dynamic sociology, and to place the age-long quest for expert social guidance in a scientific perspective. It is to introduce to the American people the social philosophy of this master of the system builders, that this book has been written.

Ward was employed by the United States Government in various scientific bureaus for the greater part of his life. Of tireless industry and great self-confidence, he accumulated a vast body of knowledge and brought it under the control of a scientific outlook and the scientific method. In his system of sociology, he not only set forth the arguments in support of a scientifically guided social order but indicated the specific equipment necessary to achieve such a result. He envisaged a National Academy of Social Science at Washington, manned by a group not unlike the "Committee on Social Trends" and their research assistants. This Academy would gather all available data on every conceivable public problem. It would indicate the general character of current social developments and the desirable economic and political policies which must control and guide government in the interest of the well-being of the people. Legislators on Capitol Hill would flock unselfishly to the Academy for advice as to what laws were needed and for aid in drafting those laws in an intelligent manner. Chance, drift, and revolution would give way before intelligence and scientific prevision, and the social order could thus be changed from one of rugged individualism and ruthless competition to a cooperative and humane system of life, called a sociocracy; in brief, from a constitutional autocracy and industrial plutocracy into a people's government—the rule of society, by society and for society.

The vision of Ward came to naught for years. The American people did not hear him because his voice was drowned in the rush for "prosperity." America, too, drifted into world anarchy, world war, and world depression. But President Roosevelt's "New Deal," as a gesture to remember the forgotten man, is a tiny fragment of Ward's sociology and a larger segment of the philosophy of the Founding Fathers. At last the United States seems to have given official recognition to the necessity of knowledge and scientific insight for intelligent government. The vision which Ward, the still unknown Darwin of sociology, wrote into his works between 1869 and 1913, has developed a vast mass of data, many specific surveys and plans under government sanction, and a complete overhauling of classical social reformism. If we drift again into something even worse than the period of 1914 to 1933, no one can say that we have not been adequately informed or powerfully warned.

It is a pleasure to commend to the attention of the public—lay and professional, radical and conservative alike—this thorough and intelligent presentation of the system of sociology and social philosophy of the founder of sociology in America—Lester F. Ward.

HARRY ELMER BARNES,
*of the New School for Social Research.*

# PREFACE

THIS IS NEITHER a biography nor another outline of knowledge served to the public, "hot and in a hurry." It is rather a book of fundamental principles that touch our lives at every point. In this survey of Ward's synthesis of knowledge which he identifies with sociology, all may watch the piecing together of the picture puzzle which constitutes the world as we travel along the path of evolution, from the star dust to man and his social domains.

These lines are being written in an era when democracy, culture, and perhaps civilization itself are in danger across the Atlantic. Even in this land of the free and the home of the brave, one hundred and sixty-three years after the American colonists shed their blood for freedom and security, many feel that they have been cheated of the fruits of their ancestors' victory. The number of afflicted and perplexed is appalling, and the tides of unemployment and general social misery are constantly threatening a social catastrophe. Why hunger in a world of plenty? What price material progress? Why should men look to force, half-measures of reform, or prayer for a way out? What is there to prevent the scourges of poverty, social tyranny, and war?

These questions fill the air, especially in America where freedom of opinion has not been abolished. But the masses, without a common rallying point, ignorant of social science, fighting shy of social planning as a foreign peril and utopian dream, wander about looking for a social philosophy to guide them. Social quacks and demagogues, with their slogans, nostrums and general stock of eloquence, are not lacking, of course, to diagnose and treat the social malady. Yet the philosophy for which the good burghers of these United States have been yearning for generations, has been right in their midst in the works of Lester F. Ward, their own Yankee Aristotle.

It has been both a labor of love and a happy privilege to resurrect this titan and place his few modest volumes beside the more pretentious works of Aristotle, Comte, and Spencer. The times are propitious for introducing Ward to his native land, for sociology is now emerging from the abstract and static stage into the applied and dynamic stage, and is ready to assume its true role as the science of sciences—the social mentor and guide.

The conservative reader may insist that Ward's exact place in history cannot yet be determined because of the illusion of the near, and that to label him another Aristotle is to damn him with loud praise. But to those who know something of their works, the reason for the analogy will be plain enough. Both were men of a similar mold—synthetic minds with the same end in view—to grasp the sorry scheme of things entire in a composite picture of nature and man. If Aristotle's work was buried for centuries in adoration, Ward's need not be glorified in oblivion. It is our sincere hope that to spread his thought will be enough to assure his recognition and fame. As the founder of sociology in the Western hemisphere he is the foil of Spencer and Sumner whose philosophy of individualism still dominates almost the whole world, while the social philosophy of Ward, the most scientific, practical, and forward looking of American thinkers is forgotten and unknown, even in his own country.

Undoubtedly, many philosophers of the chair will smile at our panegyrics and ask what Ward ever did except to utter a lot of truisms which are platitudes in the face of the original researches of objective social scientists and brilliant social metaphysicians. We can reply only, "Read Ward!" If he had achieved nothing more than carrying forward the synthesis of knowledge which Aristotle began and Comte and Spencer left unfinished, he deserves a place with the immortals. The skeptical reader may do well to listen to a master sociologist who knew Ward and his work intimately and recognized him as one of the intellectual torchbearers of all time:

When one considers the vast range of Ward's intellectual interests, the number and variety of his original contributions to science and his great power of generalization, one feels that if Aristotle had by chance been born in Illinois about the middle of the nineteenth century, his career would have resembled that of Lester F. Ward more than that of any other American of our time. Had I had the privilege of intimate association with Aristotle, he would not have made upon me a greater impression of vast knowledge and intellectual force than did Lester F. Ward.

If I should meet socially with Aristotle, the "Master of them that Know," I doubt if I would find him a bigger man than Lester F. Ward (Professor Edward Alsworth Ross, University of Wisconsin).

The neglect of Ward is one of the major intellectual crimes of the age. Although he was born a century, perhaps more, ahead of his time, and his ideas are still caviar to the general, the civilized world, where it is not yet been infected by fascism, moves today, whether consciously or not, in the shadow of his doctrine. He was so prescient ("To know is to be able to foretell," Comte said) that his grand generalizations have already appeared and been realized since his death in 1913. They are particularly marked in President Wilson's "Fourteen Points to Make the World Safe for Democracy," President Hoover's "Report of the Committee to Investigate Social Trends," and President Roosevelt's "New Deal." Fundamentally, Ward's sociology is the liberal thought of the Founding Fathers vastly expanded and set in a scientific frame to hold eternally the basic concept that the will of the people shall rule in the interest of the people so as to give them the good life, true liberty, and well-being.

As to this book itself, there is included a minimum of biographical material, for Ward's work is the thing. At the risk of protesting too much, it is neither propaganda by an alien or domestic firebrand, nor is it a heavy tome for highbrows written by a dry-as-dust pedant for others of the same tribe. Some will find it too radical or outspoken to suit their taste; others, too conservative or inhibited. But we did not write to please any particular class or sect. Although it has been done in simple nontechnical language, it has about the same relation to the average textbook on sociology that a life preserver has to a treatise on navigation.

We have no illusions about its reception by the public, and do not dream that it will compete with any tome on the sex life of Hollywood or the art and science of the crossword puzzle. It may be unfortunate, but only from the "business" point of view, that the author is not an orthodox sociologist but a sort of Bedouin who roams the great open spaces outside of academics. If any one will regard this book as an intrusion upon his preserve, we are willing to be cast to the critical lions if Ward's thought will have been brought to the attention of the people of America.

There is little to explain and interpret in Ward's crystal clear ideas, but a good deal to summarize and amplify. The aim and character of this work forbids our loading it with notes and annotations. Interpolated comments and comparisons, even if they seem to divert us, for the moment, from the main path, will prove, we hope, more valuable in the long run than extended footnotes or voluminous references. Withal, its only claim to originality lies, perhaps, in the arrangement of material.

If the reader finds this journey through sociology too long, it may be told that often we made a word do for a paragraph, and a line for a page. If the adventure seems too hurried to others, they will find compensation in traveling onward on their own account, with this as a starting point. But no matter what our labors may or may not achieve, it is a pleasant duty to acknowledge our obligations to Ward's friend and collaborator James Q. Dealey, late Professor Emeritus of Sociology at Brown University, for invaluable criticism and for his Introduction; to Dr. Harry Elmer Barnes of the New School for Social Research, for his interest in the work and for writing the Foreword; to Professor Charles A. Ellwood, Head of the Department of Sociology, Duke University, for revision of the manuscript, and to him and Professor Howard E. Jensen for writing the Editorial Note; to Mrs. Emily Palmer Cape, Ward's literary amenuensis and biographer for helpful biographical material, and to Lewis Mumford, erstwhile member of the Board of Higher Education of the City of New York; Professor Paul R. Radosavljevich of the School of Education, New York University, and Dr. Gustav F. Beck of the New York Labor Temple, for critical perusals of the manuscript. Finally, we would feel ungrateful if we failed to express our debt to those of our friends, who by their skepticism, gentle and otherwise, spurred us on to the completion of this task.

S. C.

*New York, May 15, 1939*

## ACKNOWLEDGMENTS

The AUTHOR acknowledges with thanks the permission granted by The Macmillan Company and G. P. Putnam's Sons to quote from the works of Lester F. Ward published by them. Similar acknowledgment is made to Professor Bernhard J. Stern, of Columbia University, for permission to quote from *Young Ward's Diary* and Ward's correspondence published by him; to Miss Sarah E. Simons, the only heir of Lester F. Ward and owner of the copyright of the remainder of his works; to Mrs. Emily Palmer Cape, author of the biography of Lester F. Ward, published in 1922, and to the Librarian of Brown University for access to Ward's papers and manuscripts.

# LIST OF ABBREVIATIONS

*Dynamic Sociology* . . . . . . . . . . . . . . . . . . . . . . . . . . . . *D.S.*

*Psychic Factors of Civilization* . . . . . . . . . . . . . . . . . . *Ps. F.*

*Pure Sociology* . . . . . . . . . . . . . . . . . . . . . . . . . . . . . . . *P.S.*

*Outlines of Sociology* . . . . . . . . . . . . . . . . . . . . . . . *Outlines*

*A Text Book of Sociology* . . . . . . . . . . . . . . . . . . . *Textbook*

*Applied Sociology* . . . . . . . . . . . . . . . . . . . . . . . . . *App. S.*

*Glimpses of the Cosmos* . . . . . . . . . . . . . . . . . . . *Glimpses*

*Young Ward's Diary,* ed. Bernhard J. Stern . . . . . *Diary*

*Lester F. Ward,* by Emily Palmer Cape . . . . . . . . . *Cape*

Education (manuscript, Brown University) . . . . . . . *Ed.*

# PART I

## THE MASTER-BUILDER OF SOCIOLOGY

*"He was a man, take him all in all, I shall not
look upon his like again."*

# BOOK I. THE MAN

*"Voilà un homme!"*

# Chapter I

# BIOGRAPHY

*"What is writ is writ—*
*Would it were worthier!"*—Byron

*"The whole earth is the tomb of heroic men, and their story is not graven only on stone over their clay, but abides everywhere, without a visible symbol woven into the stuff of other men's lives."*—Thucydides

A LIFE WELL WRITTEN is almost as rare as a life well spent," said the doughty Carlyle. We suffer no delusions about attempting a cynical or psychological study of Ward or trying to pander to a public taste already sated by enough eulogy and scandal. Perhaps it will prove a novelty to let his own ideas paint his full-length portrait. As for the facts of his life, we have not manufactured and therefore cannot guarantee any of them.

## GENEALOGY

Ward's biography, prosaic enough when measured by popular standards, is the story of a pioneer on the early American frontier, as well as on the later intellectual frontier. By youthful experience a wandering laborer and in maturity, a naturalist, sociologist, and teacher, his rare combination of a scientific mind and a great humane heart gave him an incandescent insight into nature and man. Will his environment explain the origin of his genius, or shall we have to poke some divining rod of heredity into his ancestral skeleton closets?

In a rare bit of autobiography, he showed his unconcern about his lineage:

I never took any interest in genealogy. My mind has always been trimmed toward the future rather than the past. Firmly convinced for most of my life that the human race has been ascending and not descending, I have cared little for my ancestors, except in a biological sense. But I have always had a horror of degeneracy, the proof of which in certain individuals, families, and even communities is manifest. Pride of ancestry is a mark of degeneracy. One of Robert G. Ingersoll's bright epigrams was that those who are most proud of their ancestors usually have nothing but ancestors to be proud of.

VIEW OF THE HOUSE IN WHICH LESTER F. WARD WAS BORN
From a Photograph

When asked if my lack of interest in genealogy was due to the fear that my ancestors might prove to be low, I always answered that it was rather from fear that they might prove to be eminent, and I, degenerate (*Glimpses,* I, lxvi).

In spite of such apprehensions, the Ward family history[1] proved that Ward, the world citizen and great commoner, was a scion of the English nobility. His mother's genealogy was never traced. The fact that she came from the old American Loomis family which boasted of Edward Everett as its famous son, seemed to be enough for the man-made world, "for men only." But his father's forbears were carefully brought to light. Foremost stands Andrew Ward, the most famous of Connecticut Yankees, who was born in 1597 in Suffolk County, England, of Andrew Ward, the fifth son of Richard Warde, Lord of the Manor of Bacon, Gorleston, and of Ann, daughter of Sir Richard Grenville. Before him there is a Captain Ward who reached England from Normandy in 1066 with William the Conqueror. Further research we leave to the genealogical head-hunters.

After crossing the ocean in 1630 with John Winthrop, later the Governor of Massachusetts, Andrew helped to subdue (read civilize) the copper-colored natives who were then recognized as the only "hundred-per-cent Americans." While engaged in founding quaint Connecticut towns, such as Stamford, Milford, and Fairfield, that restless pioneer let the Ward family cat out of the bag when he showed the roving spirit of the clan. In his will there was a provision for the payment of twenty pounds to his son Edmund "in case he ever comes back to this place." No one knows whether the errant heir returned or not, but Andrew settled down, was appointed one of five commissioners to govern the Colony of Connecticut, and attained the honor of drafting the first constitution in the New World.

In 1907 the Ward family erected a monument to his memory in Fairfield, Connecticut, where a family reunion from every corner of America was held. Lester F. Ward, the sixty-six year old grizzled veteran in the cause of social and intellectual liberty, as he stood at his ancestor's grave, harked back to the witchcraft days of New England, and sadly remarked: "And he, too, wanted to free humanity." Among Andrew's sixteen thousand descendants who were the

[1] See Rev. George Kemp, *The Genealogy of the Descendants of Andrew Ward of Fairfield, Connecticut* (New York, 1910).

blood relations of sixty children and grandchildren, are found such well-known names as Aaron Burr, General William Hull, Commodore Isaac Hull, "Fighting" Joe Wheeler, Henry Ward Beecher, Harriet Beecher Stowe, John Burroughs, Edward Everett Hale, James Freeman Clarke, and Morris K. Jessup. Good old American surnames like Lockwood, Nichols, Harris, Ogden, and Hunt hang from almost every limb of the family tree. On the whole, it is a mixed assemblage of average men and women, without any geniuses or great personages among them, and with a leaning toward ministers, teachers, scientists, and capitalists. Even art is not unrepresented—witness the light opera queen Lillian Russell, the daughter of Helen Louise Van Name, in the ninth generation of direct descent from Andrew Ward!

Whether this meagre genealogy will satisfy the blood-loving hereditarians or not, we must look to Ward's environment to solve the riddle of his personality, to learn why he chose natural science and sociology rather than business or the ministry, and whence came his inordinate love of nature, science, and the meek and the lowly.

### PARENTS

Ward's father, Justus (1788-1857), was born in Connecticut and spent his days, true to the Ward tradition, as an itinerant mechanic and jack-of-all-trades. He roamed about for years, first in New York and later in Illinois and Iowa until a merciful death gave him his first real and longest rest. The War of 1812 found him a fife major. He fought in the Battle of Buffalo, and was rewarded by the government for his services, by a land warrant for 160 acres of the virgin soil of Iowa. And so he spent the better part of his life running sawmills, doing odd jobs as a wheelright, working stone quarries as a contractor, but always going West only to return East and start back again. With a growing family heaped up in a "prairie schooner," he kept on to the end, trekking and looking for changes of luck, sites, and jobs.

Ward's mother, Silence Rolph, the daughter of a clergyman, was a refined and scholarly woman who had a flair for literature. There was little she could do in that primitive environment to improve the family fortunes except to bear her Micawber ten children in twenty-five years, over an area of half a dozen states. What with looking after the meals and the morals of her brood, always weaning a young one or expecting a new arrival, she proved her tremendous vitality by outliving her husband by twenty-two years. If Justus was the vagrant feet of the family, she was its virile head and body. There is little doubt that in their pioneer existence, where men had to be men, and women at least their peers, a goodly measure of Ward's physical strength and indomitable will was developed in him by his remarkable mother. He was her tenth and last child and was born in Joliet, Illinois, on June 18, 1841.

### BIRTHPLACE AND CHILDHOOD

When Ward's father secured a contract to build some of the locks for the Great Drainage Canal connecting Lake Michigan with the Mississippi River, he bought a stone quarry at Joliet to obtain the necessary stone. On the site of that quarry where Ward was born, now stands the Illinois State Penitentiary. For those who believe that fate lurks in inanimate things, it will be of interest to note that Ward who hated prisons even more than he loved schoolhouses, should have his birthplace connected with the penal institution remembered for housing the Chicago "anarchists" in the Haymarket affair. Ward was lucky to escape at a very early age, for when he was but one year old, the family moved East again.

Little is known of his childhood except that it was spent in the most trying hardships. Relief came only when the straitened circumstances of the Ward clan were periodically forgotten in the excitement of some fresh hegira to try a new venture in some distant state. When the father obtained a contract to build a towpath bridge extending ten miles over the swamps of the Des Plaines River, he bought a farm near the town of Cass and built himself a house and a sawmill. Ward recalls:

it was at this place that I first came to consciousness, and here are stamped on my memory all the scenes of my earliest boyhood. Here we lived until I was nine years old and here I first went to school in the school house a mile north of the Cass farm. My recollections of every detail and of the precise topography of the whole region over which I so freely roamed, is exceedingly vivid (*ibid.*, I, lxx).

In 1852, when Frank, as his family preferred to call him, was eleven, the family moved to St. Charles, Illinois, to find better social and religious opportunities. The red-cheeked, sturdy country urchin was already a millworker and "handy man" in the near-by village. Then came a brief snatch of schooling together with his brother Erastus, and then more work in a mill near their new home, further north. Frank was three and a half years younger than Erastus but was larger and could easily outwrestle him. Both spent all their time helping their father to make ends meet, and literally to keep the wolf from the door. The boys learned to fish, skate, and swim, and by selling the nuts they picked, they managed to buy a gun and feed the family with the birds and small game which they were able to shoot.

When Frank was fourteen, the family turned westward again to occupy the land deeded to his father for his war services. They traveled in a small covered wagon in which the parents slept, but the children made their beds on the ground. Two happy but hardy summers and winters were spent on the road, living on the results of the boys' hunting. Here was the life in the open which instilled in Ward's blood an eternal love of nature.

## SELF-EDUCATION

Lincoln's self-education by log fire after days of rail-splitting has grown into a world legend of the American will to succeed. Ward with far fewer opportunities than the martyred president but with greater abilities, traveled the hard road of knowledge incomparably further. In early childhood, Ward was denied even the rural education of those days, with the exception of several winters spent with the McGuffey readers in a little red schoolhouse. Since his mother, occupied with her little regiment and always on the move, could scarcely find time for tutoring, Frank and Erastus who was his inseparable companion, started out on an adventure of self-education which is without parallel in all history, and which ten long, weary years later landed Frank in college.

When Frank was sixteen, his outdoor life changed somewhat with the death of his father. The widow left the homestead in Iowa in charge of her oldest son Lorenzo and went with her younger boys to the home of her only daughter who lived in Illinois. The youngsters in the popular fashion of Alger heroes promptly abandoned the home fireside to seek their fortunes. Erastus went to work in a machine shop, and Frank became a hand for a French-Canadian farmer by the name of Smith. Finding an old French grammar lying around the farmhouse, Frank began to teach himself the language that was to become his second mother tongue. In the fall, the brothers attended a sort of grammar school where they eagerly absorbed algebra, geometry, rhetoric, and other subjects which they had not attempted, for want of a teacher. They kept bachelor's hall, pored over their few books at every spare moment and found their only relaxation in reading blood-curdling dime novels. Main Street would call them chronic sufferers from an unnatural desire to know more than was either good or necessary for them. Fortunately, Frank had the physical stamina of one in a million, and his hardy life furnished red coursing blood, and muscles of steel. With nothing in sight that gave the slightest hope of such a miracle as a college education, he strained at the leash of his circumstances like a bloodhound kept from the trail. Erastus must have been of weaker stuff, for he died in 1865 from the effects of wounds received in the Civil War.

Although books now became his great passion, Frank never stopped peering into nature's more exciting outdoor volumes. All growing things and the solemn rocks fascinated him, and he never tired of reading their history in the open, with even more pleasure than between covers of books. At an early age he already realized the universal truth in Friar Laurence's

> O mickle is the powerful grace that lies,
> In herbs, plants, stones and their true qualities.

Ward's overwhelming love of nature and a growing thirst for book knowledge stirred up in him a cosmic curiosity which seemed to sustain him in those lean years of racking toil and thwarted ambitions. Now and then, he managed to save enough pennies, literally from his meals, to buy a precious textbook or pay for a short winter school term. The promised land of a college education which alone would emancipate him from the hopeless slavery of unskilled labor, still beckoned.

He became a scientist when he was barely old enough to run in childish exuberance through the fields and woods, and when he did not even know that there were such things as botany, zoology, or biology. Many years later he wrote:

I can illustrate this from my own experience when a child with my intense desire to know the names of such things as flowers, insects, birds, fish and other animals that my companions could not give me names for. If I met anyone who would offer a name I would instantly seize upon it and never let it go . . . I even *coined* names from analogy, resemblance and association, which my brother and I freely used. These names which I never forgot seemed silly and stupid when, as a botanist, I learned the right names of those plants (*P.S.,* p. 189).

Roaming wildly over the boundless prairies of northern Iowa in the fifties, interested in every animal, bird, insect and flower I saw, but not knowing what science was, scarcely having ever heard of zoology, ornithology, entomology, or botany, without a single book on any of these subjects, and not knowing a person in the world who could give me the slightest information with regard to them, what chance was there of my becoming a naturalist? It was twenty years before I found my opportunity and then it was almost too late (*Diary,* p. ix).

Within three years he had a respectable herbarium and a collection of some hundred bird skins. His scientific career had begun, but the future international master of botany, fossil-botany and geology, who discovered the petrified forests of the West, which Poe had visioned before Ward was born, was still a raw mill-hand without education or training.

## EARLY ECONOMIC STRUGGLES

In 1858 when Frank was seventeen, he and Erastus hiked with great hardship across country from Illinois to Myersburg, Pennsylvania, to make their fortune with their brother Cyrenus Osborn, who was the only other intellectual member of the family. Cyrenus later became famous but paradoxically remained unknown, as the author of those two highly original landmarks acclaimed by Horace Greeley, Charles A. Dana, and Henry George, *A Labor Catechism of Political Economy* and *The Ancient Lowly: A History of the Working People,* both of which he printed from type set by himself. He was also a mechanical genius, and not only invented but built with his own hands, machinery for making wagon-hubs.

The younger brothers went to work in his factory as engineers and "to do every other kind of work with great expectations as to pecuniary results." After long days of toil, they eagerly mastered Loomis's *Physiology,* Ollendorff's *Greek Grammar,* and several other textbooks. While going about his work, Frank found time to learn the conjugation of all the Greek irregular verbs as well as to make headway in the study of French, German, and Latin. Although his aching body outraged by killing labor, cried out for rest, he spent the evenings studying by candlelight, aided by greater fires from within. The desire for knowledge was unconquerable, but there was no living person to give him the least help or suggestion.

After two years of valiant struggle, the factory failed. Greek tragedy has no more fateful climax than the moment when the receiver offered to pay the boys two years' wages, not in the shining silver dollars which they had expected, but in a lot of unsalable wagon-hubs! Jobless once more, Frank turned to teaching in country schools in the summer, and doing odd jobs in the winter.

His destiny seemed to be cut out for him in the same environmental pattern as that of his father. In adolescence, the son, too, became a roving unskilled hand in the great labor army. During the lean years of drudgery which followed, the whirr of sawmills and the smell of logs entered his very marrow to remain until his dying day, and to condition his social outlook and philosophy to an extent of which he himself was scarcely aware. When he later wrote with such deep feeling about the lower classes that were disinherited alike of knowledge and opportunity, he was relating the brutal facts of his own life. Was it not an ironical paradox that he, who in later years demonstrated so brilliantly that education, more than all the other social factors combined, molded the man, should himself on the threshold of manhood be practically without schooling, books and friends, spending the best formative years under conditions which would ordinarily break rather than make any man.

Ward soon discovered that poverty and the school of hard knocks, so highly recommended as blessings in disguise, were terrific handicaps. That hard work is the only road to success may be a fine Sunday school maxim, but he learned at an early age that the reckless squandering of energy just to keep body and soul together, was in reality a wasteful detour. The only hope which sustained him lay in the desperate idea that he could lift himself from the depths by going to college. Meanwhile, he was learning every day that the real difference between the upper and lower strata of society was neither a matter of luck nor heredity, but mainly one of education. In his own words:

Perhaps the most vivid impression that my early experience left on my mind was that of the difference between an educated and an uneducated person. I had had much to do with the uneducated, and I could not believe that the chasm between these and the educated people was due to any great extent to their inherent nature. . . . The influence of education and environmental conditions, took an ever stronger hold of me (*Glimpses,* III, 147-148).

In 1861, at the age of twenty, he entered his first real school, whose name, The Susquehanna Collegiate Institute of Towanda, Pennsylvania, was almost as large as its quarters. Awed by that preparatory academy which looked to him like a grand institute of learning, he felt grave doubts about the power of his tiny stock of self-acquired knowledge to open its doors. To his great surprise, he found that in Greek and Latin at least, he was far ahead of its best men. Yet all he could afford to attend, was one short fall term. In the winter, he had to teach school again, and in the following summer he went to work on a farm, careful this time, to collect his wages promptly, and in cash. Soon he saw a course at Lafayette College which was his goal, drawing near, but circumstances decided otherwise. The Civil War had broken out, and unable to resist President Lincoln's call for "300,000 more," Ward enlisted as a private in August, 1862, and was swept into the maelstrom.

## WAR EXPERIENCES

Books and ambitions were hastily cast aside, and Private Ward bravely marched off in a blue uniform to help subdue the Rebels. Five days before he left for the front, he was secretly married to his childhood sweetheart, Elizabeth Vought, the Lizzie of his early diaries. The lonely groom spent the balance of his honeymoon bivouacked under the stars, writing ardent letters to the bride he left behind. These letters, like his diaries, were written in French as an exercise in that tongue for both the young seekers of knowledge.

Ward served his country with distinction for twenty-seven months, the distinction consisting of three gunshot wounds received at the Battle of Chancellorsville, one above the right knee and one in each thigh. Before he was invalided home, his many letters from the front recorded a soldier's saga of endless marches, hunger, and dreams of home. They also showed his unabated patriotic fever in describing the enemy as ferocious savages and enemies of liberty, and his fellow Northerners, as noble saviors. Now and then, a ray of light breaks through his mass emotions. Writing of his last battle, he said:

Directly in front of me, the enemy was crowding through a gap in an old fence, and into this dense mass of grey backed humanity (?) I poured round after round. I was chuckling over this grand opportunity offered me, for thinning out the enemies of human liberty, when a silent messenger came, bringing me to the ground. Captain Swart who was holding the colors, was shot dead, and the ample folds of the glorious old flag fell gracefully over me, completely enshrouding me. But no time was to be lost. I picked up the gun and again "went in". . . . A couple more of their friendly peacemakers came whizzing along in quick succession, making a pair of holes through me, in a workmanlike manner. I took the hint and started for the rear (*Glimpses,* I, 31).

His wounds took many months to heal, but he was cured at the same time of all the illusions of war. Its glory now appeared to him in all the ugly realism of blood and muck and sweat, as legalized murder on a national scale. Though he was naturally a dynamic fighter of the most stubborn resolution, he soon recognized his enemies not in his fellowmen but in ignorance, superstition, and oppression; his weapons, no longer in the force of arms, but in knowledge—the mental dynamite which alone could change the world. Thus began his slow transformation from the stalwart partisan Republican who had little perspective of the economic causes of the war or the political battles which followed Lincoln's assassination, into a liberal mind free of all partisanship and politics, and dedicated to the emancipation of humanity on all fronts.

## GOVERNMENT SERVICE

When Ward returned from the war to the comparative peace of domestic life, he soon discovered that even a hero cannot live on cheers alone. In December, 1863, he entered the employ of the government as master of the ward called the "High School" in the Fairfax Seminary Hospital in which he had recovered from his wounds (see *Diary,* p. 126). There he enjoyed teaching which was already his forte, and spending leisure hours to study every subject which he thought might help him to enter college. He was still in the army service, and was not discharged until November, 1864. In a letter to President Lincoln (February 8, 1865, *ibid.,* pp. 160-161) in which he applied for a permanent government job, he wrote:

My necessities are great, I have no regular home, am an orphan, have no trade, am physically disqualified for any laborious occupation, and I have been out of employment nearly all winter though I have had an application on file in the War Department since December 10th, in a state of hopeless oblivion.

My motives are worthy. Though early left wholly dependent upon my own efforts, I long since resolved to give myself a thorough education. For seven years I have struggled against every form of adversity, till, by my habits of hard labor, hard study, economy, and integrity, I found myself prepared for college and in a situation which placed me on the highway to that most cherished object. But when the trumpet of war sounded, I sacrificed all to fight for my country. . . .

Three months later he wrote in his diary: "Victory! I am a clerk in the Treasury! I have won!" (*ibid.,* p. 172). Compared to his earlier years of uncreative labor, his life now became a paradise. The hope of a college education was again revived, although his meagre salary was not encouraging, and he could not even save fifty dollars, the first year (see *ibid.,* p. 200). The birth of his first and only child (b. July, 1865; d. May, 1866, *ibid.,* pp. 175-176), followed by his wife's illness, devoured any surplus out of his small salary. Being neither a politician nor a "joiner," he seemed to have little chance of promotion. Yet sheer merit pushed him upward. In his diary (see *ibid.,* pp. 316-317) he charts his rapid progress at that time as follows:

1867, January 1, left the Treasury and entered the Bureau of Statistics;
      March 9, entered college;
      July 1, promoted from first class to second;
      "   31, entered Bureau of Immigration; . . .
1869, June 18, began writing "Dynamic Sociology";
      "   30, received the degree of Bachelor of Arts;
      July 1, promoted to the third class;
      October 13, began studying law.

## COLLEGE EDUCATION

When Ward was ready to enter college at the age of twenty-six, he was a self-taught student with a remarkable avidity for languages and science. His self-education was perhaps better than most schools of his time could have given him. He had already contacted, all by himself, the outer margins of the fields of scholarship in which he was to become a world master, and had also become an active though amateur exponent of freedom of thought as opposed to religious bigotry. He felt fit to enter any university, but he had to keep his government position and could devote only his evenings to a college course. With characteristic energy, Ward, in the spring of 1867, persuaded Columbian (now George Washington) University, which long had evening classes in law and medicine, to establish also evening academic courses (see *ibid.,* p. 224).

The results of his entrance examinations were astounding to every one including himself, and he was promptly admitted to the sophomore class. The year 1867-1868 was his junior year, and two years later he took his degree of Bachelor of Arts. By majoring in botany, qualitative chemistry, and practical anatomy, he became a Master of Arts in 1872. All this time he had also been attending evening sessions in law and medicine. In 1871 he received the degree of Bachelor of Laws and a year later was admitted to the bar, and received his diploma in medicine. But he never practiced either profession because, as he bluntly put it, his "conscience would not allow it." His ambition, instead, turned to writing. Says he:

There is no profession I should like well enough to practice it. The more I consider the subject the more I am disposed to feel that my proper field is that of an author. I have made a good beginning on a book, and I find that I derive solid pleasure from it and that I have auctorial qualities. What I need now is to read the great authors and make many scientific experiments. If I could cover the other professions of medicine and theology and learn two more languages, Hebrew and Spanish, it would help me a great deal. But perhaps that is too much (*ibid.,* pp. 317-318).

He never became a minister, but otherwise carried out his entire program. In later years, he gave courses at his Alma Mater, and stimulated until his death the sentiment for transforming it into a national university.

## DOMESTIC LIFE

Throughout his preliminary studies and also during his college career, his wife was his inseparable companion and took up with him many of the subjects that he mastered. She, too, received a degree in 1869, from the Union Seminary in Washington. Two years later she died just as he was launched upon his career. Commenting many years later on this greatest tragedy in his life, he said:

This sad event threw a gloom over my life and left a blank never again completely filled. For a long time there was only a seeming of life, and the months passed in a kind of unconscious mechanical existence until my health was broken, and a determination to rally saved me from steady decline (*ibid.,* p. 318).

Still despondent, Ward wrote to the widow Rose A. Pierce (nee Simons), whom he married about a year after Lizzie's death:

I am ashamed to admit that I am in love with you so soon after the death of my darling wife who I feel must ever hold the first place in my affections. Yet this feeling exists independent of my will and of my sense of propriety. . . . I pray you however not to imagine that, in any possible event, I should for many years dream of reentering the beautiful relation from which death has so terribly dragged me (*ibid.,* p. 319).

Despite the irreparable loss of his first love, the open road of knowledge drew him with increasing force, and once begun (in 1869) he never swerved from the task of synthesizing all knowledge into sociology.

## LATER GOVERNMENT SERVICE

Now commenced in earnest a career in the government service which is without parallel in American history. Original researches in botany and geology earned him repeated promotions until he became the outstanding figure in the Smithsonian Institute, in the Biological Society of Washington, and in other national scientific bodies. He was made librarian of the Bureau of Immigration and finally became chief of the Division of Navigation and Immigration. He became distinguished for botanical research both in living and fossil forms, and was given the title of Honorary Curator of Botany and Paleobotany in the National Museum in Washington. In 1881 he was appointed geologist in the United States Geological Survey, and two years later, chief paleontologist. There seemed to be few scientific honors left to bestow upon him, yet all his scientific labors were merely stepping stones to his real goal—the establishment of social science.

## SOCIOLOGY

While Ward was making his scientific career, he was deeply interesting himself in the works of Comte and Spencer. He felt that if he became a recognized authority in one of the natural sciences, his voice would be more readily heeded in the field of sociology. Thus matured the resolution of his college days that the natural sciences should form the foundation of social science, and that a truly moral, civilized order must be based upon science. The fusion of natural and social science was in itself a stroke of genius, the eclectic knowledge of the organic and inorganic sciences involving research, travels, surveys and museum work, and the genetic inquiry into the origin and development of all the phases of man's history and achievements, leading to sociology, the science of sciences.

Accepting Spencer's theory of evolution, he disagreed almost entirely with his practical conclusions. When Ward began writing *Dynamic Sociology* in 1869 to offset Spencer's erroneous social philosophy and at the same time to produce a true synthesis of all knowledge which Spencer's synthetic philosophy was not, it was another David attacking the modern Goliath of rugged individualism, as far as fame and reputation were concerned. But in intellectual equipment and penetration, Ward was his peer. And when Ward's book was finally published in 1883, it created a sensation in the Spencerian camp, although it remained practically unknown to the public.

## THE TEACHER

Although Ward's early determination to become an author was realized fourteen years after he commenced working on his *magnum opus,* he always felt that teaching was the noblest of all the professions. Yet he had to wait until almost the close of his life to attain the ambition to teach, although he was the teacher par excellence in every page he ever wrote and in every lecture or address he ever delivered. Largely due to the influence of Professor James Q. Dealey, he was called to Brown University in 1906, to occupy the newly created chair of sociology.

After more than forty years of public service, writing and lecturing, Ward believed that he had earned the leisure, away from any daily grind, to resign all his public duties, and write his long postponed works on religion, monism, education and on the technology of sociology. His readers and auditors in every part of the world had long regarded him as their teacher and mentor, yet he had never enjoyed the prestige or opportunity of a professorship which would afford a permanent base of operations from which to spread his sociology. The Sorbonne and other great European universities had offered him that opportunity, but he surprised them by joining the comparatively tiny university in little Rhode Island, where he was content to remain for the seven remaining years of his life.

In the cloistered peace of the school walls, his age, his dignity and evident mastery of his subject, earned the immediate admiration of his pupils. The simple but stimulating form in which he presented his novel course—nothing less than the survey of all knowledge for the sake of humanity—proved to be a sort of mental electric-bath for the students who had been taking sociology as a sort of rest cure. After blocking out the entire schedule of his classroom work for a year in advance, he wrote his essential points on cards, and with the aid of a six-foot chart showing a tabular view of all knowledge (see p. 192) he so brilliantly expounded the evolution and synthesis of the sciences embraced in his concept sociology, that it became quite the thing to attend his lectures.

While teaching, he continued the lifelong habit of scientific field work, often walking fifteen to twenty miles a day in order to study the botany or geology of Rhode Island. None of his vigor and enthusiasm seemed to abate with the years. Aided by Mrs. Emily Palmer Cape, later his biographer, he found time to edit his minor works and miscellaneous papers which had been accumulating for four decades. But the shadows were gathering. His wife was bedridden in Washington during the last five years of his life, and he lived alone in a student's dormitory. Drawn near to the master, his pupils became used to dropping in on him, and much to their delight, they discovered that their professor was a very live and practical human being with an angelic disposition and an unlimited fund of knowledge and wisdom.

## DEATH

There was genuine sorrow on the college campus in the spring of 1913, when the half-masted flag announced his death in Washington, where he had been visiting his wife. There he was buried, but his remains were later removed to Watertown, New York, to lie beside her. Ward died at the age of seventy-two in the full bloom of his intellectual powers. It is hard to avoid the conclusion that he departed prematurely. Although he had crowded into the proverbial threescore and ten enough achievements to fill and satisfy many lives, it was not work which killed him. Down to the ailments that caused his death, he had never been sick for a single day. Perhaps, as some of his friends insisted, the loss of his wife's companionship during those last five years, coupled with the constant drain on his lean purse entailed by her illness, so depressed him that it shortened his years. Nevertheless, he remained the Stoic and true philosopher to the end. He often remarked that his days at the university were the happiest of his life. Was he not rid of the shackles of government service, and could he not devote his time to intellectual labor in the midst of an environment of culture? What more could any one desire?

When the news of his death seeped through the press, the eulogies by his few but tried friends were warm and widespread. No one had ever fought such a steady, disinterested and world-wide battle in the cause of human freedom in every sense of the word, as Ward had. To emancipate the fourth estate, as he called the masses, had been his aim in life. His love of the common people had been the motive for much of his opposition to Spencer's individualist philosophy, as well as for his devotion to the causes of democracy and humanitarianism. Yet, as far as the general public was concerned, it was just another old professor who had passed on. Only those who really knew him felt that it was the social Darwin, the peer of Comte, Spencer, Huxley and Haeckel, who had left them forever.

The obituaries were few but striking. Former Dean Veditz of George Washington University wrote: "His death marks the disappearance of the scientist who will unquestionably rank as one of the half dozen greatest thinkers in his field that the world has produced" (*Cape,* p. 91).

The notice which Mrs. Cape inserted in the New York and London newspapers, spoke of him as follows:

From our midst has passed a striking figure, a great soul, one who was far in advance of his age. . . . Every one who knew Dr. Ward felt that helpfulness and strength which alone shines out to the world from the soul of a true genius. His life was given to humanity; he longed to show the way of nobler living. . . . In the future when men truly begin to realize that vast amount of benefit the works of Lester F. Ward will do for humanity, his name will be as a torch which lightens the way for all toward progress (*ibid.*, p. 36).

Dr. Charles Carroll, one of Ward's pupils, in his thesis for a master's degree, thus painted the master's full-sized portrait:

Every genius is a child; every child a genius. These were almost the closing words in Dr. Ward's last lecture at Brown University. In a sense they describe the man himself, a genius with the simplicity of a child—that glorious simplicity expressed in Christ's "Unless ye shall become as little children." But in Dr. Ward it was the simplicity which comes from great knowledge, from the possession of truth,—that natural calmness which results from a complete philosophy of life.

Ward impressed his students at Brown University as a final authority. He seemed to know everything from the beginning until the final destruction of the world. Logic flowed in his words like the gentle current of a country brook in midsummer. There was no turbulence, no strain, never a hiatus; thought fitted into thought, building always upward and onward. Every lecture was a recapitulation of evolution; not of that tremendous striving of nature with the waste and failures, the trials and errors of barbarous natural selection, but the superior artificial selection which charms the reasoning minds of men. From the solemnity of great thoughts and from the simple statement of universal truths, fundamental yet transcendental in their importance, the class was called back to occasional bursts of genuine laughter. The gentle doctor was himself transformed, his face lighted up, his eyes sparkled. One might at such moments imagine what sort of a man Dr. Ward had been in his earlier years. He was old when he first came to Brown,—old but not decadent, aged but still active; his mental vision clear as in his prime. Only the body had yielded to time; his mind was still fresh and an inspiration to his students (quoted in *American Journal of Sociology,* XIX, 61-78).

Professor Edward A. Ross, who knew him intimately and can be counted as one of his disciples, said:

Few realize that Ward's daring arraignment of the supposedly perfect methods of Nature, and his justification of the ways of mind in his Psychic Factors of Civilization, published in 1893, furnishes the philosophy that lies at the base of the recent great extension of functions by contemporary governments. . . .

In association with Dr. Ward, there was an uplift like knowing mountain or sea. Like Spencer, he was a man who early conceived a disinterested life purpose and carried it through to a triumphant conclusion. His will was adamantine and he allowed nothing to divert him from the path toward his goal. For thirty-five years he labored like a Hercules at his self imposed task of proving the practicability of "telic" social progress. . . . With sentimentalists he was patient, but he never mixed with them, for he realized that what is lacking is not the will to social progress, but the way (*ibid.*).

Professor Franklin H. Giddings of Columbia University, who was not a disciple of Ward by any means, wrote:

Agreeing or disagreeing with Ward's opinion, approving or disapproving of his teachings, the thousands of students who have been stimulated by him will find here the picture of a courageous man who lived and spoke as he thought, who passionately desired the amelioration of the lot of the masses of mankind and whose kindly face and gentle speech were the expression of a kindly soul (*Cape*, p. 70).

Finally, Professor Charles A. Ellwood, now Professor of Sociology at Duke University, wrote in a similar vein:

The passing of Lester F. Ward removes from the scene of action the last of the great sociological giants of the Nineteenth Century. Professor Ward will always rank with the two great founders of our science—Comte and Spencer. In some ways the work for sociology was second only to that of Auguste Comte. If there were errors in both his premises and generalizations, as I believe there were, this fact in no wise detracts from the epoch-making character of his work, nor does it give him any lesser place than we have indicated. . . . The distinctive significance of Ward's work was . . . to get for the psychic factor in human society due recognition. . . . Ward undertook to show that the psychic factor is the dominant one in human society, that it is the factor which must receive chief attention from sociologists (*The Story of Social Philosophy*, p. 551).

## THE MAN HIMSELF

Let us introduce this reporter for the cosmos to those who thrill at meeting celebrities face to face. Ward had the magnificent muscular body of a champion athlete. A giant over six feet tall, broad-shouldered, full-chested and short-necked, his strong, open countenance was of the imperial Germanic type. His eagle's look seemed to bore right through the walls of other people's minds. In manner, he was detached and the incarnation of modesty; in conversation, there was scarcely a hint of the amazing depth and variety of his learning or of the caldrons of sympathy that boiled within him. As a young man, he had thick brown hair which later was sprinkled with silver. His eyes were bluish gray, his complexion blond and always tanned, and his teeth so white and regular that they appeared artificial. Remarking upon the slight forward projection of his head which he believed was due to early hard labor and incessant studying, Ward said:

Only conceited people are perfectly erect. The modest mind never dwells long on the appearance of the body. It is absorbed in objective contemplation or in work that always bows the head forward, and most abstracted people as well as those who lead servile lives, stoop or become more or less bent forward (*Cape*, p. 43).

In company, his tolerant smile was always saying: "I understand, therefore, I forgive." His unaggressive silence in the midst of discussion was never broken until he was invited to join, when he would masterfully put the subject in bold relief by a few well-chosen words with a breadth and vision which made the other speakers and their utterances visibly shrink.

Although he lacked the Lombrosian earmarks of genius, he was eccentric enough to amuse the general public. The funny felt hats which he bought in Paris about once in ten years; his preference for a daycoach to a Pullman car, and his refusal to allow any porter to carry his bags are not things that the world could ignore. But they were all earmarks of true democracy and independence in one who practiced what he preached. The facts that he never thought of running for public office, drank sparingly and only on social occasions, and believed that smoking did not help thinking were enough to stamp him as peculiar in the eyes of all "regular" people. How could they know that the Greek spirit of moderation (but not moderation to excess) lived again in this Yankee Aristotle?

Happily, Ward was a normal man who enjoyed the vibrant tang

of life and bubbled over, in his own quiet way, with the wit that appealed to the mind. Because of an ironclad purity (not Puritanism) which sprang from the love of all that was natural and clean, he just missed being a "good fellow." No one who knew him could imagine his harboring or uttering a foul thought. His morals and esthetics were kept as athletic as his muscles.

## THE EMOTIONAL PHILOSOPHER

In a prison-world of stupid conventions with a high outer wall of dogma and superstition, Ward kept his mind emancipated and his desires and impulses under perfect control. Like many other serious thinkers, he appeared distant and reserved, and lived and moved in solitude like an explorer who lays his course by stars still unseen. Yet he was deeply affectionate at heart, and loved companionship.

The only compensations for his lonely life were abounding health, contact with other powerful minds, and always the passion for nature. When everything else failed him, there were her quiet lanes and open hills, her boundless plains and murmuring forests, the subtle something in the common earth, to welcome him to a "purifying and perennial element."

His intellectual labors amidst economic struggles subordinated his emotional nature, and his tiny income precluded all frivolity and amusements. He rarely met any friends except at scientific meetings. One can appreciate the hidden depth of his remark as he walked one day down the hill on which stands Brown University and pointed to a quaint old mansion: "What would I not have given to be able to have had all the fine minds I have known, gather around me in a home of my own." But he never knew the luxury of servants, leisure, or wealth, and toiled all his life long for a mere crust, hard and small—so much so that all his writing had to be done in spare time so as not to interfere with the gentle art of earning his daily bread.

Commenting on Ward's emotional nature, Professor Dealey, who followed him as head of the sociology department at Brown University and who had collaborated with him in preparing the *Text Book of Sociology,* wrote to Mrs. Cape:

Ward had a deeply emotional nature, but suppressed by his close devotion to intellectual pursuits. Yet when the news of his wife's serious illness came to him, he wept like a child. This same tender-heartedness was shown in his almost bashful fondness of children, and in his sympathy with sorrowing friends. In matters of duty he had a stoic conception of obligation. He was seldom absent from his classes and was most systematic in the preparation of his lectures. He once tried to rise from a sick bed so as to meet his classes and was induced to remain only on my promise that I would lecture to them myself, so that the young men would not be disappointed. He little suspected how students enjoy "cuts" even from favorite teachers. Almost up to the time of his death he gave his lectures as usual, although he could barely put one foot before another, and could hardly carry the weight of his books (*ibid.*, p. 13).

That Ward, the cold, austere scientist, was aware of his emotional fires, and prized them above the light of his intellect, appears in a letter to Mrs. Cape in 1910:

I suppose I may be a genius in a sense; so much subconscious work. I explain it as the result of a stocked (perhaps overstocked) mind. I have acquired so much knowledge by eternally digging at things, that it is a kind of ferment in my brain, and is constantly cropping out in one shape or another. But there is a quality that I prize more than this kind of acquired genius, and that is my affective nature . . . a quality that has cost me nothing, that I was born with. I love so intensely, I am like a woman.

I attribute the warmth of my ideas to that highly emotional nature of mine. I can scarcely utter a great truth without choking with emotion. Am I bragging? I am entitled to no credit for possessing the emotional side. Still, I have always maintained that intellectual development is a condition to true emotional development. Without it, the latter is narrow, subjective, inconsistent and inseparable from egotistic interest (*ibid.*, pp. 97-98).

### THE HUMANIST

The humane tradition of which Ward was the finest exponent of his time is glowingly described in his only biography written by Mrs. Cape. Having looked deeply into his mind, she revealed the master in a much more emotional light than his staid works and personality seemed to warrant. His achievements were not due to any barren mathematical perfection of mind like in Spencer but to an extraordinary alchemy of intellect and feeling, of knowledge and wisdom. Few who met him sensed the great lover that he was—the

lover of nature, of the common people, of truth, science, and freedom—
for it was all hidden beneath a calm and silent exterior (see *ibid.,*
p. 63). He aired neither dislikes nor enthusiasms, but only expressed
convictions and advanced hypotheses. When his generous heart beat
for humanity, he was not lifted like Comte from the field of science
or the changing panorama of reality into a semireligious state of
adoration, but was urged to still greater heights of scientific achievement in the interest of mankind.

## "THERE IS A MAN"

Because he knew that there was so much to know, he detailed
in every bit of his work, the blessings of scientific knowledge and
the deadly results of ignorance, metaphysics, and superstition. He
seemed possessed to spread the truth, and for that he enjoyed laboring superhumanly. With less brains and more ambition, he might
have risen to some pinnacle of politics or pedantry, just as a fondness for cant and a readiness to exploit popular opinion might have
made his books best-sellers. He might have been, in other words,
a great many things, had he not been what he was—just himself. Not
that he had any misgivings about his own talents. Modest to a degree, often remarking that it was a hard thing to overcome an inborn
feeling of self-depreciation, he was aware of his own ability when
he wrote: "Genius without self-respect is sterile. A just estimate of
one's powers is an essential prerequisite to achievement" (*ibid.,* p. 61).

Uncompromising and far ahead of his colleagues, he refused to
indulge in gracious suavities or in the gentle art of tempering his
scientific conclusions with theological compromises. His lack of
plasticity was pure integrity. He was not born a pathological genius,
or had genius thrust upon him, but his life was a steady growth,
an application of talents which ripened into genius. His tastes were
simple, though not circumscribed. Light literature was neither light
nor literature to him. Deeply read in the classics, he found pleasure
in Kant and Schopenhauer, but none in Browning whose philosophy
seemed shallow and muddled. Neither the oracular moralism of
Tennyson nor the mellow decadence of Swinburne attracted him,
possibly because their philosophies were of a weaker fiber than his
own.

Both as a man and as a teacher of men, Ward had his faults.

Who has not? Perhaps he was too pontifical and uncompromising, as some of his friends suggested. How could he help it, alone as he was in a new and vast field of science, lifting those below and around him to his shoulders to show them the path and the goal? His gigantic intellect does not always appear symmetrically perfect to smaller minds. But we need not accept him as a superman, and it would be as unjust to sanctify him as to ignore him. Yet one cannot help saying after laying down his works, as Napoleon said when he first met Goethe: *"Voilà un homme!"*

Portrait of Lester F. Ward at the Age of 61

CHAPTER II

# ACHIEVEMENTS

*"Ward's Dynamic Sociology is America's greatest contribution to scientific philosophy."*
—J. W. Powell

*"Ideas may be classed under principles, on the one hand, and truths, on the other, and the proper opposite of a principle is a law. Truth is rather the generic term for both. My contributions are of both of these kinds."*—Ward

IT IS ALMOST impossible for anyone who has read Ward to speak of his achievements impersonally or without panegyrics. It could be very well argued without indulging in hero-worship, that Ward was more scientific than Spencer, more practical than Comte, and more psychologically minded than Marx. But only history can determine his place in the sun.

## GENIUS OR PRODIGY?

We are not dealing here with an infant prodigy or with the meteoric flight of accidental or abnormal genius. Ward was no Comte, Pascal, or Voltaire, who were all remarkable intellects at the age of seven; no Goethe, who at the age of ten, published a story in seven languages; no Bacon, who commenced his *Novum Organon* at fifteen, and no John Stuart Mill, who added astronomy and mechanics to his mastery of the classics, before he was ten. Nietzsche at twenty-one was already a professor at the University of Basle, but Ward at maturity was still a raw country bumpkin without any real schooling or evidence of great talent. Yet before he was past middle age he had founded sociology in America and made undying contributions to evolution, social psychology, feminism, government, environment, education, and humanism.

## LINGUISTIC ACCOMPLISHMENTS

Aside from his world-wide reputation as a botanist, paleobotanist, and geologist, Ward's linguistic abilities were almost uncanny. They were recognized in his appointment as a collaborator of the *Century Dictionary* and of the last supplement of *Webster's International Dic-*

*tionary.* In addition to being a Greek, Latin, and Hebrew scholar, he was a master of German, French, Italian, and Spanish, and familiar with Russian, Sanskrit, Chinese, and Japanese. Much of his main work was translated into every Continental tongue, and portions into Japanese and Hebrew.

## SUMMARY OF ACHIEVEMENTS

Ward touches knowledge at so many points that his beliefs and convictions are like widening waves of truth. Speaking of his contributions, he says with his usual honesty:

I make no claim to have greatly increased the sum of human knowledge in the sense of discovering either facts or laws, although most of my contributions to fact might be classed under the second of these heads. The discovery of facts is so easy and forms the bulk of the contributions of most men, even scientific men, that I have never considered my own work in that line of sufficient consequence to be mentioned. And yet, to those, and there are such, who consider this the most important form of human achievement, I may say that a large part of my life has been devoted to it. . . . It is only of ideas that I wish to speak, and these are of very different kinds. They might be classed under principles, on the one hand, and truths, on the other, and the proper opposite of a principle is a law. Truth is rather the generic term for both. My contributions are of both of these kinds (*Glimpses,* I, lxxix).

Although Ward himself emphasized his power of synthesizing knowledge rather than his ability to discover it, his original contributions to science and to modern evolutional and cosmic philosophy were amazing. He even anticipated, in whole or part, such brilliant discoveries as De Vries's theory of mutations, Freud's sexology, Huxley's ethical dualism, and Lenin's scheme of a social order ruling itself for its own benefit.

How many truths Ward gave to the world, may be seen from the following laws and principles which he listed as either discovered or developed in his works:

1. Synergy, the constructive principle of nature.
2. Creation, in general, including recompounding.
3. Creative synthesis (Wundt's idea expanded by me).
4. The *nisus* of nature or universal creative energy.
5. The continuity of nature resulting in the ascending series of synthetic creations.

6. The natural storage of energy.
7. Sympodial development.
8. The nature of motility, or transition from molecular to molar activity.
9. The maintenance of a difference of potential.
10. Fortuitous variation.
11. The natural origin of mind, both of feeling and of intellect.
12. Telesis, or anthropoteleology.
13. Innovation as a dynamic principle.
14. Conation, especially in society.
15. The biological imperative.
16. Gynaecocracy, or the priority and superiority of the female sex throughout nature.
17. The group sentiment of safety, or primordial social plasm.
18. The elimination of the wayward[1] "as the essential function of religion" (*ibid.,* I, lxxxi).

In routing the course of sociology, Ward set the following five milestones, each one of which is a monument to his genius:

1. The law of aggregation, as distinguished from that of evolution proper.
2. The theory of the social forces and the fundamental antithesis which they imply between feeling and function.
3. The contrast between these true social forces and the guiding influence of the intellect, embodying the application of the indirect method of conation, and the essential nature of invention, of art and of dynamic action.
4. The superiority of artificial or teleological processes over natural or genetic processes; and, finally—
5. The recognition and demonstration of the paramount necessity of the equal and universal distribution of the extant knowledge of the world, which last is the crown of the system itself (*Dynamic Sociology,* I, xxvii-xxviii).

His innate modesty did not prevent him from appraising his own accomplishments. Although he readily conceded that there were adumbrations of some of the foregoing truths, "thus far, not one of them has been systematically formulated or distinctly recognized" (*ibid.,* I, xxviii). Valuing them at their true worth, he felt that they constituted the essential elements of a great cosmic and social philosophy which was as new as anything could be new in the realm of human thought.

[1] "The conservation of social values" (Professor Charles A. Ellwood).

## PUBLICATIONS

As a writer, Ward was the peer of the best European scholars in thoroughness and productivity. The total number of his distinct publications in popular and scientific periodicals and in the proceedings of scientific bodies, amounted to nearly six hundred and these were printed and reproduced in no less than twenty-three hundred newspapers, magazines, and reports. There were also his vast researches in botany and geology recorded in nine large illustrated memoirs issued by the United States Government. Outside of his books, he wrote over eight thousand pages of articles, book reviews, and polemical matter. No other American author except the writers of dime novels or "syndicated stuff" has ever approached such fecundity. Yet his system of sociology fills only five books, and is less than half the volume of Spencer's synthetic philosophy.

## STYLE AND LUCIDITY

"The work's the thing." Ward's books are true reflections of his thought—concise, brilliant, and crystal clear. Sociology, like economics, is rarely presented in a form to stir up enthusiasm because few scientists and philosophers write in terms which are intelligible to the public. When they do, they are immediately accused of being shallow or platitudinous. As a result, sociology has been chronically suffering from the same technical jargon as philosophy. Vocabulary is mistaken for learning instead of recognized as being a smoke screen to conceal paucity of thought or lack of substantial insight. Too often, intellectual pretenders and pseudo-scientists hold their public by threads of incomprehensible speculations out of nothing into nowhere.

"The natural enemy of any subject is the professor thereof," said William James. If it loses human interest or like Greeley's handwriting is undecipherable even by its own author, it might as well be a lot of illegible hieroglyphics. Ward's sociology holds no fearsome formulas or mystical speculations but is written in plain, comprehensible language. His readers are never exposed to definitions like those of Georg Simmel, the famous German sociologist, who declared that "society is a formulation of phenomenonological correlations; a synthetic formulation in one single concept of the uniform result of uniform series of contigent events." There is a perfect excuse for the formulas of the differential calculus, but there is none for that kind of language.

It is sad but true that· most sociologists carve out their great thoughts with battle-axes. A bad style means a bad method, and that in turn causes confusing digressions and breaks in the chain of reasoning. What the reader cannot readily fathom is generally a good deal of chaos or mystery to the author himself.

Although most of his books are much less than fifty years old, it is easy to comprehend his unpopularity among sociologists of the hour who keep on inventing technical theories and finespun speculations "exclusively for the trade." Physicians, too, avoid writing prescriptions in plain English and look askance at their brethren who rely on nature more than on the pharmacopoeia.

Ward was no Huxley for style. Some may even be repelled by the words which he coined from the classics as aids to comprehension. Although he never treats sociology as a sort of short-cut to wisdom, often, a single word like synergy compresses and lights up a world of ideas. As a whole, his works are easy but not light reading. There is no sugared pap for infant minds but solid food for adults; no lyrical paragraphs or sizzling propaganda but scientific ideas embedded firmly in a scientific base. Ultimately, it is not his style but his passion for truth and the amelioration of the human race—an emotion rarely found in the most learned or "high falutin' " sociologists—that lights rockets in the reader's mind and fires in his heart.

## SIMPLICITY AND SYNTHESIS

There are times when he speaks in the grand manner described by Matthew Arnold as "the diffusion of a great poet and a noble nature, scientifically gifted, treating his serious subject with simplicity and severity." Ward's method of writing was like his thinking—a natural synthesis. Ideas would lay fallow in his mind for years, until, fertilized and quickened by some thought or event, they blossomed forth into fruitful generalizations. He was always so full of his subject that he seemed to write from the impulse of one who, as the Spanish say, "had his works in his inkstand." When it was suggested that his sociology consisted of little more than truisms, he replied: "Such fertile principles lie at the foundation of social science.

Their simplicity is like nearly all important truths, easy to understand" (*Cape*, p. 82).

Upon first dipping into his works one is tempted to exclaim as in the case of Aristotle: "Why there's nothing new here. It's all plain common sense." Which is perhaps the greatest praise for any man's thought. His work was so clear and simple because it was scientific, nothing being admitted into his system except as a hypothesis, until verified (see *P.S.*, p. 46).

Dynamic sociology may not intrigue tired or restless minds that yearn for the circus thrills of mental acrobatics or the soothing effects of darkened mysterious temples, but as social science it has a far more important mission. Ward's work is free of the tyranny of Hamlet's "words, words, words!" In the universal sweep of his ideas there is no room for merely pretty or witty words. There is no blaring argument; no window-dressing or rearrangement of material to suit prejudice or taste, and no cold-storage truths or flights into the clouds. Instead of a Shavian wit exploding into epigrams like a Roman candle, or an abstract idealism built upon the shifting sands of metaphysics, Ward's loving and tolerant humanism shines upon a scientific structure erected as far as possible upon Gibraltar-like foundations of natural law and reality.

## DYNAMIC SOCIOLOGY

Walt Whitman's comment on his *Leaves of Grass*: "Camerado, this is no book; who touches this, touches a man," applies equally well to Ward's first work *Dynamic Sociology*. Between 1869 and 1883, in fourteen long years of lonely labor, he wrote himself and all knowledge into this most important and least read of his books.

The following modest entries in his diary (1869) are highly illuminating:

June 26. I have written three pages in my book this first week (*ibid.*, p. 207).

July 4. I have written only a half-page in my book this week (*ibid.*, p. 300).

July 25. I finished the first chapter of my introduction, which I call "Nature." The second chapter of my book which I commenced Wednesday is called "Man" (*ibid.*, p. 301).

August 15. I have written 13 pages in my book, and there are now fifty pages in it (*ibid.*, p. 303).

September 19. Saturday I finished the subject of "Mind" in my book, excepting a few thoughts on instinct which I plan to write, and I brought the manuscript, of which there are at present 108 pages, home (*ibid.,* p. 305).

The heroic conditions under which the book was written are unparalled in the history of literature. In a letter to Mrs. Cape many years later, the author wrote:

I am certainly astonished at my industry that year (1870). I was studying law . . . editing the *Iconoclast* . . . and there are few days that I did not write several pages. . . . Remember that I worked at my desk from 9 till 4 every day, and we kept house and I had classes in Latin, German and French. Where could I have the time? But I got up every morning at 5:30 and often wrote or studied before breakfast (*Cape,* p. 106).

The reception of the book was so disheartening that Ward was on the verge of abandoning sociology altogether as a hopeless task and devoting his extraordinary energies exclusively to botany and geology to which he was making important contributions. It was virtually ignored until 1890 when Professor Albion W. Small, then President of Colby University, recognized its great merit, and fearlessly proclaimed it to be the most vital diagnosis and prognosis in the last two centuries of cosmic and social problems. To support his opinion, he wrote a syllabus of it for use in his classes, entitled *Introduction to the Study of Sociology: the Development of a Modern Philosophy of Society, with Special Reference to Comte, Schaffle, Bluntschli, Lieber, Lotze, Spencer, and Ward.*

Although Professor Small was later one of Ward's severest critics he wrote him as follows (December 7, 1903):

You are not only ahead of us (other American sociologists) in point of time, but we all know that you are head, shoulders, and hips above us  in many respects scientifically. You are Gulliver among the Lilliputians. . . . If there had been men ready and able to take up *Dynamic Sociology* point by point when it appeared, and to challenge it for every inch of ground, it would not have waited as long as it did for its proper recognition (*Letters of Albion W. Small to Lester F. Ward,* ed. Bernhard J. Stern, in *Social Forces,* XV, 313).

In a letter to Ward about the second edition (1896), Professor Small wrote with deep feeling:

The preface as a whole is—as you said about a recent ethical paper—a whiff out of a freer atmosphere. It is also an important contribution to history. I hope the new edition will have a *vogue*. But the phenomenal reluctance of the human mind to think impresses me more and more as I watch people devouring intellectual condiments and poisons, and refusing nutritives (*ibid.*, p. 177).

Professor Small in a critical essay (1897) upon the appearance of the second edition, again wrote with clear vision:

*Dynamic Sociology* was a startling assertion that positivism is not necessarily indifferentism, nor Manchesterism, nor fatalism. The author's positivism is so uncompromising that it was frequently construed as crass materialism. . . . A few have found so much in the work that some of them, at least, believe it will find its level among the rare monuments of human thought. It certainly anticipated all the questions of any consequence that have been discussed by sociologists since its publication, and so far as sociological contents are concerned, the trend of opinion has steadily accredited Ward's prescience. Everything considered, I would rather have written *Dynamic Sociology* than any other book that has ever appeared in America. It is a serious reflection upon the quality of thought which has been given to social questions in this country that so few men have discovered Ward's *Dynamic Sociology,* and still fewer have studied it. Men who are capable of following Ward's thought may deny that he has established his position, but they can hardly refuse to admit that he has brought the psychic factors of civilization into definiteness, permanence, and correlation which had not been evident before he wrote. . . . It is the most creditable book ever written in the United States (*ibid.,* p. 179; *American Journal of Sociology,* III, 110-111, July, 1897; *ibid.,* XIX, 77-78).

Professor Edward A. Ross describes how he became acquainted with *Dynamic Sociology* and its author, as follows:

While in bed writhing with pain, I sampled *Dynamic Sociology.* The magnificent sweep of Ward's thought made me almost forget my internal misery. . . . I stirred up others to read it, and soon Hopkins had a little band of Wardians. At the next gathering of economists in Washington . . . I beheld a tall stooped man of fifty with thick iron-gray hair and strongly moulded features, every inch a thinker (*Seventy Years of It: An Autobiography,* by E. A. Ross, p. 42).

The intellectual world had the same experience as Professor Ross, but was not always as ready to admit it. It had been long waiting for the thinker who would synthesize the generalizations of modern science with the monistic concept of nature and the collective, psychic aspects of man and society. Yet when *Dynamic Sociology* was published, it was not recognized except by a handful as a *tour de force* worthy to take high rank beside the works of Comte and Spencer.

If the book expresses a single overpowering idea, it is the idea of the universal spread of knowledge as the great panacea. Ward's faith in education becomes evangelical, based as it is upon the credo that the human mind has unlimited power, and is itself the synthesis of all the forces in the universe. Even a lightning glance into its pages is a liberal education well begun. The first volume treats of statics, and indicates the stirring panorama of the birth and development of the universe, depicting in epitome the entire process of evolution, physical, intellectual, and social. That is the scene of pure or abstract sociology. In the second volume, we enter the domain of dynamics and applied or concrete sociology. To avoid Comte's error in neglecting cosmic evolution and the still greater error of Spencer in adopting nature's passive process for man's active role, Ward literally hauls the science of human society single-handed, from metaphysical abstractions and the arid planes of piled-up data in narrow frames to the heights of practical sociology from which a moral and spiritual order becomes visible. What concerned Ward was not science or philosophy in the abstract, but science and philosophy as the means of freeing man from his bonds. *Dynamic Sociology* is not merely a brilliant dissertation upon life, but it is life itself attempting through science to answer the eternal questions: "What is going on? What does it mean? What are we going to do about it?" In his own language:

Philosophy is now undergoing another revolution, and human thought is now concentrating itself upon the practical. Men once thought for the mere pleasure of exercising the brain; philosophy was a form of amusement. They now think for a high moral purpose; philosophy has become a serious occupation. . . .

Few indeed have been the attempts to bring a recognition of law and scientific principles to bear upon this problem. *Dynamic Sociology* was at least intended to be such an attempt. . . . It is the essence of dynamic sociology to insist upon the necessity of action. The philosophies above described teach the doctrine of inaction. They are satisfied with the world as it is. They regard all evil as necessary. They treat only the natural history of man. They deny more or less absolutely, the possibility of modifying the action of what they call natural laws to the advantage of society. It is just here that dynamic sociology takes issue and it confidently claims that its position is, in the fullest sense of the term, scientific (*Glimpses,* IV, 311-313).

The drift and aim of Ward's sociology is towards the increasing extension of co-operative human agencies for the benefit of all. This would necessarily include societal ownership and control of all social possessions and achievements, the abolition of all caste and class, and the equalization of opportunity as well as intelligence. His destruction of Spencer's doctrine of laissez faire with its crown of rugged individualism, is epochmaking. As a constructive substitute for the pain economy under which present competitive society lives, Ward offers a real "New Deal" in a government under sociocracy in which social science is a governmental function. The road to that ideal society is the road of scientific education—the path of universal knowledge—which he identifies with the road to happiness.

Ward does not denounce or quarrel with the glaring faults in the social structure, but criticizes and plans and builds. He supports no schemes of mysticism, anarchism, or communism for the better life, but relies chiefly upon the panacea of scientific education to blow the vital breath of life into abstract knowledge, and create a living, dynamic sociology to fashion through the power of the social mind (public opinion) and the improved intelligence of the great mass, a civilized, happy order, truly moral, democratic and humane.

## THE PSYCHIC FACTORS OF CIVILIZATION

Ward's second book *The Psychic Factors of Civilization* (1893) is an elaboration of the most original parts of his first work. Begun while he was on a geological expedition, it was written mainly by candlelight in camp, and finished in three months. He regarded this work on the psychic factor as his best, because he wrote it to rescue mind from its sad neglect by classical psychologists and sociologists. Professor Ellwood, who developed the new science of social psychology practically founded by Ward in this book, agrees with him in placing it in the forefront of all his works. But, then, each of Ward's books has appealed as the greatest and most original to various sociologists; so perhaps all of them are right.

Its thesis that mind is the most powerful factor not only in social but also in organic evolution turned Ward from the materialistic outlook stressed in *Dynamic Sociology* to the view of spiritualistic monism. It is thus immeasurably in advance of Spencer's view of sociology as essentially static and descriptive. Ward always treated social science as utilitarian and dynamic. According to Spencer, social evolution works like natural evolution, and happiness will come to man in the natural course of events. Ward, on the contrary, regards social evolution as distinctively a product of the conscious mind and concludes that "society which is the highest product of evolution naturally depends upon mind, which is the highest property of matter."

In a relentless critique of present society, Ward marks the triumph of the psychological conception of progress over Spencer's individualistic biological conception. Ward stands with the conquest of mind over the method of nature. The postulate that the mind process is far superior to the natural process is developed as he dilates upon the ideological interpretation of history leading and fusing with the economic interpretation. He analyzes the philosophy of desire, and in the origin and meaning of the pain and pleasure economy, finds the basis for meliorism as the solution of the puzzle of pessimism and optimism. Finally, he postulates intuition as the breeding place of the plagues of human deception, analyzes the inventive faculties and genius of the intellect, and discusses the social will or collective mind of society. The peroration of the work is the thesis of the almost unknown and wholly untried doctrine of the control of society and its forces in a sociocracy, the ideal form of government.

Professor Small in his *General Sociology* (p. 82) estimates Ward's achievement in social psychology in the following true words:

Ward's distinctive effort was to get for the psychic factors in social reactions due recognition and adequate formulation. . . . He first published when the influence of Herbert Spencer was probably at its height. In sociology, that influence amounted to the obscuration of the psychic element and exaggeration of physical factors concerned in shaping social combinations. . . . While the Spencerian influence was uppermost, the tendency was to regard social progress as a sort of mechanically determined redistribution of energy which thought could neither accelerate nor retard. Against this tendency, Ward opened a crusade. He undertook to show that mind can control the conditions of human life to such an extent that it is possible to inaugurate a new and better era of progress.

*Psychic Factors of Civilization* is the first definitive study of mind-power underlying and controlling social phenomena—the book which the scientific socialists (who were not unmindful of the psychic factor but had given all their attention to the economic factor) had been hoping would be written by one of them. Its scene is the domain of human desires which collectively constitute the social forces and alone explain human achievement, for everything essentially dynamic and progressive in society, is the result of those forces. And so the plan of the book follows the paths of feeling, the dynamic agent in social evolution, and of mind, the directive agent as they crisscross, separate, and intermingle to make man and society what they are.

Thus did Ward build the superstructure of the system of sociology outlined in *Dynamic Sociology* so much the higher, while he laid the foundations deeper still. His social psychology punctured the bubble of metaphysics concerning human experience, showed the problems of man to be ultimately psychic, no matter how deeply they were embedded in the economic base, and located the forces which moved human beings, within themselves, instead of in the skies. The effect of such an analysis was a powerful protest of the age against the sterile, fantastic idea that we are impotent to change and improve our social condition, but must wait for nature to do it for us.

## OUTLINES OF SOCIOLOGY

In 1897 appeared Ward's brilliant little summary of dynamic sociology entitled *Outlines of Sociology*. It is an introductory handbook especially fitted for students whose minds are still uncluttered, and for laymen eager to know the fundamentals of the science of sciences (see *Glimpses*, V, 219). The booklet is a reprint of the twelve lectures delivered at the School of Sociology of the Hartford Society for Educational Extension, which had been published in *The American Journal of Sociology* (July 1895-May 1897). It is an eloquent synthesis of Ward's philosophy and proves by its illuminating and forceful periods that he could have been his own Huxley, if he had had the time.

When the book was translated into Spanish in 1905, Professor Small wrote to Ward as follows:

I have just received the attractive little *Compendio de Sociologia* (Madrid, 1905) by Adolfo Posado. It is not only a deserved compliment to you but it has a sort of borrowed luster shed on the whole advancing subject. I congratulate you on the cumulative evidence that you have not lived in vain. I have said over and over again that taking into consideration the whole state of knowledge and of theory at the time, I would rather have written *Dynamic Sociology* than any other book that has appeared on the subject in any language up to date. Of course, everything that you have written since was foreshadowed in these two volumes. I go back to them over and over again, and feel sure that a century from now they will be appreciated at a much higher value than they are to date. The subsequent interpretations and amplifications, like that in this little volume, will assist people who must climb over the foot hills toward the mountain instead of going directly at it in their flying machines (*Letters, Small to Ward, Social Forces,* XV, 323).

### PURE SOCIOLOGY

The most popular and mature of Ward's works, *Pure Sociology* (1903; 2d ed., 1907), was commenced on the first day of the new century and was dedicated with unconscious irony to the enlightened new era which fourteen years later was to see the most ruthless and gigantic war of all history. It is a revision and restatement of his system of sociology. Although it has often been repeated that *Dynamic Sociology* contains Ward's whole thought, it is only true by implication (Prof. Charles A. Ellwood). *Pure Sociology* shows a transition from Ward's naturalistic view of society to an almost completely cultural view. Achievement is expounded as the subject matter of sociology, and identified with invention, "the artificial modification of natural phenomena." Sociology is regarded as the science of civilization, and social progress, thus far as merely accidental in the past (because not deliberately planned) and the result of "individual telesis," not "collective telesis."

Again Ward was too modest about his work (just as he was too tolerant with that of others) when he said that his three main works thus far published were merely products of the *Zeitgeist* (see *P.S.,* p. viii). Nevertheless, *Pure Sociology* was hailed as a masterpiece by those who knew, and was soon translated into many modern languages. Russia, Argentina, and Japan still use it as a text in their universities. In the United States, the press gave it an icy stare, excepting the *New York Sun.* That well-known literary sheet reviewed in a humorous vein the book which has since been acclaimed by noted sociologists in every civilized country as one of the greatest sociological treatises of modern times.

It was undoubtedly a resounding slap at all dilettantes and pseudosocial scientists. As a source book for the study of the social forces, it required of its readers a fair knowledge of history, psychology, economics, and the natural sciences, but it furnished in return a fundamental knowledge of the essential nature, laws, and phenomena of society.

The detailed survey of its contents must be postponed to later chapters. Here may be mentioned the startling originality of its theory of women's natural superiority which formed the mainspring of the feminist movement. If Ward's analyses of the social forces were as much in the public eye as his writings on the sex question, the book would have become undoubtedly a best seller instead of a forgotten "classic."

### APPLIED SOCIOLOGY

Only another volume, one on applied sociology or "the conscious improvement of society by itself," was lacking to crown Ward's system and complete the synthesis of all knowledge which he had projected in 1869. That volume appeared in 1906 under the title *Applied Sociology* and was the flowering of all the ideas sown in his earlier works. Pure sociology is the lens through which he showed the world the social mechanism and how it worked. Applied sociology is the other end of the glass through which he exhibited what must be done to clear the road of progress and bring society into a state of civilization, and man to the full fruition and use of his powers and talents.

The public met Ward's final masterpiece with its usual air of fear and distrust. Any social theory is disconcerting enough to a mass that hides its lack of knowledge by boasting of its practicality and lack of "highbrowism." But when the theory rolls up its sleeves and threatens to go to work for a better, happier life for all under the leadership of social science, is it not enough to terrorize infant and cataleptic minds?

The central thought of *Applied Sociology* is the possibility and mode of society ruling itself, a reaction against the philosophy of despair that has dominated even the most enlightened branches of science and paralyzed the most brilliant minds. By proclaiming the efficiency of social effort, Ward shows how evolution has marched from God to nature, and now has turned a new corner, from nature to man. In the viewpoint of applied sociology, all men should have equal opportunities, for whatever the difference between native faculties may be, potentially there are talent and genius in all human beings, which need but proper circumstances to be brought out and developed. Heredity has been overstressed, while environmental influences have been incredibly neglected. By a sane balance of the two, education and not "blood" will tell, for education is the most powerful factor in social evolution.

Ward scouts Spencer's sentimental philosophy that evolution is inherently ethical and that the millennium of individual perfection and the voluntary good will of the rich and the powerful will inaugurate a happy moral order. The more practical, scientific method, says Ward, is social amelioration by which the foundations of life can be made more healthy and solid, here and now. The products of social achievement in which all will share, can be made to flow directly from planned intelligence in a system of sociocracy, and the whole of society, not a chosen few, will be lifted to a plane of consciousness and self-control. That is the basis of the new ethics which is identical with applied sociology, viz., the establishment of a surplus of pleasurable feelings over painful ones, an ethics of construction and expression instead of prohibition and repression.

Sociologists did not take kindly to the book, with the exception of the few who were rid of encrusted prejudice or curricular fetters. Professor Edward A. Ross welcomed its author as the greatest authority on fundamental social science in the world, and this work as his crowning achievement which spelled the dawn of a new era in social philosophy. The cheers of workingmen on both sides of the ocean who heard of its content were, however, sweeter music in the author's ears than any praise from fellow sociologists. The masses recognized in him the man who dared to utter social truths and stand shoulder to shoulder with the meek and the disinherited against an individualistic system of deception and oppression. While many liberal minds in Europe used the book as a torch to illuminate their ideals, America, on the whole, continued blindly to follow blind demagogues, and listen to platitudes, which coming from any one except nonentities in high office or seats of learning would have been received with gales of laughter.

The most remarkable tribute of all came from the renowned Belgian economist and sociologist, De Greef, who wrote to Ward as follows:

BRUSSELS, Oct. 1. 1906.

Dear Colleague: During my vacation I finished reading your *Applied Sociology*. It is a magnificent complement to your *Pure Sociology*. After having read these two works, my impression is that I ought to throw into the fire everything that I have ever published on sociology. We have partially followed different paths, but I am beginning to believe that you have followed the right one, and that the only good I can do now, is to save my followers from making colossal errors (*Glimpses*, VI, 232).

## GLIMPSES OF THE COSMOS

After the application of so many laudatory words to Ward's main works, we have scarcely any left for his minor papers and addresses published under the title *Glimpses of the Cosmos*. The collection forms one of the most amazing symposia of knowledge ever written and belongs with compilations like Da Vinci's *Note Books*, Voltaire's *Philosophical Dictionary*, Huxley's *Essays*, and the works of Diderot and the other Encyclopedists.

Does this again sound like hero-worship? Then let our critical readers note the keen interest in and profound knowledge of every corner of existence, shown in this intellectual treasure. Ward's voracious mental appetite is simply astounding. Nothing is too trivial, nothing too vast for him. The range of his subjects (exclusive of botany and geology which alone entitle him to undying fame) and the sweep of his mind may be gathered from his stray essays, any of which many sociologists of note would have been proud to have written. Here are a few gleaned at random:

1. Kant's Antinomies in the Light of Modern Science.
2. Professor Sumner's Social Classes.
3. Eugenics, Euthenics, and Eudemics.
4. The Use and Abuse of Wealth.
5. Spencer's Sociology.
6. The Immortality that Science Teaches.
7. Some Social and Economic Paradoxes.
8. Moral and Material Progress Contrasted.
9. The Nature of Pleasure.
10. Evolution of Chemical Elements.
11. The Essential Nature of Religion.
12. What Shall the Public Schools Teach?
13. The Struggle of Today.
14. The Course of Biological Evolution.
15. The Natural Storage of Energy.
16. What Brings out Genius?
17. Ethical Aspects of Social Science.
18. Plutocracy and Paternalism.
19. Mars and Its Lesson.
20. Genius and Woman's Intuition.

The collection was commenced with the help of Mrs. Cape, who engaged with enthusiasm upon the gigantic task of editing under Ward's supervision, thousands of letters, essays, lectures, and articles which spread over half a century. After several years of intensive labor and much selective pruning, it was planned to issue the symposium in twelve volumes. Ward's death just as the first volume went to press, and financial difficulties due to the World War, intervened, and cut the project down to six volumes. These were finally published (1913-1917) and so promptly neglected by all who could read as they ran, that they soon were out of print.

The *Glimpses* also contain autobiographical notes which furnish the history of his intellectual development. The story of each of his books is carefully recorded, and the growth of his mind can be closely followed as it kept on searching, creating, and expanding for over fifty years. Often his thoughts are hand mirrors; sometimes they are gleaming scalpels. But there is never any attempt at mere effects, never any storming of other worlds. Wherever he destroys, he also builds, and his many and varied enthusiasms are not raucous shouts but deep and moving convictions.

Our readers, too, may glimpse the cosmos as widely and as thrillingly as Ward did, if they will grasp the scheme of the evolving universe, from star dust to man and his social order. Someday, we dare not guess when, the public will discover the priceless gems hidden in these volumes. Meanwhile, nothing short of a miracle can make them as popular in this age of syncopated ideas, as the tabloid literature, the metaphysical nonsense and the hackwork of scientific quacks and compilers which overflow the bookstalls. If our efforts will lead the reader to look into the *Glimpses,* the miracle will have already happened.

## DIARIES

Possibly, the most important of Ward's writings, his diaries, like those of his immortal Greek prototype, were lost to the world. But while most of Aristotle's works were successfully hidden or carried out of Greece into oblivion, Ward's personal journals covering almost half a century without missing a day were purposely destroyed by a female relative soon after his death. The estimable lady in her sublime ignorance (or was it very human?) of what the many filing-cabinets full of "scribbling" meant for posterity, burned them all for fear that diaries in a man's own handwriting might be of too personal a nature. If Renan had seen them, he might have revised his opinion that the man who had time to keep a diary could never understand the immensity of the universe.

The only diary which escaped destruction was his youthful record between the ages of nineteen and twenty-nine (1859-1869). Originally written in French, partly as an exercise in that language, and perhaps for the purpose of secrecy, it is a marvelously frank and enticing picture by a raw country youth of the time and morals of the sixties. One reads the innermost thoughts of a son of the soil, successively millhand, farmworker, soldier, rural schoolmaster, and government clerk, which overflow in naïve adolescent passion for his boyhood love. It is an amazing true story of one who was drunk not only with life but with an overpowering ambition for knowledge and education.

In the decade covered by this diary, Ward was first and last a student. The study of Latin, Greek, French, German, and Spanish was accompanied by that of mathematics, history, botany, and the other sciences. His epic struggle to enter college and his student years in science, medicine, and law are meticulously described. Not the least interesting part of the book is the purely personal side, the story of Ward the day laborer, the most ardent of lovers, the debater, soldier, government employee, and struggling young husband and father. Poor as a church mouse, intensely human, tireless and enthusiastic, he stalks through the pages with an ambition and self-confidence that is an omen of his later achievements.

More than anything else, the diary introduces us to his love life with his Lizzie, than whom there never was a better helpmeet and truer companion. All the while, penny-pinching was not merely a miserly interest but tragic necessity, a perpetual struggle for a bare existence in which preoccupation with money was constantly over-shadowing his great love; for money meant the means of attaining the supreme goal of a college education.

Ward, the sociologist, had not yet emerged in those years, but many of the ideas developed in his works were already germinating as he debated the countryside on such questions as patriotism, progress, education, and native ability versus acquired ability. He had not yet found his life's vocation, perhaps hardly suspected it, but he was laying mighty foundations.

One can only surmise what the world lost by the destruction of his later diaries. But the juvenile record that survived is the most remarkable story of self-education and intellectual development ever written. At its close, one sees Ward's ideas and personality already expanded into a powerful mind and character, motivated by the most humane sympathies for the ignorant and the oppressed.

To read Ward's work is, in the main, to agree with them. Posterity alone can value the degree of illumination in his total vision, but, looking at his achievements, as a whole, one cannot help saying: "He was a man; take him for all in all, I shall not look upon his like again."

CHAPTER III

# A BURIED CAESAR

---

*"A sage is the instructor of a hundred sages."*—Chinese

*"The illustrious obscure."*—Shelley

*"Ward was never an iconoclast except to build better and deeper. His one desire was to help the whole human race."*—Emily Palmer Cape

*"Their bodies are buried in peace, but their name liveth for evermore."*—Ecclesiasticus

---

WE HAVE SKIMMED the story of Ward's life and achievements, a story meager in outline, but vastly rich in content. Why has he been so incredibly neglected? Is it possible that this figure of world dimensions who stands for social science as Comte stands for positivism, Spencer and Darwin for evolution, and Marx for socialism, could have been so completely forgotten? Why?

### THE FEW HONORS AT HOME

Of course, no one with Ward's accomplishments could have lived without a certain measure of recognition. As an active member of the American Association for the Advancement of Science, The American Philosophical Society, The National Liberal Reform League, The American Economic Association, The Academy of Political and Social Science, and The American Sociological Society, he received a fair share of scholastic honors in scientific circles. He was a guest at the historic dinner given for Spencer on his visit to the United States in 1882, and in 1897 he received the degree of Doctor of Laws from his Alma Mater. The universities of Chicago, West Virginia, Stanford, Brown, Columbia, Johns Hopkins, and Oxford (Central Labor College), in memory of his lectures, presented him with valuable gifts and hung his picture in their college halls beside those of the world's most famous scientists and philosophers. In 1906 he was elected president of the newly formed American Sociological Society, an event which caused as much furor among the American people as the appearance of a new edition of the *Encyclopedia Britannica* in a kindergarten.

THE OLD CHAIR
(Ward Room, Brown University)

The honors he received served to emphasize his neglect more than his acclaim. Perhaps his modesty helped to push him further back into obscurity. When he declined a bid of honorary membership in the Phi Beta Kappa fraternity, he compared such a token of fame to the accidents of birth, rank and nationality, and remarked: "Such considerations are wholly arbitrary and artificial and offer nothing upon which rational minds can lay a hold" (*Ed.*, p. 158).

## GREATER HONORS ABROAD

He was better known across the sea. William T. Harris, United States Commissioner of Education, drafted him in 1900 to represent the United States in the section on sociology at the World's Fair in Paris, and Ward became the lion of the fourth congress of L'institut international de sociologie, which met there. His paper entitled "The Mechanism of Society,"[1] which he read before a brilliant assembly of savants gathered from every corner of the globe, was promptly given an American burial in the dusty pages of the two-volume *Report of the United States Commissioner of Education for the Year 1900,* and not even the prestige of his membership in the Smithsonian Institute in Washington could disinter it. Yet nothing from the New World as profound and as scintillating had ever been heard in Europe. Fortunately, it was not altogether lost to the world, for it was later incorporated into his works (see Chapter XIII, below).

Ward also served as head of L'institut international de sociologie (1903-1905) and presided at its fifth congress in Paris. The brains of the world sat listening at his feet when he delivered the presidential address in French. But America was practically unaware of his existence, although it swelled with patriotic pride when President Theodore Roosevelt bombarded the Sorbonne with such fiery platitudes that the Continent tittered.

Unlike library-chair philosophers (Kant in all his eighty years was never further than twenty miles from his birthplace), Ward traveled extensively abroad, and became the friend of many famous scientists and thinkers, among them Spencer, De Greef, Haeckel, Gumplowicz, and Ratzenhofer. He was given the honor of being the first American to publish a review of Haeckel's *Evolution* (1879). The German

---

[1] Reprinted as "La mécanique sociale" in *Annales de l'institut de sociologie* (Paris, 1901), VII, 163-203.

lion, amazed at the American eagle's insight and vision, wrote a letter asking him for his photograph and congratulating him on his splendid achievement. When Ward later (1911) attended the Monist Congress held in Haeckel's honor, he found the head of the monistic philosophy confined to his villa in Jena with a fractured ankle. Philosophers who juggle with world ideas and planetary systems are still not spiritual enough to do without their bones. Haeckel from a hospital chair on his front porch reviewed a torchlight procession of the convention a quarter of a mile long. How the good Americans would have laughed at the parade of those funny foreigners in honor, of all things, of a *Weltanschauung!* Haeckel addressed the distinguished assembly and told about Ward's monistic views as outlined in *Dynamic Sociology*. To that assemblage, Ward was not a stray voice from a cultural wilderness, but the harbinger of a new world in the making.

In 1904 Ward was also honored by *Die Zeit,* the leading Austrian journal of sociology, which broke its iron-bound rule of printing only original articles. This time it published a translation from the *American Journal of Sociology* of Ward's essay on Gumplowicz, Austria's most famous sociologist. When Ward, in 1909, returned the compliment by reviewing his colleague's work, it was unfortunately coupled with the obituary of both Gumplowicz and his wife, who committed suicide because of incurable illness. "This was such a heroic act," Ward sadly commented, "that both of them deserved to live!"

## MARTYRDOM IN RUSSIA

Perhaps the greatest European honor came to Ward when the Czar in 1891 ordered the Russian translation of *Dynamic Sociology,* plates and all, to be burned on the public square of St. Petersburg. The imperial ukase could not send the absent author to Siberia, but it did condemn his life's work to capital punishment because of the terrifying title "dynamic" and for being "saturated with the rankest materialism." Ward was puzzled why the book which was opposed to any revolutionary mass action and breathed the loftiest idealism should have thus been summarily executed. History has proved, however, that the fears of the Little Father of all the Russians were justified. The doctrines of universal education and a people's government in Ward's innocent work, did more to help destroy the Russian autocracy than all the dynamite in Czardom.

The American press by the light of the funeral pyre of Ward's first-born creation, suddenly became aware of his existence. A more substantial recognition came from Professor Albion W. Small, who wrote him:

If the report is true that *Dynamic Sociology* has been glorified in the flames of the Russian Inquisition, you should be a happy man. Surely the two volumes contain enough to make absolutism tremble, but few men have the satisfaction of seeing their own ideas produce such effects. You will be the envy of every American "who loves his fellow men" . . . What a debt we shall owe to Russia for the eye-opener (*D.S.*, 2d ed., I, xiv)!

Another tribute was rendered in a letter by George Kennan, the famous Yankee traveler in Russia:

I most heartily congratulate you. It is not every man who achieves the distinction of having his books burned by an order of a council of ministers of the mightiest empire on earth. I have tried in my humble way to serve the cause of liberty in Russia, but I have not been able to do it with ability enough to get my writings burned. You are evidently a very dangerous man (*ibid.*, p. xii).

That settles your hash! Among some of the other authors who share with you the honor of condemnation are Lassalle, Thomas Hobbes, Louis Blanc, Herbert Spencer (Social Statics), Büchner, Haeckel, Lecky, Diderot, Neumann (History of the United States), Zola, George Finlay (History of the Byzantine and Greek Empires from 716 to 1435), Brandes, Ribot and lots of Russians. The reasons given for the condemnations, in many cases, are very funny from an American point of view (*Letters, Small to Ward, Social Forces,* XII, 166).

The natural law of compensation enabled Ward indirectly to return Russia's peculiar attention to his work. Professor Daniel De Leon, who was forced to resign the chair of political economy at Columbia University because of his radical political economy and who became the leader of the American Socialist Labor party, was an enthusiastic disciple of Ward. Ward was not a socialist, but from De Leon came the original plan for occupational representation which ‧underlies the political structure of the soviet regime later initiated by Lenin. President Wilson drew freely from Lenin's pronouncements for the "Fourteen Points to Make the World Safe for Democracy." It is doubtful, however, whether Wilson had any conscious contact with Ward's social philosophy. These facts hold a moral which the reader should enjoy finding for himself.

## NEGLECT

The slight attention given to Ward's sociology in America is the necessary consequence of the occupation with more enthralling subjects like sex, religion, politics, and first and last with the art and science of making money. Ward was popular only with audiences in labor, co-operative, and rationalist circles. So far as the general public was concerned, they would have none of him, any more than the good citizens of the eighteenth century would take to anything or anybody smacking of the sciences. When *Dynamic Sociology* first appeared in 1883 from the pen of this unknown young government clerk, it was given such a frigid reception that less than five hundred copies were sold in ten years. Ward was naturally discouraged, although he might have found solace in other neglected American authors, like Poe, Whitman, Henry James, or Jack London. They, too, arrived in their native country via Europe, and then had difficulty in passing the Americanization authorities in the intellectual port of entry. Ward's case is not so sad when compared to Thoreau's, whose library of seven hundred volumes consisting of the remainder of the edition of nine hundred copies of *A Week in Concord,* printed at his own expense and stored in his attic, was quickly exhausted when the house burned down.

Ward was also lucky to escape Walt Whitman's fate. The "good, gray poet" who, like Ward, was given a civil service position after he was wounded in the Civil War, was promptly kicked down the stairs for daring to write *Leaves of Grass.* Ward's book was possibly above the heads of his superiors, or perhaps it was not read at all. Was he already too big a man to be summarily ejected? Be that as it may, his lack of recognition is undeniably tragic. During his lifetime, it took four of the largest publishing houses in the United States to produce his few books. Since his death, they have either been buried in the flood of technology or sentimental pseudo-scientific froth which passes for sociology, or been pushed aside by the works of many sociologists who have borrowed large sections of his thought, without giving him the least credit for it.

Blessed, too, are the record makers! Encyclopedias like Chambers's and Appleton's do not even mention his name. The *Encyclopedia Americana* describes him as a geologist only. The roster of scientists in *American Men of Science* omits him except in the appendix of obituaries. The fourteenth edition of the *Encyclopedia Britannica* gives his biography as a botanist and geologist a scant two inches, but one looks in vain for his name in the article on sociology. To cap the climax, *The Encyclopedia of Social Science* (1929), the most comprehensive compendium of its kind in the world, edited though it was by an economist (Professor E. A. Seligman), does not recognize Ward's pioneering labors as the founder of sociology in America, and only in a few of the introductory articles is he included "among those present."

A search of the American magazines since Ward's death in 1913 discloses less than half a dozen critical articles, and those touch upon only portions of his system. That is all that has been published about the man in whom there converged, according to the consensus of European opinion, all the currents of the *Zeitgeist,* and whose ideas have been appropriated by the world's leading thinkers. Evidently, Ward's American public are still like those "who did not understand even when they grasped; who, like the deaf, though present, were absent" (Heraclitus).

The original manuscripts of his books are in the Congressional Library in Washington, patiently waiting, no doubt, for Macaulay's New Zealander to unearth them from the future debris of this civilization. In Brown University, there is a saddening shrine to his memory in the "Ward Room" near the furnace in the library basement. The librarian presumably finds time to keep the door locked upon his books, chair and filing cabinets, letters and manuscripts (most of them written in his own beautiful hand), all of which are literally gathering the dust of the years. But there seems little danger of anything being carried away. From behind a bookcase, the pictures of some of his intellectual kin, Spencer, Haeckel and Condorcet, peep out as if loath to disturb the eternal quiet of that forgotten shrine. The library assistants are courteous and helpful to visitors, and remember or have been told that there was a "Dr. Ward who used to teach here; his things are downstairs. You don't want to see them, do you?"

Ward's biographer comments somewhat differently upon that historic chamber:

As the years roll by and the study of the progress of the race becomes more truly from the principles underlying it, the little room containing the books and manuscripts of Ward may become a shrine for all those who loved his genius. . . . Thus do one's thoughts pass while sitting there, and as the Chinese Manchus spoke: "A sage is the instructor of a hundred sages," and true genius never impoverishes but liberates. One senses a new wealth, a quality of assurance that even though no longer in the flesh, Lester Ward shall forever inspire men to think and to stand for principles which will add to the progress and uplifting of humanity. We close the door quietly, and feel refreshed as if the memory of a great man had given us strength for finer work in life (*Cape*, pp. 207-208).

## SCHOLASTIC OBLIVION

Ward never thought of possessing either fame or leisure, or reaching the "inside" of scholastic circles, at the cost of becoming a teacher or college official who did not own his own soul. Most American teachers of sociology still smile tolerantly at the mention of his name as one who lived in the dim nineties and has been left far behind. Whether or not their memories have shrunk because of pressure by college trustees, they seem to have forgotten that Ward, practically single-handed, founded sociology in America, and that it was his ideas which first started them along the road of social science.

Although Ward has a few faithful disciples in the universities, he inspires, upon the whole, a good deal of opposition among professional sociologists. When Dr. Harry Elmer Barnes, occupying the chair of historical sociology at Smith College, edited a symposium entitled *The History and Prospects of the Social Sciences* (1926), in which not a single disciple of Ward participated, he used the following mild dedication: "To Lester Frank Ward who first clearly envisaged the importance of the social sciences in determining the destiny of man and society." Immediately, severe criticism was heard, even from such a liberal as Professor Rex Tugwell (later, one of Roosevelt's chief "brain-trusters"), who publicly warned students that if they followed in Ward's footsteps, they "might as well shut up shop."

Compensation for Ward's neglect by the scholastic world is fortunately found in the fact that the few sociologists who made Ward's work the basis of their own labors, put the study of sociology in the United States a generation ahead of that in Europe. It seems that he has had many imitators, but no rivals. There is scarcely a work on social science or its related subjects published since his death in 1913, which has not either sprung from various roots or branches of his system or which has not overlapped some tract of virgin soil which he first plowed and sowed. Curiously, hardly any of them give Ward credit for any of the major generalizations which they developed or adopted from his system.

Ward's sociology is a deep but unnamed well from which his native country has been freely drinking without as much as a simple "Thank you." A typical instance is Huxley's famous essay, "Evolution and Ethics," which unconsciously borrowed Ward's original thought. Ward modestly explained such incidents as follows:

What constantly strikes me is that ever and anon, some modern writer comes forward with the claim to the discovery of an entirely new truth. In every such case that I have thus far met with, if it really is a truth, it is one or some small part of one that I have not only stated earlier, but at least in most cases, have fully set forth, have fully analyzed and connected with other related truths, as an integral part of my system of philosophy. Such cases are not generally plagiarisms, but result from complete lack of acquaintance on the part of those who bring them forward, with me and my works. They may often emanate primarily from me, as my ideas are slowly making their way in the world, and getting in the air; and as the world becomes ripe for them, they are seized upon by brighter minds who imagine they have an original thought. Much of it, however, is due to the *Zeitgeist* itself, which is at last overtaking me (*Glimpses,* I, lxxxii-lxxxiii).

After studying Ward's achievements against the background of his time, one can hardly expect the pedantic mole-scholars and metaphysicians of our era to welcome him with open arms. The simplicity of his thought and expression; the absolute honesty of his universal mind; his refusal to spin shining nets of speculation, and his ability to remain the scientist par excellence even while rising to the heights of philosophy, have left him outside their pale. What else but neglect for such a thinker can be expected from American sociologists who ballyhoo Pareto's bible of fascism, *The Mind and Society,* as the greatest intellectual achievement of modern times, or who still glorify the reactionary social philosophy of Spencer and Sumner?

The literary sociologists, too, are frigid before Ward's system. Dr. Will Durant, wholesale purveyor of philosophy to the masses, who flirts with metaphysics only on Sundays, omits Ward from his *Story of Philosophy* because Ward uttered only "commonplaces which may have been revelations in his day, but that does not help to make them captivate us now." The worthy popularizer of knowledge satisfies his craving for captivation by confining his biographies of American philosophers to such idealists and metaphysicians as Royce, James, and Santayana, and to one liberal pedagogue, John Dewey. Strangely enough, when Dr. Durant entered the field of sociology in his *History of Civilization* (1935), he adopted Ward's synthetic method of genetic inquiry. Is there a moral attached to this?

### CAUSES OF NEGLECT

Perhaps Ward has been punished for his failure to write a popular story of sociology and for producing instead a system of fundamental social science and social philosophy. The causes of his shameful neglect, however, must be sought deeper down than in his personal traits or achievements. Undoubtedly, he lived through two phases of American history, extending from the middle of the nineteenth century into the second decade of the present century. The United States, in the fabulous forties in which he was born, had but twenty-one states and a population of only seventeen million. The telegraph and the sewing machine had just been invented, abolition was gathering momentum, Fourier's communism was being tested at Brook Farm, the women's movement was still in embryo, and Greeley's injunction "Go West, young man!" was being literally obeyed. In the beginning of that fruitful era, everything worth while seemed to have been discovered; toward the end, it was fairly certain that the new knowledge had brought the people little happiness. The panorama of the machine age was tremendous, but the details were plainly becoming more sordid and petty. The vision and the passion of the country were for big business, not for big minds or big books, and social science seemed as far away as the invisible stars.

After the Civil War, America learned of Spencer and his evolution theory through a lot of pounding press agency, but there was no one to advertise Comte and the new science of sociology. The revolutionary doctrines of Darwin and Spencer were finally accepted, but the words "social evolution" sounded too much like "social revolution" and remained as awe-inspiring as the term "communism" is today. Ward was fortunate in escaping persecution for his attachment to such a dangerous subject. His gentle colleague at Brown University, Professor E. B. Andrews, was promptly transferred to a Western college because he dared to uphold the heresy of free silver. But Ward kept his chair of sociology unmolested, although he boldly asserted that "the social process was highly dynamic, jarring perceptibly the solid structure of orthodox economics built on concepts essentially static in nature" (see Beard's *American Civilization,* I, 430). By refraining from meddling in practical politics, he not only kept his position at the university, but received no public notice whatever.

In the last two decades of the nineteenth century the structure of individualistic society, like a building which has been overloaded and outlived its usefulness, began to show wide cracks in its foundations and retaining walls. Those at the top were fearful of any radical change; the mass at the bottom, too insecure to worry about anything but self-preservation. Sociology meant giving the condition of society some thought and attention along scientific lines, and this was the last thing on earth people would worry about in the face of ever impending prosperity or starvation.

Another cause of the neglect of sociology in America was its foreign appearance. What passed for a course in sociology was first given in 1876 at Yale College by Professor William Graham Sumner, the American disciple of Spencer's individualism, who denied that it was a science altogether, and seriously defined it as "A and B putting their heads together to decide what C should be made to do for D." In 1883, when Ward's first book appeared, there was not a single department of sociology in any university. It was not until 1895 that the first chair of sociology was created at the newly founded University of Chicago, and occupied by Professor Albion W. Small.

The American Sociological Society, the first body of its kind, was organized with Ward as its president in 1905-1906. To this day, sociology is adequately taught only in a handful of institutions of learning. The rest either leave it for cursory and inadequate treatment by professors of economics, philosophy, or history, or supplant it by special studies in various branches of applied sociology.

As a result of its prolonged infancy, sociology in the United States is still in its swaddling clothes. In other words, it is, for the most part, an abstract and young science in about the same stage of development in which chemistry and physics were a century or more ago. The main obstacles to its establishment are lack of concrete application, and overspecialization. Students and teachers, as a rule, either turn their faces from the social problem or become opportunists and apologizers when they look at it squarely. They regard most social questions as chimerical, as a sort of by-product of social life which it were best to leave to the future for change and improvement. In brief, the workers in sociology, the youngest and most important of the sciences, plainly lack the courage to go to the root of any social problem. The result is that the introspectionist, the idealist, the behaviorist, and the moralist—all receive some sort of a hearing in the clash of social interests and forces, but the sociologist, the only one who is able to speak with complete authority, is looked upon either as a dangerous social rebel or as a visionary whose dreams are too impractical to be given any serious consideration.

## AGNOSTICISM

Ward's rebellion against theology in all its forms was another reason for his lack of popularity, although in the latter part of his life, his religious views became broader and more tolerant. David Hutcheson, who worked with him in the Library of Congress, and had first-hand knowledge of his lifelong devotion to the cause of science and education, said in an obituary notice: "His radical religious opinions and his serious outlook on life did not tend to make him popular; and I always felt that he never received the recognition which he ought to have had for the good work he was doing" (*Cape,* p. 58).

When Professor Small chided Ward for his blunt frankness on religious topics and suggested that a little tact might attract many more people to dynamic sociology, Ward's reply was: "I do not write for the feeble-minded" (*The Letters of Albion W. Small to Lester F. Ward*, ed. Bernhard J. Stern, *Social Forces*, XII, 165). His publishers were of the same opinion as Professor Small and even delayed the appearance of *Dynamic Sociology* because they feared that Ward's outspoken agnosticism would injure their reputation. But Ward calmly went his way and "let the people talk."

## RADICALISM

Ward did not escape the fate of every true philosopher to be derided by radicals for being too conservative, and to be feared and neglected by conservatives for being too radical. It may well have been his refusal to become a propagandist or follower of some bandwagon that buried his name and fame. Firmly convinced that no scientist or philosopher should be more than a teacher, above the battle, or do anything to interfere with his freedom of spirit, he refused to be shackled by any party or ism. Nor would he follow the intellectual plow in any field smaller than sociology, the arena of all knowledge, not even in economics, no matter how liberal and even radical were his views on economic questions.

Nevertheless, the American socialists, whose ranks he did not join, recognized him as a supreme authority in social science. Such radical leaders as Daniel De Leon, George R. Kirkpatrick, and Scott Nearing continually used the mental dynamite in his works to clear the road for the workers' movement. Although Ward believed his sociology was irreconcilable with Marxism, the Marxists themselves used his ideas as steppingstones to a people's government in a co-operative commonwealth.

Ward's popularity was not improved either by his radical economic philosophy or by his scientific principles of social progress offered to a people who did not dream of such things. Darwin's and Spencer's theory of evolution shook the religious world to its foundations, yet the church found a way to accept their teachings as eminently respectable. Only a few feeble and bigoted minds still reject man's "descent." But the number of normal people who are always trembling with fear at the mention of social change, is colossal. Ward committed the unpardonable sin of advocating, scientifically and commonsensically, that society govern itself and get rid of all its plutocratic masters. Such a man was evidently a dangerous "anarchist" or worse, and the sooner he was excommunicated and forgotten, the better.

## SIGNS OF AWAKENING

Ward does not deserve such a fate. The failure to recognize him in this crucial era as our social Darwin is sheer stupidity. His sociology is neither technical nor abstruse and can become the common knowledge of the people if there are enough of his disciples to spread it. However, there are no shadows without light, and the inert mass is showing signs of awakening. Ideas like Ward's cannot remain buried forever, and sooner or later, must rise through the pressure of inner truth and outer circumstance. Industrial and financial royalists, and suave politicians may still rule society, but judging from past history, the quiet thought of the grubbing scholar will some day fix their destiny.

Consolation is present for those who want it, in the fact that Ward's lot, compared to famous Americans is not too sad. He is relatively still unknown, but Paine, Thoreau, Whitman, and Mark Twain were branded in their day and after, as worthless rebels and apostates. Yet the spirit of progress marched on in those nonconforming "infidels," while their critics, for all their blustering little moments of venomous satisfaction, are gone forever. Ward did not happen, like Paine, to live at a time when he could help in the birth of a nation, but his achievement may far outweigh those of Paine in the scales of history. Ward was the architect and engineer who made the blueprints and laid the foundations of a new world, for the illimitable future. Such men belong with the immortals.

Current events plainly presage the departure of society in the paths laid out by dynamic sociology, in co-operation, social control, and universal scientific education. The World War and its aftermaths have already ripened many of the intellectual seeds sowed by Ward between 1883 and 1913. President Roosevelt's "New Deal" for the forgotten man, weak and futile as it is, compared to Ward's projected sociocracy, is an indication that society has begun to act in its own interests. Which again supports the timeworn platitude that great minds see far ahead of their times, and when the world finally catches up to them, they are gone and perhaps long forgotten.

Unfortunately, the fate which Ward so consistently deplored, the possession of vital knowledge by a few intellectually élite, and the disinheritance of the great mass which needed it most, ironically befell his own works. But the hope will not down that they are slumbering in the libraries merely to gather momentum for a long journey down the years to come. Anyone who cares to listen may hear in his philosophy a mighty blast from a Gabriel's horn amid the raucous shrillings of a young and already tiring civilization. He spoke decades ahead of his time, but not too soon for this post-war generation. Sooner or later, all men will have to reckon with his system or else justify their opposition to it with something more substantial than neglect or derision.

The only chance of immediately resurrecting this buried Caesar lies in a social miracle, the miracle of men beginning to use their brains collectively and in their own interest, to change the art of life from a brutal competitive shambles into a humane and psychic co-operation. How soon that will come is not in the lap of the gods but in the hands of the people.

We cannot leave these chapters with a truer picture of Ward than that contained in the words of his biographer, Mrs. Emily Palmer Cape, who looked into his mind as few others have done:

Ward was never an iconoclast except to build better and deeper. His one desire was to help the whole human race. To those who have any sincere desire and thirst to benefit the advancement of humanity, let them dwell upon the great light which has been offered to all by Lester F. Ward (from a letter to the author, 1929).

# PART II

# THE FOUNDATIONS OF SOCIOLOGY: GENESIS

*"It is the fate of human reason in speculation to build as rapidly as possible, and only when the edifice is completed, to examine the solidity of the foundations."*—Kant

## INTRODUCTORY NOTE

The approach to the temple of sociology is over the long, hard roads of science and philosophy; the entrance, through the gates of origins unlocked by the key of method (Book II). Once within the structure, the survey will follow of the foundations and structure of society, from matter, life, feeling and mind, and upward to man and society, and the mechanism and forces which move and control them (Books III-VI).

Our journey is through the sciences, and our goal is sociology, the synthesis of all the sciences. We cannot expect that abstract principles of science or methodology will fully hold the reader's interest, any more than would scattered bits of a jig-saw puzzle. But as the composite picture will take form with the unfolding of the panorama of evolution, our adventure should become more and more absorbing.

Much as the ambitious reader would like to plunge immediately into the field of the social problem, there are no magic boots to bring him there. He may chafe at the following introductory chapters as much as the young pianist rebels at five finger exercises, or the future navigator at abstract mathematics. But he must know that a drama consists of more than the last act, and that no one can make a diagnosis or prescribe a cure without a comprehensive knowledge of medicine. By mastering origins and fundamentals, we will avoid becoming social quacks and save ourselves from the world-old error of growing into the kind of social philosophers who waste their lives wandering around with spires in their arms, looking into every corner of heaven and earth for a base upon which to rest them.

Without a grasp of cosmic philosophy, just as without the knowledge of the sciences below sociology, one can have no adequate social philosophy. Sociology is not a heaven-piercing spire but an edifice with a definite base and superstructure. As such, it must be carefully surveyed, before the eagle's-eye view of the true philosopher, the sweeping outlook from the top, can be obtained.

Every real scientist and philosopher (the reader may not have felt the change, perhaps, but he is gradually becoming both), can build only upon whatever is permanent in the structure erected by his predecessors. By inquiring into the origin of things as far as possible, he can grasp the meaning of the present in the light of the past, and obtain a foothold to look into the future.

Patience, then, my readers, and onward across the field of science, philosophy, and method, the only rational approach to the temple of sociology and the domains of man's estate!

# *BOOK II.* THE SCIENTIST-PHILOSOPHER

*"It is an unfortunate circumstance that the speculating and philosophizing have to a great extent been done by persons who have not been observers of facts, while those who have extensively observed have either not found time to theorize, or have shrunk timidly from the task of drawing conclusions. . . . Shall science and philosophy, thought and things, be united or divorced?"*—Ward

*"Our first and great duty then is to bring to our studies and to our enquiries after knowledge a mind covetous of truth."*—John Locke

*"Be not satisfied with a superficial view of things, but penetrate into their matter and form, and the end they were made for."*—Marcus Aurelius

*"The empire of man over things is founded on the arts and sciences alone, for Nature is only to be commanded by obeying her."*—Francis Bacon

*"An audacious stride, a winged intellect, an eye for horizons—these are the marks of both science and poetry."*—F. J. Gould

# CHAPTER IV

# SCIENCE

---

"Science is simply knowing."—Ward

"Give thyself up with all thy soul to the search after Nature's secrets. . . . Thou shouldst, in faith, read the books of the scholars; but, above all, have constant recourse to experience. And by patient study get thyself a perfect knowledge of that other World which is Man."—F. Rabelais

"Whatever evil voices may rage, Science, secure among the powers that are eternal, will do her work and be blessed."—T. H. Huxley

---

THE ROMANTIC or metaphysical reader who deplores the lack of any comet tails upon which to fly through all knowledge, can turn back, here and now. Otherwise, he will have to stick to solid ground to avoid being lost in clouds of speculation and illusion. There will be no mirages or mystic sirens to lure the practical, realistic traveler, nor any magic carpets to shorten the journey. Compensation will be found only in the absence of technical boulders and forced marches through arid data.

## SCIENCE

The road to the temple must first be cleared of all the supernatural undergrowths which have blocked human understanding from time immemorial. To the uninformed or undeveloped mind, science may seem to be a lot of technical jargon, and philosophy a still more dull discipline. Yet science and philosophy are integral parts of everyday life, and we can no more help using them at every step, than the immortal M. Jourdain could avoid talking prose.

Science (Latin, *scire*, to know) means rational and unified knowledge of phenomena and of the relations between them. Huxley defined it as "organized common sense"; Ward, as "an *explanation* of the phenomena of the universe as presented to the senses" (*D.S.,* I, 45). It is neither a catalogue nor a storehouse of facts. Facts in themselves are static and lifeless. United by an idea or an underlying explanation of origin, sequence, and correlation, they teem with energy and become the dynamic material of science. A mass of facts or phenomena is in itself no more a science than a brick pile is a palace.

## THE HISTORY OF SCIENCE

The evolution of science runs parallel with the evolution of mind. Science is the answer which man wrested from chaos to satisfy his natural curiosity. In the infancy of the race, he experienced only dim, stark sensation, groping like a leaf toward the light. By painstaking trial and error, over countless centuries, the path was widened and the field of vision extended, until he dug himself out into the free air, and organized his knowledge into the body of science. Before increased intelligence brought science, his only recourse was to the gods or spirits created by his own imagination; his only escape, in awe and superstition. Science was already the tool of the primitive savage when he figured his chances of being alive the next day, and in its maturity, it is still the only instrument by which life is planned ahead. Contrasting science with chaos, Ward says:

The early pastoral races of the East learned much about the heavens as they lay out under the starry sky tending their flocks. But their synthetic powers wasted themselves in the fanciful grouping of the stars into constellations that possess no scientific significance. . . . It remained for science to propose any theory to explain it. . . . We thus, by a pure act of the mind, gain an orderly conception of the universe, which may be contrasted with the chaotic conceptions that formerly prevailed, or that must be entertained by any person of reflective habits unacquainted with this theory (*P.S.*, p. 52).

Time, place, and circumstances in ancient Greece combined to produce stronger intellectual curiosity as well as greater mental prowess by which pure speculation (metaphysics) was replaced by science. Socrates and Plato were turned away by their social consciousness from biology and physics to ethics and politics. Only Aristotle's mind was strong enough to combine the lines of inquiry into nature and man with the many loose threads of the imagination, and weave them into the first body of organized science. He ignited the torch of enlightenment but could carry it only a little way. Its flame flickered and almost died out before it burned again in Roman utilitarianism. At the beginning of the Christian era, the growth of speculation again relegated to the background all serious attempts at science.

In the Middle Ages the light of reason was further eclipsed by the rejuvenation of the metaphysical outlook which the Greeks thought they had forever destroyed. Science was degenerated by alchemists into a hunt for magic formulas or elixirs. But all through the centuries, its immortal seeds, buried deep in the ground, were unfolding and pushing upward. The great Renaissance saw the recovery of the Greek language, the voyages of Columbus, the decay of the Holy Roman Empire, and the invention of printing. It heard the *Zeitgeist* speak through Roger Bacon, Da Vinci, Copernicus, Francis Bacon, Galileo, Kepler, and Newton. The Greek naturalistic view of the cosmos was readopted, metaphysical concepts banished, and the rebirth of reason with its eager breath, fanned the undying flame of science to illuminate the world.

## MODERN SCIENCE

Modern science is neither a spontaneous conception nor the peculiar product of this machine age. The seeds sown in Greece over two thousand years ago had been incubating for many generations before they burst upon mankind in the eighteenth century. The science of the present is, according to Ward, the philosophical genius of antiquity applied to an enormously increased volume and complexity of new data (*P.S.*, Chapters XVIII-XIX, p. 507). That does not imply that the ancients were full-fledged scientists or that modern science is either a direct inheritance or exact reproduction of the knowledge of the past. The flashes of scientific genius of old were sparks that died almost as soon as they appeared. Whenever the ancients did discover something, they rarely knew what it was or what was to be done with it. Says Ward:

The forces of nature and the properties of substance have always existed, but they were of comparatively little use until the age of experimentation which involves the closest reasoning. The electricity that lights our houses and propels our cars was here all the time, and could just as well have been used two thousand years or four thousand years ago as now, if any one had thought out and worked out its true nature, as has so recently been done (*P.S.*, p. 6).

In the natural and physical sciences, the tidal wave of the new knowledge has swept the world out of the infantile period of ancient speculation into the mature stage of positive science. Spirits are no longer believed to control; thunder is not accepted as the wrath of the gods or gems as omens of good luck or bad. The increase of concrete knowledge has ended the age of magic and brought a basic comprehension of things.

The steady advance in science is common knowledge. The first intellectual revolution initiated by astronomy in the seventeenth and eighteenth centuries paved the way for the second one ushered in by biologic evolution. Development, as the explanation of living forms, became the chief instrument of the scientific genius of Goethe, Lamarck, Darwin, Wallace, Spencer, Huxley, and Haeckel. From biology, the study of evolution spread to every corner of knowledge to prove the universal reign of natural law, and the natural origin and development of our globe and everything upon it.

In the sciences which appertain to man, however, we have not only failed to advance very far beyond the speculations of Plato and Aristotle, but in many respects, we have not yet caught up with them. The only consolation, according to Ward, lies in the fact that science and the social order are so closely interrelated, that some day, progress in one will mean progress in the other. Besides, social science is not only the crown but also the synthesis of all the sciences; therefore, progress below must sooner or later be reflected at the top.

## THE SUBJECT MATTER OF SCIENCE

Whatever human reason can know, test, and verify, said Ward, is the subject matter of science. In the words of Spencer, its province is the knowable, not the unknowable. The solution of the problem of how many angels can dance on the point of a needle is a fine example of medieval disputation but does not belong to science. If any Unknowable, Absolute or First Cause exists, man has no instrument with which to grasp it, for his finite mind is so constructed that he is unable, try as he will, not only to solve that problem but even to state it. Science gives us knowledge of the laws of nature, a knowledge which is the only rational basis of human thought and action. It gives power to foresee, and foresight leads to action (Comte).

## THE FUNCTION AND PURPOSE OF SCIENCE

It is only when we lack positive (scientific) ideas that we resort to abstract speculation and supernatural conceptions. Science alone can teach us anything about the cosmos, and show us how to take it apart and reconstruct it. Only children, savages, or fundamentalists dig into a watch to capture the fairy that makes it tick. Scientists with adult minds know better, but they cannot do the impossible or solve the insoluble. The function of science is to explain why things happen and must necessarily happen the way they do, and not in some other way, and its methods and purpose is to use universal laws and principles in the interest of mankind. *Science is not completely positive until it is purposeful,* and that purpose, the common advantage of humanity (Ratzenhofer).

## SCIENCE IS UTILITARIAN

The common fallacy about science is that it is dry, technical, severe, and without spiritual values. The misconception is due to two other fallacies. On the one hand, the idealists claim that if men were virtuous, all would be right with the world, forgetting that the most honest and moral of men would need the right kind of knowledge to solve a single social problem. On the other hand, the scientific compilers most often remain indifferent to questions of utility or practical application and like penguins believe that the pebbles of knowledge which they have heaped up are a mansion of wisdom. Comte and Ward were two rare minds in which morals and science, the abstract and the concrete, reason and emotion, came to terms. Their conclusion is for all time, that social science must conform in aim and method to an adequate system of social morality, and serve as a cultural discipline to satisfy social needs.

Ward wrote *Dynamic Sociology* to point out the method by which the spirit of true morality, i.e., the amelioration of social conditions, could be infused into the cold and rigid body of abstract social science. In his own language:

Not until such a clew was discovered and laid hold of, as the purpose of elevating humanity furnishes, could sufficient energy or perseverance be infused into the effort to insure for it a successful issue. The conception of a universal causal dependence of phenomena when transformed into an active working principle, takes the shape of a universal theory of development or evolution. The high, utilitarian motive, focalizing all considerations in the good of man can have no other effect than to establish as the ultimate science, for the perfection of which all the other sciences exist, the science of human life, which takes the form and name of sociology (*D.S.,* I, 9).

As he put it many years later:

*All science is essentially ethical.* . . . Social science is more so than all other sciences only because it deals more directly and exclusively with the collective welfare of mankind. It seeks not merely to reduce the social friction and thus accomplish all that the old ethics has so vainly striven to secure, viz., negative moral progress, but also and chiefly to put the manifold existing and prospective wants of mankind in the way of satisfaction, and thus to bring about a progressive and unlimited train of benefits and a truly scientific or positive moral progress (*Glimpses,* V, 281).

As a true utilitarian, Ward felt that it was impossible to be a social neutral, as it were to be an artist for art's sake, or a scientist merely for the sake of science. Neither art nor science is of any value to mankind unless it can lead it out of the depths to the free human estate on the heights (see *Outlines,* p. 197; *App. S.,* p. 287). He describes utility as follows:

Here is a new or fourth category to be added to the conventional three, truth, beauty, goodness. The useful is not the same as the good, as used in this formula, but it is even more important because of universal application, while the field of ethics is a restricted one which is constantly contracting. The completed formula should then be: the true, the beautiful, the good and the useful, in which the useful is not last because least, but only because the last to be recognized (*P.S.,* p. 88).

And now comes a great paradox. Although the most fermenting element in social evolution has been the progress of science, society has done practically nothing to benefit by the remarkable resources of science for the improvement of social institutions. No greater anticlimax is imaginable, unless it is that of homeless forestry experts planting and nursing trees, without using a single piece of lumber to build a house for themselves. That is why Ward's panacea for the social problem is education, the universal spread of knowledge, so that the masses may develop a concern for scientific truth and a knowledge of how to utilize it for social needs, and thus lay the foundation of a new social order.

In glorifying science as the savior of society Ward becomes prophetic:

I deny that society has ever tried to cure itself of the disease called *Weltschmerz.* It has not arrived at that state of self-consciousness at which it has ever seriously considered the question. It is in the same state as a race of animals relative to its true condition. Some savage races are scarcely more advanced. Civilized races are waking up to these purely physical matters. They are in a state of absolute lethargy with regard to social matters. What the human race requires is to be awakened to a realization of its condition. It will find the remedy for its woes. This must be something more than the feeble plaints of a few individuals. It must amount to a complete race consciousness. If this is ever brought about, it must be by the same instrumentality that produced all other steps in human progress, viz., science (*App. S.,* p. 21).

## CLASSIFICATION OF THE SCIENCES

A system as noble in aim as science must be strong in its unity and cohesiveness. Knowledge develops under the laws of evolution in a continuous sweep. Science is the total product of that development which culminates in sociology, the synthetic fusion of all knowledge. Just as no one can live alone, and what affects one affects all, so the sciences are so closely related that a radical shift in one disturbs all the others. Which is only another way of saying that all knowledge is a unity. Knowledge which is absolutely independent is unthinkable or a figment of the imagination. Each science impinges on every other, and every phenomenon may be treated from the standpoint of all others. A human body may be regarded either as a mechanism, an animal organism, as the seat of mind power, as a social individual or as fifty cents worth of chemicals and minerals. Society, too, may be studied from the viewpoint of each of the separate sciences, but, in the last analysis, it must be investigated and treated from the rounded, synthetic aspect of sociology.

Although science is a unit, it is too vast to be handled without being arranged in subdivisions or separate sciences. All that we can know, says Ward, comes from the observation of matter and its properties, and it is that real, concrete knowledge which forms the body of the various sciences. Classification of knowledge, the sciences, is one of the most important problems of society.

The discord between the sciences is due to the same causes as the conflict between the institutions of society, viz., the failure to treat them as a synthetic unit. The grasp of the sciences as branches of a single trunk is possible only when there is a proper classification which furnishes a true conception of the nature and function of the sciences.

Aristotle was the first to chart all knowledge in detail and attempt the synthesis of the sciences, because he was the first to comprehend their unity. More than two thousand years later, Comte worked out an improved classification based upon a tremendous advance in knowledge. There followed other attempts at classification by Spencer, Bain, Wundt, Ward, Ostwald, and De Greef, all of whom furnished a panoramic view of the progress of knowledge.

## MODERN CLASSIFICATIONS

When knowledge snowballed down the centuries, it gathered new philosophical viewpoints, and consequently improved classifications (see *P.S.*, p. 69). Comte was the pioneer, and Spencer and Ward followed in his footsteps. We have added De Greef only by way of contrast to the following modern classifications:

| COMTE | SPENCER | WARD | DE GREEF |
|---|---|---|---|
| 1. Mathematics | 1. Astronomy | 1. Astronomy | 1. Economics, the science of social nutrition |
| 2. Astronomy | 2. Geology | 2. Physics | 2. Genetics, the science of population, socially organized |
| 3. Physics | 3. Biology | 3. Chemistry | 3. Esthetics |
| 4. Chemistry | 4. Psychology | 4. Biology | 4. Collective psychology, religion, metaphysics, positive philosophy |
| 5. Biology, including cerebral biology | 5. Sociology | 5. Psychology | 5. Ethics |
| 6. Sociology | 6. Ethics | 6. Sociology | 6. Law |
| 7. Ethics | | | 7. Politics |

## COMTE'S ORDER OF THE SCIENCES

French philosophic genius, in Ward's opinion, was never more brilliantly represented than by Comte's classification which served as the framework of the positive philosophy, and was itself the model for the classifications of Spencer and Ward. Spencer denied that patent fact and claimed that his own contribution was original, but

Ward indicted Spencer's ungratefulness and fully acknowledged his own debt to Comte's genius (see *ibid.,* pp. 66-69).

Comte's classification is not arbitrary but follows the order in which knowledge was evolved. Astronomy was the first to become a positive science. Then physics, chemistry, and biology left the field of speculation and became concrete and established sciences. Psychology and sociology are still, more or less, in a transitional stage. Although Comte was not an evolutionist, his arrangement of the sciences in the natural order of their development, commencing with the simplest and most general, followed by the more complex and particular, was a master stroke. With astronomy at one end and ethics at the other, he placed physics and biology between them, leaving an inner center for chemistry. Psychology was not assigned any independent position, but treated as a part of biology.

Comte was followed by Spencer in crowning the order of the sciences by ethics, and not sociology. Because the aim of mankind is a moral order, reasoned Comte, ethics belongs at the apex of the sciences, although the avowed purpose of the positive philosophy is human welfare under the rule of sociology. Only ethics, in his judgment, could synthesize the special knowledge of man's individual nature by combining the biological and the sociological viewpoint, i.e., the vital organism and the collective being.

### WARD'S CLASSIFICATION

Ward differed with Comte and assigned the leadership of the sciences to sociology, because in Ward's system it was identical with and included ethics. He clarified Comte's classification, in general, by showing there was no relationship of subject and king in what Comte called the hierarchy of the sciences, but only that of a close family kinship. Each science is not only the child of the preceding one but also the father of its successor. All the sciences are thus related and none can live alone without becoming sterile and extinct. The psychologist must work in physiology; the biologist, in physics and chemistry. The sociologist cannot pursue the study of human society without being well grounded in biology and psychology.

Sociology, although the youngest of the sciences, is the head, in the same sense that the baby is the monarch in the home. In the sciences, however, there is involved a deeper truth than mere kinship. Just as a child is not only the offspring of its parents but also of all their ancestors, so, too, each of the higher sciences is not only related to the next lower one, but is itself the synthetic product of all the compounding and recompounding that has gone before.

It will be noticed that Ward omits mathematics because, like logic, it is only a norm or gauge and not a science. Comte, however, who was a teacher of mathematics, included it in the order of the sciences, as the instrument which not only extends our knowledge of nature but enables us to follow her various perspectives. Nevertheless, Ward's classification will be found complete, with a pigeonhole, as it were, for every conceivable bit of knowledge, a fact which may be easily tested by the reader.

We leave the tradition of science with its desire to grasp the universe for what it is; to envisage the world not through clouds of myth or emotion but in the clear air of reality and reason. The will of science is the will to understand, impartially and rationally, all the realms of being and doing, and their complex mingling of values. As such, it is not a cold pavement set with sterile bricks of abstraction or technique, but the glorious approach to the temple of knowledge.

Science has had many enemies, and its life has been a continuous battle for existence. When it extended into research, it was challenged even by Comte as a mere display of intellectual energy which was bound to end in the futile search for a First Cause. Rebels against the domination of reason have always fought science as the foe of the moral and spiritual life. Science has conquered or captured its enemies, because it provides the basis for a moral and spiritual order, the foundation for a social superstructure, and the material for a philosophy or way of life.

Fortified by the grasp of science, we proceed on our journey and enter the much misunderstood and abused field of philosophy.

# Chapter V

# PHILOSOPHY

---

*"It is certain that the scientific progress of the world has been the result of thought applied to phenomena, and this surely is something very near to philosophy."*

*"It is to the theorizers—that the world is almost exclusively indebted for what it now possesses of organized science."*

*"The work of the true philosopher is preeminently the synthesis of extant knowledge."*
—Ward

*"The free man thinks of nothing so little as of death, and his wisdom is a meditation not of death, but of life."*—Spinoza

*"The discovery of what is true and the practice of what is good are the two most important objects of philosophy."*—Voltaire

---

Philosophy has been used and misused in so many senses that its true nature has been lost in confusion. At one moment, it is taken for an old and refined chaperon of science; at another, it becomes a divine intellectual taskmaster. It seeks the total perspective of all things real, and again, dreams endlessly about the supernatural and the unreal. Clear thinking makes a definition immediately necessary, but that is impossible until the aspects of philosophy as metaphysics, hypothesis, wisdom, and synthesis are examined (see *Ps. F.,* p. 9).

## PHILOSOPHY AS METAPHYSICS

In the course of the centuries, the sciences were divorced from philosophy until the latter became identified with metaphysics, the "science" of things outside of and above demonstrated knowledge.[1]

As Ward became a scientist, he gradually threw metaphysics overboard as an impediment to the search for truth. Metaphysics has the "mystical" quality of freeing the mind of such encumbrances as space, time, and the objective world, and leaving it to pursue mirages of its own creation. He regarded it as a futile and frivolous task, unworthy of respect even when it has the best intentions, for it accomplishes

[1] The great scientist Huxley thus distinguished science and philosophy: "What is commonly called science, whether mathematical, physical, or biological, consists of the answers which mankind has been able to give to the inquiry, What do I know? They furnish us with the result of the mental operations which constitute thinking, while philosophers, in the stricter sense of the term, inquire into the foundation of the first principles which those operations assume or imply."

nothing except to befog and hinder the grasp of reality, and endlessly torment the mind with inner conflict. In the final analysis, it cannot rise above an exhausting process of mental gymnastics. Just as nothing substantial comes from merely turning somersaults, so neither knowledge nor wisdom results from trying to solve insoluble problems such as "how can the mind know a supposedly external world?" or "how do we know that we know?" The result of pure speculations of this kind is to fly away into the boundless nebula of the imagination, and become forever intoxicated with superstitions and illusions.

### PHILOSOPHY AS HYPOTHESIS

However, in the sense of theory or scientific hypothesis, philosophy is a legitimate discipline which stands at the boundaries of science, carries it one step forward and seeks to solve problems by solidifying ideas too nebulous for science. As such, philosophy is the attempt (always doomed to partial failure) to think science through to its furthest implications. It may be compared to the inchoate vision of a building while science is like the knowledge of materials and construction. Science observes, records, and builds; philosophy criticizes, theorizes, plans, and co-ordinates ends.

Ward repeatedly corrects the false notion that hypothesis or speculation, in itself, is an intellectual vice. Science constantly speculates and theorizes but always in the realm of the knowable; never in the unknowable. But metaphysics, as often as not, finds itself in the country of the Mad Hatter and sees "gaseous vertebrates" wandering around outside of their skins. Yet not all metaphysical speculating is in vain, for like the dreams and visions of the poet, it often forms the nebula out of which science distills and solidifies substantial knowledge (see *D.S.*, I, 7; *Ps. F.*, p. 215).

A definition of philosophy now looms into view. It is "the explanation of the phenomena of the universe" (Comte). Undeniably, we are surrounded by wonders and mysteries. The myriad aspects of nature without, and the strange fluctuations of feeling within, all demand explanations. To find them, philosophy as hypothesis is essential.

### PHILOSOPHY AS THE LOVE OF WISDOM

In the Greek view, the aim of philosophy was to make a way of life (truth, wisdom) out of knowledge. Dynamic sociology is such a philosophy and typifies the definition of Epicurus: "The art of attaining the happy life by investigation." Such an ideal is behind Ward's sociocracy, a social order in which the soul of every man will catch flame through a scientific education and a scientific temperament inculcated by knowledge. A philosopher in that sense is far removed from Thoreau's sentimental ideal: "A philosopher is not only one who has subtle thoughts or who founds a school, but one who so loves wisdom, as to live according to its dictates, a life of simplicity, independence, magnanimity and trust."

Without science, the philosopher, lover of wisdom though he is, soon floats off on clouds of supernaturalism which are mistaken for reality, or sits splashing about in some muddy little stream enjoying the illusion that he is battling a tidal wave. The basis of all real philosophy, regarded either as theory or love of wisdom, is science alone (*P.S.,* p. 140).

### PHILOSOPHY AS SYNTHESIS

Philosophy, in the final sense, is not an independent discipline but an extension of the scientific method (see below, p. 97). The natural desire to grasp the totality of things made man feel from the earliest days that somewhere in the jig-saw puzzle of knowledge there was a composite picture of the cosmos. The desire found satisfaction in the synthetic power of philosophy which expressed itself in the synthesis of all knowledge commenced by Aristotle, developed by Comte and Spencer, and completed by Ward (*D.S.,* I, 25; II, 123).

The timeworn conflict between philosophy represented by Plato and Aristotle, and science, by Galileo and Bruno, was the result of a false antagonism. Their synthesis which resulted in dynamic sociology is not found in books but in the living world of man; not only in the mystical concept of being, but also in the social concept of doing. Philosophy in this sense is not peace with the unknowable but conquest of the knowable. As such, it is the priceless residuum in the crucible of knowledge, and constitutes the only visible hope for a happy, spiritual race.

Philosophers who are fundamentally scientists, like Comte, Spencer and Ward are the only ones who have dilated upon the synthetic power of philosophy. According to Spencer: "Knowledge of the lowest kind is un-unified knowledge; science is partially unified knowledge; philosophy is completely unified knowledge."

On the other hand, philosophers who are merely metaphysicians never make the distinctions under discussion. Their greatest joy is to destroy all other systems by a sweeping analysis dressed up in a wooly rhetoric which they adore for its own sake. Plato must have had them in mind when he said: "The result with those who may be considered the best of them, is that they are made useless to a world by the very study which they extol." True philosophers, in Plato's opinion are doers, not dreamers, because philosophy is an active culture, not a static process of the imagination. Plato knew, for he, too, was a philosopher and a dreamer.

## SCIENCE-PHILOSOPHY

Out of the synthesis arises the most valuable form of knowledge, viz., science-philosophy. Ward said that only a scientist can become a true philosopher. Science is in no way opposed to philosophy; and in the broad sense, each includes the other. His own dynamic sociology which is a social philosophy grounded in social science, is a perfect example of science-philosophy (see *ibid.*, II, 500).

Modern philosophy is largely scientific because it proceeds from facts. Ancient philosophy was mainly unscientific because it began and ended with mere assumptions. Today, every science is also a philosophy for whatever is real and valuable in it, is the result of reasoning upon facts (see *Outlines*, p. 116). Says Ward "It is certain that the scientific progress of the world has been the result of thought applied to phenomena, and this surely is something very near to philosophy" (*ibid.*, p. viii).

The works of Darwin, Tyndall, and Huxley are contributions to science; those of Plato, Spinoza, and Kant belong to philosophy. But the achievements of Aristotle, Leibnitz, Comte, Spencer, Haeckel, and Ward are in the field of science-philosophy, wherein science collects, analyzes, and handles the parts, and philosophy synthesizes and interprets the whole. Material and method thus form a perfect union when philosophy is carried on by scientists, and science by philosophers. Ward's observation upon those who have the double personality of the scientist-philosopher, applies with particular force to himself. As a theorizer and organizer of knowledge who also did invaluable scientific research, he deplored:

It is an unfortunate circumstance that the speculating and philosophizing have to a great extent, not been done by persons who have been observers of facts, while those who have extensively observed, have either not found time to theorize or have shrunk timidly from the task of drawing conclusions (*D.S.*, I, 3).

Philosophy, in Ward's view, should not remain a mere intellectual pastime or an expression of one's *Weltanschauung,* however brilliant or exalted. As an extension of science, it must descend from its intellectual throne and become every man's instrument of truth. Science has performed miracles without end, but the people have not learned that they have the social will to enjoy them. That is still the untried thesis of social science waiting to be applied as soon as science and philosophy become the property of all.

# CHAPTER VI

# METHOD

"*Method is more important than doctrine.*"—Comte

"*Application is the touchstone of all doctrine.*"—Adolphe Coste

"*They who do not feel the darkness will never look for the light. The doubt must intervene before the investigation can begin.*"—H. T. Buckle

IF THE APPROACH to science and philosophy has been long or dusty, let the intrepid adventurer take heart, for he is about to receive the golden key of method with which to open the temple.

## IMPORTANCE OF METHOD

Science and method (Greek, μέθοδος, investigation following after) are the bifocal lenses through which the universe may be seen without distortion. The tyro in knowledge, like a newly born infant, is overwhelmed by an avalanche of phenomena which are as jumbled as a printer's scattered type, and so complex that the mind is unable to handle them without confusion. The infinite burden of data must be presented in an orderly manner or it will crush the inquirer, whether layman or professional. Masquerading knowledge in robes of idealism or mysticism will not help. If it is loose and unmethodical, it rules itself out of the categories of science.

The reader may well wonder how it is possible in a short span of life even to scratch the surface of knowledge, and learn, much less reason about the myriad objects, ideas and feelings, more numerous than the grains of sand and more changeable than the winds. The senses, the emotions and the intellect, as guides to truth, are uncertain and fallible. Something more is necessary to save us from chaos, and it is found in method which sorts, correlates, and synthesizes all knowledge and experience, until the mansion of science rises from meaningless piles of facts and phenomena.

Both Aristotle and Comte expressed the paradox that method is ultimately more important than material or doctrine. The strength of a wall is not measured by the size or composition of the bricks (they may be of granite or tissue paper) but by the manner in which they are manufactured and laid. Unsystematic knowledge, however attractive or valuable, is as weak as a crumbling wall.

Method is so important, that steering even a fraction of a degree away from the true course, means landing on a strange shore or being smashed on the rocks. Aristotle, the most powerful mind of all time, was also the most powerful and useless of verbal reasoners whenever he used a purely subjective method and lost sight of the guiding star of science.

### THE SCIENTIFIC METHOD BEFORE COMTE

Yet it was Aristotle, the father of science, who laid the foundation for the scientific method with the simple act of observation. But he trusted logic and speculation more than nature and science, and never arrived at the stage of experiment. With the facts he was unsurpassable; without them he was left far behind. He was thus a dual personality: a scientist, all for moderation, and a philosopher who rode moderation to excess straight into the realms of nonsense and superstition. One undying example will do to illustrate his lack of common observation as well as the mental laziness of his hero-worshipers. His wrong guess about the number of feet on the common house fly was accepted by the world for over twenty centuries, without a single attempt to verify it.

The subjective method held sway until modern science broke through the gloom of the Dark Ages. Francis Bacon (1561-1626), who inherited some of Aristotle's genius and some of his errors, called his chief work *Novum Organon*, but there was nothing new in its inductive method. It was the revival of Aristotle's method, with the metaphysical elements omitted.

When Bacon's method was applied to research, it, too, failed. Disgusted by the errors of the metaphysical system with its a priori reasoning, he flew to the other extreme of deduction, theorized much but rarely observed or experimented. Because he essentially loved metaphysics better than science, he rejected the epochmaking discoveries of Copernicus and Kepler which were to revolutionize human thought. Yet he vitalized logic and turned induction from an inert mental process into a dynamic instrument. Much may be forgiven him for that alone.

## COMTE'S POSITIVE METHOD

Montesquieu's *L'Esprit des lois* and Adam Smith's *Wealth of Nations* paved the way for the objective, scientific method developed in the *Positive Philosophy* of Auguste Comte. These thinkers discarded the false method of making logical deductions from mere assertions, initiated concrete inductive investigations, and sounded the funeral knell of mere speculation. The effect of the transition from the theological to the scientific outlook was that of a complete intellectual revolution. The new age realized that there was something besides dogma and superstition to guide its stumbling feet, and opened its eyes wide to the matter and method of science.

The positive or scientific method is the only one which makes possible prevision of phenomena. If the wind blows according to the will of Boreas, we may beg his favor, but not calculate upon it. But it is quite another story when science enables us to predict the weather with certainty. The miracle of measuring heavenly distances and surveying the stars and the planets in their courses became a commonplace after Newton demonstrated that the general laws of celestial phenomena constituted the primary basis of human knowledge. The true nature of scientific theory in all its purity as applicable to practical knowledge in all its complexity was thus proven. Yet the science of astronomy does not include any inquiry about a First or Final Cause, for the laws of nature are treated, not as supernatural entities, but as "the relation of co-existence and succession" (Comte).

Comte, who discerned the evolution of mind before Darwin and Spencer, was the first to note that the more complex and specialized the phenomena, the less it was possible to separate method from doctrine. Method which is scientific and brings order, precision, clarity, and synthetic vision, impressed him with the necessity of a complete revision of philosophy. He regarded any suggestion, however, to restrict the scientific method to the inorganic world as absurd. He was the first modern philosopher to see the necessity of using the scientific method also in the realm of the organic and the social, in the sciences of life, man and society.

## WARD'S SYNTHETIC METHOD

Ward built his method upon Comte's basic idea of synthesis and proclaimed that science knows no insoluble problems. "What is not, may be." Following Comte, he insisted that sociology adopt the scientific method of the natural sciences. Instead of offering such vague sentiments as welfare of humanity, forces of progress and human nature, Ward argued that since sociology was a true science, subject to the same natural laws as physics, chemistry, and biology, all nebular speculations about social phenomena must be supplanted by the observation of facts and the application of the laws and principles interpreting them. That could be accomplished only by the synthetic method which gives due regard to the facts of the lower sciences and takes into account the effect of the human mind. The psychic factor can no more be omitted in the study of society than the chemical factor can be neglected in the study of life. In brief, the synthetic method includes all the phases and viewpoints of social experience, from history and the survey of present society (always along the lines of its evolution) to the minute analysis of all the factors in social evolution, particularly the psychic factor.

At the root of the synthetic method is the law of causality, the magnetic pole which keeps the mind within the bounds of reason. The same law underlies all scientific method and is founded upon the truisms (the opposites of which are unthinkable) that all effects have causes, all causes have effects, and that like causes result in like effects. To disregard it means to return to the land of metaphysics where anything is possible, because it may happen without a cause, or as the result of a supernatural will. Basal to science, however, is the fact that all phenomena have first of all a natural (material) cause. Ward expressed it in his favorite maxims: "No lotus without a stem. No tower without a base." Says he:

Neither man individually, nor society collectively, could ever take one certain step except actuated by this idea (of causality). However it may be in the domain of faith, in all real action this conception is and always has been the fundamental postulate. The invariability of nature's laws, the absolute dependence of all phenomena, these are the initial premises, the *sine qua non,* not only of all science and of all art, but of all action of whatever kind (*D.S.,* I, 65).

From Aristotle, Ward learned to seek origins and causes; to be inductive and realistic. From Plato, he inherited the faculty of "seeing things in the whole" and received deduction and synthesis. As a scientist-philosopher who first observed and then theorized, his conviction grew ever firmer that the scheme of things cannot be found in the brain but by means of it, and that truth is not intuitive, but is acquired through the examination of phenomena bound in an unbreakable chain of causality.

The synthetic method served Ward as a double-edged sword. *Science alone would have made him a mere compiler or technologist; philosophy alone, an abstract theorizer.* But the fusion of both enabled him to extract natural laws and principles from the critical observation of the social panorama. He saw human actions determined invariably by causes which lie behind and not before. Such determinism does not make us feelingless machines, as so many idealists fear, but proves that man has a certain grand courage. Weak and puny as he is, he rises to conquer the overwhelming forces of nature, succeeds in making her his slave, and compels her to give up her most precious secrets, all by means of science and the positive, synthetic method. It is only then that he begins to understand the what and the how of the universe a little more than William James's dog strapped to the vivisection table grasps of his. The inexorable conclusion is that there is one thing that man cannot and never will be able to do, and that is to abolish or suspend the law of causality. Chance, in a rational world, according to Ward, simply does not exist (see *P.S.*, pp. 151-159).

## GENETICS

Ward's methodology is an integral part of his sociology. By using genetics, the search for origins and fundamentals, to extend the scientific method, he was able to trace social phenomena to their roots, and to demonstrate that society is governed by the laws which obtain in the rest of the universe (see *ibid.*, p. 47).

The tragedy of most thinkers upon social science (not excluding Comte) is that they theorize about the ends and neglect origins. Said Kant: "It is the fate of human reason in speculation to build as rapidly as possible, and only when the edifice is completed, to examine the solidity of the foundations." Ward is equally specific:

Another of the misfortunes of human progress is, that in all departments of knowledge, the human mind and the conditions surrounding it require that the study of phenomena be commenced from the top, and that the superficial view be taken before the fundamental view can be gained. Thus not only do we find men first occupied with the problems of sociology, the highest and most complex of the sciences, but in each more simple science, as in biology, the superficial and obvious are first studied and innumerable errors formed before the most profound and recondite problems are undertaken by whose solution alone true conceptions are attainable. How great, for example, have been the error and confusion to which the study of the most highly organized living beings has led, before that of the simpler beginnings of life was commenced, which alone can yield the primary principles of organic existence (*D.S.,* I, 76)!

## GENERALIZATION

The chief instrument of the synthetic method is generalization, the only means of expressing the relation between facts. As soon as the mind reaches a view, it generalizes and adopts a larger view. By repetition of this process, phenomena are classified and correlated, and larger and larger groups are brought under uniform law. As the number of facts are increased, the underlying laws and principles are correspondingly reduced to as few as possible. Data, like millions of pennies which cannot be carried on one's back, must be exchanged or minted into larger and more valuable denominations, if they are to be used at all. Every generalization must be tested on the touchstone of ever changing fact; in that way, all knowledge was developed by generalization.

Without reasoning upon facts (that is what generalization means) there could have been no social science. In a field of phenomena as vast and complex as society, the number of facts are so bewildering that a wide induction becomes immediately unmanageable. Any attempt to handle the facts without generalizing is bound to result in confusion and finally to result in abandoning them altogether for the ancient and still honorable game of guessing, variously called speculation, metaphysics, or philosophy (see *ibid.,* p. 55).

Because nature's laws and forces are universal and uniform, generalization obtains everywhere. In chemistry, for example, higher products are obtained by compounding and recompounding, and the results are used as units for a continuation of the same process. In sociology, social data gathered by inductions in all the lesser sciences are collected, classified and grouped into units. The latter then serve as basic facts to form a still larger group, and so on and on, into the deepest and widest generalizations the human mind has ever achieved (see *P.S.,* Chapter IV). The scope of generalization is unlimited because the field of knowledge and the power of mind have no limits. Says Ward:

All unities are subordinate to some higher unity, and so on, until we arrive at the ultimate unit which constitutes the universe itself, and whose limit is infinity. This must therefore remain incomprehensible to the finite. Every approach toward it, however, furnishes a high satisfaction to the human mind, and cannot fail to place the race not only upon a higher intellectual but upon a higher material plane (*D.S.*, I, 4).

Ward's use of ethnographic parallels to prove the vital importance of generalization, is a dazzling illumination of the uniformity and universality of natural law. Since like causes produce like effects, the same or similar cultures, rites, habits, customs, and beliefs are found the world over, in as widely separated races as the Eskimos and the South Sea Islanders. Details of social evolution may vary, of course, with time, place, climate, stage of industry or other circumstance, but if one keeps on generalizing upon the known facts, a plane is ultimately reached in which all social phenomena as well as all human beings are interrelated.

## ILLUSTRATIONS OF THE SYNTHETIC METHOD

The synthetic method charts the world, physical, intellectual, and emotional, as a globe, and not as a flat, Mercator projection. Human life is not a series of watertight compartments, but an organic unity. The vessel which holds life, knowledge, understanding, is given to us in fragments. They will not put themselves together again, nor will we know what to do with them without a clear conception of the shape the vessel ought to have. Spencer believed he had that conception when he wrote his synthetic philosophy. Yet he misconceived the nature and method of synthesis when he came to sociology and made it practically an extension of biology, as if human beings were nothing more than competing animals (see p. 302).

Ward's system of dynamic sociology, on the other hand, is a complete synthesis of knowledge, which came *aus einem Gusse* and achieves a close harmony between science and philosophy, theory and practice, thought and feeling. Unlike the artist for art's sake or the philosopher for argument's sake, each of whom polishes his guns with more success than he captures his game, Ward surrendered himself wholly to the task of fusing the sciences into a unit. If the synthetic method were used more by other scientists in their chosen fields, scientific progress undoubtedly, would become as regular as the building of a brick wall, instead of being as desultory and sporadic as a forest fire.

In one of Ward's journeys abroad, he met Haeckel and Ostwald. The conversation turned upon the possibility of describing in a single word one's philosophy of life as well as the best method of helping mankind. Haeckel, the biologist and seeker of the riddle of the universe, answered: "Genesis." Ostwald, the naturalist and prober into nature's body followed with "Analysis." Ward, the sociologist, ended up with "Synthesis." Each answer was a flashlight photograph of the life and work of the speaker, but Ward's alone epitomized the co-operation of all natural forces, all science and all men to form a happy and united race.

### SYNERGY AND CREATIVE SYNTHESIS

Our method of investigation must be patterned upon nature's process, said Ward. Everything in nature goes through the stages of thesis, antithesis and synthesis—conflict, assimilation, decay, and re-birth. Taking the two words *synthesis* and *energy,* he coined the word *synergy* to denote the universal teamwork of natural forces. In his own words:

That there is a universal principle operating in every department of nature and at every stage of evolution, which is conservative, creative and constructive, has been evident to me for many years, but it required long meditation and extensive observation to discover its two-fold character of energy and mutuality, or the systematic and organic working together of the antithetical forces of nature (*P.S.,* p. 171).

To describe the use of synergy by the human mind, Ward borrowed the term *creative synthesis* from Wundt. It is met all through dynamic sociology to denote the all-conquering co-operation of nature's synthetic method and man's creative mind, a combination rarely used, but which brings into view infinite possibilities of progress.

### PRINCIPLE VERSUS LAW

The entire subject of method, particularly the distinction between law and principle, has become so knotted and confused by careless thinkers that only a master like Ward could untangle it. There is very little difference, he says, between law and theory as the latter term is used by scientists. The following differences, however, between law and principle are of great importance:

A law is the general expression of the natural sequence of uniform phenomena. It states the fact that certain phenomena uniformly take place in a certain way. It takes no account of cause, but only of the order of events. A principle, on the contrary, deals wholly with the cause, or, perhaps more correctly with the manner. . . . As principles deal with causes they must deal with forces. Gravitation . . . operates in a regular way which we call the law of gravitation. Its various applications are principles or utilize principles. . . .

Again, evolution is a law or takes place according to a law . . . but natural selection is a principle. . . . Creative synthesis is a principle of far-reaching application. . . .

A law must itself be explained. Principles alone explain. The law of gravitation is as yet unexplained. . . . The world is therefore never satisfied with laws. It demands principles (*P.S.*, pp. 169-170).

## THEORY

The ultimate importance of application does not detract from the constant value of theory. Goethe was ultrapractical when he wrote: "All theory is gray, dear friend, but the golden tree of life is green." For the practical person to deride theory is as childish as for the builder to fear engineering. Theory has been more misunderstood than law or principle. A theory may be either a pure guess or a vast induction, but it is always free and necessary, provided, of course, it is kept within the bounds of science and its method.

Society does not suffer from lack of theories but from ignorance or misuse of laws and principles. The illusion is strong that the scientist deals only in theories and the philosopher (metaphysician) only in eternal laws and principles. Yet almost all of the eternal truths of the philosopher belong to metaphysics or the supernatural, rather than to nature or science. It cannot be repeated too often that while the scientist indulges in theories based on facts, the philosopher without science theorizes without facts. Science, too, has its visions, but with increased and verified knowledge, the theory (call it vision or dream, if you like) sooner or later rises, phoenix-like, from the ashes of speculation to become the truth of a new day.

The reader need have no fear that sociology is studded with theories like a cake with raisins. Theories are compulsory, because they are manuals of action and necessary anticipations and explanations of phenomena, not only guesses or dogmatic assertions. Because knowledge has been amassed so rapidly that the mind cannot sort or correlate it fast enough to obtain an immediate explanation (principle), a theory must be had, like a temporary scaffold in a building under construction. That the coal we burn was once part of a forest of living trees, is a theory, but it is as real as the lump of coal itself. Evolution was not so long ago considered by all scientists as a theory. Today, it is an accepted fact. Ward, a most practical man, pays tribute to theory as follows:

It is to the theorizers . . . that the world is almost exclusively indebted for what it now possesses of organized science. It is the so-called philosophers who after all lead the scientific as they have always led the intellectual and the literary world. It may not be too much to say that science will some day admit that it owes more to Immanuel Kant for publishing his "Theorie des Himmels" than to Alexander von Humboldt for publishing his "Cosmos"; the one a brief but profound theory of the cosmos, the other, an extended enumeration of its then known phenomena (*D.S.*, I, 7).

### HISTORICAL PERSPECTIVE

The scientific method opens the door to new vistas in history as well as in nature. The concept of history as a story written by the finger of God, is abandoned, and generalization brings the historical perspective into view to cure the illusion of the near (see *P.S.*, p. 56).

True historical method demonstrates that focus is more important than spotlight, and that a correct range is as vital to the historian as it is to the hunter or the astronomer. To chart a city, one obtains a proper view only by rising high enough above it. As we turn the screw of the telescope of history, many of the blurs and paradoxes of the human panorama disappear. In the eagle's-eye view of the sociologist, distance affords not merely enchantment but a correct perspective. Too much proximity shows so many details that the scene is distorted into that of the worm's-eye view. Neither the man on horseback nor the dreamer in the library can do without historical perspective, as he surveys the historical terrain and observes the contour of the hills and valleys in their proper light and proportion (see *ibid.*, pp. 49-53).

## THE LAW OF PARSIMONY

In sociology, the scientific method is applied in the light of the law of parsimony which is the most fundamental and universal law of life. Economists express that law in the principle of the greatest gain for the least effort; mathematicians, in the axiom, that a straight line is the shortest distance between two given points. Spencer defined it as the law of least resistance, and Ward said it meant the greatest pleasure for the least pain. From any viewpoint, it is the most exact and rigorous of all natural laws, because it is so firmly rooted in the instinct of self-preservation (see *ibid.*, pp. 59-61).

Purely spiritual folk may deny that such a law exists, yet they will invariably seek an advantage by sacrificing some present gain for a future one, or by surrendering a lower for a higher satisfaction. The law of parsimony is as real as any law of physics and chemistry, and shutting our eyes to it will not change us into supermen or free us of its rule. If the law seems to be idle, there will always be found a disturbing cause which prevented its action (see *ibid.*, p. 61). So unerring is its effect that it is possible, for example, to develop a class of parasites by promiscuous charity. In fact, says Ward, parasitism in the organic as well as in the human world is due to an undue extension of the law of parsimony.

## PITFALLS OF METHOD

This chapter is already too long, yet it cannot be complete without noting the tragic results of some of the pitfalls of method. No language can adequately describe the consequences to mankind of a wrong method in science or philosophy. The two typical errors of analogy and formula alone explain more about confusion and misunderstanding in minds, both great and small, than any other errors.

An analogy is either an escape from facts, or an excuse for the lack of them, and can never replace correct data or generalization. An analogy used as a short cut from one science into another is doomed to failure. The significant aspects of human nature cannot be explained by any equations from physics or chemistry, nor can the laws of biology be grafted upon sociology. Analogy is the favorite and often the chief weapon, not only of the pseudo-scientist but also of the scientist who is looking for an easy way into or out of an unfamiliar or difficult field of knowledge.

The bogs of logic will engulf even the most brilliant mind which is closed against principles or which leans too far forward toward induction or deduction. No wonder that Spencer (via Huxley) defined a tragedy, as a collision between an induction and a runaway fact. Because Spencer's method was too deductive, he relied mainly upon analogies. Thus, he compared society to a leviathan, and made the colossal error of treating sociology as an analogue of animal biology, an error which wrecked his whole social philosophy upon the rocks of the laissez-faire theory.

The other equally dangerous pitfall in method is the formula, which is as great a delusion as the attempt of the cycle to explain everything. Because sociology cannot yet express its laws and principles in exact formulas and equations, the majority of people deny that it is a true science. Yet it is more important to have uniform laws and principles than mathematical symbols (see *Outlines,* p. 141). Because we are unable to weigh ideas on a scale or measure events with a yardstick, does not exclude them from the bounds of science or make them independent of natural law. Sociology is not an exact science like mathematics, nor can it be transformed into a physical science like mechanics, by the use of rigid symbols. But there is no doubt, says Ward, that with perfected knowledge, sociology will become capable of mathematical expression.

## METHOD AND SCIENTIFIC EXPRESSION

Science suffers from haphazard and imperfect method, but it has made tremendous strides although in uneven, zigzag stops like new land which is added by the action of tides or river currents (see *P.S.,* pp. 8-12). Often the arena of science resembles a skyscraper in the course of construction. Everything is chaotic; everybody is interfering with and falling over everybody else. Yet bit by bit, the preconceived scientific plan, and the precise and orderly method of operation bring order out of chaos. Of course, much time and energy would be saved if the intellect were applied to the advancement of science, instead of leaving it to nature's creeping hit-and-miss method. Science has been saved from becoming another Tower of Babel only because nothing is deemed established until it has passed through the ordeal of observation and experiment, and stood the test of criticism from every point of view.

No doubt the reader is eager to leave pure theory for concrete application, and explore the more intriguing realm of the social domain. Perhaps he has not yet discerned that science and method are as important as we have described them. But as he proceeds further into the land of sociology, he is bound to find that such abstract matters are so vital because ignorance, poverty, social despair, and happiness matter so much. Theory will cease to be abstract soon enough when confronted with society and its problems. The only means of comprehending the nature and finding the solution of those problems, the only paths to wisdom and truth, are those of science and the scientific method.

# BOOK III. THE BIOLOGIST

*"Three cosmic epochs belong to the history of life on the globe. The first was the origin of life itself. The second was the origin of soul or will in nature, that we popularly call feeling. The third was the origin of thought or pure intellect."*
—Ward

# CHAPTER VII

# THE NATURE OF MATTER

---

*"In matter is the promise and potency of all life."*—Tyndall

*"No line of demarcation can be drawn between the properties of matter and physical forces. . . . Matter is causality. Matter is power. . . . Matter is dynamic, and every time that man has touched it with the wand of reason, it has responded by satisfying a want."*

*"Matter is for man endowed with intelligence and inspired by science, a veritable lamp of Aladdin, which we need but rub, and as if by magic, all things take on the forms of utility and cast themselves at his feet."*—Ward

---

W<small>E ARE PAST</small> the approaches and have the key to the temple of sociology. But our guide is not ready to open its door until the background of the temple in the history of the earth and the universe beyond it, is examined. The task may be hard, but the reward of a synthetic grasp of nature, man and society, and their relationships, will be greater still. And though we become for the moment cosmic philosophers, the goal always remains society, and its planned control.

## THE SEARCH FOR ORIGINS

Before Ward approaches the social problem and records the glories of the mind as reflected in human achievement, he begins his system with matter, working upward to life and feeling, then through man and society. The schedule which he lays out for us is: back to sources; forward to possibilities; in other words, from cosmic to physical evolution; thence, in turn, to biologic, psychologic, and finally social evolution.

The reader may well ask: why begin with such a prosaic thing as matter when spiritual aims and thrilling events of the time beckon for attention? The answer repeated in many forms to that ever recurring question is that the desire for fundamentals is the bone and marrow of all human curiosity, from daydreams to scientific research. If one's horizon is not limited by fleshpots, or befogged by superstition, the inquiry into the nature of matter will not be a detour from the paths of science, or a futile hunt for the unknowable First Cause, as Comte believed. On the contrary, it is a necessary preparation, according to Ward, for the study of society. While the origin of origins will always remain an insoluble problem, science in its investigation of origins and foundations, continually solves questions which were once universally believed to be insoluble.

## THE COSMIC PLAN

Ward's cosmic philosophy is one of the most notable of genetic studies. Its rounded, monistic view of things dovetails into a clear-cut concept of man's place in the universe. He begins with the following postulate, that the cosmos consists of three aggregations of matter and the accompanying force of energy (*D.S.*, Chapters III-VII):

1. *Primary aggregation* (inorganic), the rough construction work and scaffolding. Its energy is chemical, and is seen in astronomy, physics, chemistry, and geology.

2. *Secondary aggregation* (organic), wherein life, feeling and mind (man) are evolved. Its energy is vital, and rises to biology, anthropology, and psychology.

3. *Tertiary aggregation* (social), wherein human association first appears and develops social structures and institutions. Its energy is social.

## THE WORKSHOP OF NATURE

Nature took the aggregations of matter (there was nothing else for her to work on) and by the process of synergy, manufactured an infinite variety of forms from relatively few elements. Ward charts the products and attributes of her labors as follows (*Glimpses*, V, 161; *Outlines*, p. 239; *P.S.*, p. 94):

SYNTHETIC CREATIONS OF NATURE

| PRODUCTS | DIFFERENTIAL ATTRIBUTES | | | |
| --- | --- | --- | --- | --- |
| | PROPERTIES | ACTIVITIES | PHENOMENA | CAUSES |
| Society | Achievement | | Social | |
| Man | Intellect | | Psychic | Telic |
| Animals | Feeling | Molar | | Conative |
| Plants | Life | | Vital | |
| Protoplasm | Motility | | | |
| Organic Compounds | | | | |
| Inorganic Compounds | Chemism | Molecular | | Efficient |
| Chemical Elements | | | Physical | |
| Universal Ether | Vibration | Radiant | | |

The unity of the cosmos and the continuity of the sciences now become clearer than ever. Each of nature's achievements results in a new creation and a fresh phase of evolution. At the bottom is the diffused ether or cosmic dust which is the seed of natural reproduction and the least powerful but most fruitful of nature's materials. Climbing up the ladder of evolution, we meet the chemical elements which are the bricks of the universe. They are more than inert blocks, however, and quickened by nature's forces, they grow in complexity until from them is developed protoplasm, "the physical basis of life" (*Outlines*, p. 239). Chemical organization can go no further than protoplasm, and evolution now takes a new turn when its activities, hitherto molecular and imperceptible to the senses, become molar and perceptible. The attributes of feeling and self-awareness are then through innumerable eons developed and expanded. Society, the latest cosmic product, evolves the novel capacity of achievement. Beyond the intelligent movements of social organization into the illimitable future, we need not peer (see *P.S.*, p. 90).

## A LAW HIGHER THAN EVOLUTION

By the use of the scientific method, as the number of known facts is increased, the number of fundamental concepts are reduced, until the supreme law of nature, the law of aggregation or organization, is reached. Our reconstruction, with Ward, of the cosmic structure (imitating nature's process of organization), is done by putting together the various aggregations of matter, commencing with the star dust and ending with the organization of society, and observing the effects of the universal energy upon the material used.

The law of organization is the one final law which was so eagerly sought by the philosophers of all time. Spencer thought it was the law of evolution which covered the physical universe as well as that of life, man and society. But Ward who was free from Spencer's fallacy that the social process was automatic, like natural development, saw in evolution only one of the manifestations of the law of organization.

## MATTER, THE ONLY REALITY

To the first question "What is the universe?" Ward offered the simple generalization that matter is the sole or comprehensive reality (see *D.S.*, I, 221). The mind is incapable of conceiving anything but

matter as having an independent existence, and no one can imagine
energy apart from matter, any more than he can see an accident in
a pure vacuum.

Ward's idea stems from Greek science. But while Aristotle's common sense at first solved the problem of matter and energy by concluding that nothing can exist without matter, he then called out the
metaphysical ghost to destroy the solution, with an aside: "Matter
itself has no existence." Only a metaphysician can handle matter
which has no substance or actuality, something so abstract according
to Aristotle that it must forever remain a possibility unrealized. God
alone is, therefore, real and actual, and the universe merely a divine
idea. To save the mind from such a dogma, the Greeks advanced
the atomic theory of matter. Call it a guess, if you like, says Ward,
but the fact remains that no one after them has advanced a better
theory.

Returning to Ward's survey of cosmic organization, or nature's
building process upon the largest possible scale, it is evident that the
masonry consists of grand aggregations of matter, not of ideas or
forces. The material is one, but it has many attributes, relations and
properties, and takes on countless forms. The urge of nature, manifested in every one of her laws, is also one, viz., to create, develop,
organize. Our comparatively insignificant little world came to its
present state through universal chemism, by the process of synergy,
the ceaseless compounding and recompounding of lower and simpler
material into higher and more complex material. The process and
its products become infinitely complicated, but the picture which remains of the birth of the cosmos, is that of matter eternally evolving
and organizing, and manifesting itself through energy. Says Ward:

The distinction between materials and forces disappears entirely
upon analysis. It is no longer metaphysical to say that we know nothing of matter except through its properties. It is only its reactions
that affect man's senses, only its properties that are utilized. But no
line of demarcation can be drawn between the properties of matter
and physical forces. . . . Matter is causality. Matter is power. . . .
Matter is dynamic and every time that man has touched it with
the wand of reason, it has responded by satisfying a want. That is
the true philosophical basis of that "historical materialism" of which
we hear so much in these days (P.S., pp. 19, 20).

## FORCE, A RELATION OF MATTER

Force or energy, like size, taste, or color is a relation or attribute of matter, and constantly changes along with it (see *D.S.*, I, 232). Both are as inseparable, even in the imagination, as sugar and its taste. Through either, one inevitably arrives at the other.

To the question what is matter or energy, there can be no answer, any more than to the puzzle of who made God. "Matter is what it seems to be," says Ward. Could anything outside the search for a First Cause be more "unphilosophical" and yet true? It is as unnecessary as it is impossible to seek what came before matter or to look for any further definition because matter is the final definition of everything. One might as well ask, "What did the alphabet consist of before it acquired any of its letters?"

## PRIMEVAL MATTER

In the beginning, infinite space was filled with matter in a homogeneous state, called star dust, cosmic dust or ether.[1] Einstein holds that matter is nothing but space held together by particles which also consist of only space. Ward's theory does not sound so bizarre. He sees energy seizing upon matter and expressing itself in two kinds of motion: one, the gravitant or pulling force; the other, the radiant or pushing force. Through synergy, the clash and the balance of forces, the primeval matter of infinite space was manufactured into our universe (see *ibid.*, pp. 232-253).

## THE CHEMICAL ELEMENTS

We pass with our guide through the earliest stages of evolution to view the development of the more complex forms of matter, viz., the chemical elements, the first permanent products of nature's crucible. Seventy-two of them were known when Ward published *Dynamic*

---

[1] Many have rejected the ether theory of space, but Ward's acceptance of it has lately been supported by the world-wide survey of cosmic radiation conducted by the Carnegie Institute of Washington under the direction of Dr. Arthur H. Compton, Nobel prize winner. He demonstrates that radiation is composed not of protons of "immaterial" light waves, but of electrically charged particles of matter coming from the farthest reaches of the cosmos. Further support of the ether theory is found in the 1933 report of the Smithsonian Institute, in which Dr. Charles G. Abbott, its secretary, states that space has been found within recent years to be pervaded with a cosmic gas which is probably made up of atoms of all the elements. Spectroscopical investigations have shown that in addition to the gas there is throughout space a tenuous cosmic dust consisting of minute material particles.

*Sociology* in 1883, and their number has now (1938) increased to ninety-three. They are molecules composed of similar atoms, but when the atoms are different, the molecules are called chemical compounds (see *ibid.,* pp. 255-299).

Atoms are composed chiefly of hydrogen and helium. Nature has been mixing the elements for so long that no further changes in the ingredients or their interaction is possible. One thing is certain, matter was finally formed on this planet according to nature's chemical and physical laws. Out of the clouds of cosmic gases were born the molecules composing our solar system. It is most probable that the chemical elements which required tremendous temperatures to change them into gases and liquids were actually evolved during the formation of the sun and the planets, out of material already existing in other forms or states of aggregation. Such is the nebular hypothesis of Kant and Laplace.

No life and little matter were possible in the solar furnace (a body 1,400,000 times as large as the earth), whose heat and light still sear and blind at a distance of a hundred million miles. In the planets, more favorable conditions prevailed. Carbon and hydrogen fused with oxygen to make a cloak of steam which obscured the sun's light. Titanic hurricanes shook the embryonic earth to its marrow, and deluges of scalding acid rains poured down to form the oceans. When the gaseous envelope cooled, condensed, and contracted, the burning elements became liquid, then molten, and finally formed the solid crust of the earth. The heavier materials sank within the waters; the lighter ones congealed upon the surface, and in time, an atmosphere of free oxygen, nitrogen, carbon dioxide and watery vapor surrounded the globe. Our infant earth was born.

The earth was composed of inorganic matter, and all its substances (molar aggregates) were formed out of chemical elements (molecular aggregates) by a simple multiplication or bubble-blowing process. Nature's synthetic method of creation which was in full swing, will be observed on higher and higher planes, as we follow evolution from the inorganic to the organic, then into the vital, and finally into the psychic and social spheres (see *ibid.,* p. 284).

Science has traveled far since Ward's *Dynamic Sociology,* but the cosmic truths in its pages still loom large and deep. New knowledge failed to lure him into metaphysical abstractions or cause him to abandon natural law and the scientific method, as it has done to many scientists and philosophers with more tender and less practical minds. He saw in the course of evolution a series of cosmic crises which marked off the turning points in the parade of the natural forces. The first occurred when inorganic matter was produced. Another and still greater crisis came with the appearance of life, when evolution turned a corner and marched forward into the realm of the organic and the vital.

# CHAPTER VIII

# THE ORIGIN OF LIFE

---

*"There can be no mind where there is no brain or nerve ganglia, no life where there is no animal, plant, protist or protoplasm."*—Ward

---

How did life originate in a world without life? What is the vital spark? Science alone offers a natural solution of those problems, while speculation continues to roam the skies for the miracle which infused a living breath into inert matter.

LIFE, "THE GREAT MYSTERY," A PROPERTY OF MATTER

Somehow, any discussion of the nature of life elicits a jargon about soul, *élan vital,* and the Unknowable. Even metaphysicians will admit the natural origin of the chemical elements, but will stubbornly deny the same origin to living matter. Ward depicts life as an evolution which can be traced backward and forward, equally with matter. If evolution is true, life had to come.

Whether life is "the sum of the functions by which death is resisted" (Bichat) or something that "presupposes an organism and a medium; the organic medium being connected with the function" (Comte), Ward regards biology, the study of life, as the preamble to any investigation of man or mind. Life is the torch lit by the universal energy; the flame of the candle, not the wax. Like all energy, it burns eagerly with one indestructible purpose, to carry on. Essentially, it is a complication of the energy of various refined and highly wrought chemical compounds, rather than an insoluble mystery to be mentioned only with bated breath.

Ward's position is that life is not an independent entity but a chemical and physical force related to matter (see *ibid.,* pp. 318-320). It is a more complete and realistic concept than Spencer's definition of life as "the continuous adjustment of internal relations to external relations," which omits the fundamental fact that life can be known only as an attribute of and in association with matter. There is no real line of demarcation between the inorganic and the organic. All matter teems with potential energy, and the only observable differences between living matter and dead matter are phenomenal, not essential. No one knows just when and where life originated on this globe, but there is no doubt that before it appeared, the earth was latent with it in every pulsation of energy. Another thing is certain, life was not created suddenly, but was evolved in the course of innumerable ages, through imperceptible changes in the primordial elements, as slowly as the dawn comes after the dead of night.

## THE SECOND COSMIC CRISIS

After the development of inorganic matter, when the storm and stress of cosmic labor had calmed down, the clouds broke and the sun shone upon the morning of creation, the flux of water, land, and air laid the pathway for the entry of the vital element. The cosmic mixture was prepared in its proper consistency; the time had come for matter to share its throne with energy. Then it was that life slowly dawned in tiny splendors to initiate the second cosmic crisis.

Superficially, the changes in evolution seem to come abruptly because they are so enormous that they look discontinuous. Yet they are necessary steps in a continuous process. To recapitulate, in Ward's words:

Three such cosmic epochs belong to the history of life on the globe. The first was the origin of life itself. The second was the origin of soul or will in nature. The third was the origin of thought or pure intellect. While I do not claim that any of the factors producing these epochs came suddenly into existence, or that any definite lines exist separating life from soul or soul from intellect, theoretically speaking, the general fact remains that they are practically distinct principles, having diverse effects, originating at widely different periods in the earth's history, and succeeding one another in the order named (*Glimpses*, IV, 218).

## PROTOPLASM

When nature worked upon the secondary aggregation of matter, it produced life through protoplasm, cells, nerves, tissues, and organs, all accompanied by a parallel development of feeling (see *D.S.*, I, 300-357). For organized forms, a higher and vastly more complex substance than the chemical elements was required, with molecules of greater size, less stability and more active properties. That demand was filled by protoplasm. Thenceforth, the principle was "no proto-plasm, no life."

Protoplasm is not a mathematical symbol, but a substance (rather a synthesis of substances) composed of elements abundantly found in nature. Its chief elements are carbon, oxygen, hydrogen, sulphur, phosphorus, sodium, potassium, chlorine, calcium, magnesium, and iron. When its chemical formula will be discovered (and that is not altogether impossible), life may be artificially manufactured. Mean-while, it is known that wherever there is life, the atoms of carbon are present. Evidently, nature, after an infinite number of hits and misses, chose carbon as the best material for the vital framework, to withstand the stress and strain of the environment (see *P.S.,* p. 116; *D.S.,* I, 335-355).

Haeckel found protoplasm in the depths of the warm Italian seas and named it plasson, while he called the microscopic organism com-posed of that elemental substance the moner. It is not an animal, but it is alive and has sensation. It is without any organs, yet it repro-duces; without any nerves, yet reacts to stimuli. It even foreshadows our social system, because it feeds upon its own kind. Says Ward: "The moner is Hero's engine; the vertebrate is the modern locomotive. The power that impels is the same in both. The observed advance is not in the force, but in the organization" (*ibid.,* p. 324).

## THE EVOLUTION OF PROTOPLASM

Protoplasm is the product of chemical organization, on the one hand, and the cause of vital organization on the other. Its power of irritation or movement (motility) evolves into bathmism, the universal growth force (see *P.S.,* pp. 118-119). With the help of protoplasm, na-ture's organizing process took on increased speed and commenced to produce more complex cell forms. A part formed a nucleus; then the clusters became new units of the second order, fit for more sub-stantial structures. Chemical organization did not stop there, but went on into the gluelike form of germs or bacteria. Much later, came the development of the lower units into various organs, vessels and strengthening timbers, all produced by the co-operative method which man has been too stupid to adopt. Integration and the concerted action of cells now grown into tissues and organs, went on apace. As the size and complexity of organs increased, means became necessary for carrying on the more complicated functions required for their existence. The further demand was supplied by feeling, out of which were evolved nerves, the brain, and finally the intellect.

No other force than life has been found to exist in any organism unless our imagination has put it there. Sensation in plants, life in animals, mind in man, and social consciousness in society, are essentially manifestations of the same natural energy. The life force is one, but it has many garments. In its infancy, it was simple irritability. Later, by the flow of sap and the circulation of blood, through respiration, nerves, ganglia and the brain, it became ever more complex, until all of nature's inventions, all of her organizing powers were concentrated and synthesized in her greatest production, the human intellect.

Life is simple, man is complex. He is protoplasm raised to the nth degree into a vital organism with a complicated machinery and many functions to satisfy many needs. Yet he is only another of nature's synthetic products, a being essentially rooted in matter, feeling, and mind. His biography begins where the history of natural evolution tapers off. The story of his lineage with the cosmos is the key to the comprehension of his place in the universe, and of the powers and possibilities of his mind to plan and to control his organized life.

# BOOK IV. THE PSYCHOLOGIST

*"The true place which mind fills in the scheme of nature is the
most important truth to be learned in the study of philosophy."*

*"Mind has two sides . . . feelings and intellect. The tendency
in all ages has been to ignore the former . . . or to sublimate
it into an intangible something called the will which no two
philosophers could agree in defining, and no one succeeded in
comprehending; while at the same time, the glories of the
intellect have been unduly extolled, and the impression created
that mind consists solely of intellect and will."*—Ward

*"Man is but a reed, and the weakest in the world, yet a think-
ing reed."*—Blaise Pascal

*"On earth there's nothing great but man; in man there's noth-
ing great but mind."*—Sir William Hamilton

# Chapter IX

# THE ORIGIN OF FEELING

---

*"Feeling came into existence as a means to the performance of function—feeling is of biologic origin."*

*"The phenomena of feeling constitute the true basis of all that part of philosophy which at all involves the interest of man. They are, in short, the foundation stones of the social science. What function is to biology, feeling is to sociology."*—Ward

*"Great thoughts come from the heart."*—Vauvenargues

---

WHEN PROTOPLASM was born, it went out to see the world and immediately showed signs of irritation. Matter was fortunate in having developed the danger signal of irritability, for without it, the jelly-like molecules of protoplasm would have been overcome by everything with which they came in contact. While man with his thinking brain is so sensitive to change that he makes martyrs of those who irritate him with new ideas, nature without any intelligence was far kinder when it evolved the new force, feeling, to preserve the existence of protoplasm.

## IRRITABILITY

Although the missing link between inorganic matter (chemism) and protoplasm (life) has not directly been discovered (such a link must have existed, because evolution is an unbroken chain), there is no such gap between life and feeling. During the prolonged period before mind was evolved, feeling was the only psychic energy in the world. Its simplest form arose from vitality, and in a series of short steps, passed through motility to sensation (see *P.S.,* p. 101).

In the case of plants, nature made sure of their survival by firm attachment to the soil, strong tissues protected by bark, and an easy method of nourishment. But what was to save the fragile, plastic protoplasm? Nature hit upon feeling to meet the new crisis. The survival of the plastic meant the survival of the fittest. Feeling was the gearing which saved the organism by solving its pressing problems of safety and nourishment (see *ibid.,* p. 120).

## FEELING, AN ATTRIBUTE OF MATTER

Just as life is the result of chemical reactions in the molecules of protoplasm, so feeling is merely another attribute of matter. According to Ward:

Feeling came into existence as a means to the performance of function, not through any foresight of the necessity for the action. Not even the simplest nutritive acts are known to be such, much less acts which conduce to higher development. The relation of feeling to function as means to end, was brought about through adaptation, and there is a sort of pre-established harmony between them. Feeling was created as an inducement to functional activity not otherwise obtainable. The fact that it furnishes such an inducement, alone explains its creation. If a means existed, it was certain to be adopted, since all means were tried.

Thus is explained the origin of feeling, and, as feeling is the initial step in the creation of mind, it also explains the origin of mind. Since, too, function is the biologic end, feeling is of biologic origin (*P.S.,* p. 126).

### FEELING, A NEGLECTED FACTOR

In examining the roots of feeling, Ward became a pioneer in the much neglected field of social psychology. Unlike the public announcements of Sumner (the disciple of Spencer's biological social science), that he had no use for psychology and preferred that his students know nothing about it, Ward forcefully decried the submergence of feeling and the exaggerated attention given to the intellectual faculty. After tracing the currents of feeling from protoplasm into the trunk lines of emotion or desire which constitute the social forces, he pointed out the fallacy that mind connotes only intellect, and feeling only something physical and biological, and therefore, low or sensual (see *D.S.,* II, 123; *P.S.,* p. 476). On the contrary, mind includes both the senses and the intellect, and therefore feeling is entitled to its proper position in nature's synthetic productions.

When he emphasized the emotional factor, he was only recognizing that man is essentially an emotional animal and not a rational one, an animal whose title to intelligence depends upon the extent to which he subordinates feeling to reason. Ward's conclusion is simple and far-reaching, for it lays the foundation for the new science of social psychology, and proves that the inquiry into origins is of vast importance to sociology:

The phenomena of feeling constitute the true basis of all that part of philosophy which at all involves the interest of man. They are, in short, the foundation stones of the social science (*D.S.,* II, 123).

When Ward followed feeling from its origin in matter up to the heights of spiritual emotion, it became clear what a tremendous universal force emotion is, and how much it can be controlled by intelligence and reason. Just as feeling undoubtedly is the motor which runs the human freight, so there is even less doubt that the intellect can direct its course. That is why Ward rests sociology squarely upon psychology, and psychology upon biology, contrary to the synthetic philosophy of Spencer who based his sociology directly upon biology and retained in his social philosophy the purely animal features of humanity. Later social psychologists may have passed Ward, but he was one of the foremost trail blazers in the primitive land of the study of human emotion.

CHAPTER X

# THE ORIGIN OF MIND

---

*"Mind dates from the dawn of the sentient property."*—Ward

*"In the evolution of the human mind, the instinct of cosmic interrogation follows hard upon the instinct of self-preservation."*—J. W. Powell

*"Die Vernunft ist weiblicher Natur: sie kann nur geben, nachdem sie empfangen hat."*
—Schopenhauer

---

THE CHAIN of evolution is our handrail, as we climb from matter to life, from life to feeling, and from feeling to mind. The path of natural development is plainly from the inert and the unseen to the dynamic and the tangible; from the instinctive and the mechanical to the intelligent and the psychic. Picking the world apart like the petals of a flower as we unfold the overlapping courses of evolution, brings us at last to thought, which is the aroma of matter. It has been truly said that nature's greatest achievement is man, and in him there is nothing great but mind.

## MIND, NOT A MIRACLE

If the metaphysicians bow before the phenomenon of life, they are prone before the "mystery" of mind. Yet the mind force is no more of a mystery to the scientist, than the falling of a pebble or the budding of a flower. What is more miraculous is the minimum of real thinking about the mind. Even a scientist like Huxley would not admit that it is a natural phenomenon, and clung to the metaphysical flotsam which he was supposed to have forever abandoned (see *P.S.,* p. 123). The biologists too, conceding that every new structure in nature is a device for the expansion and elevation of matter, seem to be paralyzed at the idea of recognizing mind as a natural creation. They are outdone only by the psychologists, who, well aware that every step in organic evolution is a link in the chain of universal cause and effect, collapse when confronted by the phenomenon of mind. They simply regard it as something independent of the past, as if it had sprung "like Minerva, full fledged from the brain of Jove" (see *Ps. F.,* p. 141).

To avoid such errors, Ward adhered to science and its methods whether he was sowing in the fields of biology and psychology or reaping in sociology. In his earlier years when he was more of a crude materialistic monist, he made his sociology a part of a universal system of philosophy. Though he never admitted that life and mind were independent in the slightest degree of the lower strata of organization, in his later life he emphasized more and more the role of intelligent activity in social evolution.

Mind is an attribute or property of matter, says Ward in his *Dynamic Sociology,* and there is no cause for resigning the study of mind unless one resigns along with it all knowledge with the doleful cry, "We cannot know; we never shall know." If thinking is a natural process, like walking or writing, we can investigate and treat it scientifically, but if mind is outside the pale of science, then thinking is a supernatural process, and all we can do is to worship it in the darkened temples of some faith.

## HOW MIND AROSE

Some pessimists may find comfort in the thought that sensation was one of nature's gross errors. Others may see a worse *faux pas* in the creation of mind to save the organism from destruction when feeling ran amok. Undoubtedly, nature's productions were not at an end when feeling was evolved as an incentive to life and an assurance of safety. For soon feeling (of course, pleasurable and alluring) took the reins of control from life and made itself a tyrannic master. Instead of a means, it became an end in itself, and threatened to wreck everything in its path.

Nature had never intended the organism to live on merely for the pleasure of living. The original purpose (function) of mind was not merely to curb feeling but to lead the organism into safe paths. Thus was intelligence evolved from elemental feeling to fill an emergency. The lowest organisms had no need of any intelligence to lead them safely through life. Sensation was a sufficient protection, but while it gave them a knowledge of the quality of the objects with which they collided, they could not know anything of their nature or properties. This knowledge which furnished them with the tremendous advantage of being able to travel about in perfect safety, was supplied by the newcomer, the intellect. In time, it became even greater than the sentient force, and was able to direct feeling. Sensation alone was insufficient to assure survival. Through natural selection, those organisms which had the power of distinguishing friend from foe, or safety from danger (the very essence of mind is the power of discrimination) lived on; the others perished (see *P.S.*, p. 477).

If Spencer is correct in saying that repetition and still more repitition is the only way to impart a new idea, we may repeat that the intellect came unwanted. Its arrival initiated the universal struggle with feeling, the battle of function against reason, which has taken on such varied forms as the warfare between nature and nurture, heredity and environment, and the individual and the race. But nature always balances her forces. The despotic tendencies of feeling, therefore, initiated that remarkable process which Ward called the elimination of the wayward; Darwin, natural selection; and Spencer, the survival of the fittest (see *ibid.*, pp. 126-133). In order to safeguard its achievements, nature put checkreins upon the runaway steed of feeling, viz., instinct in the subrational world, and intellect in man.

There are still humble, marine organisms which have lived for countless ages in just groping about. All that they have is primitive intuition or awareness, which is the deepest root of mind, and back of that, of feeling. That elemental tingling (objective feeling) is primal irritability grown up. Intuitive and egotistic, it is the forerunner of intellect, and insures the safety of the organism by distinguishing cause from effect, and furnishes the capacity to apply knowledge and experience. Those powers are the essential qualities of mind.

## INSTINCT

In the early history of organic life, feeling alone dictated survival or death. Pleasurable feelings induced the performance of acts which promoted life, while pain acted as a warning against injury and destruction. Instinct was sensation standing guard at the portals of life. As the cognitive directing force increased in power, instinct weakened. Whatever interest the organism had in living, was found in instinct, the intensive, positive sensation concerned only with pain and pleasure, and the first line in nature's defense against extinction. Out of this selfish property arose the second line of defense, viz., the indifferent and negative sensations from which true intellect was evolved.

The acts of nutrition and reproduction arising from the imperative urge of self-preservation, ripened first into instincts, then into habits, and untold ages later, acting in concert with other desires in man's world, became the social forces (see *P.S.,* p. 137). In animal life, the same instinct of self-preservation seeking its ends, developed the brain, brought speech and erect posture, and changed the brute into the human being. Nevertheless, he took along with him all his animal instincts (see *D.S.,* I, 428-429).

Before the state of rationality was reached all the other faculties were well developed. The phenomena of nature appealed to primitive man as strongly as they appeal to civilized man. But like the animal, he considered nature solely in relation to his wants and other satisfactions. His chief business was his self-preservation, and the ruling motive was fear; therefore, he feared nature (see *App. S.,* p. 50).

The social and moral instincts which developed out of primeval animal instinct are closely allied, often identical. They are founded upon three primary elements: affection, sympathy, and reason (see *D.S.,* I, 395).

## THE DEVELOPMENT OF MIND

The development of the mind force can be traced step by step into the axiom "no protoplasm, no nerves; no nerves, no mind." Before there were eyes and ears, there were sensitive areas which became nerves. The organism developed into an active machine, with sensory nerves to furnish knowledge of the external world, and motor nerves to act as assistants. Last of all, came the evolution of the brain into a powerhouse or central storage battery to control the entire system and store up energy.

With the birth of the intellect, embryonic as it was, sensation did not grow weaker, but branched out into two main trunk lines, intensive or positive feeling, and indifferent or negative feeling. These diverged and flourished in inverse proportion to each other. The first is covered by subjective psychology, and implies sensation, painful and pleasant. The second, which is either instinctive or rational, and which developed into the intellect proper, is treated in objective psychology.

## FEELING AND INTELLECT, THE TWO
## DEPARTMENTS OF MIND

In tracing the origin of mind from primordial irritability, classical psychology is of little help, for it regards almost everything from the standpoint of intellect, as if all organisms were complex and had fully developed minds. Strange to say, all the psychologists who believe that the mind has no distinct departments, including the behaviorists who have lost sight of the mind altogether, have confined their studies to feeling. To them man is a machine; every conscious act is a form of feeling, and in general, he is a mechanism of nerves and muscles which react only to physical stimuli. Long before the subject of behaviorism became a best seller in America, Ward followed the mind into its two departments, feeling and intellect, and disproved the pompous assertions that both emotion and intelligence are illusions, or at best, conditioned reflexes of the striped muscles of the stomach and larynx (see *Outlines,* p. 104).

Feeling is controlled by that part of the brain and nervous system called the subjective or affective faculty which begins with sensation and ends with sentiment. The intellect is governed exclusively by the objective or intellectual faculty, which begins with perception and ends with reason (see *Ps. F.,* pp. 2-3; *D.S.,* II, 123). Feeling is pain and pleasure; the appetites and the passions; all the propensities of man summed up in the word desire. It is the psychic force which reacts both on the organism and the environment; the great motor force, the dynamic agent in life. Intellect, reason, what is popularly called mind, is the purely directive force.

Feeling and intellect, like all other natural forces, always end in synthesis and interaction. They form a span over life, with sensation at one end and reason at the other. Between the two are reflex action, tropism and instinctive behavior. As man crosses the bridge toward reason, he develops powers of perception, judgment, memory, and imagination until he acquires the highest of all mental functions, philosophic reasoning.

### A SUMMARY OF THE EVOLUTION OF MIND

Ward does not argue; he informs and teaches. Although he wrote possibly a century ahead of his time, the world is day by day catching up to his thought. The reader who is inclined to reject Ward's theory of mind as a property of matter, should reserve his judgment until he has digested "The Status of the Mind Problem" (*Glimpses,* V, 70), one of the deepest and most comprehensive analyses and summaries of the evolution of mind in the entire literature of psychology. Some day, it may be recognized as a work of genius. Space forbids its inclusion here, but that should whet the reader's appetite all the more to acquire one of the richest of all intellectual and scientific treasures.[1]

We have been down to the foundations of the temple of sociology, seen the origin, and sensed the reality of matter and its properties, viz., life, feeling, and mind. In mind, nature has concentrated and synthesized all the forces of the universe. What has man done with that gigantic and priceless gift? This journey into his social estate will furnish the answer.

Meanwhile, we have mentioned often enough the lord of the earth, without stopping to observe or study him. What of man, and his social organization? Whence did they come? This is the cue for the next chapter.

---

[1] The American press was agog with the results of laboratory researches made by Dr. George W. Crile, who found (as Ward concluded long ago) that the brain is a dynamo which generates thought instead of electricity; that an idea is an electric current caused by the contact of the positive and negative electric charges in the brain cells (see *New York Times,* April 21, 1933).

# BOOK V. THE ANTHROPOLOGIST

*"The whole succession of men during the course of so many centuries should be considered as one Man, ever living and constantly learning."*—Blaise Pascal

> *"Many the forms of life,*
> *Wondrous and strange to see,*
> *But naught than man appears*
> *More wondrous and more strange."*—Sophocles

*"Glory to Man in the highest! for Man is the master of things."*
—Algernon Charles Swinburne

*"What a piece of work is a man! How noble in reason! how infinite in faculty! in form and moving, how express and admirable! in action, how like an angel! in apprehension, how like a god! the beauty of the world! the paragon of animals."*
—Shakespeare

# CHAPTER XI

# THE ORIGIN OF MAN

---

*"The heterogeneous condition of the human race is easily accounted for and fully explained on the simple assumption of the animal origin of man, which is now accepted by the great majority of both biologists and anthropologists."*—Ward

---

SINCE SOCIETY is composed of individuals, the origin of man is in a sense, the origin of society. But while society came through the wars of races or groups, man's origin is squarely in the animal world.

### THE ORIGIN OF MAN

The origin of man is no longer a mystery but is plainly written in nature's records. Science, unsentimentally, assigns him his true place in the sun, not as a fallen angel or as an overgrown ape, but as the highest of all animals, *homo sapiens.* The romantic and theological notions about man's origin were forever shattered by Darwinism (see *D.S.,* I, Chapter I). There is no longer the slightest doubt that the origin of all types of life, however widely separated, is a common and united one. The close affinity of all organisms, vegetable, animal, and human, among themselves and to one another, is indisputable proof of their unity and common origin. Whatever has been the history of one, has been the history of all (see *ibid.,* p. 413).

Supported by an indisputable mass of convincing evidence, science has established that man belongs to the animal family of the primates. He is related to the existing manlike apes, the gibbon, orangutan, chimpanzee and gorilla, but is not directly descended from any of them. Whether or not his lineage has been proved with scientific certainty, or whether the missing link with our animal cousins has been found or may never be literally dug up, research is continually strengthening the conclusion that our direct kinship with the animal world and through it, to the rest of the cosmos, is a fact and no longer a theory. Whatever opposition may still exist is simply due to lack of common knowledge.

## THREE PROBLEMS CONNECTED WITH MAN'S ORIGIN

On the threshold of man's emergence, Ward confronts us with the problems: Did the human race originate in one region at one time, or in several places at different times? In what part of the globe did it first appear? How old is man? (See *D.S.*, I, 441-447.)

Ward characterized all questions about "the first pair" as puerile, for in nature there is no first or last. There was no particular moment when the brute became human, any more than there was a day when some one became the first Englishman. What happened in biological as well as in social evolution was a gradual change by means of slight variations extending over long stretches of time. The evolutionary process everywhere was like the coming of dawn. Special creation would have been like turning on an electric light. Says Ward:

> Long before there was any record of tradition, the human race had spread over the entire European continent, Africa and Australia, and all the neighboring archipelagoes and islands. It has pushed northward into Kamchatka, crossed Bering Straits into Alaska, swarmed southward and occupied the whole of North America, streamed along the Cordilleras over the Isthmus of Darien and filled South America. We have scarcely any adequate idea of the successive dates of this winning of the world. Long before history dawned, man was everywhere. As Voltaire said of America, we should be no more surprised to find men there, than to find flies (*P.S.*, p. 198).

All the carefully gathered evidence points to a united human family coming from a single primordial stock. The fantastic theory of the origin of races from different types of ancestral apes (the Aryan from the chimpanzee; the Mongolian from the orangutan, and the Negro from the gorilla) may sound terribly "scientific," but it belongs to the lunatic fringe of science. Yet Gumplowicz, the famous Austrian sociologist (*Der Rassenkampf,* 1883), maintained that there were metaphorically many gardens of Eden, and that man sprang simultaneously from many hordes, in many places. The reason that races differ so much, he argued, is that they have been evolved from a large number of originally dissimilar stocks. Otherwise, it would mean that evolution had at first split humanity into a number of discordant groups, and then set about to reunite them into a single family (see *The Letters of Ludwig Gumplowicz to Lester*

*F. Ward,* ed. Bernhard J. Stern, C. L. Hirschfeld Verlag, Leipzig, 1933).

It was not until Ward visited Gumplowicz in 1903 that the latter acknowledged that Ward had changed his views on the historical reality of polygenesis (see *Die Zeit,* Vienna, IX, 86-89, August 20, 1904). What the Austrian savant had feared, Ward argued, is exactly what happened. Nature's method is that of trial and error, and she could not have hit more than once upon the same complicated manner of evolving man. Natural forces swing back and forth like a pendulum. If evolution had traveled in a straight line, life would have been extinguished long ago. In the beginning mankind was diffused; then came the reverse process of fusion. The long era of strife and wandering seems now to be drawing to a close, and the period of integration and synthesis cannot be far distant. In his own language:

The human race began as an undifferentiated group, the horde, containing all the elements of the most developed society. At length, a process of integration began, according to the principle by which all organization takes place, viz., synergy. We have the antagonistic forces at work here as everywhere, and we shall see that the entire process is identical with that which formed star systems, chemical systems, and organic forms (*P.S.,* p. 203).

As to the second problem, where man arose, mythology and philology are no longer the only sources of its solution. From human fossils and other prehistoric remains, there is little doubt that our ancestors first evolved in the tropical regions of Central Asia where nature supplied them with an abundant living, practically without any worry or labor on their part.

The third problem, about the age of man, like the question of the age of the earth, cannot be definitely answered. As long as we do not fall back on revelation or fantasy, but base our conclusions upon scientific evidence, such as there is, one guess is as good as another. A reasonable estimate is that our planet is geologically about one thousand million years old. As for man, it matters little whether he is a hundred thousand or a million years old. What is of far greater importance is his known history and background which disclose the laws and forces by which he has risen from the animal world to his present state. That knowledge which is as priceless as a miner's lamp to its owner, constitutes sociology, the science of sciences.

## THE ASCENT OF MAN

In the morning of evolution, a visitor from Mars would not have been able to guess whether the giant dinosaurs walking on their hind legs, or the small hairy tree apes that ran timidly about on all fours, would become the lords of the earth. Yet it was from the latter lowly creatures or their relatives, that man emerged. There was room at the top for a new species, and aboriginal man climbed up to take the throne. He learned how to talk, and was already human though he had no fire, no clothing and no tools. For untold ages, he was a shaggy, frightened, ungainly skulker, learning from his errors and his suffering, until his growing intelligence carried him through.

## WARD'S ORIGINAL CONTRIBUTIONS TO THE EVOLUTION THEORY

The study of man's upward climb in evolution which was mapped so brilliantly by Darwin, Haeckel, and Spencer, was also illuminated by Ward. His two original discoveries for which he received no adequate recognition, are that evolution is zigzag, made while studying the geologic history of plant and animal fossils, and the theory of mutations (chance or fortuitous variation), as the chief cause of biologic evolution, which he made in connection with his studies in botany. These novel theories were not clamped as analogies upon sociology but proved that the natural laws which govern evolution in the animal world, control social evolution, and that sociology is therefore as true a science as biology.

## EVOLUTION IS ZIGZAG

Ward's original theory that evolution is zigzag (sympodial) and not straight (monopodial) applies not only to plants and animals but also to social institutions—in fact, to all social evolution. Though it has been accepted by all students of the evolution of culture, Ward is rarely credited with it. Its argument runs that evolution cannot be symbolized by the pyramid, because evolution spreads upward and outward, and the pyramid would have to be placed unnaturally upon its apex. Not the tree portrays the true course of evolution, but the vine. In the straight type of branching, branches shoot forth at regular intervals along the main trunk which reaches from the ground to the top and gradually diminishes into a slender twig. But in the zigzag type like the grapevine and the linden tree, the trunk rises to a certain height and disappears into the first branch. The latter, which has now practically become the trunk, soon gives off a new branch, which in turn, becomes the main stem. By repetition of this process, the branching is zigzag throughout.

The course of evolution, too, is everywhere zigzag—a winding road, uphill and down dale. Whenever a new production is achieved, the course of evolution turns a corner and takes a new direction (see *P.S.*, p. 96). As each product or branch evolves, it absorbs the substance and vitality of its parent trunk and takes its place. The tree of life is sympodial; before the animals, the plant was the trunk; from the brute stemmed man, and now that he has been fully organized into society, the latter has absorbed everything below it and become the main trunk of human life.

On the plane of human history, evolution takes the same irregular course. Anthropology shows the various races in their infancy, engaged in bloody conflicts which result in a fusion of blood. Not only society as a whole, but every new race and nation is the result of such an assimilation. Only vestiges remain of the ancient races, as of primitive forms of life in geologic time. The giant saurians are now the tiny lizards in our parlor aquariums, and the colossal ferns of the coal age are represented by midget forms in our hothouses.

The wheels of evolution have ground into dust all the ancient races. The mighty Egyptians, Persians, Greeks, and Romans of old have all been swallowed up by more vigorous peoples, and the forces of evolution are already engaged upon the living ones. Every civilized nation has given its most vital elements to some colony which in time supplanted the parent nation. From England have sprung such powerful branches (most of which have already become parents on their own account) as the United States, Canada, Ireland, Australia, and South Africa, and it is only a question of time when England will have disappeared altogether. Nature, in trees as in races, is more concerned with new branching (for that spells new types and dynamic progress), than with the preservation of old and outworn stems.

## CHANCE VARIATION

Ward's second contribution to the theory of evolution is the mutation which places Darwinism in a new light. The Greeks hit upon the idea that plants and animals descended from a few ancestral types, but it remained for Darwin to prove that development came about through the slow action of sexual selection combined with the pressure of the struggle for existence. Darwin's main thesis, which still stands intact, is based upon the simple fact that all living forms (including man) were not created in their present state, but were developed out of simple forms. Ultimately, therefore, all forms of life are blood relatives. Again, while all living things are formed of the same basic substances, no two are wholly alike. The miracle of the same material developing into such widely different organisms as a flea and an elephant, a germ and a baby, is explained by· the Darwinian laws of variation and adaptation.

Variation, the result of the diversity of structure, spells survival; the lack of variation leads to stagnation and decay. In addition to the natural tendency to vary, every organism tries to adapt itself to surrounding conditions. As the environment changes, the organism changes along with it. Those that fit into the new conditions, survive and prosper; the others die out. Because slower deer are captured or killed off, and the faster ones escape, the average fleetness of each generation becomes higher or lower according to the circumstances. This natural selection in the struggle to survive, said Darwin, is the underlying explanation of the creation of species.

Ward was careful to point out that literally the term *natural selection* is misleading, and was used by Darwin merely as a parable. Nature has no intelligence, and does not select. Nor do the less fit die by chance, for chance implies an effect without a cause, whereas when the word is used by science, it means that the cause is still unknown. He has the following explanation (more comprehensive than Darwin's) for nature's selective process. The law of organization is so all-powerful, nature's material and energies are so vast, and she is so bent upon filling every nook and corner of the earth with her creations, that their almost infinite number and variety give the illusion of having been achieved by accident. Natural selection is not a weeding process by a murderous nature. Nor does it explain either the variety and charm or the dangers of the life struggle. It is a cold, automatic method, in which every organism teeming with the universal energy keeps on striving, with the result that those which are useless are ultimately submerged and buried in the grave of natural selection (see *P.S.,* pp. 240-242).

Darwin admitted that he did not know the cause of variation. But he was certain that it was not due to natural selection, for the latter merely tended to preserve the variation after it appeared, provided it was advantageous to the organism. His suggestion that sexual selection or pangenesis might be the cause was rejected by later biologists. Some of his critics went back to Lamarck's hypothesis and its support of the inheritance of acquired characteristics. Lamarck would account for the fleetness of the deer by the fact that running developed speed, and that such a trait would be passed on and amplified. Darwin and Lamarck practically neglected each other's theories, but Spencer gave their discoveries each its exact place in the field of evolution (see *D.S.,* I, 181).

Ward's conclusion is that natural selection is not the only factor in biological evolution. In fact, selection has been erroneously credited with more than it can possibly do, and has been applied as the name for a whole group of factors which lead to the elimination of certain organisms embodying certain variations. It does not explain the causes of variation or show that any particular trait causes adaptation of the organism to the environment, any more than it proves that the survival of the fittest means the survival of the best. There must be some other paramount explanation of the natural development of species, thought Ward, and found it in the mutation or "sport."

What causes one bull to be hornless in a herd of horned bulls? Variation, directly induced by the environment, does not appear competent to explain it. The mutation does. It signifies the slow inheritance but sudden emergence, according to Ward, of acquired characteristics (due to outer influences) which have become fixed in the blood stream. Small but persistent changes in the organism often become submerged and lie dormant for many generations. Then suddenly, as it seems, but in fact under the stimulus of some environmental circumstance, the old, inert trait springs to life. Nature seems to take a long leap forward in evolution in contrast to the painfully slow process of natural selection, and produces a "new" trait, organ or organism which is nothing but a chance variation. In Ward's language:

Here then we have the solution of by far the worst difficulty in the way of natural selection. The beneficial effect need not be assumed to begin at the initial stage. It need not be felt until well-formed varieties have been developed. There seems to be no flaw in this mode of solving this paramount problem, and if it is objected that it amounts to a new explanation of the origin of species, I am ready to admit it. I believe that more species are produced by fortuitous variation than by natural selection. Natural selection is not primarily the cause of the origin of *species;* its mission is far higher. It is the cause of the origin of *types of structure* (*P.S.,* p. 242).

Ward advanced this profound theory before De Vries, the famous Dutch scientist, but only the latter has been credited with it. Although it was supported by such noted biologists as Romanes, Cape, and others, Ward's name is rarely mentioned in connection with it.

Man is as much a product of the natural process as the elements of which his body is composed, or the plants and animals among which he moves. He, too, has climbed the zigzag path of evolution and through natural selection and mutation has evolved from the animal world to his present lordly state. But what has he done with his fair dominion? What has brought him to his present state? Before these questions can be answered, we must look into the origin of society, the nature of the social mechanism, and the social forces which motivate it.

# BOOK VI. THE SOCIOLOGIST

*"The high, utilitarian motive, focalizing all considerations in the good of man can have no other effect than to establish as the ultimate science, for the perfection of which all the other sciences exist, the science of human life, which takes the form and name of sociology."*—Ward

# Chapter XII

# THE ORIGIN OF SOCIETY

---

*"The genesis of society has been through the struggle of races."*—Ward

---

Despite the vast literature on social evolution, how many have any scientific notion about the origin of society? Sumner thought social origins were lost ("It seems vain to hope that from any origin the veil of mystery will ever be raised"). But Ward saw clearly the need of a genetic study of human association, when he said:

The great waves of social discussion that characterize our times and rivet public attention are only the surface manifestations of a deep current of thought that has set in strongly in the direction of a thorough investigation of fundamental social problems. . . . What is most needed is more knowledge as to the true nature and origin of society. Unless it is known how society has been developed and of what elements it is composed, it is impossible to adopt measures that will help on its natural evolution (*Glimpses,* V, 264).

## WARD'S EARLY THEORY A FALLACY

In the jungle of social phenomena, one can see the trees sooner than the forest. Here are millions upon millions of.men and women living an associated life. Is society like a seashore of human sand, or is it a synthesis greater than the sum of its units? How did they come together? Was it by divine command, by human agreement, or by invention? These questions presented themselves to Ward when he was writing his first work, but they were already ancient problems in the days of Plato and Aristotle.

His earlier solution of the problem (in *Dynamic Sociology*) was erroneous because of lack of information. Standing with Plato's and Rousseau's concept that society was an invention of superior brains, like fire and agriculture, he relied on Hobbes's argument that society arose from man's effort to protect himself; through egoism and natural selection, primitive man, essentially an unsocial being, discovered that organization was advantageous, and became a social being. Thus did Ward repeat the errors of the sociology of the seventeenth and eighteenth centuries.

Although his conclusion was wrong, many of his premises were correct. While society is not the creation of a more developed human brain, it is true that more psychic power did remove the chief barrier to indefinite expansion and enable the most favored races to spread over the face of the earth. Increasing intelligence also brought man knowledge, speech, erect posture, the idea of the family, and extension of the kinship group—things that no lower animal could have acquired.

### WARD'S LATER THEORY

Ward freely corrected his error and in his later works adequately located the origin of society in race wars. This was the original theory of Gumplowicz and Ratzenhofer which Ward developed, but he did not forget to give its authors full credit for their epochal discovery:

I do not hope to add anything to their masterly presentation of this truth, which is without question the most important contribution thus far made to the science of sociology. We at last have a true key to the solution of the question of the origin of society. It is not all, but it is the foundation of the whole, and while the edifice of sociology must be built upon it, the full recognition and comprehension will demolish all the cheap and worthless rookeries that have occupied the same ground. . . .

If I succeed in contributing anything to the subject it will consist of pointing out this truth and showing that the struggle of races is simple and typical social synergy, and that it is the particular way in which synergy as a cosmic principle operates in the social world (*P.S.*, pp. 203-204).

Ward saw the birth of society through synergy as another step in the universal process of organization, with nature using men instead of atoms and molecules for her building blocks. Society is a natural creation, mechanically evolved from races and individuals in conflict. The social process, like the chemical or the vital process, is another example of nature's teamwork of opposing forces bending backward toward separation and competition, and forward to assimilation and co-operation.

Much as Ward hated war, he could not shut his eyes to the truism that "without race conflict there can be no state and no political development, and without blending there can be no culture and no civilization" (Gumplowicz, *Rasse und Staat,* p. 31). From whatever angle we view the panorama of history, the fact stares us in the face that brotherly love has had nothing to do with the evolution of human groups.

In the infancy of the race, human contact, coupled with fresh opportunities for sexual gratification, outweighed the evils of war. Propinquity is a far more potent influence than race, Ward believed. There is something in the presence of another person that completely alters one's attitude towards him. Besides, the charm of sexual novelty enhanced the ardor of the sexes and helped to lessen the hatreds of clashing races (*P.S.,* pp. 208-211).

## THE WARS OF THE RACES

In the dawn of the race the sole basis of human adhesion was the narrow bond of animal or blood kinship. For the stranger, there were only fear and hatred. The tribe was the largest social group, and exogamy, or the duty of marrying outside of the group, was rigidly enforced. Whether the first great wars were caused by overcrowding or by the lack of food or females, the result was always that the weaker were driven out or captured, and the victors spread over the conquered territory. The conquerors who landed in isolated regions, remained unchanged; those who came in contact with new tribes, forgot about their common human origin and attacked each other with gusto. War was then a natural thing, and a social necessity, like food or shelter.

In the earliest light of history, huge tangled groups are seen engaged in gigantic battles, and the story of those conflicts fills all mythologies and historical source books. The wars of the races prove the error of Aristotle's dictum that man is a social animal. In fact, Ward argued, man descended from animals that were not even naturally gregarious. His social sense was developed after and not before he had passed through the ordeals of war and amalgamation. Man, like an infant who suffered many childhood diseases before it grew up, has had cannibalism, war, slavery, caste, competition, and tyranny in all its forms, and is now emerging into a state of civilization, with compromise, cohesion, and co-operation (see *ibid.,* p. 215). This was Ward's mature view.

## ASSIMILATION OF RACES

Present society was evolved through assimilation and amalgamation of expanding warring groups. Each of the nations that has come out of the melting pot is a synthesis of all that went into it. The nations are all branches of the sociological vine-tree, and each is a true sympode in the zigzag course of social evolution. Says Ward:

The vast and bewildering multiplicity in the races of man is the natural result of ages of race development, and it has taken place in a manner very similar to that in which the races of plants and animals have developed. Its origin is lost in the obscurity of ages of unrecorded history, and we can only judge from existing savages and the meager data of archaeology and human paleontology how the process went on. But we know that it did go on, and when at last, the light of tradition and written annals opens upon the human races, we find them engaged in titanic struggles. . . . That out of this struggle new races have sprung, and that these in turn have struggled with other races, and out of these struggles, still other races have slowly emerged, until at last down toward our own time, and within the general line of the historic races, the great leading nationalities,—French, English, German, etc.,—have been evolved (*P.S.,* pp. 76-77).

Although the road of history is strewn with the ruins of races and kingdoms which have passed away or been absorbed by stronger ones, the social process is not to be regarded as a hurricane which destroys everything in its path. While the biological principle (competition) is survival for the strongest and death to the weaker, the sociological principle (synergy) is co-operation and synthesis of conflicting elements to produce new social groups and higher types of men.

Race assimilation came about not only through wars but also as the result of peaceful phenomena like migration, intermarriage, and confederation. Through colonization, the parent group was slowly transplanted to new soil and reborn in its offspring. Thus was Troy absorbed by Greece, and Greece by Rome. Italy led the civilized world up to the sixteenth century and then gave way to Spain which in turn relinquished the sceptre to France. England became supreme in the nineteenth century, and bids fair to bow to the United States, if it has not already done so (see *ibid.,* pp. 214-215). In America, Australia, and South Africa, new races are now in the making.

Although evolution is a fact, no one in a short lifetime can wit-ness the birth of either a species or a nation. When Ward speaks of a fusion of races, he necessarily assumes an isolated and typical case of a simple form of assimilation by a single conquest. Actually, however, social evolution does not happen quite so simply. Every new race is the result of compound and complex assimilations. The conqueror may itself have been the result of a third or fourth assimila-tion, while the conquered one may have represented only a second infusion. In the case of England, for instance, five or six distinct assimilations can be traced. But the last one which welded the various elements into the English people, was the strongest of all, and engendered a high order of loyalty.

### ORIGIN OF THE STATE

The state must not be confused with government or society. So-ciety is the organization of human beings, living and working to satisfy their desires. The state is a specially organized public force to compel obedience of the law. Government is the administrative mechanism by which the will of the people is executed and controlled.

In the wake of racial wars and assimilation, followed the rise of caste and the development of patriotism, the state and government. Hostility of the warring groups became the spur to invention. Strat-egy evolved chiefs and war lords. War being what it is, the loser was always robbed of his possessions. At first, cannibalism disposed of all prisoners, but with growing intelligence and an increased nat-ural food supply, the vanquished were made slaves and put to work for the conquerors. The state evolved as the institution to protect the victor's ownership of the spoils of war which consisted of land and slaves. And so, slowly but surely, groups were solidified by power and authority, into nations and empires, and the power of government grew apace (see *P.S.*, p. 206).

### STAGES OF SOCIAL EVOLUTION

As man passed upward on his way to civilization, he went through the following stages of social evolution (see *D.S.*, I, 464):

1. The solitary life or as nearly so as was consistent with the urge to preserve the species—a theoretical period when man lived alone or in very small groups.

2. The anarchic stage when early man lived in groups for self-preservation. The rapid increase of population caused a forced association—the mind serving only selfish ends, and having moral qualities. The individual was free, but insecure from attack.

3. The present politarchic or national stage which arose when the rudimentary forms of law and government were developed, producing tribes and nations. The groups grew larger with war and conquest, and the growing power of chiefs and the paramount necessity of regulating property interests, developed the power of the state.

4. The pantarchic or cosmopolitan stage, still ahead of us, will come when humanitarian sentiments and practical interests will control. It will result from further integration of conflicting races, through the disappearance of national prejudice and interracial wars—a wholly ideal stage of superior intellect.

5. The sociocratic stage, yet to come, which completes the imperfect cycle of the previous stages. There the world will see the triumph of humanitarian sentiments and practical interests. Barriers of language, nationalism, and competitive frictions will be swept away, and all nations will be united into one vast social aggregate having a world-wide political organization.

## SOCIAL INSTITUTIONS

As the state developed, social institutions emerged. Ward lists them as follows (see *Textbook,* p. 186; *P.S.,* p. 205):

| | |
|---|---|
| 1. The caste system. | 8. Government by law. |
| 2. Slavery. | 9. The state. |
| 3. Labor, in the economic sense. | 10. Political liberty. |
| 4. The industrial system. | 11. Property. |
| 5. Property in land. | 12. The business class. |
| 6. The priesthood. | 13. The people. |
| 7. The leisure class. | 14. The nation. |

Synergy, again, is the process which explains all organization and creates all structures, both in nature and society. By the union of opposing elements, their combination and assimilation, social structures are created by a process of synthesis. Synergy underlies the cross-fertilization of cultures which is a process of equilibration. "Human institutions are all the means that have come into existence for the control and utilization of social energy." But to synergy we owe the development of law, government, religion, morals, and all social institutions.

These, then, are Ward's glimpses into the origin and development of society. There are no loose and meaningless speculations about destiny and human nature. No confused pseudo-philosophies, heavy with metaphysics, fetter our minds as we follow his survey of the natural process from the birth of suns and stars to the evolution of society, and approach the social mechanism, and the social forces by which it runs.

# Chapter XIII

# THE SOCIAL MECHANISM

---

*"Every true science must have both a dynamic and a static department. This has been sparingly recognized in biology, and distinctly so in economics by Dr. Patten, and in sociology by Comte, not by Spencer."*—Ward

---

Our guide is a true scientist-philosopher who will not be hurried. The social machine is recognized as a tiny cog in the world machine, and can be understood only with the comprehension of the cosmos and its natural laws. Ward turns us, therefore, from the minutiae of descriptive sociology into the broadest fields of cosmic philosophy (see *Outlines,* Chapter VIII; *P.S.,* Chapters X-XI). In so doing, he again demonstrates that the background of sociology is the domain of all the other sciences, and that the forces which control the universe also govern society.

## SYNERGY, THE BALANCING OF FORCES

Ward's thesis begins with the inquiry by what process natural structures are formed. Since the purpose of any structure, natural or artificial, lies in its use or function, the structure must adapt itself to its function. Adaptation is accomplished through the natural principle of synergy, or the universal opposition and balancing of forces. Synergy is the promise of all creation; the stars proclaim it, the tides support it, and man, in his individual and social life, realizes it. What exists, evolves.

## POLARITY

Synthesis typifies cosmic monism, the opposite of which is polarity,[1] or the principle of cosmic dualism. The universe is not only

---

[1] Professor Morris R. Cohen, of the University of Chicago, who follows Ward in recognizing synergy as the key to nature's process of organization, finds polarity in the following widely separated principles and phenomena (see his *Nature and Reason*):

(1) Protoplasm cannot live without continually dying (Huxley).

(2) Strife is the father of all things. The balancing of opposite forces, as in the string of the bow, gives form to things (Heraclitus).

(3) The Socratic and Platonic view of justice and other virtues as conduct according to measure, involves the idea of adjustment of opposite considerations.

(4) The relativity of form and matter determines all existence (Aristotle).

a vast unity, but it is also an arena of conflicting forces which have evolved everything, material and spiritual. The pulling, centrifugal forces of gravitation, attraction, and condensation are always and everywhere opposed to the pushing, centripetal forces of radiation, repulsion, and diffusion. When the opposing forces balance, the result is at most a static and spontaneous addition. But when one of the forces is stronger than the other, something must give way, and the result is a dynamic, fundamental change in type, i.e., an advance in the nature of an invention.

The world has always been more impressed by the conflict in polarity than by the more quiet force of co-operation in synthesis, because the former is so apparent, and the action of the latter is hidden and obscured. No choice between them is necessary, for both are used and constantly interchanged. Nature never stops trading energies. The sun gives energy to the plants in exchange for carbon, and man, taking the carbon, obtains heat and steam, and transforms the world, as if by magic, into a busy mart.

## SYNERGY AT WORK

Evolution denotes a certain predominance of the forces of attraction. But it is synergy, the golden mean, the balance of forces, which keeps evolution at work manufacturing atoms, molecules, protoplasm, organisms, and social organizations (see *D.S.*, II, 75). Each of these creations is a synthetic product of nature. Not one of them ever could have been imagined by the most powerful intellect until the laws and processes of nature were discovered, any more than a mind without a knowledge of science could ever dream that a drop of water is made up of $H_2O$.

Nature destroys, only to build. Her forces clash but continue functioning forever. If a natural force is unopposed, it is essentially centripetal and destructive. Fortunately, every force meets with resistance, otherwise nothing upon our globe could have developed or survived. The planets themselves would have left their orbits to follow a straight line and collide with the first stellar body in their path. So, too, without the opposition of the intellectual force, feeling would have wrecked all organisms through excess of desire.

(5) The mind operates effectively only when it acts like a scissors, the two blades of which (unity and polarity) move in opposite directions (Felix Adler).

(6) Hegel's dialectic.

In the arena of biology, the contending forces are those of heredity and environment. The conflict results in changes from a fixed type, and a consequent process of adaptation which makes possible a greater number of forms. In the realm of society, the struggle is between the individual and the mass, and takes the form of competition against co-operation. There, as everywhere else, synergy goes on until the milder forms of antithesis and interaction, sooner or later, lead to assimilation, co-operation, and progress.

## THE NATURAL STORAGE OF ENERGY

Through synergy, the organizing process of nature lifts ever larger masses of matter from a lower to a higher plane. At the same time it stores the unproductive forces for future use, and thus insures means of development without end. Man copies nature's method, and in the machine, has produced a device for checking and storing energy which would otherwise run to waste. When the inventor takes the electricity generated by a waterfall and concentrates it in a power machine which performs miracles at the pressing of a button, he is only imitating the natural storage of energy.

At first, energy was diffused in the clouds of chemical dust and gases which formed the starry nebulae. Then nature begins to hoard her forces, at first in the atoms and molecules of matter, each one of which is a storage battery which harbors latent currents of life, feeling and thought (see *Glimpses,* V, 142). This storage goes on and on, in the sunlight, leaf, blood, tissues, and brain, until the world becomes filled with myriad creations and activities. Greatest of all storage batteries is the human brain, a dynamo of infinite power. In society, the social forces or collective desires of all men are the gigantic batteries which concentrate psychic power and social energy.

## SOCIAL INSTITUTIONS AND SOCIAL STRUCTURES

Social institutions and social structures, too, are reservoirs of psychic power necessary for social ends, and present unlimited possibilities of achievement (see *Outlines,* pp. 171-172). The clash of psychic forces in society gives rise to social institutions, and the latter, in turn, evolve social structures. The institution of religion developed the social structure called the church; the family emerged from the institution of marriage, and the moral code arose from ethics. From the institution of property came the applied arts, and literature evolved from language (see *P.S.*, pp. 185-192).

## SOCIAL STATICS AND SOCIAL DYNAMICS

Thus far in his profound analysis, Ward keeps within the bounds of social statics (pure sociology), and touches upon processes relating only to structure and function. It is only when he comes to invention that he enters the realm of social dynamics (applied sociology). Says Ward:

Every true science must have both a dynamic and a static department. This has been sparingly recognized in biology, and distinctly so in economics by Dr. Patten, and in sociology by Comte, not by Spencer (*Outlines*, p. 168).

Almost all the sociologists after Comte, begged or muddled the vital distinction between statics and dynamics in social evolution, by asserting that dynamics referred to function, and statics to structure. Accordingly, they called astronomy a static science, and physiology, a dynamic science. In fact, however, both structure and function are within the field of statics, and physiology is as much a static science as astronomy.

Ward uses the term *dynamics* in the narrower sense of fundamental (not necessarily revolutionary) change as the result of the operation of forces—something beyond structure and function. Thus, biology was static until Lamarck, Darwin, and Wallace proved that life was in a perpetual state of flux, and initiated the science of dynamic biology. Sociology has social statics, a pure and isolated science, and social dynamics, the concrete and applied science of the world of man.

Static does not denote stagnation, but something active like a mill-pond or a river. The work of any mechanism, whether it is a world machine, a social institution, or a mechanical contrivance, is static. Anatomy and physiology, structure and function, even if they indicate some improvement, belong to statics as long as no basic or dynamic change in type (invention) results (see *ibid.*, pp. 174, 175). If the reader desires to study society at rest (social statics) he must investigate human beings as a naturalist examines plant and animal specimens in his laboratory. Of course, human beings are always doing something, yet a study of statics gives only a still life picture, as it were, of the human scene. But if he is interested in invention and progress, he must observe the steps in social development through social dynamics, and analyze and interpret society as it produces fundamental changes.

## DYNAMIC ACTION MEANS PROGRESS

Dynamic sociology is ultimately concerned with social dynamics because it treats of social progress which Ward identifies with happiness. As such, it is the only body of knowledge in the world which throws any light upon that problem of problems, the increase of human happiness (see *P.S.,* p. 221). Social progress is possible only with dynamic action (see p. 444). The social environment is. a part of nature, and therefore, an eternal battleground of forces. The forces of variation (environment) are always trying to break through the barriers set up by the forces of stability (heredity). When the break occurs, and it is advantageous to the organism, there is progress. The process of natural selection or the survival of the fittest which is the fundamental principle of dynamic biology, extends to society, where it is known as the principle of advantage. Social phenomena, which are again seen to be controlled by the same laws as organic bodies, keep on modifying, under the pressure of the principle of advantage, in order to meet the corresponding changes in the social environment.

## A CROSS SECTION OF THE SOCIAL MECHANISM

The following chart of contrasts between social statics and social dynamics furnishes an illuminating cross section of the mechanics of social evolution (see *ibid.,* p. 231).

| SOCIAL STATICS: | SOCIAL DYNAMICS: |
|---|---|
| Treats of the structure and functions of human institutions (such as government, religion, morals and marriage) by the balancing of opposing forces. | Treats of any disturbance in the balance of opposing forces, which results in a change of type in the nature of an invention, and means progress. |
| *The result is:* | *The subject is divided into:* |
| (A) Social integration. | (A) Social genetics or evolution. |
| (B) Social differentiation. | (B) Social telics, or conscious social improvement. |

*The controlling principle is:*
Synergy or the co-operation of conflicting forces, which causes development by internal organization or assimilation.

*The controlling principles are:*
1. Difference of potential, or the crossing of cultures.
2. Innovation or chance variation (impulse and invention).
3. Conation or striving which results in the transformation of the environment.

## (1) DIFFERENCE OF POTENTIAL

Ward borrowed the expression difference of potential from physics, and used it in sociology to denote the crossing of cultures or blood streams. Just as sex is nature's device for keeping up variation, so the clash and fusion of races is nature's method of creating new .types of humanity. As we have seen, nature had no other way of creating society than through war and conquest. If by some miracle, universal peace had been the early lot of man there would have been no variation of races and no social evolution. In Ward's words:

The social pendulum would have swung through a shorter and shorter arc until at last it would have come to rest. . . . Whatever may be best for the future when society shall become self-conscious and capable of devising its own means of keeping up the difference of potential, thus far, war and struggle, with all that they imply, have been the blind, unconscious means by which nature has secured this result, and by which a dynamic condition has been produced and kept up (*P.S.,* p. 240).

## (2) INNOVATION

Most human actions are merely repetitions, static and unprogressive. The more intelligence strives to produce something new or original, the nearer mankind comes to dynamic social progress. The homologue in mechanics of innovation (novelty) which constitutes the second principle of social dynamics is invention. Its homologue in biology is the "sport," when by chance variation, nature suddenly recalls germ-plasms to activity that were pushed aside in the jostling rush of heredity (see *ibid.,* p. 243).

Innovation in society may not always be beneficial. Compensation, however, is found in the law of natural selection, which Ward called the elimination of the wayward. When indulged in by the leisure class, for example, innovation may either produce useful inventions or such useless things as social teas, machine guns, or social parasites.

But there is always the instinct of workmanship to serve the desire to create something new, and keep the social scene vitally dynamic.

### (3) CONATION

The most important principle of social dynamics is conation (effort). Every human action, upon analysis, has three effects (see *ibid.,* p. 247):

1. The satisfaction of desire which is the sole purpose of all actions. The effect is static.

2. The performance of function which continues and preserves life. The effect is unconscious, unintended and static.

3. The modification of the environment which may be either unconscious or purposive. But as it causes a fundamental change in the environment, its effect is dynamic.

Even if the desire which prompts the act is unsatisfied, the will to do, the effort exerted—that is the important thing. Useless activities like pie-eating contests, writing Bible chapters on postage stamps, or filibustering for the *Congressional Record* are, in the long run, lost in the maelstrom of real human striving. In the face of Ward's generalization that the conative faculty is identical with man's will and is a natural force obeying all the Newtonian laws of motion (see *Glimpses,* IV, 218), the dogma of free will disappears into thin air as soon as the natural or causal explanation of any phenomenon is found (see *D.S.,* I, 400).

It is through the principle of conation that Ward came to the grand generalization that *while in nature the environment transforms the animal, in society it is man who transforms the environment.* In the animal world, the body is affected by the struggle for existence, but the animal exerts little or no effect upon its surroundings. The higher we ascend in the scale of life, the more intelligent and purposive the efforts at self-preservation become, until in man, many great physical and psychic activities are involved just in the effort to survive. It is different in the animal world. Birds may build nests, and beavers erect dams without appreciably changing the landscape. The lauded animal instincts seem to produce no enduring effects. Birds will often abandon their nests to build new ones in the same tree.

In the human species, there is another story. While it is true that physical activities molded the body and gave man his erect posture, high facial angle, and massive brain, the effects upon himself of the struggle to survive have gradually diminished. At the present time a reverse process of decadence has set in, and civilized man is slowly decreasing in size and weight, becoming toothless and hairless, and growing weaker in all the muscles and senses of the body. The environment, on the other hand, has never been free of his influence, and is being constantly worked over by human effort into some different form. Everything of any value in the economic sense has been created and transformed by man's hand and brain. In the attempt just to keep alive or to satisfy and to expand his desires, he has changed the earth from a wilderness into a garden or vice versa, whichever way one chooses to look at it. But fundamental change there has been and will always be, as long as man will remain an active being.

The kind and extent of the changes wrought by conation are the measure of man's material, social, and spiritual progress. The removal of obstacles which stand in the path of achievement and prevent the satisfaction of desire, is the underlying condition to social progress. When the effort is easy and unimpeded, man achieves wonders. When he has to waste all his energies to obtain bread or wage war, progress stops, and regress sets in.

Here is the climax of Ward's analysis of the social mechanism as a part of the world machine. His brilliant analysis of the cosmic process is a vast induction in which the compounding and recompounding of facts and conclusions, commencing with the evolution of the ether and ending with the integration of social forces, ends in the supreme generalization that social progress (happiness) is possible only through the intelligent operation of the social machine.

Ward points to the social machine running at full speed, and to dynamic sociology which explains and controls its operation. To the questions: Why is society so unhappy? Why is it so stupid, and inept in its own interest? Why does it not ameliorate human suffering? Ward has given the world his philosophy of the social forces, exposed the lack of social control, and the inequality of social and educational opportunity for the great mass. All of which may be summed up in the failure to apply science and the scientific method in societal affairs, and allowing society to carry on by hit or miss methods.

# Chapter XIV

# THE SOCIAL FORCES

---

*"Civilized man has made no progress with the social forces, and looks upon the passions precisely as the savage looks upon the tornado. . . . The sociologist perceives that they may, by first being studied and understood, be rendered harmless and ultimately converted into the servants of men, and harnessed as the lightning has been harnessed, to the on-going chariot of civilization."*—Ward

---

THE MODERN WORLD prides itself, and not unjustly, upon its knowledge. It knows what moves the stars and planets, and what makes atoms and molecules clash and combine. Yet the forces that move society are a great mystery. Is the social sphere harder to penetrate than the boundless skies, or can it be ignorance and superstition which have kept society from discovering what makes it function?

## THE UNKNOWN SOCIAL FORCES

Even the social engineers in charge of the social mechanism seem to know little about its motor power. They are so helpless when the machine jams or runs wild that intelligent social control seems utopian. The question must be answered why we are less the masters of the social forces, and of our own lives and fate, than we are keepers of the winds and the tides. Why has science taught us so much about the organic-physical forces which set individual wills in motion, and told us so little about the collective currents of human desires and impulses? In brief, why are the social forces as alien to the vast majority as the Einstein theory is to the Zulus? The answer lies in the lack of common knowledge about the common phenomena of the emotions, added to the false modesty and hypocritical conventions which surround the field of human desire. That has resulted in so much obscurity and confusion that even so optimistic a thinker as Ward abandoned the idea of ever dispelling them by logic, although he was certain that they could be dissolved by analysis (see *P.S.,* p. 264).

The truism that the emotions alone move mankind cannot be repeated too often. Around their expression and satisfaction endlessly revolve all of man's activities, ranging from biological gratifications

[ 159 ]

to spiritual, creative achievements. Philosophers have generally preferred to grapple with insoluble problems because they seemed refined
and intellectual, but they have almost uniformly shied at questions
connected with the passions because they regarded the feelings as
low and vulgar. Even so great a thinker as Kant left all matters
umbilical to the emotions severely alone, and refused to exchange his
exalted throne on the heights of metaphysics for the austere stand
of science in the "lower" depths of human nature.

Kant is not alone in his aloofness from social psychology. All
objective psychologists since Plato have glorified the intellect at the
expense of the feelings. The subjective psychologists, on the other
hand, who dared to investigate the motor forces of life, have been few
and far between and the names of Bain, Bentham, Carpenter, Spencer,
and Ward complete the roster of their great pioneers.

## THE IMPORTANCE OF THE SOCIAL FORCES

The result of the ignorance about the social forces is to make
society only superficially a social order. Crowded like sheep in a
pen, its members react to an environment to which they are not fully
adapted, and live in a social system which they do not control. Ward's
sociology, following that of Comte, enthroned the intellect as the
greatest force in the world, and at the same time rescued the neglected subject of feeling from its deplorable abasement. Ward is one
of the few modern philosophers who recognizes feeling as the soul
of nature latent in every atom of matter; as the transforming agency
in life which is behind all our creative impulses. In man, nature has
produced a creature, who, whether he likes to hear it or not, can
survive only *durch Hunger und durch Liebe.* By denying the worth
or the dignity of his emotions, interests, or desires, he stunts and
stalemates his life. Even if neither social nor individual life can
be carried on according to a set pattern, the highest and happiest
existence can be realized only by intelligently guiding the natural
impulses, not by ignoring or forcing them.

## DESIRE, UNIVERSAL ENERGY

The universal force is everywhere the same, whether it controls
the vital and organic machinery of life or drives the individual or
his social machine. In the social arena the universal energy becomes

a wave of mass desires (social forces) more restless than the ocean, clamoring for satisfaction. Whatever we call it—impulse, will, passion, soul, or spirit—whether it drives the bee to the flower, the leaf to the light, the male to the female, or the explorer to the ends of the earth, it is always the universal energy at work, seeking an outlet.

## OUR PSYCHIC ENERGIES

Society, as we have seen, is essentially a reservoir of stored up energies. The same psychic qualities which represent the subjective part of the individual mind, are found in the social forces. In the lower or less developed races, the psychic energy was a kind of psychic protoplasm which served to form morals, religion, the state, law, and government. In higher races, psychic energy found an outlet through the varied interests summed up in the concept culture. No matter where they function, the social forces denote human tendencies underlying behavior. They are the desires of sentient beings, the steam in the boiler which makes the engine go. As natural forces, they obey the Newtonian laws of motion (see *D.S.,* II, 95; *Outlines,* p. 142; *Ps. F.,* p. 116).

## WARD'S PIONEER SOCIAL PSYCHOLOGY

Feeling alone drives the individual to action, and feeling alone, therefore, makes society act as it does, not intellect or ideas. Elemental hungers and appetites are the only motivating forces in human life, and neither ethics nor religion, neither faith nor science, can supplant a single one of them. All the great religious systems, from Manu to Moses, and from Jesus to Mohammed, have recognized this and appealed entirely to the emotions, and not to reason.

Because feeling is the sole motive force behind all human actions, sociology (based as it is upon psychology) should primarily concern itself with the social forces, said Ward. With the zeal of the Hebrew prophets who labored to substitute ethics for magic, Ward formulated his social psychology to replace speculation and superstition in the study of the social forces. For that purpose, he located and surveyed the runaway comet of emotion in the social forces which other sociologists suspected might be somewhere about, but were chary of approaching (see *D.S.,* I, 468-706; *P.S.,* pp. 256-492; *Outlines,* Chapter VII).

Many people are aware of their own passions, but hardly conscious of the terrific pressure of the collective desires of society. Elemental hunger, love, and fear are almost forgotten in the thrill of industry, inventions, or politics. Yet the primeval demands of desire rule us all with an iron fist while we are busy compelling the physical forces of nature to obey our every whim.

If society is not a domain ruled by natural law, social science is a myth. If we are unable to control the social forces but, on the contrary, they run away with us, the hope of social planning and social progress must be abandoned. Since the intellect can control natural forces (feeling or social forces included) there should be no difficulty in shaping and directing social as well as physical phenomena. Sociology, the key to that control, now leaves the static phase for the applied, dynamic state (see *Ps. F.,* p. 2). The moment we rise from the contemplation of the individual to the study of society, we take with us the dynamic element of feeling, from the psychic into the social sphere. Says Ward:

> The social forces are human motives, and all motives, in the correct sense of the term, have feelings as their end. To attain pleasure or avoid pain is the only incentive to action. All motives are desires, and the term which expresses the aggregate of desire is will. . . . It is what I have called the dynamic agent in society (*Outlines,* p. 168).

> Besides the five external senses, there is a sixth or internal sense called the emotional sense . . . diffused throughout the body. It receives its impressions only through nerve currents transmitted from the brain. The objects producing sensations are therefore chiefly psychologic. . . . Such action is sometimes called ideation, and these products, ideas. It is these ideas which produce emotional sensations.

> This sense and this class of sensations are of primary moment to subjective psychology, although they depend upon the phenomena of objective psychology.

> The remembrance of an agreeable sensation and its attendant circumstances give rise to the representations of pleasure not presently experienced. This mental state reacted upon the emotional sense producing a special form of sensation, intensive, and essentially painful in its nature, but unlike the primary forms of pain. This sensation is called desire. . . . It is prurient in its nature, and this pruriency is satisfied by the attainment of an appropriate object which is to yield the pleasurable sensation represented. Desire is developed

*pari passu* with the organ whose function is to generate ideas, viz., the cortical layers or cerebral hemispheres. Hence, cephalization had for its earliest result the development and increase of conscious desires. . . . The leading desires were for nutrition, protection and reproduction. . . .

With the increase of desire came an increase in animal activity. This activity became a transforming agency. The effects have been great epochs in evolution or general organic progress (*Ps. F.,* pp. 126-129).

## THE SOCIAL FORCES

The reformers erroneously believe that social forces mean persons, groups, and institutions. Spencer made a still more grievous error when he failed to emphasize that life and mind were forces, and that organic, psychic, and social structures were magazines of natural energy. Ward saved the philosophy of feeling from oblivion, and almost singlehanded recovered for the "lowly" desires some of the exaggerated respect given to function (see *P.S.,* pp. 127-132). With his eyes open to the dynamic, he saw in the social forces the chief currents of social change. Freud witnessed the same changes from the side-lines of sex; Marx from the vantage point of economic pressure. Ward's outlook was from the inner or psychic (not intuitional) core of man, as it overflows into the desires and emotions which endlessly seek gratification and expansion.

Here is a bird's-eye view of the social forces, the nerves, and currents of desire in the social body, as charted by Ward (see *D.S.,* I, 472; *Outlines,* pp. 147-149; *Textbook,* p. 78):

### I. PHYSICAL OR ESSENTIAL FORCES
### (function bodily)

| 1. *Preservative Forces* | 2. *Reproductive Forces* |
|---|---|
| Epic. | Lyric. |
| They form the basis of all action and desire, and preserve and maintain individual life. | They form the basis of all efforts of nature to continue the race. |
| The chief force is hunger, which gives rise to property, slavery, labor and industry. | The chief force is love, the influence of which is internal and molding, not creative. |
| (A) *Positive* or attractive, seeking pleasure. | (A) *Direct.* The sexual desire. |

(B) *Negative* or protective, avoiding pain.

(B) *Indirect.* Affection for parents or kin.

## II. THE SPIRITUAL OR NONESSENTIAL FORCES
### (function psychically)

3. *Socializing Forces*

They are the basis of race elevation, and the chief civilizing impulses.

(A) *Emotional* or moral, seek the safe and the good.

(B) *Esthetic,* seek the beautiful.

(C) *Intellectual,* seek the true and the useful.

## THE PHYSICAL FORCES

The most intense of human hungers are those which crave protection, food, sex, and companionship, although the last is needed only by the most civilized people. Idealists may deplore that such crass physical desires are the primary motives behind human thought and action. But man is an animal, and no logic or wishful thinking can change the fact. Why try to hide it? The noblest spiritual being, despite his immortal soul and all, will become a rabid killer if starved long enough. Of course, it is intellect that crowns *homo sapiens* king of the earth, but the greater part of his mind is still occupied with basic animal appetites.

The desire just to remain alive is the greatest hunger of all, a natural force for which there is no substitute and from which there is no escape. The sex desire, unsteady and violent, is not, as popularly believed, the first object in life. Reproduction in itself is entirely secondary, and at best but a passing thing upon which no enduring human relationships have been founded.

## THE SPIRITUAL FORCES

Although Ward classes the spiritual forces as nonessential in contradistinction to the physical forces which are the essential ones, he does not belittle the former or unduly emphasize the latter. In analyzing the spiritual forces he writes his own biography in the conclusion that the intellectual forces yield the highest satisfactions. To acquire knowledge, discover truth, and pass it on to others is the most thrilling of all experiences. The desire to teach—the finest flower of the mind—is the most altrustic of all feelings, and neither demands nor expects any compensation. For the first time in nature's process, an organism takes an unselfish interest in its own operations. In the pit of his stomach, man will always remain the egoistic animal, but there is some hope in the contents of his brain-case for spirituality.

The hope of becoming truly human lies in the attainment by the spiritual forces of a greater power and speed than the physical forces. Science has already initiated a sort of rhythmic movement towards the realization of the ends of man as distinguished from the aims of nature, i.e., toward the subordination of the physical to the spiritual forces. As knowledge and the use of reason increase, animal desires and instincts are correspondingly curbed and wane. In other words, as the brute is gradually eliminated, and mind begins to have more and more control over feeling, the instincts of self-preservation and race continuance lose their grip and the spiritual forces get a firmer hold on man's life.

### PARADOXES OF THE SPIRITUAL FORCES

Mind is only a condition, but feeling is to humanity, what gravitation is to the earth. The intellect is like the rudder of a ship; it directs, but it cannot propel. If the feelings are represented by the wind and the sails, the intellect is the man at the helm. When the ship is becalmed, the helmsman, no matter how skilful, is utterly helpless. If human desire is lacking or becomes too weak, society grows as static as a painted ship upon a painted ocean.

While the intellect is a guiding agency and not a true force, feeling, the only true force, resides in the mind. Is it not then inconsistent to include the intellectual forces among the social forces? The paradox is solved by the fact that by intellect Ward means the pleasure of intellectual activity, which is a true emotion or appetite. In other words, it is not pure reason which is covered by the terms intellectual or spiritual forces, but the thirst for knowledge and the joys of intellectual achievement and teaching.

Ward notes another paradox. The physical forces which secure the continuance of life are negative and altruistic, whereas the spiritual forces which afford pleasure for its own sake are positive and egoistic. Yet the two need not change titles. Most people are wholly confused about what is coarse and refined. Instead of regarding the hunger forces which look to the preservation of life, as the most worthy (as Ward does) because they perform the first function of nature, they are stigmatized as materialistic and unworthy. At the same time the spiritual forces are glorified to the highest (see *P.S.*, pp. 257-262). This paradox is dissolved by the fact that if we measure forces by the quantity of satisfaction which they yield, the spiritual forces are far beyond the physical ones; the stings of pain and passion are always outweighed by the greater volume and duration of spiritual pleasures.

Under the law of synergy, the physical and the spiritual forces, like all opposing natural forces end in co-operation and synthesis. Society is a complex machine, and any speculation as to relative merits of feeling and intellect is as idle as any rivalry between the captain of a steamship and the engine. Feeling is the primordial constituent in life's journey, but without the force of intellect, it would get nowhere. Both must work together to bring the ship to port (see *Outlines*, p. 108). All comparisons between the physical and the spiritual forces are unjust, because the distinction between them is fundamentally qualitative, rather than quantitative.

## THE SOCIAL MIND

When the social forces concentrate in the social mind, also known as the social will or public opinion, it becomes a force of incalculable potency. The mass mind is no more of a mystery than the individual mind. Just as the individual will controls the emotions of the individual, so the social will governs the collective emotions of society (*P.S.*, p. 91). Only the social will can control the social forces, and unless it does so, society is bound to drift like an empty rowboat upon a stormy sea. That is the condition in which Ward finds present society where a small group of selfish owners direct the social forces as they desire, and practically ignore the needs and the wishes of the great mass. With rare eloquence and incandescent scientific insight, he says:

Civilized man has made no progress with the social forces, and looks upon the passions precisely as the savage looks upon the tornado. Man is only civilized in relation to the lower and simpler phenomena. . . . Manifestations of social energy are still looked upon as necessary inflictions which may be preached against but must be endured. We have no science of social psychology or sociology that teaches the true nature of human motives, desires and passions or of social wants and needs and the psychic energy working for their satisfaction. The sociologist looks upon the social forces as everybody else looks upon the physical and vital forces, and sees in them powers of nature now doing injury, or at least running to waste, and perceives that, as in the other case, they may, by first being studied and understood, be rendered harmless and ultimately converted into the servants of man, and harnessed as the lightning has been harnessed, to the on-going chariot of civilization (*P.S.*, p. 110).

Ward sees the general social problem to be the restraint of the natural forces and the expansion of social energy by means of co-operating intelligence. His enthusiastic claims for the possibiltiy of social science bringing about a moral order are justified by the inclusion in his system of sociology of the science of social psychology which demonstrates how we may control the social forces, without which control, no civilization in the true sense of the word, is possible.

Ward stood practically alone in his social psychology. In looking for the source of social evil, the emotionalists—poets and peasants, professors and proletarians—all alike, blamed everything upon some pet villain, sometimes upon the victims themselves, and then chose some favorite hero, as the savior and emancipator. It is Spencer's voice, not Ward's, which is heard in present-day sociology. Many liberals fail to pay any attention to the tottering social structure, as they keep on advising more repairs, or stagger about under the weight of mighty pinnacles of hope and sympathy for humanity, vainly seeking a solid base upon which to rest them.

We have lived by instinct long enough, says Ward. Henceforth, we must use our intellects to beat nature at her own game, by improving upon her methods. That can be done only by recognizing the existence of the social mind and giving it the reins of social control, instead of allowing social metaphysics and social emotion to sway us.

All roads lead to Rome. Ward's analyses of the social mechanism and the social forces have brought us once more to the grand generalization that mind is the greatest force in the world, and that in its collective state, it is man's most powerful instrument for social evolution. This is the capstone of Ward's dynamic sociology, as well as the foundation of his social philosophy.

# PART III

# THE TEMPLE OF SOCIOLOGY:
# *SYNTHESIS*

*"Heroes of old! I humbly lay*
*The laurel on your graves again;*
*Whatever men have done, men may—*
*The deeds you wrought are not in vain."*
　　　　　　　　　　—Austin Dobson

*"Every man may be, and at some time is, lifted to a platform*
*whence he looks beyond sense to moral and spiritual truth,*
*and in that mood deals sovereignly with matter, and strings*
*worlds like beads upon his thought."*—Emerson

# NOTE

Having surveyed the foundations of the temple of sociology (Part II: Genesis), we are now prepared for a bird's-eye view of its general structure (Part III: Synthesis). We have seen the birth of man and society against the background of the cosmos, peered into the construction and control of the social mechanism. What of these bits of the jig-saw puzzle thus far pieced together? Where is the temple itself and the social domains which have so often been mentioned? Again we urge the patient traveler onward, assuring him that the promise of this journey has not been forgotten. The adventure of synthesizing all knowledge must first be examined, and only by grasping that synthesis will sociology be comprehended. For, as we again repeat, sociology and the synthesis of all knowledge are identical. The birth of atoms and worlds may be more exciting to contemplate; the struggles of the natural forces in sex, heredity, and environment, or the conflict of the social forces in history, economics, religion, or ethics may be more thrilling for many, but the heroic attempts to fuse all knowledge into one grand science of sciences is no less intriguing when one remembers that they resulted in completing the temple of sociology.

The Greeks laid the first foundation stones of the immortal structure; Comte drew the first comprehensive plan; Spencer first traced the law of evolution through every detail, and finally, Ward strengthened the base, rounded out the edifice and crowned it with his own social philosophy. A brief study of these master builders and their achievements will afford an all-rounded aspect of social science, high above petty prejudice or emotional bias, from which one may contemplate the domain of man's estate, and study at leisure his activities in the arenas of religion, politics, history, economics, sex, heredity, education, progress, and ethics.

# BOOK *VII*. THE SYNTHESIST

*"La pensée humaine est le résumé de toutes les énergies de la nature, puisqu'elle les assimile toutes."*—Ferdinand Papillon

# Chapter XV

# POSITIVISM

---

*"The world owes to Auguste Comte a debt of gratitude which its long neglect and tardy acknowledgment of his writings have poorly repaid."*—Ward

*"Man, as the minister and interpreter of Nature, does and understands as much as his observations on the order of Nature, either with regard to things or the mind, permit him, and neither knows nor is capable of more."*—Francis Bacon

*"Man is born not to solve the problem of the universe, but to find out where the problem begins and then to restrain himself within the limits of the comprehensible."*
—Goethe

---

In choosing for study the foundation builders of the temple of sociology from the scientists and philosophers of all time, Ward singled out from the array of great names only those of Comte and Spencer. No others, however worthy, were allotted any space, because they were not synthesists. As an example, Spinoza, whose monistic philosophy attracted Ward more and more as time went on, was not therefore included. To Spinoza, man was the most important creation of nature, but he left the stars to the astronomers, the mountains and valleys to the geologists, the animals to the zoologists, and the trees and flowers to the botanists, without attempting to fuse any knowledge into a science of sciences.

### ANCIENT ATTEMPTS AT SYNTHESIS

Plato (427-347 B.C.) failed to synthesize knowledge despite his almost superhuman imagination. As the true metaphysical product of his time who was without science or its method, his thoughts were too diffuse, though world-encircling, for any synthesis. Although he went far beyond Socrates, neither of these titans was a scientific thinker or builder. Plato speculated deeper than any one before him or after him ever did, and yet failed to outline a unified system of knowledge. By reaching out for the unreality of other worlds, he destroyed any chance of setting the foundations of the temple.

Aristotle (384-322 B.C.), the intellectual sire of Comte, Spencer, and Ward, was the first man in the world to mark out the paths of the sciences and try to bring within the range of a single analysis the whole sweep of human knowledge and experience, the most unique and unparalleled enterprise in the story of mankind. With the aphorism "Men who desire to learn must first learn to doubt. Science is only the solution of doubts," Aristotle became the father of science. Although he was also a metaphysician, he was the first synthesist of all knowledge, laid the foundation of the temple, and suggested at least, the outline of the structure. He was the first to declare that the whole of nature is a connected chain; that nature (not human nature) is the basis of philosophy, and that a continuous thread may be traced throughout the ascending scale of life.

In calling Ward another Aristotle, no real comparison is possible. It is easier to scale the highest mountains than to measure lofty intellects. Aristotle who discovered so much knowledge, remained on the heights, far from the maddening crowd. Ward fused knowledge, but as a man of the people, stayed with them in the valley to show them through social science the road to emancipation, and from the lowly depths envisaged a united world and a single family of mankind, in which the forgotten common man would come into his own.

Perhaps Aristotle dared too much when he attempted to unify all knowledge, for he, too, failed. But mankind would be richer for more such failures. He ploughed virgin soil in which all men after him were to plant and to reap a glorious harvest of science. It is his argosies laden with ideas that brought to the genius of Comte, Spencer, and Ward the material for the temple of knowledge which he visioned but could not complete. They are his heirs, wealthier but not greater than he.

## ARISTOTLE'S HEIRS

Scientists like Galileo, Newton, Humboldt, and Lamarck, and philosophers like Bacon and Descartes carried on the traditions of science, but no one attempted any synthesis. Between Aristotle and Comte there were many enraptured dreamers, and many carriers of bricks and mortar for the temple. But not one of them could correlate his achievements with those of the others, so as to bring all science under a single roof. Thus, Spinoza postulated the abstract idea of unity but had few facts to support him. Humboldt, on the other hand, furnished a world of data but could not draw any basal generalizations. Spires and foundations still had to be directly connected.

Comte and Spencer were the only two thinkers who built upon the broad principles of synthesis in nature and the relativity of all her forces and materials. Their grand conception of unity was the final crown of human thought, and "was required to round out philosophy into a form of symmetry, whose outlines, at least, admit of no further improvement" (*D.S.,* I, 143).

## COMTE

Auguste Comte is the greatest thinker of modern times. His doctrine was even more important to the nineteenth century and after than Bacon's thought was to the seventeenth and eighteenth centuries. Born and reared in a devout French Catholic family that was ardently monarchical, he was educated for the quiet life of a scientist, and spent his life teaching mathematics and perfecting his positive philosophy. In his youth, he turned from religion and conservatism to the agnostic and revolutionary ideas of Saint-Simon and Benjamin Franklin, for the former of whom he served as secretary for six years. From him, Comte caught the idea of a social renovation based upon an intellectual revolution. As a result, Comte at the age of twenty-four, published a pamphlet entitled *A Plan for the Scientific Labors Necessary for Reorganizing Society,* which, to his chagrin, attracted no attention. Shutting himself in his room for a day and a night, he evolved the general conception of social science and the project of the positive philosophy which took him more than twenty-four years to develop in the immortal *Positive Philosophy* and *Positive Polity.*

After an unfortunate early marriage, he fell in love at the age of forty-five with the unhappy and remarkable Clotilde de Vaux who was separated from her husband. Her death after a single year of chaste and exquisite love, changed Comte's whole life. After he completed *Positive Philosophy* and was ready to enter upon the concrete solution of the social problem, he saw the world in a new light, and founded the new religion of humanity. Thenceforth, his answer to the question "What is God?" was "Man; the state; society." He died in 1857, two years before Darwin published his *Origin of Species.*

Ward regards Comte as the most perfect type of French intellect which has been often misjudged to be light and trivial but which is in fact a penetrating and organizing instrument (*Outlines,* p. 9). Comte, a product of the French Revolution, had the eminence of heart, mind, and character to meet the call of the ages for a synthetic philosophy, and the demand of his times for social guidance. Although he was a strict mathematician and a rigid rationalist, his emotional forces were so deep and powerful that his work seems evangelical, a combination of Aristotle, St. Paul, and Moses. For all its religious pattern, his vision of the vital importance of science for the attainment of social welfare is based upon the core of his favorite maxim: *"Savoir, c'est prédire"* (to know is to be able to foretell).

## THE POSITIVE PHILOSOPHY

Comte was the child of his century, and was brought up with the intellectual heritage which had accumulated since antiquity. The entering wedge into modern thought which he made with the positive philosophy had been prepared by the intellectual reformation initiated by Copernicus, Galileo, and Kepler, and Comte's total effect was a revolution in the world's thought. The Comtian philosophy is characterized by the subordination of the imagination to observation which specially constitutes the scientific spirit, in opposition to the theological or metaphysical spirit. As a result of emotional "thinking," political speculations in Comte's day were diverging further and further from science, and as Hobbes remarked: "Even the maxims of geometry would be disputed if men's passions were implicated in them." Comte's avowed aim, therefore, was to co-ordinate all observed facts, and gather the materials of the various sciences into a harmonious unit. In that way, the mind would be trained to form a general view of nature and life, a synthetic and dynamic outlook upon man and society.

Conditions in Comte's time were far from ripe for the great synthesis. The doctrine of evolution was still germinating. Philosophy was then an introspective study vitiated by metaphysics and the subjective method. The French Revolution which had formulated the social problem, had neither traced it to its roots nor furnished any scientific basis for its solution. It was in that troubled era that Comte wrote his immortal works, an age which greatly resembles our own, with disastrous wars threatening a civilization already weakened by the terrible scourges of industrial depression, an age filled with pessimism mixed with despair and irrational panaceas and social nostrums, while impending catastrophes or sure-fire prosperity were just around the corner.

The immediate aim of positivism was to influence the entire intellectual system by the tendency to render relative all the notions which seemed absolute, and then fuse them into a world philosophy of science. The ultimate aim was, of course, the political reorganization of society, but Comte was convinced that that would be impossible until the moral and spiritual synthesis of mankind was effected through a comprehensive system of scientific philosophy.

From his classification of the sciences rose the central idea of positivism, viz., that mind, feeling, and action must co-operate and integrate, otherwise human life cannot be sound and moral. Humanity itself, said Comte, is the real unique center, the synthesis of everything which science and philosophy reveal of truth, beauty, and goodness. This scientific synthesis unites not only all knowledge but all mankind. It also helps the mind to attain maturity, and discard, as one casts off the outworn garb of childhood, all the metaphysical fictions of the past. Ward, the true disciple of Comte, said: "We who are of age, mature out of swaddling clothes" (*Cape*, p. 96).

Positivism is composed of a philosophy and a polity which are necessarily inseparable because they constitute the basis and aim of a system wherein intellect and sociality are intimately connected. The mission of positivism is "to generalize science, and to systematize sociality." This requires a philosophy of the sciences as the basis for a new social faith, which Comte furnished in his *Positive Philosophy*. He begins with the generalization that the cosmos evolved according to natural law. It, therefore, becomes immediately necessary to isolate and demonstrate natural laws by the scientific method. Finally the mature, scientific mind is enabled to grasp the fact that politics (social life) can be regenerated by rescuing political science from the nebula of abstract feeling and speculation, and placing it on the intellectual heights of applied reason. That alone will end the chaos of fruitless dreaming which has befuddled the human race since its inception, and usher in the scientific age.

## THE LAW OF THE THREE STAGES

The cornerstones of the positive philosophy are the universal reign of natural law, the futility of seeking for any First Cause, the relativity of all things and of all knowledge, the order of the sciences, and, what was a stroke of pure genius, the law of the three stages. Illuminated by this law of mental as well as social development, the evolution of knowledge, the growth of the sciences and the march of history may be observed paralleling the evolution of the intellect.

Comte regarded social evolution as the passage of mankind through three successive states: the preparatory or theological; the transitory or metaphysical; and the final or positive state. By observing these successive stages, all the great historical phases can be explained, and thus furnish a conception of homogeneous and continuous connection of all events and phenomena, from the first signs of social organization to the most advanced conditions of mankind.

The law of the three stages unfolds the fundamental division in the human mind which has caused two irreconcilable views. The first, supernatural and metaphysical, regards everything as being done (nature is passive, man is a tool). The second, natural and scientific, views everything as actively doing (nature is active, man is a creator). All attempts to harmonize these two attitudes have served only to draw the battle line tighter, and leave the uncertain and tender-minded to build an abstract, metaphysical bridge between the two. In Comte's words:

It cannot be necessary to prove to anybody that ideas govern the world or throw it into chaos. . . . The existing order is abundantly accounted for by the existence, all at once, of three incompatible philosophies. From the study of the development of human intelligence, in all directions and through all times, the discovery arises of a great fundamental law,—that each of our leading conceptions, each branch of our knowledge, passes successively through three different theoretical conditions.

The human mind, by its nature, employs in its progress, three methods of philosophizing, the character of which is essentially different and even radically opposed, viz., the theological method, the metaphysical and the positive. Hence arise three philosophies or general systems of conceptions on the aggregate of phenomena, each of which excludes the others. The first is the necessary point of departure of the human understanding; the third is its fixed and definite state. The second is merely a state of transition (*Positive Philosophy,* by Auguste Comte, tr. by Harriet Martineau, p. 25).

So Comte sat on the heights watching *homo sapiens* passing through the stages of fetishism, polytheism, and monotheism when he looked to the heavens for all explanations; then to the metaphysical state when he began to seek the essence of things, either in the things themselves or in his inner self. Finding no real and satisfying answer in either place, man dared to examine the world about him and thus entered the positive state. There, all superstition, introspection, and treasure hunts for a First Cause are abandoned as infantile and futile, and the mind rests content with science as the discovery of relationships between phenomena. "The crown and flower of human knowledge," as Gladstone called theology, was relegated to the fairy tales of child minds and the ground cleared for the scientific reconstruction of knowledge.

The Comtian law also illuminates the development of the sciences. Astronomy is now wholly in the positive stage, but meteorology is still in the theological stage when it depends upon prayers for good weather. Scientists are no longer foolish enough to search for the cause of gravitation, but they still look for the cause of mind, or the essence of life, and indulge in an infinite number of guesses, meanwhile neglecting real observation. As for sociology, it, too, was in the theological stage, argued Comte, for most men laughed (as many still laugh) at the possibility of a science of history or of society.

Society runs the same course of development as the mind and science, and is subject to the same Comtian law. In the first stage, society is ruled by animism, magic, and the fear of the gods and spirits. Slavery and patriarchal meliorism flourish. In the second stage, man places the greatest values upon war and exploitation as he forms a close union between God and the soldier. In the third stage, now barely begun, science with its positive system of knowledge liberates the mind, so that scientific politics can work hand in hand with industry to rebuild the world upon a moral and intellectual basis.

So completely are men still in the first two stages, that ignoring all laws and conditions of social evolution, they almost universally believe that a political change can result from a change in government or the adoption of some visionary scheme, not seeing that unless the changes are fundamental, they can have no permanent effect. Man is still largely conceived in the light of ancient theology and modern individualism as external to and above the social organism, instead of being an integral part of it. The dynamic idea of man is found only in the scientific stage where the social organism is seen to have its lines of growth and development, like the human organism.

The importance of Comte's discovery was as epochal as Haeckel's formulation of the biogenetic law. Just as the latter enabled the biologist to trace the entire life history of the race in the animal embryo, so the sociologist is able to follow with the help of Comte's law, the evolution of mankind, by observing the course of development of the individual mind, which is an epitome of what the race has gone through (see *D.S.*, I, 340).

Sometimes the three stages are jumbled in the same person. There are plenty of scientific Jekylls and Hydes who serve science faithfully on week days, but bow before superstition on Sundays, who look for a First Cause in the chemical laboratory, and deride the possibility of any social science. In the physical and natural sciences, the world is today clearly in the scientific stage; in sociology and ethics, it is as plainly, in many respects, in the more primitive earlier stages. There are times and places when each of the three stages dominates the others. But find them as we may, Comte took the three stages or principles and placed them upon the broad highway of the scientific method, where they fused into the science of human society. That alone is enough to render his name immortal.[1]

## THE BIRTH OF SOCIOLOGY

Comte coined the term *sociology,* yet never wrote one. He called his synthesis of the sciences *Positive Philosophy,* and for that portion which set forth the bearing of the new knowledge on the conceptions of human nature and society, he proposed the name *sociology.* It was not merely a theory of the state or a novel view of mankind, but the true science of the associated life of humanity. It was much more than a science; it was the dynamic and applied discipline which represents in a concrete unity the whole human race and all its knowledge and experience.

Before Comte, no one had ever schemed or suspected the existence of social science governed by laws as absolute and rigorous as those governing natural phenomena. Though he laid the foundation for the new science it was not his discovery, or that of any other man. Even in prehistoric times, reflections upon nature and man must have contained sociological elements, for as soon as people were able to wonder, they began to look for explanations of everything around them. Sociology, as such, was unknown to the Greeks, although its aims and

[1] See G. H. Lewes, *Biographical History of Philosophy,* II, 784.

ideals were implicit in the ethical and political philosophy of the "good life" and the "moral man" and reached its highest peak in the *Republic*. But neither the utopian vision of Plato nor the narrower concept of Aristotle's city-state had the rich blood or the sturdy tissues needed by sociology.

Later centuries produced many dreamers and thinkers, but they were lured into dismal swamps of political and metaphysical speculation from which they never returned. Sociology under various aliases made many attempts and suffered many failures to unify and evaluate the total fund of human knowledge. Much theological straw was threshed together with golden grains of science, in the works of Aquinas, Dante, Machiavelli, Vico, Spinoza, Hobbes, Locke, Condorcet, Hume, and Rousseau. There were many acute interpretations of social phenomena, but there was also a good deal of side-stepping of fundamental problems. Philosophers were, in the main, too much concerned with the next world or with their own intuitions to pay much attention to the objective world and its problems.

Before Comte, social theory flowed in many torrents out of the past, into a seething and riotous mixture of knowledge and speculation. Traditional divisions of philosophy and sentimental versions of the human comedy came to the discovery by Montesquieu that man had an environment, and by Hume that politics was a true science. The conclusion of Condorcet and Saint-Simon that history, too, was a positive science, was shot through with currents of sociology, but neither of them co-ordinated fact and theory into a social science. There were eager minds anxious to build; there were vast piles of material and scaffolding, and much din and bustle of a sky-piercing structure in the making, but all of it had to wait for a comprehensive plan and a solid foundation. Sociology advanced steadily from chaos to order, through the realism of Aristotle, the dreams of More, the shrewd analysis of Machiavelli, and the prophecy and romance of Hobbes, Vico, and Rousseau, until it bloomed in the sociology of Comte.

Until Comte, social philosophy was like a storehouse, a sort of intellectual morgue from which antique ideas were periodically dug out for revival. He was the first modern thinker to note clearly that all social phenomena are parts of an interrelated whole and that no idea, event, person, or group stands isolated. Motivated by the ideas of his predecessors and contemporaries, he proceeded to survey and mold with the eye of a true philosopher and the method of a true scientist, the whole mass of loose sociological material. Demands for natural rights in the name of God or abstract justice, gave way to a body of scientific doctrine related to social phenomena, similar to the relation of physical science to physical subject matter. In the final analysis, Comte had the novel and realistic idea that social science was a true and exact a science as mathematics.

## COMTE'S ERRORS

Cabbages may look at kings, and any average mind can discern the dents and breaks in Comte's synthesis. His gigantic intellect was wedded to vast errors due either to his emotionalism or to his lack of positive knowledge. Had he followed the scientific method which he prescribed, he would not have become for many an idol with feet of clay (*D.S.,* I, 83). The religion of humanity took on an essentially theological aspect and brought up much pent-up mysticism, surviving from his early ideas. His aim was admirable, viz., to unify all divergent beliefs and processes through the establishment of a positive religion. It was really a system of ethics for all men, but he turned it into the worship of a new god, an abstract, symbolized humanity.

The passion for systematization led him to plan to the minutest detail the practical organization of that cult. His use of symbols and the actual adoration of some great man of the past each day of the year may strike some of us as vain or vapid, but it does not detract from his profound scheme of social reorganization. What if his texts are ornamented with scented fictions and sentimentalities? The world has waited too many weary centuries for the arrival of the thinker who could co-ordinate knowledge, to reject him because he loved humanity too well.

His other and more surprising major error was his rejection of scientific research. For fear that it may become the hunt for an unfindable First Cause, he assailed as vicious all inquiry into the intermediate causes of phenomena, such as the nature of light, heat, or electricity. While positive science was marching on, Comte was condemning the attempts to unify the sciences so as to refer concepts to fewer and fewer basic principles. What tragic irony for the father of sociology bitterly to oppose monism or the principle of continuity, and object to the reduction of the sciences to one master science!

As a consequence of this singular fallacy, Comte seems to class the law of causality itself as a metaphysical fiction, and to forget that since the most important phenomena lie hidden too deeply to be seen at once, scientific research should never be abandoned. While he was scoffing at the "vain" task of seeking the chemical constitution of the stars, it was actually being found through the spectroscope. Had Comte's concept of scientific research been accepted, said Ward, the world would not only have lost much vital knowledge, but it would have been a fatal blow to the spirit of inquiry which is the marrow of the positive philosophy (see *ibid.*, p. 90).

None of Comte's errors or weaknesses, however, marred his services to humanity in laying out the general scheme and sketching the most comprehensive laws of social development. In abandoning the theological for the scientific method, and in founding the great synthesis, he contributed much to the building of the temple of sociology. He formulated a complete social science and outlined a universal philosophy. Not even his severest critics can expect such magnificent achievements to be more or less than a basis for the future (*ibid.*, p. 142). Says Ward:

All that has been gained toward the elevation of society and toward securing the comforts and enjoyments of life has come from this source, not one item having ever been contributed to the material prosperity of the world from either teleological or ontological researches. The essential accuracy of all this cannot now be doubted and, both from the fact and for the form of its presentation, the world owes to Auguste Comte a debt of gratitude which its long neglect and tardy acknowledgement of his writings have poorly repaid (*D.S.*, I, 87).

Ward borrowed from Comte's system what was great and noble and left behind the purely sentimental which died with Comte, the individual. Social science owes to Comte as great a debt as biology or ethics owes to Aristotle, or evolution to Darwin and Spencer. No matter how far sociology has advanced beyond Comte, the world cannot fail to recognize in him the immortal genius who made that science possible.

We leave this great foundation builder of the temple, as we read once more the inscription which he wrote over its portals and which epitomize him and his life's work: "The principle—love; the foundation—order; the end—progress."

# CHAPTER XVI

# EVOLUTIONISM

---

*"By bold hypothesis, by persistence and skill in the accumulating and ordering of more facts bearing on the subject than anyone had ever brought together before . . . Darwin established, in less than a generation, Evolution as accepted fact in the minds of men. . . . The effect was truly tremendous; he revolutionized every department of study, from astronomy to history, from palaeontology to psychology, from embryology to religion. . . . The evolutionary conception is the oxygen in the air we breathe; it has worn itself into every fibre of our thought; it shapes the world we see before our eyes, one in which permanent stability is unknown, in which life is change and change is life."*
—Geoffrey West

*"And striving to be man, the worm*
*Mounts through all the spires of form."*—Emerson

*"Mr. Spencer's preëminence as a philosopher rests primarily upon two qualities, and can only come out of the union of these in one and the same mind. These qualities are first, his extensive information, and, second, his extraordinary causality. The work of the true philosopher is preëminently the synthesis of extant knowledge."*—Ward

---

IN HERBERT SPENCER (1819-1902) we meet the most famous synthetist of the sciences. He not only laid deep and solid foundations for the temple of sociology, but traced the plan of evolution for the entire structure. Nevertheless, he, too, left the task unfinished, although his contribution is entitled "the synthetic philosophy."

## SPENCER

In the first half of the nineteenth century the only social science England knew was economics. In the second half, Spencer popularized sociology for the English-speaking world as Comte did for the French in the first half.

In studying Spencer's life and works to solve the paradox of his tragic failure in sociology, Ward found that he had lived through the entire Victorian period as an only child, always ailing and pampered, never married and dwelt alone most of his life. He spent his youth as an engineer and journalist, and the rest of his life as an author and philosopher. He boasted no classical scholarship, not even a single foreign language, and he never engaged in research or experiment. Nevertheless, by the sheer power of organized thought applied to all available data, he literally forced his way into every department of knowledge, until he commanded the respect and attention of the whole world. His philosophy of evolution stirred the restless blood of all who were tired of theology with its outworn creeds and dogmas. As the philosopher of the greatest movement of modern times, viz., the advance into science, he continued Comte's immortal work in that field (see *Glimpses,* VI, 316).

Although the Spencerian social philosophy with its crown of rugged individualism was completely shattered by Ward, Ward still called him "England's greatest philosopher," and added, "and when we reach England's greatest in any achievement of mind, we have usually also reached the world's greatest" (*D.S.,* I, 139).

## THE EVOLUTION THEORY

The synthesis of all knowledge, the great integration, would have been impossible without the theory of evolution, the great unfolding. Spencer's life task was to combine into a single, unified system, the entire sweep of cosmic, physical, biological, psychical, social, and ethical science. That was possible only by observing the evolutionary process, formulating the natural law of change which underlies it and following it through the history of the cosmos from its inception in the star dust.

Probably the clearest and most brilliant epitome of evolution is to be found in the first volume of Ward's *Dynamic Sociology.* If those who run also read, they can learn from it that evolution is the law of development, of natural change and growth as opposed either to chance or special (Divine) creation. Evolution is not the doctrine that we are descended from monkeys, nor is it a dogma which tends to destroy the state, the home, or the church. It is essentially the expression of the law of causality, the idea that everything has been evolved under natural law rather than created through accident or miracle. By its light, we see the roots of humanity in the organic, and before that, in the inorganic world, and observe the universal energy weaving the future on the shuttle of the present. Finally, it explains how man grew up from the brutes and reached forth to the truly human, over paths "where the worm treads fast over the heels of the gods" (Emerson).

Evolution is not a science but a method or process which furnishes the key to the puzzle how nature works its miracles to perform, and from a chaotic, cosmic nebula has fashioned this universe. The process is a cycle of natural creation, from germination and life to decay and death, then back again to a new life. By endless repetition of the process, the universe was filled with suns, stars, and planets, pulsating with creative energy, and (at least, on this globe) throbbing with feeling and thought. Ward apostrophizes it as follows:

Not content with the conquest of nature and the subjection of its laws to human uses, man resolved to find out what he was, whence he came and what was to be his destiny. He proceeded to interrogate nature at all points, and the thousand conflicting and commingled answers that he got, all rolled together, when closely listened to, were found to spell out the talismanic word: "Evolution" (*P.S.,* p. 543).

## THE LAW OF EVOLUTION

Spencer's definition of evolution is a monolith in the foundations of modern science: "Evolution is the integration of matter and concomitant dissipation of motion, during which matter passes from a relatively indefinite, incoherent homogeneity to a relatively definite, coherent heterogeneity."

Dilating upon it, he shows that the first part of the universal law is change, the second, progress. All change is due to some motion in matter which causes it to alter its nature and position from a simple and chaotic state to a definite and orderly complexity. There is an eternal rhythm in the cosmos, in which, as motion, energy, or force is spent, matter develops, and as the latter concentrates, the former is necessarily lost. The opposite course of dissolution then sets in, in which motion is saved and matter is expanded. And so the process is reiterated without end, and the dust and ashes of natural creations are integrated and co-ordinated to make frames for new products of the universal workshop. The knowable universe thus consists of aggregates that are forever evolving. The change or evolution consists of two stages: the first, from the moment when phenomena appear out of the unknown and reach full maturity in the known; the second, when the process begins to decline and they pass back into the unknown. While man, in his short span of life is able only to observe the first stage, the second, or period of dissolution is as inevitable as death (see *D.S.,* I, 155-168).

The synthetic philosophy is Spencer's vast canvass on which he depicts the history of the cosmos: all the sciences are his pigments, and the Unknowable which he reserves for religion, is the background. The unity of his composition includes an exposition of the natural laws of physics, the indestructibility of matter, the conservation of energy, the transformability of forces, and the rhythm of motion. In the effort to synthesize, he reduced all those laws to a single law, the persistence of force. Force holds the central position in Spencer's picture of the cosmos. It is to him, the final unknowable factor, the First Cause of all phenomena.

While his definition of evolution is purely a formula of physical science (the distribution of matter and energy), it points, in spite of his strenuous denials, to a materialistic metaphysics. He also admitted in his later writings that his concept of evolution which he at first claimed covered everything in the universe was not all-inclusive.

### WARD'S CRITIQUE OF THE SYNTHETIC PHILOSOPHY

Although the fundamental dictum of Spencer's synthesis, the law of the persistence of force, is incorrect (said Ward) because matter, not force, is the basis of the cosmos, it is an improvement upon Comte's denial of the existence of force as a necessary relation of the nature and conception of mind. Comte's system, on the whole, is not founded squarely upon evolution because he substitutes for the law of causality, independent succession assumed to be uniform (see *ibid.,* pp. 157-159).

Spencer's synthetic structure, however, did not crack at the base but near the top where his false analogy between man and the animal crashed the whole edifice into the dust. Not even ethics which he placed at the apex of the sciences could save it, because beneath ethics was a sociology founded upon biological laws governing a brutal individualism. It was a top-heavy Tower of Babel that Spencer had built, and as soon as it was attacked, it collapsed and all the philosophers in the world could not put it together again. The truth and profundity in his cosmic philosophy and in the sciences of matter, life and mind are indisputable, but they could not support the fallacy of his sociology (see below, p. 302).

The collapse of the synthetic philosophy is best understood in the light of Comte's law. Incidentally, it must be noted that Spencer as stoutly denied any obligation to Comte, as Comte did to Saint-Simon. Yet, if there had been no Comte, there could have been no Spencer, for the outline and chief central positions of the evolution theory clearly came from Comte. At any rate, Spencer was in biology and psychology fully in the positive stage, but in ethics and social science, he was in all three stages at the same time, straddling the Unknowable, the static or structural concept of society, and the scientific method. He not only failed to see clearly the essential distinction between cosmic evolution and organic evolution but was unable to distinguish between organic and social evolution, both of which he regarded as one process governed by the same natural laws. Comte who was far from being a true evolutionist, perceived the possibility of social improvement through man's dynamic efforts, but Spencer, the king of the evolution theory, grew so nearsighted when he approached the social question that all he could see in society—past, present, and future—was the same deadly competitive struggle which ultimately left it to nature's law of the survival of the fittest to alter and improve man's social condition.

The reasons for Spencer's abortive synthesis are not hard to find. When the great fall, they fall from great heights. His astonishing error in failing to differentiate animal evolution from social development was fundamentally due to his straying from the path of the scientific method. Despite his vast knowledge, he remained an a priori reasoner who used that method as if it were a rigid measuring rod, and of all thinkers, committed the blunder of arguing from analogy when he came to social science. Although he knew that no argument is valid unless it is based on concrete data, he never learned how to observe, and remained a wishful and most gullible thinker who was satisfied when he could forcibly compress any argument into the frame of the law of evolution. He seemed more like a lawyer seeking authorities to support his cause, whether just or not, than a scientist who is concerned only with finding the truth. The evolution theory became a dogma in Spencer's hands, and he rarely changed an idea or listened to anything contradicting his thought. In the field of cosmic evolution where there is much speculation and little data, he remained, like Aristotle, an intellectual monarch. But where true observation and insight were needed, as in history and social evolution, Spencer has been overruled. Yet society is largely dominated by his sociology, even if the concept social evolution means to the liberal-minded scientists of today, Comte and Ward, and not Spencer,

Spencer was the king of the deductive method. It is a safe method, if the premises cover all the facts. But since his definition of evolution omitted important forms of social reality, it was unsafe and misleading. He regarded evolution as a process which runs in a straight line direct from biology into sociology. His social philosophy is, therefore, based upon the erroneous assumption that society is a purely natural formation. Surprisingly, he claimed to be an inductive thinker, though in the latter part of his life, he styled his method as "deduction fortified by induction." Professor Small characterized it more justly as "speculation fortified by illustration."

Spencer's confession is also illuminating: "All my life, I have been a thinker, not a reader, being able to say with Hobbes that if I had read as much as other men, I should have known as little." But had he read more carefully and widely, he might have written less and with more humility, and not overlooked the influence of the *Zeitgeist* on his own thought. Darwin appraised him correctly when he said:

I feel rather mean when I read Spencer. He is rather twice as ingenious and clever as myself. If he had trained himself to observe more, even at the expense of some thinking power, he would have been a wonderful man. I find that my mind is so fixed by the inductive method, that I cannot appreciate deductive reasoning. I must begin with a good body of facts and not from a principle (in which I always suspect some fallacy), and then, as much deduction as you please. This may be very narrow minded, but the result is that such parts of Spencer as I have read with care, impress my mind with the idea of his inexhaustible wealth of suggestion, but never convince me (*Life and Letters of Darwin*, II, 239, 301, 371).

Without heat or rancor, Ward concludes that Spencer failed most efficiently to complete the unification of knowledge. Like his predecessors, Spencer still lacked some of the requirements of the ideal sociologist. Nevertheless, there is little doubt that his name will retain a permanent position among the architects and builders of the temple. More than any other thinker of the nineteenth century, he popularized sociology for the English-speaking world, and made Comte's promise of a social science ruling the world assume something of the aspect of a definite program of scientific activity. In the words of one of his critics:

Spencer's sociology is one of the rungs on the ladder by which his successors have been able to climb. As no science can be completely mastered apart from its history, the student of sociology must thoroughly study the works of its two great forerunners—Comte and Spencer (cited in *The Story of Social Philosophy,* by Charles A. Ellwood, pp. 465-466).

Ward, despite his trenchant criticism of Spencer's system, displays the true nobility of the impartial, scientific spirit, in his tribute to the great philosopher. Spencer (he says) did not try to make over the universe, or revel in dreams of social perfection. Instead, he took the materials out of which the world is built, and made the most of them, in order to prepare it for the occupancy of a higher and more perfect race of men (see *D.S.,* I, 218). Ward's insight is never more incandescent and humane than in the address which he delivered in 1882 at the banquet given to Spencer on his visit to America, when he said:

It is his brain power, conceived to a large extent as impersonal, that we would recognize and honor. . . . He occupies his present exalted place in the eyes of the world, purely and solely through the force of his intellect. Unaided by human effort, and from the depths of his own mind, he has formulated the laws of the universe, not merely in the simpler and better known departments of astronomy and physics, but throughout the new and unexplored realms of life, mind and action. . . . Mr. Spencer's preeminence as a philosopher rests primarily upon two qualities, and can only come out of the union of these in one and the same mind. These qualities are first, his extensive information; and, second, his extraordinary causality. The work of the true philosopher is preëminently the synthesis of extant knowledge (*Glimpses,* III, 115).

Comte, Spencer, and Ward, in the final analysis, cannot be justly compared to one another. Each was a builder who improved the structure of his predecessor, and left his own achievement as material for the future. All of them served to establish sociology as a true science, and to fuse all the sciences into social science. Ward is not the greatest but the last in the roster of mighty system builders whose genius completed the great synthesis.

# Chapter XVII

# SOCIOLOGY

*"Sociology, under some name or other, was as inevitable as the problems of energy in physics, after the human brain turned itself loose on the phenomena in the fashion of Archimedes."*—Albion W. Small.

*"These unitary principles, forming the basis of so many systems or schools of sociology . . . all these various lines in which not only social science but all science advances, together with all others that have been or shall be followed out may be compared to so many minor streams, all tending in a given direction and converging so as ultimately to unite in one ₁great river that represents the whole science of Sociology as it will be finally established."*—Ward

In surveying the attempts to synthesize all knowledge and construct the temple of sociology, we have met its architects and builders from 400 B.C. to the beginning of the twentieth century. Ward belongs in the present century as much as in the preceding one, for he built upon Spencer's evolution theory as well as upon Comte's positive philosophy, and reached well into the present era to demonstrate that dynamic sociology means social control, and leads to a society ruled by itself.

## WARD

He not only possessed to a remarkable degree the knowledge which has accumulated since antiquity but was also a happy combination of the master of the scientific method in philosophy, the organizer in biology, the pioneer in psychology and the synthesist in sociology. Aristotle was the first to open the world's eyes to the realms of science; Comte the first modern thinker to demonstrate the relativity of knowledge and the scientific correlation of nature, man, and social science. Darwin was the pioneer who demonstrated man's biological relationship to the animal world. Spencer attempted a completely sustaining picture of development from cosmos to society. What is Ward's contribution?

Ward was a profound and practical philosopher. One of his bitter opponents, Professor Giddings, could not help saying: "Ward's ability, originality, and varied accomplishments place him in rank with Spencer and Tarde" ("Modern Sociology," *International Monthly,* II, 536-

554, November, 1900). In spite of all efforts to cast off tradition and class idealism, most sociologists have remained idealists in one form or another, whose great misfortune has been that they never mastered the natural sciences, or completely adopted the scientific method or were able to remain free-minded and practical.

Ward abandoned all metaphysical daydreams for scientific fact and theory, while, all the time, the humanitarian fires burned as strongly within him as they did in Comte. By placing sociology (not ethics) at the head of the sciences, he achieved in a natural and unforced manner the great synthesis which is sociology. His system has not only a solid base of material, physical science, but also a superstructure which holds a plan of education, a scheme of basic, social reform, and the ideal of a new social order.

### THE SYNTHESIS OF ALL KNOWLEDGE

The value of Ward's contribution to synthesis does not depend upon the accuracy of his data or the up-to-the-minute perfection of his technology. His argument is triangular. From the biological side, he proves that there are social forces working together with cosmic forces; from the psychological side, he demonstrates that mind can control nature and men; from the sociological side, he argues that education is the sure road to happiness, and that the social will is the final arbiter of our destiny. And all through his synthesis, one can follow the conflict and teamwork of natural forces; feeling and thought; from the inanimate to the animate; from the brute to civilized man; from the material to the spiritual; from despair to hope.

By amplifying the table of nature's synthetic productions, he attracted his students to the formidable task of completing the grand survey of all knowledge within a single year. He often remarked that anyone who grasped his chart of the sciences would comprehend that all-rounded projection of the cosmos and discern the value and importance of dynamic sociology (see *Cape,* pp. 148, 152; *Glimpses,* V, 150).

This tabular view of knowledge affords the composite view of nature and things which the philosophers of all time have so eagerly sought. Many have observed parts of the natural process, but few have seen it whole. Darwin found it in the struggle for existence involved in natural selection; Schopenhauer, in the will to live. Nietzsche located it in the will to power; religious philosophers, in the will to God. Spencer called it the persistence of force, but found no consistent principle like creative synthesis to explain its action.

TABULAR VIEW OF ALL KNOWLEDGE IN THE ORDER IN WHICH IT HAS BEEN EVOLVED.

| Kinds of Knowledge | | Subjects of the Sciences Products of Evolution Cosmic Structures | Differential Attributes | | | |
|---|---|---|---|---|---|---|
| Sciences | Subsciences | | Differential Properties Cosmic Functions | Activities Possessed | Phenomena Manifested | Causes Employed |
| Sociology | | Human Society | | | | |
| | Pedagogy | Knowledge | | | | |
| | Pathology | Disease | | | | |
| | Esthetology | The Fine Arts | | | | |
| | Nomology (jurisprudence) | Justice | | | | |
| | Politology, Civiology (politics) | The State | Civilization Sociism | Molar | Social | Final or Telic |
| | Ecology (economics) | Wealth, Property | | | | |
| | Theology | God, Religion | | | | |
| | Ethology (ethics) | Customs, Conduct | | | | |
| | Philology | Language | | | | |
| | Gamology (sex relations) | The Family | | | | |
| | Ethnology | Human Races | | | | |
| | Anthropology | Man | | | | |
| Psychology | | Mind | | | Psychic | |
| | Objective Psychology | Man | Intellect } Psych-ism | | | Conative |
| | Subjective Psychology | Animals | Feeling | | | |
| Biology | | Organisms | | | Vital | |
| | Zoology | Animals | Life } Zoism | | | |
| | Botany | Plants | | | | |
| | Plasmatology | Protoplasm | Motility | | | |
| Chemistry | Organic Chemistry | Organic Compounds | Chemical Affinity | | | |
| | Inorganic Chemistry | Inorganic Compounds | | Molecular | | |
| | | Chemical Elements | Chemism | | | |
| Physics | | | | | | Efficient |
| | Barology | Matter | Gravitation-attraction | | | |
| | Radiology | Electrons | Radio-activity | | Physical | |
| | Etherology | Ether | Vibration | | | |
| | Thermology | | Heat | | | |
| | Photology | | Light | | | |
| | Electrology | | Electricity | | | |
| Astronomy | | Celestial Bodies | Motion | Radiant | | |
| | Solar Astronomy | The Solar System | Orbital and Axial Revolution | | | |
| | Sidereal Astronomy | Stars | Radiation | | | |
| | Cosmical Astronomy | Nebulæ | Evolution | | | |

## SOCIOLOGY, A TRUE SCIENCE

Dynamic sociology cannot be confused with Jeffersonian democracy. It is true that the sociology of Comte's French predecessors which was wafted across the sea, impregnated the thought of the founding fathers with the humanistic doctrine of natural rights. But there was no scientific fruition of those ideas until Ward, a century later, transplanted their truths into the rich soil of dynamic social science, and transformed vague philosophical sentimentalities into scientific principles.

Nevertheless, many people still believe that sociology is not and never can be a true science. If they are right, the Zodiac should become our social guide, and chance and drift our only outlook and method. Both Comte and Ward observed clearly that cosmic law governs both man and society, and that social science is a true science because human actions are not mere accidents. Unfortunately for social progress, this view has not yet been adopted by the great majority because the totality of knowledge or human experience is for most people too immense and complicated to be grasped as a whole. While many are able to comprehend the parts, such as physical science, history, or anthropology, they cannot synthesize them. Few thinkers have had Ward's desire and ability to survey the entire field of knowledge, grasp the laws of cosmic kinship and social relationships, and weld it all into a single science.

The great opposition to sociology's claim that it is a true science is that it cannot be an exact science and is, therefore, no science at all. It is true that in spite of Plato's aphorism, "Everything which comes into being is subject to the technique of measurement," social science as an experimental, mathematical discipline is still in the making. Truth in societal phenomena is not yet deducible by exact observation, but will be arrived at in that way, more and more, as phenomena come under the wing of science.[1]

[1] In a letter to Ward (Nov. 7, 1901) Professor Small wrote: "Most of them [subscribers to the *American Journal of Sociology,* and various newspaper critics] want no sociology at all; what they think is sociology is either pure statistics with no ray of sociology to make them mean anything to anybody, or else it is a lot of sociological sugar-coated kindergarten literature" (*Social Forces,* XV, 305).

Eight years later (Nov. 29, 1909) in another letter to Ward, Professor Small wrote again: "Sociology, under some name or other, was as inevitable as the problems of energy in physics, after the human brain turned itself loose on the phenomena in the fashion of Archimedes. Instead of being a freak science, there is nothing coherent or

Because sociological data have not yet been translated into mathematical symbols is not conclusive proof that sociology is not a real science. There are no two scientific methods, the statistical or mathematical, for the physical and material universe, and the other method, unformed, loose, and unscientific, for the social and spiritual world. The worship of statistics and formulas results in much fact-finding but little interpretation. Sociology, like all the other sciences, does not deal with absolute certainties (only theology and metaphysics claim to do that) but with what is most probable. The more sociology develops (again, like every other science), the greater the area of knowledge and the smaller the field of speculation and hypothesis. The more general, simple and abstract the phenomena, the more precise are our ideas with respect to them. Mathematical propositions are the most precise, but precision is not the same thing as certainty.

We have seen the paradox in the classification of the sciences, that the truths furthest removed from the practical interests of humanity, like those of astronomy, have been the first to emerge, while the two great domains in which scarcely any great discoveries have been made or applied—those of mind and society—are nearest to what concerns man. The only compensation for such tardiness, according to Ward, is found in the fact that "psychic and social truth when it shall begin to be revealed will be far more practical than even biologic truth" (*Outlines,* p. 210).

Ward, who upheld Comte's affirmation that sociology is, in the true sense, a science, is the last of the synthesists. After him came a deluge of social surveys, special reports, and statistical curves applied to various isolated parts of the structure, until the real purpose of sociology was all but lost in mazes of specialization and standardization. Even that could not conceal the truth that society is composed of too many millions of living souls to be compressed into inert

conclusive in the social sciences at all, until everything there is, in the processes of human association, has been analyzed down to its ultimate discernible elements, and then connected up in its actual functional relations within the evolution that tells the whole story; and sociology is merely one among the possible names for that stage in scientific consciousness which insists on a scientific program which shall have this whole sweep of the phenomena in view and will not accept conclusions as final until they are conclusions which fit into a consistent account of the interworkings of all the phenomena. I think the main movement among all the American Sociologists since Dynamic Sociology appeared has had something like this as its more or less conscious motive, and I feel more sure than ever that the stars in their courses are fighting for us" (*ibid.,* p. 326).

equations or choked by meticulous pedantry. Sociology is too vast a science to be the work of a single individual. Like a Gothic cathedral, many hands and minds of many generations must help to build it. No doubt, later thinkers will add new wings and new ornamental features, but it will always be the wings and ornaments of the temple of knowledge into which all rational men must enter.

They, who still deny the title *science* to sociology because it is the least exact of all the sciences, will be found to have some other pet science as their favorite, one which furnishes data rather than principles and is a miscellany rather than a synthesis. Thus, even so clear a thinker as Professor Charles A. Beard has mistaken sociology for history and historical interpretation (see *Saturday Review of Literature,* August 17, 1935) when he asserts that the nature of sociological material precludes the use of the scientific method, and that the investigator in sociology is inside his own experiment and cannot, therefore, fail to be influenced by the material under investigation. Ergo, sociology cannot be a real science since it is filled with so much that is unscientific, and "must remain at best a humanist subject. Since there is no science of history or economics there cannot be a social science."

Much error and confusion would perhaps be avoided if our language distinguished between science in the sense of knowledge of nature and science denoting social knowledge. In English, science, as yet, refers only to the former. Excluding the nonscientific and the pseudo-scientific content which Professor Beard decries, is there a scientific kernel left to sociology or is it in the same state as chemistry, physics, or biology was in the eighteenth century? Perhaps the popular misconceptions about sociology should not be surprising. Did not Condorcet truly remark that a man who would not dare to pretend to any knowledge of physics or astronomy without having mastered it, could see nothing wrong about defending opinions on the most abstract and complicated social problems without the least study or reflection?

## A DEFINITION OF SOCIOLOGY

Like the blind Hindus in the ancient legend, each one of whom examined a different part of an elephant and then gave the most weird description of the animal, myopic thinkers and specialists have offered fallacious definitions of sociology. The cause of such errors are found in the misuse of philosophy and the lack of a broad scientific method. When one sees the mountains of philosophic material that have been piled up throughout the ages, it is surprising how little of it has been made into a permanent structure. Although philosophy is rooted in science and is coextensive with it, it does not follow that all scientific data have philosophical or sociological value. Many facts are isolated or of little account, while others bear a much deeper significance than appears on the surface. Plato's definition of a philosopher as "one who is able to grasp the immutable and the eternal" peculiarly applies to the social scientist, for the latter alone can best co-ordinate the fleeting and confusing masses of social phenomena, and from them extract the golden grains of truth. Since there is no sharp distinction between science and philosophy, in the true sense of those terms, the dry bones of social science must be animated by an infusion of the philosophic spirit.

Sociology is a science as well as a philosophy, but it is not philosophy in the popular meaning of speculation or metaphysics. One may philosophize about anything, from a blade of grass to an international war, but that does not make him a sociologist. To earn that title, one must be able to interpret by underlying laws and principles, and apply the results to actual conditions (see *ibid.*, p. 116). Many philosophers have seen large sections of life, but few have seen it whole, because their theories have been mainly reactions of their emotions to some particular phase of the human comedy. Spinoza, the pantheist, prepared the world for a spiritual renaissance; Voltaire, the Deist, cleared the intellectual ground for the French Revolution; and Kant, the philosopher, pure and complex, made mankind ready by his inquiries into the operations of the mind, for an intellectual revolution. All that was the work of geniuses, but not one of them was a sociologist. Nor does the pessimism of Schopenhauer, the individualism of Nietzsche, or the spiritualism of Gandhi make any of them a social scientist or social philosopher.

Apart from fragmentary and undeveloped conceptions of sociology, there have been various definitions reflecting a synthetic viewpoint. Ratzenhofer called it "the study of the reciprocal relationships of human beings"; Professor Small, "the study of men considered as affected by association." Ward confessed that he was almost the only sociologist who had not ventured on one or more definitions. Definitions were not needed, he said, so much as "clear explanations and definite delimitations of the field" (*ibid.,* p. x), and "a clear presentation of the scientific principles underlying it" (*Glimpses,* VI, 130).

The concept sociology (Latin, *socius,* a companion; Greek, λογι'α, an account) is in Ward's system, something more than a general discussion of social phenomena. Benjamin Kidd's eloquent thesis that religion and sociology are identical, is not an example of sociology, but of the metaphysics of a brilliant mind. Sociology of that kind, has been made the label for any emotional idea which could be coherently outlined, and even for those that cannot. So there are economists who ascribe high prices to sun spots, communism to bad teeth, and divorce scandals to eating hot pie for breakfast. They are excelled only by the medical experts who dilate learnedly upon cancer or paganism as the cause of the World War. When science is thus abandoned for pseudo-science or pure speculation, there is no limit to the nonsense in which the imagination or the misinformed mind may indulge. But why apply the label *sociology?* We may witness the marriage of astrology and anthropology or view the mad dances of graphs and cycles clad in robes of science, but why include such things in any category of science?

## THE DATA OF SOCIOLOGY

What does sociology consist of? The bricks of the temple of sociology are the data supplied by the lesser sciences (see *P.S.,* p. 15). To be a sociologist, one need not be a specialist in the sciences, but it is necessary for him to know how to find his way about in them. Ward's advice was to obtain a firm grasp of cosmic principles, including a lifelong grasp upon the law of causality, and then a working knowledge of history, economics, and the natural sciences, and one is ready to scale the heights.

Sociology may be compared to the science and art of building, and the other sciences to the individual crafts. It is not any one of the following lesser sciences, yet it is the synthesis of all of them:

1. Anthropology, the science of man.
2. Archaeology, the science of antiquity.
3. Demography, the science of social statistics.
4. Economics, the science of wealth.

5. Ethics, the science of right conduct and character.
6. Ethnology and ethnography, the sciences of the races of man.
7. History, the science of the recorded actions of man.
8. Jurisprudence, the science of laws.
9. Politics, the science of government.
10. Technology, the science of the industrial arts (see *Outlines,* pp. 66, 136).

Most sciences, at one time or another, have been confused with sociology. Thus, history deals with the details of the human adventure, but sociology alone treats of the general laws and principles which underlie history. Anthropology covers only the natural history of man, but does not include biology, psychology, or economics. Yet Spencer in his *Principles of Sociology* deals almost exclusively with matter belonging to anthropology, and only at the end of that work does he offer what could serve as merely an introduction to a handbook of sociology. As for economics, sociology travels along the same road, especially in the interpretation of history and in the study of the environment; then it takes the road of psychology and leaves economics behind.

The geologist copyrights the earth; the biologist, life. The psychologist works exclusively upon the mind, while the anthropologist digs up fossils, customs, laws, and rites to illustrate man's origin and culture. The sociologist alone is the editor of all their labors. Sitting like a forest warden in a high mountain tower, he views the social panorama through scientific lenses, sees the social forces in the human struggle on the roads of economics, psychology, history, ethics, and religion, and proceeds to extract from the scene the laws and principles underlying social phenomena.

The view is open to all, yet different minds take different attitudes and make widely separated interpretations. There are the viewpoints from (1) the mechanical, which regards society as an intricate mechanism and formulates laws and principles in terms of the quantity and direction of mechanical energy (Comte and Quetelet); (2) the biological, which considers the same phenomena in terms of organic relations (Spencer with his key phrase "Society is an organism"); (3) the psychological, developed in the works of Ratzenhofer, Gumplowicz, and Ward. Despite these varied approaches, sociology is fundamentally a single science. Whether one takes the road of method, group psychology, social analysis, social service, the environment, economics, biology, or general culture; whether he is attracted to problems of the kindergarten or of international reconstruction, as long as the method pursued is the scientific, sociology, the goal, will be found at the meeting of the roads. Says Ward:

All these various lines, together with all others that have been or shall be followed out, may be compared to so many minor streams, all tending in a given direction and converging so as ultimately to unite in one great river that represents the whole science of sociology as it will be finally established (*P.S.,* p. 14).

The burden of the ceaseless stream of the sciences which flows into sociology is not man in the abstract, but his achievements, whether for good or evil, seen from an all-sided, elevated view. The pettiness of individual contributions, like the minute accretions which after eons, form stratified rock, need not absorb our attention. Sociology is the only science that surveys human achievement and social culture as a whole, while, like geology, it incidentally examines each stratum (see *ibid.,* p. 39).

The story of man subdivides into two parts, according to whether we seek him out in his natural environment (anthropology), or whether we study his achievements (dynamic sociology). But sociology alone enters the maze of human experience, to prove that nothing has ever happened or ever can happen without impinging on man. Nothing can even be imagined that does not touch upon his problems. And so, sociology, discovering that society is a natural creation, emerges with an orderly, scientific grasp of man's place and aim in the scheme of things (see *Glimpses,* VI, 263).

## SOCIOLOGY—PURE AND APPLIED

Above the noise and strife of conflicting philosophies and methods, Ward completed the foundations and the framework of the temple of sociology. In that, he succeeded in at least two main objects: (1) to build up social science upon a definite scheme of natural laws and principles; (2) to construct a social philosophy by bounding social science and marking it off from the lesser sciences (see *Glimpses,* VI, 7). In the first part of the scheme, sociology accounts for the evolution of natural phenomena into society by the synthesis of physical, vital, and psychic causes and effects; in the second part, it enters the field of philosophy and postulates the principles of social control and social progress, and seeks to foretell and plan for the future.

It was Comte who first divided sociology into two departments or stages: the pure (abstract or static), and the applied (concrete, synthetic or dynamic). As we have seen (p. 154), statics in mechanics is the condition of equilibrium, while dynamics represents the laws of movement. The first is a necessary condition of the second, but the latter is more important to mankind. Pure sociology is a scientific study of the experiences of the race, and deals entirely with structure and function, omitting, for the time, all programs, planning or moral values. It concentrates, instead, upon truth for its own sake, upon what society is and has done, not upon what it should be or ought to do (see *P.S.,* p. 4).

Applied sociology involves the art of applying science and mechanics to the various departments of human economy. While pure sociology corresponds to the study of the positive theory of order, applied sociology is the study of the collective existence of humanity, and constitutes the positive theory of social progress. Sociology thus unites the two equally fundamental ideas of order and progress, the radical opposition of which constitutes the characteristic symptom of the profound disturbance of modern society (Comte).

Although the static conception of social organization must constitute the basis of sociology, social dynamics forms the practical and more important superstructure. Applied sociology gives social science its most decisive philosophical character by clearly developing the notion which distinguishes biology from sociology, i.e., the idea of continuous progress, or of the gradual development of humanity, under the guidance of social science.

When the science of society will be accepted as other sciences have been accepted, its influence on the life of every human being will exceed the influence of the lesser sciences, because "sociology is nearer to man and more intimately bound up with all that concerns his welfare" (*Outlines,* p. 212). This may sound to some like a prayer, and sociology like some more theory filed away between book covers, but the moment evolution brings the world to applied sociology—the stage when social science takes the chief command—man begins to use all the knowledge that he has learned and becomes truly lord of the earth.

In estimating how near to that stage we have come, Ward's opinion changed with the years. He recognized that material civilization produces problems which require a corresponding change in social science, i.e., that a science, like everything else, must grow and develop, when he said (1900): "I do not claim that sociology has as yet been established as a science. I only maintain that it is in the process of establishment, and this by the same method by which all other sciences are established" (*P.S.*, p. 8).

Seven years later sociology had appeared to him to have progressed so rapidly that he remarked: "Sociology established as a pure science is now entering upon its applied stage, which is the great practical object for which it exists" (*Glimpses*, VI, 265).

Concrete application is the touchstone of all social doctrine and the climax and realization of all sociological thinking. But this should not make the social scientist a partisan in any sense, for a partisan necessarily abandons science and becomes a "politician," or a press agent, often in spite of himself. As the most famous example, Spencer's sociology is prejudiced science, a still-life photograph of society posed by Spencer in the zoo of animal life. The difference between the descriptive and structural sociology of Spencer and the dynamic and applied sociology of Ward is the difference between a department store and an economic system (Professor Small).

## THE PURPOSE OF SOCIOLOGY

The purpose of sociology, according to Ward, is the purpose of science, to study not only what men are, but what they do. Social science has the additional and moral aim of controlling society for man's greater happiness. Yet, almost everything else under the sun has been given as its aim. The Greek thinkers whom all the intellectual world imitated, did not pay much attention to man's origin, constitution, or environment because they were too occupied, for the most part, with worrying about his immortal soul. They may be excused for their fallacious method and viewpoint which led them to lay the course of knowledge over a road of metaphysics covered with signs "This way to Heaven!" But in modern times, it is not excusable to erect sky-piercing mansions of thought concerning man and his destiny, on metaphysical foundations resting in the clouds, without raising a hand to set solid piers for them. In other words, it is a costly error to spin spiritual cables to the skies and neglect to connect man with happiness here.

After twenty-five hundred years of progress in knowledge, the forgotten species has been remembered at last, and the world can return with sociology to the ancient idea of man as the center of attraction. Sociology is the only science which has an altruistic aim, the improvement of the race from all angles and at all cost. That is no longer a polite parlor game of social reform or a vision of utopia. Social problems come before all other problems because the urge to live and the desire for happiness are recognized as the strongest of human desires. In Ward's words:

> Science is supposed to be pursued for its own sake, to increase the sum of knowledge. . . . Poets and philosophers have perceived that knowledge is power, but no one has pointed out specifically in what way knowledge operates as a power. Indeed, the practical view of science is generally condemned. . . . It is, of course, clear to all, that mathematics, physics, and chemistry have an immediate practical value in the affairs of life, but most of the other sciences,—geology, botany, zoology, ethnology, psychology, etc.,—are looked upon mainly in the light of culture, like history, literature, fine art, etc. (*Outlines,* pp. 197-198).

No science is worthy of its name, says Ward, unless it can help mankind to increase the joy of living. A synthetic philosophy like Spencer's, valuable as it is in expounding the evolution process, becomes for man rather abstract and pedantic. One is tempted to say: "Well, what of it?" To wait for the natural forces of evolution to bring happiness to humanity seems as sensible as waiting for flowers to grow in the midst of a desert. Evolution and all other knowledge of nature and man exist for the single purpose of serving mankind. It is this view which destroys the illusion that government is a glorified policeman (this was Spencer's idea of the state) and establishes sociology as the positive science of society, the instrument of social intelligence for the improvement of human existence and the promotion of general happiness.

## SOCIOLOGY AS SOCIAL ETHICS

Ward, who had "the mind of a sage, the heart of a woman and the soul of a poet," is no pious pedant because of his applied sociology, but one of the great commoners, the salt of the earth, who aimed at the loftiest spiritual values but never lost sight of the solid material base. The genius of his system is that while it is from beginning to end a hymn to science and the scientific method, it is at the same time a thrilling plea to science to increase human happiness, to minimize the quantity of human suffering so needlessly thrust upon the majority of mankind, and enlarge the volume of individual and social life.

When Ward called his era the stone age of politics and deplored the failure of society to grasp its powers of self-government, he was talking not only sociology but the social ethics which is identical with it, yet finds so little room in our conventional ethical code (see Chapter XLI). Morality is not prohibition and restraint, but happiness, health, safety and well-being—the sole aim in man's life. Applied sociology thus reflects the most benign spiritual tendencies. The climb to the heights of the moral life is impossible without a firm material base which would free the climber of all economic and social fetters. But instead of men's welfare subordinated (when it was not entirely forgotten) to the devices and institutions of society, with its customs, traditions, laws, and creeds, it should be the paramount consideration. As a result of the isolation of ethics from sociology, religion suffered from ritual sclerosis; ethics shrunk to a mere restrictive code, and sciences descended to the level of logical hockey contests.

To this day, economists, philosophers, and public-spirited men of all sorts, calmly lock themselves in their studies and make reports, evolve formulas, and split still further the finespun hairs of logic and speculation, while human beings outside their windows writhe and sweat and die in the agony of a cruel and unnecessary social struggle. Unemployment, disease, poverty, and even war can no more teach a suffering humanity the truths of sociology than the pangs of hunger can nourish the body. Though the earth is overflowing with material necessities and spiritual treasures, science remains a dismal and unknown discipline to the great mass, which continues to be ignorant, cold, and hungry.

The spiritual heights reached by the few intellectual élite are undesired and undreamed of by the vast majority. Scientific research, too, becomes unimportant, exciting as the affections of atoms or insects may be, in a social mêlée where human beings cut each others' throats or die of hunger and despair, the world over. In brief, of what earthly use are all the learned diatribes on nature, God and man, when humanity is suffering and unhappy? If this is too dark or pragmatic a picture for those who love knowledge or debate for its own sake, let them look at the world around them and see if there is any shaft of light in the social gloom except that which emanates from the ethics of sociology.

## SOCIOLOGY AS EDUCATIONAL PHILOSOPHY

In spite of the ethical aim of sociology, the peroration of Ward's synthesis is not ethics, but education. Education is the true lever of Archimedes which alone can lift man out of the ditch. As in Erasmus, the fundamental belief as well as the crowning point in Ward's system, is the idea that social progress (happiness) can come only through enlightenment for all. Again and again, he plays upon the theme that man can make his life vastly more worthy and satisfying if he would but train the same kind of intense study upon society as he has devoted to nature or to more or less meaningless trivia and abstractions. The shortest way and the surest way to better doing is more thorough knowing. Only through universal scientific education of the mass can the social will find expression. The philosophy of education furnishes the rational basis for intelligent programs of social action and lays the foundation for social control and reconstruction without class wars or bloody revolutions.

Such a program needs, of course, the support of a united people. Yet, no special individual genius or training is required. By introducing and equalizing opportunity, the present human mediocrity would begin to develop almost spontaneously those seeds of talent and genius which are latent in everybody (see p. 422). This does not ignore the impetus furnished by great men or great ideas, nor does it oppose abstract research. Even the very lowest classes have been profoundly influenced by the discoveries of Newton, Galileo, Darwin, and other world figures. But simply to wait for geniuses to move the world is a terribly slow process which may never bring relief. "Education for all!" is the battle cry of Ward's sociology. By imparting to all men all extant knowledge, they would become as wise and intelligent in societal affairs as they already are in matters relating to agriculture, hygiene, or chemistry, or in things which, in general, concern their individual well-being.

This panacea of education is in Ward's philosophy no short cut to utopia, no magic formula by which human beings could be transformed overnight into spirits of sweetness and light, but the long, hard road of knowledge. It is a new emancipation proclamation which makes its author the Lincoln not for a single race, class, or creed but for all who are disinherited of knowledge and science and opportunity. In the thesis that everything finally comes down to a conflict between emotion, ignorance, and superstition, on the one hand, and reason, knowledge, and science on the other, he furnished the impetus as well as the scientific basis for such world-wide movements as the feminist, the educational, and the peoples' movements, which have barely commenced, but have already profoundly altered the world.

## THE FRUITS OF SYNTHESIS

Although the reader has arrived at synthesis, his adventure is far from over. To give up the journey at this point would place him in the predicament of the man who knew all about the automobile and could take it apart and put it together again, but wondered what made it run without horses. All we have seen is the blueprint of the temple; we have yet to enter it and find what man has done or can do with his mansion of knowledge. Ward knew how human beings are wont to pry into every nook and corner of the globe like curious puppies, with no more real desire for social control than astronomers have to alter or improve the course of the planets. With the cry: "The twentieth century is the age of sociology; it is the age of man," Ward's epochmaking synthesis brought to the front the doctrine of the social will, the superiority of mental and conscious control over natural and unconscious control by the social forces. That has been accepted by those who know, as Ward's single and most valuable contribution to human thought, as the most powerful postulate ever made by sociology. Professor Franklin H. Giddings, one of his severest critics, characterized it as follows:

This great thought Ward apprehended, expressed, explained, illuminated and drove home to the minds of all who read his pages, as no other writer, ancient or modern, has ever done. It is his enduring and cogent contribution to sociology (quoted in "American Masters of Social Science," an essay on Ward by Prof. James Q. Dealey, p. 93).

The society that Ward foresees through the lenses of his doctrine is one which will know how, why, and where it is going. The road to that new social order is long, and there is no millennium at the end of it. Although pedants and sentimentalists may keep on fighting in the arena of sociology over pet bones of contention for the mere sake of possession, without affecting the world very much, Ward's synthesis will remain the inspiration for and the harbinger of the world movement for emancipation of all men, everywhere.

## CRITICISM OF WARD'S SYSTEM

A little over three decades have passed since Ward's system of dynamic sociology was completed, and the years have witnessed tremendous social changes. In certain respects, historical developments, especially in industry and education, have proceeded somewhat differently and more slowly than Ward anticipated. His glance into the future was, nevertheless, on the whole, an accurate one. Some critics may call him a false prophet, but his prophecies which spring from clear and acute thought must be distinguished from those of others which are the result of conceited self-reflection or pious wishes.

If Comte's system is distinguished by the absolute predominance of the moral point of view, and the rigorous subordination of the intellect to the heart, Ward adds as the supreme aim of sociology not only the elevation of mind above feelings, but of education above all, by which reason shall direct the emotions.

No one should pin wings on Ward's shoulders. Undoubtedly, there will be other and more perfect syntheses than Ward's. No science or system of philosophy can be eternal or immutable as long as the law of evolution continues to function, and knowledge and experience continue to grow. Later advances in the various sciences basic to sociology, and in social science itself, may change or tend to discredit some of his conclusions, but nothing can deprive him of the merit of having helped to lay the foundations and gone further with the superstructure of the temple of sociology, than any other thinker.

As yet, there has been little criticism of his system, as a whole. Those who were most familiar with it, like Professors Small, Ross,

Ellwood, Worms, Gumplowicz, and De Greef, accepted its foundations and pillars, even while they attacked various wings. In general, he has been taken to task for being too sure of himself and insulating his labors from those of other sociologists. In the study of the origin of society, he has been called weak. In the field of evolution, he has been accused of leaning too much to Lamarck, and away from Darwin. Psychologists have denied his theory of the dynamic agent and have taken issue with his idea that desire is the mainspring of all human action. His stress upon material achievement and upon the economic basis as the unfailing condition of spiritual progress has been called an understatement. Fault has been found with his interpretation of the functions of art and religion, his exaggeration of the importance of education, and his overpassionate love of the proletariat. But he has been so many things to so many men, that no such criticism can undermine any of the foundations of his edifice.

Again, Professor Ellwood has criticized Ward as follows: "The cross-fertilization of cultures resulting in a higher civilization was borrowed from biology, and Ward failed to show adequate psychological foundations for it. Other interpretations of the development of civilization in human history are possible. He accepted both the theories of Darwin and Lamarck as to the creation of species. While standing with Spencer's mechanical hedonism and sensationalistic psychology (he found striving at the bottom of all life processes, especially human behavior), he also accepted Spencer's general view that consciousness consists of feeling and its relations." It is not unfair to say, concludes the critic, that Ward's philosophy, psychology and sociology are a chaos of contradictions, if all his writings are considered as a whole. What saved him almost was his wide-awake, practical common sense, for it made it impossible for him to overlook any real human value. His system avoided and also cured the major error of sociology by which social theory was divorced from social practice, to the weakening of both[2] (Ellwood's *The Story of Social Philosophy*, pp. 526-552).

[2] Ward was keenly summarized by Professor Ellwood (in a letter to the author, June, 1937) as one who was aware of his undertaking to refute Herbert Spencer, and in his later years, was aware that as the foil of Sumner, he was battling against positive errors in the American social thinking of his time. But he was not a materialist. He started out as one, but he became the great opponent of practical social materialism in his insistence that mind and intelligent purposes are able to control social development. Curiously enough, Sumner, who started from the opposite end, came to be a practical

Social philosophy in the United States has, in general, followed the pattern of European sociology, just as American culture has essentially been the culture of Europe. Ward's philosophy is the rare exception, for it furnished a substantial intellectual and scientific diet, while others remained "a stimulating condiment," which starved and did not feed those hungering for social science.

A well-deserved tribute is Professor Frank W. Blackmar's:

Differ as we may from some of his points of view, object as we may to some of his conclusions, the fact remains that he was the first great sociologist, that his work is epoch-making for social science, and that his system is monumental. Sociology in its synthetic processes and its methods will change, but for years to come all writers must recognize the great lines of his system (quoted in "American Masters of Social Science," an essay on Ward by Prof. James Q. Dealey, p. 95).

### AN EXAMPLE OF WARD'S REPLY TO HIS CRITICS

Ward had no competitors in the real sense of that word and he rarely took the trouble to annihilate his critics, whether they were pseudo-scientists, metaphysicians, sociologists, or "superscientists" who borrowed his ideas and claimed them as their own. Once in a long while, he would take the guards off his mental rapier and cut through the pretense of wordy thinkers who sold themselves to the public as original thinkers, but never had an original thought of their own. His reply was always a noble task nobly done. Thus, when he saw Professor Giddings' *Principles of Sociology* hailed as a masterpiece of evolutionary social science, he broke his silence (see *Glimpses,* V, 284). It was not hard to demonstrate that the book contained little of either principles or sociology. Giddings, who like Spencer, was famous for treating social science as a sort of cadaver for social analysis, professed to agree with Ward's psychological aspect of society, but postponed that view to the last few pages of his book when he alluded only to the physical forces. Ward concluded that Giddings had not written a masterpiece of sociology, at all, but only a work on the data of sociology which was "a good text-book for undergraduates to prepare them for the study of that science."[3]

---

social materialist, because he believed that man could do little or nothing to control his own destiny.

[3] That Ward was not alone in his opinion is shown by the criticisms of Professor Giddings' works by Professor Small, himself a trenchant critic of Ward: "I size it

## THE NEGLECT OF WARD'S SYNTHESIS

A quarter of a century after Ward left his synthesis on America's doorstep, it was still waiting for recognition, although it filled the demand for a scientific, unified system of social philosophy. As we have noted, all philosophy since Plato has been couched in an imperative or theological mood, and sooner or later landed in a cloud of superstition or nebular metaphysics. Besides, the student who pored over Comte's massive positive philosophy was more often struck by some peculiarity of detail than impressed by its immortal peaks of wisdom. Others who bravely plunged into Spencer's *Synthetic Philosophy* were shocked to discover that in so far as humanity was concerned, it was neither a synthesis nor a philosophy and was, in fact, a terrific dud. And as we write these words, the world is being disillusioned about the truths of fascism which is the central thesis of Pareto's sociology founded upon an impossible logic, but ballyhooed into notoriety, as the most comprehensive synthesis since Aristotle's. The mailed fists of Europe are proving the failure of Pareto's social philosophy just as world depression and world hunger are sounding the crash of Spencer's individualistic order.

Many philosophers have furnished beads for sociology, but it remained for Ward to string them into an immortal necklace. If the world has not yet become aware of his achievements, compensation may be found in the fact that they have not been sold over the counter in sugar-coated capsules, as so many other "systems" (read nostrums) have been. The winds of time have always carried theories far ahead of knowledge. Sooner or later, there comes the synthetic mind of a Comte in method, a Darwin in biology, a Spencer in evolution, or a Ward in sociology, and brings knowledge together into a solid base upon which all the future must build. Because the sciences are not co-operating or a good deal of subjective method is being used, and science has not accomplished in a dozen generations

---

[*Inductive Sociology*] up as a somewhat stimulating condiment, but as a starvation diet if it comprises the bulk of the bill of fare" (letter from Small to Ward, Nov. 13, 1901, *Social Forces*, XV, 306).

"It is not sociology but egology. Its vanishing point is not society, but the individual. . . . It is making us feel that we have been dealing with the stage-settings, instead of the actors. . . . With this perception to the fore, our large venerable structural and functional sociology begins to look like a treatise upon the instruments of Sousa's band by a man who had not found out what they are all for" (*Science*, n.s., XV, 700-706, May 2, 1902, quoted in *ibid.*, p. 308).

or less what metaphysics, idealism, or mysticism was unable to achieve since the dawn of mind, is no cause for pessimism.

Ward's sociology appeared decades ahead of its time. Like the work of Comte, it has been much neglected and criticized, but little read. Had Ward been a propagandist who labored in a narrower field than the whole of knowledge, his works, too, might have become epochal best sellers like Henry George's *Progress and Poverty,* for example. But it seems too early to expect a synthesis like Ward's which holds so many threads of new ideas and new impulses, to do more, as yet, than stimulate those who come under its spell.

It was Aristotle who said that truth being one and the mind of man one, there ought to be in the scheme of things, a science which would give unity and articulation to the entire body of knowledge. He found that science in metaphysics, because it served man like the traveler's view from the mountain top. After Aristotle, immortality was often promised to the man who would successfully apply the proper method to the immense data of history and who would make philosophy a practical means of improving human life. What could better serve the high purpose that Aristotle set for metaphysics, or earn the promised reward, than dynamic sociology? Only he who has climbed Olympus, or who but for the grace of time and circumstance, has been the traveler "silent on a peak of Darien," can know the thrill of the new worlds which it opens to the view.

The fruits of the scientific method from Aristotle to Ward will not bloom in vain. The ground has been ploughed and the seed has been sown. Knowledge is being slowly fused into a unified, human science, as we advance step by step toward reason and co-operation and away from instinct and conflict. The age of inquiry into the abstruse and the abstract is over. The use of the obvious is at hand. Libraries are overflowing with undisputed but inert information. The time has now come to apply the vast fund of knowledge for the formulation of social policies and programs of action which will round out the great synthesis.

If this sounds utopian or visionary, let us make the most of it. Nature is never in a hurry. Man must speed up the natural process, follow the road of science into sociology and its application to human needs, if he is to save himself from his own follies and fantasies.

# PART IV

## THE DOMAINS OF SOCIOLOGY:
### *TELESIS*

*"I am determined not to laugh or weep over the actions of men, but simply to understand them."*—Spinoza

# NOTE

With the survey of the foundations of the temple of sociology completed (Part II: Genesis) and the bird's-eye view of its structure (Part III: Synthesis) fresh in our vision, we enter the domains of man's estate (Part IV: Telesis) for the last and longest stretch of our journey. No longer timid travelers, but seasoned veterans, we are ready to follow Ward out of pure sociology into the field of applied sociology.

Commencing with the outlook from the top of the temple, we first look into religion in general, and monism, the religion of a sociologist, in particular (Book VIII). The panorama of achievement, civilization, and history, illuminated by the ideological interpretation of the economic forces, next engage our attention (Books IX-X). Then, an analysis of the deadly conflict between individualism and collectivism; a glimpse into sociocracy, the ideal social system (Book XI), and a survey of liberty and truth (Book XII), and the view of the social machine at work is complete. Woman's status, her original superiority and present subjection (Book XIII), will next bring us squarely into the sex question. Thence into the realms of environment and heredity, and genius and opportunity (Book XIV), and we will arrive at the grand panacea of education (Book XV) after a retrospect along the road of social progress. A peek into the future where meliorism is seen dissolving the dilemma of pessimism and optimism (Book XVI), and we will be at our goal of a spiritual social order enlightened by the new ethics, aiming at the happiness of the mass (Book XVIII).

If the reader is able to keep an open mind, and is moved by the grand vistas of social science controlling the world, his adventure will not have been in vain. If he remains a skeptic or a pessimist in sociology, the fault will be the author's for failing to convince him of the value of social science as the leader and emancipator of mankind. Let us hope that we have kept the promise made in the Preface, and provided a summary and interpretation of dynamic sociology which forms a composite picture of the jig-saw puzzle of knowledge, and demonstrates that only social science can guide the world into the happy, free, and moral society of tomorrow.

# BOOK VIII. THE MONIST

*"This grand monistic conception is the final crown of human thought, and was required to round out philosophy into a form of symmetry, whose outlines, at least, admit of no further improvement."*—Ward

*"If it be possible to compress into a sentence all that man learns between twenty and forty, it is that all things merge into one another—good into evil, generosity into justice, religion into politics, the year into the ages, the world into the universe."*—Thomas Hardy

# CHAPTER XVIII

# RATIONALISM

---

*"The relation which the mind-force bears to these sense-forces is similar to that which the rudder operated by the pilot bears to the sails operated by the wind. Desire uninfluenced by intelligence is a true natural force and obeys the universal law of dynamics."*

*"Where the mind is filled with superstitions, supernatural causes and spiritual beings, all of which are synonymous, there can be no science, no knowledge, no attempt to control phenomena, and we revert to savagery."*

*"It is the common error of mankind to underrate the importance of his reason. Men have always allowed something else to take the place and do the work of this faculty to a great degree. . . . And this is doubtless the greatest barrier which exists to-day, to the further development of the race."*—Ward

*"Let us above all things take heed the one misfortune does not befall us. Let us not become misologues as some people become misanthropes, for no greater evil can befall men than to become haters of reason."*—Plato

*"Reason is of the very essence of humanity, and he who thinks to reason by proxy is but half a man."*—H. F. Amiel

---

RATIONALISM IS THE first cornerstone of the intellect as well as of the temple of sociology. From reason, says Ward, both science and religion have sprung. Society, the latest product of the natural process of organization, depends for true progress upon mind, which is the highest manifestation of energy. In developing that postulate Ward struck a death blow to a priori metaphysics and laid the basis for his own religion of monism (continuity).

## THE HISTORY OF RATIONALISM

The history of the rationalist philosophy is also the history of science, the struggle of clear, objective thought to break through the barriers of emotionalism and superstition. In incandescent words that reach behind all encrusted prejudice Ward says:

All this truth that science revealed had to struggle against the dense mass of primitive error which it was destined to overthrow, and the resistance was enormous. . . . Truth has never been welcome, and its utterance was for ages fraught with personal danger. . . .

Where the mind is filled with superstitions, supernatural causes and spiritual beings, all of which are synonymous, there can be no science, no knowledge, no attempt to control phenomena, and we revert to savagery. Since the scientific era began, there has been no such faith in the supernatural as exists among savages. Science was made possible by the dimunition of this kind of faith and the concomitant increase of faith in natural causes. The history of science shows that those who still possessed a large amount of the faith of primitive man, opposed science and stubbornly resisted its advance (*App. S.,* pp. 76, 88).

Since primitive times when man acquired common knowledge of how to erect a shelter, build a fire, or sail a boat, reason was developed by observation and experiment. As man grew in mentality and experience, he discovered that there was a world outside of himself, and that he could learn a great deal more about it by the scientific method than by appealing to the spirits which he imagined were all about him.

When the mind was devoid of knowledge, it was obsessed by fear and superstition. Science simply had no soil in which to take root. Logic alone did not involve the recognition of the law of causality. Early man insisted on a cause, it is true, but it was generally a final, and rarely a true cause. He demanded the reason for everything, but it was hardly ever a sufficient reason. His was the logic of emotion, of magic and supernaturalism. The development of reason had to wait for the efficient cause, which is the only cause, and for the sufficient reason, which is the only reason that science could recognize. The logic of law, causation and order, was unknown in the unrational world of the savage (see *ibid.,* p. 58).

When the mind becomes filled with real knowledge, the scientific attitude flourishes, and men are no longer satisfied with visions and fairy tales. Science, in other words, furnishes the mind with material grist, instead of with dreams and speculations.

## THE OPPOSITION TO REASON

The enemies of science are the enemies of rationalism. No one can possibly know anything about the supernatural, whether he is an ignorant savage or a cultured metaphysician. That scientific thinking has progressed to its present state in the face of so much bitter opposition must be strong proof, thought Ward, that truth is naturally rooted in man's nature.[1]

[1] Science advances but the foes of rationalism are many and powerful. In the reaction which followed the World War (Ward died in 1913), they have appeared from

## REASON

The blessed Spinoza believed that science was merely the bridge between imagination and intuition, and served only to materialize our dreams and visions; therefore, the highest effort of the mind and the highest virtue of man lay in intuitive understanding. That is directly contrary to Ward's idea that we act only in response to the demands of feeling rather than reason, but that reason is "the faculty by which the mind reaches conclusions" (*Ps. F.,* p. 28). The intellect, to him, is a unity, and its chief processes are judgment and ratiocination. The faculty of reason is the intellectual power which exerts itself in the co-ordination of perception, ideas, and psychological units (see *D.S.,* I, 404). All human actions are either rational (ideomotor and purposive) or intuitive (animal impulses) with which the reason has nothing to do (see *Ps. F.,* p. 33). There is no genetic difference between animal and human intuition, but in deference to *homo sapiens,* it is called, in his case, intuitive reason. Says Ward:

Reason is nothing else than the exercise of the intellect according to the indirect method and while that faculty is feeble and frequently misleading among the lower types of mankind, and none too strong or reliable among the higher ones, still, all men not only possess it in some degree, but they all exercise it daily and hourly and in all that they do. This fact should be recognized in any system of social science, not merely as a fact but as the prime factor in the treatment of such a science (*ibid.,* p. 236).

Because reason, not intuition, is the highest mental process, argues Ward, neither authority, imagination, experience, nor intuition can supplant objective reason in a rational world. In an irrational or unrational sphere, however, chance as well as causality rule the day. In the final analysis, the essential difference between rationalism and obscurantism depends upon whether our theories and visions can submit to critical examination, logical analysis, and verification. "When

---

behind the ramparts of Spengler's Prussian egoism, Bergson's intuitional idealism, and Pareto's fascist sociology. They have been helped by the anti-intellectual psychology of behaviorism and the successful raids of pragmatism which is an excuse for the lack of a philosophy. The seductive call to prayer, the overpowering aroma of mysticism and the promise that might is here to serve, were welcomed to deaden the fears and the pains of existence. With the obscuring of reason and realism, civilization in nazism and fascism leaped backward to the days that condemned Voltaire and martyred Socrates. But the creeds of anti-rationalism, ranging from simple theology to Spencer's Unknowable were little affected, as they stood upon intuition and inner compulsion against reason and knowledge.

speculation has done its worst, two and two will still make four"
(Samuel Johnson). Yet mankind has always taken the easiest way
out through some recess of the imagination or fled to a haven of
intuition or speculation, there to rest and dream to its heart's content. To avoid the dangers and confusions of reality, idealistic
word-spinning may be a pleasant diversion, but it is a poor substitute for thinking.

Toying with insoluble metaphysical problems may prove a grand
pastime, but it is nothing more. The human mind is finite. All
that it can ever know are things already discovered and those which
are still unknown but which can be correlated to existing knowledge.
All that it can ever grasp is the endless chain of cause and effect,
effect and cause, an infinite series of natural sequences without beginning and without end. To assume any greater mental powers is
to revert to superstition and savagery. Reason cannot rise above the
limitations of the brain, or reach above nature and her laws to enter
the supernatural and seek any First Cause. Whether one likes it or
not, the mind must be content with positive knowledge.

In upholding reason above all, Ward was not blind to the fact
that knowledge has outposts many of which are still undiscovered.
But he saw in them no fields of intuitional speculation but only the
broad highway of positive science, through the gates of the senses
and the intellect. If one can believe otherwise, he should have no
difficulty in accepting the "fact" that the Irish saint swam the Channel and carried his head in his teeth. To speculate from within alone,
or to roam time and space outside of science is as futile as letting
down empty buckets into empty wells and bringing them up overflowing with emptiness.

## EMOTIONALISM

All opposition to reason is directly related to emotion, whose
twin is intuition. In the face of reality, emotionalists, whether they
are artists, poets, romanticists, or mystics, become sleepwalkers who
meditate on shadows, write feverishly in their dreams, and then return to bed to dream some more. Nothing in their work, however
alluring, proves the existence of universal law, but all of it evidences
a feeling of universal awe. When they awaken enough to become
practical, they deliver themselves of such pearls of wisdom as: "No

rose without thorns; you cannot see through a brick wall or fly without wings; poverty will always be with us; sociology is not a science; you cannot change human nature," every one of which has been disproven by science.

Rationalism, however, does not abjure emotion in any form, for emotion is a function of mind. It is only emotion run amok that is the dire enemy of reason. When emotionalism tries to feed a starving world with prayers, fancies, esthetics or abstract ideals of love, it is as efficient as a sermon on vegetarianism to a tiger, or the printed word oats served to a horse for dinner. But the recognition of emotional values does not call for the abdication of reason.

Looking upon this earth as merely the vestibule to the next, the emotionalist claims that his reaction to the universe or to his fellow man cannot be expressed in words alone. His approach to all questions is, therefore, by the path of some outworn idealism or mysticism, essentially a form of wishful thinking which leads to the conviction that the cosmos is a fickle collection of indeterminate events, and ultimately, only a thought in the mind of the Creator.[2]

### WARD'S HYMN TO REASON

Ward's passion for the force of reason was overpowering, but was never distorted into the reason for force. Intoxicated with mind as Spinoza was with God, Ward believed, nevertheless, that "the love of a thing infinite and eternal feeds the mind with pure joy." That thing to him was the universal energy manifested in the human intellect—the most significant force in nature, man, and society.

[2] A thinker may be—in fact, he must be—a person of fine, deep feeling. But when Anatole France said: "The sciences are beneficent, they prevent men from thinking," he proved that he was intrigued by beauty and not by reason. He was unwilling to distinguish between fact and fancy, and constantly escaped from reality to some nook of his emotions. So, too, did Gissing speak for all emotionalists, and confessed how primitive and terror-stricken the mind can become when faced with the task of thinking, when he said: "I hate and fear 'science' because of my conviction that for a long time to come, if not forever, it will be the remorseless enemy of mankind, destroying all simplicity and gentleness of life, all the beauty of the world." Another emotionalist who poses as a thinker is Spengler, whose thesis that the cause of an event is the fact that it is going to happen is an ineffective blow aimed at rationalism. When he cries skeptically: "The chief historical fact is that man is a beast of prey and that war is his normal condition" he lets emotion go to his head, as much as Pareto who loves right not less, but might more. Such fundamentally emotional philosophers sacrifice both logic and reality for free will, until their work belongs with Josh Billings' mule that "looked like he thought he was thinking about something."

He was not a pragmatist who judged everything solely by its consequences, but a rationalist for whom reason opened all doors. Feeling that the reason was also the means of emancipation from frivolous and dubious pleasures as well as from vain animal activities, Ward indicted the neglect of the rational faculty. Without the least bitterness toward faith or religion, in general, his summary of the rationalistic position, when he was but twenty-eight, is epic:

It is the common error of mankind to underrate the importance of his reason. Men have always allowed something else to take the place and do the work of this faculty to a great degree. Indeed, the progress of the world has probably always been in almost exact proportion to the estimate which has been placed upon the reasoning powers. And this is doubtless the greatest barrier which exists today to the further development of the race.

Let us ask any religious devotee why he believes the doctrine of his faith. . . . He would doubtless say that the Bible taught him so. If he would "search scriptures" he would find that even that was not true. . . .

Viewed in the light of reason, no single one of these dogmas can be substantiated; every one of them is wholly unreasonable, as any thinker can easily convince himself if he has the power to divest himself of the influence of his education, and calmly pass them one by one in review before his unbiased reason.

As judging between a system of transcendentalism and one of development, between a miraculous and a rational belief, between an inexplicable and an explainable theory, there can be but one opinion. . . . It would be well for believers in the received theology to pause and inquire into the possibility of their being themselves the dupes of imposters and the victims of superstitions, whether after all, their array of authorities and great names, their whole system, may not be but little better than the mythological polytheism of the ancients ("Reason," an unpublished essay).

With greater maturity, Ward's tolerance to religion increased but he was never corralled into metaphysics, by any innate feeling of duty or by the worship of nature. His hymn to reason as the synthesis of all of nature's forces, is as near to worship as he ever came. On nature's scale, he saw man as a drop of water in an infinite ocean. But as a thinking creature, man's brain holds within it all the forces of the cosmos fused into one. Eddington's latest credo: "Mind is the first and most direct thing in our experience; all else is remote inference" is a Cartesian tenet which is found all through Ward's philosophy, without the hair-splitting supernaturalism of the idealistic scientists. By means of its unlimited power, Ward saw the mind able to subdue and control nature's mechanical forces and processes, and take evolution in hand to accelerate its speed or change its direction, as man desires. By the use of reason, he can even bring beauty and happiness into a world full of chaos, ugliness, and misery.

Philosophical idealists, on the other hand, will have little to do with reason, and construct nothing more solid than a big beautiful bubble into which they move in and leave all fact and reality outside. Their common fault is to pursue abstract values just short of the point where they might lead one to the logical conclusion of their half-truths. Thus, the primacy of the intellect has been doubted by Bergson, who attacks reason and sets up instead the creativeness of evolution. The psychological power of the unconscious mind has been advanced by Freud, and the whole system of values of modern civilization has often been rejected by opponents of rationalism, the literary pseudo-sociologists. The heresy of all these opponents consists of the fear that the mind might overcome the intensity of sensation. And what would life then be in the light of sober reason? It was Ward, who, following Comte, assigned to feeling and mind their respective positions in the social process and made clear the idea that the base was material, the motive and upbuilding force, emotional, and the only directive and progressive element that made for happiness and progress, the rational.

In thus building his system upon the true science of mind, Ward never forgot that the mind was a dual instrument controlling both the senses and the intellect (*Ps. F.,* Chapter II). He apostrophized it as follows:

The intellect thus seen in perspective across the expanse of time stands out in the foreground in a hitherto unknown clearness. All the past philosophy of mind, centering as it has upon this one faculty, however voluminous, brilliant, or profound, was incapable of thus bringing it out into bold relief. It is seen as a becoming, as a begotten child, as a product, as a reality. Nihilism, idealism and all the other 'isms of the schools are banished, and psychology as a true natural science succeeds metaphysics as astronomy succeeded astrology, chemistry alchemy, and biology the magic freaks of the mysterious archaeus (*Ps. F.,* p. 224).

## RATIONALISM AND PROGRESS

Ward ascribes the lack of social progress and the prevalence of social evil to the lack of the use of reason and its undue subordination to feeling. He always used the terms *science, truth,* and *reason* as synonymous because each reflected reality equally, and was a means of correcting the distortions of pure speculation and false idealism. As a powerful truth seeker, he announced the renaissance of the intellect to dispel the effects of the senses, and thereby placed sociology at the head of the sciences. But, as far as society itself was concerned, its failure to use reason has left man an animal, fettered and bound by nature, and made social progress a rare and limited phenomenon. Ward explains this paradox as follows:

Man's progress has been the progress of nature, a secular and cosmical movement, not the progress of art, the result of foresight and intelligent direction. In short, man has not yet ceased to be an animal, and is still under the control of external nature and not under the control of his own mind. It is natural selection that has created intellect; it is natural selection that has developed it to its present condition, and it is intellect as a product of natural selection that has guided man up to his present position. The principle of artificial selection which he has been taught by nature, and has applied to other creatures, more as an art than as a science, to his immense advantage, he has not yet thought of applying to himself. Not until he does this can he claim any true distinction from the other animals (*D.S.,* I, 15-16).

There always have existed a few minds unwilling to accept the dogmatism of the mass. There always crops out in society a more or less pronounced manifestation of rationalism as opposed to authority. While this class of views finds few open advocates, it always finds many tacit adherents, and when uttered, a large but usually irresponsible following. . . . The lowest miscreant feels that there is some fundamental wrong underlying the entire social fabric, although he cannot tell what it is. All this must be regarded as the legitimate consequence of the undue supremacy of academic ideas and teleological conceptions in society (*ibid.,* II, 24).

How long it will take to institute a rational civilization to save the present system from smashing up, no one, of course, knows. Perhaps the balancing of forces will keep the universal machine, including the social mechanism, running perpetually. What we do know, however, is that in a comparatively few moments of time, man has by means of his reason, wrested from a silent and inscrutable nature, many of her deepest secrets, and in all ways made her his willing slave. What, then, is man but mind, the greatest achievement of evolution and the most remarkable inheritance of mankind? The moment he fails to use this most powerful tool by which he can reverse the law of nature, he finds himself on the way back to savagery.

While the environment practically manufactures plants, animals, and human beings by the process of synergy, the effects that these natural products have upon the environment are remarkably different. Organisms below man do not alter surrounding conditions. Man, on the contrary, by dint of his brain power, molds the environment as he desires. What he does to it constitutes human achievement and civilization. His sole spur is to satisfy his desires and incidentally to be happy. But indirectly, he is all the while carrying out nature's object of organization. The result is that man transforms the earth and everything upon it, himself included. The greatest molding factor in that process of achievement and transformation, is education, a purely rationalistic process. Its effect, in the final analysis, is to spread knowledge, equalize opportunity and intelligence, and bring culture and happiness. Thus, rationalism, science, and education are the peaks of the philosophy of mind from which Ward's system gives us a glimpse of the world of tomorrow.

If the reader has been able by now to leave behind him some of his major prejudices, such as hero-worship, belief in hearsay; the acceptance of things or ideas merely because they are old or conventional; metaphysical habits of speculation, and purely emotional impulses and reactions, here is a supreme test. Will he continue to bow before iridescent words or ideas which excite vivid feelings, or will he shake himself loose of the grip of emotion and recognize the supremacy of reason and science? If his mind is tough enough for such an ordeal, there is no fear that he will fail to complete this journey or run off after flying banners and blaring trumpets. He may even rediscover with Ward the immortal value of reason and begin applying it individually and socially, for progress and happiness.

# CHAPTER XIX

# TELEOLOGY

*"The objects of nature are simply preservation and reproduction; the object of man is happiness, the enjoyment of his faculties, the satisfaction of his desires; and the object of sociology,—the great value that it has to society,—is the activity made necessary in order to succeed in the accomplishment of these ends."*—Ward

*"Alles Wollen entspringt aus Bedürfniss, also aus Mangel, also aus Leiden. Diesem macht die Erfüllung ein Ende."*—Schopenhauer

*"Glückseligkeit ist die Befriedigung aller unserer Neigungen."*—Kant

*"Man's work alone suggests design."*—Asa Gray

*"All sentient beings have been formed so as to enjoy, as a general rule, happiness."*
—Darwin

*"I believe first and foremost that life is not merely worthy living but intensely precious, and that the supreme object in life is to live; or, if you like to turn it round, that the great object of living is to attain more life—more in quality as well as quantity."*
—Julian S. Huxley

T HE SECOND cornerstone of the human mind as well as of the temple of sociology which dovetails into the first (rationalism) is teleology (Greek, τέλος, purpose). From the standpoint of the feelings, it is probably the most important of all, for the pressing question, "What is the object of nature, man and society?" is one that will not be put off. From the heights one sees the petty world with its countless ant-heaps, scurrying, grubbing, dying, and reproducing in a vast riot of noise and bluster. What does it all mean? Is there any purpose in the whole business of life? Why the complicated machinery of body, mind, and society? What for?

## GENESIS AND TELESIS

Ward's answer is profound and scientific. He notes that from the beginning there has been a schism in the human mind resulting in two opposite views: (1) the teleological view of the universe as the execution of a prearranged divine plan; (2) the genetic (Latin, from the Greek root γένεσις, to be born)—the evolutionary view (see *D.S.*, II, 18). The first is theological and embraces the dogmas of free will and predestination—whatever is, is the work of God and therefore good. The second is rational and scientific throughout. The two terms *genesis* and *telesis* must not be confused, however, with genetics and teleology, for genesis obtains only in nature, while telesis is possible only in man.

Man is a sort of double personality. As an animal product of nature, he has come down genetically through natural evolution, the same as the stars, the trees, and the animals. But as a rational being with an active brain, he functions teleologically, by telesis, the process of mind-power (*Outlines,* p. 180).

## TELEOLOGY—DESIGN IN NATURE

Ward regards its as a tragic commentary upon the infantile state of the human race that so many of its members still cling to the argument from design in nature as proof of an intelligence that rules the universe, but *when they come to the mind (the only place where design is possible), almost every one is in favor of carrying on the process of mind by nature's hit-or-miss method, and surrendering to fantasies and superstitions, as if the rational will and intellect of man were illusions.*

In the popular view of tender or uninformed minds,[1] all phenomena have a definite aim or purpose according to the cosmic scheme. The design hypothesis is closely linked to the belief in supernatural creation and to philosophical idealism. In the infancy of mankind, no other tenet could be expected. The savage was directly aware with certainty only of his own body, and, therefore, imputed to everything a consciousness like his own (see *D.S.,* I, 29). As he evolved into the barbarian and the civilized man, he brought his primitive notions with him. Today, believers in design think the same way that their earliest human ancestors did, and as children and savages still do. It is a comforting belief, costing little or no mental effort, to shift to the Creator the responsibilities of humanity for all social evil and human suffering, no matter how much of a confession it is that human reason is too weak to cope with human problems.

## SCIENTIFIC GENETICS

As a modern biologist, Ward could find no preordained plan or goal in evolution. From the unpopular mechanistic viewpoint, he argues upon the universal law of organization as follows:

[1] Even scientific writers like J. Arthur Thomson, J. S. Haldane, Alexander, and Lloyd Morgan must here be included, as endorsing, at least by implication, this view.

Nature's processes are not teleologic, but genetic. The cause not only always precedes the effect, but it immediately precedes it. . . . Intelligence works quite otherwise. Cause and effect are remote from each other. Means are adapted to distant ends. . . . Consciousness and intelligence are products of organization. . . . Mind is found only at the end of the series and not at the beginning of it. It is the distinctive attribute of the creature, and not of the creator. It resides in man and not in nature (*D.S.*, II, 9-11).

Nature stands to man in the relation of a whole to a part. Man is an integral part of the universe, and in order to be correctly conceived and properly studied, he must be conceived and studied as an objective phenomenon presented by nature. *"Der Mensch ist selbst Erscheinung! . . ."* In the second place, nature presents the relation of progenitor of man. . . . Nature has antedated him and has produced him. . . . In the third place, nature must be regarded as unconscious. . . . No thought, no ideas, no plan, no purpose has entered into the great cosmic movement. . . . All the great secular processes of nature, including the development of organic forms and of man, have been impelled by blind and mindless energies guided by no intelligence or conscious power either from within or from without (*ibid.*, II, 3-5).

Ward cautions us that his use of such words as object, aim, or purpose does not imply any outside plan or supervision, but is due to the poverty of the English language which lacks any other words to express a function or tendency free from supernatural control (*Ps. F.*, pp. 75-130). With that in mind, his generalizations are scientific as well as crystal clear:

1. The object of nature is function.
2. The object of the organism is desire.
3. The object of evolution is activity.
4. The object of man.is happiness.
5. The object of society is achievement.

The objects of nature are simply preservation and reproduction; the object of man is happiness, the enjoyment of his faculties, the satisfaction of his desires; and the object of sociology,—the great value that it has to society,—is the activity made necessary in order to succeed in the accomplishment of these ends (*Glimpses,* V, 10).

## DESIGN IN NATURE AN ILLUSION

According to Ward, the acceptance of a personal intelligence outside of nature would make miracles commonplace, and knowledge comparatively just a lot of vain fancies. To live in such a world, one would have to surrender his reason entirely and accept the dogma that evolution is God's handwriting in space and time, as He desires it, with man powerless to alter or direct it.

Ward's explanation of the prevalence of the belief in design in nature is that it is either accidental or the result of a mental illusion. Be that as it may, his argument has never been successfully refuted. The universal energy (he argues) which is a mechanical, natural force at work (not above or beyond, but within the cosmos) causes matter to organize and develop ever onward and upward to produce higher and more complex forms (see table of products of nature, p. 113). Through rational observation, experiment, and verification rather than emotion, the method of science has demonstrated that nature's aim is not structural perfection (that is only an incident and a means) but organization, more and higher products, material and spiritual. Says he:

Everywhere in nature genesis simulates telesis. The true scientific explanation of this is that the *nisus* of nature is in all directions and that the principle of advantage selects the advantageous course. . . . If there is a path to success it is sure to be found for all paths are tried. This secures the same result as if a directive agent had pointed out the only true path and no other had been tried. We lookers-on, after the success has been achieved, know nothing of the infinite number of failures, because they have left no record. This may be taken as the general explanation of the universal belief in teleology during the theological period of intellectual development (*P.S.,* pp. 114-115).

He points for proof of the universal reign of natural law to the very skies to which the devout look up. One may doubt the operation of the law of causality in any field, but once he admits its existence in astronomy, he closes the door upon supernaturalism anywhere. In thus looking to nature for evidence that it is not ruled by design, we must avoid becoming nature worshipers. Says Comte: "Astronomers, physicists, chemists and physiologists do not admire, neither do they blame their respective phenomena; they observe them" (*P.S.,* p. 5).

### ADAPTATION NO PROOF OF DESIGN

The argument from design finds its stronghold in biological adaptation. What stronger evidence of design can be produced than the intricate structure of the human hand, for example? The scientist, however, is not hypnotized by the beauty or marvels of nature, and digging deeper into the facts, finds that evidence of adaptation is merely an illusion due to nature's wasteful method of trial and error. Her process of selection is not selective at all, but so labored and stupid that the final product, whether organ or organism, may look like the last step in a preconceived plan; but it is nothing of the kind.

Nature is an eternal becoming, a ceaseless striving. If there is a single germ of life anywhere, the universal energy will find it and lavish everything upon it, whether the resulting development is normal or a monstrosity. Overbreeding or insane overproduction is the rule in nature, rather than the exception. No intelligence could ever be guilty of such waste and carnage as the production and fate of the 50,000,000 animal spores of a single fern; the 730,000 seeds of a mustard plant, or the 200,000,000 eggs of a star fish. The progeny of any one of them would, if unchecked, soon fill and overrun the entire globe. The fact that one house fly can reproduce 5,598,720,000,000 in less time than it takes to breed a single baby is evidence of extravagance which cannot possibly come from any intelligence.

Ward's argument is that things have adapted themselves in nature. What we see exists of necessity as the result of definite causes. Adaptation is brought about by the material forces of nature which are within and not without the universe. There is no evidence, says he, of any intelligence anywhere in the cosmos except that which emanates from the mind of man (see *ibid.*, II, 19-26). In his words:

The necessitarian sees no reason for astonishment that there should be a perfect adaptation in many important circumstances, since it is the circumstances themselves that adapt. No one would be astonished to see a sphere come from a spherical mold or wonder that it is not a cube or prism. . . . Most of the examples that have been brought forward establishing the operation of a designing intelligence and benevolent intent in the universe are either cases of a natural or genetic adaptation, or they are mere coincidences (*D.S.*, II, 49-50).

## MAN'S OBJECT IS HAPPINESS

If nature has no conscious aim, man has a very definite one. Ward indulges in none of the sentimental and theological solutions of the problem which are so varied that they would be comical if they were not fraught with such tragic results of supernaturalism. From the sentimental viewpoint man has been depicted in the depths, a miserable sinning worm grovelling at the feet of the Maker, and on the heights, as an overlord of the globe especially created for his preserve. Science has no such delusions. The cocky little sapient creature has the same aim as the rest of the animal world, viz., to satisfy his needs and desires, in a word, happiness. This "lowly" goal can be lifted to the highest plane, as the level of desire is raised. But the physical and material needs will ever remain, and their satisfaction is not only the first law of nature but the main purpose of human life.

### "HUMAN NATURE" NO PROOF OF DESIGN IN NATURE

In every analysis of human aims, the subjective method, sooner or later, brings out the smoke screen of "human nature." While it is a camouflage which deserves as much space at least as the weather did in Mark Twain's immortal chapter devoted exclusively to that subject, one is tempted to add his indignant "We talk about it, but why don't we do something about it!"

The concept human nature serves as a convenient escape for those who need it, but it should never be mistaken for an entity or finished structure in which to hide our errors and prejudices. All that is meant by calling a thing natural is that it follows the law of its being. It is as natural for a dog to bark as it is for a diplomat to lie; that is what we have learned to expect. Human nature is neither an independent attribute, a human faculty, nor a biological inheritance. It is purely the result of human contacts and of the classifications of human motives (see *ibid.*, II, 335).

Human nature contains unselfish as well as selfish elements. The proper social conditions or motivation can subordinate egoism to altruism and transform human nature accordingly. Despite the popular belief to the contrary, it is, in fact, being changed by the environment at every step. Although each of us has a distinct physical, chemical, and psychic individuality, our group habits and social attitudes are no more eternal or unchangeable than are plants and animals. In brief, we are in a continuous state of flux in our social attitudes, as is amply proved by the antislavery, the women's, the labor, and the youth movements, all of which exhibit distinct changes in human nature.

### HEDONISM

The fundamental law of self-preservation is bound up with the universal law of parsimony by which every organism seeks the greatest pleasure for the least pain. With these laws as his compass, Ward traced the current of human desire from elemental sensitivity to social movements. He came to the inevitable conclusion that man's constant aim in life is to satisfy the ceaseless claims of feeling. His supreme object is not, as Montaigne thought, to cultivate the art of living, but simply to live. The life urge does not point to destinies in the stars, but is inherent in man's biological make-up. In striving to survive and carry on, he approaches the goal of happiness (in the measure that he is able to fulfill his desires), as naturally and as unconsciously as the leaf bends toward the light (*P.S.,* p. 129).

To those who labor under the fallacy that this is Epicureanism, a vile philosophy of a pagan sensualist, it may be told that the much maligned Epicurus stood for nothing low or voluptuous. He advocated, instead, a full and glorious life in which pleasure is only a means to an end; wealth is a limitation upon desire, and sensual joys are avoided because they last but a moment and wane by repetition, whereas intellectual and other spiritual pleasures increase and endure. Epicurus, the "sensual" philosopher who taught that temperate people are prudent ones, inscribed over the entrance to his olive gardens: "Enter, stranger; here all is fair. Pleasure lords the day." The stranger, however, learned to his surprise, that pleasure there meant the health of mind and body, and that bread dipped in water was the daily fare.

Not all the great philosophers of Greece were hedonists, for the ancient thinkers, being all too human, used their own lives as models for their ideals. Plato, the outstanding spiritualistic philosopher who also believed that man was not actuated by any other motive than that of securing the most pleasure at the least expense of pain, preached that there was even a higher purpose in life than good citizenship, viz., to be a philosopher. Aristotle, on the other hand, was equally certain that reason was man's highest function and his greatest source of happiness; that the highest good was the life (like his own) of the scholar and thinker who pursued knowledge for its own sake.

Ward was a true hedonist. Happiness, to him, consisted of doing something, not being something or having something. In other words, a life of activity and well-doing (not inertia and well-being) is the most exalted state of happiness. Pleasure is not the sense of what promotes life but the feeling of life itself; the play and movement of all that is virile and dynamic in man. We strive after pleasure because we desire life, and living is essentially an exercise of energy. Happiness consists not of success, but of achievement—the realization of one's life work and the finding of one's natural place in the social scheme. And so he follows in the steps of Aristotle, who over two thousand years ago said: "The good of man must be the end of the science of politics . . . to secure the good of one person only is better than nothing; but to secure the good of a nation or a state is a nobler and more divine achievement."

Ward's concept of man's object in life is thus a synthesis of Plato's and Aristotle's best thought. Looking at life with open eyes, he advocates living to the highest degree but withal a life of reason. Why should not everybody have contagious enthusiasms for the enjoyment of life, with an overwhelming desire that all share in it? If the reader still thinks that hedonism spells sensuality, let him turn to Spinoza, whose precise and austere morals hailed the joy of life in these words:

Nothing but a gloomy and sad superstition forbids enjoyment. For why is it more seemly to extinguish hunger and thirst than to drive away melancholy? . . . It is the part of a wise man to refresh and invigorate himself with moderate and pleasant eating and drinking, with sweet scents and the beauty of green plants; with ornament; with music, with sports, with the theatre and with all things of this kind which one man can enjoy without hurting another. To make use of things, therefore, and to delight in them as much as possible (provided we do not disgust ourselves with them, which is not delighting in them), is the part of a wise man (*Ethics,* IV, 45, note).

The simplicity of Ward's credo of happiness for all, because happiness is the realization of the object of human life, is the high mark of its truth. The average man is always much more interested in the gnawing of his own hungers than he is in social questions. Mankind cannot be sliced like an apple into two parts (as Spencer tried to do), the physical and the intellectual. Human beings are first of all biological organisms with the necessary numbers of wants and desires. Anything, therefore, which does not satisfy in some measure some human want or desire is dry rot, and any science which does not help to find the way to happiness is so much learned rubbish, said Ward.

No one with these ideas could have any taste for the hemlock. Ward recognized that life's table is filled with better things than dry crusts, and that the days which make man happy, also make him wise. When he seems to be praising sensuous pleasures, he is really preaching achievement. Human life cannot be the theologian's hell or the ascetic's heaven, he protests. Men have as much right to be happy as they have to live. Pleasure means the highest good; best denotes the greatest pleasure. This has universally been accepted as true for the animal world, and it is equally true of humanity (*Outlines,* p. 98).

To any one who fears that hedonism may lead to spiritual bankruptcy, Ward has the following consoling reply: Happiness is not asceticism. The Oriental doctrine that happiness is a myth; that desire is conceived in sin and exercised in error, and that the only satisfaction in life is to avoid pain, is an utter denial of life. The view that life is a sort of balance, a negative state of peace, is abnormal. Only the scientific outlook can grasp the importance of using all of nature's gifts to the utmost, not only as a challenge to loneliness and despair, but as steppingstones to achievement for the individual and for society, i.e., to a loftier and happier life for all.

Great men are not always wise men. Often, their asceticism is the product of an unhealthy emotional pessimism. The failure of the philosophical systems of Kant, Schopenhauer, and Spencer was due to the crashing of their emotional selves. Boilers, too, have exploded under too much pressure, but that is no reason to deny the use of steam. The credos of such noble characters as Tolstoy and Gandhi, on the other hand, are the fears of disenchanted emotionalists who see in life nothing but the conquest of desire.

"The earth is bad," wails Anatole France; "it is without feeling. But man is good because he suffers. He has derived everything, even his genius, from his pain." Which bit of wisdom is on a par with the definition of joy as the removal of new shoes from old bunions. It is idealism again weeping over life and making the same error when it believes that genius comes through starvation, and art from freezing in garrets. Ward dilates upon the subject of happiness somewhat differently:

Happiness in the popular restricted sense is the experiencing of the higher emotional pleasures afforded by the gratification of social, esthetic, moral and intellectual tastes. New wants of a spiritual nature come thick and fast upon one another as soon as the coarser necessities of existence are fully supplied. It is really true, as the pessimists claim, that there is no possibility of satisfying all desires, for if they could all be at once conceived to be satisfied, new ones would immediately arise demanding satisfaction. Yet the degree of happiness depends upon the relative proportion of them that can be silenced, and upon the nature and refinement of the tastes that can be gratified. Therefore, provided the means of supplying wants can be secured, the greater the number and the higher the rank of such wants, the higher the state of happiness attainable. The problem of social science is to point out in what way the most complete and universal satisfaction of human desires can be attained, and this is one with the problem of greatest happiness (*Ps. F.*, p. 74).

Like all philosophers, Ward does not omit painting his own full-length portrait, when he suggests that the intellectual life yields the most pleasure; that the discovery and teaching of truth is still more exalted and thrilling, and that unhappiness comes from the inability to harmonize instincts and emotions with the activities of dynamic reason (see *ibid.*, p. 104). Thus, our guide, who has sometimes been branded as an ignoble materialist is, in fact, the champion of the life of the intellect; of a spiritual existence in which one can enjoy to the utmost the bounties of nature and the fruits of man's wisdom.

## THE OBJECT OF SOCIETY

The object of society is achievement. Metaphysicians have invented the comforting illusion that man is working out his destiny, and is moving in society toward some righteous end, but social science rejects it entirely. The sociologist sees man functioning under the cosmic urge to achieve, not independently of or beyond the rest of the universe, but strictly along and within nature's process of organization. Whether we consent to it or not, we are all part of nature, and there is no evidence of any promised rewards or punishments waiting for us at the end of the road. Man's associated life, too, is a dynamic activity, an unbroken chain of growth and development and the result of the conflict and teamwork of natural forces. The impulse to achieve is his only incentive; the achievements themselves his only compensation. The object of the individual (and he calls upon society to help him) is to attain happiness. The object of society functioning through the individual is to achieve, i.e., to attain the inventions, discoveries, and spiritual treasures of his fertile brain.

The individual can find happiness directly, but society, which necessarily can act only through its members, must seek it indirectly. But from any point of view, the aim of society is achievement, while the problem of society and the mission of sociology are the organization of human happiness (see *D.S.*, II, 153-157).

The co-operative habits of the human species give an increased importance to the principles underlying its activities. Animated more than any other organism by high and complex needs and desires, man finally begins to make collective efforts in the direction of happiness. Society, like the individual, in trying to achieve, also causes widespread and dynamic changes in the environment. These changes, taken together, whether they are the result of unconscious or planned changes, constitute civilization. Witness the Oriental civilizations which, although the oldest in the world, are so socially inert that they have made scarcely any advance in science or in the art of life, in bringing general happiness to its members. Contemplating one's navel for years may bring the peace of Nirvana, but the process hardly produces either knowledge or bread. As for the Western world, although it is still in the throes of competition, individualism, and depression, its dynamic powers of achievement seem still virile enough to carry it through.

No one can justly call Ward's teleological philosophy either vulgar or Utopian. By the light of its principles, one may see pleasure or the normal exercise of human faculties, riding with the ideal and the spiritual on the swift back of reality. If life is gay and pleasant, virtue will find its reward not only in achievement, but in what is more important, in the increase of happiness for all. A forthright look at life, eye to eye, and it is clear that happiness comes not through denial or suppression but from positive expression and satisfaction. It is not better to travel than to arrive. The poor, the afflicted, and the ignorant are never essentially happier than the rich, the well, and the educated (see *Ps. F.,* p. 69). When one stops to note that the concept of happiness expresses the ultimate purpose of the entire organization of life to secure for everyone not only the bare necessities but all the leisure, luxury, and freedom that life has to give, any sentimental objection to the hedonist philosophy should at once disappear.

Ennui, pessimism, and asceticism are forever banished in the program of sociology which calls for social progress (happiness) to change life from a pain economy into a pleasure economy, and human beings from miserable, fighting animals into experts in the art of life. It is time to make this planet a happy one, from pole to pole, for everybody, says Ward. Sociology, the leader in this latest movement, is not a solemn dirge but the paean of joyous life: "Life is short, art is long. Long live life and art for all!"

# Chapter XX

# RELIGION

---

*"Religion is the embodied and organized state of the emotions; it represents the combined forces of human feeling. It is reason applied to life, the social instinct of race safety."*—Ward

*"The intellect should always be the servant of the heart, never its slave."*—Comte

*"To love justice, to long for the right; to love mercy, truth, liberty, to wage relentless war against slavery in all its forms; to love the beautiful in art, in nature, to make others happy, to discard error, to destroy prejudice, to cultivate hope, to see the calm beyond the storm, the dawn beyond the night:—this is the religion of reason, the creed of science; this satisfies the brain and heart."*—Robert G. Ingersoll

*"Religion cannot live nobly without science or without morals."*—Havelock Ellis

---

It MAY HAVE BEEN a prudent man or one who wanted peace at any price who promised never to discuss sex, politics, or religion with his friends. But for the sociologist, no subject is taboo. We, therefore, come to the survey of religion, the third cornerstone of mind and sociology.

## THE TWO ASPECTS OF RELIGION

Whether the present era is regarded as the beginning or the end of civilization, religion is a social phenomenon to be studied like any other, instead of being held sacrosanct as a divine revelation. Its two aspects must immediately be distinguished, however, for there is religion, and there are religions. Great conflicts and confusion have resulted from the unfortunate use of the term to cover two entirely different concepts: (1) a creed based upon theological ideas springing from the belief in a Supreme Being; (2) the true core of religion, which is the sense of the mysterious, insatiable human curiosity, free of dogma or superstition.

In the first sense, religion is wholly supernatural. There is no natural religion, and the best it has achieved is a philosophical theism. In the second sense, it is a keystone in the social arch; the basis of all social spirituality; the bond which links the divergent tendencies of human beings into a human synthesis.

## DEFINITION OF RELIGION

"The somewhat vague and exceedingly ambiguous name of religion," said Ward, "has been applied to many things" (*D.S.*, II, 252). Few thinkers have accepted his novel theory that the essential core of religion, true religiosity, is a product of the rational faculty, but their definitions are not as comprehensive and real as his. Kant holds that religion has for its sole basis the idea of immortality. The anthropologists claim it is the belief in spiritual beings (Tylor); or mere sensations of fear, the recognition that there are other beings more powerful than man (Lubbock). Spencer defines religion as something which passes the sphere of experience, and, therefore, belongs to the Unknowable. Yet, from the practical point of view, he agrees with Tylor (see *ibid.*, p. 259). To Freud, the psychologist, religion is "an obsessional neurosis of humanity" which originated in the Oedipus complex (*The Future of an Illusion,* by Sigmund Freud, 1928). In the eyes of mystics and metaphysicians (Santayana, Whitehead), religion is poetry mistaking itself for reality, or what a man does with his solitude. Einstein, the physicist, defines it as follows:

To know that what is impenetrable to us really exists, manifesting itself as the highest wisdom and the most radiant beauty which our dull faculties can comprehend only in their most primitive forms,— this knowledge, this feeling, is the center of true religiousness. In this sense, and in this sense only, I belong in the ranks of devoutly religious men (*Living Philosophies,* 1931, p. 6).

To Ward, the scientist-philosopher, religion had the same meaning as to Einstein and more. *It is not an illusion,* for it is one of man's reactions to the exterior world. His definition is: "the embodied and organized state of the emotions; it represents the combined forces of human feeling" (*D.S.*, I, 11); "it is reason applied to life" (*Outlines,* p. 27); "the social instinct of race safety" (*P.S.*, p. 134; *App. S.*, pp. 53-63). In asserting the original idea that it is a product of reason he says:

If I have described something that has hitherto escaped attention, I am quite willing another shall give it a name. But that I have outlined a chapter still to be written in the history of life, of mind, and of man, I shall remain convinced until clearly shown to be in error ("The Essential Nature of Religion," *Glimpses,* VI, 32).

## THE EVOLUTION OF RELIGION

Ward well knew the difficulty of analyzing religion. Most often its external garb seems to have become a part of its amorphous body. But enveloped in mystery as the religious sentiment has always been, he finds it ever active in the evolution of society, and "to those who understand its nature, its workings can be seen at all stages" (*ibid.,* VI, 14).

When man started on his upward climb, he was without religion. Then he worshipped everything, animate and inanimate, including his own person. With increasing intelligence and culture came idealism and the reverence for higher things of the spirit which many confuse with primitive fears and tribal religion. In time, the bolder minds revolted against the gods, and monotheism was evolved.

Like all social institutions, it did not arise spontaneously but was a product of evolution. Three explanations of its origin have been offered: (1) the belief in spiritual beings was implanted by God in man's being; (2) from the assumption that there exist supernatural powers, invisible and immaterial, but in other respects like man, which control all phenomena; (3) from deductions based upon experiences manifested in dreams, trances, epileptic fits and the like, and observations from reflections in water, shadows, echoes, thunder, lightning, and similar phenomena.

Since religion was not common to all the early races, the second and third of the foregoing theories must be accepted as the most probable ones. But whether fetishism, animism, ancestor worship, or magic is found at the root of religion, there is little doubt that it received its first impulse from fear and the urge for protection from a hostile environment.

The fire-belching volcanoes, the crashing thunder, and the dazzling lightning were enough to terrorize him into centering all his hopes and despairs around some idol or temple in which lay salvation from the awful Unknown. From those fears were born all the superstitions of religion with its fetishes, miracles, magic, and revelations. Only with a more developed rationality was the Unknown changed into the Unknowable, and the host of supernatural beings merged into one divine entity (see *D.S.,* I, 195).

Ward takes the position that it was a necessity of the condition of things that religion should have arisen as it did. The evolution of animals or creatures without intellects into rational beings constitutes, to him, an all-sufficient explanation of the genesis and evolution of religion. To follow the development of mind from instinct and reflex emotion into complete rationality, is also to trace the growth of religion from its roots of fear and restraint into a mighty social structure.

What else could have happened to man's infantile mind with its minimum of correct information, inability to reason abstractly or speculate about remote causes? What interested primitive man amid the mysteries that surrounded him was to remain alive and safe. His reason had but one mandate: "Live and satisfy desire at any cost!"

## RELIGION AND THE GROUP SENTIMENT OF SAFETY

Blind obedience to desire often proved dangerous, but man was saved by the group sentiment of safety, says Ward, which was developed to warn him against all race-destroying acts. In the name of religion, a Chinese wall of "musts" and "don'ts" was built up. The guardians in charge—the chiefs, medicine men, and other self-appointed emissaries of the supernatural forces—performed their mission exceedingly well and inculcated a fear of the gods which was kept alive by the promise of the most terrible penalties, mainly in the hereafter.

Ward's theory of the nature of religion, law, and morality was, thus, that they were devices to restrain the individual and hold him in his place. In *Dynamic Sociology* he regarded them as having no socially adaptive value, and only as being negatively socially valuable. In his later works, however, his view of religion changed. Although he did not see it as a progressive force or factor in social evolution, he came to appreciate its value as a conservative force—an instinct of race safety, whose purpose is to prevent the elimination of the wayward in human society (Professor Charles Ellwood). He even spoke of it (1898) as "the force of social gravitation that holds the social world in its orbit."

## RELIGION, THE PRODUCT OF REASON

After centuries of conflict and debate, the question what is the purpose of religion remains for most people a moot one. Have creeds of millions of human beings been merely fears, mental aberrations, or emotional outlets? Is there any value in its essential element, or does it merely mark the period during which mankind developed from frightened, credulous creatures into knowing, thinking beings? It was never a natural instinct in man. According to Ward, the paradox is that while its dominant driving force was feeling, it was a product of the rational faculty, developed to restrain unsafe actions (see *Glimpses,* VI, 23). Yet it did not arise merely for the protection of the individual from evil. It had a much higher function, viz., to combat the tendencies to violate the laws of nature and jeopardize the race. What instinct is to the plant and animal world, religion is to mankind. In his own words:

> In modern phrase, religion is a mechanism for social control, and in the absence of government, the fear of spiritual beings was the only means to the restraint of the wayward tendencies. . . . My thesis is that religion is a substitute in the rational world for instinct in the subrational world (*ibid.,* p. 14).

> It is not true, as Benjamin Kidd maintains in his *Social Evolution,* that religion and reason are opposed, or that religion proceeds from an "unreasoning," or, as he expresses it, an "ultra-rational" sanction. Religion is rational, through and through. It is not to be compared to instinct, such as both animals and men possess, adapted to produce such automatic activities as result in the safety and healthy development of races. On the contrary, it often and usually impels man to do just those things which his instincts and his natural propensities would never dictate. It counteracts the animal nature of man, and is one of those things which distinctively mark him off from the animal world. It could be easily shown that this is precisely the role that reason plays. everywhere, and it is the failure to perceive this that has led many political economists and others into the gravest of errors in philosophizing about man (*Outlines,* p. 28).

### RELIGION AND THE SOCIAL PROBLEM

Early in his life of toil Ward was struck by religion's neglect of the social problem (see *D.S.,* I, 14). He remarked upon the tendency of the institution of religion to side with nature against man, and with the rich against the poor, as follows:

> Man has thus far been chiefly engaged in a struggle for existence. His struggle for liberty, of which human history is chiefly the record, has consisted simply in so many assertions of the claims of feeling against function. . . . Human progress has consisted in the reluctant concession of such of these claims and demands as did not threaten existence.

Throughout Western Europe and America, this struggle is chiefly over. The ruling class is at the feet of Demos and the power of the priesthood is broken. . . . But a new set of rulers have come forward. The owners of the means of subsistence now dictate to the masses. The "labor question" of to-day is essentially utilitarian, and economists are just beginning to understand that their science is dynamic, and that "consumption," i.e., enjoyment, i.e., feeling, constitutes its true basis. To all of which religion, from its very nature, is opposed (*Glimpses,* VI, 29-30).

Religion in its essence, had nothing to do with sympathy or any other kind of 'pathy. It deals with function, not feeling, and simply serves Dame Nature in her great cosmic scheme of preserving, perpetuating and increasing life. If to these can be added the perfectionment of living beings, this is only because such perfectionment is a means to the supreme end. It has no reference to the deepening or heightening of the quality of sentiment. Anything in existing relations that seems to contradict this statement is something superadded to religion itself,—some late graft upon the original stock,—and belongs to a modern period (*ibid.,* p. 27).

Thus far, it is science, Ward says, which has taken responsibility for social conditions from the Deity and placed it where it belongs, upon the shoulders of man. Science is a creed for our thinking, a schedule for our achievements, and a guide for our perplexities. The true scientist is not interested in merely revealing truth but in using it for the conquest of nature and the control of the environment for the benefit of humanity. Human needs determine the direction of science, and its doctrines find no place in any dull catalogue of banal things or glamorous fictions but touch the vitals of man's existence at every point. To those who fear that this is "materialism," Ward brings the comforting thought that his concept of science as opposed to superstition is of the highest immateriality and spiritual character (see *D.S.,* II, 23-24).

## SUPERSTITION UNMASKED

Although Ward became, as the years passed, more and more the spiritualistic monist and less and less the crass materialist, he never lost sight of science as his guiding star. When he fought or exposed vitalism and idealism, he tore the mask from superstition garbed as science. Putting Bergson and his metaphysics, for example, on a spit, he turned them neatly before the open fire of his analysis. What emerged was Bergsonism, a potpourri of eloquent and confused mystical "science" which was for years hailed as brilliant philosophy. Ward mercifully destroyed it in a few short paragraphs, and for once, his criticism did not spare anybody's feelings, when he wrote:

Articles in the magazines and scientific journals contain glints of my principles by writers who suppose they are saying something very original and brilliant. . . . Sometimes an author of high standing and great eminence comes forward with a work that focuses the attention of the thinking world, in which, along with much, of course, that is new and original, and often with considerable that is questionable or positively untrue, these ideas upon which I have been ringing the changes for thirty years, are served up as something wholly new to the world. I will refer to the most signal example within my knowledge, the *Creative Evolution* of Henry Bergson.

It was an attempt to prolong the metaphysical stage of the celebrated *trois états* of his great countryman, Auguste Comte, whom he does not once mention, far into the positive stage or era of science. That this attempt has been successful, I emphatically deny (*Glimpses,* I, lxxxiii).

After stripping Bergson of all claims to science, Ward left him a bare supernaturalist, with a style, and nothing more. Bergson's argument from intuition, in effect, is stand on your head and see the world. The *élan vital* which he offers as a substitute for theological dogma, is our old friend, the universal energy, dressed up for the occasion in the robes of the intuitional philosophy. His scientific pretensions are on a par with those of astronomers before Copernicus, or biologists before Lamarck. Bergson deprecates intelligence, individual and social; abjures science and reality, glorifies instinct, and performs all the other rites of the mystic. He assumes that the law of causality applies only to occasions where phenomena repeat themselves, and since events in history and psychology never (?) recur, the law of causality must be excluded from those fields! And so, with a wave of his metaphysical wand of logic, he solves the riddle of life by asserting that the art of life is altogether free from any relationships to the exterior world. To accept such dogmas as free will, intuition, and design is to indulge in a form of mental exercise which tends to make the mind irrational and incapable of appreciating any real knowledge (see *D.S.,* II, 550). It is no wonder that endless antiscientific speculations parading as religion, which to him seemed antisocial, made Ward thus speak so bitterly in his first work:

Throughout all time past, the mass of mankind has been carried along by the power of sentiment. It has never been deeply moved, at least directly, by that of intellect. Hence we see that the psychical agencies that have stirred up mankind have been chiefly of a religious nature. . . . The immense success with which religious reformers have met, has been due to the almost irresistible power of their emotional nature, and never to their intellectual supremacy. . . .

Not only has the world thus far been ruled by passion and not by intellect, but the rulers of the world have had to be, in order to win that distinction, not merely enthusiasts and fanatics, but in the majority of cases, insane persons, in a certain legitimate acceptance of that term. . . . The strange truth is that instead of having been guided and impelled by intellect and reason throughout all the years of history, we have been ruled and swayed by the magnetic passions of epileptics and monomaniacs (*D.S.,* I, 11-12).

It is a fair speculation how much higher the human mind would have risen in its efforts to comprehend the natural universe, had no such explanation as a supernatural being or a personal God ever suggested itself. . . . Upon the whole, we must conclude that there is no direction in which the belief in spiritual beings has advanced the temporal interests of mankind, and that therefore, such belief, if it is of any advantage to the race, must be so in virtue of gains which it is to bring in a future state of existence,—a field of discussion which, of course, lies outside the province of this work and of all scientific investigation (*ibid.,* pp. 286-287).

## RELIGION AND SCIENCE

Ward banished all supernaturalism from his works and stood by the scientific hypothesis because it bore the plainest earmarks of truth (see *ibid.,* pp. 158, 221). His thesis is plain: science necessarily rests upon matter, which is the most basic of all the items of experience. Knowledge is association, and scientific knowledge is the name for the broad scheme of associated sensations and ideas. The only way to know anything at all about our mental states is to bring them within the scope of material science, i.e., the laws of matter and the realm of physics, chemistry, and psychology. He, accordingly, concludes that science and superstition are worlds apart (see *ibid.,* II, 304-305).

Man has groped into the mêlée of experience and emerged with two methods. The first sought to control the simpler and more superficial phenomena which are subject to invariable laws of nature. The second aimed at governing the more occult phenomena. Under the spur of the first method, he created civilization. Under the impulse of the second, he erected the religious structure. One by one, the more obscure regions occupied by faith have been proved to be under the dominion of the fixed laws of nature, and were captured by science. Religion has, therefore, been compelled to retreat from, and finally abandon, one dogmatic position after another. The entire terrain of astronomy, physics, chemistry, and biology now belongs to science. The fields of moral and social phenomena are still arenas of conflict. But when science will capture these last strongholds, says Ward, religion, the core of true religiosity, will still remain.

In his earlier years Ward regarded Spencer's reconciliation between science and religion by assigning the knowable world to the former, and the unknowable to the latter, as an invitation to both science and religion to join hands in the avowal of a common ignorance (see *ibid.*, I, 156, 196; II, 269). Later in life Ward recognized in the essential nature of religion something that transcends any war with science and which is subject to a reconciliation far more complete than any other. Taking the broadest possible philosophic view, he declared that since science and religion started out from the same rational base, no rational mind could doubt that they will arrive at the same goal (see *Textbook*, pp. 157-158). Both are the products of reason; both are attempts to explain the universe. In his own honest words:

Will science finally swallow up religion, assume its functions and stand wholly in its stead? We can only answer these questions by noting the history of science thus far, by considering its long series of conquests and the steady but orderly recoil of religion, as the guarantees of safety were one after another placed in its hands. Noting this, and comparing the condition of the vanguard of civilization with that of its dark beginning, it seems impossible to doubt, not that religion is ever to disappear, but that it will ultimately put all confidence in reason and cease to raise its voice against the realization on the part of man of the fullest capabilities of his nature (*Glimpses*, VI, 31).

## THE FUTURE OF RELIGION

Although we have used the word *religion* indiscriminately in both its meanings, the reader will not fail to differentiate between the essential nature of religion, and what it has become in the hands of its emotional votaries. In Ward's final view, religion as the noblest and highest of human feelings, will live as long as life itself. Realizing the immense importance of religiosity, he saw its development entering upon a new stage. Instead of aiming at the next world, it will join hands with social science in the betterment of this. Religious education will gradually outgrow all supernaturalism, free itself from the last vestiges of myth, legend and superstition, and engage in a humanistic tradition which teaches that nature is helpful, life is good, the sunshine is warm and cheerful, and the flowers both of nature and friendship, worth cultivating. Withal, Ward sees no reason why both science and religion cannot lead mankind in the march of achievement toward a spiritual and happy civilization.

Whether the purified form of the religious sentiment in the new society will flourish, as Ward predicted, or whether it will be absorbed by science or reappear under a different name, is in the lap of the future. Meanwhile, sociology stands for the principle that too little science, and too little religiosity, not too much, will enslave us. The fear that science, too, is a dogma accepted on faith, should not impede our search for truth as it has done to so many "pure" philosophers and "scientific" metaphysicians. The hope of the brave traveler through knowledge lies not in the continuation of superstition or the attainment of a peaceful state of inertia, but in the continued conquest by reason of which both religion and science are products, of ever more unexplored fields, especially those of mind and society, in the interest of human happiness.

# CHAPTER XXI

# MONISM, THE RELIGION OF
# A SOCIOLOGIST

---

*"We may even go so far as to maintain that matter is spirit, but not in the sense that it is endowed with intelligence and will. The view that matter and spirit are the same is true monism; and I believe it is true science, but it means only that the material world contains all the elements of intelligence, and will and can and does take that form when organized in the appointed way and to the required degree."*

*"Nature is not only a becoming, it is a striving. The universal energy never ceases to act and its ceaseless activity constantly creates. . . . It is not matter but collision that constitutes the only cause. This eternal pelting of atoms, this driving of the elements, this pressure at every point, this struggle of all created things . . . it is the soul of the universe, the spirit of nature, the "First Cause" of both religion and science,—it is God."*—Ward

*"The world is my country; to do good is my religion."*—Thomas Paine

*"We should be constantly losing sight of the power and majesty of Nature if we persisted in studying it in detail without a conception of its unity."*—Pliny the Elder

---

THE RELIGION of Ward, the individual, is no more important than that of any other man. The religion of Ward, the sociologist, however, with its foundations of science, continuity and meliorism, is of vast importance to the student of social science.

## WARD'S RELIGIOUS LIFE

Beginning in adolescence as a devout believer, he grew, with increasing scientific knowledge, into a devout unbeliever, so to speak. As editor of and almost sole contributor to the *Iconoclast,* he preached in early manhood that religion was a reactionary agency, founded upon fear and thriving upon error and superstition (see *Diary,* pp. 171, 202, 218, 251-252, 275-276). When Professor Small, in 1890, gently chided Ward who was then almost fifty, for antagonizing the public by his undue frankness on religion, and suggested that Ward would make many more converts to dynamic sociology if he toned down the religious note, Ward fiercely replied: "I do not write for the feeble minded" (*Letters of Albion W. Small to Lester F. Ward,* ed. Bernhard J. Stern, in *Social Forces,* XII, 165, December, 1933).

Ward's religious views took the general course of so many other thinkers: religious training in youth followed by agnosticism in early manhood and middle age, and ending with a refined feeling of true religiosity. In his first work he is an iconoclastic, scientific materialist, throughout. In his later ones he is almost a disciple of Spinoza's pantheism. He has not retreated from his former position because he is still the scientist par excellence before the philosopher, but he has made vast strides in advance by concentrating and fusing his thought. Decrying, as he always did, the purely theological and supernatural in religion, he stressed with renewed fervor the moral and melioristic phases of monism. Every atom and molecule evidenced to him the existence of mind, a world-soul which represents a striving in every direction. Evolution was not merely the Spencerian redistribution of matter, motion, and force, but the creative, organizing process of nature. In his own language:

We may even go so far as to maintain that matter *is* spirit, but not in the sense that it is endowed with intelligence and will. The view that matter and spirit are the same is true monism and I believe it is true science, but it means only that the material world contains all the elements of intelligence, and will and can and does take that form when organized in the appointed way and to the required degree (*App. S.,* p. 89).

Deeper study and more mature experience only strengthened the "essential element of religion" within Ward, the reverence and sense of cosmic unity with nature and his fellow-men. With the passing of the years, too, the conviction grew apace that there was no need or place for supernaturalism (in the popular sense) in an intelligent world; that omnipotence existed only in the universal energy, and goodness within the hearts of mankind.

### WARD THE SCIENTIST, A GREAT BELIEVER

Ward's claim that scientific thought is not cold or "materialistic" but passionately unites mankind with a common bond of truth, is borne out by his own emotional life. Although he concentrated on the intellectual phase, he was so sensitive that "the immensity of space, the tremendous waves and the sublime, starry heavens" seen on a sea voyage, impressed him with a sense of cosmic unity which filled him with life and infinite joy (see *Cape,* pp. 50, 183).

His emotional nature readily accepted the natural effect of prayer. At Brown University he attended and enjoyed the daily chapel service, while he was preaching as well as practicing the maxim "to work is to pray." Remembering the dictum of Machiavelli: "Let no man be so silly as to believe that if his house falls upon his head, God will save it without any other prop, for he will die beneath the ruins," Ward himself never prayed. Yet he firmly believed that "the sense of aspiration and thoughts voluntarily made toward Truth and Beauty, strengthened man's finer character" (*ibid.*, p. 111). Stripping prayer and religion of all superstitious elements, he declared with almost messianic enthusiasm:

> The day will come when every church spire will loom up as a center of education. Every bit of knowledge shall be offered to all, and we may call them "Halls of Science" (*ibid.*, p. 106).

> The day is coming when fine church buildings will be used more than one day in the week, and for an even higher object than that to which they are now devoted. . . . There is a law in biology which is called the law of vicarious function, by which an organ which has outlived the purpose for which it was originally created, is not destroyed or abandoned, but is, as it were, remodeled and adapted to a new and useful purpose. . . . And so it will be in the great social metamorphosis. The handsome buildings which have so admirably served their purpose during this larval state of social development, will, figuratively speaking, become the wings on which the full fledged human psyche shall rise into the pure atmosphere of intellectual freedom (from an unpublished lecture, "The Solution of the Great Social Problem," 1893).

So have spoken all the free minds and great hearts of the ages, who visioned an enlightened world in which every servant of God will become a minister of humanity and a teacher of the truths of science.

All through his life, he fiercely attacked superstition as "an enemy to the human race" (see *Cape,* pp. 29-30). Though he opposed all theologies, he was never the enemy of religion, for his own life's work was a signal act of faith, faith in the possibility of human development and happiness. Such a creed was a constant spur to higher planes of conduct, free from any irrational reactions to blind emotion. His fundamental monistic concept that the spiritual was the attribute as well as the goal of the material made him the great believer who sought the spiritual heritage of man, not in the clouds or in the imagination, but in the material world of man and society.

In spite of this scientific attitude, Ward was essentially religious, though free from the fictions and errors which are the very flesh and bone of theology, as the crowd knows it. Even the tragic picture of man's weary trek across the pages of history did not turn his head to heaven for solace. If he leaned too close to adoration, it was to adoration of intellectual power. When he was but twenty-five he had already written:

After what I have said in proof of the superior importance of intellectual over moral culture, it will not be a matter of surprise that I should claim for it the equal supremacy over religious culture. I regard the principles of religion as much above the things of time and sense as Heaven is higher than earth or God than man. If the truths of eternity are anything, they are everything. I only differ with the majority of mankind in the mode of testifying my perception of their majesty and striving to gain admittance to their glories. While others would leap at one bound from the earth to Heaven, I would approach the courts of the Infinite through the channels prepared by his wisdom (from an unpublished essay, 1866: "The Importance of Intellectual Culture").

## GOD

Ward's fundamentally religious nature is further proved by his concept of God, not as a supernatural power, but as a convenient symbol for grasping under a single head all the activities of the universal energy in their relation to man. In an exalted panegyric Ward spoke with true reverence but without superstitious awe as follows:

Nature is not only a becoming, it is a striving. The universal energy never ceases to act and its ceaseless activity constantly creates. The quantity of matter, mass and motion in the universe is unchangeable, everything else changes—position, direction, velocity, path, combination, form. To say with Schopenhauer that matter is causality involves an elipsis. It is not matter but *collision* that constitutes the only *cause*. This eternal pelting of atoms, this driving of the elements, this pressure at every point, this struggle of all created things, this universal nisus of nature, pushing into existence all material forms and storing itself up in them as properties, as life, as feeling, as thought, this is the hylozoism of the philosophers, the self-activity of Hegel, the will of Schopenhauer, the atom-soul of Haeckel; it is the soul of the universe, the spirit of nature, the "First Cause" of both religion and science—it is God (*P.S.,* p. 136).

## THE SOUL

His concept of soul is equally noble, while remaining within the bounds of science. Although he does not regard it as an entity, a sort of gaseous vertebrate as Haeckel ironically described it, he sees soul, like mind, as a part of the universal energy, as desire incarnate, the endless striving and reaching of man, a natural force which emerges from the universal energy—cosmic soul (see *ibid.,* pp. 140-141).

Ward had no recurrent periods of agnosticism and faith, but often his work seems to have that appearance because he never forgets science, and never buries his sense of religiosity. Thus, even in his first work, in which his agnosticism seems to be paramount, the truly religious note still rings clear in the scientific atmosphere:

In nature, there is beauty, there is grandeur, there is activity, there is even life, but mind there is none. The universe is insensible. Nature has no soul although within her are all the elements of sensibility and all the materials of intelligence. For mind is merely a relation. Thought is a mode of material activity. Intellect is a brainwave. To secure it only requires an appropriate form. One revolution of the wheel of organization evolved the living vegetable world; another culminated in the creation of sentient beings. Higher and higher has arisen the type, finer and finer has grown the product, till brain has become the ruling force, and man has emerged from that darkness which hitherto had never permitted nature to contemplate herself. This highest product of evolution, and which may properly be called spirit, has been described as that which "sleeps in the stone, dreams in the animal, awakes in the man" (*D.S.,* II, 74).

## IMMORTALITY

Ward treated the problem of immortality from the same scientific standpoint as the other phases of religion. He knew that vast numbers oppressed by the seeming futility of existence have always worried that life is fleeting, death certain, and achievement, fame, and happiness but passing things. If the travail of existence is to end in an eternal sleep, what sense or meaning is there to life? Is it merely for the purpose of destruction that the universe has been evolved, and man allowed to see the light of day for only a brief moment?

To such sentimental fears, Ward, speaking with the voice of science, has the assuring comfort that man is not erased by death from the cosmic slate, for achievement, not the achiever, is immortal, and he lives on forever in the ripples which he has made in the ocean of life.

The belief in survival of the body or soul is wholly unnecessary to support the fundamental postulate that the law of causality outlives all the transient things of the earth. Human beings pass away, but the effect of their lives never dies. The establishment of physical mortality is more important for human progress than the continuance of the belief in immortality. For, with the former is coupled not only the abolition of another superstition, but the acceptance of a positive belief in the worth of human life, and in the intrinsic value of man's deeds.

Like Christian salvation, the immortality of achievement (social immortality) is personal. While only those who achieve it, may attain it, everybody may aspire to and in some degree realize it (see *P.S.*, p. 43). Since the average man accomplishes little that is worth while, he is not much interested by social or ideal survival which necessarily precludes personal survival. Nevertheless, the immortality of achievement concerns everybody, for there is no one so low or inefficient that he does not in some measure affect his world.

Everything survives which gives worth and dignity to life, i.e., the participation by everyone in the conquest of his environment and in the spread of knowledge and happiness. With such a creed, our petty selves need not cringe before the infinite universe. It will endure forever, and our achievements, no matter how insignificant, will be a part of it (see *Glimpses,* IV, 59-63).

The immortality which science thus teaches is itself a spur to achievement. Perhaps the survival of one's deeds may not sound so thrilling as a conscious life beyond the grave, but a little sober thought will show that the former is a source of inspiration for all who have social consciousness and are interested in the happiness of mankind; the latter, a vain and selfish hope. Says Ward:

Science is not skeptical as to the immortality of the soul. Science postulates the immortality not of the human soul alone, but of the soul of the least atom of matter. Consciousness results from the eternal activities of the universe, is their highest and grandest product, and not one atom nor one atomic movement is ever lost. The immortality of science is the eternity of matter and its motions in the production of phenomena, and science will always object to all unphilosophical attempts to confound phenomena with these (*Glimpses,* IV, 58).

It is something to have learned that there exist, have always existed and will ever continue to exist, the indestructible and unchangeable elements and powers out of which, through similar processes, equal and perhaps far superior results may be accomplished. This is the immortality that science teaches, the faith that inspires the genuine student of nature, and this pure and ennobling sense of truth he would scorn to barter for the selfish and illusory hope of an eternity of personal existence (*ibid.,* IV, 63).

## MONISM (CONTINUITY)

Reason and science, rationalism and teleology, these are the main pillars of Ward's religious structure. Capping it all is monism (or continuity as he preferred to call it), "like a dome of many colored glass that stains the white radiance of eternity." It was the creed of his sensitive heart and mind that loved nature even more than mankind. No sentiment, this, unalloyed and unattached, but a feeling of close kinship with all the universe. Fundamentally, it is but another expression of the cosmic law of attraction and cohesion which holds out the promise that some day men, too, will come near enough to unite into an inseparable whole.

Continuity is a faith in the cosmic energy without any personal or supernatural significance, yet with more true religion in it than many churches, perhaps, can offer. In his own life Ward made it the basis of an all-embracing social creed. It is, in sum, the belief in natural law, in human capacity and in social progress as parts of a synthetic, dynamic view of the universe. It is in such a religion that Ward found his ideal of a natural, joyous life rooted in loving kindness to all, tolerating no injustice and knowing no fear, and spurring human achievement to enlarge the genius and multiply the desires and satisfactions of all men.

As distinguished from dualism, monism is that explanation of the cosmos which finds unity in all things, "the one in the many" (Spinoza). Everything in the universe is related to everything else, so that the slightest disturbance in a single atom anywhere, forever affects all the other atoms. Which is another way of saying that our world and everything within it are relative bits of a single cosmic pattern.

Ward was necessarily a monist. No sociologist who accepted evolution as a fact and who identified the totality of things with matter, and with mind as its chief attribute, could be anything else. He rejected the common dualism which places the mind force in eternal opposition to the material universe, for he no more could believe in two worlds in one than he could see disembodied spirits filling the air.

The history of monism is also the history of science. Both have their roots in the brilliant speculations of the early Greek philosophers which came to maturity in the thought of Spinoza, Haeckel, Comte, and Spencer. The same urge of unification which sought the fundamental relationship between all things, led Thales to postulate water as the essence of the universe, the texture of the "oneness" so endlessly pursued through the ages. Pythagoras thought it was number and harmony; Xenophon, matter. Spinoza found it in the universal substance of which matter is one side, and spirit, the other.

Although not all of us can follow Spinoza's pantheism up to the throne of the Almighty, his principle of continuity which is the source of Ward's, is sound science and philosophy. It was Spinoza who repaired the break in the concept of a continuous universe, with the postulate that God as well as matter had the attribute of extension, and so Spinoza showed the connection of the material universe with the spiritual universe.

Speaking of Comte and Spencer who built upon the broad principle of the absolute unity of nature, Ward indirectly describes his own contribution to monism, as follows:

This grand *monistic* conception is the final crown of human thought, and was required to round out philosophy into a form of symmetry, whose outlines, at least, admit of no further improvement (*D.S.*, I, 143).

Comte turned to dualism because he feared that monism meant another search for a First Cause. Ward dissolved such a fear by the argument that basal to the cosmos are matter and energy whose cause is unknown, but the effects of which are uniform and inexorable in the universal reign of natural law. Comte's position is surprising because it is the idealist and fundamentalist in philosophy who leans to dualism, either because he assumes phenomena to be caused by a power outside of and above nature, or because he regards nature as a conscious intelligence moving the cosmos to a preordained end (see *ibid.,* II, 18-34). The scientist, on the contrary, can see no divine design anywhere and one naturally expects him to be a monist. He views nature as dynamic and creative throughout, while the dualist, being at bottom a theologian, regards nature as passive clay in the hands of the Creator. When it comes to social science, the dualist seems to be more successful in taking the social mechanism apart than in putting it together again, often having spare parts left over which he uses in building his dual world.

## THE UNITY OF ALL THINGS

Science, from Aristotle's day to the present, has furnished increasing evidence that the source of the elements of universal life is one and not many; that matter and energy are essentially a unit, and that all of nature's forces are manifestations of one force, the universal energy. Ward, from his earliest work, argued that the organic and inorganic are one, and that the truths of science and philosophy ultimately merge into one doctrine of the true, the good, the beautiful and the useful, i.e., dynamic sociology.

In general, Ward saw heights and depths as one. At the top, all knowledge, thoughts, and feelings merge. All things pass into each other, and all opposites appear as views of the same thing. Everything in the universe strives toward unity; but as soon as that is attained, it is immediately subordinated to a higher unity. The highest or final unity is unthinkable, because it is, again, a First Cause, but every approach to the ultimate unity furnishes a high satisfaction to the mind (*ibid.,* I, 3-4).

Monism proves the amazing unity of all truths. Going straight ahead brings one to the starting point. There are no dual truths or plural worlds or universes. "Truth is one but man and his books have tried to give it many names," says the Hindu. A glance at Ward's table of all knowledge (see p. 192) reminds us again that there are no breaks in nature's process or in the sciences which man has formulated from its study.

## THE UNITY OF NATURE AND OF MAN

Ward regards the human race, too, as a unity. In the course of many ages, the human germ plasms have been so completely pooled that each individual is related to every other. No item of experience, no event or object, no race or sect can be isolated. For humanity, there is only one body of knowledge called science which is controlled by natural law. That does not mean that the laws of nature apply equally everywhere. One can scarcely use the laws of geology to study hard-headed people. There are general laws in the natural world, and special laws in the psychic and social spheres. But all laws point to a single universal process, the law of organization which manifests itself in society, the same as it does everywhere else in the cosmos, through synergy and creative synthesis. The physicist has demonstrated that temperature, pressure, and volume of gases are interrelated; the biologist and the sociologist, that all nature and all men are basically united. Everything, everywhere, is both cause and effect—links in infinite series of links—in short, a part of infinite causation (see *ibid.,* I, 66).

In achieving the synthesis of all knowledge Ward, like Spinoza, reasoned according to the rigid scientific method of the geometer, while, with the spiritual courage of the true philosopher, he pointed out the continuity of nature, man and society, and echoed Pascal's famous thought: "The whole succession of men, during the long series of ages, should be considered as one man, who continues to live and who continually learns."

No matter how miserably human beings have failed to recognize their common origin and common aims, monism furnishes a telescope through which they can gaze at the universe from its inception to the present moment. Especially is it valuable in the study of society, for the monistic principle is a synthesizing and co-operating one. Society is not a series of aggregate divisions of human beings, but a real unity. Every phase of associated life—economic, political, ethical, artistic, religious, or scientific—is a function or a part of every other phase. Each human expression of energy undergoes development in a close correlation with every other human activity, until the cosmic truth appears that nothing in the universe, within man or outside of him, has any existence, meaning or value, standing alone.

Economic production, art, education, research—every human endeavor tends to become international. The globe is fast losing its appearance of a mass of pigeonholes for different races, castes, nations, creeds, and ideas. All of them, once worlds apart, are being slowly drawn together and welded into one grand scheme of organization (see *Outlines*, p. 233). The Hebrew Chasidim chanted to their heavenly father: "Northward, You; southward, You; eastward, You; westward, You. Everywhere, only You, You, You." St. Gregory said: "Man has in him something of all the creatures; he has being in common with the minerals; life, with the vegetables, sensation, with the animals, and intelligence, with the angels." Ward, too, was permeated by the spirit of universal kinship. Speaking of quotations from great authors which he placed at chapter headings in some of his works, he remarked: "Although difficult of accomplishment and little appreciated by readers . . . these glimpses of truth dropped along the wayside of time, impress me as nothing else can, with the continuity of human thought, and the universal striving of man after unity" (*Glimpses*, I, li).

## THE RELIGION OF CONTINUITY

The existence of conflicting religious sects, said Ward, is enough to prove that thus far, at least, religion has failed to bind humanity together. As is the case with the various sciences, each religion may contain much truth, but unless there is an underlying philosophy which connects and explains them synthetically, there is no coherent structure. Bricks are not a house, and very often are used only as missiles.

Faithful churchgoers may wonder at a religion which has for its object the love of man, and for its basis the universal energy, i.e., the continuity of the universe. But here it is. Instead of relating itself to a Creator, it recognizes the cosmic energy as the all-pervading power, present alike in the sunset and the cyclone, in the press that prints this page and in the minds that will read it. The sentimentalist may call it love; the esthete, beauty; the moralist, truth; the believer, God; and the monist, the universal energy; but fundamentally those terms denote the same thing.

Ward accepts the creed of continuity because it educes our love of nature, that love which is the last stopping place of all true religion (see *Cape,* p. 76). It is a creed which is not necessarily opposed to the underlying ethics of any other religion. Continuity extends into a humanistic tradition which expresses the well-being and improvement of society as its most active principle (see *Glimpses,* III, 31-32).

## THE RELIGIONS OF COMTE AND WARD CONTRASTED

Ward, unlike Comte, never deified dynamic sociology, nor was he obsessed by continuity as Comte was by humanism, or Spencer by the Unknowable. Says Ward:

I am in the habit of considering sociology as a science, not a religion, cult or program of action, and therefore, "Christian sociology" sounds to me about as would "Christian mathematics," "Mohammedan biology" or "Buddhistic chemistry," for it is no better than Christian astronomy, biology and geography used to be in the days when such things were recognized; it is a rather poor article (*Glimpses,* V, 194-195).

Comte, on the contrary, worshiped mankind as the great collective life of which human beings are the units, a life which exists apart from individuals, just as the body has an existence apart from thought which is dependent upon the material of which the body is composed. The collective life is the Supreme Being, he said, the only one we can know, and therefore, the only one we can worship. It is not the Supreme Being of the universe, but only of our world, and hence it is synonymous with morals, our relations not to God, but to man. In the old theological systems, morality was inculcated with the view of a world to come; in the new, the view is to the general progress and happiness of the race, in this. That was Comte's religion.

Comte defined religion as the harmony proper to human life, individual and collective, constituting for the soul a normal consensus similar to that of health for the body. It is a religion that gathers into its bosom all the tendencies of our nature, active, affectionate, and intelligent, and presides over politics, art, and philosophy. It rests on the permanent combination of two conditions, love and faith; the heart and the mind; intellect and morals. It is different from all other religions, because it is a religion of humanity, which ultimately is based upon a fusion of science and ethics.

Ward, in combating the view that religion would pass into ethics, maintained that religion had a grand mission all its own: "As it began in awe and fear of nature, it will end in awe and love of nature" (*Cape*, p. 110). In his own method of teaching, he brought the Bible into his classroom in Brown University, and fitted its ancient cosmogony into the frame of modern science, as far as possible. He found so much consolation in continuity that he intended to call his *magnum opus* which he never found time to write: "Monism, the True Quietism, or the Continuity of Nature, the only Faith that can satisfy the Emancipated Soul" (*ibid.*, p. 21).

Ward's faith would sublimate theology to the higher reaches of feeling induced by the scientific study and control of nature and of men. The usual reaction of the faithful to his God is that of a loyal slave to an omnipotent master. The response of the rationalist and monist, said Ward, is the same as his reaction to life, that of a free, clear-eyed traveler who sees the cosmos as a whole, forever changing, without beginning and without end, and whose restless soul is satisfied by the thrill of the universal panorama of which he is a dynamic part (see *ibid.*, p. 188).

Monism goes farther than adoration of nature. The principle of continuity concentrates in the rational mind not upon any concept of godhood but in the ecstacy of creative human achievement for social ends. To live to the highest and fullest extent is to merge one's personality with the eternal stream of evolution, and help achieve social continuity. Man does everything to multiply his powers and enlarge and refine his faculties, because of his natural urge to continue the natural process, i.e., the urge to achieve.

The third pillar of the religion of continuity is, therefore, the love of society, not the love of mankind in the abstract. It is the dynamic desire to effect human happiness on a high spiritual plane and supports the maxim that to do good is above being good. This faith has much in common with modern humanism, yet Ward did not adopt the humanist cult which was too academic, too Puritan, and too definite a reversion to the outworn theological past to take the place of dynamic sociology.

To Ward, religion could never be an individual salvation, but always a social one, so much did the ignorance and the suffering of the mass touch him. The shift to that kind of a creed is already noticeable, and biblical authority and religious sanctions are slowly but surely giving way to scientific and factual authority and sanctions (see *Recent Social Trends in the United States,* 1933). The gospel of the Bible is being replaced by the gospel of society. For many people it may prove a great wrench to cast off ancient dogmas and superstitions, but for all informed and active minds, it should be only another step forward. For it is a faith without miracle or mysticism, one which belongs to all time and to all men, that partakes of Buddha, the humanitarian moralist, Confucius, the wise agnostic, and Jesus, the gentlest of human beings, and stands solidly upon the principles of social science and social ethics.

In spite of the World War and world depressions since Ward's death, it should be clear to the thinking reader that sociology as the body of the new religion of science is within the grasp of every man. Through the eyes of social science, one sees the human kind as neither wholly superstitious nor entirely rationalistic, but as a composite mass slowly finding itself, tired of endless bickerings about God and other worlds, and determined more and more to make this vale of tears a little less moist and a good deal more happy. It may take many years for such a faith to be organized, but it is coming as fast as knowledge and intelligence can make it come. The strange confusion of impotent and dying creeds and the growing curiosity of large sections of the people about the possibility of leading a happy, free, and active life, presage the quick ripening of the new creed. Perhaps it will be called by some other name than religion, or look altogether different from what Ward pictured it. One thing seems certain, monism, the gospel of science and society, is slowly spreading with the development of civilization. Man is learning to recognize and control the eternal unchangeable laws of the cosmos which work in society through him. To be aware of the fact that no one is utterly independent and yet is the inheritor of all that has come before him, will inspire all to contribute to life's continuous flow.

# BOOK IX. THE PHILOSOPHER OF HISTORY

*"The history of man, if it should ever be written, would be an account of what man has done."*—Ward

# Chapter XXII

# ACHIEVEMENT AND
# CIVILIZATION

---

*"The environment transforms the animal, while man transforms the environment."*

*"Sociology is concerned with social activities. . . . The platforms of previous ages become the steps in the great staircase of civilization, and these steps remain unmoved, and are perpetuated by human history."*

*"Civilization consists in the utilization of the materials and forces of nature, but the efficiency of the human race depends absolutely upon food, clothing, shelter, fuel, leisure and liberty."*—Ward

*"L'histoire de la civilisation peut se résumer en six mots: plus on sait, plus on peut."*
—Edmond About

---

Having traced man's origin and development from the nebulae to society, and viewed from the depths of feeling and the heights of intellect his aim in life as well as the nature of his faith, we turn to a closer inspection of his activities. What has he done for himself and for civilization? What are the influences that make his history?

## CIVILIZATION

In Ward's analysis, achievement is synonymous with civilization. While neither is the result of any prearranged scheme, both are the incidental, often the accidental, consequences of the quest for happiness. Civilization has been treated from too many sentimental and pseudo-sociological standpoints, either as a victory of mind over matter, or as the altar upon which mankind has sacrificed health, liberty, and happiness. Ward does not regard it as a spiritual state evolved from man's inner being but as the result of his conquest of the materials and forces of nature, upon the highest tread of the grand, ascending staircase of evolution (see *P.S.*, p. 18).

## MAN, THE ENVIRONMENT MOLDER

Of all the animals, man rose to the top because he developed a mind strong enough to conquer and mold his environment. He was not only a tool user but a toolmaker, and his workbench was the world, with all nature as his material.

Abstract speculations, innate genius or divine destiny—neither one nor all of these brought about civilization. Only human activities due to a growing intellectual power initiated that miracle in the primitive wilderness. From behind a rampart of such unique inventions as language, tools, fire, and the arts, primitive man defied and conquered nature. By extracting energy from the earth, air, and waters, he not only modified his body and his mind, but also the entire world. No animal could have done that, because animals are prisoners of the environment. Man with his active brain became free to rise above his surroundings and mold them like putty. Besides, his real achievements are of an intellectual, and therefore spiritual and permanent character, while those of the lower animals are material, mechanical and transitory. Ward expressed this distinction between human achievement (civilization) and animal achievement (evolution) in the illuminating generalization that *the environment transforms the animal, but man alone transforms the environment.*

## ACHIEVEMENT AND NATURE

Everybody achieves. Even the most primitive races have contributed something towards modifying or adapting their environment. Civilization began in that adaptation. If human needs could have been satisfied by manna falling from the skies, there might have been a primitive Eden, but no achievement, and, therefore, no civilization. Remarking upon the necessity and effect of human effort, Ward said:

It is human activity that transforms the environment in the interest of man. It is that *interest* which is in the nature of a force, and which in fact constitutes the social forces, that has accomplished everything in the social world. . . . Just as the biotic form of this universal force pushes life into every crack and cranny, so the generalized social energy of human interest rears everywhere social structures that are the same in all ages and races, as far as concerns their essential nature (*P.S.,* pp. 21-22).

## ACHIEVEMENT, FEELING, AND FUNCTION

In the survey of social evolution Ward concentrates upon two main aspects: (1) feeling (the social forces), the dynamic agent which works mechanically towards the natural ends of the individual and consciously under the guidance of the intellect, towards social or collective ends; (2) the urge to material achievement, as the basis for a moral, spiritual order.

Again we see feeling playing the leading role—now in the drama of civilization. Reason and intellect are subordinated, and the emotions and their satisfaction which find expression in the striving for happiness again hold the center of the stage. With the advent of mind, the directive agent, all functions including that of reproduction, become means instead of ends in themselves (see *Outlines,* p. 96). The aim of nature is biological; the tendency of the organism is psychic. From nature's standpoint, feeling is a means to function, and the individual a mere cipher in the sum of social evolution. From the opposite standpoint of the individual, however, function is a means to feeling, and the organism, not the mass, is paramount.

The world-old conflict between man and nature thus reappears. If nature in its only concern to reproduce and preserve the species seems to have the last word, man is no less egoistic in his urge to play the role of achiever. That urge is all-important in the scheme of sociology, for in satisfying it, or trying to, man has created the myriad phenomena which constitute the subject matter of the sciences and the substratum of sociology, and has brought civilization (see *Ps. F.,* p. 128). The Crusades, for instance, although barren of direct result, were the result of deep human feeling, and in the long run had a beneficial effect, much more so than if Europe had remained at home (see *P.S.,* p. 533).

### DIRECT AND INDIRECT ACHIEVEMENT

Animals satisfy their wants by direct action; human beings, because they have minds, by indirect action. Despite his brain power, however, man is no more concerned with the result of his actions than the brute is. Human achievement has been, thus far at least, as unconscious and spontaneous as breathing. One does not marry to found a family, or dine to save the race. But while he keeps on grubbing and squandering his energies for wealth or a mere crust, or for power or fame, he keeps on creating and inventing (see *Glimpses,* II, 275). In so doing, he changes the earth along with himself. His success or failure is of little importance except as his activities produce a lasting effect upon the environment, and through the arts and sciences lift him out of the gloom of savagery into the light of civilization (see *D.S.,* II, 108).

## INTELLECT, INVENTION, AND CIVILIZATION

The chief ingredient (not the motive) in the fermenting process of civilization, is mental power. The greater the intelligence, the more opportunity there is for the satisfaction of desire, either through the mechanism of invention or through scientific discovery. Most often, civilization is the result of a combination of both, or else it veers into artistic creation, and that union of ideas and vision which is called philosophy. But whatever its source or tendency, the outstanding feature of civilization is invention.

All inventions are man's complex modifications of simple natural forces by which he has annihilated space, conquered time, and speeded up the wheels of evolution. Although many look for signs of spirituality in civilization, few realize that spiritual heights cannot be reached except over the hard, cold steps of inventions, from tools and weapons to complicated machines, mechanical as well as social (see *P.S.,* p. 18).

Invention has wrought little change in man himself as compared to its effects upon his environment. He is no more fleet of foot, keen of vision, or strong of muscle than he was ten or twenty thousand years ago. Nor is he more or less loving, jealous, or spiteful than in prehistoric times. It is only in his culture that he has grown, due to the increased exercise of his brain power in devising and using new tools and instruments—all of which spell civilization.

In an apostrophe to invention, and indirectly to the intellect as the only true guide of civilization, Ward says:

Thus has invention not only satisfied a thousand wants but it has created many thousands more; and not only has it satisfied old wants and created new ones, but it has also satisfied these latter and thereby contributed in an incalculable degree to the fullness of life or volume of existence, which alone constitutes social progress (*ibid.,* pp. 524-525).

## THE HISTORY OF INVENTION

The evolution of achievement was no spontaneous process. The arts and sciences germinated during all the earlier centuries to develop into modern technology. From the dawn of history down to the fifteenth century, man dreamed, stirred, and finally awoke, possessed in succession of such means to conquer nature, as knowledge of fire, bow and arrow, wheel, sail, plow, clock, compass, smelter, printing press, and gunpowder.

Printing was the turning point of the modern age. Improved ships, new lands, new inventions, and discoveries swiftly followed. The telescope, microscope, thermometer, camera, clock and watch in the sixteenth century were rivaled by the steam engine in the seventeenth. The use of steam was second in importance only to printing. The eighteenth century brought the loom, the spinning jenny, and the other mechanical devices which ushered in the age of machinofacture and the Industrial Revolution. With the introduction of electricity in the nineteenth century came another avalanche of inventions which sowed knowledge and scattered human beings to all the corners of the earth.

The formulation of the laws of evolution blazed the trail for the new sciences of mind and society (see *ibid.*, p. 543). Each step in civilization developed into the next through a quickening of the tempo of invention and discovery. Only in social science did the power of mind seem to falter, as if it were fearful of entering the only field where its force was needed and where it could serve humanity most.

## INDIVIDUAL ACHIEVEMENT

Demagogues, statesmen, and pedants usually tackle the problem of achievement from their own limited viewpoints instead of from the broad standpoint of sociology, the only science which is primarily concerned with individual achievement (see *ibid.*, Chapter XIX). The story of mankind proves that in order to conquer the environment, man needed more than a knowledge of how to use nature's gifts of wood and stone, or how to exploit the inventions by which he had learned to obtain the necessities of life. He had to develop intuitive reason and intellectual foresight which led to the scientific method. Nature was always a surprisingly weak opponent and quickly became a docile slave, once the proper method of attack was mastered.

It is only because of the scientific method that individual achievement was able to advance so far since Plato, long before Christ, dreamed of the ideal republic of man, or Roger Bacon in the thirteenth century foresaw the invention of the steamboat, the telescope, the automobile, and the aeroplane. All progress in the approach to Plato's Utopia or toward the realization of Bacon's vision has been due entirely to the incessant and untiring labor of individuals in the fields of science and invention.

The story of civilization is the story of achievement, and that in turn is identical with the advance of science. Before recorded history, mankind already enjoyed such tools as the decimal system, the sun dial, the moral code, and the knowledge of mathematics which built the pyramids. They also knew language, literature, astronomy, domestication of animals, agriculture, navigation, mining, medicine, and manufacture. Woman was the pioneer in invention, but both sexes blundered through all the errors which constituted human experience. The earliest Greeks possessed bows and arrows, spindles, plows, sailboats, chariots, locks, turning-lathes, and balances, and arrived at the stage of fabrics, oils, wine, papyrus, metal work, and fine ornaments. They lived on their cows and sheep, yet strangely knew nothing of the natural miracle of changing milk into cheese or butter.

## THE PROCESSION OF THE SCIENCES

Astronomy was the earliest science, and medicine men and priests were its first votaries. The Babylonians knew the difference between the fixed stars and the planets, and were able to calculate, with amazing accuracy, the length of the years and the dates of eclipses. In 2000 B.C. the Chinese had instruments to measure time, mark the midday sun and figure the angular distances of stars. Between the third and the seventh centuries B.C., there was such a vast mass of loose and isolated bits of knowledge that students of antiquity are inclined to claim that all we moderns have accomplished has been to revive ancient truths (see *ibid.,* pp. 531-532).

Ever spreading, the stream of knowledge and invention flowed down the centuries, from Asia Minor into Greece and Italy, thence into western and northern Europe. The world's greatest collection of geniuses flowered for a cosmic moment in the glory that was Greece, where philosophy brought the human mind to its highest pinnacle. Then came, in turn, the Roman Empire, Christianity, and the Dark Ages, followed by the revival of knowledge and the dawn of modern science.

The immortal threads of science were not destroyed in the nebula of antiquity or in the gloom of the Middle Ages. The Saracens invented the pendulum and the process of making paper; the Chinese, the compass and the art of printing. Undying human energy nursed the seeds of ancient knowledge through the cold ground until they

bloomed in the heliocentric system of De Gusa and the immortal discoveries of Copernicus, Kepler, and Newton.

## THE COURSE OF CIVILIZATION

In following the course of civilization Ward singled out the
achievements of the European races. The English took and kept the
lead longer than any other nation because it achieved the most, and
was the repository of the highest culture. The fact that it was mainly a
material culture is unimportant since the English people possessed the
most social efficiency and spread it almost over the entire globe (see
*ibid.,* pp. 238-239). Although like other progressive people, they never
hesitated to use force or to make detours from the paths of strict ethics,
their achievement was not due to the ruthless principle of might makes
right, but essentially to their greater ability to conquer nature and
develop and exploit its resources to the ends of the earth.

The Orientals, on the other hand, have been the most backward
of races. Despite the genius of Confucius whose guiding social principle was that wisdom is preferable to violence, China after thousands
of years is still, for the greater part, the China of old. It was not
immune to civilization but simply shut its doors against it. Neither
Chinese art nor ethics and philosophy could take the place of achievement. So, too, have Buddha's creed of renunciation and Christ's
doctrines of atonement and the golden rule failed as substitutes for
achievement in producing civilization. Looking at history with open
eyes, Ward says:

Sociology is concerned with social *activities.* It is a study of action,
i.e., of *phenomena,* of how the various social products have been
created. . . . Viewed from the evolutionary standpoint, the highest
types of men stand on an elevated platform, which man and nature
working together have erected in the long course of the ages. This is
true of all times. The most advanced of any age stand on the shoulders,
as it were, of those of the preceding age; only with each succeeding
age, the platform is raised a degree higher. The platforms of previous
ages become the steps in the great staircase of civilization, and these
steps remain unmoved, and are perpetuated by human history (*ibid.,*
p. 16).

## SOCIAL INVENTION

All the achievements and inventions that have been mentioned thus
far were individual and mechanical, i.e., incidental and unconscious.

None were socially planned or socially utilized. Dynamic sociology is a plea to socialize science and invention to serve the needs of all; to harness the social will and to modify and to improve social conditions in the same way that mechanical inventions have altered and improved the physical conditions of mankind.

It cannot be denied that thus far social inertia and the lack of social invention have been outstanding. The only consolation, says Ward, is found in the fact that there has arisen the artificial eman-cipation of a part of society from the restraints of the environment, analogous to the domestication of animals. As a result, psychic energy can be liberated on a large scale and allowed to expand itself upon moral, cultural, and spiritual things instead of in the everlasting strug-gle for existence (*ibid.,* p. 510). Is it too much to expect, he asks, that the social art, when it will be applied to society with the same care that the mechanical arts have been applied, will be the most important and beneficial invention the world has ever seen?

## THE ESTHETIC FORCES

And what of art? Abstract science, like abstract ideas, could not have built civilization without applied science, which is art. The sub-ject of art cannot be dismissed with the truism that beauty is in the eye of the beholder (*ibid.,* p. 435). To do so inevitably lands one in the bottomless pit of metaphysics and prevents any clear and just view of the esthetic forces which form part of the spiritual forces in society.

## ART AND SCIENCE

Sociology does not recognize art for art's sake any more than science for science's sake. If art does not tend to serve humanity, it is a sterile and useless process. Science is knowledge. Art is science applied to man's needs. A science which is so pure or abstract that it cannot be applied as a human art is vain erudition and useless pedantry (see *D.S.,* I, 59).

Art is not an escape from life but its expression and application. It cannot be torn loose from its social framework, any more than eco-nomics, politics, or religion can be isolated in a pure state. The esthete often develops into a worshiper of abstract beauty to whom it matters little that a thing is devoid of human interest or is even antisocial. He forgets, in the intoxication of beauty, that there is a material world about him of which he and his art are integral parts. The scientist, too, has his visions of beauty, and if he steps outside the bounds of science to realize them, he makes the same error as the artist. While esthetes like Nietzsche mistake art as the only justification for life, sociology sees in achievement, prosaic as it may sound, a still higher reason for art.

The advance of science, as we have seen, presents a panorama of what man has done with the forces and materials of nature in the building up of civilization. The popular idea that science deals with truth and intellect while art belongs to beauty and emotion, is a fallacy. Both science and art equally are products of the intellectual faculty. Even the simplest and most primitive of human arts, such as digging into the ground with a stick, is impossible without science, viz., the knowledge of the physical principles involved which make the act effective. While every art consists of the application of science, the converse is not true; science is not an art. Mathematics is not the same as engineering, nor is astronomy identical with navigation.

Whistler's aphorism that art is fundamentally brains is a sociological truth. That every art is artificial (no pun intended) is also a truism. Art does not exist in nature, except in the sense that the statue is hidden in the virgin block of marble. Science enables the mind to chip away the unwanted parts and release the artistic masterpiece. Whether we dig a ditch, manufacture a lens, paint a picture, or compose a song, science directs every step (see *Outlines,* pp. 255-265).

## ART AND ACHIEVEMENT

Achievement is the product of art and science, the two sides of the golden coin of mind. Under the law of synergy, both cooperate to produce civilization. For the expressive arts we go to the artist who by his creative imagination reproduces and interprets the world as it impresses him. But for knowledge of truth and reality, of the ways and means of conquering nature, we must appeal to the scientist.

The love and creation of beauty is itself a typical social force. In proportion as science supplies our material wants and makes our social relations secure, the rigor and austerity of existence is embellished by the charm and thrill of the esthetic forces (see *D.S.,* I, 674).

Art is the beautiful way of doing things, and civilization adds the efficiency of science to the process, creates new wants, and in satisfying them, produces new arts. Science offers wide outlets for esthetic impulses until on the heights of achievement, the artist and the scientist stand side by side, and often they are one. Both exercise the same faculties to synthesize art, science, and philosophy into the culture of the greatest of all arts, the social art, the art of living.[1]

## THE SOCIAL ART

The art of collective living is the social art, and its products are the beauty of a happy social order and the joy of achieving together. The pure esthete is rarely concerned with any such things, but the true artist cannot avoid being a true sociologist, often in spite of himself. Imagination and intellectual force which are at the core of both art and invention, are synonyms for the concrete beauty of a happy social system as well as for the universal hunger for abstract beauty. Ruskin, Edward Bellamy, William Morris, and Samuel Butler were fine painters as well as ardent social reformers who sought to realize the beauties of the social art. The development by society of the reach and content of the individual life through co-operation was recognized by them as the apex of art, second to none in satisfying the appetite for a beautiful world.

## THE INTELLECTUAL FORCES

Among the spiritual forces, neither esthetics nor morals outweighs the power and importance of the intellect, not because art and morality are less desirable but because the intellectual forces, more than any others, help to achieve. In other words, the intellect is the distinctive characteristic of social evolution, notwithstanding the truism that man is an emotional being and that there is nothing that he will not do to avoid the pain of thinking.

It is because of its powers of imagination that the intellect is the greatest force in the world—in fact, the sum total of all the forces in the universe. The freeman is the one with a free mind. In the mind, not in the emotions; in science, invention, and art, not in

---

[1] See Hendrik Van Loon's *The Arts* (1937), where Veblen's "instinct of workmanship" and the idea that the arts and the crafts should be regarded as one are clearly developed. The author does not fail to advise the art of living as the greatest art of all. We wonder if he has read Ward.

superstition, speculation, or metaphysics, is found the nearest approach to real freedom which is the *sine qua non* of unlimited human achievement (see *Glimpses*, V, 164).

The mind force is superior to all the other forces in the universe because it alone employs the true economy of action. By its indirect method, it converts means into ends in the same manner that the lumberjack delivers logs to the mill. Although he is unable to move them directly, he does it indirectly by the use of his mind, as he dumps them, one by one, into the moving stream. The idea developed in his gray matter has overcome nature's obstacles and harnessed her mighty forces to achieve for him an otherwise impossible task.

Dynamic sociology is the only science which refuses to follow the mechanical method of nature and wait for the miracle of the timbers of knowledge and achievement throwing themselves into the stream of time. Thinking by itself is not enough; dynamic, intelligent action is necessary. The lumberman must do something to put into operation the genial idea of floating his logs downstream. The world has never been disturbed by theories alone. Until Franklin's kite brought down the lightning, and Darwin's inductions were verified, their genius counted for little. The lively interest which urges man to explore, migrate, invent, and search for knowledge and spread the truth, is as vital to society as the delivery of the logs upon the bosom of the river is to the people waiting for them to build homes and cities.

The intellect alone directs achievement like a traffic officer at the crossroads. By a kind of vortex motion, the mind changes the mode of movement of physical bodies so that they pour into channels of human advantage instead of running to waste or destruction (see *P.S.*, p. 544). If desire is the motor of achievement, the intellect sits like a detached controller in a high tower, impersonally viewing the tangled human web and guiding the emotional and obstinate little human machines.

In biology, the mind force spells survival. In ethics and politics, it makes possible the wisely chosen good. That was the dictum of Aristotle, the first one to regard reason as an actuality. Six hundred years later, St. Augustine made the intellect the logical support of Christian faith. Twelve hundred years later still, Descartes called reason the instrument of truth. Leaping across the years, we come to

Ward's definition of the knowing faculty as one which enables man to cogitate, understand, believe, and reason. He saw that the higher mental faculties are derivative and nonadvantageous (though nonetheless desirable), for they represent the surplus that has accumulated over and above what is demanded for the essentials of life (see *Outlines*, p. 111).

## THE HEIGHTS OF INTELLECT

When the purely biological ends of life have been accomplished, the mind turns to other things than food, clothing, and shelter. The inventive faculty then begins to function, and the intellect is free, at last, to reach forth to the heights of inventive genius, to roam the universe for its own sake and pleasure (see *P.S.*, pp. 490-493).

The mind also attains philosophic genius which has the largest stock of knowledge, uses reason most of all, and, by its synthetic wisdom, permanently emancipates itself. Scientific genius is also close at hand, and differs from philosophical genius only in that the former treats of the relations between phenomena, while the latter deals with the broadest possible generalizations drawn from those relations.

The vast importance of scientific genius can be plainly discerned in the labors of the world's great scientists. When Copernicus discovered that the planets revolved about the sun, it may not have been of the slightest "practical" consequence to the man in the street. Nevertheless, it was of tremendous intellectual and spiritual value to all mankind that the earth was dethroned as the center of the universe, that man's superegoism was shattered forever, and that the erroneous belief in his own importance was removed to make room for a sane, balanced view of his relation to nature.

## THE SPECULATIVE FACULTY

On a free, high plane, the mind speculates and theorizes. It dreams and imagines as naturally as the heart pumps the blood. When the speculative intellect goes out into the world and lives upon facts and their relationships, its powers become unlimited. Science decries speculation only when the mind feeds upon fictions, but when the imagination stands upon reality, the mind becomes prophetic and is able to create what Ward calls "the poetic idea." Poesis is the creative, synthetic process of the intellect applied to all the sciences and practical arts. It is the faculty which co-ordinates the distorted and isolated impressions of the senses, and discarding the trial-and-error process of nature, furnishes the only certain method by which truth may be obtained (see *ibid.*, pp. 84-89). Poetry, in this sense, is next to prophecy. A perfect example is Emerson's epitome of evolution written before Darwin:

> A subtle chain of countless rings
> The next unto the farthest brings;
> The eye reads omens where it goes,
> And speaks all languages the rose;
> And striving to be man, the worm
> Mounts through all the spires of form.
> (Quoted in *ibid.*, p. 87.)

In line with the ancient fallacy that science lacks moral values, are the more modern errors that civilization can have no spirituality, and that sociology, therefore, has nothing to do with the poetic faculty. Social science does not challenge poetry or laugh at theories and daydreams, except when speculation opposes science, distorts or abandons reality, and substitutes superstition in its place. If the poet cannot rise above abstract emotion, he is ready to become the enemy of knowledge and progress. Only when he uses the imagination as a telescope to bring nearer distant and elusive truths, does he serve as a true seer (see *ibid.*, p. 85). It is that speculative faculty with its genius for theory, from the austere regions of mathematics to the glowing heights of ethics and humanism, which has opened the road to the world's spiritual treasures without which material achievement alone would have no value (see *Ps. F.*, p. 221).

### THE SPIRITUAL GOAL OF CIVILIZATION

In analyzing the esthetic and intellectual forces (the moral forces will be surveyed at the end of our journey), we have left the material social forces far behind, like the foundation which has been lost sight of when the structure begins to rise. After all, the goal of civilization is a spiritual one whether we are consciously striving toward such an end, or not. But just as thought is the bloom of matter, so is spiritual achievement the flower of material activity. Dynamic sociology, often miscalled materialistic because it takes a determined stand for a healthy material base, stresses the socializing and civilizing effects of the intellectual forces which lead straight to a spiritual order. Only by providing economic opportunity, education, and leisure for all, can the seeds of the spiritual flowers of life germinate. Merely because the spiritual springs from the material, is no reason for neglecting the latter, and giving all our attention directly to the former. More inventions, more knowledge, more achievement, all mean more leisure for a fuller and happier life, and more chance to attain the sweet, ripe fruits of civilization and step into the wider outlook and the deeper life.

To neglect material achievement is ultimately to push back the spiritual goal of man. Only the Oriental mystic believes that "it is better to walk than to run; to stand than to walk; to sit than to stand, and to lie than to sit." It is he who looks contemptuously at Western civilization with its insane rush for achievement, and himself welcomes Nirvana. Opposition to achievement springs mainly from the gloomy idea that ignorance is bliss, and that human suffering is the result of science, invention or discovery. The spiritualist who abjures material civilization is close kin to the soothsayer who would cure a toothache by cutting off the head. Why is it necessary in order to avoid rationalizing human life to descend to a nerveless, animal state or to leave knowledge behind and fly off into metaphysical clouds?

It is paradoxical that the failure to grasp the importance of achievement (civilization) or to make the most of it in any scheme of life, has been largely due to the fallacy of regarding civilization either as exclusively material or spiritual, but never as both. Wealth seems to be the main condition of progress because human welfare is so largely dependent upon it in the social structure. Without the necessities of life, which money alone can buy, no one could exist very long. Yet the achievements that have elevated man consisted neither of necessities nor luxuries. He has risen in evolution because of the means he was able to use, viz., invention, methods, principles, arts, devices, institutions, and systems, all products of the intellect (see *P.S.,* pp. 19-25). Note the paradox: wealth, which is material, is transient and worthless; true achievement, which is spiritual, is noble, enduring, and life sustaining, and yet depends in great measure upon wealth.

Achievement, despite the autointoxicating fallacy that sitting buried in thought is the road to bliss, tends to develop high, psychic motives. With material civilization achieved, the mind supplants the stomach. The craving for art, science, and truth in general, as strong as the pangs of hunger or love, will not be denied (see *ibid.,* pp. 40-42). Under the influences of these higher desires, man's ambition leans to contributing something to the immortal stream of achievement. The student burns the midnight oil, the explorer sails the seven seas and the thinker probes the cosmos. Are they merely bubbles in a ceaseless current inflated to their fullest extent only to burst and pass away? Is the idealistic and metaphysical viewpoint that "all is vanity" correct and just?

The love of reward or the fleeting moment of fame is not to be compared to the ecstacy of creative achievement. All through the ages, men of genius have often refused to allow their best work to be given to the world until long after they were dead—witness Leibnitz, Descartes, Helvetius, and Mark Twain. The noblest and most enduring of man's treasures were not created to order or born out of sheer egoism or the lust for wealth, but always under the unselfish drive to discover and achieve, and enrich the world. If this is true of individual achievement in a society where the chief end is individual wealth and power, what could man not accomplish if achievement were socialized and became the collective concern of society, as a whole?

## THE PHILOSOPHY OF ACHIEVEMENT

Ward's philosophy of achievement is the challenge to the fatalistic, materialistic creed of individualism, on the one hand, and to the nebulous dreams of an impossible spiritual perfection upon an imperfect material base, on the other. His thumping social truths brought into focus the psychic factor and the transforming effect of man's mind upon the environment. That generalization synthesized Locke's psychology of sensation and Schopenhauer's theory of the will, and crowned them with an original and invigorating call for the social will to reform society from the bottom up. This philosophy of achievement is the apex of the great synthesis, and standing upon material achievement, looks to the heights of spirituality to attain the happiness for all which is the supreme aim of mankind.

Man's object in life is happiness, and happiness comes only through achievement. Ward visualizes human energy at work not for fame or wealth, but in the interest of happiness in a spiritual, civilized order. A truly civilized society (and that can be only a socially achieving one) will put a premium on intellectual attainments, not upon physical skill; upon spiritual productions, not upon material ones. Some day, under the guidance of social science, men will acquire enough intelligence to achieve their best together on a higher plane than competition and individual profit; to achieve as a social duty, not as an individual investment. That is the hope and the promise of Ward's sociology. It is also the unavoidable conclusion of the sweep of science and history by which a new civilization will begin, as different from the old and the present as slavery and feudalism are different from freedom and democracy.

# Chapter XXIII

# THE IDEOLOGICAL
# INTERPRETATION
# OF HISTORY

---

*"The affections, the inclinations, the passions, constitute the principal motor forces of human life."*—Comte

*"The ideological interpretation of history does not conflict with the economic interpretation."*

*"Only world ideas rule the world."*—Ward

---

WHICH OF THE social forces moves mankind the most in achieving? Has history, the story of achievement, any pattern? Whose is the hand that writes it, chance or evolution, man or God? Does history make man, or man, history? If the latter, is he motivated by ideas or actions? The philosophy of civilization cannot be grasped unless these questions are answered, and the problem of historical interpretation solved.

## HISTORY

To the sociologist, history is but another step in cosmic evolution, a cyclorama of events in vast perspective; the arc in the curve of social evolution; the dynamic story of achievement in man's endless pursuit of happiness.

History is not sociology, says Ward. Once the former's function of compiling data has been performed, the latter takes its place. The historian furnishes the facts, and the sociologist uses them as mountain peaks from which to discover the origins, and causes and explanations of the human scene, and then looks ahead into the future. History is thus an essential step toward establishing the science of sociology (see *P.S.*, pp. 56-57).

History has often been confused with the philosophy of history, which has given every philosopher an excuse to view the human comedy through his own pet lenses. Plato saw the world as essential harmony; Kant, as a moral order; Hegel, as a coherent, self-evolving consciousness; Schopenhauer, as will, forever striving and failing;

[ 276 ]

Ward, as the endless process of organization. History has also been variously interpreted to be the biography of great men (Carlyle); past politics (Freeman); social evolution due chiefly to the economic factor (Marx); social evolution, mainly as the consequence of the fermentation of world ideas (Ward).

## INTERPRETATIONS OF HISTORY

The effusions of idealists and theologians in the historical field lie wholly beyond the limits of any valid interpretation, for they make history an escape for their emotional bias, or regard it as too complicated a process for analysis, and treat it without the scientific method. The sociologist reads the page of history altogether differently. To him, it is neither God's finger moving across time and space, nor man's record of intrigues, wars, and tyrannies. It is the story of man's activities, a drama of the people's struggle for existence, the adventures of spawning masses, of slaves, serfs, and freemen caught in the wheels of the social forces. From the nightmare of lusts and battles of human beings entangled in webs of rites, customs, and laws, the sociologist attempts to pick out the fundamental factors which control the human scene.

As Comte suggested, every historical interpretation reflects the state of the current social mind. The Oriental thinks in terms of supernatural ethics. Classical antiquity had its mythology, and Christianity, its supernatural dualism. The modern age with its skeptical rationalism and scientific outlook is far in advance of historical compilation and achieves a perspective reflected in two main scientific viewpoints: the economic, generally miscalled the materialistic, and the ideological or psychological. There are other concepts such as the theological or spiritual, and the metaphysical or idealistic, but they are altogether outside the pale of science and belong entirely to metaphysics and speculation.

## THE HEROIC INTERPRETATIONS

Whether God or one of his children is the particular hero, the most popular but most erroneous concept of history is that of the hero-worshipers. Ward corrects it by the simple fact that ideas and circumstances mold all human beings, the hero included, and not vice versa. The truly great are the master builders of civilization—

the scientists, philosophers, inventors, and artists whose achievements disturb the world-old fear of change by creating doubts, advancing new truths and opening the sluice gates of knowledge. Around them swarm hosts of little antlike people who lead armies, corner markets and pile up wealth, all of which lasts only a little while. In a few moments of history, the immortal streams of intellectual achievement flow over the remains of heroes, heroics, and spent ambitions, together with the decadent social systems in which they moved.

Once in a long while, conditions create a man chosen by no one, but far ahead of his time, who is a dreamer and an organizer, a scientist and a philosopher; who is ignored or derided until events catch up to his ideas, often long after he is dead and forgotten. Meanwhile public adoration is heaped upon the mediocrities, the swaggering militarists or industrial barons who have been jerked up into the seats of the mighty. The fact that the undeserving usually receive the rewards of fame, stamps the "great man" theory of history as absurd.

Spencer was the first to shatter the heroic "drum and trumpet" idea of history. Then Ward buried the fragments by his analysis of the social forces. His researches into the problem of genius (see p. 409) stressed the futility of interpreting history merely through the actions of individuals. Ward exposed the fallacy (even more clearly than Spencer did) of glorifying the ruler or the master, and belittling the slave, the serf or the citizen. Such a historical method overlooks the growth of art, invention, and other achievements of the race, and considers only men, and not social forces, forgetting that men are only the pawns moved around by the social forces on the chess board of history (see *App. S.*, pp. 130-133, 149).

## THE MATERIALISTIC CONCEPTION

The materialistic, as distinguished from the economic, interpretation of history is the approach from the standpoint of the natural sciences. Thus, Hobbes deduced history from the laws of motion and the position of matter in space and time, and Feuerbach argued for the difference between the food-quality chemistry of the roast beef of England and the potatoes of Ireland, as the determining factor of political conflict between those countries. Buckle, Condorcet, and Comte believed that the influence of geography, climate, and minerology was a more vital historical factor than the achievements of all the soldiers and kings who ever lived. They related history, therefore, directly to the advance of natural science, and regarded man as conditioned upon the physical effects of nature.

Ward's ideological concept of history completely overshadows the materialistic theory. Racial or physical conditions are undoubtedly conditioning factors in social evolution, but they have never determined the general character of historical phenomena, he argued. The main factor must be sought elsewhere than in the natural and material field. The materialistic interpretation is only a partial truth. While it points to a basis for the historical process, it does not furnish the most accurate measuring rod or the great approximation of cause and effect above that base. Ward's study of all the factors (see p. 422) brought him to the conclusion that the influence of education alone was greater than that of all the other environmental factors put together.

As the sociologist above all, he takes the broadest possible view that education is the most certain road to social change, more so than any alteration in the climate or geography, or in the economic mode of production. By giving the people the truths of science and eliminating the world errors which fill their minds, Ward believes they would soon realize the means of self-emancipation from the bonds of nature as well as of men. In short, put a people in the correct mental attitude, give them fundamental knowledge, and they will write a new history (see *ibid.*, p. 82).

## ECONOMIC DETERMINISM

The economic interpretation of history sees man making his own history, chiefly as the result of his method of production. It claims that economic forces are the foundations; all the other social forces merely effects or superstructure. It is not ideas or beliefs which determine social existence and mold the political and economic forms of any age, but it is the latter which determine ideas and beliefs, and fashion the economic and political framework of society. In other words, the roots of objective social forces cannot be traced upwards into ideas or ideals, but must be sought below in the humble regions of economic production. All people are primarily influenced by their occupations and economic environment, and, according to this theory, all history is the story of social class struggles.

From the standpoint of philosophy, economic determinism recognizes the priority of matter over mind, and claims that the role of ideas, sentiments, and all mental and psychic factors are necessarily secondary and indirect. Mind, which is a manifestation of matter, can only influence social evolution indirectly by setting material forces in motion. There is an interaction, of course, between the material and the psychological social forces, but the intellectual factor is superstructure, and not foundation. As a corollary, the mental activities of man are only a function of his economic life, just as the individual mind is a function of the individual body. Ideas, therefore, are nothing but reflections of economic conditions. In order to correct a wrong ideology, it is necessary, first of all, to correct the basic economic system of production. It is that base and its changes more than any other thing, which make history, from the viewpoint of the economic determinist.

## THE IDEOLOGICAL CONCEPT OF HISTORY

Ward did not love the economic interpretation of history less, but the ideological concept more. His profound conviction that mind force was the most powerful of all the forces in the universe suggested to him that while the premises of economic determinism were true, its conclusion did not tell the whole story. There was a sequel in the effect of world ideas, which had to be accounted for to complete the underlying explanation of the historical process.

It is true, Ward admitted wholeheartedly, that no healthy, happy society is possible without a sound economic foundation. While radical economists have explained a great deal about the historical process, it is to be deplored from the wider sociological viewpoint, says he, that they did not pay much attention to the reaction of the mind force upon the economic factor. In their stress upon the subordination of mind to matter they opened a wider chasm between the intellectual and the economic forces than really exists.

The ideological interpretation which is infinitely removed from philosophical idealism, has for its thesis that economics and politics so often regarded as "first causes," have something deeper beneath them, viz., the force of world ideas. Therefore, the character of any society, i.e., its history and evolution, depends in the final analysis upon the quantity of truth in the collective ideas of its members (*App. S.,* pp. 40, 82).

The evolution of mankind corresponds chiefly, according to Ward, to the development of thought. The same idea appears in Comte, as follows:

> Every considerable change historically . . . has been preceded by a change of proportional extent, in the state of their knowledge, or in their prevalent beliefs. . . . From this accumulated evidence, we are justified in concluding that the order of human progression in all respects will be a corollary deducible from the order of progression in the intellectual convictions of mankind; that is, from the law of the successive transformations of religion and science.

Ward's interpretation of history is not one thoroughly deterministic, and is thus not conditioned by a chain of economic causes and effects which make all events inevitable because they lie outside of conscious, wilful, dynamic human action. Minds, he said, are not merely mirrors of the processes of nature, nor is history a grand and inviolable design over which society has no voluntary control. Deeper analysis of the historical process makes it clear that history is not a preconceived pattern at all, but a process of social control; not a matter of one causal chain but a dynamic interaction of social currents wherein each force is only partly, but not entirely responsible for what follows.

Accepting the materialist and economic concepts of history as far as he can (and he, too, is a realist and a scientist even while he bows before the power of the intellect), Ward argues that the economic concept claims too much when it conceives the entire social process in terms of merely a part. The scientific warrant for economic determinism lies in the fact that the economic interpretation is a phase of a still wider concept which must make due allowance for the influence of the mind force.

To summarize Ward's argument: the main forces which make history lie in human desire. Desire induces action. World ideas rest upon desire (interest or feeling), not upon knowledge. No one can argue mankind out of any world views, once it has become aware of them, because those views are social life belts or bulwarks of race safety. Neither abstract ideas nor intellectual forces can directly cause any events. Ideas must first be translated through the emotions into dynamic action, just as light must first give heat, in order to move anything. Universal beliefs spring from the feelings. The latter are based upon the group or race instinct of safety and are not necessarily rooted in economic conditions. In his own words:

It is just the element of interest that links beliefs to desires and reconciles the ideological and economic interpretations of history; for economics, by its very definition of value, is based on desires and their satisfaction. . . . The belief or idea is not a force. . . . The force lies in the desire. The belief does not cause the desire. The reverse is much nearer the truth (*ibid.*, p. 45).

The achievers in history are the personifications of social ideals that have permeated the social mind. The sum of world views constitutes the *Zeitgeist* or consensus of opinion. The influence of those collective ideas has been so much neglected that the mind seems to have become a forgotten factor among the social forces. World views rest above all doubt and difference, and consist of universal concepts, such as democracy and monogamy. Such ideas tolerate no opposition because they have become hardened into accepted universal beliefs and act as the mainsprings of social action.

As a striking example of the molding power of world views, Ward points to the Oriental civilizations. Not long ago, the Western world erroneously thought that all Asiatics were intellectually inferior. That fallacy has been dispelled by the discovery that the great difference between them and their white brothers consists only in widely separated world views. The East lives in an abstract world of being; the West, in a practical world of doing. Any change in their respective ideologies would fundamentally change their histories. In fact, that has already happened, says Ward, with Japan (*ibid.*, p. 49). After his death, the same result has appeared in China.

Ward's appeal to social consciousness based upon correct universal principles, or world ideas, is a new emancipation declaration. He sees in the infinite force of mind not only the chief instrument of social emancipation, but also the main factor in human history. Education, through which correct world views become bred into the very blood and bone of man, is the chief method by which history can be made to serve man's needs. If that is too distant a goal, we must console ourselves that neither history nor science is in a hurry, and that the goal when attained, will be a real and permanent one.

If the radical reader will insist that Ward is after all a bourgeois who will not see the economic factor in its full light, he should remember that Ward's entire social philosophy is a fighting program of social reconstruction, and that his glorification of the intellect is not an appeal to disregard the economic factor but to give it due attention. What distinguishes him from so many other liberals is his ability to recognize and synthesize the social implications (psychological as well as economic) of all historical material. Hegel was afraid to change the word into the deed. But Ward's insight drives him to a fearless but humane dynamic philosophy of life, a philosophy which is slowly transforming the world from a material to a moral order, because evolution and progress are the necessary results of knowledge and reason.

## THE RECONCILIATION BETWEEN ECONOMICS AND PSYCHOLOGY

The reconciliation between the economic and the ideological concepts of history has no relation to the backwoods debate: "Which is more important, the chicken or the egg?" Ward doubts whether the economic factor alone can furnish the all-sufficient philosophy of life. Although he finds in economics a revolutionary tradition, it is but a single element, though a vital one, in a more comprehensive conception of society. As one who saw with telescopic eye the panorama of history, and thought in terms of synthesis, Ward recognized economics as an integral part of sociology, and, accordingly, interpreted history as the result chiefly of ideology. In other words, he saw the historical process as neither economic nor psychological; it is sociological. To believe otherwise, is either to fall into Spencer's error that pitted man against the state, or to sail away in the nebulae of metaphysics where there are no such things as social science or social forces, at all.

Although Ward did not regard his system of sociology as reconcilable with Marxism, he saw a reconciliation possible between the economic and the ideological interpretations of history. The best solution, he said, is the widest and the deepest—the synthesis which correlates numberless facts, and linking economics and psychology—the atom and the mind, in one all-embracing formula, demonstrates that man can make his own history not only out of the data of economics but also out of the collective ideas of mankind.

Our quest for an interpretation of history is over. If sociology is a dynamic science, then mind, the directive agent, must stand like a captain at the helm. If world errors instead of world truths still fill the minds of men, it is all the more reason why Ward's trumpet call to the social will to take charge of society should be heeded and why all men, all forces, and all opinions should co-operate to write a new page in the history of mankind.

# *BOOK X:* THE ECONOMIST

*"There are two distinct kinds of economics which may be called biological economics (the economics of life) and psychological economics (the economics of mind)."*—Ward

*"Act from affection; think in order to act."*—Comte

# CHAPTER XXIV

# THE ECONOMIC FORCES

---

*"The wealth a man has is a means to freedom; the wealth he pursues is a means to slavery."*—J. J. Rousseau

*"Wealth is a good servant but a bad master."*—Alexandre Dumas, fils

*"All social processes that can be called economic have their origin in exploitation."*
—Ward

---

FROM THE TURRETS of history and from the heights of psychology we catch a bird's-eye view of man's achievements and the social forces which motivate them. Is not a worm's-eye view of the economic forces at the roots of the social process, next in order? Ward's faith in the power and supremacy of mind is so strong, however, that he takes the bird's-eye view also of the economic forces. Raising the lens of his mental telescope, he studies economics from the elevation of reason and becomes the pioneer social psychologist of his time who understood economics.

## THE MATERIAL BASIS OF LIFE

Ward looks to the rational faculty for guidance in the social art, yet never loses sight of the truism that the foundation of human life is material. Granted that man does not live by bread alone (after he has the bread), no one can ignore the physical bases of existence, no matter to what heights the intellect may soar to contemplate them.

Again and again, Ward stresses the fact that the economic factor is neither crass nor ignoble. Industry is the subjugation of nature by man; his taking what he needs from her bountiful stores, and making it over, as he pleases. Anything which tends to fulfill man's desires is, therefore, an economic necessity, whether it is bread, art, science, or education, because it lessens the danger of extinction, and is to that extent, noble and elevating.

These fundamental truths do not hide the fact that the individual and society have ultimately the same goal—heights, not depths. Economic security means a stronger and better mental foundation. The mental factor in the final analysis is objective in social evolution, while the economic is the base of operations.

Ward bowed before the intellect, but he never believed that we could rise above material conditions by thinking alone. Men, driven by hunger, will always sack the bakeries, not the libraries. Food is a god that has never been blasphemed, and logic, reason, and beauty are all mute in his presence. We have not yet reached the stage where physical or temporal interests can be neglected. Man, the child of nature, is subject first of all, to nature's rigorous biologic law. In his efforts to survive, he will become a slave driver, or a killer, if necessary. As yet, the higher moral and spiritual pleasures are subservient to the lower ones, because all emotion, thought, and achievement still flow into one great current, the instinct of self-preservation (see *D.S.*, I, 597; *Glimpses*, VI, 136).

## SLAVERY

The historical roots of the economic forces which insured man's survival can be traced back to ancient chattel slavery. Long before recorded history, the human being was largely a human tool. Originally a vegetarian, he was forced by hunger to become a cannibal. By the time his food supply improved and he became intelligent enough to make his prisoners into slaves instead of steaks, he had acquired economic wisdom. After that, slavery was regarded as a beneficent institution because it produced a surplus over and above the expense of its upkeep (see *P.S.*, p. 267).

In antiquity, labor was practically synonymous with slavery. Plato's view of both as equally disgraceful institutions is representative of the still extant idea that society exists only for the benefit of an élite minority, and that the great majority, the lower or laboring classes, are born to toil for the benefit of the upper classes so that they may have the time and the means to rule the world.

Although the ruling or aristocratic classes furnished almost all achievement (except that which required physical labor, of course), there is something wrong in Plato's genial picture. No pen can adequately describe the brutal history of early slavery, or as it should be called, primitive labor. There was no escape from it but death, or the miracle of Aristotle's vision: "If the weaver's shuttles were to weave of themselves, then there would be no use either of apprentices for the master workers or slaves for the lords."

Aristotle's dream has come true, and we have machinery without end. Although slavery is now universally condemned, sociology regards human bondage in its time and place in the past, as a beneficial institution. Distinctly cruel and unjust as it was, it furnished the only school of experience in which humanity could develop those habits of industry without which material civilization could not have been built up.

Of course, with greater intellectual development, the acquired habit to sweat and strain grows weaker, and the primitive, natural "right to be lazy" again comes to the front. In a really civilized world slavery in all its forms will become useless and die out, as cannibalism did, and as war and competition will in time disappear.

## LABOR

Ward strongly emphasized the idea that from the standpoint of social science, the one word which conveys the supremacy of man over nature and his superiority over all other living forms, is labor (see *D.S.*, I, 475).

The earliest struggles for existence did not involve labor in the true sense of the word. Man was not born with a grubbing or toiling instinct. In his natural state he was too lazy to be roused into full activity even by his personal needs. It was only the sting of the master's lash on his back, the cry of "Work! Work!" which constantly dinned into his ears, and the promise of rewards in the hereafter, that literally drove him to build civilization. The human beasts of burden rarely revolted because they were not aware of their servile condition. Slavery continued until it became cheaper to have ostensibly free men toil for a small share of the product. Under feudalism, the human horse was let loose to work upon the land, with a long chain that tied him to a stake in the soil. When modern machinery was invented, the serfs were liberated from the land and compelled by hunger to scramble for jobs. They had nothing to sell but their labor power, and thenceforth became proletarian "hands" in the mines, mills, fields, and factories of the descendants of the ancient and medieval war lords, patricians, and barons who now were known as captains of industry and finance. The laborer was the same bondsman as of yore, but he had different tools and a new master (see *P.S.*, p. 270).

## PROPERTY

Slavery and labor—in fact, all the economic forces—are closely bound up with the institution of private property. In the early communal or protosocial stage of society, when no such thing as individual ownership existed, property was impossible. Whatever anyone then had was his by virtue of possession, and not as a matter of right. The idea of owning anything that was in the hands of another, developed in a much later stage (see *ibid.,* pp. 273-278).

When man ceased being a wanderer and settled down, property rights in land arose, at first communal, then private. The "genius" who fenced off a part of the earth and challenged the rest of the world to fight him for it, is the ancestor of all rugged individualists. All later forms of ownership grew out of property in land and slaves. The conquering chief parcelled out the fallen enemy's territory among his own favorite sons and friends, and laid the basis of the feudal system. The land was never given away outright, but title was retained by the original owner and his heirs, through many ingenious devices. As for property in chattels, it originated in production beyond immediate needs, viz., the surplus which could be sold or bartered.

Property, in the historical meaning of the word, was impossible until the state and the law were evolved to protect its sacred rights and make it the leading agency of social evolution. Especially did the possession of land contribute to social development, because land ownership furnished the incentive to work, and induced thrift and social stability. The curse of landlordism, no less than that of war and slavery, played one of the chief roles in the drama of civilization. The ascetic renounces any good in property as he does in sex or in life in general. But it is only the abuse of human rights and the waywardness of human emotions uncontrolled by reason, says Ward, that make property or wealth an end in itself and the cause of so much conflict and misery.

## MONEY

The adoption of money as a medium of exchange, blended at a stroke all forms of property into one, and made the possession or control of gold the chief aim of all civilized people. The great majority since then has regarded any suggestion to abolish money or change the system of production with equal alarm, as sheer lunacy, or, to put it mildly, as a dangerous attack upon the foundations of society.

Again, the sociologist recognizing the curse of acquisitive lusts cannot accept the popular fallacy that money is intrinsically evil. The biblical sage did not say "money is the root of all evil" (I Timothy 6:10), but "the love of money is the root of all evil." The mad rush for gold, like all human striving, has had its compensation in social evolution. The darkest corners of the globe were penetrated, and every historic race was developed in the race for wealth. As a factor in human achievement, money has had no rival, and if one recoils at the ugly mess it has caused, no one can neglect its history.

Ward extols the necessity for wealth, upon the simple ground that it affords leisure for invention and other social achievements. Patently, the search for truth cannot succeed unless the means of subsistence are fully provided for (see *Glimpses*, IV, 49). Society itself cannot do much for its members unless it first has wealth. Money, like war, cannibalism, and property, was a steppingstone upon which man in his weary climb to civilization erected many altars and made many sacrifices, but advanced from inertia to achievement, from darkness to enlightenment (see *P.S.*, p. 278).

## PRODUCTION

Society lives in and through production. Under slavery, production was fitful, and since the greater share of the product was appropriated and generally wasted by the parasitic master, a slave system never produced much in excess of actual needs. Neither a slave-owning nation nor an agricultural or mining country without extensive machinery has ever grown rich. A real surplus, meaning wealth, is possible only under machinofacture (*ibid.*, p. 279).

From the viewpoint of sociology, production is the most important economic process because achievement—the satisfaction of desire, and the enjoyment of life—is dependent upon the product of labor. Those products are many and multiply with the increase of production. Aside from the sated rich for whom money cannot buy either happiness or escape from ennui, every person is always needing something which money can buy.

Production is of such far-reaching import that the stage of social evolution can be gauged by the method and the tools of production.

The following chart of social evolution, from ancient slavery to the ideal co-operative system, which Ward used in his classes in sociology, still lies mouldering in the Ward Room at Brown University:

## THE CO-OPERATIVE COMMONWEALTH

| CLASS | The World Market The Trust Steam and Electricity | CONSCIOUSNESS |
|---|---|---|
| WAGE | CAPITALISM Machinofacture Printing Press Gunpowder and Fire Arms | WAGE |
| SERFDOM | CIVILIZATION Plowshare Sword Armor Axe Smelting of Iron | SERFDOM |
| SLAVERY | BARBARISM Cereals Copper Tools Domestication ot Animals Pottery Brick Buildings | SLAVERY |
| CANNIBALISM | SAVAGERY Bow and Arrow Baskets Wood and Stone Implements Art and Language Fishing Fire | CANNIBALISM |

## DISTRIBUTION

The problem of distribution involves everybody. The social problem does not spring from too much production, but from too little distribution. Insufficient consumption of economic goods is due to the inability of the producers (who are also the majority of the consumers) to buy back the product. That is the economic paradox which flows from unjust and unequal distribution (see *ibid.,* pp. 278-282).

According to Ward, the growth of production is a social need, if for no other reason than to enlarge the distribution of wealth and so broaden the means of enjoying life. Besides, more production leads to lower prices and the increased ability of the producers to repurchase the product. Every economic depression adds to the proof that when the laborer receives one dollar for producing something which the owner offers for sale at two dollars, the result is superabundance of products on the one hand, and abject need, on the other.

The ancient slave owned nothing, not even his own body. The modern wage earner, likewise possesses nothing except his labor power. He does not own the tools of production any more than a horse has title to his harness. According to the iron law of wages which acts on the same principle as the iron law of prices, the worker never receives more than an approximate living wage. If he is able to save anything at all and tries to climb out of his class, his wages are automatically reduced. If he weakens in the struggle for existence and fails to sustain himself, the economic law will spontaneously increase his earnings. The horse must be fed to pull the load.

Whatever the worker receives, therefore, above the pittance necessary to keep him going, is essentially a transgression of the law of wages. The surplus is happily, or ironically, called by Ward "social distribution" and the "socialization of wealth." The workers' demand for a greater share of the product is always at first denied, and is granted only when the demand becomes insistent enough. Ward dryly notes that in spite of a smug benevolence, the owners never admit that the workers were entitled in the first place to the granted increase (see *ibid.,* p. 280).

In stressing the process of distribution Ward's sociology proved independently of the propaganda of the labor movement, that the age of production has matured and settled down, and that the era of distribution has arrived and clamors for attention. While production is according to up-to-the-minute technique, distribution, the apex of the social problem, is medieval and lags far behind. Its solution lies much deeper than any mere increase of wages. The individualistic system, however, marches blindly through more wars, panics, and depressions, afraid to change the method of distribution radically, and content to look for salvation to new markets and new makeshifts to keep up the present system.

Hope for social progress, nevertheless, lies in the fact that the social forces cannot be forever prevented from functioning. Co-operative movements, government job insurance, workers' pensions, minimum wage laws, and other beginnings of a planned economy are already harbingers of the passing of the outworn system of distribution and the dawn of a new order of socialization.

## CONSUMPTION

Economics has nothing to do with the consumption of products. Sociology, on the other hand, begins with consumption, where economics leave off (see *ibid.,* p. 282). Because all men are consumers, social science is primarily interested not only in the producers but in all other social classes.

Consumption, in the sociological sense, implies the satisfaction of human desire. Desire is the dynamic factor in social evolution. Thus, the sociologists' concept of value is not measured by any arbitrary gold or silver or other standard, but by the quantity and quality of pleasure which the product yields to the consumer. Animals and the lower sorts of human beings live only to eat. Man's degree of culture may be measured by the time and effort spent upon the preparation and consumption of food and other material necessities.

Again, Ward reminds us that sociology does not stop with the economic forces in the abstract and subjective science of social statics but proceeds into the applied and objective science of human welfare (applied sociology). There it finds beneficent only those forces which tend to fill human needs and afford pleasure to all. Says he:

To the power of production there is practically no limit, and all that is needed to place in the possession of every member of society every object of his desire, is the power to purchase it. . . . It is therefore useless to talk of increasing production except by the increase of the power to consume. The problem is no longer how to increase production, but how to increase consumption; not the desire to consume, for that already exists . . . *but the opportunity to earn.* That the reduction of the hours of labor is one of the means to that end is certainly clear. The discovery of other means and of the best way to put every means into practice seems to me to constitute the chief economic problem of our times (*Glimpses,* IV, 164-165).

## ECONOMIC PARADOXES

To measure the distance which Ward traveled beyond the old and beaten paths of conventional economics, one must glance only at the theories, laws, and principles which he distilled from the study of the social forces. Appreciating with fine satire how conservative and reactionary minds that apologize for the existing order would be shocked by his thumping economic truths, he labeled them economic paradoxes (*ibid.,* IV, 155; *Ps. F.,* p. 278; *P.S.,* p. 452):

1. Reforms are chiefly advocated by those who have no interest in them.
2. Subsistence increases more rapidly than population.
3. Competition raises prices and rates.
4. Free competition is possible only under social regulation.
5. The evils of private monopoly can be prevented only by resorting to public monopoly.
6. Because of self-interest, individuals cannot be depended to act in their own interest. The consumer will not encourage better production. Competition results in deterioration.
7. The interests of the individual are rarely the same as that of the community.
8. Market values and social values are not identical.
9. Public service will secure better talent than private enterprise, for the same outlay.
10. In an increasing number of cases, the hope of gain is not the best motive.
11. Private enterprise, through aggressive competition, is a monopoly that taxes the people more heavily than does the state.
12. The prosperity of the community depends as much upon the mode of consumption of wealth as upon the produced quantity.
13. The social effects of taxation are more important than the fiscal effects.
14. Wages are drawn from products and not from capital. The wage fund theory is a myth.
15. The increase of wages results in the increase of profits.
16. Prices fall as wages rise.
17. Diminished hours of labor bring increased production.
18. Reduction of the time worked enhances wages received.
19. A man working alone earns the same as when his wife and children also work.

Ward notes that two major paradoxes cap the foregoing. The first is that the owners, the nonproducers, are intelligent and class conscious and co-operate with each other. As industry is centralized, they form trusts and combinations, and reduce competition to a minimum. But the workers who are the producers are less intelligent and class conscious than their masters, and fiercely competing among themselves, co-operate less and less (see *D.S.,* I, 594-595).

The second and greater paradox is that there is so much food that millions starve; so much cotton that humanity is in rags; so much leather that untold numbers must walk barefoot. Yet all the people have to do to obtain the necessities as well as the luxuries of life is to take charge of society and conduct it for their own benefit (sociocracy).

How vast and profound is Ward's grasp of the social problem may be gathered from his economic paradoxes and his all-rounded view of the economic forces, the biologic as well as the psychologic outlook. If his economic philosophy in the frame of social science were given to the people, the social problem would be well on its way to solution. Economics would then cease to be the dismal, biological discipline that it has been for ages, and assume its true character as a humane science rooted in the productive forces but reaching upward through spiritual forces of the intellect to bear the fruit of economic security and social well-being.

Chapter XXV

# THE PSYCHOLOGICAL BASIS
# OF ECONOMICS

---

*"L'homme n'est ni ange, ni bête; et le malheur veut que qui veut faire l'ange fait la bête.*—Pascal

*"To make a man a machine is to make him anything but productive."*—J. B. Clark

*"Nature may be called practical, but not economical; man economical, but not always practical."*—Ward

---

THE MULTITUDES who avoid the musty corridors of economics and run from its dry formulas can scarcely be blamed. The very word *economics* suggests a dreary compilation of graphs and statistics, and the public shuns the subject as much as the student who promptly forgets it all, the day after graduation.

### ECONOMICS AND SOCIOLOGY

Ward was the first American sociologist to suggest rebuilding the foundations of economic science by extending the biological base into the realms of psychology. Sociology, he argued, is almost the opposite of economics, because the former considers the advantage not only of the producers, but of society as a whole. The radicals who are aflame with the idea that economics is the most important of all the sciences because it treats of the manner and means of earning a living, are really arguing that the tail is the most vital part of the dog because it is the tail which keeps on wagging (see *Outlines,* p. 14).

Ward's stand was that the science of economics from the viewpoint of the human synthesis does not ultimately deal with matter alone, but with matter under the control of mind. Economic forces are not necessarily or eternally automatic, even though they are natural forces which cannot be supplanted by more refined forces. It is true, argues Ward, that the foundation of economics is physical science (man cannot live by ideas and ideals alone), but eventually reason must take charge of the economic process in order to accomplish by indirect means (social telesis or intelligent planning) what no natural force could do by direct means.

[ 296 ]

Spencer was wrong in believing that economics is the child of biology. It is the offspring of psychology, said Ward, as truly as man is the heir of his animal ancestors. If economics is a true science, the mind, and not the biologic law of might makes right, must control. Sociology is essentially psychic. Economics is a part of the data of sociology. Therefore, economics, too, is fundamentally psychic. It is not merely a cold and narrow-gauged science of profits and losses, but a human, dynamic study of conscious and planned production, distribution, and consumption of the means of life (see *Ps. F.,* Chapter XXXII; *D.S.,* I, 483-597; *P.S.,* pp. 266, 471; *Glimpses,* IV, 298).

## BIOLOGICAL ECONOMICS

The conflicting and confusing viewpoints in economics are due to the same old error of seeing only parts or distortions of the truth. It is enough to dishearten the student when he follows the currents of theory and meets Spencer's rugged individualism, with biological laws trying to explain social change, or Tarde's theory of the law of imitation as the underlying dynamic force. Why have such eminent sociologists failed to take sufficiently into consideration the final and supreme influence of the psychological factor? Are they not doing the same thing to the field of sociology as the blind Hindus did to the elephant which they learnedly described according to the portions of its body that they managed to touch?

Comte in France and Ward in America were among the few sociologists who saw distinctly that there are two kinds of economics, viz., the biological economics of nature, and the psychological economics of mankind. The former embraces organic nature, animal life, and the struggle for survival through the law of the strong. To the latter belong the actions of man as a rational being; as the master of nature and of society by virtue of his intellect.

## THE ERROR OF MALTHUS

One of the gravest errors of biological economics is found in the Malthusian theory that the race is prematurely doomed to starvation, because population runs ahead of the food supply. The least thought given to the supremacy of mind over the physical forces of nature at once proves that the human mind is powerful enough to save the world from any such calamity. Not only can overpopulation be prevented by mechanical means, but inventions continually increase economic productivity, leaving a surplus instead of causing a deficit. Sociologists today cannot possibly be as wrong as Malthus was, unless they regard society as an arena of clashing physical appetites without the possibility of intellectual control.

The pessimistic Malthusian doctrine which quickened the dormant genius of Darwin, clearly applies to the animal world alone. When man, because of his superior brain power, ascended the throne of the animal kingdom, he harnessed the economic forces to do his bidding without coercion and compensation, and has since compelled them to produce more than enough to satisfy his needs (see *Glimpses*, IV, 366).

Man economizes because his brain adopts economical and rational methods. Nature alone wastes and spends recklessly (see *D.S.*, II, 494). Her sowing, as Asa Gray so abundantly proved, is a scattering at random, and the product is often abnormal. Whenever man follows nature's method, he, too, creates ideas and institutions which are parasitical or monstrous. Ward's grand generalization that the environment transforms the organism, but that man alone can transform the environment, assumes greater visibility in the light of psychological economics and the story of human labor. Nature really produces nothing in the politico-economic sense of the word. Man, on the other hand, does not have to leave anything to nature, and by the use of his mind, produces everything that he needs for life and happiness. With the appearance of a surplus beyond his needs, biological economics abdicates and yields its scepter to psychological economics, and the belly-philosophy surrenders to the force of brain power.

### PSYCHOLOGICAL ECONOMICS

Seeing further and clearer than the classical economists, Ward takes the broad view that social institutions are so many methods of the psychic force to check the natural force of competition. Ethics, law, and government are means adopted by reason for suppressing the animal nature of man and for chaining his inherited biological egoisms (see *Ps. F.*, p. 261). If, in spite of civilization and a developed rationality, society allows competition and monopoly to tyrannize over it, society is guilty of an immoral act. Deception and brute force do not help mankind, and civilization cannot flourish unless competition and biological economics are supplanted by co-operation and psychological economics.  Therefore, until the force of reason is recognized, a true science of economics is impossible.

Radical as well as doctrinaire schools of economics have neglected the intellectual factor because they believe that ideas and events are shaped mainly by pressure of the economic or some other factor exclusive of the mind.  But the mind force is being taken into account more and more as the notion of co-operation and synthesis seeps through the social strata.  Leaning too much to the economic influence would lead to the abandonment of social science for a one-sided view of the social forces.  There is no question that the natural force of gravitation retards a horse pulling a load up hill, but neither the muscular power of the animal nor the mind power of the driver can be ignored.  It is true that bread comes before ideas, but that does not shut from view the still greater truth that ideas can make it possible to produce more and better bread for all.  Which is but another way of saying that the most important factor in economics as well as in social science is the power of the human mind.  Material conditions are the foundations; intellectual development, the structure.  Without both, there can be no mansion of society.

No clearer, more profound or brilliant summary of the cause of social evil has ever been offered to this heedless world than Ward's:

The most prominent fact in social life is the economic struggle for existence.  Some who consider themselves highly scientific maintain that this is natural and proper and they base their claim on the admitted fact that a similar struggle for existence has always gone on in the organic world, and that through it organic evolution has been accomplished.  This, they say, is nature's method, and all attempts artificially to thwart nature's plans emanate from sentimentalism and end in failure. . . .

The view above stated ignores the intellectual factor which completely reverses the biologic law.  The whole effect of intelligence has been to do away with the struggle for existence.  The industrial arts and civilization in its entirety have been the result of the successful conflict of mind with nature.  The law of nature has been neutralized in the physical world and civilization is the result.  It is still in force in the social and especially in the economic world, but this is because the method of mind has not yet been applied to these departments of nature. . . . The existing competitive system in society is the consequence.  Whenever society becomes sufficiently intelligent to grapple with the social forces as it has with the physical forces they will yield as readily and come as fully under its control. The world sustains now the same relation to the social forces that it did to the physical before there was any form of art whatever, i.e., the equivalent of the lowest known state of savagery" (*App. Soc.*, pp. 319-320).

If all that Ward's dynamic sociology had accomplished was to announce the freedom of the mind from the bondage of competition and the biologic law, it would be enough to make his name immortal. His economic principles are trumpet blasts in the ears of the dozing human giant, rousing him to cast off the stupor of the brutal biologic law in the struggle for survival. Must mankind be forever content to live upon the level of the helpless beasts which spend their lives hunting for food and safety? Must the mechanical process of nature and the uncontrolled emotions of man forever bar the art and application of thinking? If Ward's reply is propaganda, let us make the most of it, for it is social science calling upon society to use its brains for its own benefit and control its own social forces—economics, intellectual, and moral.

# BOOK XI. THE SOCIOCRAT

*"I have never yet had the good fortune to hear any valid
reason alleged why that corporation of individuals we call the
State may not do what voluntary effort fails in doing, either
from want of intelligence or lack of will."*—T. H. Huxley

*"Men are born unequal. The great benefit offered them by
society is to lessen this inequality as much as possible by giving
all men security, property, education, and help in time of need."*
—Joseph Joubert

# Chapter XXVI

# INDIVIDUALISM AND
# COLLECTIVISM

---

*"The fallacy of the reasoning for laissez faire belongs to the class of 'fool's puzzles,' like Zeno's proof of the impossibility of motion, or the feat of the woman of Ephesus who carried her calf each day from the time of its birth till it became an ox."*

*"It is not the doctrine of inactivity, of the folding of arms that naturally and legitimately flows from a full comprehension of the law of evolution, but a gospel of action . . . of man as a great and potent cause in the world."*—Ward

*"The interest of the individual is always to be found in the common interest. He who would hold himself apart risks his own destruction; justice for others is charity for ourselves."*—Montesquieu

---

We enter the inner domains of society where government and politics present us with a view of another of man's whited sepulchers. The paradox immediately presses for a solution why such vast strides have been made in material civilization and so little progress in self-government. Society, despite any labels of democracy, is living almost entirely under competition, individualism, and capitalism (these terms are used as synonyms), but it is evolving towards co-operation and socialization, also used here synonymously. Politically, almost the whole world is a democracy or nearly so, while industrially, it is highly developed, but an autocracy which belongs in the stone age. Why?

## INDIVIDUALISM

Ward's analysis and critique of individualism is ever green, and should prove valuable both to the reader who believes individualism is gone, and to the one who is certain that it is here to stay, because it is the best possible system, and only needs a little patching and tinkering to make it run smoothly for all. Ward regarded it as unjust, unnatural, and a blot on civilization, as a fallacy which he saw no hope of dislodging except by means of education. Though the philosophy of individualism has permeated the thought of all the ages, it came to maturity in Herbert Spencer, the sire of "rugged" individualism, upon whom his attack is centered. Whether Spencer is regarded as a social metaphysician or as a philosophical anarchist, his argument unmistakably runs as follows: The social order must imitate the competitive process of nature. There is nothing wrong in a social system in which property rights are as sacred and more so than human rights; it is all the method of natural selection, even the stranglehold which the system has upon present society (see *Outlines*, p. 94; *Glimpses*, VI, 312).

To Spencer, the Sanskrit aphorism, "as one piece of wood and another piece of wood may meet together in the ocean, and having met, may part again, such like is the meeting of human beings," is an eternal truth. He regards the state as a policeman who is watching a street brawl and turns his back to let the "best" man win. The social problem can be solved, according to Spencer, only by application to the problem of the individual. Society can best regulate its affairs, therefore, by letting its members fight it out among themselves, and itself do nothing to interfere; for nothing that society could do would abolish human misery. Only better, higher types of individuals through self-improvement will bring about a better social system.

Spencer treats economic law as a natural necessity, not as a man-made discipline. Social relations are as rigid and as fixed as the Rock of Gibraltar; and social evolution, civilization, and human happiness and well-being are parts of the unconscious cosmic process. Social progress is the same as natural evolution. Human progress is inevitable because evolution is inherently ethical, and nature tends toward improvement. Science, in general, can never be anything but a gospel of inaction, when applied to man's life. Nature made us as we are, for better or for worse, and nothing we know or do can change human nature. It is futile to try to abolish poverty, disease or war, before nature is ready to abolish them. Neither legislation nor force (so ends the Spencerian argument) can rid society of those evils. Therefore, laissez faire, let things alone, mind your own business, and wait for the perfection of human nature to bring about social changes.

### THE PHILOSOPHY OF LAISSEZ FAIRE

Spencer's sympathy for the ignorant and the oppressed becomes rugged, indeed, when he blames them for their own plight. He feels certain that if only the discontented could be induced to improve their own characters, nature would solve the social problem by weeding out the weak and fostering the strong. He, therefore, concludes that noble character can come solely through individual initiative and free competition.

The laissez-faire philosophy was not the discovery of Spencer or any other thinker, ancient or modern, but originated in man's acquisitive instinct brought along from his animal ancestors. The stronger impulse of self-preservation drove him into the primitive communal, co-operative form of life which lasted until about 4000 B.C., when individualism based upon private property took its place. Thenceforth, it was every man for himself, and the devil take the hindmost. The new system became so firmly intrenched that it was given the high honor of a natural order ordained by God. Capitalism, its latest offspring, is still regarded by untold millions of people as eternal and unchangeable, the best possible system of an all-merciful Creator.

It was more than a mere flaw in the synthetic philosophy which caused it to topple into the dust. Spencer's sociology is so inconsistent with the rest of his evolutional structure that it destroyed the value of the entire synthesis which Spencer believed he had found through the law of evolution. In *First Principles,* social development like all other development is shown to proceed strictly from the indefinite to the definite state; from the simple to the complex, from chaos to coherence and order. But in his *Principles of Sociology,* he departs from the formula of evolution and argues that social development is based upon the survival of the fittest, and Lamarck's principle of the inheritance of useful characteristics.

When he comes to treat of social organization, Spencer leaves evolution far behind. Society is a superorganism, a real entity, he says, and this analogy finally destroys his synthesis. Society, he argues, is like a biological organism because of similarities which outweigh such differences as continuous growth, increasing complexity and dependence of parts, and possible independent life of the whole and individual parts. Every society has a system of nutrition, circulation, and regulation (like any organism), with a central system of nerve control.

In the end, his leaning to laissez-faire individualism bred in his blood from early Victorian ideals, becomes stronger even than his adherence to evolution and the organic analogy. Militarism requires government, he argues, but under industry, government slowly disappears or becomes voluntary co-operation. Economic life grows so complicated that it cannot submit to any governmental regulation without ending in disaster. Ergo, natural liberty, unrestricted freedom alone can bring progress. The government which governs least is best, and no political or other authority should try any of the following: (1) establish any church or religion; (2) relieve the poor and unemployed, or help the weak; (3) establish free public schools, compel education, supervise public sanitation or provide post offices. And so, though he divides sociology as Comte did, into social statics (the balancing of a perfect state) and social dynamics (the forces that make for progress), Spencer is certain that "the course of civilization could not have been other than it has been." Finally, his formula of universal evolution led him to emphasize nature's mechanical rather than man's psychological process, and to try and convince his readers that social evolution is an automatic process in which man's mind can do nothing to accelerate or retard the mechanically determined distribution of matter and energy which produces social phenomena. But he goes even further in disregarding the role of mind and asserts that if conscious, intelligent planning could affect the social process, the evolution of the militant type to the industrial type of man was natural and inevitable. While automatic forces made primitive mankind militant, the industrial stage taught man enough about controlling nature to enable him to make things. Industry depended upon voluntary compulsion; the state let the individual loose and thus undermined authority and the caste system which had developed under militarism. Everyone in seeking his own interest necessarily seeks the benefit of society. Thus takes place the transition from status to contract, from slavery to freedom, and results in a state of industry which establishes peace and democracy. Therefore, again and always, laissez faire!

## THE SOURCES OF SPENCER'S FALLACY

How explain the paradox of Spencer, the scientist in physical and biological evolution, suddenly becoming a metaphysician in whatever touches upon social evolution? What caused his synthetic philosophy to part the way between two irreconcilable methods of living, the individualistic and the collective? What made him, despite his extreme libertarianism, regard society as a machine of the gods which can only be described but not controlled?

Great men fall from great heights. Spencer's tragic error in believing that nature alone could do man's work in social evolution, while man was powerless to do any of nature's, belongs, says Ward, to the "class of 'fool's puzzles,' like Zeno's proof of the impossibility of motion, or the feat of the woman of Ephesus who carried her calf each day from the time of its birth till it became an ox" (*P.S.*, p. 21).

Ward found in Spencer's biography the source of the greatest of all social fallacies, individualism. Spencer was a child of his place and time and could not rise above them. His social philosophy was the full-blown product of the naturalism of the nineteenth century, a philosophy which rested entirely upon faith in blind nature, and represented perfectly the complacency of stolid Victorian England. Society, to him, was not a whit more than the individuals who composed it. The individual is supreme, and society and social laws are only matters of convenience without any real status. These ideas flowed naturally from this lonely bachelor and respectable burgher who never knew the sting of toil or poverty and whose last twenty years were so poisoned by illness and drugs that he said: "If pessimism means that you would rather not have lived, then I am a pessimist."

Pampered in childhood and youth, brought up in cotton wool, well educated (chiefly in mathematics and the physical sciences), and amply protected from the brunt of the economic struggle, he had (as Heine said of Kant) "no life and no history." He was a sort of Jekyll and Hyde personality, according to Ward, and hated anything ignoble but strenuously upheld a social order which stunted and degraded the individual. With one hand, he opened wide the gates of knowledge to let in the evolution theory to explain the development of the world up to the point of social organization; with the other, he shut out every bit of the evolution formula in social life which would take us beyond the animal struggle for existence and out of the natural process. Ward even looked at Spencer's physiognomy for a clue to the riddle of Spencer's personality (see *Glimpses,* VI, 162). The lower portion indicated a bigot who might claim to be open to conviction but who would like to see the man who could convince him! The sharp nose, tightly drawn lips, hard mouth, and belligerent chin were all the features of an uncompromising dogmatist who was ready to kill anybody for a difference of opinion. The upper part, on the contrary, showed the enormous mental development of an intellectual giant who was also a liberal man of the world.

The same irreconcilable elements appeared in Spencer's social philosophy. Its static and individualistic features came from the atmosphere of his early life where he carried over biological principles into sociology and made them the basis of his social creed. In so doing, Spencer stood the pyramid of the sciences upon its apex, and rested sociology upon biology, so that biologic (animal) principles, charitably called natural, appeared to rule the human world.

When Ward's critique threw the synthetic philosophy into a heap, it was Spencer and not sociology that crashed (see *D.S.*, I, 209). Ward then set the pyramid upright upon its base, and made sociology rest upon psychology, the laws of society upon the laws of mind.

## WARD AND SPENCER CONTRASTED

The same competitive industrial age gave birth to Spencer's philosophy of individualism as to Ward's philosophy of collectivism. The former had the stifling effect of a wet blanket upon all utilitarian tendencies; the latter fanned the smoldering fires of the social will into a white heat. Only widely dissimilar environments could have produced in these two intellectual titans such opposite views. Spencer's youth was spent as a cloistered student of mathematics and engineering; Ward's, as a penniless, itinerant laborer who trained himself in the natural sciences and experienced poverty and toil without end. Spencer's concept of the social mechanism was as unbending as his surveyor's rod. To Ward, society was a living, ever changing phenomenon impelled by molding forces no less vital and dynamic than nature's, to knead both men and circumstances, like so much putty, into any desired form.

Spencer (said Ward) fell back on nature as if the human mind did not exist, and worshiped her as if he had never heard of social forces or social science. One might think that he loved animals more than men, so much did he stress the biological and shun the psychic and social aspects of man's life. The result left man confessing his inability (as if he were a fish or a horse) to modify or control his social condition, and looking to heredity and a mythical, acquired altruism to produce a nobler society.

When Spencer in 1883 received a copy of *Dynamic Sociology,* he wrote to Ward as follows:

I infer that you have a good deal more faith in the effects of right theory upon social practice than I have. The time may come when scientific conclusions will sway men's social conduct in a considerable degree. But, as you are probably aware, and as I said very emphatically when in America, I regard social progress as mainly a question of character, and not of knowledge or enlightenment. The inherited and organized natures of individuals, only little modifiable in the life of a generation, essentially determine, for the time being the type of social organization in spite of any teaching, spite even of bitter experience (*Glimpses,* III, 213).

Ward characterized Spencer's dogmatic and fatalistic theory as sounding "more like the wail of a Tacitus over a crumbling empire, than the firm voice of a philosopher who is making an epoch" (see *ibid.,* V, 60). For, it was crystal clear to him that Spencer failed to recognize the difference between organic evolution or progress under the law of nature, on the one hand, and social evolution or development under the law of mind, on the other, and treated both as the same natural process. Accordingly, he looked upon all social reform as social coercion, even if it took the form of a compulsory education law, the prohibition of child labor or regulations against unsanitary factory conditions. In the hope of achieving a better society through free competition Spencer attempted the impossible task of elevating the dogma of might is right into a just and advantageous principle of social progress.

From the earliest days of his childhood, Ward, on the other hand, never lost faith in the principle of co-operation. His sociology commenced in psychology, while Spencer's tapered off in biology. Life, to Ward, was a spiritual (psychic) phenomenon based upon the material, but in the final analysis ruled by the mind force. There was nothing, therefore, which man could not accomplish for his own happiness, with the use of that most powerful tool.

## MAN VERSUS NATURE

The foundation of Ward's victory over Spencer is the principle that man is active, but nature is passive. Nothing can be more wholesome and practical than the advice of Spencer's great intellect: "Observe nature!" Yet nothing is more harmful to mankind than his second suggestion: "Imitate nature!" To obey the latter would be as fatal to human progress or happiness as the All-Fools'-Day optimism

that there is nothing we need do collectively to solve the social problem, or the sickly pessimism which is equally certain that nothing
we might do, could possibly help.

In Ward's view of nature and man, the moment we enter the
field of human achievement, we are in the midst of dynamic social
forces which are controllable by human effort, and have left the unconscious, automatic forces of nature outside in the field of biology
and physics. By the use of mind, we become true masters of nature
and no longer helpless slaves. But it is not the individual mind which
can achieve that. The social mind at once destroys the boast of individualism that each and every man is all sufficient unto himself,
a sort of God in miniature. It is only when his collective mind force
takes charge of vital, psychic and social phenomena that he can claim
to have risen out of the material and animal stage and reached the
human and spiritual stage of development (see *ibid.,* III, 376).

Spencer's gross fallacy was to accept the popular belief that nature
was the active element in man's life, and that man was merely her
passive subject or toy. The king of evolutionists, in failing to see that
the opposite is true, put himself in the position of the man who
had never seen a railroad and thought that if he bought a ticket and
merely sat in the depot long enough, it would bring him to his
destination.

Ranging with an eagle's eye over the vast expanse of social phenomena, Ward unerringly placed his finger upon competition as
the fundamental fault in the individualistic philosophy. He was practically the only American thinker to note that social evil was due to
the glorification of the natural forces and the corresponding neglect
of the psychic forces; in other words, to the lack of social co-operation
and control. In his devastating assault upon individualism, his words
ring with increasing prophetic power, as time passes:

Why cry *"Laissez faire!"* as if society would ever work out its own
progress? As well say to all inventors: Cease trying to control nature,
let it alone and it will control itself; it will, if left undisturbed, work
out, in its own good time, all the cotton-gins, reaping machines, printing presses and sand blasts that are needed (*D.S.,* I, 53).

No progressive race has ever been content with the natural. There
are philosophers who cry *"laissez faire!"* but every step that man has
taken in advance, every invention he has made, all art, all applied
science, all achievement, all material civilization, has been the result

of his persistent refusal to let things alone. . . . This ecclesiastical *laissez-faire* policy, often with great power behind it, certainly retarded the march of the conquering host of science and art, but nothing could repress it, and it went on with its succession of triumphs that have placed the historic races where we find them today (*P.S.*, pp. 511-512).

It is not the doctrine of inactivity, of the folding of the arms that naturally and legitimately flows from a full comprehension of the law of evolution, but a gospel of action . . . of man as a great and potent cause in the world.

Nature is first to be observed, but, having been learned, the laws of nature become the property and servants of man, and he is not to imitate the methods by which nature accomplishes results, but must direct the forces of nature into channels of his own advantage, and utilize for his own good all the powers of the universe.

The true crown of a system of scientific philosophy is not an ethics which seeks to restrain and circumscribe activity, but a sociology which aims at the liberation of action through the directive agency of intelligence (*Glimpses*, VI, 62-63).

In his stand with man against nature, mind over matter, and collectivism against individualism, Ward expresses the conviction in many forms, that man is able to be the complete master of himself. Nature cares nothing about material, and will sacrifice numberless organisms, if need be, to save a single one. She shoots, as it were, with a 20-inch cannon at a million birds, and prizes the lone survivor as the best and the fittest. The idea that there is any selection in nature's method under the law of competition is wholly false. Only the mind through its telic power is able to select.

In so far as man has progressed at all, he has done so by gaining little by little the mastery in this struggle with the iron law of nature. In the physical world he has accomplished this through invention from which have resulted the arts. Every artificial form that serves a human purpose, is a triumph of mind over the physical forces of nature in ceaseless and aimless competition. In the social world it is human institutions,—religion, government, law, marriage, customs,—that have been thought out and adopted to restrain the unbridled individualism that has always menaced society. And finally, the ethical code and the moral law are simply the means employed by reason, intelligence and refined sensibility to suppress and crush out the animal nature of man (*Outlines*, p. 258).

## COMPETITION, A NATURAL AND SOCIAL EVIL

Ward destroyed the Spencerian dogma with its aura of sanctity that competition is good and beneficent because it is the order of nature. He demonstrated, on the contrary, that it is a social evil— a social, not a natural category which changes with time, place, and circumstance. Material civilization, it is true, has gone on even under competition, but the attendant evils have been too great to be regarded merely as incidental or temporary. The animal monopoly of the strong simply cannot be transferred to human beings, for evolution tends away from the cruel and wasteful method of natural selection and survival, and in society adopts an entirely different process (see *Outlines,* p. 225).

There is a great deal of evidence in all the realms of nature below man that competition is also a natural evil. Instead of a developing force, it is a dam which prevents maximum development and keeps all forms of life at a low level. As soon as the pressure of competition is slackened or removed, great progress follows. Such has been the case with cereals, fruit trees, domestic animals, and all other organisms that man by the aid of his intellect has freed from the biologic law (see *Ps. F.,* p. 260). Whatever nature gains in the flood tide of competition, is lost in the ebb. The best that can be obtained under competition is far inferior to that which is achieved by co-operation (see *Outlines,* p. 258).

The same thing is true in the social field. Competition, contrary to popular belief, is not the life of trade, nor does it furnish the only incentive to human effort or initiative (see *P.S.,* p. 544). Achievement under a competitive regime inevitably spawns such monstrosities as unemployment, poverty, and war. The direct effect of individual initiative in industry is to check production by choking circulation and distribution. Thus, the economic machinery of individualism may create plenty, but the social mechanism of co-operation is needed to distribute it and make that plenty available to the masses. The gnawing economic paradox of hunger caused by too much food, can be solved only by the social art (a co-operative process) liberating for the common good all the latent creative forces in society. Mankind then no longer can be deprived of the necessities of life, while wealth and luxury are accumulated in the hands of a tiny minority. Such a social problem, Ward concludes, is a social anomaly (see *Outlines*, p. 291).

## SPENCER'S SUPREME FALLACY

Spencer's intrinsic contradiction which undermines his whole social philosophy lies in his admission that social evolution is organic evolution expanded (differentiation) and his stubborn insistence that the reverse process of social co-operation (integration) which is naturally advantageous to mankind is a myth (see *D.S.*, II, 397). Says Ward:

The existing "social unrest" of which we are hearing so much is due in the main to the imperfect state of social integration at which the world has arrived, and its sole remedy must be through more and more complete integration. The present social movement is wholly in this direction. Mr. Spencer saw the movement, but he misinterpreted it. He saw in it "the coming slavery," instead of the coming liberation of mankind.

The movement toward collectivism, which no one with his eyes open can fail to see taking place, in spite of all that the philosophers may say, is really a true social evolution, proceeding on natural principles, and aiming at the same end as all other forms of social progress,—the good of mankind. If Mr. Spencer had seen this, he might have made his sociology not only symmetrical in itself, but harmonious with his entire scheme of philosophy, of which it would have become the natural culmination and true crown (*Glimpses*, VI, 177).

In pursuing to its logical end Spencer's analogy of society as a kind of leviathan which encircles the globe, which Spencer made the foundation and apex of his argument for individualism and laissez faire, one is bound to come to co-operation and collectivism. Ward quickly proves the fallacy of the entire analogy when he points out that society can be correctly compared only to a mechanism. Human society, basically rational, is generally distinct from animal groupings which are essentially instinctive (see *Outlines*, pp. 92-94; *Glimpses*, VI, 312).

If Spencer is right, the social leviathan is a very low and primitive kind of organism, with little feeling and no brain (see *Outlines*, p. 62). By denying altogether that a social consciousness exists Spencer completely misses the point that in an animal organism the brain operates to check the parts to the advantage of the body, but that in society, the minds of the individual members seek to compel the social body to act for their benefit. In brief, he dilates upon the biological truth that the co-operation of parts is a benefit to the whole, but ignores the sociological truth that the concerted action of its members is advantageous to society.

## COLLECTIVISM

The moral equivalent of individualism is collectivism, social achievement. As men become more civilized and leave behind that part of nature which is "red in tooth and claw," social assimilation leans toward the less destructive and more constructive processes of co-operation rather than isolation and competition, and looks to fusion instead of diffusion of human interests.

The stone age and the cave man are no more. Plants and animals have no other means of preserving their existence than through deadly strife and struggle, although mutual aid plays no small part in their lives, but man is able to help himself through social organization and pooling of effort. Individuals, if given the chance, will find a religious joy in forgetting more of their own petty interests, and sharing in the life of the community. The ant heap and the beehive are, after all, better (moral and successful) models for human society than the wolf pack. If the present social system makes any claim to civilization, it will have to supplant the ruthless wars of individuals as of nations, for land and markets and gold, by peaceful competition in a collectivism wherein the common good is the first duty of the individual, and the good of the individual the first duty of the state.

No one need fear that the removal of competition will bring a worse evil in paternalism or over-government. Says Ward:

Modern society is suffering from the very opposite of paternalism,— from under-government, from the failure of government to keep pace with the change which civilization has wrought in substituting intellectual for physical qualities as the workers of injustice. . . .

All the evils of society are the result of the free flow of natural propensities. The acquisitive faculty need not be condemned; it cannot be suppressed, but it can and should be directed into harmless ways and restricted to useful purposes. . . . The true function of government is not to fetter but to liberate the forces of society; not to diminish but to increase their effectiveness. Unbridled competition destroys itself. The only competition that endures is that which goes on under judicious regulation (*Glimpses*, V, 235).

The individualist system has become so ingrained and inbred in people's minds that the slightest approach to co-operation or collectivism is denounced as the most terrible "ism." Omitting those whose interests have riveted them to the present system, the number who hold fast to the tenets of competition is amazing. Spencer himself was a high-minded lover of liberty and humanity who wanted everyone to have the right to do as he pleased, provided he did not infringe on the equal freedom of anyone else. This included the right of private property and all which it implies. He condemned all aggressions of individuals and nations, and, even more than Comte, stressed the necessity of social order: "The possibility of a high social state fundamentally depends upon the cessation of war, i.e., of wholesale cannibalism." But Spencer's remedy was that of a vegetarian picnic for tigers in a jungle; the development in natural evolution of peaceful industry and voluntary co-operation. The solution of the social problem lies only in the spread of the voluntary co-operative movement, not in any militant type of social reform like socialism or the co-operative movement because that seeks the regimentation of society and is directly contrary to the natural order. Such doctrine is surprising from one who, as a champion of the cause of humanity, said (in closing his *Principles of Ethics*):

There exist few who . . . look forward through increasing changes now progressive, now retrogressive, to the evolution of a Humanity adjusted to the requirements of its life. And along with this belief there arises, in an increasing number, the desire to further the development. . . . Hereafter, the highest ambition of the beneficent will be to have a share,—even though an utterly inappreciable and unknown share,—in "the making of Man." Experience occasionally shows that there may arise extreme interest in pursuing entirely unselfish ends; and, as time goes on, there will be more and more of those whose unselfish end will be the further evolution of Humanity.

Coming from one who spoke as a sociologist, Spencer's vision of altruism arising from voluntary philanthropy and co-operation is only an emotional effusion, for his strongest feeling is one of fear that the removal of competition will put humanity in irons. Ward's opinion is directly to the contrary. Individual activities under the full play of natural motives will remain most important in any scheme of life. But friendly rivalry and honest emulation, legitimate, harmless, and powerful, are quite different from brutal competition and natural selection of human beings.

In answering the question how true individualism may be secured without the loss of individual freedom or initiative, Ward remarks:

Herein lies a social paradox. This will never bring itself about. The tendencies are strongly in the opposite direction. Competition is growing more and more aggressive, heated and ephemeral. Combination is growing more and more universal, powerful and permanent. This is the result of the most complete *laissez faire* policy. The paradox therefore is that *individual freedom can only come through social regulation.* The co-operative effects of the rule of mind which annihilate competition, can only be overcome by that still higher form of co-operation which shall stay the lower form and set free the normal faculties of man. Free competition that shall be both innocent and beneficial may be secured to a limited extent in this way and in no other way (*Ps. F.,* p. 275).

Referring to the charge that state interference with private initiative, in general, is despotism, Ward says:

Nothing is more obvious today than the signal inability of capital and private enterprise to take care of themselves unaided by the state, and while they are incessantly denouncing "paternalism,"—by which they mean the claim of the defenseless laborer and artisan to a share in this lavish state protection,—they are all the while besieging legislatures for relief from their own incompetency, and "pleading the baby act" through a trained body of lawyers and lobbyists. The dispensing of national pap to this class should rather be called "maternalism" to which a square, open and dignified paternalism would be infinitely preferable (*Glimpses,* V, 240).

## SPENCER'S AMERICAN DISCIPLE

Spencer's individualism found a fertile soil in America. A famous, typical disciple was William Graham Sumner, professor of sociology at Yale University, who is still regarded as a master of masters in the social sciences. His reputation as an original thinker is world-wide, yet his laissez-faire philosophy is essentially Spencer's except as to public education and a few government functions. Sumner's interpretation of society is not a physical and biological one like Spencer's, but one in terms of social functions and social customs, the result of the influence upon him of Darwin's theory. Ultimately, Sumner accepts natural selection and the struggle for existence as the method of social evolution, as much as Spencer did.

His concern for the social problem and his sympathy for human suffering may be gauged by his well-known challenge to the unemployed: "If they don't have jobs, why don't they try and take mine away from me?" The poor and the lowly, in his opinion, are merely intruders in an otherwise perfect world which is a noble creation of natural forces. Nature forever provides one's station in life. Wealth and success are insignias of industry and virtue, but poverty is undeniable proof of indolence or corruption. Social classes are a myth and should not exist, for people can be nice to each other, if they only want to. The state must increase opportunity but never meddle with the distribution of wealth in industry. Though classes are inevitable, he argued, they "simply result from the different degrees of success with which men have availed themselves of the chances which were presented to them." There is, therefore, no natural equality in society and no trend toward equality. As to democracy, says Sumner, "it is impossible to discuss or criticize it. It is glorified for popularity and is a subject of dithyrambic rhetoric. No one treats it with complete candor and sincerity. No one dares to analyze it as he would aristocracy or autocracy. He would get nowhere and would only incur abuses."

We linger with Sumner's American brand of Spencer's laissez faire because it is their social philosophy and not Ward's that has the ear of the American people. Sumner would make a perfect disciple in many respects of the fascist Pareto. Neither of them even mentions Comte or Ward, and the attitude of both toward the social problem is practically the same. Spencer, Sumner, and Pareto, all want to make sociology a pure, abstract science divorced from social application, and for that purpose, each piled up mountains of facts with only a grain or two of psychology for their interpretation. Society cannot be led or controlled by itself; nevertheless, it is necessary to develop a science of society free from bias arising from any practical moral or social problems. These three social philosophers condemned all forms of socialization, trade unionism, social legislation, government control, and even child labor laws.

Sumner believed, of course, that laissez faire and natural liberty are the only levers of social progress. He regarded the organization of human society as largely a work of nature, and seriously remarked: "We can judge of the amount of serious attention which is due to plans for 'reorganizing society,' to get rid of alleged error and inconveniences in it. We might as well plan to reorganize our globe by redistributing the elements in it."

He tried, in sum, "to assimilate the cultural processes of human society to the blind forces of nature" (Ellwood). Social phenomena are no different from natural or biological phenomena, said Sumner. Sociology should be developed as a more or less exact science; in fact, as a purely natural science. Accordingly, he had faith only in automatic natural forces, and distrusted human intelligence, especially when it entered the field of collectivism. Art, science, and philosophy should not be trusted, he urges, but only natural competition whose vast impersonal forces have always accomplished everything that is expedient and successful.

Sumner treated the process of social development as a mechanical one, without the possibility of intelligent plan or control by the human mind. The industrial system, he believed, is mainly "automatic and instinctive in its operation"; so are our forms of government, religion, family, the very earth itself. In his own words:

All the life of human beings, in all ages and stages of culture, is primarily controlled by a vast mass of folkways handed down from the earliest existence of the race, having the nature of the ways of other animals, only the topmost layers of which are subject to change and control, and have been somewhat modified by human philosophy, ethics and religion, or by the acts of intelligent reflection.

His sociology conforming to his individualistic leanings and background is mainly concerned with a materialistic evolution which inquires into the relation of man to the earth, the uniformity of human nature, the belief in spiritual beings, and man's ruling motives of hunger, sex, vanity, and fear. From all of his pedantry and philosophy, he comes to this surprising sense of defeat:

If this poor old world is as bad as they say, one more reflection may check the zeal of the headlong reformer. It is, at any rate, a tough old world. It has taken the trend and curvature and all its twists and tangles from a long course of formation. All its wry and crooked gnarls and knobs are therefore, stiff and stubborn. If we puny men, by our arts can do anything at all to straighten them, it will only be by modifying the tendencies of some of the forces at work, so that, after sufficient time, their action may be changed a little, and slowly the lines of movement be modified. This effort, however, can at most be only slight, and it will take a long time. In the meantime, spontaneous forces will be at work, compared with which our efforts are like those of a man trying to deflect a river, and these forces will have changed the whole problem before our interferences have time to make themselves felt (quoted in Ellwood's *The Story of Social Philosophy,* p. 523).

Sumner's dogmas support Ward's axiom that many minds begin as social rebels and end as social conservatives. Their later views become set because the pace of thought advancing with the times is too swift for them and they take pride in defending their earlier but long outworn ideas. Spencer and Sumner modified their social outlook backwards, and their social philosophy never squared itself with the times or social conditions.

Competition opposed to co-operation, intelligence against force, reaction versus progress, all these are suggested in the historical panorama. How have the sociological titans reacted to them? Marx, from the field of economics, saw the rising star of the workers and called upon them to unite because they had a world to gain and nothing to lose but their chains. Spencer in his ivory tower of evolution and Sumner on his balcony of folkways, sat calmly waiting for nature to evolve a happy world of benevolent individuals who would improve their characters and become just and moral enough to save society. As for Comte's scientific sociology, it seemed to have been buried beneath an avalanche of sentimentality and formula. And so reaction, social metaphysics, and fascism overshadowed social science, and Spencer and Sumner hid Ward and dynamic sociology from view.

The spirit of Ward's time was ready for a new social horizon; his age, ripe for a social Darwin. At the present time there is a universal cry for a united front against war and poverty and social despair; for a "third party," a people's party. That demand, Ward anticipated by decades in his philosophy of collectivism, his call for social control by the social mind, and his plan for a sociocratic state.

# Chapter XXVII

# SOCIOCRACY: THE IDEAL GOVERNMENT

*"Why should not society as a whole, and all mankind from the highest to the lowest, profit by the brilliant achievement of the élite of mankind? . . . The great world movement of socialization is nothing else than the gradual recognition of this by society in its collective capacity."*

*"Sociocracy means a government by society, or the art which corresponds to the science of sociology. The great social problem must be solved by society itself."*

*"If with the relative handful who at present possess opportunities, we have such results as we now see, what may we not expect when this favored class is made co-extensive with the entire population?"*—Ward

*"Government, of whatever sort, is made for the people and not the people for the government."*—d'Holbach

*"Live for others: Family, Country, Humanity. Live openly."*—Comte

IT IS GENERALLY ADMITTED that social science thus far in its career has not been much of a success. The practical results garnered from politics, economics, history, and anthropology have been astonishingly small. Sociology has been led astray by the false philosophy of nominalism, the refusal to face reality. Autocracy is in the saddle everywhere in one form or another, and the sciences of government and the social art, in general, are practically in the stone age.

Ward's constructive contribution is not a stroke of heaven-sent genius but the scientific form which government must take in social evolution, if force and emotion are not forever to bar the use of mind and reason. He suggests no new political form, no purely industrial state, but sociocracy, the rule of society, by society, and for society, a true democracy controlled by social science. It is neither spontaneous nor inevitable, and only the collective will of the people, intelligently expressed and applied, can bring it about.

## AUTOCRACY

In clearing the path to sociocracy Ward chose Hegel's idea of the Prussian state as the typical autocracy which is the negation of true government. Hegel (1770-1831), the high priest of metaphysical idealism, regarded the state as a divine creation. Though he said, "Only one of my pupils understood me, and he misunderstood me," he regarded the state as the realization of the moral idea, the absolute aim or reason in itself, and therefore, the absolute master of the individual. Man's first duty was to be a member of the state, and any tendency towards democracy was not only nonsense but high treason. This Prussian philosophy (it was not Nietzsche's vision, at all) fertilized all individualistic thought with the dogma that science is a contemptible thing and that "the state is the march of God through the world."

In Hegel, one finds an ancestral mixture of Spencer, Sumner, and Pareto. The state to him is an organism, social classes are necessary, and neither slaves nor animals have any rights. As for war, he believed that it was the only means of preserving the power and integrity of the state. With such a political credo he flourished as the successful politician who was always careful to be found on the popular and winning side of the political arena (see *Glimpses*, V, 128).

Ward's critique of Hegel is brief and annihilating. The state is not the metaphysical ogre which Hegel depicted, but has the more modest task of presiding over the anarchy in society which enrolled it as a watchman. The anarchy is the general struggle of man against man. The individual seems free, but the idea of the state, carried to the extreme by Hegel, represents the complete enslavement of all its subjects.

## COMTE'S POSITIVE STATE

Comte's concept of the scientific or positive state is the very opposite of Hegel's. Democracy has the historical mission, said Comte, of overthrowing in the name of the people, the feudal system which stands for the spiritual despotism of the church, and the political tyranny of rulers. Comte, too, saw the bare political principles of democracy as negative, implying no true social order, but rather the incarnation of laissez faire. While the aim of democracy is of great moral value, the methods of achieving and maintaining it must be reconstructed—a prophetic insight for one who wrote in 1835. For the ideal but practical, new democratic state, Comte coined the word *sociocracy*.

The seer often errs when he begins to solidify his vision. Like Spencer, he became over-optimistic and appealed to men's moral sense, especially to the altruism of the wealthy, to regenerate society and to solve the social problem. Comte did not even mind giving the capitalists great power; in fact, he was most anxious to have them use it, provided they would act as servants of the common good. Which sounds much like trusting the cat with the milk.

Comte's ideal government is neither individualistic nor collectivist. It consists of a dictatorship of three wise men who represent the technological, the temporal, and the spiritual spheres. Final veto rests in the spiritual officer in whom alone are found wisdom, philosophy, and moral ends. The temporal power, however, acts according to the laws of nature expressed through the social forces, and is guided in all things by social science.

Unlike Plato, who finally conceded that the perfect state can exist only in heaven, Comte was convinced that he had projected in his positive state, a foolproof system in which scientific thinkers would act as spiritual chiefs and establish politics as an exact science. Industrial chiefs would realize the noblest of political theories through moral principles, and make the state a sort of technocracy ruled by social engineers. He never suspected that his hard-boiled French and English readers might fear to be governed by a corporation of salaried scholars. Ward, on the contrary, rejected the naïve idea that government should be entrusted only to experts and specialists, for social problems require synthesis and co-ordination, both in the mind and in the legislative hall. Their solution is not the result merely of expert technique, but of a combination of natural law and social science applied to actual conditions.

Comte was fundamentally right in believing that unless sociologists controlled the state, the social problem would never be solved. The first step toward the ideal government, therefore, was to indicate just what the social sciences are, and what they have to contribute to the knowledge of human problems and social progress. Comte insisted that the present order is the result of defective knowledge, neglect of moral teaching, and of anarchical habits of egoistic living. To erect the ideal state, the temple of humanity, there must be a consensus of organized philosophy, reformed morality, and permanent nonsupernatural religion. Capital must be moralized, the marriage institution renovated, and every other institution spiritualized by the awakening of the sympathetic instincts enlisted in the service of humanity. To lead and control the positive state, Comte offered his philosophy of science which is a scheme of education, a method of government, a school of wisdom, and a form of religion— in brief, a synthesis of mind, feeling and action, crowned by the religion of humanity.

Comte's passion for humanity was fused with positive science to pour the concrete base for the positive state. All that may appear visionary and especially insecure in its economic supports. The capstone may seem too close to emotionalism and too near to the heavens of ritual to fit a scientific structure. But the edifice is so solid, the builder's genius for perspective so vast, and his humanistic purpose so profound, that one may overlook his landing heart first in sentimentality when he reached the top. His exalted moral aim which manifests itself in every brick and tier of the positive order will never grow faint as long as men remain human:

To pray to humanity is at once to love, to reason and to act. It offers the best type of life, and life, in its noblest aspects consists of one long prayer. Live for others,—for family, country, humanity. Act from affection, and think in order to act. See to foresee; predict, in order to control.

After Comte came the development of capitalism and the worldwide individualistic system. Too engrossed in scrambling and fighting either for a bare existence or for more wealth and power, the world little realized that it was passing through an industrial revolution. Comte's plan of the scientific state was left mouldering in his dusty tomes, and society went on floundering in the whirlpools of free competition. The cornerstones of Comte's ideal state—"the principle, love; the base, order; the end, progress"—have been reproduced in one form or another in all later theories of government. No new social system came as a result of his philosophy, and the world kept on waiting for the new direction and more practical organization required for a better social system projected in Ward's scheme of sociocracy.

## WARD'S COLLECTIVISM

In 1883, the year of Marx's death, Ward came upon the American scene with his *Dynamic Sociology*. In his doctrine of the social will, he pointed out the widening crack in the existing individualistic system, and the necessity of building a collectivist order in which human life would be above dollars, and the interest of society above that of any one of its members. His argument has the simplicity of all great truths. We cannot live alone, any more than by chance or drift. "There can be no virtue without deliberation and election" (Seneca). By himself, the individual is a letter in a vast alphabet. In co-operation with his fellows, he spells words and expresses ideas which rock the world.

The principle of the god-intoxicated Spinoza, "reasoning is not the reward of virtue but virtue itself," appears again in the mind-intoxicated Ward, who held fast to the doctrine that we must think and act together, if we are to think or act at all. The socialization of life is the *sine qua non* of any social order ruled by intelligence, and not by tyranny. When social science will replace social meta-physics, then will socialization rescue us "from the rapacious jaws of human egoism under the crafty leadership of a developed and in-structed rational faculty" (see *Ps. F.,* p. 320).

Collectivism (not individualism) is the natural social process, ar-gued Ward, because it is the extension into the social domain of nature's synthetic method. No natural force, no idea, no man, and no group can function by itself. Civilization (social progress) is pos-sible only through the concerted action of society, as a unit. Human beings are not absolutely free agents, but are moved by social forces. As in a watch, the little wheels make a hundred revolutions while the big wheel makes only one, so we find the mainsprings of social evolution in the vast, collective aspects of human achievement rather than in the relatively petty and more numerous activities of individ-uals. Whatever affects all the people is the concern of all. Whatever moves any one of them, moves all.

## SOCIALIZED ACHIEVEMENT

The foundation of a sociocracy is collective, socialized action. In-dividual achievement is due to invention and scientific research into the domain of the physical forces. Social achievement consists of in-vention and discovery in the domain of the social forces. Early achievements, of both kinds, were always empirical, a series of pay-as-you-go experiences without any fundamental plan. Under the in-fluence of the developing collective consciousness, however, individual achievements are, one by one, becoming socialized through co-operative action. The benefits are easily seen. Says Ward:

The question is being seriously asked why society as a whole, and all mankind from the highest to the lowest, should not profit by the brilliant achievements of the élite of mankind. Inventors and scientific discoverers are generous, and if they could dictate the policy of the world, the results would be freely distributed and completely socialized. As it is, society only secures so much as cannot be prevented from filtering through the economic sieve which is often very fine. The great world movement of socialization is nothing else than the gradual recognition of this by society in its collective capacity, and the tardy, often fitful, inconsistent and uneven, but yet sure and steady determination ultimately to claim and to have its full share in the achievement of the human race (*P.S.,* p. 571).

Ward recognized the ideal state of sociocracy essentially as a form of collectivism, and possible only through a just distribution of the products of all labor or effort. Unsocialized individualism is simply the appropriation of the fruits of achievement. The reason that so much has been achieved in society and yet so little progress or happiness enjoyed by the mass, is that achievement has been mainly individual, rather than social. The benefits of labor, of inventions, and all other achievements have gone to a very few instead of to the many or to all. The world, as a whole, still believes and acts upon the fallacy that men are born either rich or poor, are fated to occupy high or low positions in life, and that since human nature cannot be changed, things as they are have been ordained from above, and "what are you going to do about it?"

Our social system is so arranged, says Ward, that the worthless command the pay, while the worthy are unjustly neglected. Very often, the inventors, the true leaders and greatest achievers in society, receive nothing, and almost everything goes to a predatory few, resulting for the former in underpaid labor, prolonged drudgery, misery, or premature death (see *D.S.,* I, 79). His own true words ring out an indictment of individualism to which there is no defense:

The whole history of the world shows that those who have achieved have received no reward. The rewards for their achievement have fallen to persons who have achieved nothing. They have simply for the most part, profited by some accident of position in a complex, badly organized society, whereby they have been permitted to claim and appropriate the fruits of the achievement of others. But no one would insist that these fruits should all go to those who had made them possible. . . . They are few in number and soon pass away. They would be the last to claim an undue share. They work for all mankind and for all time, and all they ask is that all mankind shall forever benefit by their work (*App. S.,* p. 22).

## THE CHOICE BETWEEN COMPETITION AND CO-OPERATION

Enough has been learned about society and its mechanism for men to be able to plan and build together, reasoned Ward. The choice lies between order and chaos, education and force, intelligence and emotion. Shall it be property or peace, competition or progress, for all? The war between them is without compromise, and no one can sit on the fence and claim to be in either or both fields at the same time. Ward was not blind to the fact that even more than the people hate strife, they fear co-operation; more than they dislike poverty and social chaos, they shy at social planning. Fearful of any social change, the great mass sticks in the individualistic morass. They fear to think of any co-operative system required for a life of abundance and happiness to which the achievements of civilization naturally entitle them, and so hate to give up their familiar habits, customs, and institutions to which the individualist system has enured them.

The study of sociology, apart from any propaganda, should convince any open, rational mind that in the light of social evolution, individualism and its god, individual achievement, are but landmarks on the road to socialization and collectivism; not eternal monuments but merely way stations in history, just as slavery and feudalism were. Even democracy is not the last word in political life. To go forward and not backward, we must "disbelieve that nothing can ever be devised more perfect than was established by our forefathers" (Jefferson).

## THE COST OF INDIVIDUALISM

As has been noted, the basis of individualism does not consist of technics or technology but in the erroneous principle that man is naturally a beast of prey, and that the world naturally consists of riders and horses. The fundamental thesis of collectivism, on the other hand, is the substitution of life values, of spiritual and social values, for wealth and individual values. Competition is the greatest obstacle to human progress because it is antivital as well as anti-social. Ward is no anemic parlor liberal who is always looking for a pencil to add up the mounting costs of the competitive order. Speaking of the price we pay for human exploitation, he says:

These are great and serious evils, compared with which, all the crimes, recognized as such, that would be committed if no government existed would be as trifles. The underpaid labor, the prolonged and groveling drudgery, the wasted strength, the misery and squalor, the diseases resulting, and the premature deaths that would be prevented by a just distribution of the products of labor, would in a single year outweigh all the so-called crime of a century for the prevention of which it is said, government alone exists.

This vast theatre of woe is regarded as wholly outside the juris-diction of government, while the most strenuous efforts are put forth to detect and punish the perpetrators of the least of the ordinary recog-nized crimes. This ignoring of great evils while so violently striking at small ones is the mark of an effete civilization, and warns us of the approaching dotage of the age (*Ps. F.,* p. 320).

## SOCIOCRACY

We turn from our political democracy to sociocracy, as one turns from disease and suffering to health and joy. The word *sociocracy* does not, of course, sound as inspiring as Lincoln's Emancipation Proclamation: "This nation shall have a new birth of freedom, that government of the people, by the people, for the people, shall not perish from the earth." But sociocracy connotes the same principle, and has the additional virtue of being a form of government based upon and controlled by social science. Without Lincoln's middle-class ideology which would have everyone become a prosperous employer of labor, sociocracy preaches no turning back of the clock to the simple life of the pre-machine age; no mere reformistic tinkering with the social mechanism, and no vague, sentimental, and impos-sible democratic ideals in the midst of a brutal, competitive order.

Ward first used the word *sociocracy* (a term he borrowed from Comte) in a paper read in 1881 before the Anthropological Society of Washington (see *Glimpses,* II, 334; *D.S.,* I, 60, 137). In 1893 he elaborated upon the idea as follows:

The term designed to note a state of society or form of govern-ment in advance of any hitherto attained, was sociocracy, meaning a government by society, or the art which corresponds to the science of sociology. The great social problem must be solved by society itself, when it shall have become conscious of itself, conscious of its power and sufficiently intelligent to exercise that power, in the execution of its own will. This presupposes a wider acquaintance on the part of the individual member of society of the true principles of social science, and a fearless application of those principles by the collective mind of society as embodied in its form of government, in the interest of the whole social organism ("The Great Social Problem," an unpublished paper, at Brown University).

Still later, he defined sociocracy as "the general social art, the scientific control of the social forces by the collective mind of society for its advantage, in strict homology with the practical arts of the industrial world" (*Outlines,* p. 292). Such a conception of the coming social order is beyond the paternalism of Comte and the individualism of Spencer, far above state-capitalism and socio-capitalism, and would put the state to work as the only and most powerful agent in the accomplishment of social ends (see *Ps. F.,* Chapter XVIII; *Glimpses,* II, p. 352).

There is no intention in Ward's postulate to draw the detailed and finished plans of any new and ideal social system. The ideal is always the goal, approached but never fully achieved, and can serve only as a standard of measurement by which to evaluate the existing social order. All that the sociologist can do is to use his science as a compass toward the goal. The aim of sociocracy is the moral, intellectual, spiritual life put above the material and animal life. In a sociocratic state, the infinite worth of every man would be reflected in unlimited possibilities of socialized achievement in a democratic form, without classes or parties. Such a system could fulfill the first obligation of society to its members—to give them sustenance, security, and happiness, and not leave it to God to bless the rich and let the poor shift for themselves.

## THE SOCIAL MIND

Ward knew too well that sociocracy, based as it is upon a life of reason and system of scientific planning, would be bitterly opposed by the obstinacy and laziness of the human species that always yearns for some convenient escape from the danger of thinking. Psychologists are still loath to recognize the existence of any such thing as the social mind; although labeled "public opinion," it is always under their noses. The difference between the individual mind which the psychologists have placed on a pedestal, and the social mind which they profess not to see, is that when the social mind begins to work the quantity and quality of the psychic force it employs are as far superior to that which the individual mind exerts, as the lifting power of a dozen men is greater than the sum of their individual powers (see *Glimpses,* III, 369).

It must have occurred to the reader as often at least as it has failed to occur to the individualists, to ask: if man is master of the forces of nature, why can he not also master the forces of society? His power by virtue of his mind, over the illimitable universal energy is unquestionable, yet his lack of control over the social forces through the use of his collective feelings and intellect, narrow and limited as they are, is just as plain. Ward explains the paradox as follows:

Just because nature is a domain of rigid law, man's destiny is in his own hands. Any law that he can comprehend he can control. He cannot increase or diminish the powers of nature, but he can direct them. He can increase or diminish the amount of power that is to be exerted at any given point. He can focalize the rays of the sun; he can divert the course of the rivers; he can direct the currents of the air; he can vary temperatures; he can change water to steam and set the steam to work in propelling machinery or ships or railroad trains; he can utilize electricity. His power over nature is unlimited. He can make it his servant and appropriate to his own use all the mighty forces of the universe (*Outlines,* p. 25).

There is little doubt, he adds, that if society were aware that it had a mind or a will of its own, it could act as shrewdly and ingeniously as the individual has always acted in his own self-preservation. Ward's simple question why society cannot imitate the methods of the individual has never been satisfactorily answered by the individualists (see *ibid.,* p. 186-187). What is to stop it from mapping out a field of operations for the realization of its own interests in the same manner that any intelligent and keen-sighted individual would? (See *D.S.,* II, 249.)

Ward sees the mind in its collective state, as the real monarch of all it surveys. Instead of worshipping nature or the unknowable, sociology points out nature's deficiencies and seeks to direct her processes by the rational or telic method of mind. If the natural process aims to build higher by destroying the weak, the social mind can beat nature at her own game, by supplanting the destructive, competitive method by the co-operative and collective method. Nobler and happier human beings can be developed not merely by nursing the unfit, but by abolishing the competitive motive which breeds the misfits and the failures. Social evolution has already (because of the introduction of social science) become marked by two forward drifts. The first is toward the reduction of competition, and the corresponding interference with the operation of natural forces. The second is toward the growing supremacy of the telic or sociological method of development, over the instinctive or biologic method (see *ibid.*, p. 376).

## SOCIAL TELESIS

In studying social achievement and projecting the idea of a sociocracy Ward approached the subject with the detachment of an anthropologist surveying a cannibal country. In an age when almost every American economist and sociologist was straining himself to the utmost to uphold the individualist order as a just and divine creation, Ward not only bared the cruel absurdities of the system but offered constructive social planning, i.e., social telesis. He received no adequate recognition for his concept of the social will. Even coining the expression "social telesis" was not credited to him but to the late Professor Franklin H. Giddings, conservative evolutionist and philosophical individualist.[1]

The argument from social telesis is not strictly an original one. No great truth is. Any child of grammar school age and intelligence can easily grasp it. Comprehension alone is not enough, said Ward. The social will to put opinions, beliefs, and knowledge into action is what ultimately counts. The rule of the people through the social mind is inevitable only if the people will "do something about it." Just as illness is not a necessary condition of health, so individualism is not a necessary tread in the grand staircase of social evolution.

Ward's thesis was too simple to receive much attention. The human being, he argued, is an animal with a mind who sometimes tries to control his emotions but rarely his environment. Yet man has enough knowledge to mold or create any environment he chooses.

[1] See "The Practical Application of Sociology: Social Telesis," by Herbert N. Shenton, Syracuse University, 1928.

The brutal and unnecessary struggle for existence continues, however, fiercer than ever, because he still relies upon animal instincts and natural processes. If he were not so stubborn a being, he could transfer the struggle to the human or psychic plane, and make the natural process a social process, and the animal instinct a human idea. Then the individual would grow more socialized, and society more individualized. To all of which, the world has in the main turned a deaf ear.

Social telesis is important only if it leads to progress. Ward's analysis is again simple and direct. All human activities proceed from feeling; if the effect of any act is progressive, it is because feeling is guided by intellect; if intellect does not enter, the result is static or reactionary. The only means by which social progress can come, i.e., by which man's condition has ever been or ever can be improved is "the utilization of the materials and forces that exist in nature" (see *D.S.*, I, 18). The adjustment and application of these means to the universal end of happiness is social telesis or the social art.

Since all human effort is expended upon means, the art of life occupies every moment of man's time. By applying social science to social improvement (through legislation and education) social telesis becomes identical with applied sociology, the science of the future, and begins to look to aims and ends. Civilization, social achievement, and social telesis thus merge into sociology, a synthetic philosophy and a way of life.

The possibilities of social achievement through social telesis are practically unlimited and make men not only class conscious but also socially conscious. If the individualistic system seems impregnable, there is an increasing number of legal and extralegal interferences by the state (from income taxes to various uses of the police power of government) which presage the coming of social telesis and social control. As yet, society even in its present low state of individualism, is neither brainless nor defenseless, but simply unconscious of its own psychic powers.

## SOCIOCRACY AND SOCIALISM

Socialists (today the term may be used in the generic sense to include Communists) have often claimed that sociocracy is the same as socialism. "The truth is," says Professor Ellwood (*The Story of So-*

*cial Philosophy)*, "that sociocracy is such a broad term that it could be used to designate many conceptions of a socialized government, and of the diffusion of the results of achievement to all classes."

Ward mapped the differences between the three chief concepts of government as follows (see *Outlines*, pp. 292-293):

| *Individualism* | *Socialism* | *Sociocracy* |
| --- | --- | --- |
| 1. Creates artificial inequalities. | 1. Creates artificial equalities. | 1. Recognizes natural inequalities, and aims to abolish artificial inequalities. Removes all artificial barriers raised by individualism and once more places society in the free current of natural law. |
| 2. Confers benefits on those only who have the ability to obtain them by superior cunning, intelligence or the accident of position. | 2. Confers the same benefits on all alike. Aims to secure equality of fruition. | 2. Confers benefits in strict proportion to merit, but insists upon equality of opportunity as the only means of determining merit. |

In an early criticism of doctrinaire socialism in which he again revealed his supreme faith in the panacea of education, Ward said:

It is high time for socialists to perceive that, as a rule, they are working at the roof instead of at the foundation of the structure which they desire to erect. Not that much of the material which they are now elaborating will not "come in play" when society is ready to use it, but that their time would be better spent in working out the basal principles which will render social reform possible. Present attempts in this direction consist essentially in seeking to attain progress or even happiness *directly* as ends, without employing the necessary means. Their failure is, therefore, as certain as their efforts are premature (*D.S.*, II, 597-598).

Comte's concept *sociocracy* (before Marxian socialism was born) had no connection with socialism. But no one can criticize any Socialist who appropriates the term *sociocracy*. As Ward used it, it was not identified with modern socialism, for Ward's ideal government would retain present democratic forms of the state, and abstain from all dictatorships as well as any autocratic or class rule.

Although Ward often felt that the socialist movement was either too dogmatic or too optimistic, his belief in the fundamental tenet of co-operation and social control remained unshakeable. Among the leaders of the American socialist movement, Daniel De Leon, Scott Nearing, and George R. Kirkpatrick, who fought so bravely in the early years of this century to gain support for their propaganda among the masses, constantly borrowed from his dynamic sociology, and did not find social science at all harmful to Marxism (*Ps. F.,* p. 330).[2]

## SOCIOCRACY LOOKS AT PLUTOCRACY

Democracy has not been lost sight of in our journey through government. The very core of sociocracy is democracy, political and industrial. Ward clearly saw the defeat of all democratic principles by the stranglehold which plutocracy had upon the American people. America, in spite of its universal suffrage, political parties, and patriotism, was an aristocracy of wealth and a domain of "big business"—something that its founding fathers never dreamed the land would become for which they led their children through a bloody revolution. Like President Wilson, Ward found that America had a dual government—a minor one by the Congress, the President, and the judiciary, and a major one by the great plutocratic class. In Ward's words:

The *laissez faire, laissez passer* principle put forth at a time when government was in the hands of a small ruling class bent on their own aggrandizement, and always true for many kinds of social activity, has become under democracy the bulwark of the so-called money-power, and the only hope of the classes in their effort to exploit the masses (*Glimpses,* VI, 58).

[2] To what extremes, however, propaganda and emotionalism can go may be seen in the latest work of a radical on the various types of government—Albert Weisbord's *The Conquest of Power* (New York, 1937). A single quotation will suffice: "Welfare-liberalism in the United States found in the sociological writings of Lester F. Ward, an American variation of Comte, a mass of arguments to further its case of national control and social meliorism. Ward's opinions, it is true, have much that would heartily commend them to fascists today. But it is not with those possible interpretations that we shall deal now. There were at the time no elements in the United States that could reach these fascist conclusions, and it was not the conservative but the ordinary liberal city petty bourgeoisie that drew comfort from his writings. Against the slogan 'Laissez faire' Ward proposed that of 'Faire Marcher.' Similarly, sociologists who stem from Lester Ward's 'sociocracy,' historians who follow Seligman's 'economic interpretation,' and pragmatists who look like materialists, in short, all these chickens offering substitutes for socialism, naturally form fine ideological prototypes for the fascist birds of prey" (p. 701).

Ward's remedy for the plutocratic tyranny is not to exchange it for some other form of autocracy, but to let the people rule and institute real democracy. That does not mean that sociology has any general objection to present forms of representative government. Whatever its faults or deficiencies, the theory of government has always been right at heart and essentially benevolent. "The king can do no wrong" is an ethical as well as a political maxim. How can the father of all his people do anything to injure his own? (see *P.S.*, pp. 549-555). A democracy (no king is needed because each citizen is supposed to be a sovereign) has solved the moral aspect of government through the system of representation (see *Outlines*, p. 280). Why, then, has democracy failed? Why are so many of its votaries cold and hungry?

Ward did not have to join any radical propaganda group to see that democracy has, thus far, remained an abstract ideal. It has not failed for the reason that it has not yet been tried. Politically, the citizens of a democracy are self-governing. Socially, their lives are in the hands of those whose wealth and power dictate the kind of politics, industry, and bread, if any, that those free citizens may enjoy. Democracy with plutocracy pulling the strings is a sad Punch-and-Judy travesty upon free government (see *D.S.*, II, 407).

Faith in parliamentary methods is fast declining because democracy has become powerless to fulfill its primary duty of protecting and caring for its citizens. That is why men run amok after schemes of direct action, even if the leaders are insane dictators. There was a time in Europe when society was unable to save its members from highway robbers and pirates. Today the law insures personal safety, but that does not spell democracy. Hungry people will commit every crime to obtain food. Rapacious people, the modern plutocratic brigands, now use subtler methods to take their toll, although the labels of democracy camouflage every road (see *Glimpses*, V, 235).

It is not the fault of democracy that public opinion upon vital social problems so often coincides with that of the reigning financial or industrial monarchs. Cunning leaders are the manufacturers of public opinion for private benefit, and ply their trade everywhere. The masses, ignorant and easily swayed, soon come to regard all government as their bitter enemy, and do not know who their exploiters are, or how to get rid of them (see *Outlines*, pp. 276-278). Democracy cannot thrive upon such ignorance, but must be educated to its duties and opportunities. What the present system needs, Ward concludes, is to abolish the golden idol, "to do away with the present oligarchy of brains, and to establish a true democracy of ideas based upon an equal chance for all" (*Glimpses,* IV, 37).

They who deny that plutocracy is the real ruler of democratic countries, wholly disregard, says Ward, the amount of tribute, for example, that the people pay for the necessities of life. It is common knowledge that if a business, no matter how "successful" financially, is vicious or injurious, it is socially a failure. Why is it not true also of a state or nation? In national or international affairs it is not a question whether a policy will bring profit to the state (the plutocratic owners) but whether it will benefit the people (see *Outlines,* p. 286). Economic and social activities are not ends in themselves for any government, because no government should be in business for any kind of profit. Although the democratic state is still playing the role of soldier and policeman, democracy does very little to prevent the people from being robbed at every step. Says Ward:

It is known to all political economists that the prices of most of the staple commodities consumed by mankind have no necessary relation to the cost of producing them and placing them in the hands of the consumer. It is always the highest price that the consumer will pay, rather than do without. Let us suppose that price to be on the average, double what it would cost to produce, transport, exchange and deliver the goods. Is there any member of society who would prefer to pay two dollars for what is thus fairly worth only one? The individual cannot correct this state of things. No democracy can correct it. But a government that really represented the interests of society would no more tolerate it than an individual would a continual extortion of money on part of another without an equivalent (*Ps. F.,* p. 327).

As a true social scientist, Ward would not bar any plutocrat from a sociocracy but would have him join in the work for the common good. In suggesting that homage be paid to work rather than to wealth, Ward counsels:

Let every man be esteemed, not for what he has, but for what he has done, and possession, now so often a barrier to labor, will become its most valuable auxiliary. It is the obvious duty of the well-to-do classes to avert the impending crisis by defying custom, eschewing luxury and idleness, and taking hold with will and energy of the active duties of life. They claim to constitute a superior class, and they are in a position to make good this claim; not in the sense of natural superiority, but by means of the superior facilities they enjoy for making their native powers effective. Let them demonstrate this superiority by the unstinted development of those powers, and their industrial exercise and no one will dispute their title to the means employed (*Glimpses,* IV, 54).

## PATRIOTISM, NATIONALISM, AND POLITICAL PARTIES

When Ward looks at such handmaidens of plutocracy as "my country right or wrong," nationalism, hatred of everything foreign, patriotism, and political parties, he recognizes the agencies by which (despite Lincoln's aphorism to the contrary) all the people are fooled all the time. Society with its gullibility and infantile activities seems to be in the cocoon stage, or else its members use their spinal cords instead of their brains, in all things which require reasoning.

Nationalism descends to a religion of fear and hatred. In its view, all minority beliefs and opposition to things as they are, are treason. Anything that challenges existing law and order or which expresses any sympathy with other people or other ideas is anathema. The sheer lunacy of such dogma is equalled by party politics. Modern politics bears as much resemblance to the proud and honorary civic duty which the Greeks understood by that word, as a modern hobo bears to Plato. Elections are sham battles carried on to mask the real struggle for mastery that goes on behind the scenes, between various economic and political interests, but never the people's. The successful political party considers itself the government. The loser looks, for a moment, like a hostile invader repulsed; yet no social change or upheaval follows. The spoils of victory are amicably shared by both contestants. At the next election the position of the parties may be exchanged or reversed, but no one protests; proving again that most political issues, so called, are so many drums which are beaten to befuddle the sovereign citizens and shut out any real social questions which affect them in their daily lives.

There is no essential difference between the various political parties. The only party, said Ward, should be the people itself. As things are, politicians keep shifting from one party to another, and often straddle both, as their interest requires. Consulting sheep-like voters on election day, most of whom are incapable of expressing a rational opinion upon any important subject, does not constitute a democracy. Without sufficient intelligence to grasp or solve the complicated social questions of the day the masses remain nationalists, patriots, and fiery partisans, fighting the masters' battles, and shouting for flag and country while they are being snared into some new war or forced into another social crisis. No man needs a political party to tell him when he is hungry. In a sociocracy, i.e., a social and economic as well as political democracy, parties would be impossible and unnecessary, and the ceaseless chatter of politicians and demagogues trying to cheer up the people with vain promises and eloquent phrases would no longer be heard.

Politicians often blurt out the truth, generally, long after social scientists have discovered what is going on under the noses of the people. Thus President Theodore Roosevelt said (July 27, 1912): "The crooked control of both of the old parties by the beneficiaries of political and business privilege renders it hopeless to expect any far-reaching and fundamental service from either." Ward, two decades before that remark, analyzed the fundamental objection to parties as follows:

How does society differ from the people? If the phrase "the people" really meant the people, the difference would be less. But "the people" stands simply for the majority of qualified electors, no matter how small that majority may be. All democratic governments are largely party governments. . . . The contestants care nothing for any issues and merely use them to gain an advantage and win an election. From the standpoint of society this is child's play. A very slight awakening of the social consciousness will banish it and substitute something more business-like. Once get rid of this puerile gaming spirit and have attention drawn to the real interests of society, and it will be seen that upon nearly all important questions, all parties and all citizens are agreed, and that there is no need of this partisan strain upon the public energies (*Ps. F.,* pp. 324-325).

## HOW WILL SOCIOCRACY COME?

The specters of force and revolution frighten many minds already touched deeply by scenes of exploitation and misery. Again Comte's immortal aphorism that method is more important than doctrine looms into view. Ward soothes the troubled souls who have the common aim of a reorganized society, but who cannot agree on the method of reaching the promised land with his conclusion that no violent social upheaval is needed to usher in the new system. The force of public opinion would be enough.

If the people collectively would assert their right to own and control society and all its products, Ward repeated, no government would dare to enforce any of the injustices daily heaped upon them. Once the seeds of social change are planted, "sooner or later they must spring up, grow and bear their fruit" (*ibid.*, p. 329).

It is rash to predict just how sociocracy will come. But if history and social science mean anything, we can judge the future by interpreting the past and studying the present. The individualist regime, Ward argues, is just as capable of developing smoothly and peacefully into a sociocracy, as autocracy passed into limited monarchy, or as the latter, often without even a change of name, evolved into political democracy. Despite all ruling dictators, charlatans, and lunatics (often the same person) and notwithstanding the growth of individualism with its necessary attendants, militarism and economic depression, the slower and more quiet methods of social evolution seem to be the only rational means, according to Ward, of bringing about the new social order.

When competition will give way to co-operation, the social order, by whatever name it will then be called, will be altogether unlike our present political state. While society is now industrial, the government is political in form, and there is no democratic state machinery for industry. Society has become mature, but the people neither own nor control it. Ward feels certain of the future when he prophesies that when social consciousness will dawn upon the people, they will only have to stretch forth their hands to possess the world they have built up (see *Ps. F.*, p. 312). In an unpublished essay he says:

This ideal solution will be realized through a long series of slight advances which constitute true social progress, which will take place in strict proportion to the increase and diffusion of sound knowledge of the true nature of man and society ("The Great Social Problem," 1893).

### ATTRACTIVE LEGISLATION

In Ward's opinion the two chief means of approaching sociocracy are attractive legislation and attractive labor. The first is the substitute for force and direct action; the second for grinding toil and hopeless economic slavery. He does not mean the game of legislation as it is now played by selfish politicians but the scientific process of regulation, telic and voluntary, which he, therefore, qualified as attractive. Sociology developing a clear appreciation of the needs of society, is the only means of furnishing the agenda of enlightened government: "What do the people need? How can we give it to them?"

With any such questions, the present lawmaking bodies are, as is common knowledge, not overconcerned. Instead of planning for the satisfaction of human needs, they are chiefly occupied with the interests of small minorities, and, as a matter of self-preservation, with pacifying the exploited and often outraged public with all sorts of pap. The man-eating tigers of plutocracy are carefully and severely let alone. Only now and then is there an attempt to exterminate some of the fleas in the pelt of the royal beasts—an act which draws the applause of a large section of the populace who believe that at last the state is doing something for their safety and happiness.

Legislators, most of them lobbyists, find their greatest delight, especially in the United States, in passing more prohibitory laws to hold the masses in check, or to legalize immoral and unsocial acts in the name of business. The results for social progress are as valueless as calling a convention to pass a resolution that everybody shall immediately become prosperous and happy. Said Ward:

Most of the attempts to control the social forces have thus far been made according to the coercive method, and this illustrates in a remarkable manner, the infantile state of the science of sociology. We are living in the "stone age" of the art of government. We shall not emerge from it until the principle of "attractive legislation" is thoroughly understood and applied. . . .

The existing laws on nearly all subjects are prohibitory, compulsory and penal. They appeal to the fear of punishment as the sole deterrent. Very rarely do they promise reward. When the principle of "attractive legislation" is fully understood and put in operation by competent legislators, it will be seen that this supposed "necessary evil" will be in a great measure removed. Instead of continually damming the stream of human desire, as has been so often done in the past, until it finally bursts over all its barriers and whelms everything in the ruin of political revolution, men will learn to direct it into channels not only innocent, but useful (D.S., I, 40).

The collective actions of society when compared to individual activities are like those of an ocean liner running on schedule compared to the drifting of an iceberg. How many states have typified the steamer, and how many the derelict? The English have accomplished more legislation in the interest of the masses than any other people (see *P.S.*, p. 558). The Continent, on the other hand, has seen more collective action in regard to railroads, public works, and the like. In the United States, there has been little more than a struggle for political majorities and control of political parties in the interest of their financial and industrial owners. And all the while and everywhere, individualism is sanctified as the ideal system, and the existence of social classes is suavely denied amidst an increasingly bitter class struggle. All that is heard are the voices of reactionaries and conservatives uttering their "social principles," feebly echoed by so-called liberals and reformers, all of which matches the ignorance of lawmakers and judges who rarely know the origin or causes of the human misery parading before them (see *ibid.*, pp. 568-569).

If government is a true art, so is social legislation. Ward calls it attractive because it is akin to the individual ingenuity which underlies invention (see *P.S.*, p. 570; *Ps. F.*, p. 306). How can ignorant, blundering or selfish legislators be compared to any body of inventors? Can the labors of any law factories be put in the same category with any achievement of the social art? The corrupt, incompetent or half-blind political agencies of the individualistic system, from top to bottom, can by no stretch of the imagination be included within the scope of true or attractive legislation. The collective consciousness of society has not yet been aroused enough to create anything beyond a House of Congress or a Parliament. Nobody can seriously contend that those bodies represent the will and needs of all the people. It is just because society has not acted the role of a creator or inventor, that it has failed under individualism to develop a system of government which would care for its people as an individual cares for his household (see *D.S.*, I, 38; *App. S.*, p. 339).

## ATTRACTIVE LABOR

Side by side with attractive legislation as the way to social emancipation and self-rule, Ward puts attractive labor. The idea that labor should be pleasant rather than obnoxious is not original with him. Fourier, Comte, Mill, Ratzenhofer, and Veblen, every sociologist who has seen the worker as well as the product, has mourned the slavery attending labor in the individualistic system. The never ending threat to the great mass has always been: "Work at any price, under any conditions, or starve!"

In a sociocracy the social art would not only provide the means of existence for all, but also see to it that no one should be obliged to do any disagreeable work or to which he is not fitted. Thus would creative talents and energies be fostered and developed into achievement, instead of being shunted or destroyed (see *App. S.,* p. 334). Besides, special material incentives to labor would no longer be necessary, for abundance would guarantee to all the fulfillment of their needs. Labor would then be a joyous privilege instead of a heavy burden, and the role of the state, as the exploiter of its citizens, would forever disappear.

## A NATIONAL ACADEMY OF SOCIAL SCIENCE

Attractive labor is still only a vision, but attractive legislation has already been put into practice to a slight, but nevertheless heartening, extent. Ward was the first American sociologist to propose a central national university which would be an academy of sociology manned by the ablest social scientists and their research assistants (see *Glimpses,* IV, 324). The faculty would be chosen by a commission of the most eminent scholars of the land, without regard to politics or personal bias. The chief subject would be instruction in the abstract and applied art and science of government. The academy would act as a clearing house for all social questions and problems, much as a great university does for education, or a medical center for health, and would mark out the general trend of social evolution and the most desirable social policies to be pursued in the interests of the people.

Government itself, being still in the empirical stage and far inferior to the inventive art, would have to attend the academy before it could properly function in the social art (see *D.S.,* II, 251). The growing intelligence of the masses is making the state positively anxious to allay the people's fears and satisfy their needs and desires (see *Ps. F.,* pp. 300-304). Governments in democratic countries, Ward adds, have become so sensitive to the will of their wards that a single adverse vote in a Parliament or Congress is enough to retire the reigning administration, or cause the resignation of the dissenters.

Ward's vision of the national academy was of one without professional philosophers immersed in abstract speculation and sitting high on a pedestal of pure science. Nor would there be any expert opinion for sale, since the state would be the only bidder. Graduates of the academy would fill all administrative posts in the government service. Politics would be integrated with social research, and all public employees would receive a thorough training in the theory and practice of government before entering the public service (see *Glimpses*, IV, 324-325).

## READY FOR SOCIOCRACY

Sociocracy was not a dream of Ward's. He felt that the times were ripe for a new social order, and that social evolution had come to a stage when only sociocracy could make for social progress, without any special preparation on the part of society. The aim of individualism is to give society as little as possible in return for as much as possible. It is not hard to grasp the idea that society is not an unmined treasure to be exploited or despoiled by individuals, but is like a tender mother who lives only to serve her children, without stint and without reward, except their well-being.

The social stage is set for her true role which selfish individualism has not allowed her to play. Production is already a fully developed collectivist process. Only distribution of the product remains individualistic. By taking distribution out of private hands and making it a public, social process, said Ward, the social arena could be immediately transformed from a scene of brutal competition into a humane co-operation. The citizen in the present regime is far from being a free member of a true democracy. Why not emancipate him by giving him the opportunities which are due him? Ward answers:

I look upon existing humanity as I look upon a pristine vegetation. The whole struggling mass is held by the relentless laws of competition in a condition far below its possibilities. Just as what might be grain is mere grass, just as the potential greening is a diminutive crab-apple, so the potential giants of the intellectual world may now be the hewers of wood and drawers of water. . . .

If, with the relative handful who at present possess opportunities, we have such results as we now see, what may we not expect when this favored class is made co-extensive with the entire population? . . .

In a country like ours, where all power resides in the opinions of the people, we have only to suppose them to possess a clear conception of their interests and of the measures necessary to secure them, in order to see such measures adopted and enforced. While legislation cannot successfully be applied to the alteration of the great laws of nature, such as those of heredity, I regard the work of creating opportunities, by which gifted individuals can utilize their powers, as simply in the nature of police regulation, capable of being conducted by any body politic (*Glimpses,* IV, 42-43).

## GESTURES TOWARD SOCIOCRACY

A concrete program is what people want, long before theories and fundamentals. Such a program of equal economic and social opportunity (not equal income or wages), can be supplied only by society. Yet it has done practically nothing in the way of collective research, invention or planning. The slightest effort in that direction is immediately denounced as rank heresy and treason. But there are omens and harbingers that Ward's plan for a national academy of social science is being realized.

The theories of yesterday are the facts of today. In the gradual crumbling of the individualistic system, as well as in the rising tide of co-operation, the signs of the new society are already visible. More than a decade after Ward's death, the "Social Trends Commission" appointed by that rugged individualist President Hoover, found the path of collectivism clearly marked out in the current history of the United States (see Foreword by Harry Elmer Barnes; his article in the *New York World-Telegram,* January 7, 1933; and Charles A. Beard's *Character of the Social Sciences,* 1933). The monumental report of that commission of eminent sociologists, none of whom was a radical, followed by President Roosevelt's attempted reforms, weak and superficial as they were, are nevertheless portents that "the age of individualism and laissez faire in economy and government is closing, and a new age of collectivism is emerging" (Commission on Social Studies of the American Historical Association, 1934).

Ward's idea has further been applied, although without recognizing him as its author, in the opening of a school of public affairs conducted by sociologists, as a laboratory for the study of government through direct contact between students and government officials (*New York Times,* March 21, 1934). President Roosevelt has even appointed a "National Resources Committee" whose slogan is that an ounce of foresight is worth pounds of hindsight, and which is to investigate how we are to use our heads to preserve and exploit our fundamental resources to solve the problem of technological evolution. Agencies will be set up to study inventions, their progress and potential effects. Ward's basic idea of social science as a government function constantly crops up.[1] In the mouths of noted men of the day, it sounds terrifically original. One illustration will suffice: Professor Arthur H. Compton argues for research work by the universities for information which will increase the welfare of mankind ("Can Science Point the Way?" *Forum*, XCVII, 272-276, May, 1937). Such efforts will be fruitless unless there is a direct linkage with the public agencies. The following sounds like a transcript from Ward:

Would it be too much to suggest that each department of the government should have associated with it a permanent non-political group of investigators, who, acting in an advisory capacity, would

[1] The basic idea of a scientific government has been expounded in the plan of the American Psychiatric Association for a mental consultation service for statesmen. This recognizes the fact that lessons derived from the study of mental diseases apply also to the mass, and that in the clash between labor and capital, pacifist and chauvinist, or radical and conservative, each human unit is apt to act and think in a non-rational way, unless it has knowledge of underlying causes (see *New York Herald-Tribune*, May 4, 1937).

Dr. Alexis Carrel, surgeon and Nobel Prize winner, in a recent address at Dartmouth College adopted Ward's idea of synthetic education and a central institute of learning and research, without, of course, mentioning Ward, or perhaps, being aware of his pioneer achievements. Dr. Carrel said that the solution of the social problem rests ultimately upon science, and that there must be established throughout the world a true science of man, based upon profound knowledge of the body and mind alike. The following is from the press report of his remarks:

"The spiritual is within reach of the scientific method," he said, "and to attempt to improve the human person is far from being Utopian."

Dr. Carrel charged that industrial civilization had committed the sin of almost exclusively developing specialists, men incapable of the "strenuous mental efforts" necessary to synthesize all the data within the consciousness of the individual.

"Minds endowed with universalistic tendencies alone have the power to solve the problems of modern society," he declared.

"The specialists of physiology, medicine, pedagogy, politics, economics or other human activities have proved their incapacity to solve the problem that concerns man as a whole."

The proposed "Institutes of Psychobiology," Dr. Carrel stated, "should be scientific centers where spiritual as well as material values would be studied."

"In order to weld biology, psychology, sociology and economics," he said, "such minds (the specialists') will have to be organized into a center of synthetic thought, a focus of collective investigation of human problems. In fact, into an institute for the construction of the civilized."

"As far as I am concerned," Dr. Carrel concluded, "I intend to devote the rest of my life to the problem of developing man in his organic and spiritual entirety. For the quality of life is more important than life itself. We must now use theoretical and applied science, not for the satisfaction of curiosity, but for the betterment of truly civilized man" (*New York Times*, Oct. 11, 1937).

keep the department administrators informed regarding possible and desirable courses of action?

The effectiveness of organized research in opening the world to our understanding, in guiding the development of our great industries and in shaping the attack on disease can leave no doubt about the value of such a measure. Industry cannot afford to operate without the value of its research laboratories. Why not permanent institutes of government research?

The power of the scientific method is established. The procedure for its effective application is well understood. Utopia as seen by Plato, was a world led by rulers guided by reasonable knowledge. May we not find in a more adequate extension of scientific study of human problems the way to approach that goal?[2]

In a crowd of paralytics a man on crutches is regarded as a flying ace. Among individualists the slightest gesture toward sociocracy is indicted as revolution. Although President Roosevelt's "Brain Trust" filled the American air with frantic efforts to bring back prosperity to the richest country on earth, the old hit or miss, chance and drift methods of rugged individualism still flourish. Financial interests, politics, taxes, tariffs, and all the other dams in the individualistic order prevent the varied streams of benefit to the masses from uniting to achieve a collectivist system.

The United States has boasted of social experiments on a large scale, such as the liquor prohibition law and the National Recovery Act, both comparatively short-lived. Let the reader judge for himself whether those legislative fiascoes were examples of the social art and expression of the social will. Nonetheless, President Roosevelt's "New Deal," frankly intended as a new lease of life for the individualistic system, is an embryonic type of social telesis. It may not be a single step nearer to sociocracy, but it is looking in that direction, intended to secure the "twofold end of increasing the sum total of social efficiency and social improvement" (*App. S.*, p. 339).

## MEANWHILE—

Meanwhile, it is sad but true that sociology has so little to do with social evolution. A race which has medical science without end but

[2] Dr. Harry Elmer Barnes, commenting upon this in the *New York World-Telegram* (May 11, 1937), remarked: "This sounds promising until we recall that over fifty years ago Lester F. Ward made exactly the same proposal. If we let another half century go by without doing something about it there may be neither government nor research."

also has masses suffering from preventable and curable maladies, would be no less astounding. Almost all social achievement down to the present has been either accidental or automatic. When society does something for its own benefit, it is generally done unconsciously, as it were, and is carried out mainly by individual enterprise. Now and then, perhaps under the impetus of a war or other major calamity, society becomes aware of its own existence, and asserts itself in socialized action. No wonder that Spurgeon exclaimed when a slight earthquake was felt in England: "Thank God! My old country is moving at last!" But outside of such extraordinary situations, society has drifted with the stream, and the amount of its social planning has been like scattered tiny ripples in a boundless sea.

Yet, it is undeniable that social science is gaining ground, and teaching the world the simple idea that the world for man, is society. The wider world is nature, but society is nature transformed by human achievement. Society has become the most important part of the world. It is not merely a collection, but an aggregate of human beings connected by relations imposed upon them by the social forces. The control of those forces by the collective will of society is the task of the social art in a sociocracy.

Sociocracy, like democracy, has not failed as many skeptics and social fundamentalists would have it, for it, too, has never been tried. The two causes of social inertia, the rivalry between the government and the people, and the general lack of opportunity and cohesion in the masses, still cry out for correction.

If the public is still unaware of Ward's pioneering labors in political economy and government, some of his fellow sociologists are not unmindful of his profound and original thought. Says Professor U. G. Weatherly in a symposium, *Social Progress:*

What Adam Smith did for the laissez-faire principle, Lester F. Ward has done for the doctrine of effort. Ward was more than a scientific investigator in the field of social forces; he had something of the character of an evangelist and a prophet. . . . There remains in his conception of telic social development an element of truth which makes it an outstanding contribution to the philosophy of progress (pp. 103-104).

# *BOOK XII.* THE LIBERAL

*"To surrender Freedom is to surrender manhood; it is to sur-*
*render human rights and even human duties."*—J. J. Rousseau

Chapter XXVIII

# LIBERTY

---

*"To be deprived of rights is the same thing as to be deprived of property. The first step toward taking away liberty or life is to take away property. It is but a step from penury to slavery."*

*"What must be, will be, but everything depends on the manner of its being. The problem of today is how to help on a certain evolution by averting an otherwise equally certain revolution."*—Ward

*"Neither one person, nor any number of persons, is warranted in saying to another human creature of ripe years, that he shall not do with his life for his own benefit what he chooses to do with it."*—John Stuart Mill

*"Liberty and life walk hand in hand."*—Michel de l'Hôpital

*"All that the world can give without Liberty hath no taste."*—Lord Halifax

*"Men are born free and equal in rights, and so they remain. The natural and imperscriptible rights of men are Liberty, Property, Security, and the withstanding of oppression."*—Declaration of the Rights of Man, Art. 1

---

Ward's gospel of liberty which came from the depths of a great heart and a great mind is a monument in our journey. It should be especially welcome to all who hold a distinctively American social philosophy, for it is essentially the concept of the Founding Fathers. Implying as it does, not only physical freedom but also mental freedom, it embraces the right to leisure, education, truth, and, above all, the equal opportunity to attain those precious things, the opportunity which is the *sine qua non* of any social freedom. In the final analysis, Ward sees liberty and truth as conditions of each other, the two sides of the golden coin of civilization, neither of which can be imagined to exist without the other.

## CHANGING CONCEPTS OF LIBERTY

It is an ancient truism that restless *homo sapiens* clamors for bread and asks for knowledge, but must always have liberty. That he cannot live by bread alone is only half the truth. There is something of the universal energy in him that makes his independence as necessary as his daily sustenance.

The *Weltanschauung* of antiquity was that mankind consisted of hunters and game; kings and high priests who were God's anointed, with the nobility as their lackeys, and the rest of the people, decreed by a natural division into caste and class to be the servants or slaves of their "betters." Between Aristotle's view that liberty was meant only for the rich and the noble, and the modern ideal of freedom for all alike, there stretches a bridge over which humanity is plodding its weary way. In the Dark Ages, when superstition dimmed the light of reason, oppression was the outstanding social feature for the greater part of the people. The few who had wealth or political power had all. The feudal system which kept the masses in ignorance and subjection and used its church powers to side with the lords and barons against the serfs and peasants, had no room for any such sacrilegious nonsense as temporal liberty, but promised salvation in heaven.

The new era of enlightenment brought little novelty into the concept of freedom. While philosophers like Spinoza wisely discussed emancipation from slavish lusts and sought the peace which comes from understanding (the union of mind with infinite nature), the social forces were transforming the serf into an industrial hand without leisure or opportunity for education, and perverting the last remnants of liberty into a meaningless freedom of personal movement. To this day, the delusion common among intellectuals is that force means physical force, forgetting that even propaganda and opinion foisted upon innocent minds are methods of force and enslavement. This brings one to the question, which is preferable, security without freedom, or freedom without security? That is not a conundrum or a rhetorical question, but the very core of the social problem. Recognizing that freedom of movement is far from being the whole of liberty, Ward says: "The system of artificial props, bolsterings and scaffoldings has grown so perfect as to make exertion needless for the protected class, and hopeless for the neglected mass" (*Glimpses,* V, 236).

### LIBERTY AND GOVERNMENT

The philosophic libertarian regards government as a vicious violation of natural law, and as an odious tyrannical force that should be resisted at all cost. He therefore demands unrestricted freedom for the individual. The sociologist, on the contrary, though he may dream of a future state of human perfection through evolution, applies his practical mind to reality, and feels certain that we are far from being able to live without organized government. He analyzes the ruling power into its component parts of restraint, protection, accommodation, and improvement (see *D.S.*, II, 231). The aboriginal man was as free as a bird, but as soon as he started to climb to civilization, he had to give up most of his liberties for the good of the group to which he belonged, in exchange for safety and protection. The sacrifice was worth the price, claims Ward (see *ibid.*, I, 32-33).

It was the restraining hand of society which allowed mankind to survive and spread over the entire globe. Government is an advantageous invention of social evolution, and not merely something to be tolerated as a necessary evil. Men may do evil things without end, but humanity is not evil. Governments may be bad, but government, as the great link in the socializing process is good, because it preserves society and all its achievements. Says Ward:

> The great *plexus* of rules which constitutes the civil, the social, and the moral codes, has been woven in just this way. . . . The exact method of their adoption or enforcement is quite immaterial. They have grown up in society, have been the results of human sagacity, cunning or intelligence, have been devised by the victims of these same attributes, and have become binding upon all members of society. It is to these three codes that civilized society owes its protection of rights and its immunity from arbitrary violence (*ibid.*, I, 514).

## LIBERTY AND PROPERTY

The problem of liberty is a phase of the problem of property. "Life, liberty and the pursuit of happiness" (the friends of Jefferson who wrote these immortal words into the Declaration of Independence, tried to have him substitute the word *property* for the word *happiness*) may be summed up in the term *property*. The social history of the United States supports the axiom "no property, no liberty." It was Daniel Webster who said (1820): "The freest government, if it could exist, would not be long acceptable if the tendency of the laws was to create a rapid accumulation of property into a few hands and to render the great mass of the population dependent and penniless." Ward's view (1883) was still more sweeping: "To be deprived of rights is the same thing as to be deprived of property. The first step toward taking away liberty or life is to take away property. It is but a step from penury to slavery" (*ibid.*, I, 519).[1]

[1] Ward has been borne out by history. At the end of the nineteenth century, one-tenth of the American people owned five-tenths of the national wealth. By the

Rebelling magnificently, not against property, but against the concentration of private property and the consequent expropriation of the poor and the ignorant, Ward decries the gradual disappearance of liberty. Why is it logical, he asks, to make robbery illegal, but allow aggrandizement by intellectual force aided by legal fictions and deceptions? (see *Glimpses*, IV, 70). Since society is just as acquisitive in civilization as it was in barbarism, and continues to deprive unrepresented classes of their rights, liberty is possible only when the ogre of greed has been destroyed and the worship of private property has been shifted to more worthy institutions. Says Ward:

The degree to which the citizen is protected in the secure enjoyment of his possessions is a fair measure of the state of civilization, but this protection must apply as rigidly to the poor man's possessions as to those of the rich man. In the present system, the latter is not only encouraged, but actually tempted to exploit the former. Every trust, every monopoly, every carelessly granted franchise, has or may have this effect, and the time has arrived, when a part at least of this paternal solicitude on the part of the government should be diverted from the monopolistic element and bestowed upon the general public. If we must have paternalism, there should be no partiality shown in the family (*Glimpses*, V, 240).

## LIBERTY VIA CO-OPERATION

Individual liberty in an individualistic system is impossible, argues Ward. Social philosophy is tending away from the primitive and utopian ideal of natural rights underlying absolute personal liberty and drawing nearer to the mature and practical ideal of liberty shared by all in a collective order. What if social control does restrict the rights of the individual? The restrictions are insignificant when com-

year 1934, when almost one-third of the population was unemployed or on public relief, and the other two-thirds in the doldrums of a terrific crisis, the increase and concentration of incomes had progressed to such an extent, that according to a reliable research, "11,653,000 families with incomes of less than $1500 received a total of about 10 billion dollars. At the other extreme, the 36,000 families having income in excess of $75,000 possessed an aggregate income of 9.8 billion dollars. Thus it appears that 0.1 percent of the families at the top received practically as much as 42 percent of the families at the botton of the scale" (*America's Capacity to Consume*, The Brookings Institution, 1934).

But not all liberals agree with Ward. Thus, such a lover of liberty as the late Judge Oliver Wendell Holmes, Jr., of the august Supreme Court of the United States, remained so obsessed by the irresistible power of property that he took Spencer's naïve view of social evolution, and remarked: "I believe that the whole regeneration which so many seem to expect cannot be effected appreciably by tinkering with the institution of property, but only by taking in hand life, and trying to build a new race."

pared to the cruelties that individuals inflict upon each other in the competitive system. The doctrine of equal freedom for all, whether uttered by extreme anarchists or rugged individualists, has no meaning unless society collectively prevents the individual from exploiting his neighbors (see *P.S.*, p. 567). It is not the unbridled competitive forces in society, but the controlled co-operative forces which liberate the physical and spiritual energies and enable them to function freely (see *App. S.*, pp. 128-130).

The faithful disciples of individualism will have none of these generalizations, and keep on prating about initiative, incentive, and regimentation. Sociologists look a little deeper, and note that the first important consequence of the group instinct of self-preservation which evolved into the social mind, was to check competition and to open the road to monopoly. Just as a virile weed which invades a virgin field drives out every indigenous plant, so in a social system without a strong, regulative apparatus, the forces of competition, if unchecked, will destroy the more refined and delicate elements which give variety to social culture and make social liberty possible.

When co-operation and collectivism are accused of stifling personal liberty, Ward asks what liberty is there left for the average individuals in the competitive state. The present condition of society proves that without collective action they have little peace or liberty, and no security. Only as co-operation is adopted, does society take out of the greedy hands of individual initiative, the things which concern the group. Such matters, for example, as the punishment of individual crimes, the collection of revenue and finance, and the coining of money, have become affairs of the state in comparatively recent times (see *P.S.*, p. 564). Society survives, not because, as Nietzsche believed, man is weak and puerile, but because civil justice takes the place of natural justice, and mutual aid and co-operation gradually supplant conflict and competition (see *ibid.*, p. 557).

## CASTE AND CLASS

We stop with Ward to examine the scaffoldings for the temple consisting of caste and class, which were left standing after the structure was completed and have become dangerous social obstructions to liberty. Those divisions of society are neither arbitrary nor accidental or identical. Landlords, for example, are a class because they are united by a common interest in the economic field. The nobility, on the other hand, is a caste fused by inheritance.

The reader who does not believe that social classes exist in a democracy would do well to note how liberty or the lack of it, since antiquity, has always been tied up with the same castes. In India, the Brahminic caste is the same as those clergy the world over, who call themselves "the lords spiritual." The Kshatriyas are the ancestral prototypes of the soldiery and the nobility, the lords temporal. The ancient merchants or Vaisyas are the sires of the modern commoners or bourgeoisie. Finally, the Sudras are the forefathers of the present artisans or laboring class (see *Glimpses,* VI, 340).

## LIBERTY IN THE POSITIVE STATE

In Comte's positive state, order, progress, and liberty depend upon the co-operation of four classes: (1) woman, to represent humanity; (2) labor, to exploit natural resources; (3) directors, to administer social wealth and to act as political rulers; (4) philosophers, thinkers, and priests in the religion of humanity, to serve as educators, counsellors, and interpreters of history.

Ward cuts still deeper than Comte into the social strata and finds only two great classes, the intelligent owners and the propertyless, ignorant workers. "How could liberty thrive in the face of such a schism?" he asks. What does it profit to have wealth, armies and politics without end, if the mass of people is entangled in a crushing social machine? Of what value is knowledge, science, art; of what importance is the sign of political democracy over the front door of the temple of society, if social and industrial classes are engaged within in a mortal struggle? Can fish in a pond of sharks be considered free?

## SOCIAL FREEDOM IS SOCIAL JUSTICE

In a brilliant survey and analysis of the struggle for liberty Ward depicts its four stages: national, political, economic, and social. National freedom was achieved when the warring races in ancient and prehistoric times were amalgamated into compact units. Political freedom took much longer to arrive, but it has already spread over most of the civilized globe. Economic and social freedom are now in the making, a final struggle which Ward described in his address at a historic Thomas Paine anniversary dinner (January 29, 1912), in these memorable words:

There is another struggle that is very intimately associated with the economic one, and that is the great important struggle of today. I call it the social struggle. When men were in the political struggle, they imagined that when their political rights should be attained, the millennium would be here. But they found it was nothing of the kind. There was another great struggle to be gone through, the economico-social struggle, the struggle of today, which is in the direction of a contest for the attainment of social and economic equality. It is the effort on the part of the fourth estate which used to be called the proletariat, the working classes, the mass of mankind, to secure social emancipation (*Glimpses*, VI, 369).

Ward observed the social unrest everywhere and felt that it will cease only when society becomes intelligent enough to want social freedom and social justice as strongly as it desired political freedom and political justice in the past. In his own words:

The present social inequalities exist for the same reason that civil and political unequalities once existed. They can be removed by an extension of the same policy by which the former were removed. The attempt to do this will be attacked and denounced, as was the other, but the principle involved is the same. And after social justice shall have been attained and shall become the settled policy of society, no one will any more dare to question it than to question civil justice (*App. S.*, p. 24).

Military and royal oppression have been overthrown. Slavery, serfdom, feudalism have disappeared. The power of the nobility and the priesthood has been broken. The civilized world is democratic, no matter by what name its governments are called. The people rule themselves by their sovereign votes. And yet, never in the history of the world was there manifested greater unrest or greater dissatisfaction with the state of things. National freedom and political freedom have been achieved. Social freedom remains to be achieved (*ibid.*, p. 27).

### HOW WILL LIBERTY COME?

Must liberty be taken by force or can it be evolved by education? We have labeled sociocracy and social liberty as ideals only because they are still so remote from actual conditions, not because they are difficult to attain. Ward's educational philosophy is umbilical to his gospel of human liberty. Social classes can be abolished, he argues, only when the ignorant mass will grow conscious through education, not through starvation or war. Complete social freedom is possible only with complete mental freedom.

Ward often spoke of the people taking what was rightfully theirs, yet the acceptance of force in advance of its inevitable necessity, was to him the very negation of rational action. Where Marx chose to fight for human emancipation with the weapons of class warfare and economic cataclysm, Ward advised the masses, no less resolutely, to educate themselves, wake up to their own interests and by collective effort make force unnecessary. By fighting with the weapons of education, there is a strong possibility of transforming utopian visions into a practical, working reality.

While Ward is convinced that education is the only means of gaining a permanent victory over tyranny and oppression, he often foresees the probable use of force. It was no timid pedant speaking when he said in an extemporaneous address, "Education and Progress," delivered at the Central Labor College, Oxford (1909):

What do we hear all over the world? Nothing but the subterranean roar of the great mass of mankind, infinitely larger numerically than all the other classes put together. That class is rumbling and seething and working, and coming to consciousness; and when they do come to consciousness, they will take the reins of power in their hands, and then will have been abolished the last of all the social classes (*Glimpses*, VI, 340).

Yet, even when his words flame with social revolt, he always returns to the panacea of education:

No matter how grievous the wrongs to be suffered, or how loud the protestations of philanthropists, it will all avail nothing until the victim class is represented and its voice is heard. To be represented is to be clothed with power. This shows that rights can only be obtained by force, that the only way to secure justice is to enforce it, and that human right and natural right are essentially one.

All attempts to soften the human heart must fail. Without assuming to dictate what human nature ought to be, the only rational course is to recognize what it is, and act accordingly. Instead of trying to dissuade men from taking away the property of others, society must render it impossible for them to do so. The proper way to induce men to desist from unjust action is to make it for their own interest to do so, and teach them in an unmistakable manner that it is so. This is the work of intelligence and education (*D.S.*, I, 518).

Convinced with the passing of the years that the choice lay between education and force, Ward summed up the methods of social change as follows: "What must be, will be, but everything depends on the manner of its being. The problem of today is how to help on a certain evolution by averting an otherwise equally certain revolution" (*Glimpses,* IV, 315).

Guns and dynamite may be powerful arguments for peace or liberty, but the method and purpose of sociology are to substitute human reason and intelligence for homicidal paraphernalia. Ward's thought and aim are dynamic throughout, and he does not find the alternative to bloodshed in some form of Fabian pacifism with hands folded in watching and waiting. But why civil war when, in the instrument of public opinion or the social will, there is the most powerful of revolutionary forces?

Upheaval and destruction are never necessary when the reason for force is overcome by the force of reason; in other words, when education and intelligence are given a chance. Society, for instance, can attack from all angles the evils of exploitation and unjust distribution exactly as any man would, without fear or bias, attack his personal problems. Does this, again, sound like a platitude? It is nevertheless a vital and sadly neglected truth. Ward expands it as follows:

> Whatever society demands it must and always will endeavor to supply. If it fails at first, it will continue to try until success at last crowns its efforts. Higher and higher types of statesmanship will follow the advancing intelligence of mankind, until, one by one, the difficult social problems will be solved. It is useless to maintain that the functions of government are necessarily limited to the few that have thus far been undertaken. . . .
> This country is today fully ripe for a series of important national reforms which cannot be made because a comparatively small number of influential citizens oppose them. Conservatism, fear of disapproval and general timidity before the people who are recognized as the real government, characterize the legislation of all modern nations.
> Our Declaration of Independence which recites that government derives its just powers from the "consent" of the governed has already been outgrown. It is no longer the consent, but the positively known will of the governed from which government now derives its powers (*Ps. F.,* pp. 303-304).

Above all, the working people should realize that the government is their own, and will be just what they make it. . . . If they are to secure from government that protection which forms its only claim to exist, they must throw off all party allegiance. They need no revolutionary schemes of socialism, communism or anarchy. The present machinery of government, especially in this country, is all they could wish. They have only to take possession of it and operate it in their own interest.

The true solution of the great social problem of this age is to be found in the ultimate establishment of a genuine people's government, with ample power to protect society against all forms of injustice, from whatever source, coupled with a warm and dutiful regard for the true interests of each and all, the poor as well as the rich. . . . This conception of government gets rid entirely of the paternal, the patriarchal, the personal element, and becomes nothing more nor less than the effective expression of the public will, the active agency by which society consciously and intelligently governs its own conduct (*Glimpses*, IV, 71).

Man's attempts at freeing himself from his bonds are pitiful but not hopeless. Human nature is changing toward the full recognition of the fact that everyone is entitled to all desirable opportunities in life, including the necessary leisure and knowledge to realize them. The fundamental concept of co-operation is bringing the people ever nearer to asserting their rights to own and dispose of their own lives, freely and unhampered, not in competition, but in a collective unity. With bread and education assured, the vital element of liberty will not be lacking. Meanwhile, the ignorant and the hungry, the stolid and the complacent, subjected masses can only dream of liberty, when they are not dreaming of bread or gold, instead. All that opportunity, security, life itself means for them is a vision of the truth that shall make them free.

# Chapter XXIX

# TRUTH

---

*"In the present state of the world the wheels of human progress are in large measure clogged by various impediments and obstructions. These consist mainly in error in one or the other of its many forms and in those repressive social structures which are its natural product. Only through the removal of the greater part of both error and its resultant institutions can that degree of liberation be attained which shall render possible the mobilization of society, or social movement."*

*"It is often said that ideas rule the world; but this is true only of world ideas. The highest and brightest ideas, the most important thoughts of any age or people, have scarcely any influence upon the world. This is because such ideas are always confined to a very few of the most developed minds and are not shared by the mass of mankind—but any idea that permeates the whole mass and becomes the thought of society itself, sways the mass and shapes the action of society in its entirety."*

*"The discovery of truth leads to achievement; it does not necessarily lead to improvement. . . . Applied sociology aims at the complete social transformation which will follow the assimilation of discovered truth."*—Ward

*"My only desire is to know the truth, my only fear to cling to error."*—George Eliot

*"However you look at it, truth is at once the most sublime, the most simple, the most difficult, and yet the most natural of all things."*—Madame de Sévigné

*"Whatever retards a spirit of inquiry is favorable to error; whatever promotes it is favorable to truth."*—Robert Hall

*"Is it not strange that the race of man should have gone forward so far and so well when all the while most of what it was thinking and believing was not true?"*
—H. F. Amiel

*"If truth cannot save Man, nothing can."*—John M. Robertson

---

THE MEEK and the disinherited of truth as well as property are fortunate in having Ward as their champion. In his liberalism, there are no abstract speculations about human rights, no sentimental gestures of protest. In his philosophy of truth, there is only a forthright scientific conviction that error, especially error of world-wide dimensions, is the jailor of humanity; truth alone, the great liberator.

## FREEDOM THROUGH TRUTH

The core of his argument is that freedom consists in the conscious choice of action, which in turn depends upon the kind and quantity of truth (knowledge) we possess. Although the bonds of poverty may cut more cruelly than all the others, we can be free only to the extent that we know what is true.

As a raw youth struggling desperately to free himself from the crushing weight of ignorance that he felt kept him imprisoned in the laboring class, Ward already discovered the importance of truth. Said he:

> I have always labored against my natural proneness to indorse popular errors. Freedom and independence of thought and opinion is one of the surest tests, as well of a sound intellect as of proper education.
>
> There are some persons who cannot really be said to have an idea of their own. . . . This mental apathy is perhaps more fatal to the spread of ideas than the want of talent or genius itself (*Diary*, pp. 103, 212).

In his maturer years he exposed the deadening effect of a barren educational and cultural environment, such as he himself had lived in. He instinctively took the part of the underdog, because he had learned from bitter personal experience how much poverty and exploitation owed to ignorance and error. When he analyzed the elements of achievement and expounded the laws of biological statics and the universal growth force of nature, Ward formulated an undying gospel of liberty:

> I only faintly perceived the connection between the principle there laid down and that which I had always defended on the human plane. And yet, the substantial identity of the two ideas is plain. The essential thing in both is latent power, suppressed energy, lost labor, waste caused by obstructions to normal activities.
>
> The forces of nature are, as it were, chained. The channels are everywhere choked. The new gospel, therefor, to which I found myself committed, was a gospel of liberation. Nature does not consist in the mere coddling of the weak. It consists in freeing the strong. It is emancipation. It becomes a practical question and not a futile speculation (*App. S.,* pp. 127-128).

Such truth, any truth, as the basis of liberty, may sound strange to squirrel souls that live on treadmills, but dynamic sociology is essentially a philosophy of achievement for free, rational, and informed minds. Ward tolerantly notes how the unfailing paths of nature, reason, and truth are avoided or unwanted by most people. Yet truth is neither anodynal nor anesthetic, and its severely minded pursuit is not without consoling compensations. It strengthens the spirit, teaches humility, and gives us our proper place and proportion in the universe.

The enemies of liberty have always known that their most dangerous foe is truth. That is why they have consistently spiked the wheels of education and dammed the avenues of progress with all the errors man's fertile brain is heir to. Sociology demands the removal of such errors and calls upon society for an organized movement toward happiness through the universal spread of correct information and opinion. In Ward's words:

In the present state of the world the wheels of human progress are in large measure clogged by the various impediments and obstructions that have been described. These consist mainly in error in one or the other of its many forms and in those repressive social structures which are its natural product. Only through the removal of the greater part of both the error and its resultant institutions can that degree of liberation be attained which shall render possible the mobilization of society, or social movement (*App. S.,* p. 110).

### WHAT IS TRUTH?

What is the priceless gem of truth which is higher than goodness and more precious than life itself? Pilate did not wait for an answer to his question, "What is truth?" but science has waited and labored patiently, and by its answer forged the keys to all human dungeons.

Truth, says Donne, stands on a hill, and he that would reach her

about must and about must go
and what the hill's suddenness resists, win so.

The logicians define truth as the relation of agreement or disagreement of individual or group ideas. Spencer calls it the actual correspondence of subjective and objective relations; George Henry Lewes, simple identity. Ward sees truth when the thought and object are the same under varying external aspects, in which case the superstitions of supernatural causes and effects are necessarily absent (see *D.S.,* II, 416; *Ps. F.,* p. 27).

There is nothing ineffable and mysterious supporting the conviction that truth should prevail. But how achieve it? Aristotle said: "No one is able to attain truth adequately, while on the other hand, we do not collectively fail, but everyone says something true about the nature of things." The pragmatist's idea that truth is that which works is a fallacy because its workability has to be determined without a criterion. Truth does not necessarily come with experience, or through the senses or the intellect alone. And when we grasp a truth, it is only a steppingstone to another truth. Says Ward:

Truth is no longer a privileged commodity; it is the common property of all who want it. The pursuit of knowledge is no longer the pursuit of a phantom. It is a safe investment of time and talent. . . . Since all causes consist of real and tangible circumstances, they can in most cases be reproduced or prevented in future according as they produce beneficial or injurious results. If we can create the same conditions, we may be sure of the same result; if we can break up these conditions, we can avoid the result (*D.S.,* II, 43).

Ward never wavered for an instant from the position that truth is possible only through science and the scientific method. Yet he was practical enough to discern the incandescent power of mass opinion, the social mind, to grasp truth:

Everybody knows how, on many great political and judicial questions, the slow detail and careful technicality of legislators and judges do violence to truth and justice, while the public mind has seen the justice of the case from the first, and suffers sore disappointment at the manner in which the truth has been smothered under the forms of logic and of law (*ibid.,* II, 327).

## REASON, SCIENCE, AND TRUTH

Truth is relative. Nothing in and of itself alone is true, whether it is sensation, thought, or experience. The Greek ideal of truth as an opinionless impassibility is a useless ideal. But the truths of science furnish positive opinions and knowledge of the universal laws of nature, and free man from the terrifying darkness of ignorance (see *P.S.,* p. 89).

Man has enthroned error instead of truth, and reason is the only liberator from that tyranny. Reason alone makes the knowledge of common things exact, orderly, and translatable into correct ideas, as the basis for dynamic action. When man learns to know, he clothes his naked reason. His hope for the future lies not in scientific specialists selling expert opinion to a stupid mass, but in a generally educated race interested in and controlled by science (see *D.S.,* II, Chapter XIV; *P.S.,* pp. 144, 195).

Without the material of science, especially the knowledge of evolution, there could have been no truth. With science, the march of evolution along the paths of discovery in astronomy, physics, and biology, has now reached the domains of psychology and social science. The sciences that were earliest brought to light were furthest from human interests. That is why they contained the least amount of error. The two nearest and most important to man, the science of mind and the science of society, are shot through and through with error (see *Outlines*, pp. 208-210).

In the knowledge and application by the intellect of natural laws, Ward argues, lie the solution of doubt and the possibility of removing error. Science as a whole is the revolutionary means of abolishing error and instituting truth. Pain is no substitute for truth. The bits of knowledge that man acquired through the misery he suffered because of his ignorance of natural laws and social forces, were acquired at too high a price.

The reconstruction of the social order, the solution of the social problem, is a task which cannot be completed until the mind becomes as hungry for truth as it is now avid for wealth. That change would be the greatest upheaval in human history, far more important than any political overturn, for it would bring about a complete change of vision, spirit, and method; an altered pattern of life in the arrival of the scientific and rational age.

## ERROR IS ACTIVE IGNORANCE

Needless to say, reason, science, and truth are, as yet, merely timid experiments. The enemies of science are many and well organized, and they are never modest about claiming to be the legitimate pioneers who built up civilization. To name a single one of them, the idealist asserts that while man's eternal quest has been for truth, the method pursued has been wrong, for a jot of intuition or imagination is worth a mountain of facts and figures. This and similar widespread errors do not denote the void of ignorance but the boulders of misinformation and misjudgment which it is almost impossible to dislodge from the human mind. Error is not a desert; it is a jungle.

The ignorance of the human race has been so active that it has developed and elevated world-wide errors into so-called universal truths. The mind has made endless deductions, but error, which is a false deduction, has resulted as often as truth, which is a correct deduction. Given the same reasoning powers, truth or falsity will depend solely upon the amount of correct knowledge put into the mind (see *App. S.,* Chapter VI).

Society has enough mental food or knowledge to carry on, argues Ward. Its most vital need is to eliminate error. In the form of superstition, the masses love it passionately, dote on their emotional fancies and stubborn beliefs more than on anything else on earth, and will defend them to the last.

## THE ERRORS OF GREAT MINDS

Faith alone does not result in truth, for faith often denotes a state of mind which prevents the discovery or use of truth. It is much easier to wipe out despotism or change the map of the world than it is to rid the mind of superstition and error. For ages, mankind believed everything that is now disbelieved. Comets were taken for omens of disaster, and evolution was denied successively in astronomy, chemistry, geology, biology, and psychology, with as much vehemence as it is now being fought in sociology. The only consolation is, that for want of facts, the greatest minds have harbored the greatest errors, and done the same thing as lesser minds, i.e., indulged in pure guesses and fancies.

Thus, Aristotle, the father of science, never doubted anything in the modern sense of the term. He believed, for example, that the brain was bloodless and without sensation; birds and insects should be grouped together; semen was a foam derived from the most thoroughly cooked foods; and that if animals faced north during conception a female would be born; if south, a male. Such nonsense is not far removed from the palmistry, numerology, astrology, and other superstitions of today. It is matched by the belief of both Plato and Hippocrates, and accepted by Galen, five hundred years later, that liquids when swallowed went to the lungs. Kepler was certain that each of the planets whose motion his mathematical genius discovered had a guiding spirit. Cuvier, Owen, and Agassiz had supreme faith in the divine creation of organisms, although they spent their lives discovering organic structure. Kant admitted the truth of determinism in history, but clung to the doctrine of arbitrary individual free will. Faraday, a world master in chemistry, kept science and metaphysics in different pockets, to be used as occasion suited him. Descartes, one of the most powerful intellects in all history, devoutly believed in the divine creation of Adam and Eve, and of all the planetary bodies exactly as he saw them. As far as common truths are concerned, the world stood for ages, as it were, around a horse and gravely disputed the number of its teeth, without having the sense to look into its mouth.

## WORLD ERRORS

"Nothing is so firmly believed," said Montaigne, "as what we least know." The slightest research into error discloses that it is so powerful and dynamic that nothing has ever been too foolish or shocking for human credulity as long as it was dictated by the logic of some dominant feeling or idea. In the face of individual errors expanded into world errors, it is a miracle that any truth at all has survived. In other words, when one views the mountains of superstitions which completely overshadow the quantity of truths mined from the treasures of science, or takes stock of the fallacies and illusions piled up by man on his own back, civilization, such as it is, seems a miracle (*ibid.*, p. 71).

Ward groups the main world errors as follows (*ibid.*, p. 72):

1. The sacrifice of human victims, often accompanied by the destruction of property, of which modern funerals are an example.

2. The erection of costly tombs and mausoleums. Modern tombstones are not as expensive as the pyramids which cost the lives of hundreds of thousands of slaves over a period of twenty years, but belong to the same class of errors.

3. Self-mutilation and similar attempts to please the gods, surviving in modern dress styles.

4. Superstition. The groups of customs and practices which restrict liberty of action and fill the mind with ungrounded fears, embrace all the other world errors.

5. Asceticism. This is thoroughly egoistic, and in its milder forms, like Puritanism, is dangerous to health, and destructive of liberty.

6. Zoolatry, or animal totemism. To this day, in India, the destruction of vermin, snakes, etc., is strictly forbidden because they are worshipped or regarded as holy.

7. Witchcraft. The belief in the existence of emissaries of the Evil One was accepted by Luther, John Wesley, and Blackstone, and still survives.

8. Persecution. Savages never doubted anything, and, therefore, were never persecuted. But civilization sacrificed numberless heretics in the name of religion.

9. Resistance to truth. Opposition to science is the most serious of errors. The utterance of truth was for ages fraught with grave personal danger, and still carries severe penalties.

10. Obscurantism, really a more subtle form of persecution. "It is only in the prohibited books," said Helvetius, "that the truth is found." From the Pope's Index Expurgatorius to the smut-hound censorship of our day, this error has been glorified by religious and moral fervor.

In the wake of these major errors have followed other fallacies which are still here in many guises. To list them all would fill volumes. We cite a few discussed by Ward:

(a) The general illusion of the near, taken for farsightedness and wisdom.

(b) The absolute efficacy of prayer.

(c) Emotion arises from sin and leads to depravity.

(d) Science stands for what is crass and sensual. It has no room for spiritual values.

(e) Instinct is more important than reason.

(f) Nature is superior to mind.

(g) Under competition or individualism, there is incentive to achievement and progress. Under co-operation and collectivism, incentive is destroyed.

(h) The male sex is primary, the stronger and more intelligently endowed by nature, and always will be the superior sex.

(i) Human beings are great only because of noble birth, high office, much wealth or other circumstances; heredity is, therefore, the chief molding influence of mankind.

(j) Race, climate, wealth, and other environmental conditions far exceed in potency the effect of education.

(k) Ignorance is bliss.

(l) Happiness is the denial of desire; desire is the denial of wisdom.

(m) Human nature is heaven-sent and cannot be changed. We have always had competition, poverty, war, greed, and lust, and always will.

(n) Certain institutions like democracy, marriage, the competitive order, and the money system are holy, eternal, or unchangeable.

(o) To live in a civilized country is to be civilized. Civilization is a national or territorial condition, not a personal or social one.

(p) The culture of a few will do for the masses.

(q) Specialization leads to truth.

(r) A complex style, ponderous dogma, and brilliant eloquence indicate depth and knowledge.

(s) Trivia and inconsequentials, even in knowledge, are important to mankind.

## WORLD ERRORS SURVIVE

Not only are world errors defended by many an honored and otherwise progressive mind, but despite all scientific advance, not a single one of them has thus far been removed (*ibid.*, pp. 80-83). The result is that the number of persons who know the truths of science, and whose minds are emancipated enough to think independently, is so pitifully small that they are lonely indeed, if not outright social pariahs. Converse with people for five minutes, advises Ward, and you will discover that most of their minds are like bundles of straw which are bound tightly by stout cords of cults, conventions, and superstitions. Is it surprising that social truths are practically unknown or ignored, or that the human mind, for the most part, is drugged with error?

## SOCIOLOGICAL TRUTHS

Culling a few of Ward's generalizations in dynamic sociology and contrasting their constructive meaning with the world errors and illusions throws a dazzling light upon the profundity and liberalizing force of his thought:

1. The universe is governed by natural law and controlled by natural forces.

2. The comprehension of the world, from its origin into the future, is possible only through science and the scientific method. Instinct or revelation will not do.

3. Organization is the supreme law of the universe. Evolution is the method by which matter, life, feeling, mind, man, and society were developed.

4. Feeling is the only motor force; mind, the only directive force. The social forces, the collective desires of society, cause all social movements. The social mind directs them.

5. The object of nature is organization. The aim of man is happiness. The purpose of society is achievement.

6. Achievement tends toward co-operation, and away from competition.

7. Mind is at the botton of history and above the economic forces.

8. Liberty is impossible without truth, education, leisure, and economic security.

9. The ideal society, sociocracy, is possible here and now, but will not come until society takes charge of its own affairs, for its own benefit.

10. Woman, constituting one half of the human race, suffers from an inferiority complex bred by men. She is by nature the original and superior sex, and must be allowed to achieve equally with man.

11. There is no personal god, free will, or immortality. The religion of science, truth, humanity, is enough for any man.

12. Environment is more important than heredity, and more neglected. Talent and genius can be bred by education through opportunity.

13. Morality spells progress, and progress means happiness. None of them are possible without the rule of reason.

14. Pessimism and optimism are the wrong ways out of the social miasma. Meliorism is the only true goal of progress; education, the initial approach.

15. In education, the great panacea, lies the solution of the social problem.

When one surveys the human scene in the light of social science, hope springs eternal that the future holds achievement and progress in store for all, and that ignorance and error cannot forever remain blissful ideals. To the pressing questions—"Has all truth died?" and "Have we any real desire to be free?" let the reader turn to his own stock of knowledge, beliefs or opinions, for an answer. Is he an enslaved dogmatist or a free and enlightened being? Are his views reached by straight thinking upon substantial facts or through personal interest and emotion? A truthful and fearless response will perhaps indicate how much or how little he has been emancipated by his journey through the domains of sociology.

As a jealous lover and guardian of truth and liberty, Ward never felt discouraged because humanity has not yet been freed of its errors. What if the great masses still regard social science or science, in general, as some dusty dream of "highbrows" and dreamers who are vainly trying to change human nature? World errors can still be replaced by universal truth, if only those who have been disinherited of knowledge will receive their rightful inheritance. "Away with myths and legends for adult minds," cries Ward, "with childish and corroding fears and superstitions in all their enticing and monstrous forms. Sociology proclaims truth, the truths of science, as the great liberator of mankind, and the truth shall make them free!"

# BOOK XIII. THE FEMINIST

*"The inequality of rights between men and women has no other source than the law of the strongest."*—John Stuart Mill

*"Die Mutter ist früher als der Sohn."*—Bachofen

*"To Lester F. Ward, sociologist and humanitarian, one of the world's greatest men; a creative thinker to whose wide knowledge and power of vision we are indebted for a new grasp of the nature and processes of society, and to whom all women are especially bound in honor and gratitude for his gynaecocentric theory of life, than which nothing more important to humanity has been advanced since the theory of evolution, and nothing more important to women has ever been given to the world."*—Charlotte Perkins Gilman

# CHAPTER XXX

# THE SEX FORCES

---

*"For the sociologist, love is not a sentiment in the popular sense; it is a* principle, *the second of the great powers that propel the social machinery."*

*"Natural love is the original form of all love, and all other forms are derivatives of it."*—Ward

---

Our JOURNEY, THUS FAR, seems to have been through "man-made" fields. Although woman is tacitly included in the term *man,* Ward has no doubt that she who constitutes one half of the human race has been infinitely neglected and excluded from social achievement as an inferior being. Is the mother of the race really of a lower order, or is she, as Ward demonstrates, the originally superior sex that has been debased to an inferior state? What are the forces that have made her what she is today?

### WARD'S SEX PHILOSOPHY

In a conventional and hypocrital world Ward's clean, moral sex views are highly refreshing. The fear and general reactionary views of sex are even worse than those about the social forces. Ethics and religion have fettered sex with so many prohibitions that love is furtively regarded by millions of people as a sin, and the body and its appetites as sensual and ignoble. Dynamic sociology sharply contradicts those false and narrow outlooks, and rescues the sex force from degradation by blind or unhappy people. So-called moralists have decided that purity means modesty and asceticism, and that the sex problem involves questions only of individual ethics and self-control; ergo, the less said about the entire subject, especially in public, the better (see *P.S.,* Chapter XIV).

Fortunately, the greater part of Ward's sex philosophy is contained in *Pure Sociology,* a title which must have kept away the moral snoopers and censors. Nothing that our virile strongly sexed guide wrote about love and sex can be ascribed to any personal inhibitions, this despite the handicap of an extremely puritanical environment in his adolescent years. It was an unforgivable sin in his circle for young people even to read a textbook of physiology (see *Diary,* p. 45). Yet he developed a truly emancipated mind, although he never came to believe that man had advanced far enough to risk anarchy in sex, any more than in government. He discovered soon enough that the sex forces were natural forces to be studied, analyzed, and controlled like any others. Maturity and research further convinced him that love is purely psychic (although described generally as a physical feeling because its sensations fill every fibre of the body), a psychic phenomenon whose limits are boundless, ranging from the animal sex urge to the widest reaches of unselfish love for nature and humanity.

## SEX AND MODESTY

Since nature is amoral, where did modesty come from? Primitive man lived as innocently as the animals, and his sex desires were as unassuming as all natural functions. Clothes, not nudity, made him uncomfortable and ashamed. Sexual immorality increased, in time, in inverse ratio to the quantity of clothes worn—compare the Spartan woman who went undressed before male audiences and the dissolute women of the French Court in the eighteenth century who were swathed in clothing.

Ward's thesis on sex is scientific and startlingly original. In the instincts of love and the group sentiment of safety, nature has provided surer safeguards for the race than man wrote into all his codes. It was the masculine sex that introduced immorality in society. In the dawn of the race, the female was queen and did the selecting in courtship and marriage. Later, when the male dethroned her, and did the selecting, marriage became a matter of seizure and rape, and involved hiding the female from the eyes of the world. Modesty arose when she fell in with his wishes, and grew bashful and retiring. Its vestiges are still found in the modern elopement and honeymoon. Yet the great majority, in the name of this false and exaggerated sense of modesty which they believe is an emanation of the Divine, have distorted and expurgated the true story of mankind (see *D.S.,* I, 632).

## LOVE, A NOBLE, NATURAL FORCE

Pessimists in sex like Tolstoy, Schopenhauer, and Weininger who saw only the shadows and were for erasing the picture of life as a blot upon a perfect universe, did not affect Ward's scientific view. He regarded love as a natural desire, whose expression is not a matter of taste or caprice, but the perennial flow of an irrepressible stream of feeling which constitutes the very essence of biological life (see *P.S.,* pp. 387-389). Defining the sex force as "the great life tonic of the world, the sublimest and most exalted as well as the purest and noblest of impulses," he added:

No one feels that he is in duty bound to propagate the race. Nature is greater than man and has arranged for the preservation of the species of the human race, *"durch Hunger und durch Liebe"* (*Cape,* p. 123).

I have a profound contempt for the life of mere animal existence which does not reflect on the glories of love, but takes them as simple passing waves, to be satisfied, if possible, and gotten rid of as soon as possible, as something rather bad in themselves. It is a part of that slavery to function which belongs to a pain economy.

I sometimes have this thought come over me, hard to express, but great: I imagine that there was not and never had been any taboos on love or sex, or the body, or the great organs of reproduction, and that all the feelings from that source were looked upon the same as those from sight or sound (art, music) over which cultivated people so rave, although they do not yield a tithe of the joy that comes from love. Imagine the whole enlightened, cultivated, reflecting, thinking world thus freed from this incubus of the sex taboo, what a glorious thing this great source of joy would be. . . . One emancipated from the slavery to function can look upon life ("the phylogenetic forces") as not only "life mitigating" forces, or "forces of race elevation" (*Outlines,* p. 155), but as truly esthetic forces and the most effective of sources of happiness (*ibid.,* p. 93).

## THE SEX FORCES ARE SUBORDINATE

Long before Havelock Ellis published *Studies in the Psychology of Sex* (1897-1910), Ward argued that the sex force is not supreme in the scheme of life, and is subordinate to the hunger forces. It is not, as many imagine, the only source of sympathy, art, or achievement, but it is only one of the social forces which have driven man to civilization. Civilization is the result of a trinity of forces centered in the stomach, the loins, and the brain. The desire to reproduce is a part of the universal energy latent in every atom of matter, but it dwindles down to its true proportion when placed beside the hunger forces.

Civilization, from the viewpoint of achievement and social progress, owes nothing to the sex forces, for their influence is creative and not molding. The hunger forces deal with the hard and practical side of life and incessantly urge their way forward, but the love forces are a part of nature itself, conservative before social innovation, and wholly indifferent to all signs of progress (see *D.S.*, I, 598). The sex force is really a supplement to the hunger force. All living forms have one great urge, to feed themselves, and reproduction is a specialized form of nutrition through the renewal of the body, a mode of growth outside the organism (see *P.S.*, pp. 290-304). Upon deeper analysis, reproduction is found to be the embyro of the feeling of altruism. When the life process is carried over by reproduction into another individual, the organism has someone else to worry about than itself.

Ward's prophecy that the time is coming when sex will become less important in the social scheme of things was supported, years later, by Freud, as follows:

One is probably right in supposing that the importance of sexuality as a source of pleasurable sensation, i.e., as a means of fulfilling the purpose of life, has perceptibly decreased. Sometimes, one imagines one perceives that it is not only the operation of culture, but something in the nature of the function itself that denies us full satisfaction and urges us in other directions. This may be an error; it is hard to decide (Freud, *Civilization and Its Discontents*, p. 76).

### NATURAL LOVE

There is in nature and man, an unbroken current of the love force, said Ward. Natural love, or sex desire, is the trunk; all other feelings of love, friendship, and sympathy are the branches. Almost all thinkers have missed this simple truth and have thought of love as dual, one kind for the body, and another for the spirit. Ward sees the sex passion beneath all love, including the feeling of ecstacy in the presence of beauty or of the infinite—Plato's Eros (see *D.S.*, I, 610-611). Sensual love is, therefore, on the same plane as intellectual and spiritual love. Says he:

Love is a great desire, the greatest of all desires, passing into passion and lust. And when we rise into the higher, intellectual fields, we have what we call inspiration, while in the practical world we have ambition. In other words, what I mean by desire is the great NISUS of all organic life that creates or produces pleasure (*Glimpses, V, 7*).

What advantage is it to man to find out the nature of desire, the great principle or power that underlies all organic life? What benefit can that be to man? This only: if we can learn something about those desires—the great leading ones—that actuate humanity and society as a whole, we may be able to do something in the domain of life and mind and man, as we have done in the domain of mechanics and physics. We may be able to deduce the laws according to which humanity is actuated (*ibid.,* p. 9).

## ROMANTIC LOVE

Human association began with the propagating couple, and all the later forms—kinship, hordes, clans, gentes, tribes, states, and nations—together with the romantic, conjugal, maternal, and humanistic phases of love are the products of the sex passion, the primitive call to life (see *P.S.,* p. 390).

Romantic love is natural love with a sugar coating, a refinement and rationalization of the sex urge, which matured in the chivalry of medievalism. The Dark Ages suppressed intellectual activities but intensified the emotional currents centered in the religious fervor which burned in the monasteries of Europe. When the Crusades took the flower of manhood to the Holy Land, absence made hearts grow fonder. Natural love was sublimated into a romantic ideal sustained by her wearing "his" colors, and his singing "her" charms in foreign lands.

The immortal Cervantes in *Don Quixote* exposed the absurd extremes to which romantic love could go, but the sociologist sees deeper than the literary genius. What if the cavalier's serenade does sound inane? Is it not nature's voice commanding reproduction? Even in the more sober modern times, romanticism is still present in some form as a necessary stage setting in the theater of love, to make the sex function more attractive.

## CONJUGAL LOVE

Nature's resources are unlimited. The evolutionary process did not stop with romantic love. Something more stable to assure race preservation was needed, and it was found in conjugal love (monogamy). Marriage is a relationship which requires a certain amount of character and tolerance, despite the popular idea that it is a state of martyrdom which destroys all romance. One can easily comprehend the conflict between natural love, the biological imperative, and conjugal love, the social imperative. The Latin races are not the only ones who comment upon the meeting of their wives and their sweethearts. The sex passion cares nothing about any social aspects but seeks what it wants, thus unconsciously promoting race vigor and symmetry. But ultimately, as nature always bows to man, sex desire submits to the impulse of the social force and founds homes and families. Thus, the sex relations of married people exert a powerful influence on them, and through them, upon society.

Conjugal love is not the result of any romantic "love at first sight," but of the natural principle of propinquity. "A mastiff dog may love a puppy cur for no more reason than that the twain have been tied together" (Tennyson). Mere proximity to another, which Ward called "the sanctity of the second person," creates an attachment often wholly disproportionate to real worth. Nevertheless, living together in marriage is not only a physical union but also a spiritual and social union in which love of one's mate is more important, socially, than self-love, and of course far more noble.

Under monogamy, conjugal love approaches the equality of the sexes. Of course, when the wife was the husband's chattel, there could be no more equality, friction, or infelicity, and no less, than between the horse and its master. When the marriage institution ripened, unavoidable conflicts between individual wills were solved by marital adaptability. As couples grow old together, the bonds of propinquity become stronger until they develop into indissoluble ties. Monogamy is the result of social experience, and has proved more beneficial to the race than polygyny or polyandry. Despite all criticisms, marriage is also more socially efficient than natural and romantic love, because the marriage relation is a powerful spur to achievement. The physical and mental condition of a married person is best for social effectiveness. The flesh and the spirit have been somewhat calmed by the satisfactions of conjugal love, and the energies released for important achievements. Civilization has, in the long run, advanced further, i.e., society has achieved most, under monogamy. That is a generalization which is far more valuable in sociology than any moral precept concerning marriage (see *ibid.*, p. 403).

## MATERNAL LOVE

Maternal love is not a social instinct, says Ward, but like natural love, is a biological feeling (see *ibid.,* p. 412). Among the lower animals, there are impulses which take the place of maternal love, such as the bird's true instinct to hatch its eggs. The love of children has often been confused with the love of kin, and with the general feeling of sympathy in the human breast. Sympathy is the basis of our moral nature and is the product of a high rational faculty (see p. 527). Maternal affection, a sentiment inherited from and close to animal life, was developed in the mother by the laws of survival and advantage. It is highly characteristic of the mammals, and is directly connected with the function of suckling the young. Ward anticipated Freud by declaring that because the mammary system is a part of the sexual organization, maternal love is an outgrowth of the sex impulse. While Ward stressed the mother's pleasure in nursing, Freud emphasized the thrill felt by the child.

As a social force, maternal love in the human race has functioned in a more or less negative fashion. As sex equality approaches, mother love becomes less biological and is diverted into other channels, there to play a nobler part than that of feeding and caring for the young. Only when woman will be recognized as the social equal of man, Ward concludes, will the full effect of the maternal passion emerge to embellish and spiritualize the art and life of society as never before.

## LOVE OF KIN

The love of kin is founded on altruism, and is probably an exclusively human attribute. It is the social feeling of sympathy for others, operating freely and unselfishly (see *ibid.,* p. 315). As the evolution of the natural feeling of attachment which existed in every member of the original horde for every other member, it expanded into love of all kin. In the matriarchal system under which mankind lived for the greater part of its history, all members of the group considered themselves brothers and sisters, and that primary blood bond (basically sexual) persisted, until its value in social evolution became of vast importance.

The dynamic quality of the love of kin is found also in its negative aspects, the correlative race hatred which is often more powerful than the positive feeling. The light of natural, romantic, and conjugal love also has its shadows of dislike and jealousy, and maternal love is mixed with intense hatred of everything that threatens the offspring. But it is only the conflicts resulting from racial friction that have had wide social effects and have helped to build up, through war and race assimilation, the foundations of organized society.

Man's life seems to be consumed by sex because the sex force is regarded unscientifically, and its effects exaggerated, said Ward. The civilized, rational view sees it only as a phase of a more ample experience. With increasing knowledge enjoyed by all, attention will be increasingly directed to the moral, intellectual, and esthetic forces. Judging from the influence of reason over emotion, the time must come when the energies of man will no longer be spent upon the sex passion, as such, or even upon the problem of raising a family. That does not imply that the sex forces will be destroyed or exchanged for others, any more than humanity will dispense with eating after the struggle for bread will have been done away with. The currents of sex desire can be directed into other channels which need those reservoirs of energy. The vigor and beauty of natural love in all its manifestations will ever remain, but will be made to flow through other realms than the exacting and consuming field of sex desire.

# CHAPTER XXXI

# WOMAN'S ORIGINAL
# SUPERIORITY

---

*"I am tired of this one-sided civilization, this half-built society, of this false chivalry, this mock modesty, this pretended regard which one sex assumes for the other, while loads of putrid prejudice hang upon woman's neck."*

*"Woman is the unchanging trunk of the great genealogic tree, while man, with all his vaunted superiority is but a branch, a grafted scion. . . . Woman is the race, and the race can be raised up only as she is raised up. There is no fixed rule by which nature has intended that one sex should excel the other, any more than there is any fixed point beyond which either cannot develop further. Nature has no intentions, and evolution has no limits. True science teaches that the elevation of woman is the only sure road to the evolution of man."*

*"Civilization demands this revolution. . . . Woman is half of mankind. Civilization and progress have hitherto been carried forward by the male half alone. It is high time that all the forces of society were brought into action, and it is especially necessary that those vast, complementary forces which woman alone can yield be given free rein and the whole machinery of society be set into full and harmonious operation."—*Ward

---

WARD WAS DRAWN TO THE feminine question early in his career because it was part and parcel of the social question. His studies in sex were therefore only a prelude to the feminist movement which his writings initiated in America.

## WARD'S FEMINIST PHILOSOPHY

One of the most brilliant and profound theses in all sociology, the importance of which can be compared only to that of Darwinism, is Ward's theory that woman is not a lower being than man, but on the contrary is his superior in nature. By a careful survey of the history of her who is still believed to be sin and mystery incarnate, he came, without any saccharine or foggy sentimentality, to the conclusion that she owes her present subordinate state, physical, mental, and social, to the treatment received at the hands of her lord and master (see *D.S.*, I, 642-644; *P.S.*, Chapter XIV; *App. S.*, pp. 231-232). His attack with the aid of all the sciences upon the universal fallacy of woman's place in the sun, opened the road to her emancipation. Of course, this theory which he advanced with Messianic fervor, was bitterly opposed by both sexes. Nor did the intellectual and scientific world, with the exception of such savants as August Weismann, David Starr Jordan, and Havelock Ellis, warm to his argument.

What his sex theory needed most was a hearing. Only a small band of disciples who founded the suffragette movement accepted the theory, but to this day it is looked upon askance by all respectable and conservative folk. When the world will be ready to listen to Ward as it finally did to Darwin, Ward's philosophy of feminism will be saved from the fate of many great truths to be vehemently attacked and denied, long before they are given a hearing (see *P.S.,* p. 291).

Among the few women who grasped the full significance of Ward's solution of the woman problem was Charlotte Perkins Gilman, who dedicated her neglected work *The Man-Made World* (1911) as follows:

To Lester F. Ward, sociologist and humanitarian, one of the world's great men; a creative thinker to whose wide knowledge and power of vision we are indebted for a new grasp of the nature and processes of society, and to whom all women are especially bound in honour and gratitude for his gynaecocentric theory of life, than which nothing more important to humanity has been advanced since the theory of evolution, and nothing more important to women has ever been given to the world.

## THE THEORY OF MALE SUPERIORITY

The universally dominant masculine view of the sexes is that the male came first in the organic scheme of life, and that all things center about him. The female was secondary, an accidental factor that served as a breeding machine, which is inferior to the male sex in every respect. Nature's evidence of that seems to be irrefutable. Biology reveals that the male animal is larger, stronger, and more complete than the female. In the human race she is generally weaker, smaller, and mentally less endowed than he is. In achievement she dwindles by comparison, for there are few women among the world's great artists, authors, scientists, or philosophers. Civilization, as a whole, has been the result of man's work, and woman had to be content with her subordinate place as wife and mother. To believe otherwise, thus ends the masculine argument, would be to fly in the face of all facts.

## THE THEORY OF FEMALE SUPERIORITY

The male theory is a fallacy, Ward counters. It is founded on the illusion of the near and is the result of tradition, convention, and prejudice. The female theory is based upon facts that are not upon the surface but which are, nevertheless, easily accessible. Femaleness is primary and basic in nature; maleness is secondary and accidental. The female is by nature the dominant one, because all female animals were (and most of them still are) superior to the males. But in the human race, she was deposed from her throne by the male's brute force, and from her exalted position as the stronger and brainier of the sexes, she has been forced down to her present lowly status.

Ward found that the boasted male superiority applies only to a relatively small number of animal genera and families, and is the result of specialization due to causes that have no relation to the general scheme of life. From any comprehensive view, the female is the racial type and the conserving element, while the male is merely the sex type or fertilizing element. She is the base and the trunk of the human tree; he is the agent of variation and branching. Primitive races knew this when they worshipped only the mother as representative of the group, and recognized descent only through her. If theologians were as consistent as the savage children of nature, God would be depicted as a woman.

## THE ORIGIN AND DEVELOPMENT OF THE MALE

In support of his theory Ward begins with a biological survey of sex. It is neither a basic invention of nature nor a primal necessity in evolution. Nature did not start her vital organizing process with two sexes, but only with one, the female. For a long time, life went on without the help of the masterful male. Before he appeared the living world was well developed and continued by fusion, division of cells, spore formations, and virgin reproduction. Because the results were as monotonous as leaves on a tree, nature evolved the male as a fertilizing instrument to assure variety, i.e., rejuvenation, new blood, and a greater diversity of form and quality. Much later still, under the operation of the law of advantage, the male became an independent organism, and has never stopped boasting about it. Having found an additional sex advantageous, nature proceeded to safeguard bisexual reproduction, especially in human beings, by attaching heavy penalties to inbreeding and the reversion to the single strain method.

The evolution of the male can be traced all through primitive life. In most cases, he is only a tiny appendix to the female, a sac filled with male seed. In barnacles, for example, the husband is a parasite that lives in the valves of the female shell, and she carries around from two to seven of his kind for the sole purpose of reproducing. If this seems like a deviation from the title of this chapter, it must be remembered that woman's changing status can be comprehended only by studying her ancestors in the lower and more formative types of organisms. As we descend the scale of life, it becomes clearer that the female is nature's superior sex, for she grows larger and more commanding, while her mate decreases in size and strength and finally disappears altogether. Below the vertebrates, she is the queen, while he is relatively unimportant.

Thus, all male bees are drones. The only mosquito the public knows is the female, for the males die out in the early spring after their sexual task has been completed. In certain spider families (*nephila chrysogasier*) the female is more than thirteen hundred times the size of the male, and he is considered so worthless that he is devoured by the bride after the marriage is consummated.[1]

## FEMALE SELECTION

Ward's theory follows research in sexual selection, but Ward commenced where Darwin left off. When the latter speaks of courtship or mating in the animal world, he always means nature's exclusive method of selection by the female. Ward believes that Darwin's discovery of sexual selection is at least as important as that of natural

---

[1] Professor Jacques Loeb has induced reproduction of a frog without the help of a male. And as we write this (March, 1936), the American press is ringing with the feat of the Harvard University biologist, Dr. Gregory Pincus, who put a rabbit's ovum into a test tube and fertilized it with a salt solution. The resulting embryo was then transplanted into a female rabbit, which in due course gave birth without having seen the male of her choice or contributed anything of herself to the offspring. While the social possibilities of ectogenesis (birth without a father) are startling, it must be noted how much nature thinks of the male, for all animals reproduced by stimulating ova by heat or salt, are females.

selection (see *Glimpses,* IV, 216). It was her monopoly of the right to choose her mate which, in time, developed the male, as she desired him, from a primeval sex organ into an independent organism. Heredity preserved the physical and psychical characteristics of those males whom she preferred, but she herself remained essentially unchanged.

The female, misnamed the passive sex, was always so certain that the male would obey nature's command and seek her out that she used all her powers to guard and regulate heredity qualities. Since nature had only one motive, to procreate, she made the female instinctively choose the males of her liking (see *P.S.,* p. 325). Even when the male animals attained greater brain power, size, and strength than the female, those advantages were not used to attack her, but to combat other males for her favors. As for the offspring, the female alone still defends them. It is the mother hen that cares for her brood while the cock struts around with his lady friends. A male animal that risks its life to protect the home and the young, is a rarity.

## MALE EFFLORESCENCE

Male superiority among animals never consisted of anything more than the development of secondary or sexual characteristics like muscles, hair, coloration, and the like. The superiority resulting from this male efflorescence, as Ward called it, was a sham, for those flowery adornments did not indicate any real supremacy. The fact is that below the human species, the female is still queen in all the serious and essential affairs of life. There is no male rule, despite his gaudiness. In Ward's own language:

Nevertheless it represents organic evolution of which both sexes have partaken. Its chief value lies in the fact that in lifting the male from nothing to his present state, it has elevated all species and all life, and placed the organic world on a higher plane. The apparent male superiority in some birds and mammals instead of indicating arrested development in the female, indicates over-development in the male. . . . It has been shown that even the typical secondary sexual characters crop out to a limited extent also in the females (*ibid.,* pp. 331-332).

In 1888 Ward, in a popular address adorned by a humorous vein so as to attract the public to his novel thesis, said:

Throughout all the earlier stages man has been the complete slave of woman and under the most abject bondage to her. There was a time in our history (I am speaking only to gentlemen now) when we were scarcely of any account at all. As compared to our female companions we were utterly insignificant in size. When we were bees we were called drones and treated with the utmost contempt by our wives, who called themselves queens, and as mayflies we were not allowed to take any nourishment, and had no mouths, teeth or stomachs for that purpose. Hence we could only enjoy the society of our wives for a single day and then die of starvation.

When we finally got a little backbone and became successively fish and frogs and snakes, we fared a little better, but even as birds we were sometimes subjected to great indignities, such as that of the American ostrich, where the gentleman is required to sit upon and hatch out the eggs and rear the brood, while the lady goes to the polls.

Then the women picked out the biggest and strongest, and none but these large, powerful handsome fellows could get anywhere near a woman (still speaking metaphorically). These predominant qualities were thus transmitted to the progeny and a race of these picked men was thus produced. . . . Bye and bye the women got somewhat higher ideas and began picking the smartest fellows as well as the best looking. Ah! What a mistake! Slavery is incompatible with intelligence, and cunning was soon used as a means of throwing off the yoke. Brains were also transmitted and they predominated in male heads according to the law that confined antlers, tusks and spurs to that sex (*Glimpses*, IV, 127).

## THE FEMALE DETHRONED

Female devolution began when the male was transformed through her selective preferences into a colorful dandy as well as a brutal but chivalrous "he-man." In the human race, his title to supremacy is based upon his increased size and strength, and upon the religious edict that he was created first, and impliedly supplied the life-giving element. Science, however, discloses a different story. In animals as well as in mankind, when through male efflorescence he became the gaudier and the more powerful, he alone exercised sexual selection and affected her as she had affected him when she was the chooser. Her body and spirit, thenceforth, became molded in his image. He transferred to her most of his ornamental characters, for he no longer needed beauty and color to win her, and now sought those things in her. His superior strength was enough to dethrone her, and about the beginning of the historical period, she became the clinging vine and the parasitic camp follower, and practically exchanged places with him. Says Ward:

A new selection on the part of the men of the most beautiful wives has made a race of beautiful women. . . . The inference was that whatever man is he has been made through millions of years of sexual preference, by the female of his own species and the anthropoid and the other species from which he has sprung, and that it would be unfair for him to kick down the ladder by which he has climbed (*ibid.,* IV, 128).

The chief event that initiated her downfall in primitive society was the knowledge gained by the male, that childbirth was the result of sexual intercourse. There are still savage races alive today that attribute pregnancy to witchcraft. When the truth about the results of cohabitation dawned upon the primitive father, he found an excuse for claiming the chief honor of parentage, in the rite of the *couvade,* which is still practiced in various parts of the world. It consists in the man simulating her pains of childbirth. When the local medicine man is through treating both of them, the man waits for her recovery, and then rises from his "sick-bed" to point proudly to the baby to which he alone had given birth.

### VIRTUE

Under the matriarchate, the man was a puppet dangling from the woman's apron strings. But when he exercised equal dominion with her over their children, a comparison of strength became inevitable. As long as she had ruled and done the sexual selecting, her virtue was absolute. No man ever dreamed of forcing her any more than the male animal has ever forced an unwilling female. But when he assumed tyrannical mastery, he lost all respect for her natural wishes and feelings.

Primitive, man-ruled society then became patriarchal and polygamous. Female virtue was a thing of the past. True virtue, as Ward argues, does not mean mere refusal of sex relations, but willful selection by the female, her refusal to cohabit not only with the unfit but also with the fit, under circumstances undesirable to her. Thenceforth womanhood, so glibly called glorious and divine by

chivalrous men, was debased by her male adorers into a live commodity governed by supply and demand, forced to offer herself for
sale, in one way or another, for the privilege of remaining alive. She
became his chattel, and did all the menial work of the camp, while
he loafed or hunted or went to war. In time she lost her physical
prowess equally with her spirit and mental forces, and became a
hopeless drudge or clinging vine, often both at the same time.

## THE MAN-MADE WORLD

Ward takes the broad view that women's lowly status is due to
centuries upon centuries of subjection, and not to any inherent differences between the sexes. To keep her debased, the invention by the
man-made world of an aura of mysterious evil power that surrounds
her, is outdone only by the exaggerations of her intuition, lack of
reasoning power, and natural impediments. The misunderstanding
and misrepresentation of her rights and powers expanded on a world-
wide scale. Any desire on her part for equality or emancipation was
branded as unnatural and dangerous because it would develop a
race of female monstrosities, contrary to the laws of God and man.
Even modern high-minded advocates of social progress could see nothing wrong in the conventional relation of the sexes or in woman's
position in the world (see *ibid.*, IV, 227). Admitting her present
inferiorities, Ward argues that the cause of her lowly condition is
not what it seems to be. It is, in brief, her compulsory parasitic condition and not her natural inferiority that arrested her development
and evolved traits and characteristics, which, aided by her own sense
of inferiority, have since kept her debased (see *P.S.*, p. 376).

## WOMAN, THE EVIL ONE

Ward deplores but explains the gigantic errors and illusions in
which woman as a human being, like man, was all but lost from
view. In all the myths and legends of the race, the male rule has
seen to it that woman should be regarded as a puzzling creature, partly
divine and partly satanic, born only to love and to be loved. Male
prejudice has libeled her from time immemorial. Early Christianity
believed she was a creation of the Evil One. In Hebrew theology
she is excluded from heaven. Yahweh and his angels are all males,
but the imps are female, descended as they are from a rib of Adam.

The Mohammedan believes that woman has no soul, that she is like a snake, charming and venomous. The traditional epics of all Oriental literature, all Greek, Roman, and medieval thought, and much of the outlook of the Renaissance, teem with slurs and vilifications of woman as an evil being endowed with some sort of supernatural power; at best an incomprehensible and dangerous creature of a lower order.

Modern times did not abate her vilification. Rousseau, like Comte, thought of her only as a servile and loving consolation for man. Nietzsche warned us of her: "Thou goest to woman? Remember thy whip. Women are always cats and birds, or in the best case, cows."[2]

## THE SUBJECTION OF WOMAN

Ward treats her great subjection as a historical fact, and not as a theory. The evidence to support him is overwhelming, from the fall of the matriarchate down to the latest slander. Her story is a tragedy which darkens the history of all time (see *ibid.*, p. 346). Spencer bemoaned her brutal treatment which is utterly beyond the imagination, but Ward objects to this libel upon the brutes and says:

Far too many human sins are attributed to the brute that still lurks in man, but in this case, it is flagrantly unjust to do this, since no male brute maltreats the female, and the abuse of females by males is an exclusively human virtue (*ibid.*, p. 347).

The persecution of the Jew, the Negro, and the Mongol and the ostracism of the tramp or the leper have not been more vicious or deep-rooted than the mistreatment of woman. Inferior races and socially lower classes have often obtained some ray of hope, but for

[2] Even the liberal George Bernard Shaw has not hesitated to add to the slander by remarking: "The Eternal Feminine draws us ever upward and on—without getting us a step farther. Woman is the pursuer and the contriver; man, the pursued and disposed of."

As an example of what the brilliant best-selling literati think of women, the latest (John Erskine, *The Influence of Women,—and Its Cure*, 1936) shows irritation with the "weaker" sex, and seriously asserts under a camouflage of light and airy wit, that "society can get along perfectly without women except in that one matter of child-bearing." From across the sea, Professor Anthony M. Ludovici, Professor of Philosophy, London University, is a perfect model of male bombast. After a great deal of indictment and fulmination, he assures us that he has solved the riddle of woman as follows: Man is fundamentally a sadist and woman a masochist. Only by demanding service, sacrifice and surrender of her, can she be made normal and happy. All of which is on a par with Aristotle's profound idea that woman is a weaker being whose courage and virtue consist only in obedience, and whose silence is her chief glory.

women, there was none at all. Her bondage, like that of the slaves in Greece, was regarded as perfectly natural, and she herself was made to believe it, and look upon any criticism of her status as sheer blasphemy.

Anthropology reveals that in the golden age of woman's primitive dignity, she and her mate were both free. All property was held in common, both sexes shared in the labor of the group, and there was no motive for either to subject the other. She was queen, and ruled society until shortly before the dissolution of tribal communities. All history up to that time reflected her natural superiority and domination. In Homeric Greece, some of the chief gods were female, and all Greek children took the name of their mothers.

Then the matriarchate broke up in Greece about 1300 B.C. (see *Cape,* p. 128). Communal life disappeared; the women were carried off and enslaved to do all the hard labor. The ancient goddesses were replaced by male gods whose main attribute was physical strength.

When the economic foundations of clan life were undermined, the lands went to the strongest chiefs who acquired their own plots of ground, farm tools, and other means of production, and private property commenced to develop. Since property thenceforth belonged to the man, the father right was set up so that his wealth could be handed down to his heirs, and in order that no mistake be made as to who were his children, he compelled his wife to be absolutely faithful, while he remained a disciple of the double standard of sex morals.

Woman revolted, but she was outnumbered and defeated, as told in the legend of the Amazons. She remained a chattel and sexual commodity. To the free Greek of antiquity a wife was something better than a dog and a little dearer than a horse. She lived a harem life restricted to the management of the home, and of course, the bearing of children. In Sparta, "the perfect state," women were trained equally with men, but the master of the household loaned them to his visitors as freely as he would lend his dog. Was Aristotle justified in defining woman as "an unfinished male" any more than the leading English encyclopedia more than two thousand years later which described her as "the female of man; see man"?

Woman has had to overcome the incubus of the ages and live down her reputation as a temptress and destroyer of purity. In savagery her physical and mental powers were already stunted; in civilization they were further drained and inhibited. For countless generations, it was impossible for her to live on an equal footing with man. The handicaps imposed upon her were so great that she had no more opportunity to rise to man's status than a horse had to sit with the driver.

Conditions, laws, habits, and conventions continued to fix and exaggerate her inequality. For doing practically all of the manual labor, she received no more compensation or better food than a domestic animal. Even in modern days her wages for the same work as man's have always been arbitrarily less than his. When the laissez-faire system expanded political rights, she was still treated as man's private property and given scarcely any rights at all. When she rebelled and wrested some rights from his unwilling hands, she was expected to think and in all things act like her lord and master. In short, woman has been universally treated as the chattel of her father or husband, both of whom could legally drive and abuse her as if she were a beast of burden. Only during the last two centuries has she compelled society to give her some relief from being classed, as she was in the laws of many countries, the United States included, with infants, criminals, and lunatics.

Ward applied woman's status as a yardstick of civilization. Long before the Nazis were born, he placed Germany at the bottom of the scale, despite its *Kultur,* because of the attitude of the German people to womanhood, best typified by Frederick the Great: "Woman, go back into the house. An honest woman should keep indoors." The views of France, on the other hand, are civilized, said Ward, and far ahead of the Code Napoleon whose author not only approved of polygamy but believed that a husband should have absolute power of life and death over the actions and person of his spouse.

Nothing except the advance of civilization and her own efforts served to liberate her to the slightest extent. The belief that her salvation is to be found in marriage and the home is not supported by history. From the wife purchase in Homer's time to the modern marriage of convenience, the holy state of wedlock has tightened the bonds all the more. Undoubtedly it was of great importance in social evolution, as it secured variation and new blood strains for the promotion of social vigor. But as a benefit to woman, marriage was negligible, for it is an economic arrangement upon the basis of sex relations, and cannot be divorced from property relations. The true concept family appears in the Latin meaning of the word, servants or slaves. In the matriarchal regime there could be no family in the modern sense, because it could not be determined who was the father of any particular child (see *P.S.*, p. 351). When paternity became fixed and the male usurped the female throne, the children along with the mother, became the man's property, and the patriarch owned the lives and persons of his wives and children. Under those circumstances, true marriage was as impossible as in a harem of seals. All through the ages, the burden of unremitting toil was never removed from her shoulders whether she was slave, concubine, or wife. She was for all purposes her husband's property, bound to obey him or suffer the severest penalties. Modern conditions eased her bonds, but did not remove them.

The only help that woman has ever received has been from mother nature. To prevent promiscuity and race destruction, the group instinct of safety hedged marriage with all kinds of taboos, including the veiling and hiding of women from the sight of men. Although monogamy was a socially beneficent institution, prostitution (essentially a sterile form of marriage)—an economic rather than a purely immoral phenomenon—was never abolished by the marriage state. Since the reproductive forces are irrepressible, and there must be a limit to the number of children, in view of the ever important question of the food supply, promiscuity is the solution. On the other hand, race vigor has been kept up by group marriages, marriages by capture (of which the modern wedding tour is a vestige), and rape in which entire hordes engage. The result was always a leveling up of the race. Says Ward:

1. The women of any race will freely accept the men of a race which they regard as higher than their own.
2. The women of any race will vehemently reject the men of a race which they regard as lower than their own.
3. The men of any race will greatly prefer the women of a race which they regard as higher than their own.
4. The men of any race, in default of women of a higher race, will be content with women of a lower race (*ibid.*, p. 359).

In such generalizations is found an explanation of the inhuman "lynch law" by which white races seek to justify their running amok when men of a different color dare to cohabit with a white woman. Man-made laws, based upon a distortion of the clean and beneficent laws of nature, have never helped womankind (see *ibid.,* pp. 357-360). Only the emancipation of man will free woman of her ancient bondage. Free together, the sexes can make marriage a true copartnership, in which the personal element will be independent, the social element dependent, and the obligation reciprocal.

## WOMAN'S LACK OF ACHIEVEMENT

Ward does not deny that woman is conspicuous by her absence from achievement, especially in the arts and sciences. But when the arrogant male sex derides woman's weaker mental powers and her lack of achievement, the fact that she has been forcibly discouraged from using her brains is completely overlooked. He may be inferiority-haunted, but it is she who pays the price for his unnatural feeling. Brought up to be servile and dependent, she has actually been made unfit to achieve equally with him, and then dubbed superemotional, brainless, and infantile in the bargain.

How could her talents flourish when she was never given a chance to develop? If both thinking and achievement were made taboo for her, how could she contribute to the world's treasures? Whatever privileges she gained were grudgingly given to her as gifts, and not as matters of right. Until lately, she was shut out from all fields of commerce, art, and science, and whatever sparks of genius she possessed were smothered. When she did achieve something, it was done by more or less indirect means; by tact and finesse or through erotic outbursts of talent rather than by the steady, healthy force of free effort.

Grant Allen, among others, fiercely attacked Ward's position, and maintained that woman is naturally the intellectually inferior, since she relies mainly upon animal intuition rather than upon the reasoning faculty. Ward replied (see *Glimpses,* IV, 222) that female instinct was developed because of the dangers that beset her, and served to protect her young, guard her virtue, and detect her mate's infidelities. She had to think fast, or go under, and it did not take her long to learn the bitter lesson that the woman who deliberates is lost. Yet her mind, unaccustomed as it is to close reasoning, often comes nearer to correct conclusions than her spouse's more brilliant and logical intellect (see *D.S.,* II, 327).

Considering the resources of society, the omission of the female factor is shocking, claims Ward. Not only has she not dared to raise her voice about the laws that control her life and the lives of her children, but the prevalent male view (largely shared by her) has served as a wet blanket upon all her ambitions and creative powers (see *App. S.,* p. 231). He has been given some sort of mental food by way of education, while all she received was mental pap and assurances that all she needed was love, romance, and chivalry.

Education is for all, and its only limit is mental capacity. At a time when there were no institutions of higher learning for women anywhere in the United States, Ward wrote in his unpublished work "Education":

As to the education of women, there is but one thing to be ascertained. This is, whether women have minds. The true educationalist knows no sex any more than he knows rank, color or stature. He sees only mind. Show that men have a right to knowledge and you have shown that women have the same right. . . .

I am tired of this one-sided civilization, this half-built society, of this false chivalry, this mock modesty, this pretended regard which one sex assumes for the other, while loads of putrid prejudice hang upon woman's neck (pp. 163-180).

Man throws her lack of achievement constantly into woman's face, as conclusive proof of her natural inferiority. But her life has suffered from indoor occupations, lack of training and opportunity, and an unbearable mountain-load of legal restrictions and social burdens. Sheltered and surrounded by the trivia of domestic life, she could not help becoming more flippant and superficial than her mate, whose contacts and experience were so much broader.

The fact that woman was almost exclusively the inventor in primitive ages but has achieved less and less as time went on, is not a welcome truth to the male world. Ward asked the straightforward question: "Was it not her subjection that was the cause of her lack of achievement?" In view of her abuse, discrimination, and lack of incentive and opportunity, it is a wonder that she achieved anything at all. The masculine world simply monopolized all human activities except the drudgery that it was pleased to call "woman's work." In Ward's own words:

John Stuart Mill justly said that women had had no chance to show what they could do; that they were not professionally trained for anything as men are; that they were therefore virtually all amateurs, and that the only just comparison would be of all women with amateur men. Such a comparison would certainly be creditable to women, for it may be said of amateur men much more truly than of women as a whole, that they have accomplished nothing in the work of the world (*Glimpses,* VI, 355).

## WOMAN'S EMANCIPATION

Comte's ideas upon womanhood in comparison with Ward's are amazingly backward. The least suggestion of female emancipation sounds to Comte like rank anarchy. He construes her mission in life to be strictly the office of sentiment, for she is the symbol of affection, as man is of force. And so Comte believes that she ought not to work except in her domestic sphere; that man is bound to support her and she, in turn, must obey him implicitly, and quotes Aristotle's discovery that "woman's force is best shown in surmounting the difficulty of obedience."

Ward, on the contrary, was the first American philosopher to advocate woman's right to equal opportunities with man (see *Cape,* pp. 132-134). His pioneer labors in her behalf gave the necessary scientific impetus to the feminist movement, and put the United States in the front rank of civilized nations. His demand that society return to nature's view of woman as the original, superior sex, and restore her, not to her ancient throne, but to her position as a free, achieving human being beside her spouse—this demand virtually sounded the knell of a social revolution heard round the world. Said Ward:

Civilization demands this revolution. . . . Woman is half of mankind. Civilization and progress have hitherto been carried forward by the male half alone. Labor and production are now also suffering from the same cause. It is high time that all the forces of society were brought into action, and it is especially necessary that those vast, complementary forces which woman alone can yield be given free rein, and the whole machinery of society be set into full and harmonious operation (*D.S.,* I, 657).

If women were the recognized social equals of men, we should see a very different state of society from that which now exists . . . men and women wearing nearly or quite the same kind of dress . . . performing substantially the same duties . . . pastimes, recreations and pleasures. If the equality of the sexes were recognized, we should see both sexes educated alike . . . both accorded the same rights, not only in political affairs. Under the head of rights may be ranged all the sexual inequalities, still higher rights. It is the right to themselves, the right of controlling their own persons, the possession of their own bodies (*ibid.,* pp. 650-655).

## THE FUTURE OF WOMAN

Both in his sex philosophy and in his philosophy of progress, Ward came to the same conclusion that in a sociocracy, society will be able to return to the fundamentals of the free, natural life, without discarding any acquired knowledge and experience. With the return of the golden age of co-operation, sex will inexorably take on a new meaning, and woman will be regarded as the social equal of man. Ward's piercing analysis was not made in vain. Cultural progress owes him much for working a change in the world's sex ideas. Though woman has had to combat all the organized forces of society, the future belongs to her. And in that future she will not be less feminine but more of a human being whose moral and intellectual beauty will come, as it does now in man, before physical charm or fictitious virtue.

In an article entitled "The Exemption of Women from Labor," Ward replied to the plea for the complete abstinence of woman from bread-winning labor, as follows:

The effort of a fully self-conscious intelligence as it exists in the most enlightened types of mankind is to preserve all that is best in woman, to heighten to the utmost that aesthetic attribute through which she has ennobled man and made him what he is. . . . The progress of civilization has wrought a change in the aesthetic tastes of mankind, and while physical beauty has lost none of its charm, moral and intellectual beauty have come to hold the first place, and true companionship can only be found in the harmonious union of these three. Such a combination in woman can only be secured through a life of interested activity which unites the exercise of all the faculties with the acquirement of both knowledge and the good things of this world. Agreeable productive labor is the highest and only true source of happiness and worth, whether for man or woman (*Glimpses,* V, 108).

Although woman has barely begun to throw off her fetters, she has wrested from a reluctant male world within a brief century the opportunities to advance from domestic into social relationships. While men are still polite to her in public places, and exploit her mercilessly at home and at work, the idea is gaining ground that she is neither an incubator nor an altar. Comte's suggestion that she must be treated as a loving child is disappearing as the doors of achievement are opening to her and the feminization of society in the fundamental and not in the conventional sense is gathering speed. The woman's movement, no less than the labor or the people's movements, constitutes a step forward into a new world whose future is already visible. The downward curve of her flight across the pages of history surely can go no further; the upward trend is already marked. Soon both sexes will stand upon a higher plane than either has ever occupied, free to rule themselves. The philosophy of Tolstoy and Weininger that woman should become man, is fading out. Woman's progress has become a harbinger of a world of two sexes, instead of one.

The details and adjustments of woman's future position in society belong to the future. Nothing that is really fine and worthy in her will be destroyed by social progress, but the essentially feminine will be gathered into a complete and enduring human synthesis with the essentially masculine. Kant's prophecy that woman will never give up her secret becomes sheer nonsense as sociology penetrates into the scientific aspects of both man and woman as parts of the social synthesis. Ward's thought is truly prophetic when he says:

Accepting evolution as we must, recognizing heredity as the distinctive attribute of the female sex, it becomes clear that it must be from the steady advance of woman rather than from the uncertain fluctuations of man that the sure and solid progress of the future is to come. The attempt to move the whole race forward by elevating only the sex that represents the principle of instability has long enough been tried. . . . The way to civilize the race is to civilize woman. And now, thanks to science, we see why this is so.

Woman is the unchanging trunk of the great genealogic tree, while man, with all his vaunted superiority is but a branch, a grafted scion, as it were, whose acquired qualities die with the individual, while those of woman are handed on to futurity. Woman *is* the race, and the race can be raised up only as she is raised up. There is no fixed rule by which nature has intended that one sex should excel the other, any more than there is any fixed point beyond which either cannot further develop. Nature has no intentions, and evolution has no limits. True science teaches that the elevation of woman is the only sure road to the evolution of man (*Glimpses,* IV, 138-139).

Such is the practically unknown story of woman's debasement from the position that nature gave her as mother and queen of the race. Such is the world error of male superiority which has kept her in subjection. Like the force of individualism, male supremacy has attained the proportions of a social structure, but both are already crumbling before the sweeping advance of social science.

The truth will never recede before the superficial and the apparent. Ward surveyed the mountain of facts concerning sex, and opened the world's eyes to new vistas lying beyond male prejudice and sex dogma. The genius of initiating the new view of womanhood belongs to him. For that alone, many would place his name beside Darwin and Spencer in biology, and Freud and Ellis in sexology.

# BOOK XIV. THE ENVIRONMENTALIST

*"My researches show that nurture is more important than nature. There are 19 causes which favor the production of savants in any country, and heredity is only one of them."*
—Alphonse de Candolle

*"The equalization of opportunity means the equalization of intelligence, and not until this is attained is there any virtue or any hope in schemes for the equalization of the material resources of society."*—Ward

*"The welfare of mankind primarily depends on the correct knowledge of the world in which we live and of human nature."*—William Graham Sumner

Chapter XXXII

# HEREDITY AND
# ENVIRONMENT

---

*"The environment represents opposition, not an active antagonism. It is man that is active. His will guided by his intellect is ever pressing against the environment, and compels the very powers that at first opposed his progress to serve his interests and supplement his own powers. It is this that constitutes civilization."*

*"If left to itself the mind will receive only the germs that float about at random. Different kinds of weeds will spring up. . . . Such is the environment of nature. But the seed may be carefully selected and only the most useful kinds allowed to grow."*—Ward

---

AFTER SEEING WHAT nature and man have done to and for the female, we enter the human laboratory to note how both men and women are molded by the forces of heredity and environment. Wherein lies the improvement and happiness of the race, in biology or education? in nature or nurture? in eugenics or opportunity? That is the question which society must solve, fundamentally and finally.

To the sociologist, race is more important than nation, class, sect, or individual. Since the biological and psychological bases determine the social superstructure, we must inquire into man's inner structure (heredity) as well as his surroundings (environment) and learn how each may be employed to build a better and happier social order.

### THE HEREDITY FETISH

Had Ward contributed to the survey of the relationship between man and nature the sole discovery that nature and the hereditary forces have been glorified and exaggerated at the expense of man and the environmental forces, he would deserve our eternal gratitude. Other sociologists have shed little light on such problems as: What must we do to raise the general physical and spiritual level of mankind? What kind of human beings does nature develop when she is let alone? What can we achieve in the production of human material by taking charge of nature's process? The reason is that almost everybody believes that heredity is the more important because it is an unchangeable force flowing from the Creator, while environment or the effect of outer circumstances upon human life is secondary and transient, and comparatively negligible, in effect.

How can conditions, as varied and uncertain as the play of a frisky kitten, have any permanent effect upon human evolution? ask both layman and scientist. The biologist who worships heredity does exactly what the layman does when he worships God; when he takes the easiest way out and solves the problem of human development by referring everything—causes, materials, forces, and results— to an all-wise and all-powerful Creator.

## ENVIRONMENT

Ward never denies or belittles the natural power of heredity. But he is one of the few sociologists to take up the cudgels for the effects of the environment. He sees it as man's occupation, education, family, milieu—the things that he sees, hears, does, and thinks. It is as passive and as pliable as putty, and without it, we would be the eternal and powerless slaves of nature, doomed to go through life with only what we brought into it from the great beyond. If, however, the environmental forces can influence the natural process, then man is truly the monarch of all he surveys, and by making his own environment, he can practically recreate himself and all the world with him (see *App. S.,* Chapter VIII).

### HEREDITY IS THE TOTAL OF PAST ENVIRONMENTS

Because of the influence of religion and the worship of natural forces as the expressions of supernatural power, individualistic society has held mainly to the view that men are impotent clay in the hands of an omnipotent nature or divinity, and that social evolution is unchangeable and uncontrollable by any act of man. Ward wrote *Applied Sociology* to offset the depressing effect of such a credo, and to show that heredity is not a spontaneous, immutable force, but the sum total of past environments. Nature furnishes the material; man is the master builder.

As we trace back the history of life, the force of heredity becomes deeper rooted, says Ward. As we go forward, it appears weaker and less stable. In plants, heredity is stronger than in animals because nature took so much longer to affix the hereditary factors in the vegetable kingdom. The more animals are susceptible to the forces of the environment the weaker becomes the force of heredity. In human beings, heredity is constantly challenged by the force of outer circumstances, until heredity itself seems to depend upon the influence of the environment instead of upon any mysterious forces of transmission. The belief is justified, says Ward, that the entire path of heredity, physical as well as mental, is not of its own making, but is one that is trodden out by circumstances, i.e., experiences in the environment (see *Glimpses,* IV, 252).

## VARIATION AND ENVIRONMENT

Ward's study of biological variation leads to the conclusion that environment plays a much more important role in biological evolution than is commonly assigned to it. All things, living and non-living, are composed of the same atoms. The natural laws which underlie their combination to form different substances are also constant. What then determines whether those atoms will develop into a rock, a tree, or a man?

Ward was one of the first scientist-philosophers to express dissatisfaction with the theory of natural selection as a complete explanation of the origin of species, and to supplement that theory by the hypothesis of variation. Natural selection stresses survival, not variation, and does not answer the question why there are departures from type.

The law of heredity is simplicity itself—like begets like. But its deeper significance lies in the fact that no two species or organisms, even of the same kind, are exactly alike. Nature insists on variety but manufactures it, Ward claims, not in the sex germs, but in the host of minute differences in the environment. Outer stimuli, no two of which are alike, impinge on the organism with the regularity of water dropping upon a stone. The organism seeks to adapt itself to every new condition in two ways: (1) by the natural method of evolution; (2) through the artificial results of its own acts. Adaptation is the most powerful means of overcoming obstacles to survival. The more sensitive the organism, the more readily it takes the outer impressions, as if they were rays of light on a photographer's plate. Variation is due wholly to environment and results in the myriad kinds, shapes, colors, qualities, and properties which make up the universal panorama.

Ward and De Vries, as we have seen (see p. 39), independently of each other, discovered mutations or chance variations. Ward alone saw the value to sociology of that theory—evolution proceeding by leaps and bounds through the influence of the environment to produce a variation. Darwin paid little attention to "sports" or monstrosities because they did not seem to be of any importance in evolution. But Ward's theory of mutations opened the door to the amazing possibility of producing improved species through artificial means instead of by the slow method of nature. Variations which appear so suddenly that they seem to be the result of a jump or short circuit of the hereditary force are really the effects of environmental influences stored up in past heredities, and then released (see *P.S.*, pp. 241-243, 499-500).[1]

## ARE ACQUIRED CHARACTERISTICS INHERITED?

The question whether human traits and talents are inherited or whether they must be acquired anew by each person from his experience in the environment is of paramount importance. Lamarck's answer was that structure follows function. The organization of a fish speaks of water; that of a bird, no less plainly of the air. The human foot implies the existence of solid ground, and the eye does the same for light. By stretching to reach for its dinner of leaves, the giraffe's neck grows longer and becomes an inheritable characteristic. Every organism has the urge to fit itself into surrounding conditions. Thus, sea animals discarded their fins for feet, and their gills for lungs, when they left the sea to live on land, and developed wings when they tried to fly. All such acquired characters were inherited.

[1] Ward appears to be right in choosing the environment as a satisfactory medium for research rather than the heredity bodies in the sex cells. All of those bodies belonging to two billion people of the next generation could be packed into a one gallon pitcher, and "the heredity substance of both eggs and sperm together would form just one tablet of the size of an aspirin tablet" (*Out of the Night*, by H. J. Muller, 1936).

Research (after Ward) dug into those tiny universes and brought to light the infinitesimal particles, the self-propagating genes or atoms of heredity which lie within the visible chromosomes or color bodies of the sex cells. But no one yet knows why the genes should keep on dividing indefinitely and still retain their properties, or why they should hand down the spark of life and evolve into different organisms. Scientists have developed a frog without the aid of a father, and a starfish without the help of a mother, but they have not yet discovered how a seemingly lifeless speck in a sex cell can start the current of life flowing into matter, and pass its own properties onward.

Darwin, on the other hand, differed from Lamarck and laid greater stress upon the force of natural selection. Only the giraffes with the longer necks survived; the short-necked one starved and died out, said Darwin. With him stood Weismann and his germ plasm theory, Mendel with his famous experiments in plant and animal breeding, and in general, those scientists who believed in the importance of mental heredity, the invariability of the social future, and the necessarily slow nature of progress. Opposed to them and siding with Lamarck were those who emphasized the vital importance of habits and institutions, and who believed that progress is cataclysmic because the organism is plastic.

Ward's analysis of Weismann's germ plasm theory shattered the neo-Darwinian position and uncovered the absurdity of Weismann's denial of heredity to acquired characteristics. He divides the organism into two parts that never can meet: (1) the germ plasm or immortal and unchangeable sex cells; (2) the somaplasm or the perishable and constantly changing body cells. No physical qualities that were not already in the sex cells from which a person is born, said Weismann (Galton believed the same about mental conditions), could possibly be acquired by the individual in his lifetime. Of course, Weismann did not altogether deny that new traits could be evolved, but he felt certain that they would be due to internal causes, independent of conditions outside the sex cells. To him, the universe outside the organism, in general, and the body in particular, was nature's medium of insuring the continuance of life. The body is merely a protective storehouse for the sex cells (see *Glimpses,* IV, 246, 385; V, 117).

To believe that these cells can reproduce only themselves and not change or give birth to body cells would lead to the strange conclusion, says Ward, that the seed of every person is the same as that of his ancestors back to the mythical Adam. It is not at all certain that body cells cannot develop into sex cells, or at least directly modify them. Training, education, experience, habit, all may cause changes in the body due to contact with the environment and so affect the sex cells that those changes will be transmitted in the blood stream.[2]

[2] A young plant leans to the light as naturally as a child sees through its elders. A chick one day old will run to the cover of the mother's wing when the hawk's shadow is seen from above, and a kitten with eyes barely opened will arch its back at the first dog it meets. A bell rung three hundred times will teach a mouse

Weismann never did explain by an iota of fact how variations occur. He even denied that secondary sexual characteristics are the result of natural selection, but assumed that they are due to an essential maleness or femaleness in the sex cells. Such rigid theories blinded him to the plain fact that changes and exchanges were constantly going on in nature and man. New characteristics are being created outside the sex cells at every step. The human clay pile is continually being molded by outer circumstances.

Weismann asserts that since internal conditions alone are responsible for the development of the embryo, every individual is born with a ready-made set of mental and physical traits. If this is so, replies Ward, a child's future would be relatively unimportant, for whatever characters it acquired in life and whatever changes it underwent through experience would not be transmitted, but would die with the body. The hereditarians base their conclusions upon Weissmann and insist that criminals are born not made. If you cannot bring genius with you from the mother's womb, you will be a mediocrity or worse, no matter what your training or general environment will be. Since nature is supreme and almighty, man is powerless to change the course and method of heredity any more than he can make a silk purse out of a sow's ear.[3]

---

to run to its dinner, but its offspring can be taught the same trick after the bell rings only five to ten times.

[3] Modern science has produced silk from plants. Who knows what it will produce from animal matter? Since Ward's death, experiments have effected miracles equal to that of the sow's-ear-silk-purse. Professor H. J. Muller of the University of Texas (now at Leningrad University) subjected the sex cells of fruit flies to X-rays and radium, working directly upon the chromosomes which carry the genes or hereditary characters of the insect. He produced one hundred distinct mutations, made evolution work 15,000 per cent faster than it does in nature, and in a single year obtained physical modifications which would have taken nature at least one hundred and fifty years to produce. Flies (many of them monstrosities) were practically created with numerous surprising variations of organ, size, form, color, and function, and a definite technique for increasing the number of genes in the fly's sex cells was discovered. "Man should be able to improve vastly upon nature's results," said Dr. Muller, "now that he knows more about the way of the gene" (New York Times, March 29, 1936).

The 1937 meeting of the British Association for Advancement of Science, Sir Edward Poulton delivering the presidential address, was reported as follows by the New York Times (Sept. 2, 1937):

"Recent evidence of the existence of 'prophetic instincts' among living creatures of the lower orders on an evolutionary scale offers incontrovertible proof in favor of Darwin's theory of natural selection as the underlying cause in the process of evolution. . . . These prophetic instincts, which enable the larva of certain insects to avoid future dangers and prepare in advance elaborate defenses against natural

## TENDENCIES ARE INHERITED

Ward vigorously opposes the bombastic attitude of the hereditarians in the field of human evolution which insists that "it can't
be done." Human conditions and circumstances, they claim, are as
uncertain as the wind; the forces of heredity are as stable and reliable as
nature herself. But, asks Ward, who can believe that genius, for example, can be traced back to the sex cells of some super-Adam in an
unbroken chain of descent? Training and education, surely, have had

---

enemies that they have never met, Sir Edward declared, settle at last the long-
standing controversy between the two great schools of evolution—namely Darwin's
and Lamarck's—in favor of the former.

"The followers of Lamarck regard the evolutionary process as largely determined
by the inheritance of acquired characters. The Darwinians hold that organic evolution is the result of natural selection by elimination of the unfit and the survival of
the fittest."

" 'I would ask any believer in Lamarckian evolution or in the theory of un-
concious memory residing in the germ cell how it would be possible to explain
these prophetic instincts, adapted not to meet but to avoid future experience, except
by the operation of natural selection,' said Sir Edward, continuing:

" 'I venture to bring forward certain observations opposed to a belief in Lamarckian evolution by means of inherited experience. In the relationship between
enemy and prey, there is very commonly no opportunity for the latter to learn by
experience. The wonderfully elaborate adaptations by which sedentary insects are
hidden from enemies have been evolved, not by experience of enemies but by avoidance of enemies. . . .' Sir Edward summed up present views on non-inheritance
of acquired characters by quoting from an address of Professor Ray Lankester at a
previous meeting of the association, as follows:

"Educability can be transmitted; it is a congenital character. But the results of
education cannot be transmitted. In each generation they have to be acquired afresh."

"On the other hand, the nerve mechanisms of instinct are transmitted and owe
their inferiority as compared with the results of education to the very fact that
they are not acquired by the individual in relation to his particular needs, but have
arisen by the selection of congenital variation in a long series of preceding generations.

"The effect of Lamarck's laws on hereditary transmission of acquired characteristics would be this: a past of indefinite duration is powerless to control the present,
while a brief history of the present can readily control the future.

"The vital conclusion that the results of education cannot be transmitted by
heredity deeply concerns human life," Sir Edward said. However, he added that
"while it was now accepted by nearly all biologists, it is not appreciated as it ought
to be by the general public. . . . Yet any human being transported as a baby from
his own country to another and brought up there among the natives will learn
to speak as they speak. All the past generations, however many, during which his
ancestors spoke the language of his birthplace will count for nothing, will not
retard his acquisition of another tongue or modify it in any way." . . . Sir Edward
concluded his notable address, as follows:

"If, as we are all coming to believe, the hidden powers within are inherited
while the results of their development are not, then there is no easing of the burden
with the passage of time, but each generation afresh must bear the heavy responsibility
of conducting this development in the best way so that its successor may be able to
meet the changing and at this time, the increasing needs."

something to do with the qualities and talents of mankind, at least more than hereditarians will admit. Granting that there is no direct evidence that our social heritage, i.e., our knowledge, skill, art, and culture, has been inherited in the same way as our biological heritage. Yet, while knowledge must be acquired by everyone for himself, there is an inheritance of tendencies along the road laid down in the brain (see *Glimpses,* IV, 252).

The inclination of the Arab is to be a wanderer, of the New Yorker, to be a city dweller. In a family of ministers and scholars, the chances are that the offspring will not have business as a prime ambition. Although no child directly inherits the manual or mental skill of its parents, adaptability is transmitted all along the line. The children of musicians are not necessarily musicians, but the capacity for mastering music is generally inherited in musical families. Tendencies are inherited by entire nations. The ethical cast of the Hebrew, the talent for music and sculpture in the Italians, and the German leaning toward philosophy are indisputable evidence of inherited tendencies.

## CO-OPERATION OF HEREDITY AND ENVIRONMENT

Just as seed, soil, and air play their roles in the synthetic process of producing a flower, so the sex cells, the physical body, and the environment interact to fashion the human being. The bald question which is more important, environment or heredity, is meaningless. The real problem is not their comparative importance, but the degree in which either operates in any given case. Nature and man toss them back and forth in an unceasing game of conflict, co-operation, and synergy. The interaction of heredity and environment, like the balancing of all other forces, brings about a teamwork of energies which mold all organisms, including man. Says Ward:

The role of the environment is not to produce or to determine civilization. It is not an active agent but a passive condition. It represents opposition which is not an active antagonism. It is in the nature of a passive obstruction to man's activities. It is man that is active. His will guided by his intellect is ever pressing against the environment. In the more advanced stages, he transforms it, utilizes it, subjects it to his service, and compels the very powers that at first opposed his progress to serve his interests and supplement his own powers. It is this that constitutes civilization, and to the original natural environment, there is now added an artificial environment of his own creation. This is of far greater vital importance to him than his natural environment, the physical world into which he is born. Yet to this human action, the environment opposes its *reaction*, and it is this interaction of man and his environment, or *synergy* that accomplishes the results (*App. S.*, p. 131).

The earth itself is obviously closely related to man. In the Rocky Mountains, his struggle with the natural environment determines the trend of his whole being. In a large city, he is generally of a different type—physically and intellectually. And so with all the other factors which constitute the environment. It is fair to conclude that the environment alters the intellectual and hereditary development and vice versa, in a continual organic interplay of forces.

It is as yet impossible to draw any line between the respective domains of heredity and environment, because we do not know definitely which particular part of the sex cells represents a corresponding special characteristic of brain or body. All characteristics seem to be due to both factors in co-operation—to heredity, because it covers the germinal material and causes changes in the organism which are parallel with any alteration of that material; and to environment, because the characteristics are conditioned upon development, and are affected by every modification in the surroundings.

## NATURE AND NURTURE

To say that any human trait is directly present in the sex cells would be as true as observing that Shakespeare can be found in the dictionary. Inheritance brings everybody certain abilities, but the environment alone decides whether the ability will be used to write a poem or shoot a gun. Heredity is the canvas and the brush. Environment decides what shall be painted, a comic strip or a Mona Lisa. Admittedly, the natural force of heredity cannot be changed or abolished. But, claims Ward, it can be directed and controlled. While that is being gradually achieved by science, the environment becomes more evident in nurture, the nursing of nature's forces and materials in the interests of man. Nurture is a process or function of the universal energy which is coiled up like an electric spring in the box of circumstance, waiting only to be released by human hands to change everything, including the force of heredity. Heredity may be compared to gravitation, and environment to the ball tossed into the air. Gravitation is not abolished when the ball travels upward, but is held in check according to the force exerted.

## THE SOCIOLOGICAL IMPORTANCE OF THE ENVIRONMENT

Thus far, mankind has acted as if the best chance for solving its problems lay in improving the natural environment rather than the economic or social environment. Wars, depressions, and a general feeling of insecurity have evidenced the failure of such a method. Sociology alone can free us of any obsession that heredity is an overpowering fate which pursues man from before the cradle until after the grave. Sociology studies and treats heredity like any natural force, and concentrates its attention more and more upon the neglected factor of the environment.

The argument from heredity is that nothing stimulates achievement as much as the thought that all our achievements, large or small, will be transmitted to posterity. Since none of our efforts outlives us (here is the cue for the entry of the rugged individualist), anything we may do to improve society is futile, for everything must be left to nature and the chances of direct survival. Ergo, concludes the hereditarian, do nothing about social conditions, since nothing can be done.

Only one whose eyes are shut to science and history can fail to note the utter bankruptcy of thought and action which is latent in such a defeatist creed. The heredity fetish is being constantly discredited by human development through environmental influences such as intermarriage, contacts with alien races, economic reform, and, above all, education. Owen, the sociologist, and not Rousseau, the romanticist, was right. Man's character is not made *for* him, but *by* him. His pride and his fall are due not to what he brings into the world at birth, but to what he does with himself and his world, after that.

And so Ward once more lifts the curtain on the human Punch-and-Judy show to exhibit the figures which are not moved by remote control, by inherited genius or inherited sin, but by the direct influences of knowledge, science, economics, and education. Gradually, it becomes clear that we need no longer pray for a good inheritance or blindly try to adapt ourselves to nature, but that we can compel the natural world to adapt itself and its forces to us. We discover, in other words, that man can make his own history and his own environment out of the material furnished by nature, outside of the sex cells.

Ward's study of the environment (discussed in detail in the next chapter) does not lead him to behaviorism, or to Locke's position that the mind at birth is a blank slate upon which only conditions may write, and necessarily remains so because man is molded solely by his physical reactions and not by his ideas. To Ward, the simile of Locke's *tabula rasa* limps badly and the only correct analogy is to call the brain a virgin, unseeded soil. The quality of the soil is heredity. The character of the seeds may vary greatly, but that many seeds will fall upon it is certain, for the air is full of them. These represent experience. In Ward's words:

If left entirely to itself, such a mind will receive only the germs that float about at random, and become stocked with all manner of germs comparable to molds and algae. Different kinds of weeds will spring up, choke out one another, and leave the mastery to those that possess the greatest vitality, although they may be coarse, noxious and worthless. Such is the environment of nature.

But the seed may be carefully selected and only the most useful kinds allowed to grow. Careful tillage may destroy the low, useless growths and leave the useful plants to flourish without competition and bear rich and abundant fruit. This is nurture and represents a favorable educational environment. Where careful nurture is applied to a rich soil we have the condition of talent or even of genius (*App. S.*, p. 237).

Sociology has done away with an imaginary, transcendental world, ruled by hereditary forces, a world which we can no more affect than we can move the Alps with our bare hands. Through science, however, both the forces of heredity and environment, of nature and of nurture, can be controlled, to the advantage of mankind. Nature and her forces are eternal, but in one of them, the human mind, she has evolved a power which is able to subject all the other forces to its will. By the mind force applied to the improvement of the environment, we can fashion mankind as we desire, and mold the social domain nearer to our heart's desire.

# CHAPTER XXXIII

# GENIUS

---

*"Le génie est dans les choses et non dans l'homme. L'homme n'est que l'accident qui permet au génie de se dégager."*—Alfred Odin

*"Only when genius is married to science can the highest results be produced."*—Herbert Spencer

*"This exalted faculty of invention, both in its mental and its physical aspects—is susceptible of cultivation in the same manner and to the same degree as all other human faculties. It can be increased by education to any desired degree."*—Ward

---

Our journey through heredity and environment has brought us to the enticing field of genius. If man is able to adapt nature to him, by controlling the environment and his own mold, why can he not create conditions in which genius will flourish as abundantly as any plant? The affirmative answer forms the basis of Ward's philosophy of genius.

### THE "MYSTERY" OF GENIUS

By transferring the subject of human talents from the sentimental and metaphysical "divine-gifts-of-the-man-in-a-million" stage to the scientific fields of heredity and environment, Ward removes the saccharine adoration and awe-inspiring mystery with which the subject of genius has been surrounded. What is genius? Goethe said it was application; Weininger, memory. Ward defines it as "the focalization of psychic power," just plain brains (see *Cape,* p. 92; *P.S.,* p. 36). As his study of its social implications deepened, his concept of it grew wider:

Genius is something more than intelligence, intelligence is intellect plus knowledge. Genius is intellect plus character. Ability is intelligence plus character. The difference between ability and genius is the unknown quantity that we are seeking (*App. S.,* p. 115).

We are not concerned here with abnormal or pathological talent. Children of six who compose symphonies or chess problems are not unimpeachable witnesses to the inheritance of genius. Nor is eccentricity evidence of genius, abnormal or otherwise. Genius and insanity are not related, and each has a different origin.[1] What if Kant was unable to write unless he could look out of his window at a ruined tower, or Hawthorne had to cut up bits of paper, or Edgar Saltus did his best work only when he wore a blue dressing gown and was surrounded by white cats? Ward explains personal peculiarities of emancipated minds by the fact that the exercise of the intellect for many ages developed talents of a high order which were literally invested in disinterested and nonadvantageous activities. Such minds finally become independent, differ from the average type, and develop eccentricities which are analogous to the erratic coloration acquired by animals under domestication. Says he:

The real élite of mankind, not the wealthy or the influential, but those who use their reason most and who possess the largest stock of both knowledge and ideas, will not slavishly follow the herd, and do just such things as lead the mass of mankind to look upon them with suspicion. They rise above both gain and fashion, and persistently violate the code of social action and rules of propriety (*P.S.,* p. 503).

## THE ORIGIN AND DEVELOPMENT OF GENIUS

If Weismann, Galton, and the other hereditarians are right, genius is not an acquired characteristic but is strictly and essentially a product of heredity. Following that conclusion from its source to its legitimate end, one comes to the *reductio ad absurdum* that all extant genius was contained full grown in the sex cells of the "first" propagating couple.

Ward believes that genius, like other human qualities, is made, not born. Cases of "sports," of some overwhelming genius unlike anyone in his ancestry, are ascribable to a special concentration of the piled-up abilities of a long line of ancestors. The result may be as astonishing as coming across a one-horned bull. One thing is certain: genius is neither an accident nor a miracle but the result of definite causes, which, according to Ward, are principally environmental, and only secondarily hereditarian (see *ibid.,* p. 442).

Genius appears in all the paths and products of mind force, through inventions, art, science, and philosophy (see *Ps. F.,* Part II). In the earlier stages of human development, when action was chiefly

[1] Insanity is traceable in less than 5 per cent of the families of geniuses (see *A Study of British Genius,* by Havelock Ellis, 2d ed., p. 172).

instinctive, genius was egoistic. Later, when the intellect became fully developed, the passion arose for achievement for its own sake (see *P.S.*, p. 495). In scientific genius ("retrospective prophecy") and philosophic genius, the pleasure of discovering and spreading the truth is its own greatest reward.

## GENIUS AND FAME

Fame is often mistaken for genius, and the conceptions of greatness are dim and confused. Are they great who fill high offices, possess much wealth, win great battles, swim the English Channel, or copy Genesis on the back of a postage stamp? Napoleon was neithei a true genius nor the greatest man of his time, yet he is perhaps the most famous man in history. Popular heroes are rarely able people, and hardly the great minds or the progressive spirits needed for permanent achievement. Those who fill the headlines of the daily press are generally famous characters who would have made the world happier if they had never been born. Besides, the famous in history are at best mere pawns on the social chessboard, and one set of men is as good as another for the social forces which move them around.[2] Says Ward:

The above is true of all public functionaries. Their high position is mistaken for superior ability. . . . It often happens that a statesman is regarded as absolutely indispensable and as the savior of his country, when in fact he has only ordinary abilities but happens to hold a high place at a critical period. Sometimes there is afforded proof that he was not really needed, as in the case of Bismarck.

[2] Ward's contemporary, the eminent sociologist Charles Horton Cooley, late professor of sociology in the University of Michigan, was one of the few who agreed with Ward's concept of genius: "Genius is that aptitude for greatness that is born in a man; fame is the recognition by men that greatness has been achieved. Between the two lie early nurture and training, schools, the influence of friends and books, opportunities, and in short the whole working of organized society upon the individual. One is biological, the other social; to produce geniuses is a function of race, to allot fame is a function of history" (*Sociological Theory and Social Research,* 1930, p. 121).

"The relation between genius and fame is fairly well represented by the comparison of a farmer sowing mixed seeds in a furrow which traverses a great variety of ground. Here many come up and flourish, there none, and there again, only those of a certain sort. The seed-bag is the race, the soil historical conditions other than race, the seeds genius, and the crop fame. That the amount of natural ability produced from a given stock is approximately constant is certainly the simplest supposition and it would seem reasonable to accept it until the contrary is shown (*ibid.,* pp. 158-159).

After he steps down, the country goes on as before. The superiority even of military officers is usually exaggerated (*App. S.,* pp. 134-135).

## THE DISTRIBUTION OF GENIUS

Aside from the proportion of the subnormal, the mediocre, and the talented in society, what is the output of genius? Is Comte's estimate of only 558 great men in all history in the seven fields of religion, philosophy, poetry, statesmanship, war, industry, and science a correct one? Or is Professor Giddings' computation to be accepted that in the twenty-two centuries between the age of Pericles and the middle of the nineteenth century there was but one distinguished, though not necessarily talented, person for every four hundred and fifty thousand people?

Galton, speaking for England, concluded that for high-grade talent, there were two hundred and fifty (at least fifty years old) in every million of population or one to every four thousand males. Ward adopts the figures in Odin's *Genèse des grands hommes* (1895) of about two geniuses in every one hundred thousand population, but concludes that by reasonable improvement in the environment, genius could be multiplied at least a hundredfold to run two hundred to every one hundred thousand, or one to every five hundred (see *App. S.,* Chapter X).

## THE METHOD OF INVESTIGATING GENIUS

The layman, without scientific method, is apt to select some one factor which strikes him as having done most to produce genius and neglect all the other factors. The sociologist uses the scientific method and puts many biographies of noted people under his mental microscope to examine the influences which contributed to their make-up. The statistical method employed in such inquiries was broadened into a science by Quetelet (1835) and used by Galton (1869), de Candolle (1873), and Odin (1895).

Odin's survey of genius which struck Ward as the most accurate and far-reaching embraced a wider range than any other, both in number investigated (sixteen thousand famous French men and women of letters, from 1300 to 1825, of whom 6,832 were selected for minute biographical study) and in the number of social strata that were probed (see *ibid.,* p. 207). Odin also showed that what was true for

French-speaking countries was also true for other lands, and what applied to men of letters, applied equally to the famous in other fields (see *ibid.,* pp. 210-211).

## GENIUS DOES NOT COME FROM THE LOWER CLASSES

Method may be more important than doctrine, but the results of Odin's investigation were so far reaching that the method is almost forgotten. He proved that more than three-quarters of French literary talent sprang from the nobility, government officials, and liberal professions. The fewest came from working men, though they were the most prolific in numbers. In Odin's own words:

What is specially striking is the prodigious superiority of the first three classes over the last two, and especially of the nobility over the hand workmen, the first having had at least two hundred times as many chances as the second to give birth to men of letters of talent (*ibid.,* pp. 209-210).

The following are representative figures drawn by Odin from a minute study of a smaller group of eminent French men of letters, which also show the fecundity of genius and talent, relative to population (*ibid.,* p. 208):

| Social Classes | Talent Only | | Genius | | Number Relative to Population |
|---|---|---|---|---|---|
| | Number | Per Cent | Number | Per Cent | |
| Nobility | 125.0 | 24.5 | 34.0 | 30.4 | 159.0 |
| Government officials | 157.5 | 30.8 | 29.5 | 26.3 | 62.0 |
| Liberal professions | 116.5 | 22.8 | 27.0 | 24.1 | 24.0 |
| Bourgeoisie | 62.0 | 12.1 | 10.5 | 9.4 | 7.0 |
| Manual laborers | 50.0 | 9.8 | 11.0 | 9.8 | 0.8 |
| *Total* | 511.0 | | 112.0 | | |

In the face of such results, no one can help asking why the working class which constitutes 80 per cent of the population should contribute less than 10 per cent of the eminent men. Why should a high-born personage have nearly two hundred times the chances to become famous that one lowly born has, assuming their native talents to be the same, while for the middle class, the chances are only one to twenty-eight? Why are the lower classes, in the vernacular, so "out of luck"? Ward's answer is that genius is mainly a question of opportunity, something that the poor and the lowly are entirely lacking (see *ibid.*, p. 129).

## GENIUS AND OPPORTUNITY

Ward accepts Galton's generalization that "no man can attain eminence unless he possesses innate ability of a high order," but rejects the assertion that "few who possess these very high abilities can fail in achieving them." By the latter belief, Galton deprives the environment of its force, becomes the sire of all the hereditarians, and avoids the whole sociological problem: given equally high ability, what conditions of nurture will accelerate their development, and what conditions will retard them?

The only solution of the problem of genius, said Ward, lies in the environment. Genius is not in men, but in things. Hostile conditions throttle it, but it thrives under favorable circumstances; it all depends upon opportunity. If Shakespeare had been cast among the Zulus, he might have become one of their leaders, but never the genius who understood humanity so well. Had Caesar been a laborer, his innate talents would have been of little avail to make him a great historical figure. Men are the pens with which the environment writes history. They are the levers that release the accumulated energy of the social forces. The fallacy of the worshipers of heredity and heroes is that they mistake the levers for the motor power; the pens for the writers.[3]

## TO WHAT ENVIRONMENTAL FACTORS IS GENIUS DUE?

Research into the phenomena of genius is necessary in formulating a theory of social progress, and deciding whether progress is biological (inheritable) or sociological (environmental). The influences which make men and write their history, for better or for worse are: (1) the material environment or physical heredity which changes very little; (2) the biological inheritance which changes slowly and

[3] Lincoln became a sociologist for a moment when he said: "I have not made events; events have made me." Great men, like small men, are the creations of their environments, no less than any other phenomena in the social sphere. Inventions are not absolute strokes of genius, but the syntheses of achievements in time, place and circumstance. Witness the needs of an age filled by simultaneous but independent inventions and discoveries, such as those of Leibnitz and Newton (the calculus), Darwin and Wallace (natural selection), Ward and De Vries (theory of mutations), Goebel, Swann, and Edison (the incandescent lamp), and Adams and Leverrier (the planet Neptune).

develops racial and individual characteristics; (3) the cultural environment (civilization) which produces the social heritage and changes
rapidly.

Since all men are products chiefly of the environment, genius ori-
ginates in the physical, racial, religious, economic, and educational
influences in which it is born and bred. These will now be briefly
surveyed (see *ibid.*, Chapter IX).

## THE PHYSICAL ENVIRONMENT

The physical environment is the warp through which the shuttle
of the social forces carries the threads to be woven into human characteristics. A barren rock becomes the magic city of Athens. A
cowherd blooms into a genius. Is not the earth itself (its soil, climate, and geography), the basic cause of such marvels, asked Buckle,
and devoted his life to the answer. Ward does not deny the physical
environment any more than he neglects to note the effects of the
economic forces, but he sees both as subordinate to the psychological
factor. Geography and climate are undoubtedly conditioning factors,
but their effects cannot compare with the force of ideas or the compelling urge of human desire seeking satisfaction.

## THE LOCAL ENVIRONMENT

In his study of the local environment Ward destroys the fallacy
that genius comes from the farm and not from the big city. Aristotle
was right when he said that man was a political animal, literally a
city-dwelling animal. The material and cultural conditions of large
centers of population, although popularly believed to be hectic and
abnormal, supply the necessary stimuli to develop potential genius.
Odin's analysis shows that the literary fecundity of French cities is
almost thirteen times that of the hinterland; that of Paris is nine
times as much as the rest of France, and more than thirty-five times
that of rural districts. Farm folk or country-bred people are not
healthier, more virile or more talented than the nervous, spoiled
children of the big city. It is a question of education, not of locality.
The great majority of the 6,832 great men whose lives Odin investigated, came from large cities (see *ibid.*, p. 169).[4]

[4] The city urchin is more intelligent than his country cousin. By transplanting
children into an urban environment, their intelligence quotient can be raised (see

## THE ECONOMIC ENVIRONMENT

The tremendous influence of the economic factor has scarcely been realized '(see *ibid.,* p. 198). Statistics show that the longevity of the rich is about twice that of the poor. The mortality of infants born in poverty is about six times as high as that of children born in wealth (see *ibid.,* p. 322). The chance for the development of genius is never so small as when it has the misfortune to be born in a poor family. The following is the result of Odin's research into the economic origin of French eminence (see *ibid.,* p. 203):

| PERIOD | RICH | POOR |
|---|---|---|
| 1300-1500. | 24 | 1 |
| 1500-1600. | 81 | 4 |
| 1600-1700. | 157 | 9 |
| 1700-1800. | 227 | 32 |
| 1800-1825. | 73 | 11 |
| *Total*. | 562 | 57 |

At the same rate, in the nineteenth century, the rich would give 292 geniuses for every 44 coming from the poor. Odin's survey was made by dividing the talented men of letters into two classes: the wealthy, whose early lives were free of economic pressure; and the poor, who spent their formative years struggling for bread. By simple calculation, the chances of the rich to succeed in literature were found to be thirty-seven times as great as those of the poor endowed with the same measure of innate talent. Only 9 per cent of the literary men investigated were of limited means; the rest were safely beyond the border line of the economic problem. Since the poor comprised over 80 per cent of the population, the fact is that a tiny but wealthy 3 per cent minority furnished 91 per cent of the talent, and the vast but poor majority contributed the other 9 per cent. De Candolle's figures for talented men of science run to about the same proportions.

## THE RACIAL, RELIGIOUS, AND SOCIAL ENVIRONMENTS

Racial environment is not as important as is commonly believed, said Ward (see *ibid.,* p. 156). Greece, for example, gave the world

Report of Frederick Osborn, Secretary of the Galton Society, *Literary Digest,* June 3, 1933).

the greatest host of geniuses in history, not because of an improved heredity or racial superiority, but because of environmental influence, mainly education and training. So too the religious influence may have lasting effects, but it is not a vital factor. How else explain the many eminent men who were agnostics or heretics? Wherever genius has come from the clergy, the surroundings have been more or less free and altogether friendly to enlightenment. If the Protestant Church had adopted the practice of celibacy, the achievements of hundreds of great men, among them Agassiz, Emerson, Hobbes, Ben Jonson, Swift, Addison, Jenner, Lessing, and Hallam who were sons of clergymen, would have been lost to the world (see *ibid.*, pp. 161, 204).[5]

As for the social environment, its influence is so closely connected with that of the economic and the educational factors that it requires no independent treatment.

### THE EDUCATIONAL ENVIRONMENT

Ward's final conclusion is that neither the physical factor nor any other except education can account for genius (see *ibid.*, pp. 148-221). When he wrote *Dynamic Sociology* he was unacquainted with the sociological literature of opportunity. Great was his joy in later years to find in the works of de Candolle and Odin ample corroboration of his own opinions which had been based mainly upon personal observation.

In 1891 de Candolle sent Ward a list of twenty factors (including heredity) which favor the development of scientists in any country (see *ibid.*, p. 145). Ward's studies compelled him to conclude that education was a more important factor than all the other nineteen combined. Opportunity without education (intellectual centers, material wealth, and prolonged study) is an empty shell; with it, the other influences may be controlled to an extraordinary extent. The rest of the factors have definite roles, but they are minor ones and much less important than is generally believed.

[5] Ward's conclusions are buttressed by later researches. In Professor J. McKeen Cattell's biographical compilation, *American Men of Science* (1906), which covered the lives of 13,500 prominent scientists, only 1,189 were chosen as truly distinguished. Of these, 75 per cent were either irreligious or indifferent to religion, and of the remainder, 216 were members of liberal denominations. It seems that the more liberal their religion, the greater the number of famous scientists.

Ward marshals his facts to show that genius is greatly dependent upon education. For example, in Odin's study, 811 out of 827 French men of letters had been thoroughly educated in their youth. In fact, 98 per cent of French talent was well educated. The figures prove that an educated person has fifty-two times the chance to succeed, other things being equal, than an uneducated person has. Education, not poverty or privation, is the powerful magnet that draws out and develops genius (see *Glimpses*, VI, 290).

## SELF-MADE AND PRIVILEGED MEN

The hereditarians play what they believe is their last trump when they point to self-made and privileged men as examples of genius who seem to have no relation to any environmental influence at all. Ward simply questions the existence of such individuals (see *App. S.*, p. 261). All self-made men have been well educated, and, in general, have had favorable circumstances to pave their way. Such has been the case with the sons of the upper and middle classes, e.g., Descartes, Newton, Voltaire, Goethe, Hugo, and Darwin, as well as with the children of the shopkeepers and handicrafters included in the lower classes, and among whom there are Rabelais, Spinoza, Molière, Rousseau, Kant, Heine, Carlyle, and Dickens. All of them were comparatively well-to-do and were helped into fame by necessary training. As an example of wishful thinking to the contrary, there is the familiar argument that Spencer's genius was self-made. But it falls upon the slightest analysis of his biography (see *ibid.*, p. 252). Says Ward:

Those who have succeeded in bursting the conventional bonds of society, have usually done so at such an immense cost in energy that their future work is rendered crude and well-nigh valueless. Such is the character of most of the results accomplished by so-called self-made men (*Glimpses*, IV, 39).

## GENIUS NOT A PRODUCT OF ADVERSITY

There is no greater fallacy, said Ward, than the popular view that favorable circumstances stifle genius but adverse ones breed it. All important human achievements have been accomplished by the privileged classes because they did not have to waste themselves in the struggle for existence.

Ward refutes Huxley's "exceptional man" theory of "the glorious sports of nature," and says:

The three classes who have made all the contributions to the world's advancement have performed only "a labor of love." These are the mechanical inventor, the scientific discoverer and the philosophic thinker. . . . The greatest results that have been achieved by this class (inventors and discoverers) have come from men of leisure and of means, who were wholly free from embarrassment,—of hardship and opposition (*D.S.*, I, 78).[6]

[6] Ward's grand generalization that education is the most powerful yeast in the brewing vat of humanity has been supported by such authoritative American sociologists as Professors Charles H. Cooley and J. McKeen Cattell, while in England thinkers like Havelock Ellis and John M. Robertson came substantially to the same conclusion, although they stressed the environment generally, rather than education particularly (see *App. S.*, pp. 211-223).

Cattell's essay, "A Statistical Study of Eminent Men," *Popular Science Monthly*, LXII, 359 (1903), raked the fatalistic dogma of the hereditarians with a broadside from which they have never recovered. Without depriving heredity of the first word, he refused to take the veto power from the environment. If a white pine seed, he argued, is dropped on New England rocks, only a small bush will grow up, but if planted in the rich soil of the South, a majestic tree will rise. Human beings are just as dependent as plants upon outer conditions.

In two later researches ("A Statistical Study of American Men of Science," 1906; "A Study of the Distribution of 1000 Leading American Men of Science," 1910), Cattell found that in America, men of different nationalities contributed to the roster of science in unequal measure. The inequality, however, was not due to any racial differences, but to the social and economic factors. It is not likely, he concluded, that such vast differences in family stocks exist, as lead one part of the United States to produce one hundred times as many scientists as another. The main factors in intellectual achievement are wealth, opportunity, social traditions, and ideals. What a child or man can do depends upon his native ability; what he actually does depends upon his environment.

Based upon an analysis (as of 1850) of the occupations of the parents of 685 famous American scientists, Cattell obtained results which seem to dovetail exactly into the generalizations of Odin, De Candolle, and Ward. Fathers who were professional men, a class that constituted only 3.1 per cent of the population, produced 43.1 per cent of America's eminent men of science. Farmers, comprising 44.1 per cent of the population, furnished 21.2 per cent. The merchants and manufacturers, a class that numbered 34.1 per cent of the population contributed 35.7 per cent. Not a single famous scientist came from the home of a working man! Galton discovered the same fact in the lives of the leading ninety-six English scientists but saw nothing startling or noteworthy in it (see *App. S.*, 144-145).

Havelock Ellis (*A Study of British Genius*, 1926) ploughed over thirty thousand famous lives taken from *The Dictionary of National Biography* and selected for special study 975 men and 55 women. The result was the same: eminence was due to environment. English genius came almost entirely from the middle class, while the poor or laboring classes showed a marked progressive decline in contributing to the roster of the famous.

In *The American Journal of Sociology* (March, 1925) appeared the result of an investigation made by S. S. Visher into the genius in the families of American clergymen. On the basis of the 1870 census, he computed that forty-eight thousand

None of the facts or arguments here presented has deterred the worshipers of heredity from continuing to beat their tom-toms and chant their hymns to "blue-blood." The beginning and the end of their views is that the nobility and the members of royal families are great men and women, an assertion that does not seem to find much support in the thin, pale blood of royalty.

One of the chief protagonists of the hereditarians, Frederick Adams

---

unskilled laborers would contribute, on the average, only one notable son to *Who's Who in America* for the year 1922-1923. Clergymen's families produced the greatest number of famous sons; then came the families of businessmen, farmers, skilled workers, and semiskilled laborers, in the order named.

Professor Jerome Davis, of Yale University, in his *Contemporary Social Movements* (1930), made a survey of the lives of 163 outstanding communist leaders in Russia. The overwhelming majority, it appeared, were born in cities of over ten thousand population and had access to educational facilities of at least high-school rank; 60 per cent were born outside the peasants and workers. Apparently, the educational factor is just as valuable for revolutionary leadership, as for any other.

In 1930, in research done by President Glenn Frank of the University of Wisconsin, he computed that out of each million people without schooling, only six attained distinction. With elementary schooling, the number rose to 24; with high-school education, to 622; and with a college education, to 5,768!

In an article entitled "Fame and Social Origin" (*Social Forces*, March, 1936, p. 354) Joseph Schneider described the results of a research by Professor Raymond Pearl, the eminent American biologist, who surveyed the lives of the parents of the most famous men in history in order to find evidence that the eugenic method of improving the race by selective breeding can claim no support from the science of genetics. By using the biographical material in the 11th edition of the *Encyclopedia Britannica,* he obtained the same result as Galton, but differed strongly with him on its interpretation.

The parents under investigation turned out to be average men and women without any special accomplishments. Even in exceptional cases, where a parent was a famous person, it was not proven that the son's talents were inherited. Heredity and environment (the latter meaning opportunity, i.e., early nurture, education, wealth, position, influence) are only limiting factors which determine who may become famous, not who will.

Using the English *Dictionary of National Biography,* Mr. Schneider arrives at the same conclusion as all the other scientific studies of genius have reached, that the number of famous men who emanate from the various social classes is inversely proportionate to their number in the total population. The well-to-do and professional classes which never exceeded 5 per cent of the population, have always produced about 50 per cent of all eminent men, or ten times their quota. The laboring classes, on the other hand, have contributed only about 10 per cent, although they constitute the bulk of the people in every country.

In a later paper ("Social Class, Historical Circumstances and Fame," *The American Journal of Sociology,* July, 1937) the same author demonstrated that the total number of persons who become famous in an area at any given time is determined by historical circumstances and situations. Contrary to the views of the hereditarians, the decline in the absolute and relative number of eminent men of genius produced by the English working classes after 1800 is apparently not due to biological deterioration, but to a curtailment of opportunity.

Woods, shudders in the most refined style at the mention of such crass things as environment, opportunity, or the common people. Besides, he believes that royal families produce more geniuses proportionately than any other families, and that this fecundity of talent is due to natural and mental selection (see his "The Law of Diminishing Environmental Influences," *Popular Science Monthly,* April, 1910).

His thesis is bold and to the point:

Experimentally and statistically, there is not a grain of proof that ordinary environment can alter the salient mental and moral traits in any measurable degree from what they were predetermined to be through innate influences.

Mr. Woods argues for all hereditarians when he asserts that the lower we descend in the scale of life, the easier it becomes to modify plants and animals by changing the environment. But when we reach the human brain and nerve tissues, the environment affects them "at the minimum of efficiency," which to any hereditarian in good standing, means plain zero. Man is essentially, therefore, what he is at birth and nothing more. This is the beginning and the end of the gospel of genius according to heredity.

All men and women carry the seed of genius, says Ward; only opportunity is needed for its full development. The manifestation of genius depends, therefore, upon social conditions. The problem of society is to find this talent in the masses and utilize it first in abolishing poverty and ignorance which stunt the individual, and secondly, in developing human resources through education. Those are the final aims of applied sociology.

If education, as Ward feels certain, is the chief factor in the environment, and it can evolve a talented mass—not supernormal geniuses among countless mediocrities—there is hope for social progress. The most precious possession of society is not the gifted man in a million, but the average normal person. But to bring his dormant seeds of talent to fruition, society must provide him with proper and equal opportunity. This is the climax of Ward's study of genius; the hope and the promise of social science.

# Chapter XXXIV

# INHERITANCE AND
# OPPORTUNITY

---

*"For an indefinite period yet to come, society will continue to be recruited from the base. . . . So far as the native capacity, the potential quality, the 'promise and potency' of a higher life are concerned, these swarming, spawning millions, the bottom layer of society . . . are by nature the peers of the boasted 'aristocracy of brains' that now dominates society and looks down upon them, and the equals in all but privilege of the most enlightened teachers of eugenics."*

*"It narrows down, then, to one point, that the great demand of the world is knowledge. . . . The great problem is the equalization of intelligence. I know of no other problem of applied sociology that society can solve until this one is solved."*—Ward

*"Our little lives are driven eddies of the dust of chance in the gust of circumstance."*
—George M. Gould

---

THE PROBLEM of human improvement, physical and spiritual (even the individualists do not deny the need of it), fluctuates between two attitudes: eugenics and opportunity, heredity and environment. Dynamic sociology stands squarely with the latter and says: "Genius is universal; opportunity is rare. Equalize opportunity and you also equalize intelligence. In so doing, you put society on the road to solve its problems, not only how to provide for a better future, but also for a happier life in the present."

## EUGENICS

Ward sympathetically examined the method of eugenics and found it visionary and unscientific. Sir Francis Galton, who founded the eugenics movement (1883), denied altogether the possibility of improving the human species and promoting genius by altering the environment. Commencing with the premise of the dire need of a finer race, he leaped over all questions of external conditions and took refuge from the perplexing social problem in the safe and conservative sex cells. There was the ideal breeding place for perfect human beings with their traits and talents provided for in advance. Why look elsewhere? Eugenics was the shorter and surer method of producing a world of healthy, intelligent, and gifted people, and not the uncertain and painfully slow and roundabout method of attempting to change social conditions.

[ 422 ]

The naïve but alluring argument of eugenics stands upon the dependable and eternal laws of heredity which work alike in all environments, in city or farm, in a moist or a dry climate, under conditions of good nurture or in the most wretched surroundings. Men are born, not made, whether they are kings or peasants, saints or sinners. Ergo, if men only knew the laws of heredity, they would soon have not only a biological aristocracy of perfect human specimens, but also an intellectual aristocracy of mental giants. Is not selective breeding of far greater importance and efficiency than trying to alter the foundation or superstructure of society through legislative co-operation, redistribution of wealth, and equalization of opportunity and intelligence?

## SOCIOLOGY AND EUGENICS

Ward regards eugenics as a gospel rather than a science. It is the royal road to perfection and runs parallel to the other royal road to learning. Both are impracticable and illusive. He has no quarrel with negative eugenics which seeks to eliminate reproduction of the unfit. But positive eugenics is a short cut to progress, an attempt to legislate a human stud farm into existence by mating picked couples, clearly a makeshift of social reform under a cloak of science.

Admitting that the laws of heredity can neither be altered nor supplanted, the easier and more feasible method, says Ward, is to adjust the environment so as to allow the hereditary forces to operate freely under improved conditions. As a preliminary to any real test of eugenics, a great many basic reforms would first have to be carried out, such as the abolition of overwork, bad living conditions, general exploitation, and poverty. In sum, an environment would have to be provided that would not sap vitality or lower morale, but would allow free play of all human faculties. When the human plant will be given surroundings in which it can unfold and thrive without being stunted or mutilated, then it will be timely to seek the origin and cure of all human imperfections in the hidden chambers of the sex cells, says Ward.

If eugenics is right, and intelligence comes only through heredity, how did such movements as democracy, antislavery, or feminism come about? The theory that by encouraging eugenic marriages the world would be instantly improved has broken down too often. Nothing in the ancestry of Shakespeare, Keats, or Lincoln foreshadowed their arrival. Nor do the family trees of Bach, Galton, or Darwin prove that genius is inherited. Even the history of degenerate families like the Jukes, the Zeros, or the Kallikaks are not unimpeachable proof that their evil traits were transmitted by inheritance or that they could not be eliminated by changes in the environment.[1]

## EDUCATION AND EUGENICS

Our bodies (the biological heritage) have not changed to any great extent during the historical period. But our knowledge (the social heritage) has undergone a most stupendous expansion. The eugenist who can not see environment, especially education, as the most powerful instrument of progress, is of course blind to the chasm between the upper and lower classes, i.e., between talent and mediocrity. What separates them is not a difference in blood but a difference in opportunity, chiefly educational.

Ward's rousing rebuttal of eugenics is that improvement is possible only through equalization of opportunity—education, knowledge —which is the indirect way of advancing the general level of intelligence and ability. A people informed in natural and social science will have a quickened imagination and social consciousness sufficiently strong to serve as the best guides for the sex function. An intelligent society will have the same antipathy to unfitness and mismating as all now have to disease or degeneracy. People differ by nature more in their tastes than in their abilities. The exceptional person can no more be selected in advance than a career can be chosen for an infant with any certainty of success. All that can be done is to equalize opportunity for all. That will prevent inefficiency

[1] The heredity principle of like begets like upon which eugenics must stand or fall, has not been found to be solid ground for a better race movement. Inferior parents may have a superior child, and superior parents often bear mediocre children. Heredity is the synthesis of traits developed by past environments and never a facsimile of the mating pair or their immediate ancestors. To those who believe that all the feeble-minded come from idiotic parents, it may be told that prohibiting marriages between mental defectives has prevented the birth of only 11 per cent of the feeble-minded (see H. S. Jennings, *Biological Basis of Human Nature*, 1930). That babies today have fifteen years more expectation of life than their grandfathers had (Sir George Newman) is due to improved environmental conditions. It is not so much the unfit as the uneducated and the ignorant who overbreed.

and mismatching in sex as well as in all other phases of human life (see *App. S.*, p. 276).

## EUGENICS AND SOCIAL STRATA

The thumping truths of dynamic sociology correct the fallacy of eugenics that social classes have a sound biological basis. Eugenics sees nothing wrong or unnatural in a social ladder on which the ablest are at the top and the less able ones at the bottom. On the contrary, that is regarded as the order of nature (see *Glimpses*, VI, 387). Eugenics, like individualism, insists that there must be social classes, horses and riders, for that is nature's plan. That is why people are born either stupid or brilliant, and there is nothing much that can be done about it.

Ward looks upon the view that humanity consists mainly of subnormal beings as a grievous slander upon the race. That view is illustrated in the diagram to the right.

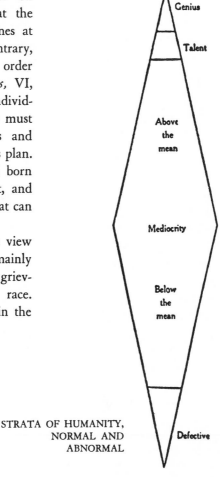

STRATA OF HUMANITY, NORMAL AND ABNORMAL

Psychologists outside the eugenics movement deny that the above distribution is true for mentality, and assert that the bulk of humanity is in a normal state. They would therefore widen the figure into a topshape. Ward claims[2] that it would still exaggerate the number of defectives and incompetents in society, and that the correct diagram is the following which depicts the great mass as normal (see *ibid.*, VI, 389):

Genius 1/10th of 1 per cent

(Latent genius and talent scattered somewhat equally throughout the mass, amounting to at least 50 per cent, needing only to be called out.)

Normal minded 99.4 per cent

(Transition from defectives to normal not gradual but abrupt, the latter sound, the former pathologic.)

Defectives 1/2 of 1 per cent

## CRIME AND SOCIETY

Much of Ward's argument upon genius and opportunity was the result of personal observation in travels abroad. He saw the Italian people, for example, descendants of the brave Romans, sinking into the same decadence as the Spaniards. He heard European criminologists preaching: "True, we have many poor and many criminals, but they have always been with us. They are God's unfortunates who have inherited criminal tendencies." He read their tomes on genius and insanity, the inheritance of evil traits, and crime and criminals, in which those subjects were treated from every point of view except that of the environment. Ward saw clearly how wrong that was, how ignorance, poverty, and crime were an inseparable trinity. He denied that the poor and the criminal classes were beg-

---

[2] Striking support of Ward's position is found in *Genetics* by the noted biologist, H. S. Jennings (1935), who says: "Looking at the population from the standpoint of vigor, efficiency and general fitness for life and its functions, it might be divided roughly into three groups. Forming a small percentage of all are the superior individuals. . . . At the other extreme in the scale is the small group of the very defective, the weak and inefficient . . . the paupers and criminals and defectives. Between these two lies the large mediocre class, composing perhaps 95 per cent of the population, having a very great variety of gene combinations."

gars, thieves, or numbskulls, but suggested that they owed their physical and mental make-up to social conditions. The pseudo-scientists and others who refused to recognize the real causes of human misery and degradation were no better to Ward than the witch doctors and medicine men of old who ascribed plagues and famines to the anger of the spirits.

## THE ARTIFICIAL PRODUCTION OF GENIUS BY INCREASING OPPORTUNITY

Ward's deduction that genius flows from opportunity grew firmer as time went on. Only education can increase the average fecundity of genius and remove the glaring social inequalities which are due to faults in the environment. Only man's failure to improve the environment prevents the ratio of such increase from being sustained until he can approach the condition of excellence which eugenics demands.

When Ward was but twenty-one and had not yet seen the inside of a real school, he was already a full-fledged environmentalist (see *Diary*, p. 68). In 1869, the year in which he began his *Dynamic Sociology*, he already could write such sound sociology, sophomoric though it sounds, as the following:

Only princes or prelates or nobles aspired to mental culture. The great masses of mankind were doomed to a condition of dark and hopeless ignorance. To those who suppose that rank or title or high birth embraces all there is of talent in man, this circumstance will doubtless seem of small importance. But he who recognizes that God and nature have done as much for the lower as for the higher classes of our artificial society, that thousands of Newtons and Franklins and Websters have lived and died in obscurity for want of the means of arousing their slumbering talents into action, can see in the extension of the facilities of intellectual improvement to the masses of mankind, the consummation of a progressive movement as much grander than that of manuscript literature as the number which it affects is greater ("The Invention of the Printing Press," *ibid.*, p. 299).

## GENIUS EVERYWHERE

Ward urges no facile equalitarianism to standardize mankind and reduce personality to a symmetrical democracy of ciphers. Of course, there are insolvable differences in capacity and creative ability, but why should such differences be exploited at the expense of the great majority? Why cannot all human talent be put to work for the common benefit of all? The answer is that thus far eminence and genius have centered around a few great names. Talent has been regarded as a rare gem; mediocrity or less as the normal condition. In the present social order, the great God is success, and genius merely one of his minor servants. Sociology demands the abdication of the oligarchy of brains and the dethronement of fame (see *Glimpses,* IV, 34-43). High intelligence, but not necessarily the highest, combined with a beneficial environment can achieve greater results and earn true eminence for a far greater number than the highest innate intelligence with less favorable opportunities.

Why search for genius? The germs of excellence, Ward argues, are present in every human being. The rare thing is not ability, but opportunity. Enormous quantities of hidden, creative mental force are waiting to be liberated. The few geniuses whom society hugs to its bosom, instead of being the object of frenzied adoration, should be proof that for every one of them that has risen into the limelight, thousands have gone down to oblivion in the struggle with circumstances.

Humanity is like a mass of growing plants. Nature (heredity) needs no help or urging to do its part. But man (environment) must cultivate the soil and take care of all the surrounding conditions of air, light, and moisture, or nothing of value or beauty will result. What might be grain will remain mere grass. In society, those who might become giants of the intellectual world, will die stunted sons of toil, average nonentities, unknown and unsung. Culture and civilization have been produced virtually by the handful who have had opportunity. What may not society expect when all men will be favored equally with such blessings as leisure, education, and freedom?

The emotional and intellectual nature of man, as far as achievement is concerned, is like the constant flow of electricity, a fixed quantity which no one can change or diminish. The sociologist, like the electrician, should give his whole attention to the environmental conditions, the wiring and regulation of the current which is always at hand (see *App. S.,* p. 129). As things are, however, the flow of genius is continually interrupted and diverted by lack of opportunity.

Ward agrees with Huxley that the most important object of education is to spread a net over society which will catch the big fish. But

Ward adds: "The only kind of net that can do this is the kind that extends absolutely equal opportunities to all the members of society" (*ibid.*, p. 266). If eugenics is the only method of improving the race, and ability is inheritable outright, geniuses can be bred like chickens or horses. That leaves the task of social evolution to nature, and man can sit back like a gardener who idly waits for flowers to bloom, without his doing anything to cultivate the soil.

Often Ward's own genius impressed some of his students as innate, and, therefore, as a strong argument against his passionate faith in the power of the environment. When asked whether his lowly origin and severe economic struggle did not refute his own doctrine that external conditions make the man, Ward replied: "No, it is true I have accomplished a certain amount, but who knows what I might have done if my mind had not put forth so much effort and time on the daily necessities of life?" (*Cape*, p. 50).

The fact that famous men have fought their way up from the ranks only increases the likelihood that had their earlier days been spent under more favorable conditions, their number as well as their achievements would have been far greater. The untold numbers who were trodden underfoot or left far behind in the mad rush of the successful ones, would also have had a chance. Ward describes the tragedy of his self-education as follows:

As Professor Cooley says: "A man can hardly fix his ambition upon a literary career when he is perfectly unaware, as millions are, that such a thing as a literary career exists." It is the same with a scientific career. I know this from my own experience. Roaming wildly over the boundless prairies of northern Iowa in the fifties, interested in every animal, bird, insect and flower I saw, but not knowing what science was, scarcely having ever heard of zoology, ornithology, entomology or botany, without a single book on any of those subjects, and not knowing a person in the world who could give me the slightest information with regard to them, what chance was there of my becoming a naturalist? It was 20 years before I found my opportunity, and then it was almost too late. A clear view of a congenial field is the one fundamental circumstance in any one's career (*App. S.*, pp. 275-276).

## OPPORTUNITY FOR THE LOWLY

The present individualistic system presents a grim paradox. Society is divided into two classes: the upper, well-informed, well-to-do and class conscious; the lower, ignorant, poor, and not at all class conscious. The system creaks and totters because it is weak at the bottom, the people lacking opportunity and having no abilities developed. It would be putting the cart before the horse (as the hereditarians do) to try saving society by working for the improvement of the upper social strata. No tree can be nurtured by applying moisture or new soil to the branches instead of to the roots.

The only method by which genius can be increased is to recruit it from the base. The long and arduous process of educating the masses instead of seeking great leaders or supermen among the favored few, is the wiser course, according to Ward, because it is bound to develop latent talents. It is better for society to have all of its members educated than to have a few informed and powerful minds ruling a sodden mass. Great leaders do not make history or bring progress. An improved environment, humane conditions, and opportunity do (see *ibid.*, p. 24).

Looking back into history to catch the reflection of the future, the hope that intelligence will change decadent slum dwellers into happy, high-grade free dwellers on the heights does not seem so fantastic. The caste system developed the brains of a small minority that had leisure. The resulting surplus of psychic power went to build up civilization, at the expense of the ignorant and nonleisured classes. About eight centuries ago, the leveling process began. When the feudal system broke up, the caste system was destroyed. The qualities of the higher types of men were diffused through all the lower strata of society. Progress was neither impeded thereby, nor the tone of culture lowered. On the contrary, the enlargement of opportunities given to the submerged nine-tenths was more than compensated by the wider field thus opened for the selection and development of more talented human material. Ward supports the view that the lower classes have the virility and potential genius worth salvaging in the catastrophic rush of material civilization, in these eloquent words:

For an indefinite period yet to come, society will continue to be recruited from the base. The swarming and spawning millions of the lower ranks will continue in the future as in the past to swamp all the fruits of intelligence and compel society to assimilate this mass of crude material as best it can.

This is commonly looked upon as deplorable and it is said that society is doomed to hopeless degeneracy. Is it possible to take any other view? I think it is, and the only consolation, and the only hope, lies in the truth that, so far as the native capacity, the potential quality, the "promise and potency" of a higher life are concerned, those swarming, spawning millions, the bottom layer of society, the proletariat, the working classes, the "hewers of wood and drawers of water," nay, even the denizens of the slums,—that all these are by nature the peers of the boasted "aristocracy of brains" that now dominates society and looks down upon them, and the equals in all but privilege of the most enlightened teachers of eugenics (*Glimpses,* VI, 397).

## ALL MINDS ARE POTENTIALLY THE SAME

It is often asked how equality of opportunity is possible when human beings are so different in sex, race, color, creed, class, and physical and mental equipment. Ward's answer is that there are no inborn inequalities of any kind which can prevent the equalization of opportunity. By the grand generalization of "intellectual egalitarianism" he sought to remove at a stroke all the timeworn accretions of prejudices based upon biological and psychological differences in mankind (see *App. S.,* p. 95).

Social inequality is due chiefly to mental inequality. Inborn mental superiority is a fiction. The words *inferior* and *superior* make everyone think of mental caliber. The social philosophy of our age revolves around those distinctions as a pivot, no less than around the inequalities of wealth. So steeped is the public mind in the worship of mental brilliancy, that those who do not have it are considered naturally inferior. But our social organization gives potential genius little opportunity to assert itself, and the number of able and intelligent people remains sadly limited. The resulting state of social and intellectual snobbery is one of the reasons for the demoralization of the individualistic regime; it is "the out-Nietzsche-ing of Nietzsche."

It must always be remembered that Ward looks upon mind and human achievement as only means toward the supreme aim of happiness. He recognizes the intellect as the most effective of all social agencies, but notes the surprising fact is that all intellects are potentially the same. Humanity, in other words, is one family with the same amount of latent ability, talent, and genius. This does not mean that people have identical mental powers, but that they have the same capacity for development, and are, therefore, equal in possibilities. Regardless of race, class, color, or nationality, human beings are seeds sown in time and place. Some take root and others do not, and their degree of development depends upon the surrounding conditions and circumstances (see *ibid.*, Chapter VII).

Ward's argument reverses Rousseau's dictum: "Man is born free but everywhere he is in chains." Man is fettered from birth, and gradually is freeing himself of the gyves of the environment. Not the least of those fetters is the stock of erroneous ideas by which he is made to support every species of fraud and chicanery. To understand is to forgive, and Ward explains the plight of the people as follows:

The general fact remains that in the world at large, a few dominate society and make it, if not an "aristocracy of brains," at least an oligarchy of intelligence. These false and narrow ideas which make the mass of mankind dependent upon a few enlightened citizens and keep them in subjection, in poverty, toil and misery, are, of course, the result of the emptiness of their minds,—in a word, to the limited amount and poor quality of the knowledge they possess. They reason as well as they can with the materials they have. Their conclusions are as in the case of the savage, either false or practically useless as guides to action (*ibid.*, pp. 94-95).

The claim that a superior intelligence entitles anybody to a superior social status does not differ in any respect from the principle that might makes right, which underlies the social philosophy of the totalitarian or fascist state. It is easily traced to the vicious barbarous doctrine that the physically strongest men had the God-given right to the handsomest women, the finest cattle, the choicest food, and, of course, the autocratic power to rule their fellows (*ibid.*, p. 23).

The mental endowment of the man of the stone age was no worse than that of the twentieth-century free and cultured citizenry. The intellectual improvement that has taken place in the interval between the two, has been solely due to advances in the technique of thinking and to the increase in knowledge, but not to any more or better kind of brain power.[3] The contrary idea is not only a fallacy, but a positively immoral idea. Men are ready to gaze squarely into heaven or hell, but they tremble at any suggestion that there are essentially and naturally no superior races, no chosen people, and no mental and social inferiors.

[3] Here is the scientific core of Jefferson's "all men are created free and equal." If there is any truth in the historic Declaration of Independence, it expresses only a latent identity of powers and an equal right to opportunity.

## CIRCUMSTANCES FASHION THE MIND

It is an ancient truism that man is a creature of circumstances, but few have paid much attention to its application to the development of mind power. Even many scientists still believe that circumstances, as compared to heredity, scarcely affect mental development (see *ibid.*, pp. 267 *et seq.*).

Ward regarded the brain as a dynamo, but to make it clear how it is molded by the environment, he compared men's intellects to receptacles of various shapes and sizes for the storing of knowledge. The contents are dissimilar in kind and quantity, but the boxes are of the same material. What is put into them are the things and qualities acquired through education and experience, and may range from cobblestones to pure diamonds. Thus far, so much care has been lavished upon the material and size of the boxes, that the contents which alone represent the real differences between intellects are neglected.

Eugenics asserts that the kind of receptacle one is born with is what counts, not what is later put into it. Dynamic sociology vigorously combats such a fatalistic view. Knowledge (the subjective environment, as Ward calls it), the action of mind upon matter, that is the vital factor in the molding of our mental as well as physical qualities (see *D.S.*, II, 321).

## THE FICTION OF RACE SUPERIORITY

Each major error of the human race seems to vie for magnitude and devastating effect with all the others. The fallacy of race superiority has outdone that of intellectual aristocracy and caused unbelievable misery and bloodshed. Sociology cannot find that any races are superior. There is no better or nobler blood; there are no inferior races or peoples, only undeveloped and stunted ones. The same thing is true of individuals. The college professor and the man with the hoe differ mentally only in training and equipment, not in the constitution or latent power of their brains. What separates them is education, a thing which no one can inherit but which all may acquire. Analagously, all men may become athletes, but those who have the best environment, the best food and training, will excel. The half-starved slum-dwellers who would be champions will fall far behind, though the blood of kings flows in their veins (see *App. S.*, p. 236).

There are no valid racial differences beyond the superficial bodily variations, and even the latter are being gradually removed by a common environment, argued Ward. Galton's theory of racial uniqueness is a muddled fiction (see *Cape,* p. 135). Racial stock or "blood" is a purely passive factor, which denotes merely the hereditary material out of which the forces of the environment mold human beings of great diversity. The real race problem is not what any particular people has in the way of hereditary equipment, but what society can do with the equipment, such as it is.

The theory of pure races is a guess, and a wrong guess in the face of science. No one-hundred-per-cent American exists, any more than a one-hundred-per-cent European, Englishman, Frenchman, German, Italian, Spaniard, or Slav. The colored race has the same natural capacity for knowledge and achievement that the white race has. Quatrefages foresaw and advocated the intermarriage of all races, and Benjamin Kidd doubted the superiority of the white over any other race (see *App. S.,* p. 108). Tylor, Lubbock, and other anthropologists of note flatly denied Aristotle's dictum that low races have degenerated from higher ones. Science has proved that human beings are not decadent apes, no matter how much men will make monkeys of themselves.[2]

[2] Albert Edward Wiggam may be cited as one of the shining examples of American literary scientists whose best sellers once flooded the book mart and still have a large following. Slums are made by "slum people," he asserts, and you cannot get Lincolns out of log cabins or geniuses out of fools. He even honors Ward by mentioning him as the dominant sociologist of the "past generation," but refutes his philosophy of the environment with the lone example of the life of Christ.

The best scientific authorities agree with Ward. The Boas school of anthropology, for example, has found that such differences as appear in cultural achievements are due to opportunities of various kinds. So, too, Professor A. M. Tozzer in his *Social Origins and Social Continuities* (1925) says that there is no evidence to prove that savages are fundamentally different in mind, body or estate from the sophisticated products of civilization. Similarly, Professor Friederich Hertz in *Race and Civilization* (1929) maintains that races do not vary in innate ability and that the theory of supermen and predestined inferiors is almost dead.

Races are superior only by virtue of the environment. Given the same cultural opportunities, the Hottentot will do quite as well as the American or the European; the Negro and the Mongolian will prove the equal in native ability of the descendants of any of the passengers on the *Mayflower.* The biological differences in mentality, physique, and temperament which so many believe are insurmountable, are relatively unimportant. Besides they tend toward extinction or general identity. It is the cultural differences that are the most vital, and they are mainly the products of the environment. Nordics, Orientals, Anglo-Saxons, all are alike in intellectual power, yet all differ culturally because of different training and environments (see address by Prof. Robert D. McKenzie, of the University of Washington, *New York*

## THE ERROR OF CLASSES

The fundamental error of the hereditarian's position brings us to another of man's whited sepulchers, viz., class superiority. The bias and false pride of class so prevalent among the intellectual aristocracy and *nouveaux riches* are mercilessly exposed by Ward. To the wisdom

---

*Times,* Aug. 6, 1928). Said J. B. S. Haldane at the 1934 Congress of Anthropological and Ethnological Sciences: "Knowledge of a man's ancestry throws little light on his capabilities. Whatever innate differences in ability may exist between races, they are clearly of an overlapping type. . . . . It is already certain that some Negroes can reach higher cultural levels than most of the whites" (see *New York Times,* Aug. 3, 1934).

The popular idea that the height of the brow is an index to brain power has been completely exploded by Dr. Ales Hrdlicka, Curator of Anthropology at the Smithsonian Institute (see *New York Times,* April 22, 1933). A high or a low brow has little to do with a person's intelligence. Among racial groups the white race has the lowest forehead.

If mental power were reflected in the height of the brow, the Alaskan Eskimo would rate as the world's supreme intellectual, for his forehead averages nearly 9 per cent higher than the American's. The position of the hair line is merely a racial inheritance and not an index of the brains behind it. Dr. Hrdlicka has demonstrated that there are no measurable differences between four groups of American foreheads, viz., of illiterate mountaineers, national academicians, scientists, and old American stock. Evidently, physical highbrows are no more intellectual than physical lowbrows, unless education and training make them so. The value of the argument from heredity as compared to scientific research into the environment becomes crystal clear at the slightest examination of the "blue-blood" dogma. Said Gobineau, one of the forefathers of the Nazi madness (1853): "Everything great, noble and fruitful in the work of man on this earth, in science, art and civilization, is derived from a single starting point; it belongs to one family alone, the different branches of which have ruled in all civilized countries. This was the 'Aryan race.' "

The German anthropologists, in order to investigate the "Aryan" theory, and to prove incidentally that the Teutons were the first and finest of all races, began to measure heads, but forgot to plumb them. The elusive Aryan, as a result of such investigations, has been revealed as Asiatic, then European; first a round-head, then a long-head; blond as well as dark; a Celt, Scandinavian, Slav, and German successively, all of this, of course, because the Aryan is wholly a fiction.

The cheer leaders of the Nordics and Aryans still carry on exuberantly. The voices of Madison Grant *(The Passing of the Great Race)* and Houston Chamberlain *(The Foundations of Civilization in the Nineteenth Century)* as well as those of the players of the heredity game themselves (it is unfortunate that Ward did not live to hear Hitler, Mussolini, or the witch doctors of Central Africa), are still heard hysterically insisting that there are pure races, comparable to the races of animals or species of plants. Science, however, is proving almost daily that no such thing as a pure race ever existed. The so-called Aryan, Nordic, Anglo-Saxon, American, and Jewish races are not races at all, in the real sense of the word. In *We Europeans: A Survey of the Racial Problems* by Julian S. Huxley and A. C. Haddon (1936), the authors suggest dropping the idea of race altogether and substituting the study of ethnic groups and nations by means of anthropology, the fascinating science of man.

For thousands of years, waves of humanity washed back and forth over Europe and Asia. If ever there was a "pure" race, it was lost after each conquest and

of Confucius: "By nature we nearly resemble one another," and that of Buckle: "Human progress is not one of internal power, but of external advantage," Ward contributed:

One class is the intellectual equal of another in the sense that individuals selected at random from one class are as likely to prove capable of a high state of development as if taken from another. The chances for the discovery of native genius are the same in all classes, whether we look among the high-born and rich, the middle classes or the poor and lowly (*Glimpses,* IV, 37).

Differences between human beings (Ward never tires of repeating) in intellect as well as emotion are quantitative, not qualitative. The causes of those differences lie in the environment and not in the sex cells. Therefore, the chasms which separate the rich from the poor, or the economic baron from the economic peon are wholly artificial. In Ward's words:

I have come to the conclusion that there is no difference in the native capacity of mankind so far as classes are concerned; that all mankind are equal; that the brain power of the world is the same at every level; even the lowest slaves and serfs that have ever existed on the globe have the same power for exercising their faculties, the same faculties as those who have had them under control, those who have owned them, those who have whipped and flogged them, those who have robbed them of their rights and liberty,—there is no difference (*Glimpses,* VI, 338).[3]

assimilation. After many centuries of interbreeding, no one then could have said, and no one today can say, just what a race is. The Royal Anthropological Committee in Great Britain has been trying in vain since 1934 to frame a definition of race. A race is an abstraction. We are all mongrels in spite of the hectic hereditarians. As proved by Professor Franz Boas and his disciples, the physical characters of immigrants have changed after the first generation in the new American environment. It may be hard for eugenists to believe that nurture can triumph so easily over nature, but it becomes entirely credible when it is recalled that heredity means the synthesis of past environmental influences.

Professor H. J. Muller, who, like all other responsible geneticists, sees "race-science" as a rash on the body of fascism which points straight to helplessness and regression to barbarism, says: "There is no scientific basis for the conclusion that the socially lower classes, or technically less advanced races, really have a genetically inferior equipment."

[3] The fallacy of class distinction can be traced back to Plato's and Aristotle's division of society into two categories, the creative and intelligent men born to rule, and the toiling and dull ones, born to obey. This autocratic and arbitrary division can be followed straight into the latest best seller of the heredity fetishists like Dr. Alexis Carrel (*Man the Unknown,* 1935) whose ideal hero-worshiping society is to be governed by experts because the people are unfit to rule. How far can it be from such doctrine to the fundamental Nazi dogma: "What the Jew believes is immaterial; the fault lies with the race."

## THE MYTH OF SEX SUPERIORITY

A no less damaging error than mental, racial, and class superiority is the fiction of male superiority. Sociologically, there is no difference between man and woman. Male dominance is a fact, but his superior position is due to environmental causes, not to the laws of heredity. The hereditarians, however, conclude from her lack of achievement that she is of an inferior material, but Ward, as we have seen, has shown that it is due to her subjection and lack of opportunity. Says he:

The universal prevalence of the androcentric world view, shared by men and women alike, acts as a wet blanket on all the genial fire of the female sex. Let this once be removed and woman's true relation to society be generally perceived, and all this will be changed. We have no conception of the real amount of talent or of genius possessed by women. It is probably not greatly inferior to that of man even now, and a few generations of enlightened opinion on the subject, if shared by both sexes, would perhaps show that the difference is qualitative only. If this is so, the gain in developing it would be greater than that of merely doubling the number of social agents, for women will strike out according to their natural inclinations and cultivate fields that men would never have cultivated. They will thus add to the breadth, even if they do not add to the depth of the world's progress (*App. S.*, p. 232).[4]

## THE EQUALIZATION OF INTELLIGENCE

Equality of opportunity is important, Ward stressed, only because it leads to education and the equalization of intelligence. Society is a gigantic reservoir of psychic forces whose flow has been dammed by ignorance due to lack of opportunity. How soon the infantile minded mass would mature and bring about a different society, if only the superabundant knowledge now possessed by a few were acquired by all! The unequal distribution of knowledge is a greater curse to

[4] Again, Ward's generalizations have received surprising corroboration from other scientists. For example, Professor Margaret Meade, a fieldworker in ethnology (*Sex and Temperament in Three Primitive Societies,* 1935), riddled all popular theories about characteristics that are either innately human or innately masculine or feminine. The author furnishes much data to show which of man's traits are of biological origin and which derive from the social structure characteristics. Traits which our culture is inclined to refer to as masculine or feminine have no real basis in sex differences at all, but are the result of the molding of human nature by the environment. This, following the unmasking of such fallacies as man is by nature competitive; men and women naturally differ; man is dominant and aggressive, and woman is the passive servant of his desires, seems to lend weight to the belief that human beings are the most gullible and stupid of all living creatures.

mankind, repeats Ward, than the unequal distribution of wealth. The fact is that a small number of intelligent people have taken power over the vast ignorant and misinformed majority. Deploring but also explaining the abyss between those who have knowledge, leisure, and opportunity and those who have none of those blessings, Ward says:

It is not the idler, but the toiler, the real producer of wealth, who has none (leisure) while the man who has wealth is usually a man of leisure,—at least he has rarely or never acquired it through labor in creating it. The former occupies his position solely in consequence of his *relative* ignorance, the latter occupies his solely in consequence of his relative intelligence. Knowledge is power, and power has ever been wielded for self-aggrandizement, and must ever be so wielded. To prevent inequality of advantages there must be equality of power, i.e., equality of knowledge (*D.S.,* II, 602).

Not a single one of the injustices suffered by the people (and that means, of course, only the poor and the ignorant) would continue another day, argued Ward, if knowledge were equally spread. Such superstitions as one must be born with luck or ability; our brains need improvement; people cannot be all alike; the better minds and the better people are born to govern the weaker and inferior ones, would disappear if intelligence were equalized. In brief, if a sufficient number of people were to know the truths of science, the complete social distribution of the products of human effort would take place without delay (see *App. S.,* pp. 294-295). Ward's words ring with true prophecy when he says:

There is no use talking about the equalization of wealth. Much of the discussion about "equal rights" is utterly hollow. There can be no equality and no justice, not to speak of equity, so long as society is composed of members, equally endowed by nature, a few of whom only possess the social heritage of truth and ideas of all past ages, while the great mass are shut out from all the light that human achievement has shed upon the world. The equalization of opportunity means the equalization of intelligence, and not until this is attained is there any virtue or any hope in schemes for the equalization of the material resources of society (*ibid.,* p. 281).

I know of no other problem of applied sociology that society can solve until this one (the maximum equalization of intelligence) is solved. Most of the others would solve themselves long before this received its complete solution. An approximate solution of the primary question would naturally and automatically put the great majority of all other social problems in the way of at least ultimate solution (*ibid.*, p. 314).

It narrows down, then, to one point, that the great demand of the world is knowledge. . . . The great problem is the equalization of intelligence to put all knowledge in possession of every human being. . . . I have coined a new word in the English language and I hope it will be carried to the ends of the earth. I call this the principle of intellectual egalitarianism, the principle that no matter what class of society you may select from,—taking a corresponding number from each,—the individuals from all classes of society will be equal in their native capacity for knowledge (*Glimpses*, VI, 337).

## NATURAL INEQUALITIES NO OBSTACLE

There is nothing that can permanently stand in the way of equalizing intelligence, claimed Ward. Man's natural inequalities can do no harm for they merely provide the variety of personality and achievements which makes the world tolerable and interesting. Only social inequalities obstruct human progress, and they are evils which social science can remove.

If it is argued that even after the equal distribution of knowledge there would still exist an inequality of intelligence because of differences in natural ability, Ward has the following consoling answer (see *D.S.*, II, 601). The differences in men's native capacities are small when compared to the differences in the extent of their knowledge. Humanity is a mediocre mass, with a few below average intelligence, and a tiny percentage above the average. The great bulk of mankind is fully witted and able to take care of itself, if only given the chance. From this great bulk of mediocrity have come most of the famous names in history. Average minds with will power and ambition plus opportunity will contribute more to achievement than geniuses and mental supermen. But even the most powerful minds often lack ambition and incentive, and need spurs to achievement.

## THE RISE OF THE SUBMERGED

All this discussion, the reader may well say, is rather utopian and theoretical. Ward's practical mind is aware of such an indictment, but his faith in education is so strong that nothing can blur his vision of the rise of the numberless millions of the submerged to claim their birthright of intelligence and opportunity. This champion of the underdog minces no words:

The history of social classes furnishes to the philosophical student of society the most convincing proof that the lower grades of mankind have never occupied those positions on account of any inherent incapacity to occupy higher ones. Throughout antiquity and well down through the Middle Ages, the great mass of mankind were slaves. A little later they were serfs bound to the soil. Finally, with the abolition of slavery, the fall of the feudal system and the establishment of the industrial system, this great mass took the form of a proletariat, the fourth estate, considered of so little consequence that they are seldom mentioned by the great historians of Europe.

Even at the close of the 18th century, when the greatest of all political revolutions occurred, it was only the third estate that was at all in evidence,—the business class, bourgeoisie or social mesoderm. This class has been looked down upon and considered inferior, and only the lords spiritual and temporal were regarded as capable of controlling social and national affairs. This class is now at the top. It has furnished the world's brains for two centuries, and if there is any intellectual inferiority, it is to be found in the poor remnant that still calls itself the nobility in some countries (*App. S.,* pp. 97-98).

What is actually taking place, concludes Ward, is the gradual elevation of the completely submerged nine-tenths. Soon, in the most civilized countries, there will be only a submerged one-tenth. Even that seemingly hopeless stratum is bound to rise with proper opportunity, because there is nothing inherently inferior about it (see *ibid.,* p. 100). With prophetic vision, Ward adopts Comte's view of the equivalency of races and pictures the final blending of all classes and all races into one human family, in which

the less forceful elements will enter as modifiers. They represent qualities that in moderate proportions will improve and enrich the whole. The final great united world-race will be comparable to a composite photograph in which certain striking faces dominate the group but in which may also be detected the softening influences of faces characterized by those refining moral qualities which reflect the soul rather than the intellect (*ibid.,* p. 108).

## THE SIGNIFICANCE OF THE ENVIRONMENTAL PHILOSOPHY

Ward's philosophy of the environment demonstrated that man is the creature of external conditions, and that nature is biologic and constant while nurture is social and variable—a complex of needs and desires. The crowning generalization is that man and his environment react upon each other, and that he writes his own history, changes his own nature, and creates his own environment as he desires it. Nature's forces and materials which are the only things he has to work with and work on, are incredibly malleable in his hands, and human nature is equally changeable. If he so chooses, he can take a hand in evolution and substitute human selection for natural selection. But while science furnishes the knowledge to do so, his own future depends largely upon the universal distribution of that knowledge.

Withal, Ward's philosophy always points to our return to nature not as helpless primitives but as proud possessors of scientific knowledge. He tells the nature worshipers and all who believe that the natural is superior to the artificial, that the natural condition of happiness (which is all that is implied in a return to nature) is possible only through such artificial means as education and the conquest of the environment. For that, Ward has been dubbed a crass materialist, although in his dynamic sociology matter grows of less importance and mind rises to dominance as man takes charge of the environment. Science tells of breath-taking miracles in plumbing the furthest reaches of space inside the atom and into the infinite ether. But the story is supplemented by that of sociology which reveals the still greater miracle of the power and the possibilities of the mind.

Ward's apothesis of knowledge and his demand for more talent have stood the test of time, but still have to be tried on a large scale. The philosophy of the environment is the only one that pays real attention to the question of genius. Genius, it finds, is not cowardly, but it is not a war tank which can lay its own road. While it is brave enough, it is modest and shrinks from all obstacles. Real merit is often unable to create its own opportunities, and as often falls in the sheer struggle for existence. Education is the only soil, says Ward, in which genius may flourish; toil and misery, ignorance, and lack of opportunity are the rocks under which it is crushed.

Such is the pith and substance of the environmental philosophy. All sorts and conditions of men, creeds, and philosophies may subscribe to it—from the natural and physical scientist to the theologian and metaphysician. If virtue is ultimately to triumph by the power of God's grace, the meek will inherit the earth only when they become the strong—strong with the power of knowledge and intelligence. Both religion and science can meet on common ground in dynamic sociology to build for perpetual peace and good will and find the brotherhood of man, if they will only turn from the dogmas of heredity to the realities of the environment.

We turn from Ward's pages to the world outside with many misgivings, yet with much hope. Around us is every conceivable kind of makeshift and nostrum to ease the plight of humanity. The remedies of education and equalization of intelligence and opportunity seem to be carefully avoided or neglected. The social will abdicates to everything except science, as material conditions are put above intellectual and spiritual considerations. The better or more fit do not survive or rise in our individualistic order, and the characteristics which lead to fame and fortune are not always the most desirable. If Ward's guidance in the fields of heredity, genius, opportunity, and education (all of which may be summed up in the concept of environment) will leave anything in the reader's mind, it will be the absolute necessity of first improving the environment. That will call for inculcating society with a philosophy of life which is natural, scientific, and moral. That, again, is the task of a planned order, the hope and the promise of social science, and the duty of all who are socially conscious.

# *BOOK XV*. THE EDUCATIONALIST

*"The totality of human actions is governed by the totality of human knowledge."*—H. T. Buckle

*"Quiconque ouvre une école, ferme une prison."*—Victor Hugo

*"Nothing uproots or prevents superstition better than a sound education."*—Fenelon

# CHAPTER XXXV

# PROGRESS

---

*"Progress is not automatic. . . . The world only grows better, because people wish that it should, and take the right steps to make it better."*—John Morley

*"Le progrès est le développement de l'ordre."*—Comte

*"The business of life is to go forwards."*—Samuel Johnson

*"When I assert that all the control that can ever be exerted over mankind must in the future as in the past, emanate from the side of feeling and not of intellect, and promise a mitigation of the hardships of existence, at the same time, I unqualifiedly maintain that all the true progress which has in fact taken place in the world, has come from the side of intellect and not of feeling."*

*"Thus far social progress has in a certain manner taken care of itself, but in the near future it will have to be cared for."*—Ward

*"No doubts have been fixed to the improvement of the human faculties. The perfectibility of man is absolutely indefinite. The progress of this perfection, henceforth above the control of every power that would impede it, has no other limit than the duration of the globe upon which nature has placed us."*—Condorcet

---

THE END of our journey through the temple of sociology looms into view. As we look backward and forward along the path of evolution as far as the mental eye can reach, the arc of man's progress becomes plainly visible. Ward's philosophy of progress is founded upon the premise that knowledge, science, sociology, all exist for man's happiness; that social progress is identical with happiness, and education is the initial step toward that chief aim in life. There are no esoteric discussions *à la* Spengler of cycles of progress and catastrophes, but a keen vision of the purpose of life and the means of achieving it.

## EVOLUTION AND PROGRESS

The basic idea of progress in evolution is that of an advance. An impartial glance at the course of nature's organizing process reveals a progressive world. The universal energy which shaped the past and will mold the future, despite all pessimism and without any sentimental or metaphysical implications, spells progress. Nothing in the universe is ever finished, and force and matter are eternally occupied with the supreme task of building, destroying, rebuilding, and organizing.

While the quantity of matter and motion is fixed, the forms of matter and the modes of motion are infinitely variable. Progress is inherent in matter itself.

## THE TWOFOLD CONCEPT OF PROGRESS

Ward approaches the idea of progress from a wider angle than either Comte or Spencer, and sees progress divided into two sharply defined, but not necessarily antagonistic, parts (*P.S.*, pp. 544-545). He epitomizes them as follows:

| GENETIC PROGRESS | TELIC PROGRESS |
|---|---|
| in nature: evolution. | in man: institution. |
| 1. It connotes development. | 1. It connotes dynamic social change. |
| 2. It creates higher and more complex products out of lower and simpler material. | 2. It has nothing to do with evolution except as a happier state may be said to be an advance over an unhappy one. |
| 3. It has nothing to do with misery or happiness. | 3. Its sole aim is happiness. |
| 4. It is foreign to any values, intelligence or morality. | 4. It connotes values and is based upon reason and morals. |
| 5. As an unconscious growth, it is static, negative, and mechanical—a natural process, automatic and involuntary. | 5. As a planned process, it is dynamic, positive and psychic—a rational process, conscious and voluntary. |
| 6. It applies to nature, and also to man when his actions are unconscious or reflex. | 6. It applies to man alone because only he has rational intelligence (mind). |

## GENETIC PROGRESS

In man's early history, progress was passive, the same as in natural evolution. He lived only for survival, and expended all his energy in the mechanical, automatic struggle of life. In civilization, progress is still the same process. Now and then, under the stimulus of some crisis or catastrophe, man becomes for a moment a conscious, intelligent planner toward a fixed purpose. But when the emergency passes, he generally settles back into the same routine of mechanical action. Genetic progress is all he can expect, and that is all that the great majority believes is possible. Telic progress has scarcely begun, and is almost entirely unknown (*D.S.*, I, 43; *Outlines*, pp. 223-224). The general notion of social evolution is that society has no mind or will of its own, and that so far as social improvement is concerned, we are still savages, helpless before the forces of nature. Says Ward:

Social progress is either genetic or telic. Progress below the human plane is altogether genetic and is called development. In the early human stages it is mainly genetic, but begins to be telic. In the later stages it is chiefly telic. The transition from genetic to telic progress is wholly due and exactly proportionate to the development of the intellectual faculty (*Outlines*, p. 179).

## TELIC PROGRESS

Again Ward reminds us that the lack of telic action is the fault of individualism, and that the human mind has not yet abdicated. If it will take charge of the natural process, it can transform it into telesis, an artificial process, in its application to the forces that control social phenomena (see *ibid.*, p. 216). Up to this point, nature has done everything, using man only as a blind instrument. If she had to wait for man to exercise his will or intelligence, not even genetic progress would have been possible. But when he begins to use his reason to control the natural forces in social evolution, he becomes the agent of telic progress, and the possibilities of human happiness first appear.

Telesis, courageous and constructive as it is, is easy to achieve. The materials of nature are around us in such abundance that all we have to do is stretch out our hands for them. Says Ward: "Matter is for man, endowed with intelligence and inspired by science, a veritable lamp of Aladdin, which he need but rub, and as if by magic, all things take on the forms of utility and cast themselves at his feet" (*P.S.*, p. 225).

The method of civilization is invention, and that passes into arts and institutions (see *ibid.*, p. 25). It is striving or the process of conation which is at the root of civilization. Intensive thought or moral reflection has little to do with it. Conation is either direct and genetic, or indirect and telic. The force of intellect only appears in the telic, and its effects constitute social progress—no longer a growth, but with the advent of mind power, a true manufacture (see *ibid.*, p. 231).

The lack of intelligence shown by society in the conduct of its vital affairs makes one wonder why there is so little suffering in the world, not so much. Whatever society has accomplished for its own benefit has been done with the greatest possible friction and expenditure of energy, instead of the least. Man has had sense enough to apply the energy extracted from nature to light his homes and to drive the wheels of industry, but he has failed to utilize the far stronger currents of the social intellect and the social will through which the needs of society could be satisfied and the chariot of civilization driven into a safe and happy course (see *ibid.*, p. 107). If the knowledge of the laws of nature, by which this orderly universe has been evolved out of chaos, were used to control the social forces, the gain for humanity would be stupendous. A dynamics of mind and a mechanics of society, once established, would end the era of speculation and doubt, and change the struggle for existence into a humane and social co-operation (see *Outlines*, pp. 211-212).

In the final analysis, telic progress is neither the product of intellect alone nor of pure emotion, but a synthesis of both. It is not bodies or souls that are the objects of progress, but human beings. To the complaint of metaphysics and idealism that the thought of thousands of years has not yet reached the inner chambers of the human soul, and that man is still living on the surface, too occupied with material achievement to look within himself, sociology replies that that is true only to the extent that man has feared or neglected to use his intellect and has substituted his emotions for the rational process, or has let nature do his work and his thinking for him. What can be expected of him in the way of true social progress when almost his entire efforts in life are spent on the struggle for bread or the battle for wealth? Says Ward:

There are two kinds of telic progress, or telesis, individual and collective. The former is the principal kind thus far employed. The latter is as yet so rare as to be almost theoretical. Society itself must be looked upon as mainly unconscious. Its operations are the result of the combined activities of its members. . . . This is individual telesis. It constitutes almost the only social progress that has thus far taken place (*ibid.*, 181-182).

Ward wrote his system of sociology for the purpose of demonstrating that the chief aim of man is happiness and that he can achieve it only through the use of reason. Society's most important function is not to expand or "succeed," but to care for its members. That is true morality and true social progress. It will not come spontaneously but through three well-defined and connected stages: (1) pure science, establishing laws governing phenomena; (2) applied science, perceiving utilities; (3) social telesis, making the necessary adjustments to secure useful ends (see *Ps. F.,* p. 306).

Above all, social development comes as the result of the mind force exerting its power upon the material environment and influencing mankind. All the currents of Ward's argument flow finally into the illimitable ocean of the mind force. In so far as man has made any progress whatever, Ward repeats in many forms all through his system, he has done so by his mind conquering the iron law of nature. The ethical code and the moral law are the final means employed by the intellect to suppress and destroy the animal nature of man.

## SPENCER'S MISCONCEPTION OF PROGRESS

In opposing Ward's entire philosophy of progress Spencer confused genetic progress (evolution) with telic progress, and popularized the idea that natural forces made human progress inevitable. Standing upon the general law of evolution, Spencer saw the balancing of energy moving inevitably forward to man's adapting himself to conditions, and toward ultimate happiness, if nothing (not even man himself) interfered with nature's process. In other words, genetic progress and individual telesis (to use Ward's terminology) are the only ones possible for man, said Spencer, for human or social progress is only another phase of the mechanical redistribution of energy, like the action of a machine which can "read" manuscript and set type. All that we can do to help nature is to speed up her action by improving our characters so that benevolence may correct all social evils. And it is this gigantic fallacy which so wantonly exaggerates the physical elements and obscures or entirely omits the psychic element and which, despite Ward's destructive criticism, still rules civilization.

In proving that Spencer's philosophy never got beyond the static and genetic states, Ward supplied the missing science of social dynamics. Although impulsive or static actions are the more universal and natural because they serve the end of preserving life, the rarer dynamic and artificial actions of the intellect serve the great purpose of individual utility, viz., the increase of human happiness (see *D.S.,* II, 161). Spencer, too, desired happiness for mankind, but the cure he suggested is worse than the disease. Like the Indian who admitted that the grass grew but firmly denied that the giant redwoods had

ever been other than they were, Spencer clearly saw the surface movements of social events (did he not warn against socialism as "the
coming slavery"?) but stoutly insisted that there were no currents
underneath for man to control (see *P.S.,* p. 11).

Before Ward, sociology furnished few clews to the relationship between civilization and progress. Condorcet's brilliant phrase, "the
present is pregnant with the future," and Comte's profound principle,
"progress depends on order as its essential basis," were just vague
enough to omit the explanation of how social progress occurs (*P.S.,*
p. 223). Ward transferred the subject of utilitarianism and human
happiness from the speculative into the scientific field, from emotion
to reason. Believing that a happy people is a moral people, and that
whatever increases the total of happiness or reduces human misery, is
progress, he defined it as success in harmonizing natural phenomena
with human advantage.

In one of Ward's frequent travels abroad, he visited Gumplowicz,
the leader of the Austrian sociologists and staunch disciple of Spencer.
Invading the peaceful villa of his colleague, Ward spent two days convincing him that Spencer's social philosophy of progress was a huge
error. The same discussion in many forms is still going on everywhere. On one side, are the individualists who assume that whatever
is, is a product of nature and, therefore, inevitable and right. On the
other, are the social scientists who believe that whatever is, is nature
only partially realized and, therefore, that improvement is always possible through rational endeavor.

Recognizing that telic progress is not yet established but a mere
theory, Ward deplores the blind opposition to it through all history:

Progress in unfolding the truths of the universe has taken place in
the order of their remoteness from human interests. The ones earliest
brought to light were farthest from man and least useful to him.
Astronomical truth was less valuable than physical, and physical than
vital.

There are two great domains in which scarcely any wide discoveries have yet been made. These are the domains of mind and
society. Psychic and social truth, when it shall begin to be revealed,
will be far more practical than even biologic truth. The leading
propositions in both these fields are today chiefly in the stage of theory.
To exert any influence, they must be *established* (*Outlines,* p. 210).

## IS SOCIAL PROGRESS INEVITABLE?

The practical-minded Ward is fully aware that social progress is possible but not necessarily inevitable. It depends upon human intelligence and human effort. Only genetic progress (evolution) is inevitable because it is inherent in matter and energy. But the social forces work for man's benefit only when the social mind works, and they are inert when it is asleep. Knowledge is always needed to rouse man into action. This thought is the climax of Ward's dynamic sociology which advocates civilization as a movement from intuition to objectivity, from emotion to reason, from life as an economy of pain and suffering, to life as an economy of pleasure and happiness.

Comte said that progress in and by itself was no benefit to humanity unless progress tended to the consolidation of order to form the new scientific state. On the other hand, he added, no true social order can be established unless it is fully compatible with progress. Ward, in the enthusiasm of youth, emphasized almost exclusively the problem of social progress. In maturity, he came to appreciate also the problem of social order and the means of preserving it. But he never forgot that mankind boasts of ancient errors and superstitions, and clings to outworn fetishes. The number of persons who believe that social improvement is possible (not to speak of being inevitable) is pitifully small. Who expects, in the same degree, any changes in worship or funerals, in the marriage institution or courts of justice, or finally, in the basic conditions of the people?

Had Ward survived the World War, he could not have spoken with greater prevision of the post-war "New Deal" than he did in 1883 when he said:

Thus far, social progress has in a certain awkward manner taken care of itself, but in the near future it will have to be cared for. To do this, and maintain the dynamic condition against all the hostile forces which thicken with every new advance, is the real problem of sociology considered as applied science (*D.S.*, I, 706).

Progress is not automatic in the sense that if we were all to be cast into a deep slumber for the space of a generation, we should arouse to find ourselves in a greatly improved social state. The world only grows better, even in the moderate degree in which it grows better, because people wish that it should, and take the right steps to make it better (John Morley, quoted in *P.S.*, p. 21).

## FEELING, INTELLECT, AND PROGRESS

In a brilliant analysis Ward probes deeply into the nature and possibility of social progress as the result of the co-operation of feeling and intellect. The old psychology always subordinated the emotions to the intellect, but Comte stressed the dominance of the feelings over reason. Ward agreed that man is moved only by his emotions, and uses his mental eyes only to see the way. If feeling alone dictated human activities, society would be endlessly involved in a struggle of conflicting individual desires that would wreck the social order. Intellect saves the day by providing ways and means of attaining ends, and by showing the individual the advantages of self-restraint and co-operation over competition and the biologic law of the jungle. The intellect also can work out regulations, laws, customs, ideals, and principles to guide the energies of the physical feelings into higher and safer spheres.

Ward now expresses a startling paradox. Although feeling actuated the evolution of moral codes, religious systems, and even civilization, it is unable to ameliorate social conditions to the slightest degree. When impulse challenges, the decision is not always with truth and justice, but always with those who are moved with the strongest feelings.

Neither the god-intoxicated philosophy of Spinoza nor the sublime ideas of all the mystics, esthetes, and poets of the past or present, have ever done anything of importance for the regeneration of society. Bread does not come from precepts or ideals, or happiness from abstract visions. Philosophy and metaphysics may flatter the mind with "brilliant" solutions, yet for all their parade of logic and fine words, they give but a dusty answer to the sore and afflicted. Says Ward:

All reform which it is hoped to bring about by argument, persuasion or any of the means available to the philosopher, must hold forth moral rather than intellectual inducements. To succeed, it must follow in the path of all previous efforts of the kind, of the religious systems of Manu, Zoroaster, Confucius, Jesus and Mohammed. Any one of these systems, if attempted to be put into effect in Europe or America today, would fail at its inception. The condition of society is at all times so bad, the degree of suffering witnessed everywhere so great, and the amount of sympathy thereby excited and constantly experienced in society is so intense, that there has never been an age when there did not exist a deep-seated demand for some improvement of the existing state of things (*D.S.*, I, 13).

When I assert that all the control that can ever be exerted over mankind must, in the future as in the past, emanate from the side of feeling and not of intellect, and promise a mitigation of the hardships of existence, at the same time I unqualifiedly maintain that all the true progress which has in fact taken place in the world, has come from the side of intellect and not of feeling (*ibid.*, p. 15).

The great oversight of the classical schools of philosophy was to regard feeling from the sole viewpoint of object or function. "Is man's only object in life to reproduce and pass away?" they asked, and failed to see that nature (genetic progress) had no other object for the rational being than to satisfy his desires. So far as human happiness is concerned, the social forces, operating as they do under the laws of evolution, bring only genetic progress, negative and passive (see *P.S.*, p. 471; *D.S.*, I, 56).

Ward does not deny progress in the past, but it has been an unconscious, accidental progress, not a planned intelligent one. Telic progress which is identical with happiness is due to the extrinsic factor of intellectual force which is as effective as the speed of lightning in comparison with the slow trial and error method of natural evolution. In Ward's words:

So long as society remains the unconscious product of the individual demands of each age, so long will the organized social state continue to be found out of accord with and lagging behind the real spirit of the age, often so intolerably as to require more or less violent convulsions and social revolutions. But if ever an ideal social organization shall come to be a clearly defined conscious individual want, it will be possible to establish one that will have elements of flexibility sufficient to render it more or less permanent. But here, as everywhere else, under the dominion of the psychic forces, the individual aim or object of man, happiness or some improvement in his personal condition, must be put vividly before him as the loadstone of desire and motive to action (*Ps. F.*, p. 101).

The heights of intellect are connected with the feelings of pain and pleasure found in the lower physical strata. With every advance in structure of the organism, the capacity for feeling correspondingly increases. Function is always fixed in quantity, but feeling grows with development. Accordingly, there has been a steady rise in the price

be exchanged for a complex but enlightened state. As he was once truly happy in a state of anarchy, so will he again be happy when he shall again attain to a state of anarchy. But the difference will be that the former was the unconscious anarchy of ignorance while the latter will be the conscious anarchy of intelligence (*D.S.*, II, 234).

## SOCIAL AND MORAL PROGRESS

Social progress is moral progress, says Ward. Contrast can be made only between material improvement and moral advance. Civilization, social achievement, individual happiness, and social progress are all synonymous of moral progress. Although the aim of social science is ethical throughout, it has done little, thus far, to accomplish its purpose. The chief reason for its backwardness is that social progress, not being an automatic or natural process but essentially a product of reason, has had little thought spent upon it. Ward sees clearly the tragic neglect of the very object of man's individual and collective existence:

The great moral and religious systems have been grand successes in so far as exerting an extraordinary influence and absolute control over the wills and acts of men is concerned. They have been signal and complete failures in so far as the amelioration of the condition of society is concerned. While it is impossible to discern what would have existed in the world if they had not, it is possible, on the other hand, to trace to their direct influence an enormous amount of unquestionable evil, and that mixed with but a small quantity of demonstrable good. . . .

There has been progress in civilization just as there has been progress in organic life, because the highest and best has been selected and preserved, and the lowest and poorest has perished. . . . In short, man has not yet ceased to be an animal, and is still under the control of external nature and not under the control of his own mind (*D.S.*, I, 14).

The reason why material progress is so far ahead of moral (social) progress becomes even plainer, continues Ward, as we contemplate the variety and intensity of human desires which find expression in actions intended to secure their satisfaction. These actions have incidentally, but with marvelous effect, wrought changes on this planet far greater than would have been possible for any irrational or mindless creature to accomplish (see *Ps. F.*, p. 90). The initial wants of man were for subsistence (demands of the body) and communication (demands of reason). The results that followed the hunt for subsistence, were invention, hunting, fishing, agriculture, manufacturing, and the arts (see *D.S.*, II, 179, 189).

The need of communication for human beings who were interdependent evolved the artificial process of language which much later developed writing and printing. Everything which increased the ratio of the artificial over the natural was a civilizing influence. Civilization finally came as a social achievement, as the artificial adjustment of objects so as to fulfill man's desires. Those who still believe that man was happier without civilization confuse animal contentment with human happiness, and inertia with achievement. A lack of desire is negative, like the absence of pain, but it denotes paralysis sooner than well-being. Happiness is positive; it is the aim and motive of all animal and human life, and what promotes it, is moral.

Nature is the whole; man, only a part of the unconscious cosmic process of organization. He begins as her pupil but ends as her master. Their relationship is clearly depicted in Ward's argument upon the nature of progress as follows:

Society can and should undertake seriously the artificial improvement of its condition upon scientific principles strictly analogous to those by which the rude conditions of nature have been improved upon in the process which we call civilization . . . and to adopt an aggressive reform policy guided entirely by scientific foresight rendered possible by intelligent acquaintance with the fundamental laws of human action (*D.S.*, II, 2).

Physical realities have, one by one, been stripped of their masks and dragged before the light. Once caught, they have been tamed, trained, and put to man's service. To this alone is due all our brilliant material civilization. Vital laws have been gingerly invaded, but with proportionate results. Psychic laws have long received attention, but from so false a standpoint that little more than the natural results have been achieved. Moral laws have stood absolutely still, if they have not gone backward, as the "moral science" writers admit, because the *appearance* of a *free will* has not yet given way to the *reality* of a *dependent will*. Social laws have received scarcely any attention, and, as a consequence, society as a whole has undergone no improvement, although the vastly disproportionate extent to which physical progress, due to the discovery of physical truth, has overlapped and overgrown it, makes the social stagnation another paradox to thousands who mistake material progress for social progress (*ibid.*, I, 52).

Moral progress has faltered because society has not used sociology for the diagnosis and cure of its ills. Material development and knowledge are up to the minute, but moral and spiritual development in society at large, and the social system which is the frame that holds all our progress since we left the treetops and the caves, present a crazy-quilt system rather than a rational order. We produce everything with such ingenuity that a visitor from Mars would take us for gods, but we use the products of our knowledge in a social order which belongs in the Dark Ages.[1]

These thoughts do not prove Ward to be a pessimist but a very profound thinker. His faith that moral progress will sooner or later arrive is a part of his insight into the unlimited power of the mind. History has confirmed his scientific optimism. The nineteenth century was the age of natural science. The twentieth will be a laboratory for research in human happiness. Although it still presents a scene of confusion and little has been accomplished, it is not because mankind is so decadent that moral progress is no longer possible, but because the method of applying reason to social phenomena is young and still in the probing and experimental stage.

Ward's philosophy of progress is a spiritual one founded upon a scientific study of the material base. It is the long-time view of the cosmic thinker who deals with eons, not a lifetime; with evolution, not generations. But it is also the view of the warm-hearted, clear-eyed sociologist who does not turn away from squalor and misery. His love of all human beings, great and small, as drops in the ceaseless stream of nature, the continuity of which brings the soul contentment, is the love that one has for a child, helpless and irresponsible but full of possibilities. In that squawking, fighting and impossible little shaver, he discerns the future civilized *homo sapiens* whose rational faculty will transform the battleground of society into a human estate, and the struggling, unhappy mass into a co-operating, happy order.

With the passionate demand that intelligence must lead, Ward revised the accepted story of mankind and wrote a new and elevating

[1] As Dr. Harry Elmer Barnes puts it: "If society wakes up in time and closes the gulf by bringing our institutions up to date, we may literally 'inherit the earth.' If we go on as we have so far in the twentieth century, there is not even a gambling chance of preserving civilization for more than another generation."

chapter in man's history. His theory of the social will is one of the boldest ever advanced in this world of doubts and fears. His dynamic concept of society which includes the principles of achievement, the environment, social control and social progress will some day rank as the most important contribution to the intellectual and social history of mankind.

CHAPTER XXXVI

# EDUCATION, THE GREAT PANACEA

---

*"The distribution of knowledge underlies all social reform. . . . The economic conditions constitute the end. The equalization of opportunity is the tangible, realizable means. I reduced the economic conditions to the bed-rock of human happiness, and I called the equalization of opportunity education (in "Dynamic Sociology"), but surely, the whole trend, drift and logic of this work have been to pile up the evidence that all influences, all environments and all opportunities converge to this one focal point, resolve themselves into and constitute education."*—Ward

---

Our guide has mentioned education, the great social panacea often enough, and here we are at last. The reader may wonder why it is found next to progress. Since Ward regarded education as the initial step toward progress (happiness), the sequence is both logical and natural.

## THE GREAT PANACEA

Few scientists or philosophers who spend their lives adding some more pebbles to the mountain of knowledge, or putting new colors into more clouds of speculation, have paid much attention to the question of social progress. So far as the aspiration and suffering of the masses are concerned, the worthy savants when they think about such things at all, feel certain of one thing—that if only their ideas were followed, everything would right itself. Kant's forward vision of universal peace, Haeckel's backward look into natural creation and Darwin's and Spencer's analysis of human origins are invaluable in the history of intellectual development, but they did not bring mankind a single step nearer to a better or happier life. Something more than knowledge and deep thinking was needed. Ward found it in education. By the synthesis of his theories of education and the equalization of opportunity and intelligence, he took his place in the front rank of the world's social philosophers. Education as the first and final remedy for the evils of society is not only man's deadliest weapon against dogma or reaction, but also the strongest instrument for the reconstruction of society. That is Ward's thesis.

His recurring stress upon education as a cure-all is a projection of his youthful struggles to extricate himself from the social morass. He knew too well from personal experience what social loss and individual maladjustment followed one barren of education, and never forgot what it meant to be hungry for knowledge. As a raw youth of twenty, he commented upon the vital truth of Jefferson's dictum "a nation that expects to remain ignorant in a state of civilization, expects what never was and never will be," as follows:

It is justly said that the great difference between the happiness, the independence and the prosperity of our nation and that of others, is due principally to the general diffusion of the means of education throughout its territories. These provisions wield a great influence over domestic affairs, and as our politics are governed, to a great extent, by domestic matters, they have a powerful effect in shaping the principles of our nation's government (*Diary*, p. 68).

Ward's philosophy of education owed much to Comte, for whom education was the most important function of the spiritual power and the foundation of all its other operations. Unlike Marx, who was convinced that education as a method, by itself, could not bring social progress, "not even if we wait for centuries or geological eras," Ward was certain that in the final analysis, education alone could open the doors to human happiness.

In defining education (Latin, *educire*, to bring or lead out) he added that the world had enough brains with which fundamentally to improve social conditions and evolve a moral civilization, but that the distribution of extant knowledge, equally and impartially, is vitally necessary (see *D.S.*, Vol. II, Chapters XIII-XIV; *App. S.*, Chapters VII, IX, XIII). His conception of education was not of a single factor among the many which enter into social evolution, but of the entire pattern of life.

Some day the world will marvel why our civilization, with so much knowledge and means for education, should have remained so profoundly ignorant of the causes and remedies of social evil. Whatever progress has been achieved, says Ward, has been due to the labors of the educated men and women who have increased the stock of knowledge and spread it over the globe. They are the true promoters of civilization and the benefactors of mankind. The resources of society are buried human talents and energies. Knowledge, the social heritage, has. fallen into the hands of a few privileged persons, on account of social inequalities (see *App. S.*, p. 300). To return the priceless inheritance to its rightful owners, the common people, is the mission of sociology. That is why Ward put education even before economic reform which he so often demonstrated was basal to spiritual progress. In his words:

Of all the panaceas that have been so freely offered for the perfectionment of the social state, there is none that reaches back so far or down so deep or out so broad as that of the increase and diffusion of knowledge among men. But the increase of knowledge, the discovery of wholly new truths, is attended with such a charm that it may be trusted to take care of itself. *The great social duty, therefore, is the universal diffusion of all the most important knowledge now extant in the world* (*Glimpses*, VI, 33).

The distribution of knowledge underlies all social reform. So long as capital and labor are the respective symbols of intelligence and ignorance, the present iniquity in the distribution of wealth must continue (*D.S.*, II, 598).

The economic aspect is of course the final test. . . . We are here dealing with the opportunity to achieve. The whole difficulty with the discussion of social questions has always been this haste to deal with the end, this impatience with everything that relates to the means. . . . The entire series of means are so related and dependent, that whatever affects any one affects all above it. . . . The rude comparison made of a row of bricks stood on end, of which it is only necessary to touch the first one to see them all fall in succession, is a perfect illustration of the process and one within the comprehension of all. . . .

The economic conditions constitute the end. . . . The equalization of opportunity is the tangible, realizable means. . . . I reduced the economic conditions to the bed-rock of human happiness, and I called the equalization of opportunity education (in "Dynamic Sociology"), but surely, the whole trend, drift and logic of this work have been to pile up the evidence that all influences, all environments and all opportunities converge to this one focal point, resolve themselves into and constitute education (*App. S.*, pp. 279-280).

## EDUCATION AND HAPPINESS

In one of the widest and most profound generalizations of all science-philosophy, Ward with mathematical precision traces the path of happiness as follows (see *D.S.*, II, 108):

(A) *Happiness* is the aim of man; the excess of pleasure over pain; enjoyment over discomfort.

(B) *Progress* is the state by which happiness is increased; the success in harmonizing natural phenomena with human advantage; the direct means to happiness, and the primary means to the ultimate end.

(C) *Dynamic Action* is the right action which leads to happiness; the employment of the intellect or the inventive and indirect method; the direct means to progress and the secondary means to the ultimate end.

(D) *Dynamic Opinion* is the correct view of the relation of man to the universe; the direct means to dynamic action, and the third means to the ultimate end. Right action comes from correct opinion.

(E) *Knowledge* is correct opinion; acquaintance with the environment; the direct means to dynamic opinion, and the fourth means to the ultimate end.

(F) *Education,* the universal distribution of extant knowledge is the direct means to knowledge and the initial means to the ultimate end.

### (A) HAPPINESS IS THE AIM OF HUMAN LIFE

Because education involves not only the discovery of truth but also its dissemination, Ward argues, it furnishes the highest and most exalted of all pleasures (see *Outlines,* p. 106). Happiness is not only the normal state of the healthy mind but increases with the flow of achievement. The aim of sociology is the organization of happiness, the love of pleasure, and the avoidance of pain. Its attainment means not only the satisfaction but also the increase and improvement of desire. The individual seeks happiness directly, but society can obtain it only indirectly.

The end is happiness; the means is progress. Progress is good because it spells happiness. If we ask what is happiness good for, there is no answer. Happiness is good, not as a means to something, but for what it is in itself. The concept civilization is identical with progress only if it means the gradual lessening of the tyranny of nature and the ascendency of the rule of mind, says Ward. In that sense, civilization is not pelf or glory, wealth or size, but spiritual treasures based upon those material necessities which make life more pleasant and tolerable. It means art, science, and philosophy; the forms for the expression and application of great truths to human needs; the complete subordination of the cosmic and the animal points of view to the human and the moral point of view (see *ibid.*, II, 473).

## (B) PROGRESS IS THE DIRECT MEANS TO HAPPINESS

Progress means whatever increases the sum of human happiness. Animal life is always limited by the walls of circumstances. But even with his developed brain power, man is dissatisfied. Progress in the final analysis, therefore, consists of the removal of all barriers to happiness by the artificial means called thought, reason, intellect. But how can that be achieved?

## (C) DYNAMIC ACTION IS THE DIRECT MEANS TO PROGRESS

Progress flows directly from dynamic action. Since progress is an artificial phenomenon, it can come only through human intervention. All impulses are static and involuntary, and have created the social order. Dynamic acts, on the other hand, originate in true intellectual effort, and they alone bring about social progress. The question now arises: what is the basis of dynamic action? The answer is found in the analysis of human actions, and the phenomena upon which they are expected (see *ibid.*, II, 106, 314). The further we go back into human history, the more predominant are man's impulsive actions. Deliberation, which first appeared in animal sagacity, has not as yet been developed to any great extent. Society seems to deprecate all such impulsive acts as love, hunger, ambition, and the like. At the same time it upholds the moral code in theory, but violates it in practice. As to deliberative acts, either moral or unmoral, man has no faculty which enables him to distinguish right from wrong. Conscience cannot be relied upon. Since it can perform only an intellectual and not a mystical judgment of what is right, conscience is nothing more than the rational faculty of mind. Only those rational actions which are the result of correct interpretations of phenomena, and involve the application of correctly perceived principles of natural ends to human ends, are progressive. The rest are stumbling blocks in the path of progress.

### (D) DYNAMIC OPINION IS THE DIRECT MEANS TO DYNAMIC ACTION

Opinion (belief, idea, judgment) is the direct means to progressive action. The axiom that principles rule the world means that opinion guides all human action. What men do depends directly on the views they entertain. The value of any act, however, depends upon two qualities in the views that motivate the act, viz., (1) correctness; (2) importance of subject matter.

As to the first, it is not unanimity of opinion or the general acceptance of a fact which steers action into progressive channels. Because millions of people believe in witchcraft or individualism, for example, is no final evidence of its correctness. Most thinking is emotional and wishful. "The wish should never have the remotest connection with the thought," said Ward. Cold calculation (scientific thought) must be our sole guide, for opinion based on emotions are as likely to be false as true.

As for the second quality, the importance of subject matter, it must be remembered that opinions are held not by any act of the will. Can a Roman Catholic compel himself by his own will power to accept the heresies of Luther (see *ibid.,* II, 421)? Opinions are products of education and human experience, over which the will has no jurisdiction. Hence the futility of coercing humanity to accept any particular opinion. Dogmas demand only loyalty. Mankind either fears the truth and refuses to think or else it is unable to think rationally. The only comfort is that the process of rationalization has never been seriously tried on any large scale, and that man is still to rise from a creature of circumstances—of feeling and animal instincts— into one of thought and reason.

### (E) KNOWLEDGE IS THE DIRECT MEANS TO DYNAMIC OPINION

Knowledge is the immediate data of opinion. Since man cannot think rationally by any act of the will, he must resort to intelligence, which is intellect plus knowledge. In the average mind, present intellectual capacity is far in excess of the amount of useful knowledge. Knowledge, in turn, is in advance of its general distribution. The net result is that general intelligence is far below present possibilities.

The field of knowledge is infinite. We are like children playing on the seashore, thrilled with finding new shells of truth. Yet, we leave the vast ocean unexplored. Like children too, we often do not know the difference between actual experience and imaginary experience; between truth and error. Only within the last two centuries has mankind, through science, commenced to clean house of accumulated illusions and superstitions, use real knowledge to rebuild the world, and plan for the future. "To know is to be able to foretell" (Comte).

Social progress, the improvement of man's lot, calls for straight thinking and the development of a scientific attitude. The kind of government or social life we enjoy depends upon our intelligence, and that, in turn, upon the reality and the application of our knowledge. This places the responsibility squarely upon society to ascertain, organize, and spread knowledge.

### (F) EDUCATION IS THE DIRECT MEANS TO KNOWLEDGE

All the paths leading to happiness converge and meet in the goal of education. The secret of transforming the social order, such as evolution has made it, into a moral and progressive state, lies in education, which connotes correct knowledge of the means to be employed. The principles of education constitute a creed, the first article of which is that all progress (civilization, happiness) is the result of the utilization of the forces and materials of nature; the second, that the chief means of attaining progress is the scientific education of all members of society. Education, in sum, is the only available means of setting the progressive wheels of society in motion; the only lever to which the power is to be applied. In Ward's words:

Give society education strictly held within the assigned limits, and all things else will be added. Even the philosophy required to co-ordinate existing knowledge would be certain to come in time ("Solution of the Great Social Problem," unpublished, 1893).

Coupled with this grand generalization is the desire to teach. It is one of the noblest human instincts that we cannot feel within us the full joy and power of any great conviction without earnestly striving to pass it on to others. The artist, too, thrills at exhibiting his work. And if propaganda has a religious fervor, the spreading of truth by teaching is not only a social instinct but a social duty.

Ward's vast induction closes with this question: Why learn anything if not to continue the conquest of nature, the satisfaction of wants and the realization of one's self upon ever higher planes? Why cherish spiritual treasures, if not to share them with the world? Why suffer, if not to learn by the experience, and plan to prevent further misery?

Has mankind heard Ward's answer that society must spread correct information to all, and let knowledge guide the forces of desire and achievement? Has it grasped the synthesis of education, happiness, and progress? Only the few, the wisest of the wise, have caught a glimpse of the infinite power of education to mold and control the opinions, ideas, beliefs, and actions of humanity. Socrates knew that evil springs from ignorance, not from sin; Kant, that in education lies the great secret of perfecting human nature; Jefferson, that no people can be ignorant and free at the same time.

## DOES EDUCATION, THE INDIRECT METHOD, LEAD TO HAPPINESS?

Mankind has suffered so much that it cannot be blamed for looking with suspicion upon all social panaceas. Without denying the cultural value of education, many warmhearted intellectual people look to ethics, eugenics, or social revolution as the way out. Why wait upon such a tedious evolutionary process as education? Will it ever be possible to connect such a remote means to the end of happiness which is needed as quickly as food or liberty? Why not try something which will produce immediate results?

Ward quickly disposes of such enticing doubts (see *D.S.,* II, 541). Practical as they sound, the demands of direct action in any form defeat themselves, while the apparently slow, indirect process is the only one that can win through. For the way of direct action is the way of nature, of the animal and the savage, instinctive and impulsive. The indirect method, on the contrary, is the method of man and his mind. Which can serve us better, the canal built by human ingenuity that runs in a comparatively straight line to its destination, or the meandering stream of nature which twists and turns without any goal at all?

Education is the best lever of progress. The very remoteness of education from the goal of happiness is proof of its high efficiency, argues Ward. To those who believe it is cumbersome or too long a lever to move the desired object, he points out a paradox. The longer the lever, the more weight is thrown upon it across the fulcrum; the greater is the force exerted. Its length does not steal the pressure, but, on the contrary, multiplies it many times over. Archimedes knew that when he offered to lift the earth if he only had a lever long enough. In sum, any direct means to attain happiness is a short lever which is powerless to accomplish its purpose. Exhortation, prayer, individualism, force, autointoxication, none of these direct attempts at happiness has ever attained or can ever attain its object. Only knowledge and its application—the long way round—can move the world forward to the supreme goal of happiness.

## THE KINDS OF EDUCATION

The field of education is so vast that a lifetime can be wasted in acquiring the least worth while, while neglecting the most important knowledge. Ward classified the various kinds of education as follows (see *ibid.*, II, 559-568):

1. *The education of experience,* founded on the method of trial and error. Who can believe that stumbling in the dark is the only way to go forward? We have sufficient knowledge to act with open eyes, according to plan.

2. *The education of discipline,* a form of mental gymnastics which is the false method of learning to think by thinking. Contact with objective reality is necessary (see *App. S.,* p. 307).

3. *The education of culture* puts nonessential knowledge ahead of practical and dynamic knowledge. Man cannot live only by esthetics and other refined accomplishments, much as they are desirable.

4. *The education of research,* the discovery of truth, is essential, but unless it is given to all, it is as useless as feeding a few, and then locking the food in a vault.

5. *The education of information,* the most necessary and worth while, seeks to extend to all the most important extant knowledge.

Ward's ideal of education follows that of Socrates—the diffusion of knowledge. The concept should be broadened, however, to include Aristotle's concept of education, i.e., not only the training of intelligence but also the training of character, the inculcation of habits and emotions, and finally the art and science of how to be happy.

As an appendix to his concept, Ward offers three cardinal principles: (A) knowledge, not mental capacity, is essential; (B) education should be the exclusive task of society; it must be socialized; (C) education should be universal and compulsory.

## (A) KNOWLEDGE, NOT MENTAL CAPACITY, IS ESSENTIAL

The curse of the educational system is the time and labor spent in polishing the mental grindstone instead of giving it something substantial to work on. Mental acrobatics, mathematics, logic, these have been the lures of even the greatest thinkers. Comte's emphasis on the cultivation of the sciences as the basis of education is noble and correct, but when he apostrophizes positive logic and mathematics because they provide a natural field for the exercise of the deductive method, he wanders far afield.

Ward decries the exaggeration of the importance of mental capacity. If one seeks, for example, to increase the quantity of a chemical compound, he would not keep on adding to one element and neglect the others. That is exactly what has happened in man's psychic and intellectual development. The already mature brain is carefully trained and exercised, but its contents are neglected (see *D.S.*, II, 481). It is Ward's achievement to have observed that the differences in intellectual ability between various races, classes, and individuals are small when compared to the differences in the knowledge they have. Not the crudity or the weakness of intellects, but their terrible lack of knowledge, the world over, is the main cause of human misery.

To fill the mind with correct information does not mean cramming or forcing the brain. Vital, knowledge-giving studies are always pursued with pleasure. The easiest strain on the human system is the acquisition of truth. Says Ward:

The normal mind is hungry for truth and when fed with it, it devours it with a relish and digests it without effort. That which wears out the young mind is the perpetual straining after an ideal intellectual development, the taxing of the wits in the solution of valueless puzzles, the memorizing of long lists of meaningless names to "lead out" the faculties, and all the other "tricks" of the teacher's trade which it is supposed necessary to learn in order to "get an education." The psychological principle upon which all so-called over-brain-work rests is the essential difficultness of all unnatural mental action. The studies that wear out the brain are those that are forced upon it against its natural promptings (*ibid.*, II, 569-570).

## (B) EDUCATION SHOULD BE SOCIALIZED

Can anything be clearer than the doctrine that education, a process which affects all of society, should be carried on exclusively by society? Yet Spencer's objection is still heard that parents are the best teachers, that the three R's are enough for the common people who want no more, and that to extend and socialize education would be to expand unduly the functions of government.

Ward shatters the objection by noting that government is not an extraneous power to be constantly held in check, as though it existed by and for itself alone. The fear of public ownership and control is a selfish fear. The function of controlling railroads, telegraphs, the post office, education, or health, is best performed by society, for things which affect the social weal should not be left to private interests. Whatever the state does is accomplished more economically and more efficiently than if done by private persons for private profit. In his own language:

The scientific mind appears to be peculiarly adapted to faithful service in situations where great practical interests are involved. Though making no professions of philanthropic principles, scientific men really have the welfare of society more at heart than many who talk loudly of social reform. They only ask an opportunity to apply scientific principles to great things, and when this is offered, they, as a rule, devote themselves completely and unreservedly to their work.

Science is ill-adapted to the feverish sentiments and methods that obtain in nearly all departments of private life. Science cannot be hurried. Forced to make haste, it is in danger of degenerating into charlatanism. It must also be independent. No one can influence it or warp its conclusions. There is no substitute for exact truth. All this applies to educational work. Education is essentially a scientific labor, and this in the highest sense. It is not only the science of sciences, but the art of arts. For all these special characteristics of all scientific work, the service of the state is admirably adapted (*ibid.,* II, 583-584).

The function of deciding what to teach should not be entrusted to parents, children, or individual teachers, but to society. It is the only competent tribunal to make such a vital decision (see *ibid.,* II, 591). If education is to mean anything more than charity, it must be public and co-operative. In private schools, all students are generally models of ambition and scholarship, according to the school reports.

Civilized nations boast of their public school systems, but such systems are far from a complete socialization of education. There are still too many private donations, bequests, and foundations (see *P.S.*, pp. 573-574). Despite many private endowments, society, as a whole, has hardly stepped out of the elementary schools. Most students receive only a few meagre tools with which an education may be acquired, and there they stop.

In the United States, state universities are gradually superseding older privately owned colleges, but there are few real universities which are anything more than training academies for young people or which offer opportunities for research to all who desire it. In Europe, education is generally socialized and freed from the laws of supply and demand, the only human endeavor no longer conducted on "business" principles. Ward was optimistic enough about his own country to say:

The action of society in inaugurating and carrying on a great educational system, however defective we may consider that system to be, is undoubtedly the most promising form thus far taken by collective achievement. It means much even now, but for the future, it means nothing less than the complete social appropriation of individual achievement which has civilized the world. It is the crowning act in the long list of acts that we have only partially and imperfectly considered, constituting the socialization of achievement (*ibid.*, p. 575).

### (C) EDUCATION SHOULD BE UNIVERSAL AND COMPULSORY

Ward dispels the world illusion that education is a dangerous social remedy for the masses. No one need have any fears about education if he realizes that by educating and elevating the lowly, the rest of society is elevated. Plato thought there was no sense in turning stones into gold unless one knew what to do with it. Ward believed that if only a comparative few possessed the truth, education would be of little social value. It is not more knowledge that we need, for what there is still lies fallow in the heads of the intellectual élite. What is much more necessary is to distribute extant knowledge to all. The tragedy of its unequal distribution evokes the following from Ward:

Of the gain thus made (by discovery of truth and artificial appliances) nothing is ever lost. But when we come to the actual utilization of the products of discovery, invention, and handicraft, we find this under the control of the opposite class of forces. The power to produce either knowledge or wealth is controlled by man, exercised when it can serve his purposes, checked or arrested when it no longer does this. But the power to possess—the ability to obtain the truth discovered or the commodity wrought—is controlled by natural laws and depends upon the thousand accidents of life—the conflicting wills of men, the passions of avarice and ambition, the vicissitudes of fortune, the uncertainties of climate and seasons, the circumstances of birth and social station, the interests and caprices of nations and rulers.

Of what use is discovered truth to the millions whose minds it can never reach? . . . The industrial system is out of order and we live in a pathological state of society. The vast accumulations of goods at the mills, avail nothing to the half-clad men and women who are shivering by thousands in the streets and while vainly watching for the opportunity to earn the wherewithal to be clothed. The storehouse of grain held by the speculator against a rise in prices has no value to the famished communities who would gladly pay for it in value of some form (*Glimpses,* IV, 12-13).

Thus, Ward comes once more to the conclusion that the deficiencies of backward regions are deficiencies of knowledge, and that the chief errors and evils of the world arise from ignorance (see *D.S.,* II, 481). The principal quality of all ideas is not their brilliancy, depth or complexity, but the quantity of mental dynamite or truth which they contain for release. Therefore, the progressive character of any age or people, said Ward, depends upon the truth embodied in its universal or world views.

Paradoxically, the universal opinions which dominate mankind are so firmly fixed that no contrary opinion is ever allowed to enter. The reason, as we have seen, is that such ideas ultimately rest upon interest or feeling, and not upon reason or intellect. No one can argue or reason human beings out of any fixed emotion or belief, observes Ward, even by mountains of logic or proof (see *App. S.,* p. 45). The only way in which such views can be changed is by the indirect method of modifying the underlying feelings, interests, and desires. That, in turn, is possible only by education.

To illustrate the consequences of mass error, Ward once more turns to the vital field of economics, where the battle lines between capital and labor are sharply drawn. The intelligent employing class has a correct idea of the class struggle and its own interests, and therefore co-operates with its own kind. The ignorant working class on the contrary functions individually and on the whole, competitively, and generally turns over to the capitalists without any real equivalent, the greater part of the product of its labor. In Ward's language:

> In modern times, the capitalists are able to perpetuate their hold upon labor by establishing influential organs and molding public opinion. The laborers have few, if any, such avenues of communication. . . . Those who are able to read at all, therefore, read the organs of the capitalists, and unable to penetrate their sophisms, and hearing only the one side, they acquiesce in and even defend their views.
> This genuine cooperation on the part of the capitalists does not go by that name. It is simply recognized as the only proper and successful way to do business, and such it really is. But any attempt on the part of the laboring classes to cooperate on the same principle and for the same object is loudly denounced as a sort of crime against society! The laborer is actually made to believe that it is so, and the state frequently steps in to punish it, as such (*D.S.*, II, 603).

Ward observes the great swarming mass of thoughtless humanity filled with vague and confused derivative ideas, eagerly devouring light gossip, current rumor, and trivial daily news and events, and upon that experience, boldly expressing positive opinions upon the most complex and puzzling questions. They know little or nothing of nature and science, and live almost an unconscious existence, as it were, leaving the world no better or happier for all their efforts (see *ibid.*, II, p. 505).

The unhappy condition of the poor, Ward continues, is due as much to their erroneous stock of opinions as to their definite lack of knowledge. The only gleam of hope is in the leveling-up process which has been going on for about eight hundred years (see *P.S.*, p. 446). Yet the social conditions which breed error and ignorance are still highly deplorable. No truer words were ever uttered by any lover of humanity than Ward's:

The mass of mankind have no time, disposition or ability to examine their opinions. They are like children. Their leaders are parents to them in all matters of opinion. They assume to tell them what is true, and they can only believe. If the teachers are themselves ignorant, so much the worse for truth, but it makes no difference with the acceptance of opinions. They are formed in the same manner, whether true or false (*D.S.*, II, 425).

The great struggle which the human race in common with every other species has had to make for its existence, has kept down every extraneous influence. The strife for food, clothing and shelter has swallowed up all other considerations. Man's constant warfare against the enemies drawn down upon him by his own error, has ever stood in his way when he has aspired to look upward for an inspiration. So long as man regarded the sun as a great fire-god . . . there was no hope of his pausing to investigate the nature and constitution of that celestial body. . . . So long as he is compelled to toil from morning till night to obtain sufficient to eat and to wear, he cannot stop to ponder over deep and weighty themes of science or philosophy, much less can he find time to read, study and investigate whereby alone his mind can be awakened (*ibid.*, II, 431).

Contrary to the belief of the Dark Ages, opinions are not produced or held by the will. Science, knowledge, and truth—the words are synonymous—constitute the foundations of all belief and opinion. The effect of opinions is directly in proportion to their truth. If one believes that the world is about to end, or regards the natural forces as a host of animated spirits, his individual and social conduct will undoubtedly be affected (see *ibid*, II, 459).

Repetition, and still more repetition, but all to nail down neglected and unpopular truths. To Ward, education does not mean the same thing as it does to the vast majority of the pedagogues engaged in polishing young minds. It is the first step in the most vital of social arts, i.e., the control by society of its own affairs. The real mission of education, "the loftiest flight of the inventive faculty," is to acquire and spread truth. That, as we have seen, means exactly one thing: to impart to all people, to all mankind, an equal amount of existing essential (scientific) knowledge (see *Glimpses*, VI, 337). There is no substitute, no other means, and no other method.

## EDUCATION AND THE SUBMERGED

The education of the poor and lowly, of the great masses, submerged and partially free, is a worthier and more important social need than any "brain trust" to do the thinking for everybody, or of any eugenic supermen to do the eating for everyone. Ward's appeal for universal education is a fitting peroration to his social philosophy:

A system of education, to be worthy of the name, must be framed for the great proletariat. Most systems of education seem designed exclusively for the sons of the wealthy gentry, who are supposed to have nothing else to do in life but seek the highest culture, in the most approved and fashionable ways. But the great mass, too, need educating. They need the real, solid meat of education in the most concentrated form assimilable. They have strong mental stomachs, and little time. They cannot afford to take slow winding paths; they must move directly through. Culture they can get along without. Failures are dead losses. For them every step should count (*D.S.*, II, 629-630).

Left to chance there are a thousand ways in which the influence of civilization is escaped. In sweeping down through the ages, it has only skimmed the surface of society. The great, the exceptionally talented, the influential, the fortunately circumstanced, the heirs of plenty and of leisure, such alone have reaped its advantages. The mass has scarcely felt its breath. In more recent times, civilization has been more generally diffused, but in this, chance has still ruled supreme.

Modern civilization is wholly unsystematic. Those to whose lot it has chanced to fall, have received it in proportion to their opportunities. A large proportion of the inhabitants of the civilized world are still uncivilized. In every large city there exist throngs of true barbarians—nay savages, that make the great bulk of the pauper, beggar and criminal classes of every country. The total cost of supporting, punishing and guarding against them constitutes half the charge of all legitimate government. Yet this so-called "heathen population" have normal faculties and developed brains.

Just as poverty in the midst of wealth aggravates its evils, so ignorance in the midst of intelligence is intensified by the contrast. So long as society has this burden on its shoulders, it cannot progress in refinement. It must cling to a large part of its old crudeness, as a protection against its unassimilated membership. The presence of these classes in the midst of civilization tends powerfully to lower the condition of the latter and clog its advance. The need of ridding itself of these classes, therefore, becomes twofold, and since they cannot be annihilated and will not civilize themselves, the importance of undertaking their artificial civilization is doubly great (*ibid.,* II, 594-596).

To the criticism that education would be wasted and impossible for the submerged classes, he patiently repeats that it is they who are the salt of the earth and who will finally inherit it. The roar of dissatisfaction which we hear round the world is the subterranean rumbling of the masses. And because genius is latent in its lowest depths, Ward pins his hope for social progress upon the unthinking and "unwashed" swarm whose day is dawning. His concern for the meek of the earth swells through his eloquent periods:

The denizens of the slums are the same kind of people as the inhabitants of the most respectable quarters. They are not fools by any means, but men and women with normal minds, susceptible, if surrounded by the same influences, of becoming as capable and intelligent people as any. As to the criminals, they are the geniuses of the slums. Society has forced them into this field and they are making the best use they can of their native abilities. Punishment does not reform and make good citizens of them. They go back with more bitter hatred of society than before, and they finally justify their attacks upon it, realizing that it is responsible for their condition.

But there is no need of having any slums. . . . Just as you cannot tame a full grown wild animal but must take the young and surround them with the proper conditions, so it is necessary to apply this principle to wild men and take them in their youth. . . . There is no other class in society whose education is half so important as this lowest and most dangerous class. Society ought to have and will one day have, the wit to devise means of reaching this class without its becoming a very heavy charge. It must apply scientific principles that will render·the work automatic and self-executing, but whatever the cost, it is a work that must be done, and which, when done, will a thousand times repay the cost (*App. S.,* pp. 312-313).

Ward can find no adequate reason why a mechanic, for example, should not have the same education as a white-collar worker or a professional man. In his manuscript, "Education" (pp. 158, 386), he foresees the time when it will no longer be a disgrace to labor; when every order of intellect will also be able to perform mechanical work, and when the workingman and the farmer will be men of culture. Says he:

Then labor will be recreation instead of drudgery. At the lathe and the plow will be digested and organized the ideas which will be received from the library and lecture hall, when mind and body will share alike the working hours, when the hands and the head will neither be overtasked, nor neglected.[1]

Ward's analysis of mind and social progress brought him to reduce the social problem to the following aim of education with which he closed his first and greatest work:

Whether the social system shall always be left to nature, always be genetic and spontaneous and be allowed to drift listlessly on, intrusted to the by-no-means always progressive influences which have developed it and brought it to its present condition, or whether it shall be regarded as a proper subject of art, treated as other natural products have been treated by human intelligence, and made as much superior to nature in this only proper sense of the word, as other artificial productions are superior to natural ones (*D.S.*, II, 632-633).

Is a social philosophy all that is necessary in education? What of the tragedy of mis-education? What of the correct principles and methods of education?

---

[1] There seems to be no exaggeration at all in the assertion of H. G. Wells and Julian Huxley in *The Science of Life* (p. 1469) that the progress of the world depends upon an understanding and competent minority of about a million people in all the world, and that the remaining fifteen hundred million in the civilized countries have remained practically what they were a thousand years ago.

# Chapter XXXVII

# THE PRINCIPLES AND METHODS
# OF EDUCATION

---

*"The great aim of education should be to furnish the proper materials for thought. Instruction should embrace the most suggestive truths. . . . What is really required is knowledge,—truth apprehended by the intellect, of the materials and forces of nature. . . . The only important knowledge is science."*—Ward

*"That man I think has had a liberal education . . . whose mind is stored with a knowledge of the great and fundamental truths of Nature, and of the laws of her operations."*—Thomas H. Huxley

---

WARD WAS A DUAL personality, a teacher as well as a philosopher. As the years pass, his principles and methods of education are being adopted with scarcely a word of recognition. He was one of the first educators in America to practice and preach the duty of the teacher to base his policies upon a thorough analysis of social phenomena. In so doing, he formulated the relationship between education and social science, and laid the foundation for a new system of education in which the teacher shapes the policies of the school, and at the same time takes his place in the front rank of social philosophers and social achievers.

## AN EPITOME OF EDUCATION

The following epitome of Ward's science and philosophy of education will give the reader an immediate bird's-eye view of what he has already surveyed and what lies ahead (see *D.S.*, II, 471, 484, 549-571):

### PRINCIPLES OF EDUCATION

I. Society may improve itself in two ways: (1) by increasing the amount of intellect; (2) by increasing the amount of knowledge.

II. The first method is that proposed by eugenics or the artificial selection and reproduction of human beings. The second method is that of applied sociology, or the rational change in the environment, by giving the intellect more and better material to work upon, i.e., by increasing knowledge.

III. Intellect is mental capacity—innate ability.

IV. Intelligence is intellect plus knowledge. Whatever increases knowledge develops the intellect.

V. Talent is intermediate between genius and intelligence, and depends upon intellectual power rather than the quantity of knowledge possessed.

VI. Genius is the special application of intellectual power in certain directions.

VII. Wisdom is intellect plus knowledge, and presupposes the possession and proper application of knowledge to human affairs.

VIII. Equal intelligence does not mean equal intellects. Intelligence will vary with the amount of useful and authentic knowledge. The mind absorbs error as easily as it does truth.

IX. The value of experience, i.e., the quantity of knowledge derived from the environment, determines the kind and quantity of intelligence.

X. Education is trivial or important, and leads to wisdom and progress or to error and reaction, according to the material which the mind acquires, i.e., according to whether the mind is rich in scientific knowledge or overladen with dogmas and fictions.

XI. Education means the distribution of useful knowledge equally among all. It does not imply the exercise or training of the mind to make it strong, brilliant, or clever.

XII. The degree of intellectual capacity (the quantity of brains) is amply sufficient in the present civilized races to conduct a moral and civilized order.

XIII. The more knowledge, the more "brains." The amount of useful knowledge possessed by the average mind is far below its intellectual capacity, and thus keeps the degree of intelligence correspondingly below what it might be.

XIV. The actual amount of present knowledge, though still below man's ability to utilize it, is sufficient if equally distributed, to elevate mankind to a relatively high position, and to awaken society to complete consciousness.

XV. The origination of knowledge, though slow and difficult, is easier and more rapid than any possible increase of intellectual power can be and may be made to keep pace with the intellect in the future without any difficulty.

XVI. The most important and feasible thing, therefore, is the thorough distribution of the great body of valuable knowledge already extant.

XVII. Knowledge implies laws and principles, which are the most important things to be taught.

XVIII. Real knowledge is knowledge of nature, environment, science, and literature.

XIX. There are two principles in the guidance of what to teach—generality and practicality.

XX. The aim of the state should be to see that each person is engaged in what he is best fitted for by nature, and equipped by a full knowledge of the scope of science and art, so that he may be free to do what he prefers and enjoys. Society should not allow the young to choose between a trade and an education. They should have a trade *and* an education.

## EDUCATION—WARD OR SPENCER?

The contrast between the educational theories of Ward and Spencer illuminates the differences between their social philosophies. Education—its theory and practice—is a reflection of social outlook. A glance into Ward's and Spencer's ideas upon education proves how inexorably those ideas are correlated to sociocracy and individualism, respectively.

The source of their viewpoints is clearly traceable to their environments. Ward was reared in poverty, far from any seats of learning. He was the youngest of ten children and always had the companionship of boys and girls. Untutored by anybody, and practically self-taught until the age of twenty-five, he never forgot what it meant to be deprived of wealth as well as knowledge—without friends, books, or teachers. At an early age, he learned how to farm, tend farm animals, and search for specimens of plants and rocks. He slept in the open, hunted in the forests, and trekked the plains. Unpolished and without any books or learning, he spent years among simple, uncouth and callous-handed sons of toil and discovered keen intellects. He was a true son of the soil who climbed to great intellectual heights —a patient, brilliant observer, student and reader, but never a dry book in human form.

Spencer's life was altogether different. Brought up in a well-to-do middle-class family, he was sheltered from all, and lived in the midst of opportunities for education. There was never anything to stand in the way of his philosophical bent, and he grew up a thinker par excellence. He was never a reader or researcher, and his theories were all colored by his extreme individualistic and evolutionary principles. As the oldest and only survivor of nine children, he was tutored at home, and chiefly by relatives who were marked for generations by extreme conservatism in politics and nonconformity in religion.

Here follows the result of his widely separated views on education when set opposite those of Ward:

### SPENCER ON EDUCATION

1. Education is no panacea but a reform which must move equally with other reforms and in all things follow nature's system and method.

2. Society, like mind, is an organism. Happiness comes only through individual growth and adaptation.

3. Social statics and the passive adaptation of the cosmic process to man, should be emphasized. Social progress is possible only under the laws of evolution which apply equally to nature, animals, and man.

4. Social improvement can come only through the increase of sympathy by progressive adaptation of the character of men. Evolution occurs through the inheritance of acquired characteristics. Natural selection alone will accomplish social improvement.

5. The unit or individual determines the mass, through individual action and competition.

6. The function of the state is negative, to administer justice.

### WARD ON EDUCATION

1. Education is the great panacea and the only way out of social stagnation and misery. It is not above social science but a part of it.

2. Society may have started as a growth but it has now become a mechanism, artificially (rationally) controlled. Happiness is a product manufactured by man's intelligence.

3. Social dynamics should be stressed. Social progress is an artificial, telic process. The world can be changed by man.

4. Education is the chief method of improving society and the only sure road to meliorism. Social improvement depends only indirectly upon the inheritance of acquired characteristics and the force of natural selection. Direct dependence must be placed on social opportunity and social environment.

5. The mass determines the unit or individual, through control by society and co-operation.

6. The function of the state is positive, to minister to the happi-

Education is a private, individual function, and the state should neither provide for it nor control it. The law of equal freedom applies. There should be no national or socialized education. The initiative and foresight of individuals will provide.

7. The plan of education is an individualistic one and is controlled by the law of supply and demand. Education depends on the strength of the parental instincts. Under no circumstances should the state usurp the functions of the parents. No child has a right to education, and the state should not meddle in such private matters. If children are not adapted, the evolutionary law will settle the problem in the interests of society. It is more humane to let the inferior perish.

8. Education is not an active factor in the scheme of evolution.

9. The purpose of education is the preparation for life by the individual. Man must be adapted to nature and the environment. The aim of education is an individual one, to evolve fine characters and noble individuals.

10. The curriculum of education must be organized in support of the aim of education as a preparation for life.

ness of the people. Education is a social function and should be compulsory, universal, and socialized.

7. The plan of education is a social one and cannot be regulated by supply and demand. It is the business of the state and should be provided for all alike. Every child has a right to education. Knowledge will help to evolve a world where there will be no inferiors fit to perish.

8. Education is an active factor in evolution and is the mainspring of all progress. It is the piston of civilization.

9. The purpose of education is a social one, to achieve the good society by making its members happy. The environment must be adapted to man through knowledge (the subjective environment). Man can make both nature and the environment serve him.

10. Education is not a drawing out but a mental feeding for the purpose of growth and achievement. It consists therefore not only of science (knowledge of the environment) but of such other knowledge as adds to man's enjoyment.

## WARD, THE MASTER BUILDER IN EDUCATION

Ward who wrote the greatest original work on education of the nineteenth century and left the manuscript to molder in the files (now in the Ward Room) at Brown University, regards Spencer's famous *Education* as merely a treatise on home training rather than on education. Spencer's postulate that parents are generally qualified to instruct their children in what is most important for them to know, Ward says, is altogether unsound. "There never was a time when children of twelve years could not instruct their parents in the most important branches, and this fact grows more noticeable as the methods of education improve" (*ibid.*, II, 556).

The drift of the times has been steadily away from Spencer's theories of education and toward Ward's. The trend of education thus follows the trend of social evolution. But like democracy and social control, education has not yet been fully tried. One thing is clear, the world is moving forward to co-operation and sociocracy. In that new system, education is bound to be as different from what it is now, as co-operation is different from competition.

## CRITIQUE OF PRESENT EDUCATION

Ward's criticisms of the educational system is also an incisive analysis of the social foundations and superstructure, but throughout his critique he immediately builds wherever he destroys. The necessity of a scientific education and the universal spread of knowledge is always in the van of his argument, and he never forgets the aim and purpose of education as the *sine qua non* of human happiness. His main attack upon education in the individualistic order is as follows:

1. Education leans to culture more than to science.
2. The education of information is not put first.
3. Education is not well balanced between books and objects.
4. It fails to teach invention.
5. It is blighted by specialization.
6. The courses of study are not synthesized.
7. Education must be a practical process. Knowledge should be taught in three curriculums: (1) the general, dealing with the widest generalizations; (2) the special, continuing the reduction of generality and allowing freedom for the teacher to choose students and subjects

according to talent; (3) the technical, giving room for specialization and electives.

8. Teaching should be in the hands of both men and women.

9. There should be methods for determining mental fitness, by intelligence and performance tests.

10. Reading, writing, and mathematics must remain the primary tools of education.

11. Education should be conferred by schools, by literature, and by objects.

12. While observation, experimentation, and the teaching of the concrete before the abstract, are important, books and scientific treatises are of inestimable value. Translations of foreign books may be used instead of the originals.

13. There should be formulated by educational experts, a uniform system of grading for the entire country, varied perhaps, to a slight degree, by particular circumstances of localities.

14. A treatise on the matter and method of educational procedure should be published at public expense and made public to all.

15. The method of education should be telic, planned like all other social activities. That method must utilize the emotions and the intellect by extending knowledge to them equally. Such differences as would then remain would be natural differences, and not artificial ones.

16. There should be a national university.

## EDUCATION MUST LEAN TO SCIENCE MORE THAN TO CULTURE

The thesis that scientific knowledge is the most important of all, stems from Comte.[1] Ward was convinced that unless education is

---

[1] George Henry Lewes in his *Philosophy of the Sciences* (pp. 16-17) quotes Comte as follows: "The establishment of the positive philosophy will be the presiding and influencing agent in the general reconstruction of our system of education. Already, indeed, all enlightened minds unanimously recognize the necessity of discarding our European system of education, which is still essentially theological, metaphysical and literary, and substituting for it a positive education in harmony with the spirit of the age, and suited to the wants of modern civilization. . . .

"A general education absolutely requires an *ensemble* of positive conceptions upon all the great elements of natural phenomena. It is an *ensemble* of this sort, on a scale more or less extensive, that must henceforth become even among the popular masses, the permanent basis of all human combinations; that must, in a word, give the general tone to the minds of posterity."

scientific, it is comparatively worthless. To search the depths of the mind or to hunt for the infinite may be more exciting than to look into test tubes or scientific books, but fundamental principles culled by science from nature are far more valuable than any kind or quantity of metaphysical disputation, ethical grounding, or mental exercise.[2]

As a tyro of twenty-five, Ward already saw deeply into the need, first of all, of a scientific education, when he wrote in his unpublished essay, "The Importance of Intellectual Culture" (1866), as follows:

Moral, called mental culture, leads to abstract sophistries and invalidity. Religious, to the exclusion of intellectual training, degenerates into morbid asceticism or bigoted fanaticism. Neither serves to accelerate in the smallest degree the onward march of civilization, and as progress in one direction or the other is the great law of creation, they both operate to drag the world backward upon the foreign hedges of atheism and idolatry or into the miry clay of credulity and superstition.

A generation later (1893), in another unpublished lecture, "Solution of the Great Social Problem," he said:

We may imagine the creeds of the world supplanted by a similar faith in the progressive principle here formulated. The energies heretofore so powerfully directed to ecclesiastical work would then be directed to educational work. The school would fill the place now occupied by the church. The scientific lecture would supersede the sermon, and the study of normal objects and of standard scientific works would form a substitute for the study of sacred writings.

Time and maturer thought convinced him all the more, that true culture is founded only upon the study of science, something which is within the reach of all. But the ability to grasp the truths of nature must not be confused with the ability to discover them. What has taken many centuries for great minds to wrest from nature, can now be attained by the average school child in a few hours (see *App. S.,* p. 102). Even original research does not require extraordinary talents. Anything which is so involved that it cannot be readily comprehended is of little importance. Fine-spun theory is not knowledge, and the process of abstract reasoning soon becomes reasoning about nothing at all—a discipline as valuable for the mind as an empty stomach imagining that it is digesting something. Subjects that make pupils think—

---

[2] Honest John Morley knew that well when he said: "Where it is a duty to worship the sun, it is pretty sure to be a crime to examine the laws of heat."

and thinking is the highest and purest of pleasures—are certain to be the most interesting and the most easily absorbed. If the mind is fed on husks, it naturally grows lean and tired. As he said in his unpublished "Education" (p. 575):

The great aim of education should be to furnish the proper materials for thought. Instruction should embrace the most suggestive truths. The more important and comprehensive the knowledge is which a student is acquiring, the more likely it will be to exercise his thinking powers, and the more thoroughly he exercises these, the more knowledge he will acquire.

All important knowledge is the direct testimony of nature—original and scientific. Therefore, said Ward, knowledge of the forces and materials of nature is the education worth while (see *Cape,* pp. 76-77). If the student is not kept in the dark as to the nature and purpose of education, but is informed early in life that its goal is the further conquest of nature for the increased happiness of the human race, he may learn something about organic and social development, of the victory of mind over matter, of what has happened in the world, and what it all means for the future of mankind. That is what Ward taught his classes from the tabular view of all knowledge (p. 192). He always believed that what shall be taught was more important than how it should be taught.

The mind, he said, is naturally hungry for real food. In 1909, when he delivered an address at the Oxford Labor College entitled "Education and Progress" (see *Glimpses,* VI, 330), he was astonished that his audience of workingmen heckled him not about wages or hours of labor but about the origin of the universe, of life on this planet, and similar problems. "Such are the questions that present themselves to the laboring classes as soon as they begin to receive a little real education" (*Cape,* p. 189). Says Ward:

What is really required is *knowledge*—truth apprehended by the intellect. Intelligent mind fortified with knowledge is the only reliable form of the directive force. The only proper knowledge for this purpose is that which can be acquired of the materials and forces of nature. The first element of a truly progressive system is *popular scientific education* (*D.S.,* I, 21).

The only safe knowledge is the knowledge of *things*. Knowledge of *thoughts* is unreliable, because thoughts themselves as often consist in errors as in truths. The only real knowledge is knowledge of *nature*. The only important knowledge is science (*ibid.*, I, 70).

Ward deplores the system of education which wanders far afield into sham intellectual problems or mock tournaments of logic and polemics—of wrangling, debate, and disputation—all offered as a vital part of education. Even the Greek geniuses who were grand reasoners and sometimes good observers, went wrong and sterile whenever they reasoned insufficiently. When they erred, it was only for lack of proper and sufficient observation and knowledge. Proficiency in abstract thinking or mental acrobatics could not supply that deficiency. Ward, too, observed the futility of just mastering mathematics, or pursuing memory training, or having what is generally known as a brilliant mind (see *ibid.*, I, 103, 106). In words that have not yet been heeded in a world where education is partly a business, he said:

What each one needs and what the schools shall not fail to provide is such a conception of life and such a general knowledge of the world that each one may intelligently choose, duly appreciate and wisely pursue his own special vocation. This object can not be pursued by drilling him in details; it can only be obtained by a comprehensive indication of all the great truths of human knowledge.

The educational method must be comprehensive at the expense of minutiae. Absolute mastery cannot be expected in the brief time allowed for education. Above a certain point, its specialty will rob it of its utility. And no amount of school drilling will secure such complete mastery of anything that it will not require practical experience to render it serviceable.

There is something so totally distinct in the process of memorizing from that of reasoning, that while engaged in the former, the mind may be wholly free from the latter. Yet the former is the greater drain upon the intellect. When exercising the memory, therefore, to its full extent, as the student must usually do, he finds it exceedingly difficult to apply the fact he is learning to the deduction of laws and principles. The consequence is that the true lessons which he should have been learning at school, never reach his mind until years, or at least months afterwards, after the fan of time has winnowed away the chaff which clouded his mind, and enabled him to see the real meaning of all he has been learning.

He then finds that what he spent the greater part of his time in studying and conning at school, is of no use to him, but only the general truth of which it is but a spray, but which had been so dense from first to last, that he never got gleams of its source. But where one person ever derives this late advantage from what he has been taught, there are hundreds that never wake from the delusion that it was all for mental discipline, and where one of these general truths thus comes out at length from the fogs of confusion, there are many more which never dawn on the pupil's consciousness (*Ed.,* p. 573).

## THE EDUCATION OF INFORMATION SHOULD DOMINATE

To Ward, scientific knowledge, the education of information, came before all other knowledge. Quality alone must count. One may know many facts without having much knowledge, for real knowledge is deep and broad and is of a fundamental nature (*ibid.,* pp. 556, 630). The education of experience cannot give the student an insight approaching that of the mind possessed of natural science. The pursuit of knowledge is not the same thing as the pursuit of life, as Nietzsche believed, and Bergson expanded into the error that intuition is above knowledge. Experience is not the best teacher, for one cannot learn from what has happened to him unless he has developed the power of reflection and can check up his experiences with those of others. Truth is an ideal; thinking is a synthetic process. Experience never furnishes truth, and intuition is only sometimes right. Nothing but a creative faculty can educe truth from fact (see *P.S.,* p. 89).

Ward's simple conclusion is that the primary basis of opinion is the experience of the senses. Education confined to sermons, dead languages or mathematics fails to furnish the important facts for generalizations upon vital subjects. First of all, he says, a knowledge of nature, especially of the environment is conducive to correct opinion. Such knowledge (the education of information) creates a desire for more knowledge, for only the ignorant are content to remain so.[3]

The knowledge generally possessed by mankind springs from trivial emotions and prejudices. Few have any practical, fundamental truths, and the last thing one expects to find in their busy brains is any knowledge of the environment. Lacking any scientific information, their minds are soon filled with mere beliefs or assumptions based upon all

[3] The great Newton with the true modesty of science remarked: "I do not know what I may appear to the world; but to myself I seem to have been only like a boy, playing on the seashore, and diverting myself in now and then finding a smoother pebble or a prettier shell than ordinary, whilst the great ocean of truth lay all undiscovered before me."

kinds of hearsay and illusions. Whatever real knowledge they have is distorted by errors which creep in during transmission. The first duty of society, therefore, according to Ward, is to acquaint its members with their surroundings so that they may grasp and co-ordinate phenomena according to underlying laws and principles. The latter has been done by dynamic sociology. The former is the task of education.

The failure to acquire a fundamental education of information results as follows, says Ward:

Men are still continually dashing blindly against the barriers which the environment presents to their free activities. Empirical knowledge has afforded them a superficial view of the world and their relations to it. But below lie hidden truths, whose meagre manifestations at the surface are almost always wrongly interpreted, and from which conclusions precisely the reverse of the truth are frequently drawn. Actions based on these conclusions lead men into innumerable pitfalls and entail anguish and suffering where immediate destruction is escaped (*D.S.*, II, 16).

### EDUCATION BALANCED BETWEEN BOOKS AND OBJECTS

Education must be perfectly balanced between knowledge of the environment and knowledge contained in books, which is only another example of synergy, the teamwork of forces. Although Ward studied nature at first hand, his passion for books was unbounded. The inscription "Read and you will know," which he came across as a boy in some old textbook, inspired him more than all the refined literature which later came his way. To know meant for him direct contact with every phase of the environment, a scientific knowledge of nature. Yet he once drily remarked on the paradox of scientific investigators who held books in contempt, but kept on writing more of them (see *ibid.*, II, 630). In his own words:

The greatest vehicle for the conveyance to millions of the knowledge of the truths established by the few, is letters. . . . All knowledge must first have been acquired by drawing information from the objects about us. . . . Years may be necessary to learn from nature what books will teach in a few hours (*Ed.*, p. 207).

The study of objects and literature are both necessary, indispensably and equally so. They will be found to be mutually dependent upon each other.  Observation and experiment constitute the growth and manufacture of knowledge, while literature represents the world's commerce of ideas.  Literature is the grand leveler, science, the grand leader.  The former embraces the toiling millions; the latter inspires the heroic few.  The one labors for the immediate present, the other, for the distant future (*ibid.*, p. 411).

Ward felt that young people learn too much from books and hearsay, and too little from use of their own senses in nature's school.  The less "training," at least before the age of ten or twelve, the better, he recommended.  In the present school system, the study of nature is generally pushed to the rear, although it is far more important than studies from classical history or mythology.  Neither the rocks and shells nor the flowers and animals can lie or exaggerate.  Nature must be our first and last teacher.  Drawing upon his own experiences, Ward observed:

The country boy, roaming through fields and forests, little dreams that he is all this time acquiring scientific knowledge of the most useful kind, and he is apt to imagine a little later when he begins to feel the need of an "education," that all the time thus spent has gone to waste.  But if he presses on, and at last gets that education and enters any of the great avenues of science, he will come at length to see that those rustic days were the richest of his life, and that it is to them that he owes the breadth and volume of his subsequently developed nature (*Glimpses,* V, 31-32).

One of the greatest mistakes made by parents as well as by teachers is to measure a child's future ability or usefulness by its precocity in learning its lessons at school.  The kindergarten should be expanded or extended so that all book learning until about the age of twelve would be abolished.  During the receptive stage of the child's mind,

education should consist in placing the child in such situations that the things which it is most important that it should know will be constantly appealing to the senses.  It is such impressions that are to constitute the basis of all future ideas, opinions and actions. . . .
This much neglected point of view is one for parents and educators, nay, even for legislators and social reformers, to consider.  Something must be done to enrich the lifelessness and attenuated atmosphere of the more populous centers. . . . Recreations from business only tend to relieve the strain upon adult life, leaving the foundations of the evil untouched.  The remedy must be applied earlier and the mental and physical constitution of the race must be given that touch of

nature which makes the whole world kin by teaching all, the high as well as the low, that they are the children of the Earth, the common Mother of all that lives and feels and thinks (*ibid.*, pp. 30, 32).

Commenting on courses of study, Ward placed the concrete before the abstract, especially in the teaching of natural science. Personal experience should be used wherever possible. While specimens, collections, and museums are necessary, original research need not be included in the general curriculum. Nor is mathematics so very important, because when it is "too exclusively pursued, it destroys both the reason and the judgment and consists in prolonged thinking about *nothing*" (*App. S.*, p. 311). As for history, while valuable enough, learning it does not train the judgment unless it is that kind of history which through sociology, studies the laws and principles underlying social phenomena (see *ibid.*, p. 312).

Ward's criticism of mere book learning is not founded upon any distaste for the library. Because he saw the danger of knowledge becoming specialized and descending into a second-hand process, he was keenly aware of how much reading predominates observation. That led him to advocate teaching invention as a social necessity, and to affirm resolutely that the social art, the art of life, can be learned only by observing, grasping, and applying the laws and principles of nature.

Nevertheless, he always prized literature—writing of a descriptive, explanatory or interpretative nature—as invaluable to education. He warned against making artistic writing a fetish, or preferring rhapsody to sober truth. Loving the gems of the intellect, he felt nevertheless that what is called polite classic literature consists in adroit ways of saying nothing beautifully. Rhetoric generally conceals more than it reveals (see *D.S.*, II, 500).[4]

### EDUCATION SHOULD TEACH INVENTION

Is it not tragic, asks Ward, that the greatest part of invention, the most useful of all forms and products of thought, should be lost for

[4] The result of the faults in our educational system has been illustrated by Professor W. H. Kilpatrick, of Teacher's College, Columbia University (*New York Times*, May 3, 1936), in his report that two-thirds of the New York City schools are creating antisocial character through autocratic instruction and the failure to teach students as personalities. In other words, the ordinary school is run largely upon an antidemocratic and antisocial basis. Instead of learning to think and how to live in the society of his fellows, the student generally learns to hate books, school, and teachers. Memorizing facts does not help in the slightest.

want of opportunity? And it is education alone that can furnish the opportunity. Until now, that highest and most complex function of the mind called invention has been left to chance. From now on, Ward insisted, it must be treated as a science, and its method inculcated through systematic training. The faculty of invention which uses all knowledge, of nature, books, art, and science, can be cultivated in the same manner and to the same degree as any other human faculty. Says he:

The world has moved by virtue of what has been done in it, and only indirectly by what has been known. It is no secret that a large part of what now passes for education, both of the lower and of the higher kind, is thus sterile. To give it results is to give it life, and the introduction of the element of work is literally breathing into a moribund system the breath of life. . . .

To those who can rise to the contemplation of society as a conscious organism of the highest and most complex character, and who understand what its progress consists in, it must be obvious that the most eminently practical of all things is the subjugation of nature to man. Thus far, this has been accomplished empirically, at haphazard, and, as it were, by accident. The educational training of the mind and hand together on a grand scale in the public schools, through the conscious action of nationalities throughout the civilized world, is the first effort ever made by society to lift the work of civilization out of the empirical groove and place it upon the high plane of systematic science. And if the movement continues, there is no cause to doubt that we shall see, upon a scale commensurate with civilization itself, all the difference which has ever attended the transfer of any human art from the stage of raw empiricism to that of organized science (*Glimpses*, IV, 102-104).

### THE BLIGHT OF SPECIALIZATION

Ward stressed specialization as one of the blights upon the system of education, by which the vocational and the technical elements crowd out the cultural ones. In coddling the specialist we make the same mistake that the Schoolmen did when they confused erudition that dries up the soul, with wisdom which expands it. Grammar school children are specialized in figuring interest and discount, but they acquire no clear idea what mathematics means. High-school children are specialized in knowledge of battles and reigns of kings, without absorbing any fundamentals of the movements of history and its forces. Facts, large and small, mountains upon mountains of them, are the specialist's joy, but he has nothing to do with syntheses, generalizations, and cosmic truths. The hope of the future lies not in scientific specialists, but in a generally educated public that travels the broad highway of science instead of some narrow-gauged specialty, which practically bars out the view of all other subjects. Says Ward:

The same principle which makes a special student arrogant, makes a general student humble. But this same humility, far from deterring him from making a proper use of his knowledge, aids him in doing so and prevents him from making an improper use of it (*Ed.*, p. 554).

## THE COURSES OF STUDY ARE NOT SYNTHESIZED

From his classification of the sciences, Ward deduced the necessity of unifying and integrating the various courses of study. On every social question which involves a knowledge of the sciences below sociology, very few even educated people learn enough to synthesize their knowledge. The fault is with the educational method which takes no account of the natural succession of phenomena, or the dependence and evolution of the sciences, but teaches bits of the jigsaw puzzle of knowledge, without giving a picture of the whole.

Something like double the progress would be made by pupils of all grades, if an exact logical method were adopted in the order of their studies, so that every new subject would naturally grow out of the preceding one. Such a program in education would follow the dynamic program of sociology, i.e., the serial arrangement of the sciences. Only by this method can the pleasure of following up a logical chain of causally connected truths plow its groove in the plastic young brain (see *App. S.*, pp. 302-305). But it seems to be the last thing thought of in school or college, and then it is postponed for more important· matters.

Space forbids that we touch upon more than a few of the main criticisms of education in the individualistic system.[5] Enough has

---

[5] Even the universities in America are not exempt from the glaring faults of the educational system. Although the advance of learning has made the university the most complex and the most sensitive of institutions, there are courses which look like polite dancing lessons and afternoon teas. It is not unusual to meet with doctorates in hotel management and high degrees for theses on "The Essence of Motherhood," "Child Guidance Correlated with Thermodynamics," "The Scientific Reconstruction of Character," and "The Technique of Janitor's Work." The degree of bachelor of arts is given for courses in wrestling, judo and self-defense; food etiquette and hospitality; gymnastics and dancing for men, and retail advertising, and the degree of bachelor of science for courses in drugstore practice, principles of coaching, and home laundering

been shown to indicate Ward's view that education should not be made a forcible cramming of knowledge like a dental filling, or the sharpening of the mind as if it were a razor. It is a process which should give the student a dynamic, synthetic view of nature, man and society and enable him to think for himself. In other words, science is the only method, and nature the chief source and material of any scientific scheme of education. Facts are bricks, static and inert. Method alone is dynamic. Give the student a fundamental knowledge of laws and principles, and he is able to build his own mansion of understanding. It is general, not special, knowledge which is most important. Learning a mass of details at the beginning of any subject is fatal, for that is generally the end of the study. To tyros and minds devoid of fundamentals, the vast number of· facts and phenomena present a scene of chaos. Memorizing is not the solution to the problem of conquering knowledge. To the student of social science (and everybody should always be one), the eagle's-eye view, the all-round aspect and the synthetic treatment are the phases of true education.

## FUNDAMENTALS OF TEACHING

Ward was a teacher in the best sense of the word, all his life. He was more interested in creating a demand for knowledge than supplying it, though he did not neglect the latter. He proposed three distinct curriculums: (1) general and practical knowledge; (2) truths of greater depth and difficulties; (3) elective courses for those who have successfully passed the first two. He had room for never ending study under the principle "everything that has been made by man should be known to all men" (see *D.S.*, II, 621-623).

By general knowledge, he did not imply abstract or difficult knowledge. General truths are simple because they are concrete and treat

---

(*Universities, American, English and German,* by Abraham Flexner, 1930). America even has professors of police administration, and biography. One can become a master of arts or doctor of philosophy by writing theses on "Administration Problems of the High School Cafeteria," "Public School Plumbing Equipment," "Concerning Our Girls and What They Tell Us," "The Intelligence of Orphan Children in Texas," "An Analysis of Paring Knives in Terms of Time and Material Wastes in Paring Potatoes," "Style Cycles in Women's Undergarments," "The Bacterial Content of Cotton Underwear in Texas," and anything else your heart desires. There are schools of journalism, schools of business, schools for secretaries, advertising, merchandise control, barbering, optometry, and most anything you can pay for.

of phenomena. To acquire facts of science requires no more than the ordinary intellectual powers of an average man. By practicality, Ward did not mean the ogre of technical knowledge. Technology and artistic education simply teach how to do things, while the education of information deals wholly with knowledge of things, objects, laws, and phenomena. Both are necessary, but the latter is more vital in social progress.

The equipment of scholarship is not all there is to education and teaching. As early as 1870, Ward wished that every impediment were swept away and that teachers and pupils could meet in some genial clime, as it were, on a bare plain under the open skies, without a building, program, or ceremony, and together look straight into each other's minds and into nature, and then begin the real work of education. Such a task is not visionary or impossible. All important truths are easily grasped. The facts may be many and elusive, but when acquired they are simple and intelligible, often too straightforward and reasonable to satisfy the average mind which is ever intent on the easiest way, but ever yearning for thrills and mysteries. In remarking upon man's stupidity in rejecting truth and clamoring for everything else Ward says:

Nature is too reasonable for the human mind. The very simplicity of true explanations leads to their rejection. This is very apparent in all the organic sciences but equally so in the more complex sciences of biology and sociology. The epigenetic or monistic theories are more simple and reasonable than the dualistic or teleological ones. The truer the theory, the more reasonable and simple. The lesson is to distrust all mystical and profound and far-fetched theories.

One of the commonest criticisms of a newly presented truth is that it is too crude. All direct presentations of natural truth are first thus attacked. The world demands that truth shall first be cooked and seasoned for the public palate. . . . The truth is a live, not an artificial concoction, and confection kills it and renders it either error or nothing. It must not only be crude but nude to be effective. Clothed in specious garments, it is masked, and instead of truth it becomes falsehood and deception (from an untitled and unpublished paper at Brown University).

Those who fear that the load of truth is too much for the human mind should note Ward's generalization that while the capacity to acquire knowledge increases in an arithmetical or some lower ratio, the quantity of knowledge increases in a geometrical or some higher ratio (see *Glimpses,* IV, 88). That is no ground for despair. Individual or racial differences in savagery as in civilization spring from lack of true information rather than from any disability to grasp the quantity or quality of truth. Malthus feared the destruction of civilization because of lack of food. Ward with much better reason feared for the future because of lack of knowledge. While Malthus is wrong because through birth control as well as machinery the food supply can be easily balanced with the number of people, there is no invention imaginable which can automatically educate anybody. Because truth is easily comprehensible, Dante's "Give the people light and they will find their way" becomes in dynamic sociology whose basic principle is that knowledge, not brains, is necessary: "Give the people knowledge, and they will not need to search for the way, but will be able to lay their own road to the future."[6]

[6] The opinions of two good Americans on the subject of education illustrate how Ward anticipated by more than a generation the liberal thought of this country on many vital topics. The late President Faunce of Brown University, where the ink is slowly fading from Ward's unpublished manuscript on education, said in the public press (January 6, 1928):

"Most Americans do value education as a business asset, but not as the entrance into the joy of intellectual experience or acquaintance with the best that has been said and done in the past. They value it not as an experience but as a tool. Possibly, Americans value everything in that way, always for the sake of something just around the corner. The sense of tomorrow is an amazing part in our American life. Never was there a people so careless of the past and even so careless of the present except as a stepping-stone into a tomorrow which shall bring wealth and dynamic and material progress."

President Robert M. Hutchins, of the University of Chicago, is likewise remarkably frank, when he says:

"The character of education is determined by the character of society. Love of money and the desire for freedom to pursue it, are the current ideals of the United States. The consequences of these ideals in American education have been to emphasize vocational education, to base the curriculum on obsolescent knowledge, to omit the consideration of moral questions, and to sacrifice intellectual development in favor of vocational techniques and the acquisition of information. The educational system reconstructed according to the ideal of the common good as determined in the light of reason, will have as its primary object the cultivation of the intellectual virtues. . . . The graduates of a university so organized and so conducted (to exclude informational and vocational courses, and where professors and students join in studying fundamental problems, those of natural science, social science and metaphysics or philosophy) should after three years of study have some rational conception of the common good and of the methods of achieving it" (*The American Journal of Sociology,* July, 1937).

President Hutchins' latest word on American education is that despite America's world beating and most extensive and elaborate educational system, its people, even those with the highest degrees, are still uneducated:

"They may have acquired a good deal of information much of which is useless to

Ward's idea of education is entirely utilitarian and dynamic. He not only emphasized the necessity of a knowledge of the physical and natural sciences in order to comprehend the social sciences, but he urged a redirection of the whole process of education. The noblest human values are associated with learning and the fundamentals of the art of living. There can be no grasp of either without a scientific education which flows out of a dynamic, scientific outlook upon life.

Koheleth's "He that increaseth knowledge increaseth sorrow" is a fallacy by an ancient prophet who knew little about knowledge. Knowledge, said Ward, is power and happiness. The man who carries knowledge gracefully, has acquired new energy, new hope, and the greatest instrument for happiness. Ward enriched the world forever with that idea infinitely multiplied when applied to society.

Perhaps our journey should end here. Education, which is the entrance to happiness, is also the exit for social evil. But like life itself, sociology cannot say "Finis" when it arrives at education. The emotions, i.e., the spiritualization of ideas, have still to be reckoned with. And so we travel on to meet the dilemma of pessimism and optimism and its solution in meliorism.

---

them because changing conditions have rendered it archaic," he said, "but they have not learned to think, as their pitiful efforts to read, write and speak make apparent."

"Our people have little knowledge and much opinion," he said. "They do not suspect that there is a difference between the two. The fundamental questions of human life and human society they have never faced. They would not know how to go about trying to face them.

"Yet the great practical issues of our time are not new. They are the persistent problems that have always existed because man is man, living in this world. The nature of the world and man provides the clue to the difficulties that seem about to overwhelm us.

"We confront these difficulties today with little real assistance from our education, because they revolve around basic questions affecting the ends of political and economic organizations, questions that neither technology, nor science, nor naturalism as we apply it, can answer. Only the attempt to understand nature can help us to answer them.

"Attempting to understand nature does involve a reconstruction of the course of study. We must first determine whether a subject is important enough to be taught. This we cannot do by job analysis, by finding out what jobs our pupils are going to perform when they leave us and training them to go through the motions employed in them. That is a conventional way to proceed."

"Asserting that 'no books that are any good appear in the elementary or high school curriculum,' Dr. Hutchins charged that 'the text-book racket has despoiled us of our intellectual heritage.'

"In the colleges and universities the situation is little better," he added. "It is perfectly possible to graduate from a good American college without reading a single great book in its entirety" (*New York Times,* Oct. 10, 1937).

# BOOK XVI. THE MELIORIST

*"Optimism may be said to be the thesis, pessimism, the antithesis, and meliorism the synthesis of man's relation to the universe. The optimist says: do nothing because there is nothing to do. The pessimist says: do nothing because nothing can be done. The meliorist says: do something, because there is much to do, and it can be done."*—Ward

# Chapter XXXVIII

# PESSIMISM AND OPTIMISM

---

*"When a man is perfectly content with the state he is in, which is when he is perfectly without any uneasiness, what industry, what action, what will is there left?"*
—John Locke

*"We are now in the transition stage from this pain economy to a pleasure economy."*
—Simon N. Patten

*"Rational optimism and pessimism are products of the naked reason than which no guide is more unsafe. The true guide, the true Moses that is to lead man out of the wilderness is* Science. . . . *The only science that can teach man to know how and why he is subjected to all these woes, and then he may see a way of escaping them, is social science."*—Ward

*"Despair is the greatest of our errors."*—Vauvenargues

*"Those only are happy who have their minds fixed on some object other than their own happiness."*—John Stuart Mill

*"We have dreams; we have at present undisciplined but ever-increasing power. Can we doubt that presently our race will more than realize our boldest imaginations, that it will achieve utility and peace, that it will live—in a world made more splendid and lovely than any palace or garden that we know, going on from strength to strength in an ever-widening circle of adventure and achievement?"*—H. G. Wells

---

THE VARIEGATED REACTIONS to the human comedy make its contemplation a thrilling experience. Everybody feels that there is something wrong with the social organization, but not many know the cause. Yet all of us are either confirmed pessimists or optimists, or a mixture of both. Sociology asks the pregnant question why one must necessarily either sink into inertia and despair or soar away upon a rosy cloud, certain that somehow, somewhere, tomorrow or a century later, all will be well. Why do so many contemplate the social scene with mingled feelings of hope and chagrin, while their opinions waver up and down like elevator indexes? What is the rational, the scientific attitude toward life?

## PESSIMISM

Large sections of society suffer from (perhaps enjoy) pessimism. Its seeming wisdom is due to the soothing effect upon troubled minds and outraged hearts. No thinking person, however, can either altogether deny the indictment by pessimism or for a moment join in a plea of guilt, and accept it as a working philosophy of life. Hurt and disappointed by his contact with reality, the pessimist mounts the barricades of human limitations, reads his shattering charges, and angrily asks why there should be famine in a world of plenty. Receiving no satisfactory answer, he becomes a disenchanted prophet and turns his face away from the suffering which surrounds him, feeling that since all human effort can end only in frustration the wisest thing is to do nothing. Unable to bear the glare of reality, he retires behind closed shutters to become a sleeping partner in human affairs, wraps himself in robes of mystery, abstraction or doleful irony, and consoles himself that all things being always the same, nothing can be expected of the future to remedy the increasing woes of mankind (see *App. S.,* pp. 19-20). Thus are born and mature the pessimist and all his kin. The hard straight road of science is renounced for darkened corners where one may sit in peace and bewail man's fate. The will to live is abandoned, and mankind is advised to return to nature and the quiet of the cave. Wealth and machines are roundly cursed as incarnations of the Evil One, and the only solace is generally announced in the return to the Divine Essence.

Any such philosophy, says Ward, is a wearing thin of the mind, a decay of the natural, dynamic impulses of life. It is the rejection of the forward, rational outlook for the backward, emotional view that liberty is merely the right to stand still, civilization an incurable disease, and progress a new tyranny. What is missed by the pessimists is the power of the human mind and the possibilities of science. And so they continue to accept life either as an immense affliction upon man who is the victim of an inscrutable malignity, or else as the service of an apprenticeship for the world to come.[1]

## THE REFUTATION OF PESSIMISM

Dynamic sociology quickly picks the flaws in the unnatural and unscientific viewpoint of pessimism. Life is not a continuous pain, as

[1] The philosophy of despair is matched only by that of the artist (like Anatole France) who regards humanity as a menagerie of which he refuses to become the keeper. Esthetes and idealists, in general, treat the social problem as insolvable, and stand with the brilliant author of *Penguin Island,* when he says: "I have had no plan; I have observed no rule. I have simply gone straight on, musing as a child might muse, pursuing my path, if not joyfully, at all events with a light heart, trying never to be dismayed at the sinister sights wherewith life essayed to daunt me" (*The Opinions of Anatole France,* by N. Segur, 1928).

the pessimist claims, nor is pleasure merely the relief from pain. That might be true if the joys of life were like taking off a tight shoe, or health only the result of curing some ailment. In fact, the intervals between the states of pain are filled with vibrant pleasures. The pessimist is wrong when he claims that the best we can hope for is occasional respite from pain followed by a larger dose of new suffering. All desire is pain, but satisfaction is a positive pleasure. Man has the means to live and enjoy life, and if he but wills it, he can make life a surplus of pleasures over pains.

Taking his stand upon the principles of organic evolution, Ward argues that pleasure means life, and pain, death; therefore, the object, nay, the duty of man is to pursue the former and avoid the latter. The opposite, pessimistic attitude opens wide the door to most world errors, that find support in asceticism, orientalism, and the other isms which disregard the real basis of evil and waste themselves bemoaning the sufferings of humanity. Pessimism must be cured in the same way that a mental physician cures phobias, by investigation and analysis (see *Ps. F.*, pp. 40, 43, 58). Nature, Ward finds, is indifferent to any pain or pleasure, for feeling is only a means to function. That is evident enough in the animal world in which the struggle for survival is a war to the death. But in the human race, the concept humane implies the avoidance of pain. Yet pain, unpleasant as it may be, has an important biological function, the protection of the organism. If the power to feel pain is removed, it means the end of life. Pain is the guaranty of life. But life itself is essentially pleasant, no matter how much misery mankind suffers because of his stupid or irrational actions, his frequent prayer for annihilation, or his mad rushing about as an escape from his suffering. Life is worth living, but the philosophy that to live is to suffer, and that there can be no relief except in death is a false and destructive philosophy.

The pessimist blames the world for his woes, like a child striking back at the object over which it has stumbled. To hide from life in some ivory tower or in a secret chamber of the mind is no more sensible than the child's anger. The Stoic who avoids the pains of life, thinks it is the height of morality to cry for no one, carry nobody's burdens, evade all possible discomfort, and please only himself, is only a postgraduate pessimist.

## NATURAL AND SOCIAL OPTIMISM

What is the way out of pessimism? First of all, through nature, answers Ward. Nature alone spells health and buoyant optimism. The joy of living is the will to live, a natural impulse which springs directly from the instinct of self-preservation. That instinct and natural optimism are conditions of each other, and constitute the sound, normal view of things, the virile outlook upon life, and ultimately the faith in nature and her eternal laws and forces (see *ibid.*, p. 66).

Natural optimism, unfortunately, is often made the excuse for a false social optimism which takes a distorted view of the human comedy or shuts its eyes altogether to the social mêlée. Ward deplores the fact that so many good men and true sit on their own minds, so to speak, and complacently wait for progress and happiness to come along from somewhere and liberate them, somehow. Their naïve faith is like that of drunken men who patiently cling to lampposts and wait for their homes to reel past so that they may step in and retire. It has been said that a pessimist is a man who has met an optimist. Perhaps the optimist, when he becomes a social optimist and looks at the world through rosy glasses, is one who must have had the sadder experience of meeting a pessimist. The smiling, eternal joy dispenser is as futile as the ailing grouch who wears mental blinders and claims to have special powers of vision. Here it may be told that a social scientist is a man who has met both an optimist and a pessimist.

Ward notes the paradox that the pessimist in world views is generally an optimist in his personal life, while the cosmic optimist is mostly a pessimist in his individual life. Thus, the wealthy who have every incentive to be hopeful, are fatalists and defeatists when it comes to the social problem. But the poor whose circumstances one would expect should make them confirmed pessimists are often social optimists, jolly beggars all.

In Western civilization, the great majority are optimists, says Ward, but in the East where mysticism has such a firm hold, the bulk of opinion is pessimistic, with a quiescent outlook upon the world which lives for them only in the dead past. The Occident with its dynamic philosophy of achievement always sees new turns in the road ahead. Prosperity is "just around the corner" say its "happy warriors," yet its social optimism is just as huge a failure as the pessimism of the

Orient that accepts everything as fate. The greater part of mankind, West and East, lives under the spell of some form of social metaphysics or theology which, without openly favoring any social class, preaches and engenders a benign resignation which is highly favorable to various kinds of exploitation, and in the end stands in the path of social progress (see *ibid.*, pp. 158-165).

Probing deeper into the social comedy, Ward saw that the condition of mankind from the standpoint of emotion or morals alone, will not bear analysis. Says he:

The optimistic theory is based either upon willful blindness or inexcusable ignorance. . . . Absolute optimism as well as the whole dogma of predestination, would, if logically pursued, put an end to all individual effort whatever, since all efforts result from a recognition, conscious or unconscious, of the necessity of certain effects following certain causes.

The practical evil of qualified optimism which consists in the belief that the widespread adaptation which all admit to exist in nature is in all respects perfect, arises from a general indisposition to seek to improve that which is already conceived to be perfect (*D.S.*, II, 47-48).

## SCIENTIFIC OPTIMISM

What, then, is to save us from the two horns of the dilemma, from pessimism and social optimism, from the self-intoxicating illusions of a Browning that this is the best of all possible worlds, and the sentimental pessimism of a Schopenhauer that it is the worst? In neither view is there any basis for a significant change in the condition of mankind, one way or the other. Again, the sociologist, standing on the infinite power of the intellect, on man's adaptability to a shifting environment and his ability to recognize in the past and present the reflection of the future, comes forward with social science to prove that yesterday and today are the materials for tomorrow, that social progress can be made to flow from social evolution, and press forward to a new social order (see *P.S.*, p. 221). The liberator from the bonds of pessimism as well as false optimism is science. In Ward's own words:

A little reason corrupts and neutralizes the optimistic impulses and produces that false and mongrel optimism that teaches the folding of the arms and the gospel of inaction. More reason penetrates to the dark reality and ends in pessimism and the gospel of despair or nirvana. But it is possible to probe still deeper and to find again the hope that characterizes the first blind sub-rational or ultra-rational struggle for existence. Rational optimism and pessimism are products of the naked reason, than which no guide is more unsafe. The true guide, the Moses that is to lead man out of the wilderness, is *science*. The naked reason must be clothed. Man must learn to *know*. He must learn how and why he is subjected to all these woes, and then he may see a way of escaping them. The only science that can teach this is social science (*P.S.*, pp. 143-144).

The optimism of science is founded upon the power of mind force to bring about social progress. Material progress, vast as it has been, is much less impressive than intellectual or psychic progress, which is truly unlimited. Much of what the immortal Greek geniuses believed sounds comical to any schoolboy of the present, so much has the stock of exact knowledge and the achievements built upon it advanced since the days of Plato and Aristotle. Because man has not acquired the proper knowledge or sufficiently used his mind or in the words of Faust "has used it to be more brutal than any brute," is no cause for pessimism.

## PROGRESS AND SCIENTIFIC OPTIMISM

On the contrary, a dynamic outlook and a scientific, rational program of action would make for a more rapid rate of social progress, says Ward. As dynamic sociology is applied, the mass of mankind will have a chance through education and opportunity to achieve happiness, as they never had before. Life is a collective process, and man as an individual is the most helpless of animals. Sociology, the only science which has for its object the organization of human happiness, inevitably makes for true scientific optimism and true social progress.

In the synthetic view of man's history, there is no Spenglerian moaning about decadence and cycles ending in disaster. Progress is not a spiral, nor civilization a disease. The stupidity and disorganization of society are curable, says Ward. Whether one feels optimistic or the contrary, he cannot grasp the real nature of progress unless he considers the relation that man in the social state bears to the universe of which he is a part. In Ward's words:

That cosmos must be contemplated as wholly unintelligent and wholly passive. Man must regard himself as in full possession of authority to subjugate it . . . to his own personal use. . . . The universe is in a certain sense fortuitous. While there is a cause for all things, there is no intelligent reason why anything should be as it is. That this little planet of ours happens to be peopled with life is merely an accident, or rather the convergence of a number of accidents. . . . No one therefore conceives that there can be any life or intelligence on the other planets or the sun. Think of the optimism that is required to make out a favorable case from such facts!

If we contemplate the earth itself, we find an analogous state of things. The period that man has inhabited the earth is very small compared with what we know its age to be. The crust of earth seems to have been fully formed not less than 100,000,000 years ago. . . . The most extravagant estimates of man's entire historic and prehistoric existence do not go back 500,000 years. More probable ones stop at 200,000. . . . Intelligence never reached the point at which it could furnish a record until within at most 25,000 years of our present epoch, and authentic records are confined to the past forty or fifty centuries. Thus only one fortieth or one fiftieth of the little span of man's existence belongs to the age of culture, however rude. And what is there to be said in favor of the condition of the world even at its best? Read human history. . . . There is what we call human progress but what is it but a rhythmic and only partial success in rendering a worse condition a trifle better? Even this is accidental and may go backward instead of forward (*Outlines,* pp. 30-33).

Whether the cosmic and human drama is to have a happy ending or not, one thing is certain, concludes Ward, that we are still far from the climax. In fact, the play has scarcely begun. Despite his scientific generalizations which have no room for any supernatural intelligence, social evolution seems on the whole to be going upwards and tending toward improvement. Man himself has not changed relatively during the last five thousand years, nor very much for thousands of years before that, but his environment is constantly being transformed. Science and machinofacture are the greatest of historic achievements, and the world has advanced a good deal since inventions were anathema as the works of Satan. Evidently man has groped his way out of primeval darkness and collected a few ideas on the way, which fairly indicate his future course.

To justify his scientific optimism, Ward takes us to review, for a moment, the panorama of evolution. In the cosmos at large as well as in the human race, the series of steps has thus far been an ascending one (see *P.S.,* p. 448; *App. S.,* p. 84). Even pessimists who have or are bad livers will cheer up a little when they hear that no devolution is as yet visible. The passing of ideas, nations, or empires is no more a sign of decadence than the death of old people is a sign of the decline of humanity. Behind man, there lie eons of savagery and animalism that still have to be eliminated from the blood. Is it any wonder that he has scarcely commenced to be human? By looking back into the past, the present assumes more just proportions, and the future becomes more visible. The conclusion is inevitable that scientific optimism is the only possible state of mind for any informed and rational being.

### OUR INFANTILE GLOBE

Looking at the cosmos as a screen upon which is thrown the universal picture of organization, Ward points that whatever may be the final doom of our universe, it (including our globe) is in a state of progress, still rejoicing in the morning of evolution. Unless some cosmic catastrophe intervenes, our home on earth is assured for at least some millions of years. In the light of astro-physics, the earth is a newly born infant (see *P.S.*, pp. 38-40). It is the merest speck in the galaxies of universes flying with unthinkable speed over paths of immeasurable extent, in which there are thousands of millions of stars, compared to which our sun is as insignificant as a grain of sand in the desert. Modern science has opened up a wide perspective in which man looks like a mere atom. If the age of the earth is estimated arbitrarily at one hundred million years, and we construct, as one of Haeckel's pupils did, a clock dial of the cosmic day which covers the life of the universe, it appears that by giving each geological period its proper allotment of hours and minutes, the traditional six thousand odd years of the Bible period covers only six seconds (see *ibid.*, p. 40; *Glimpses*, VI, 253).

By taking the age of the earth at seventy-two million years, Ward gave a proportionate span of three million years to each hour of the cosmic clock. Assuming the human period to have lasted twenty-five thousand years, man is only thirty seconds old, and the historic period covers less than five seconds of the cosmic day![2]

Is the world senile or has it just been born? Is there any cause for

---

[2] After Ward, the late Professor James Harvey Robinson made the illustration still more striking by crowding man's biography into twelve hours, each hour representing twenty thousand years and each minute 333 1/3 years. Assuming that mankind is now living at high noon, the ancient Greeks are not quite seven minutes old. At one minute before noon, Bacon wrote his *Advancement of Learning*, and the steam engine was invented only half a minute ago.

pessimism or does progress lie ahead on a road that we have seen but hardly touched? Man and his institutions have lived comparatively only for a split second. The human race has been conscious of itself only about ten thousand years, and somewhat human for less than five thousand years. Its most valuable achievements were accomplished in less than two thousand years, and its greatest work, only in the last two hundred years. It is the age of matter that is drawing to a close. The age of mind is just dawning (see *Glimpses,* VI, 258).

Only a hundred years ago, all our grains and vegetables were either accidental or incidental developments of selection from wild, native plants. Our great-grandfathers lived essentially, as far as external conditions were concerned, in about the same way as their ancestors did six thousand years ago. The races which bred Goethe, Laplace, Shakespeare, and Spencer, were only a few centuries ago, warlike barbarians. Wholesale exterminations of conquered peoples, starvation, torture, witchcraft, hanging of starved peasants for stealing food—such things seem part of a dreadful nightmare rather than a recent leaf from man's biography (see *P.S.,* pp. 448 *et seq.*).

Scientific optimism is justified in believing that just as the preceding century occupied itself mainly with mechanical and scientific achievement, the present century will devote itself chiefly to moral and social progress. The mind reels at the thought what the use of reason will accomplish for man in the next two hundred or two thousand years. What he has thus far learned about the world and what he has done with his knowledge, are mere trifles. How brief is the history of the steamboat, the factory, the telephone, or the airplane in comparison with that of the amoeba or the horse. Progress as the result of mental energy advances in a geometrical ratio, both in quantity and in quality, and puts to shame the spontaneous processes of nature which jog along in an arithmetical ratio, or less. Here Ward liked to quote Condorcet:

No doubts have been fixed to the improvement of the human faculties. The perfectibility of man is absolutely indefinite. The progress of this perfection, henceforth above the control of every power that would impede it, has no other limit than the duration of the globe upon which nature has placed us.

To those who tremble before social change, it should be evident that the course of history has arrived at the point of fusion and integration. We are living upon the brink of the greatest advance the world has ever seen. Blood and culture are gradually becoming cosmopolitan, and the time is not far distant when there will be but one race, a world family inhabiting the entire civilized globe. In spite of social, racial, and religious conflicts still raging everywhere, the signs of the approaching new age may be seen. It is not a mere fancy, but the crest of the wave of evolution, and the irresistible result of all that has gone before. It will be a period in which the races of man will all be assimilated, and which will last several million years at least. "Let anyone attempt to figure to himself the possibilities involved in such a truth" (*ibid.,* p. 220).

Although his scientific optimism is a voice that has been lost in the wilderness, and progress is still a shuffling crawl or a leap in the dark, events since Ward's death prove that time and events are following his call for social action. Sociology is slowly but surely entering the stage of concrete application. When one considers what society has accomplished in spending all its energies upon means and scarcely any upon ends, staggering along with the hit-or-miss, trial-and-error method, speculating in cloudy nebulas, competing and killing and destroying instead of planning and building together, it is not hard to foresee what social progress would be if the methods of social science were put to work full force for social improvement.

Ward's denomination of progress up to the present as accidental, and under the control of social science as artificial, is an inspired description of the difference between natural evolution and social evolution, between the method of nature and the method of man; between the intelligent and the mechanical; between disheartening individualistic pessimism and enlightening social optimism.

The optimistic smile amid the crudities of the social shambles is as inane and futile as the pessimistic frown of surrender to fate. Both evidence the failure to note the ascending curve of progress, and neither is any remedy for social evil which requires for its conquest and cure the collective intelligence of society. To remain inert, steeped in panic because the sun will some day together with the planets explode in star dust from which they came, is as suicidal for any rational being as to sit idle and wait in complete confidence for something, miracle or windfall, to come and save us. What then is to be done? What is the real solution of the puzzle of pessimism and optimism?

# CHAPTER XXXIX

# MELIORISM

---

*"In her general attitude towards life, George Eliot was neither optimist nor pessimist. She held to the middle term, which she invented for herself, of 'meliorist'."*
—J. W. Cross

*"The greatest possible happiness of the greatest possible number is the foundation of morals and legislation."*—Jeremy Bentham

*"The nobler a soul is the more objects of compassion it hath."*—Francis Bacon

*"All great thoughts come from the heart."*—Vauvenargues. *"But they must go round by the head."*—Lord Morley

*"The fundamental doctrine of modern social life is the subordination of politics to moral aims."*—Auguste Comte

*"Do I seem to say: 'Let us eat and drink, for to-morrow we die'? Far from it; on the contrary I say: 'Let us take hands and help, for this day we are alive together'."*
—W. K. Clifford

*"The only means by which the condition of mankind ever has been or ever can be improved, is the utilization of the materials and the forces that exist in nature."*—Ward

---

W ARD LOOKS upon pessimism as highly demoralizing and unscientific, and finds the only rational, satisfying solution in meliorism (see *D.S.*, II, 468). It is to his undying fame that he gave the world not only the scientific view of society but also made such a moving appeal for scientific meliorism, against the pessimism of the individualistic philosophy, as well as against the optimism of idealism and metaphysics.

## THE HORNS OF THE HUMAN DILEMMA

The rationalization of the human comedy is so depressing to most people, any basic change in society involves so much effort, waste, and suffering, that only a small part of what is gained in the flood is retained in the ebb tide (see *ibid.*, I, 75). The sentimental reader, however, need not be crushed by the sight of human failure and woe. Life is neither a tragedy nor a comedy, but an object of study and a field for achievement. Man is neither a god nor a devil, and life and men are always worthy of improvement. When one folds his arms and resigns himself to fate, he is lost (see *Outlines*, p. 35). And when, without employment, he lives in constant hope that some rich relative will leave

him a fortune, he is equally lost. Ward completes the analogy by introducing the meliorist as a man who knows that unearned fortunes do
not fall into laps, and therefore rolls up his sleeves, and goes to work.

## MELIORISM

Ward's specific for *Weltschmerz* is not a magic draught. Meliorism
is the solution for what seems a baffling problem: What can minimize
human suffering and enhance human happiness? No one need choose
between the horns of the dilemma offered by pessimism and optimism,
counsels Ward. The restless skepticism that questions everything,
even the methods of nature, is good. The scientific optimism which
views progress as possible and unlimited is helpful. But the conviction
that the only way out of the human impasse is planned, dynamic
social action to ameliorate the condition of mankind is the only rational
way to treat the social problem (see *Ps. F.*, pp. 69-70). Ward did not
discover meliorism any more than he originated sociology. The modern
notion of a continuous amelioration in human affairs which began in
the thought of Abbé de Saint-Pierre in 1737, flourished during the
revolutions of the eighteenth and nineteenth centuries, received a scientific basis from the doctrine of evolution, and reached its maturity in
Comte and Ward.

The pessimist, consciously or unconsciously, reasons that the business of life is hopelessly insolvent and is being run at a loss. To try
and keep it going seems to him a struggle for something less than zero,
a perpetual and hopeless deficit. Then comes the sociologist to his
aid with a plan of reorganization which, by asserting the claims of
feeling, seeks to obtain a surplus of joys over sorrows, and of pleasures
over pains (see *App. S.*, p. 36).

Ward's thesis is that nature is passive, but man is active. Both
pessimism and optimism are passive states of mind; meliorism is the
active state. In his own words:

Optimism may be said to be the thesis, pessimism the antithesis,
and meliorism the synthesis of man's relation to the universe. The
optimist says: Do nothing because there is nothing to do. The pessimist says: Do nothing because nothing can be done. The meliorist
says: Do something, because there is much to do, and it can be done
(*Outlines,* p. 26).

## MELIORISM IS SCIENTIFIC

Ward is always the strict utilitarian. To point to the achievements of science and scientists as the reason for patiently waiting for nature to send along social improvement, would be an anticlimax in view of the chaos and suffering which permeates the social strata. Says Ward, quoting Huxley, a true meliorist:

"If there is no hope of a large improvement of the condition of the greater part of the human family; if it is true that the increase of knowledge, the winning of a greater dominion over Nature which is its consequence, and the wealth that follows upon that dominion, are to make no difference in the extent and the intensity of want, with its concomitant physical and moral degradation among the masses of the people, I should hail the advent of a kindly comet which would sweep the whole affair away as a desirable consummation" (quoted in *P.S.*, p. 143).

The pessimists are like desert travelers who search for water with a divining rod. Having no fundamental laws and principles of science with which to locate and direct the deep currents of the social forces, they are doomed to failure from the beginning. Confronted with the argument from meliorism, the pessimist will turn away despondently, to think that anyone can believe in the possibility of social science solving the insolvable riddle of society.

Meliorism leaves us the idea that it is possible to learn enough about the history and conduct of man and men to guide us in deliberate programs of progress. Science tells us what took place in the past, and so makes us familiar with the factors of human evolution and human improvement. Meliorism is practical and possible, here and now, in the exact proportion to our knowledge and application of social science to social phenomena.

It is lack of common knowledge and not human weakness that causes the great social evils to flourish, says Ward. The remedy consists, first, in acquiring and spreading the necessary knowledge, and then in applying to societal affairs the same principles which govern and obtain in individual affairs, by which the art of life is conducted. Before there can be any improvement, however, society must act, in all things, as an individual would act now, and manifest conscious intelligence in the positive pursuit of well-being and happiness (see *Glimpses*, IV, 29-30).

Science and the scientific method are the foundations of meliorism. The road of social progress stretches from primitive life when the social unit was the group, and all individuals were practically its slaves. The emergence of the intellect first taught the individual his right to a place in the sun. Finally, mankind ran amok and developed a system of individualism which, in competitive conflicts, outdid the animal world. Now, social science has been developed to interpret man's relations to nature and to society, and to furnish the true mental attitude of meliorism to save mankind from the crashing of individualism.

## MELIORISM AND HUMANISM

Meliorism is more than humanism, charity, or benevolence. The chain of feeling that runs from impulse and sentimentality to reason and applied science is paralleled by another that stretches from almsgiving through the broadest forms of philanthropy, into the deep-laid principles of meliorism. If meliorism were just another ethical principle directing us to help our fellows, it would be satisfied with alleviating present suffering. But since it is part of a dynamic social science, it aims to create new social conditions in which suffering will be at a minimum. And so it is ready to sacrifice temporary enjoyments for greater future benefits, and the pleasures of the few favored ones for the happiness of the great mass (see D.S., II, 468).

While Comte's positive philosophy ended in the religion of humanity and demanded a new untheological spiritual power to govern, Ward's dynamic sociology stressed the need of education leading to concerted action to ameliorate social conditions. The spiritual element is always latent in society, but dynamic action is needed to bring it out in full force. Comte's philosophy which stood for education no less than Ward's, emphasized the fostering of the social sentiments by appeals to the universal history of the race, and the commemoration of the heroic figures of history, in daily rituals. Ward's suggestions for social reform, motivated by the same moral aim as Comte's, are less sentimental and more practical.

Ward takes the position of meliorism because it demands a fuller and broader life for all. The pessimist may continue to preach: "To me life is an evil thing, the more of it, the worse" but to the meliorist, life is good and beautiful, and the more of it, the better, no matter what fools and knaves are doing to spoil it. The earth is not a vale of tears but a place in which one should be as happy as possible, in the short span of life. Human suffering is not a cardinal virtue of the individual, but a dire and unnecessary sin of society. Life is good because it is desirable, and in the enjoyment of it, we move onward and upward to higher desires and nobler ideals. New faculties can be developed, which in turn yield fresh and undreamed of pleasures—the thrill of wisdom, the exercise of the moral sentiments, intellectual faculties, and artistic powers.

## MELIORISM IS APPLIED ETHICS

Morality and present civilization are not identical; neither are material progress and spiritual progress. Morality rests ultimately upon sane, healthy impulses and general intelligence, while civilization embraces ideas relating to the building up of life and society. Dynamic achievement and ethical ideals approach each other and merge only on the plane of meliorism.

In the final analysis, meliorism means moral or spiritual progress. Ethics stands for the removal of social evils, the improvement of the race, and the extension of material benefits to all. In short, as Huxley said, it is the *sine qua non* of happiness. There is only one test in looking for the better in anything, said Ward, and that is the sociological (ethical) test which seeks to discover the degree of satisfaction that the thing yields. What is more agreeable is better; what is less so, is worse. That is the final proof of utility and at the same time, the basis of economics. Social improvement is not only the passage out of a pain economy into a pleasure economy, but also from one that yields only the satisfaction of physical needs, to one that fills out the moral, spiritual demands of life.

To the pessimist and his twin brother, the social optimist, meliorism points out that although under the operation of the competitive laws of nature, it seems a waste of breath to urge peace, justice, and a humane social system, there is little doubt that the moral force is growing stronger and gradually mitigating the severity of the natural process. We need not expect utopia, for mitigation is all that is in sight.

The eager minds that look forward to the day when reason shall dethrone emotion will be sadly disappointed at the thought that the day will never come. Renouncing the hope of a purely intellectual regime of mankind; admitting the fact that feeling alone drives the social machine, for good or for evil, it becomes the duty of man to apply himself to the only task remaining, i.e., to discover how the existing conditions of society may be ameliorated (see *D.S.*, I, 13). Sociology in coming to that conclusion has made safe the continued exercise of feeling on a human plane:

The new motor (of feeling) is a powerful one, and it is necessary to apply the brakes. But they have been successfully applied, and the train, now for the first time laden with human freight, is safely speeding on (*P.S.*, p. 135).

The scientific optimism that permeates meliorism cannot tolerate or move in any paths of laissez faire (see *ibid.*, p. 231). In the face of man's power over nature, including his own lot, the individualist philosophy stands utterly bankrupt. The meliorist is surprised to see man slumbering peacefully amid the ruins of his failures, or else fighting desperately for mere existence, wretched and naked, in a world of wealth and beauty. What room is there for any philosophy of "Mind your own business" or "There is nothing to be done about it" in such a social arena? Both the philosophies of competition and inaction in a world of dynamic human beings are anomalies.

To Socrates' "Know thyself," Plato's "Control thyself," and Christ's "Give thyself" must be added Ward's "Help thyself." Meliorism is not a call to a bloody revolution but a plea for the methods of science and education to change the miserable conditions of human life. Tennyson's song about the parliament of man, and Browning's classical bedtime story: "God's in his heaven; all's right with the world," have moved nothing and nobody. But the least sign of dynamic activity, Ward remarks, in any movement for universal education, for attractive legislation and attractive labor, or for the equalization of opportunity, and society begins to ferment.

Meliorism is no mere belly philosophy of hungry rebels. It is the result of a scientific analysis of social reality, and is at once a social truth and a social faith with a practical program for the achievement of a new and happy social system.

## MELIORISM AND THE WORLD OF TOMORROW

The immediate remedy for the social patient is meliorism; the physician is society itself, with the help of dynamic social science. Most people fear those words as much as the Russian Czar did when he burned *Dynamic Sociology* at the stake. Yet there are no splashes of red in the picture that meliorism presents. The progress it advocates is a true evolutionary progress, a plan to lay the ghosts of hunger, competition, ignorance, and despair; a disturbance of the balance of the social forces, not a kinetic explosion and disruption of everything in sight. Society, in Ward's view, is an incubator, not a torpedo. Progress via meliorism is like the birth of a chick rather than like the uprooting of a tree.

No one therefore need tremble at sociology and meliorism. If there is any danger of a social eruption when general discontent becomes too great, the catastrophe can be avoided by the amelioration of social conditions. Unless education is the means relied upon to bring about the emancipation of the people, and meliorism is put into operation without delay, the social forces, dammed by ignorance, may burst asunder like the gases and lava imprisoned in a volcano. Says Ward:

It would seem to be the duty of all who recognize the laws that have operated to produce the movement to do what can be done to check its wayward tendencies, as far as possible, to keep it within the normal channels of safe and healthy development. If this is not done, those who are likely to suffer by its ravages are certain to resist its whole current until, no longer capable of restraint, it will burst forth in open revolution. What must be, will be, but everything depends upon the manner of its being. The problem of today is how to help on a certain evolution by averting an otherwise equally certain revolution (*Glimpses*, IV, 315).[1]

Under meliorism, Ward states, labor will be humanized, the people will receive the benefits of material progress, and the hitherto strange idea of the government making the welfare of the masses its first duty, will be taken from the musty pages of books and put into practice, through education and economic security. Only as human "hands" will become free and enlightened human beings, will the timeworn differences between citizens and slaves, serfs and lords, privileged and commoners, leisure class and working class, disappear in the current of free achievement. The amelioration of social conditions will uplift the masses by their own effort, and that will be the greatest revolution

---

[1] "Two things, said Kant, fill me with breathless awe;
The starry heavens and the moral law.
But I know a thing more awful and obscure—
The long, long patience of the plundered poor."—Edwin Markham.

of all time (see *ibid.*, V, 219-220; VI, 397). With evolution as a guide and meliorism as the motive power, the organization of all forces and materials toward the object of happiness will be ready to advance.

Ward's vision of meliorism is a glorious one. Everywhere, it will be possible to have beautiful cities filled with cultural and artistic treasures, with gardens and sunshine for all. Machinery will do all manual labor, and education will be incessant and progressive. Human energy is no longer wasted in unpleasant, uncreative toil in a cruel, crushing environment, but is replaced by creative effort and invention in a humane milieu. Hand in hand with the increase in pleasure and the decrease in pain, investigation into the problems of life will go on. Ugliness and disease will grow as rare as beauty and natural health are now. Though ours will be still a common earth inhabited by common people, it will look more like the Eden befitting the home of intelligent beings than the busy mart and bloody battlefield in which the grubbing mass now mills and struggles.

Does this strike the reader as utopian? Then let him look once more at what science has done for the natural and the physical world, for the wilderness and the jungles in which savagery and barbarism flourished not so very long ago. Why cannot science be applied to the social world with the same degree of success? When intelligence, not force, and science, not superstition, will work for the improvement of social conditions, the social order of tomorrow may be as much in advance of that of today as the present civilization is an improvement upon the social life in the early centuries of the Christian era.

Looking back, the feeling is strong that man is ready to take charge of his own estate, solve the problem of the mass in order to solve that of the individual, and usher in a real civilization through the amelioration of social conditions and the spread of education. Where he has in the past struggled blindly toward the light, he will in the future emerge from the fog and gloom of superstition and speculation to walk solidly together with his fellows on the road to the future. With science as his guide, the common, average man will have the opportunity to climb the heights now open only to the educated and the all powerful. And above those heights, new peaks of desire and achievement will rise.

We have gloried, not unjustly, in the achievements of the past. But civilization is only a day old, and the future holds still greater things in store for us, if only we will use our intelligence to reach those treasures through rationalism, co-operation, and meliorism.

# BOOK XVII. THE MORALIST

*"Ethical teaching is in the main misdirected and ineffective. The positive side of ethics is lost sight of in the prominence on the negative side. The object has been not to increase happiness but to mitigate suffering. . . . . Ethics is not only not a science, but is only an expression for the imperfection of the social order, an imperfection which, theoretically at least, is removable."*

*"The great object of action is to do something. Conduct only aims to* avoid *doing."*—Ward

*"It is not enough to be ready to do our duty; we must know it."*
—Guizot

*"The evolution of morals is a fact patent to any student of human nature and human history, for the operation of this stupendous law persists alike in the worlds of matter and of mind."*—Eden Phillpotts

# CHAPTER LX

# THE ETHICAL FORCES

*"The moral world is still in the stone-boat stage of its history, dragging its heavy body over the rugged field of human life with the utmost friction and the smallest ethical economy."*

*"Men do not want to know that their life is capable of analysis into simple physical principles. . . . Every rational analysis of human action tends to ground it in egoism and assimilate it to animal action. Very few want to know such truths."*—Ward

W E TURN to the right for the moral outlook from the temple. "Thou shalt not" signs are everywhere pointing to an invisible path of righteousness, in the midst of a social domain which presents anything but a moral scene. The air is filled with stern commands to obey God's word on pain of suffering or death. Ward finds two insurmountable difficulties with those commands, viz., they are nonexistent and if they did exist, obedience would be impossible. The only true ethics, according to Ward, is human ethics, the observing of the laws of nature which make for man's welfare and happiness.

## THE BACKGROUND OF WARD'S ETHICS

Ward's moral philosophy is grounded in the ethics of the ancient Greeks, of Spinoza, Comte, and Spencer. More than three thousand years ago, the social prophets of Egypt were already demanding more and better moral conduct, and warned the world that "God decrees death to him who doeth what is hated, and life to him that doeth things that are loved." The Greeks came nearest to the modern scientific concept of a nonreligious morality. Nor has there ever been a moral code as tender and merciful to the poor and the afflicted as that of ancient Israel.

Aristotle's immortal ethics was solicitous chiefly for the good of the state. Morality was in his philosophy an integral part of politics (social science) and the only path to the good life. As for Socrates, the chain of morals forged by his wisdom has never been broken. The highest good, he said, is virtue, not a divine gift, but useful human knowledge wisely employed. Virtue alone leads to happiness. Happiness does not consist of desire, but lies in a certain ideal of perfection, viz., becoming more virtuous and enabling others to do the same. Then comes the Socratic anticlimax: happiness can be achieved only by obeying the inner command planted within us by God.

Plato thinks that virtue is essentially a matter of intelligence, but like Socrates, cancels all that is scientific in the idea by concluding that intelligence is the ladder upon which man climbs back to the Divine Essence whence he came. Plato's genius, nevertheless, was too vast for his ideas to be wholly metaphysical. Justice, which is the basis of the good life, he argued, is possible only for the good members of a good state. His social and educational theory furnishes the method by which the state would lead its citizens to knowledge, which is the condition of virtue. Nevertheless, Plato did not believe that the practice of virtue could be taught to humanity at large, or that ethics was an independent science.

As all roads lead to Rome, so we return to Aristotle, the greatest intellectual power of all time, who believes that ethics and sociology are identical. Only in a good state can there be virtuous citizens. Reason is the cornerstone of morals and the crown of all the sciences. But the father of science vacillated between heavenly and worldly ethics. At one moment, the metaphysician in him found a set of absolute and eternal virtues outside of and beyond human experience. In the next, he was again the practical scientist who found that "virtue is a moral habit based upon a life of deliberation and expressed in the observance of a rational mean." Human actions, he added, are not merely right or wrong, but also ugly or beautiful. Moral fervor cannot reform conduct; sooner will knowledge organized on the basis of science, accomplish the ends of virtue.

Good taste and the happy medium in all things, occupy in Aristotle's system the place reserved by the metaphysicians for the narrower concept of innate conscience. He scarcely pays any attention to inward motive as a moral censor, because he does not seem to believe in any moral imperative, or place the will in the skies instead of inside man's brain. A wrongdoer, he said, is one who is ignorant of what is right. The Greeks had the same word to express the respective concepts sinning, and missing the mark; habit, and virtue. No abstract good will or divine urge, but knowledge and positive deeds are necessary for the moral life. Right in morals meant to Aristotle the same as right in mathematics—what was fit or correct; what worked out the proper result. Just as a draughtsman must observe the laws of perspective, so man, having no inborn moral consciousness, must follow the natural laws of conduct in order to make life precise and happy.

Modern ethics is not as frank or as utilitarian as Greek ethics, because the new world is more fettered than the old, by theological dogmas. Religion still looks as it has always looked at the problem, through supernatural spectacles. True to the tenet "Give me a doctrine and I will find reasons for it" (Chrysippus), the believer assumes that the world is a moral order in which evil either does not exist, or is a correlative of good. Anyhow, man's suffering is his own fault, and no doubt, is inflicted upon him for his own good.

The exalted ethics of Spinoza is far in advance of the conventional, formal ethics of theology. He regards morality as *scientia intuitiva*. The discovery of nature's laws furnishes us with material science, but only the study of man's deeper inner nature, unrelated to outer circumstance, can reveal the nature of morals. Kant, too, saw the moral mandate written in the stars and buried deep in man's breast. Like Spinoza, he sought to formulate a science of "pure" ethics unrelated to practical life, but failed as miserably as if it had been tried by some simple village priest.

Modern scientists have often let the theological cat in through the backdoor when they came to the question of morals. Thus, Huxley, king of agnostics, insisted that evolution was inherently and essentially ethical. Westermarck, another titan of science, believes that moral ideas are grounded in feelings of resentment and gratitude, and that all concepts of right and wrong are based on emotions of approval or dissapproval. He therefore locates the source of morals in the emotions through introspection.

Spencer's ethics, too, wandered so far from the path of science into the nebulae of speculation, that Ward justly remarked that the immortality of the author of the synthetic philosophy would rest securely on his cosmic evolution, and that it was of slight importance whether *Principles of Ethics* had ever been written, or not. This, despite Spencer's estimate that his ethical philosophy was the capstone of his synthetic system (see *Glimpses*, V, 38; VI, 307).

Nevertheless, Spencer asserted that the purpose of his synthetic philosophy was to find the principles of right and wrong, and furnish a scientific basis for ethics. Unlike Comte, Spencer sought new sanctions for conduct in natural conditions, and his natural morality is analogous to Voltaire's natural religion. Spencer's error consisted in basing ethics upon biology, said Ward, who depicted ethics as an extension of psychology into social science where it merged into applied sociology.

## ETHICS NOT A SCIENCE

Ward's sociology is ethical throughout. The purpose of all science is ethical. Yet ethics is clearly not a science, and those who have elevated it into a science have built upon shifting sands. Says Ward:

The ethical problem is misunderstood. Ethical teaching is in the main misdirected and ineffective. The positive side of ethics is lost sight of in the prominence of its negative side. The object has been not to increase happiness but to mitigate suffering. This has always been the principal form of doing good. Even where it is sought to confer pleasure, it is only upon isolated individuals. In fact, the ethical method has been applied only to special cases, and not to underlying conditions. It is superficial and temporary, not fundamental and lasting. . . . Its effect is always static, never dynamic. This desultory beneficence has been erected into a creed and inculcated as the great duty. By many, it is regarded as the supreme end of life, and philosophers have characterized it as the highest aim of science. The only two philosophical systems claiming to be universal, viz., those of Comte and Spencer, both make ethics the last, highest and most important of the sciences.

I have been compelled to conclude that, except in so far as it means the discovery of ways to diminish social friction, ethics not only is not a science, but is only an expression for the imperfection of the social order, an imperfection which, theoretically at least, is removable (*ibid.,* V, 274-275).

## WHAT IS MORAL CONDUCT?

Perhaps the reader is still wondering just what is moral conduct. Sociology postulates that man has no innate will for good, nor is he a being whose soul is naturally incorruptible. Social evil standing grimly in front of all moral speculation is evidence enough that this world is not essentially a moral order. Man, like the rest of animate nature, is entirely unmoral. He becomes moral or immoral as a result of his activities and surroundings. Not a single moral precept— neither the golden rule of god-men nor the moral codes of good men—

even when bolstered by the fear of hell fire or the promise of heavenly rewards, has ever brought about the slightest improvement in human conduct. Again, Ward notes the supreme domination of feeling behind human conduct. Says he:

The great object of action is to *do* something. Conduct only aims to *avoid doing,* either to avoid interfering with the "pursuit of ends" by others, or to prevent others from pursuing such ends, or to do some benefit for another, whereby he is prevented from doing the necessary acts for rendering an equivalent, or to do him an injury, whereby he is prevented, to that extent, from pursuing his natural ends. . . . The pathological state of society to which all moral considerations are directed is the consequence of this complicated network of human pursuits which, in the nature of things, must frequently clash (*D.S.,* II, 376-377).

The exploitation of a human being, an animal, or a natural resource is equally based upon and measured by the same psychological criterion. Has an equal amount of benefit been exchanged for sacrifice? Or, has either party given pain for pleasure? That in all cases will determine whether the act has been moral or immoral (see *Glimpses,* V, 271-272). In Ward's own language:

The practical and the useful are at the bottom the agreeable, or at least a surplus of the agreeable over the disagreeable. Moral philosophers agree that the end of ethics is the *good,* as distinguished from that of science, which is the true, and from that of art, which is the beautiful. But what is the good but the useful, the practical, the agreeable? To cause happiness or relieve suffering is the real purpose of moral conduct. This is what is meant by "doing good," and many who deny that pleasure is the end of conduct, work unceasingly to give pleasure to others.

This, too, is the meaning of virtue—conduct which in the long run is believed to yield a surplus of enjoyment, while vice although yielding a present pleasure of a low order and short duration, is believed to be followed by pains that more than counterbalance this, either to the agent himself or to others (*ibid.,* V, 272).

## SCIENCE AND ETHICS

The purpose of science is to establish moral values, not to abolish them. The mission of sociology is to make possible a morality which will be positive, constructive, and enlightening. The common enemies of sociology and ethics are not the material forces, but dogmas and superstitions. The ethical code which the world believed for ages was handed down from heaven is found by science to come from human behavior and experience, and to be rooted in primitive fear forces. Instead of morality being lodged from above in the human breast and acting through the mysterious conscience, science discovers that morality, growing weaker as knowledge increases, is replaced by applied social science.

Moral character depends entirely upon the environment. When social conditions become adapted to human needs and desires, and the pains of living are reduced as the pleasures of existence increase, the true character of morals looms into view. Social progress then follows, not through restraints or prohibitions, but through healthy, free, and creative activities. The acceptance of social science and natural law as bases of human action may be a bitter pill for one to swallow who clings to the belief in divine ethics, but no one can ascribe the evil in society either to fate or accident. The struggles between the individual and the group, instinct and reason, egoism and altruism, and heredity and environment, are clearly due to something else than innate wickedness or the work of Satan.

## THE ETHICAL FORCES

To follow Ward's abandonment of theological and metaphysical ethics is not to fall into anarchism or naturalism but to admit the same scientific method and viewpoint in human behavior as in all the other phases of the human scene. In seeking the origin of morality and tracing the current of the moral forces Ward discovered new truths and had to revise old ones. As Pasteur did in medicine and Freud in psychology, Ward demonstrated in sociology that to discover the origin of the ailment is also to discover its cure.

Good and evil are neither inherent in nature nor innate in man. Nor are they blessings and afflictions imposed by the Creator. Sociology sees society neither as a moral order nor as a hopeless exhibition of the law of the strong, but as the field of the social and ethical forces. Although ethics is not a true science, the ethical forces are real enough. Yet of the civilizing or spiritual social forces—moral, esthetic, and intellectual—the moral are the least important (see *P.S.*, p. 417). At best, morality is a thin veneer upon the social body. "Scratch a Russian and you will find a Tartar" is a sociological truism. In the crowd, the restraints of civilized life are removed, and the true character of the civilized man as an enlightened savage comes to the surface (see *ibid.,* p. 92).

In tracing ethics back to its roots in psychology and biology Ward uncovers two grand divisions, race morality and individual morality. The first is identical with primitive ethics, is based on custom, has its source in the animal instinct of self-preservation, and expands into group feeling and group thinking. The second springs from man's rational faculty and emerges in altruism, the deepest and highest of human motives.

## RACE MORALITY

When the animal is in danger, it reacts instinctively to save itself and does the things which man often ineffectually tries to do by use of his reason. Race morality, from its inception, has had nothing to do with any question of right or wrong, since it is entirely confined to the more important problem of life or death (see *ibid.,* pp. 418 *et seq.; App. S.,* p. 28). The group instinct of survival which Ward called the social imperative was the result of collective experience and was evolved to offset the waywardness of individual feeling which ran amok. The restraints that the primitive animal was forced to practice in order to survive, became its instincts and constitute the morals of the animal kingdom. But the restraints which the human group imposed upon its members formed the foundations of the institutions of religion, ethics, law and government, in all of which the chief factor was custom. Many ancient languages have the same word for law and custom. Originally, all customs were beneficial because they helped to preserve life, but in time many departed from their purpose. Because of severe penalties attached to their breach, it often becomes hard to distinguish whether they are immoral because of a disregard of prohibitions in the moral or religious code or because of the instinct that they are biologically injurious to the race.

## THE PROHIBITIONS OF ETHICS

The real meaning of the term *prohibition* has been lost in confusion. The naïve belief that legislation, for example, can make men moral is based upon the ancient fallacy that right conduct results only from fear. Fear is the source of the false, conventional ethics which dams the liberation of social energy instead of expanding and satisfying human desires, as constructive ethics (applied sociology) does.

The moral censors of the day, self-appointed one-hundred-per-cent moral purists, would do well to note Ward's axiom that social forces cannot be destroyed or made to flow into unnatural channels. So far as moral conduct is concerned, nature is our best guardian—which does not imply the return to any primitive state, but the creation of a natural, healthy environment. Social needs are properly fulfilled through social science; requiring man's active application to the ultimate object of morals, viz., the well-being and happiness of humanity, social science is fully in accord with nature's scheme. But moral codes, in spite of their terrifying penalties, have all been failures because they sought to impose virtue by force and paid no attention to the vital needs of the race. Public opinion, the social mind, based upon race morals is the only means by which the moral forces can be controlled. Says Ward:

Any human rule made in opposition to those natural laws is as incapable of enforcement as the pope's bull against the comet, while human rules in harmony with them do not in the least facilitate or affect their normal operation. . . . The prevailing idea is that anyone might conduct himself immorally if he preferred, and that pure *principle* is all that prevents the majority of mankind from doing so. Such ideas legitimately flow from the free-will doctrine and other kindred errors that pervade the moral teaching which we all receive. The truth is that men are compelled to conduct themselves according to the established standards of propriety. . . . It is a code which enforces itself and therefore requires no priesthood and no manual. And strangely enough, where alone *laissez faire* is sound doctrine, we find the *laissez-faire* school calling loudly for "regulation" (*D.S.,* II, 372-373).

Conventional or formal ethics is the attempt, generally by religious authority, to preserve primitive race morality by prohibition and commands. It is, however, no longer needed in civilization. Many acts now regarded as detrimental to the race such as cannibalism, theft, and slavery were once, in the infancy of mankind, beneficial to race preservation and were therefore treated as moral. Today, from the same standpoint of race safety, such acts are universally and naturally condemned because they are no longer necessary for the well-being or preservation of society, but on the contrary, are positive menaces.[1] The

[1] For example, science does not oppose polygamy because it is immoral, but because it is injurious to society. There may be a future state in society when bigamy will not

converse is also true. Society has written into its codes many prohibitions which have been found in time to be unnatural and absurd because they have outgrown their usefulness, and are no longer adapted to the needs or interests of society.

## ETHICS AND SOCIAL FRICTION

The savage knew no better than to obey his natural instinct of self-preservation, and for that purpose, practiced what appears today as the most absurd rites and customs. The civilized man does the same thing when he stubbornly clings to moral laws and institutions founded on restraints that are harmful to the race, something of which the untutored children of nature could not be guilty. In its stand on prohibitions in the interest of morals, modern ethics is positively indecent.

The moral cure is often worse than the social disease, for the ethics which is founded on restraint stands like a barrier on the road to human progress. Ward envisages a new social order controlled by social science when men will find joy in sharing as much as in possessing; in the exercise of their natural faculties as much as in the conformation to dogmatic fictitious criteria of virtue. A uniform moral code should be as impossible as a uniform diet. Any order which disregards the fundamental diversity of mankind is itself unnatural and immoral.

If ethics were a science, it would be a science of social friction. The essence of the ethical idea as preached the world over is that of a check-rein upon human effort. The degree of correspondence between man and the environment, notwithstanding his cunning and wisdom, is not large enough to prevent a great deal of friction which entails so much suffering and prevents so much happiness that it defeats the very purpose of all morality (see *D.S.*, II, 15).

Moral progress consists not in putting more moral precepts or laws into books and codes, but in removing the frictions and their causes from the social machinery. That can be done only by satisfying the individual's needs and desires and giving him the leisure and opportunity to function as a free and creative intelligent being. In that way will the smooth, energetic movements of the social mechanism and all its parts become possible (see *Glimpses*, V, 270-281).

---

be a crime provided the parties find mutual pleasure in the arrangement and no race deterioration is involved. That is the opinion not only of Ward, but also of every progressive sociologist.

That human suffering and discomfort can be minimized and overcome by intelligent effort is certain, for all evil is relative, and none of its underlying propensities are essentially bad. Any force, natural or artificial, is good or bad according to where and how it is spent. Human desires seeking their satisfaction through appropriate actions, constitute the only good from the standpoint of sociology. The ethical reformer and the sociologist should join in making the same demand for the removal of all social friction, because that would not only enlarge the progressive powers of society, but also increase the happiness and make possible the spiritual growth of its members. As Ward says:

The moral progress of the world has consisted, and must continue to consist, in a similar series of steps in reducing the friction of society. When we look back over the history of the world and realize how much better it is than it once was, especially in public life, it looks as if we had come a long way; but when day after day we scan the heads of the newspapers and note the ever-recurring horrors of our present state, we are compelled to admit that the moral world is still in the stone-boat stage of its history, dragging its heavy body over the rugged field of human life with the utmost friction and the smallest ethical economy. It is the painfulness of this feature of life that so arouses the quickened sympathies of mankind, and lends such an intense interest to all ethical questions (*ibid.,* V, 274).

## INDIVIDUAL MORALITY

Individual morality, unlike race morality, is grounded in altruism and has nothing to do with the egoistic group instinct to survive (see *P.S.,* pp. 422-426). Although race morality is of primary importance because the race is paramount to the individual, whatever social progress society has achieved has been the result of altruistic action.

Ward analyzes altruism into three elements: (1) affection for kin; (2) reasoning that it is more advantageous to co-operate and forebear than to compete and retaliate; (3) sympathy. The last named element is the pith of the golden rule, and is a purely rational product, despite any metaphysical arguments to the contrary. Of course, feeling is needed to motivate the individual into doing any altruistic act, but pure altruism, like pure morals, is like light without heat, and cannot move anything.

In its widest aspect altruism is the love of mankind. Everything that is enduring in the philosophy of the noblest spirits of the ages from Confucius, Buddha, and Hillel to Jesus and onward, has been essentially altruistic. Civilization can be gauged by the extent to which men are roused into altruism or remain indifferent to human misery, near or far (see *D.S.*, II, 448).

Reason by itself, no matter to what heights of genius it may soar, is self-centered and egoistic and cannot elevate man into a moral being. Unaided by sympathy, such products of the rational faculty as competition, slavery, or war would increase human misery apparently beyond the hope of alleviation. But with altruism, the narrower ripples of sympathy for immediate blood relatives broaden out into an all-embracing sentiment and form great waves of feeling for all mankind. On the higher planes of endeavor, the egoistic acts of individuals expand through altruism until the best minds and the warmest hearts, investigators, inventors, and discoverers, are unselfishly engaged in their work for posterity. In man's infancy, his sympathies were repressed either by fear and ignorance or by the direct conflict with the moral code foisted upon him. As race morals weakened and faded out, individual morals (altruism) springing from the deep wells of human feeling, developed and grew stronger.

## ETHICAL DUALISM

Moral feelings take different courses, but often converge. In primitive life, there was little real sympathy. When kinship developed its bond, loyalty became twofold: one to the race, founded on the fear of destruction and the group sentiment of race preservation; the other, to individuals, founded on altruism. The two loyalties will remain in conflict until the causes of race prejudice and national animosity will be removed (see *P.S.*, pp. 426-431).

When society was evolved out of the assimilation of warring races, altruism in the form of patriotism was developed in the new people that rose, phoenix-like, from the ashes of the conquered group. Love of country resembled the original blood bond, but it was, under the circumstances, dual in its nature, with hatred for all aliens, and love for all countrymen. Citizens of the world whose sympathies run beyond national boundaries have always been a rarity. Until their numbers increase, ethics will have two loves: (1) the narrow circle of blood relatives, race or nation, representing the present; (2) the fainter sentiment of love for all mankind, representing the illimitable future. It is the latter which Ward named ethical monism (*ibid.*, p. 430).

## ETHICAL MONISM

Ethical monism is still a rare phenomenon. Only the synthesis by emancipated minds of the dual ties to race and kin, on the one hand, and to humanity on the other, can make it better known. Such a combination of sentiments which denote a universal altruism comparable only to the true love of nature, has been felt and advocated by all truly moral as well as scientific minds. It is a pure, unselfish feeling, far above awe, admiration, or curiosity. As it proves that we are all integral parts of an infinite universe, it is the high point of spirituality. Under its influence, the mind acts in harmony with the rhythm of the cosmos, and the ethical monist or lover of nature, far from being a Don Quixote or a sentimental dreamer, absorbs and retains the purest essence of true morality, to be expressed and expended wherever possible.

Ward's monistic system of scientific ethics runs from the individual instinct for safety developed through race morality, fuses with individual altruism, and returns to nature through the widest channels of sympathy in which moral restraints and prohibitions are abandoned for the positive love of nature and the dynamic love of man. No organized religion and no individualistic system has ever accepted such an ethical philosophy. Opposition to it has always come from those pure and simple moralists who demand that no one shall substitute the private judgment of science for the divine command of God. Very often, the theologian, the metaphysician, and the abstract moralist have combined to use ethics to fan the dying embers of religious conflict. Yet no two of them, even if they have the most judicial habits of mind, have ever agreed upon what is moral or immoral, or right or wrong (see *D.S.*, II, 279-283).

The highest product of evolution is morality, the emergence in man of spirituality. But morality is something more, from the scientific viewpoint, than an intuitive sentiment or a spark from the Infinite struck in the imagination. A moral world is a healthy world and a happy world in which altruism or the religion of humanity directs all human action, and wherein the morality which binds and restrains is relegated to the limbo of outworn fears and fetishes. Social science is ready to usher in a new order with a new, constructive ethics of meliorism (applied sociology) and free the world from the ancient prohibitions of primitive race morality. In that new ethics will be found the means and method of solving the social problem.

# Chapter LXI

# THE NEW ETHICS

---

*"The fundamental assumption of the old ethics is that there is something essentially evil in human nature. . . . This knowledge of the psychic and social forces constitutes the basis of the new ethics. But it seems folly to call it ethics. The real science to which all these ethical considerations belong is social science, . . . a true constructive science."*—Ward

*"The old and the new stand side by side and admit of being compared; when the energies of all men are searched by fear and by hope; when the historic glories of the old can be compensated by the rich possibilities of the new era."*—Emerson

*"The ultimate problem on the side of pure Science is: 'What is worth doing?' The ultimate practical problem is: 'How may the thing worth doing be done?' "*—Albion W. Small

*"The ground of duty rests on no ancient code, but solely on the experience of what, after long ages of sore testing, man has come to feel to be the best for man."*—Edward Clodd

---

THE PROBLEM of society is not an ethical problem in the popular sense of the words, but a social one. Emerging from the depressing prohibitions of formal ethics into the heartening arena of social achievement where ethics becomes identical with applied sociology, is like leaving a dark prison for a sunlit field. Instead of restraining moral mandates imposed upon human beings already enmeshed in circumstances, life is again free, and faces nature and man with all its creative impulses, ready to serve humanity.

## ETHICS IS APPLIED SOCIOLOGY

Why have the fears and compulsions which underlie the old ethics been allowed to rule mankind so long and clog the road to social progress? The new ethics which comes with a happy and, therefore, spiritual life has nothing to do with religion or irreligion, but embraces the best elements of race morality, is wide enough to encompass the rational mean, and deep enough to absorb the idea of co-operation and mutual sacrifice. Yet the new ethics is so rarely met with that it is always described as an ideal or a vision.

Thus far in man's history, says Ward, morality has been the twin bed of religion upon which mankind was lulled into obedience with promises of heavenly rewards, while in the world outside the oppression and slaughter of human beings by each other never stopped. Prayers and persuasion have always been as ineffective as anathemas and threats of dire punishment to make society a moral organization. In Ward's language:

The sterile, old or negative ethics does not recognize the reason as a factor. It does not attempt to direct the destructive elements of social activity. It treats them as only baneful, and wages a crusade against them. It invents such epithets as vice, sin, immorality, and seeks to stamp these out. It denounces, anathematizes, condemns or else it pleads, expostulates and exhorts. All this, if separated from the influence of example and personal magnetism, is without effect. As well might King Canute command the sea to retire (*Glimpses*, V, 280).

Sociology takes the scientific view of ethics, but it is a novel attitude for encrusted minds that look only backward. Knowing the course and method to be pursued in accomplishing worthy social changes, social science removes morals from the plane of speculation to the domain of objective science, where it belongs. Ethics is thus recast from a metaphysical and theological mold into a scientific mold. Man is regarded as a unit of the cosmic aggregate, as one with an active intelligence, and is no longer thrown upon the mercies of the supernatural, or eternally blamed for his sins.

For the first time since the golden days of primitive life, man is recognized as a free individual having rights and duties arising from the environment and conforming to natural forces. The source of his morality is found in the synthesis of the Socratic view of knowledge as virtue, and the Aristotelian principle of reason as the foundation of the good life. Ward goes an important step further than those titanic Greek thinkers when he says:

The fundamental assumption of the old ethics is that there is something essentially evil in human nature. Its whole purpose is to destroy this evil element. No other science is wholly destructive. Nothing that is such can be a science. . . . But all true science is essentially constructive. Where, then, is the fundamental fallacy which must lurk somewhere in the current moral philosophy? It lies in the very assumption of evil propensities. They underlie the social world and belong to the nature of man. They would never have been planted there if they had not been necessary to his development. They are evils only in so far as they conflict with individual or social interests. . . . If man only knew fire is something that destroys, that would be classed as an evil agency. . . . The attitude changes in proportion as the knowledge of the nature of the agent increases. Strange as it may seem, the natural forces about which man knows least are those that reside within him. The latest sciences to be developed are those of mind and society—psychology and sociology. . . .

This knowledge of the psychic and social forces constitutes the basis of the new ethics. But it seems folly to call it ethics. The real science to which all these ethical considerations belong is *social science* —a true constructive science (*Glimpses*, V, 275-276).

Morality, said Comte, is impotent in the attainment of ends unless there is a genuine science of society. Moral ends should not be mistaken for scientific means, and it is futile to deal with either of them isolated from the other. If sociology acts as a signal designed to touch off the sympathetic emotions, the feelings that are aroused are the same every-where and for everybody. The science of human society, a science in-tended to help mankind at every step, should not mean different things for different people, but like medicine must essentially serve its very nature, as a means of curing human ailments.

Sociology stands squarely upon the brotherhood principle, but it goes beyond mere lip service and labors to discover and apply the means of realizing its doctrines. It puts on its working clothes, so to speak, and emerges as the new ethics. It is the sociologist who regards moral progress as possible, and then offers a constructive plan and a solid foundation for the structure (see *ibid.*, V, 281). Yet, unless the ghosts of fear are banished, and society is rebuilt upon a scientific (which necessarily means a moral) base, the present order of hungry animals in the guise of men, stalking and destroying each other, will retain their present morals of restraint, and expect no other.

In a flash of revealing analysis Ward demonstrates that the Greeks were correct in defining moral as practical. Practical virtue to the Greek moral philosophers consisted of the golden mean, while theoret-ical virtue lay in a life devoted to wisdom. The real object of morality, in Ward's view, is social efficiency, with sentiment, not sentimentality, as its foundation. So, too, did the moralists of Greece believe that "the good of the body is the primary condition of the good of the soul." In the widest sense, self-love is the highest love, for it indirectly includes preservation of the race. But what can the masses who feel, but do not think or reason, know of true ethics? Says Ward:

Criticism of received beliefs is always sweet to a considerable number who rejoice at the overthrow of the leaders of opinion or the fall of paragons of morality. And this it is which often renders the peace of society insecure. The established code of morals is dimly felt by the lower classes to be, in some respects, radically unsound. The broad contrast between men's nominal beliefs, as spoken, and their real beliefs, as acted, is apparent even to children. The standard of conduct is so much higher than that which the controllers of conduct can themselves live up to, resulting always in the punishment of the poor and the weak for the same transgressions as are daily committed with impunity by the rich and influential, that the lowest miscreant feels that there is some fundamental wrong underlying the entire social fabric, although he cannot tell what it is. All this must be regarded as the legitimate consequence of the undue supremacy of dogmatic ideas and teleological conceptions in society (*D.S.,* II, 24).

## THE NEW ETHICS AND HEDONISM

The new ethics keeps in the forefront the fact that the purpose of human life is the satisfaction of desire at the least possible cost. Only that is moral and spiritual which helps in the fulfillment of the natural aim of life. If this sounds shocking to the sensitive reader, Ward reminds him that there is scarcely a single important principle of science which did not at first jar the world's opinions and prejudices to their foundations. Science continues to seek and impart the truth, no matter whom that hurts, and it has no concern either with the nicety or rigor of its conclusions, or with its effect upon established doctrine. Says he:

While in the physical sciences every attempt to go back to fundamental principles is deemed highly proper and praiseworthy, the original truths upon which society and morality rest can not be laid bare and stated plainly for fear of shocking the morbid sense of the civilized world. . . . Therefore most thinkers are obliged to refrain from promulgating the real truths that underlie society and conduct, through fear of actually obstructing the progress of the world. . . .

The primary laws of human action, upon which both social and moral science rest, can not be stated in the simple language of science. The objection that the explanation is too simple to be true, which is often made in the less involved sciences, is particularly apt to be made in these most involved sciences. Men do not want to know that their life is capable of analysis into simple physical principles. They prefer to contemplate themselves as something entirely preternatural. The science of human conduct is particularly objectionable. Every rational analysis of human action tends to ground it in egoism and assimilate it to animal action. Very few want to know such truths. That the most disinterested action should result from the effort of the actor to experience pleasure is a truth repugnant to the cultured mind. It belongs to the list of unwelcome truths, like that of the genetic development of the race from a less highly organized state (*ibid.*, I, 76-77).

In one of his rare self-appraising moments, when his ultra-modesty was put aside, he said:

I am the only one who has fully worked out the philosophy of life on scientific principles; shown what feeling (pleasure and pain) means, and explained on biological principles the "origin of evil" and of good, too; in fact, put ethics on a sound, scientific basis. Without this, I do not wonder that thinking minds go wild and run to mysticism. It is to them all a great mystery (*Cape*, pp. 123-124).

The duty of the state is not over, said Ward, when it provides food, shelter, and clothing for the people. There still remains the general problem of making it possible for them to live with a minimum of pain and a maximum of pleasure; of enabling every man to magnify the volume of life and realize himself to an increasing extent. In other words, the important function of spreading knowledge and widening mental and spiritual horizons, and the endless possibilities of individual and social achievement must not be omitted. The ethical means the useful; that is why all science is ethical. And because feeling underlies morality, pain and pleasure furnish the only valid tests of moral quality (see *Glimpses*, V, 271). Can anything be plainer and more real than Ward's:

Pleasure means life and pain means death. This new element is nothing more or less than the *moral* element. No such element exists in Nature outside of this class of beings. Nature is wholly *unmoral*. To Nature at large, the moral world is nothing. To the sentient world it is everything (*Outlines*, p. 98).

While formal ethics denies the claims of feeling, the new ethics stresses the tragic loss at which the social art is conducted, with the debits of pain far exceeding the credits of pleasure. Is it possible to acquire a surplus of joys, or is mankind to be forever doomed to misery and pessimism? The purpose of dynamic sociology is first to show how the long standing deficit of human suffering is to be gotten rid of, and then how to accumulate the greatest possible quantity of profits in happiness. Increased knowledge might produce more material achievement popularly called progress, but only the new ethics, or as it should be properly called, applied sociology, can point the way to elevate feeling, eliminate pain and increase the joys of life, and bring about a truly moral state. Sociology is the only instrument by which the two seemingly conflicting problems of achievement and improvement can be brought into close harmony to prove the mechanical dependence of each upon the other, and show how they can fuse into social ethics.

That ethics is bound up with feeling and thus determines all human action was demonstrated all through his works. In his first book he summed it up as follows:

The "pure morals" of Kant and the "absolute ethics" of Spencer can never be fully realized, and can only be approximately realized through a complete *organization of human action*. The wholly unorganized, independent and sporadic character of human pursuits at the present time, is the cause of the constant conflicts of interests in society, and is that which causes a moral quality to exist. Moral conduct, though necessary to prevent worse evils, is in itself a serious evil. Every departure from the direction of the propelling force of an action is made at the expense of the results accomplished.

Moral conduct is in reality conduct in a very irregular line. The path of *rectitude* is a crooked path, and the distance lost in following it counts heavily against the progress of the world, yet less heavily than would the jars and collisions which a failure to follow it would inevitably produce. . . . Proceeding upon the direct method, success of this great ethical movement from the earliest historic periods has been only temporary and local. . . . At this late day, we still find ourselves at the foot of the ladder, and we must begin, if at all, where Confucius and Manu began (*D.S.*, II, 377-379).

The explanation of the paradox of feeling is the simple fact that the object of human life is not moral perfection but happiness, the fulfillment of desire. It is happiness that produces morality for the human being, not vice versa. Morality is simply the safeguard at the social mechanism which is operated for the direct purpose of achievement and with the indirect object of bringing happiness to the individual. Ward emphasizes again and again the necessity of shifting ethics permanently from the emotional to the rational side of life, from the theological to the scientific. No abstract, negative, or metaphysical aspect of the human scene can give us the proper slant on right and wrong; only positive, dynamic, and applied scientific tendencies can do this.

Abstract (formal) ethics claims to have the same aim as sociology, i.e., the amelioration of existence, but its methods are entirely different. The former seeks to control conduct by a direct appeal to that emanation of the Divine called conscience. The latter makes its appeal to humanity for help and guidance come true by the effective influence of proper circumstances and environment. That method belongs to applied sociology—the social art combined with social justice.

The abstract moralist is so busy exhorting people to be good and to do right that he forgets to tell them how that can be accomplished (see *Ps. F.,* p. 114). Somehow, he always preaches the restraint of the natural forces, but never their expression or control. Sociology, on the contrary, claims that crime, for example, is a disease which can be cured only by social science. The removal of the causes of crime or any other social evil cannot be effected by moral catechisms presented to hungry or brutalized slum dwellers. A leaflet about the wonders of astronomy, Ward suggested, is of greater interest to a prisoner than a sheaf of moral tracts.

While he was still trying to get into college, and before he commenced writing *Dynamic Sociology,* Ward had the grand generalization clearly in mind that education is the initial step to happiness, social progress, and a moral order. We can find no more scientific and loftier summary of the moral question than the following which he wrote at the age of twenty-five, when he was still a believer, looking at science:

The world labors under a grave and serious error. It has generally been supposed that our duties to our fellow men and to our Maker are more vitally important than the mere acquisition of knowledge. So usually we devote ourselves more to moral than to intellectual culture. This position, however sound it may seem, is as false in logic as it is pernicious in effect.

To say that mental culture is the highest moral action may be a paradox to the moralist, but none the less, a great and important truth. When we descend into the abstract principles of moral science and endeavor to investigate the laws of right and wrong, we soon find ourselves engaged in meshes of doubt and bewilderment. . . . In the midst of this maze of bewildering testimony, we pause and ask ourselves the question whether morals are not, after all, the result of education and tradition alone. Teach morality! Whose morality will you teach? You say it is right; I say it is wrong. But you insist that many wise men agree with you. I retort that as many agree with me. . . . Far be it from me to belittle the vast importance of correct moral principles. But opinions of men on questions of right and wrong may be changed or new ones formed by the logic of circumstances, but they admit of no demonstration.

The intellectual faculties are the only ones capable of expansion and development, and to these, there is no limit. Mental researches are the only ones in which there can be any final human solution, and these are as countless as the sands of time.

Moral culture leads to abstract sophistries and invalidity. Religious culture, to the exclusion of intellectual training, degenerates into morbid asceticism or bigoted fanaticism. Neither serves to accelerate in the smallest degree the onward march of civilization.

The great panacea for all our doubts and dangers is the thorough and universal education of the mental powers. With a lofty and polished intellect, the moral and religious natures will shape themselves right. Show me a man with an intellect, refined, lofty, and ennobled by service in the vast field of science, art, and letters, and I will show you one of exceptional moral character and a profound respecter of the sublime and imperishable truths of Him who spoke as never man spoke. Show me an intelligent people and I will show you a moral and religious people. Show me a land of school-houses, and I will show you a land of churches (from "The Importance of Intellectual Culture," an unpublished address, 1866).

## PRIVATIVE ETHICS

Analyzing the social order as it is, Ward finds ethics split into two sharply defined divisions, viz., privative or negative ethics, and positive or constructive ethics. The first is the one always in the public eye because it is educed by the universal surplus of pain over pleasure. Privation is so widespread that it is accepted even by most of the sufferers as their natural condition and destiny. It is sad but true that the idea hardly ever strikes them that man was not born to suffer, and that he has already acquired enough knowledge to do away with the competitive struggle for existence and abolish the state of ignorance from which all his misery flows. Ward's hope as well as his prophecy is that if society were to apply its collective mind to the social problem, happiness would in time become the natural condition of mankind, instead of the great exception (see *App. S.,* pp. 319-321).

Privative ethics opens the family closet of society and reveals an appalling number of skeletons. Most human beings have little or no incentive to be moral. The present system is such that because material conditions are insufficient to maintain them, a great number is constantly being killed off by disease, poverty and war. Thus, the average longevity of the wealthy classes is about fifty-five years, but that of the poor is only about twenty-eight years. The mortality of infants in the families of the rich is less than 6 per cent, but among the poor it is between 30 and 40 per cent (see *ibid.,* pp. 321-322).

These and similar facts prove to Ward that the individualistic order is inherently immoral, and its system of morality, vicious and inhuman. It is impossible to seek individual advantage through competition and disregard the effects upon society. The very essence of true ethics is to act with an eye upon the consequences to others. The method of individualism is the opposite; it is egoism incarnate. It even adds insult to injury when it begins to blame the poor and the ignorant for their plight and miserable condition.

Comte and Spencer sincerely believed that the voluntary benevolence of the rich and powerful could be depended upon to abolish social injustice and social suffering.[1] Ward makes no plea to those in power to feed or release their hands. Nor does he beg the poor and afflicted to be either moral or patient. To leave the questions of bread, employment, politics, sex, population, heredity, environment, or education to the caprice or sympathies of private individuals, or to the tender mercies of public charity seems to him to be as futile as begging a hawk to become a vegetarian. His rousing call in the name of positive ethics for dynamic action is unmistakable:

Reformers tacitly assume that 60 or 80 per cent of the members of society are and must always remain objects of charity, "the weaker members of the community." Yet on any kind of theory of social equality or social justice, society belongs to them. They are the big end of society. Thus far, the tail has been wagging the dog. . . .

[1] Even at this late day when so many believe that laissez faire is gone forever, President Roosevelt, who favors dressing the wolf of individualism in sheep's clothing and filing down his fangs, continues to exhort industrial and financial barons to *create jobs* for the unemployed in order to solve the problem of a recurring or permanent economic depression.

When the problem of equalization of intelligence shall have been solved and society awakes from its long and fitful sleep, it will all be over, like a horrid nightmare, and the world will be thankful that it was only a dream. Mankind want no fatherly oversight of the privileged classes, nor any other form of patronizing hypocrisy. They only want power—the power that is theirs of right and which lies within their grasp. They have only to reach out and take it. The victims of privative ethics are in the immense majority. They constitute society. They are the heirs of all the ages. They have only to rouse and enter upon their patrimony that the genius of all lands and of all time has generously bequeathed to them (*App. S.,* p. 326).

## DECEPTION

Privative ethics, like a cancer, has spread deeply into the social body. The moral bankruptcy of individualism is closely related to its industrial and economic bankruptcy. Character has become molded, on the one hand, to the profit motive, militarism, and a general system of exploitation, and on the other, to a submissive obedience to authority that dulls the moral sensibilities. Cruelty and deception finally acquire haloes of success, and develop into supreme virtues. While the air is literally full of noble moral preachments, the gentle art of fooling the public goes merrily on. The upper and shrewder classes, moral and respectable of course, see to it that deception is not unmasked as cruelty in its ugliest form, an imitation of the predatory brutes that devour the weak and the innocent,—all of which is one more example of man's inhumanity to man.

Falsehood appears to be the warp and woof of the social fabric. The animal's struggle for mere existence is allowed, nay urged, to be carried over full strength into the human domain. The ruse and cunning, the common necessary tools of the beasts, become the chief and unnecessary instruments of *homo sapiens* to outdo his fellows. How is morality at all possible under such circumstances? In other words, how can morality live under the same roof with competition, poverty, or despair?

To the upholders of the individualist system of "get all you can and keep all you get," the only known spur to achievement is the fear of want and the lust for gain. Those are the ends that justify all means. If all is fair in love and war, what nobler or greater war is there than the struggle for existence? The idea of a social order without competition or a deadly struggle for existence serving as an economic and moral incentive, is as inconceivable to them as a war without ammunition.

Dynamic sociology dissipates the view that our social world is unchangeable because it is the best one possible, "human nature" being what it is, and demonstrates how false and infantile is such a philosophy. The fact is that three out of the five principal social classes have been almost exempted from the wear and tear of economic conflict, and have been the main achievers, though without any incentive of hunger or acquisitiveness (see *ibid.,* p. 321). But argue as one will, it is plain that the natural (animal) law of acquisition is as strong as ever. The only progress society has made toward a moral order has been to soften here and there the hardships of exploitation while it consoled itself with the cold comfort that in the competitive system, the means justify the ends. And so, society has substituted for a blow in the dark all sorts of legal steps in the full light of day, and instead of piracy and brigandage, there are complicated laws, combinations, and monopolies which are so strongly established that it may require a general social upheaval to overthrow them.

To maintain such an outwardly "moral" system, the keen minds and bold spirits that control the individualistic system have spread exploitation by every available form of deception, misrepresentation and chicanery masked as strategy, and service of man and God. The effect has been to strengthen the conclusion that the entire physical, social and moral struggle has been due to the law of competition. In so far as man has progressed at all beyond the animal stage, he has done so by triumphing over individual lust which seeks possession for its own sake, by fair means or foul. Human institutions, including morals and religion, are so many ways of meeting and checking this ogre of competition. Moral laws are the means adopted by reason for chaining the competitive egoism which we have inherited from our animal ancestors. The fittest to survive are not the best or the moral but only the strongest, the fit in view of the surrounding circumstances. Yet the law of survival in the struggle for existence has always had a certain moral flavor attached to it as if those who survived were favored by God for their righteous achievements.

Ward's comments on human deception bite like acid. He finds it everywhere, in home, church, business, and government. A moment's conversation with a stranger, he confesses, will usually show that he is trying to deceive you about something "and if you do not discover this, it is generally because he has succeeded." Fashionable society is a sham. Quackery reigns in the professions, and charlatanism in scientific bodies. Falsehood is everywhere, "and as you look out a car window, the rocks and trees are placarded all over with lies" (*P.S.*, p. 488). Notwithstanding all the cant about the dignity of labor, to work with one's hands is regarded as degrading, and those who do so are generally denied all social position. To avoid social abasement, the more "genteel" occupations are made the ambition of every man, woman, and child who wants to succeed in life. "The effect is to throng the 'learned professions' with aspirants to this honor" (*Ps. F.*, p. 272).

Lifting the world-old curtain of smugness which has covered the ancient and honorable legal profession, Ward throws the spotlight upon the advocates of justice and unmasks them in two brief paragraphs:

I used to smile when I heard good and simple country dames say that lawyers lived by lying, and I "studied law," acquired that profession, and was duly admitted to the bar. But long before the end I had learned that the good country dames were right and I was wrong. I was openly taught by the senior professor that my business was to gain my case, and that I was not to be the judge of the justice of the case. I need scarcely add that I have never pleaded a case (*P.S.*, p. 488).

There is, for example, scarcely a doubt that if nine out of every ten members of the legal profession were eliminated entirely from it and turnd into some useful occupation, the ends of justice would thereby be immensely the gainer and thousands of laborers would be added to the industrial pursuits. But this is the class whom the masses intrust with the framing of their laws, and as long as they continue to do so, they must pay the penalty of their stupidity (*Ps. F.*, p. 167).

In every country where wealth is the chief social ideal, and individual success the most honorable ambition in life, laissez faire still goes hand in hand with organized religion, negative ethics, party politics, lack of education, and a legal sanction of the exploitation of the individual for the benefit of private masters. Anyone who fails to practice a certain amount of deception (at least within the law) is regarded as a dreamer and a fool (see *D.S.,* I, 511-512). The principle of *caveat emptor* is turned into an ethical principle and is matched for sheer ingenuity by the art of salesmanship which consists in selling a man something that he does not want at several times its value and many times the amount he can afford to pay. The whole current economic system seems to be a means of allowing knaves to enrich themselves at the expense of the public, through monopoly, graft, and the other pet methods of the competitive system, all of which is sanctimoniously covered by the magic word "business," and is deemed moral from every viewpoint.

The offspring of deception is easily recognized in the ruse, in diplomacy and in "business ability." The necessary components of success are found in the peculiar talents which help to commercialize and pervert art, science, philosophy, and religion, and foster superstition and hypocrisy everywhere. The moral fibre is thus weakened, and law, justice, and human rights are subordinated to force, legal camouflage, and property rights.

Deception has become a powerful social institution in which the timidity of the legislators, courts, editors, teachers, and other important social leaders is outstanding. Kings of industry and finance bring on international wars in order to obtain or retain new markets, and call it national honor, protecting investments and making the flag follow the dollar. Society, says Ward, is really living in the stone age, or before. We no longer need to trap animals for our dinner, but we still hunt human beings more cleverly than the savages did, for our cunning has been intensified and refined by civilization, and there are constantly new methods invented for the grand chase. "You can't live by morals," says the civilized huntsman, "you must outwit and get the best of your stupider brothers if you want to survive and prosper" (see *D.S.,* I, 503). And so we have kept the verb "to lie" an active one, while we have not yet found one for truth telling.

In the face of universal deception and cruelty are there still optimists naïve enough, asks Ward, to believe that society is a moral order? Though we pretend to have abolished outright force, the swindle and the racket, the "legal" exploitation of woman, workers, and weaker nations, advertising and other "business methods," booms and monopolies aided by law and patriotism—all these means and methods prove the contrary, and emphasize a system whose dominant principle is "Whatever is, is right" (see *P.S.*, p. 486; *Ps. F.*, p. 167).

In every human activity, business, politics, social life in general, real morality is tabu just as it is in war, and deception rules. Politics has descended from its position as the highest duty of the citizen to a source of profit to a large section of the population. A public opinion that fosters deception is created through special laws and the clever supervision of school, church, and press (see *P.S.*, pp. 487-488). Society becomes one mass of auto-suggestion, hypocrisy, and sheer stupid cruelty and is as far from having any moral sense or moral purpose as a hungry tiger.

## TRUTH

The lame defense in all apologetics for the individualist system is that humanity is naturally imperfect, that absolute truth is impossible for finite beings, and that truth must be tempered with a certain amount of deception. After all, competition is an instinct, and "business is business." But sociology does not demand either absolute truth or absolute perfection in mankind. Relative truth is all that can be expected, but that does not mean a perversion or neglect of natural principles and natural forces so as to set up a system which lacks even the natural justice and collective spirit of an animal pack.

Telling the truth is as much an untried experience as reasoning. The will to face the truth is an impossible ordeal for most people. Men have learned that they must work (or get others to work for them) or die, but not that they must tell and live the truth in order to survive. On the contrary, the vast majority find consolation in the credo that ignorance is bliss, and that what one does not know cannot hurt him. Yet, as we have seen, correct opinions are vitally necessary for the satisfaction of desire, a state which is directly connected with achievement, civilization, and morality. A really educated person, one who holds correct opinions, is a rarity. As for the truth-seeker, he is generally eyed with suspicion as a freak and dangerous character. Ward emphasized with all the power he possessed that until society becomes permeated with the truths of nature and the experiences of science; until the liars who lead are thrown from their saddles and men who know and speak the truth are put into their places, morality will remain an abstract ideal, and formal ethics our only code of conduct.

Again, Ward's analysis brings him to education, the great panacea. Says he:

It is often said that ideas rule the world; but this is true only of world ideas. The highest and brightest ideas, the most important thoughts of any age or people, have scarcely any influence upon the world. This is because such ideas are alwas confined to a very few of the most developed minds and are not shared by the mass of mankind. . . . But any idea that permeates the whole mass and becomes the thought of society itself, sways the mass and shapes the action of society in its entirety (*App. S.,* p. 41).

Most of the progress due to ideas is of that superficial kind which merely produces material civilization through the conquest of nature and does not penetrate to the lower strata of society at all. This is because the truth is possessed by only a minute fraction of society. It therefore has great economic value but little social value. What the progress of the world would be if all this truth were socially appropriated no one can foresee, but its effect would probably be proportional to the number possessing it (*ibid.,* p. 83).

## POSITIVE ETHICS

The aim of social science is to build a moral order, not a sensual or a materialistic order. In planning for that end, it asks the simple question why all people cannot be happy and healthy, inhabiting houses and cities which are spacious, beautiful, and inspiring, with full opportunity for work, education, individual development, and communal satisfaction. Moral reform outside of the frame of sociology has never accomplished anything permanent toward laying the foundations for any such system which would provide the physical and mental well-being and satisfy the deepest human impulses. Why?

Ward's answer that it is due to the failure of society to adopt a system of positive ethics may sound trite, but it goes right to the roots of the social problem. "What price morality?" he asks. Is there no way out of the social miasma of deception and cruelty inherent in the cut-throat competitive order except through theological dogma? Does not a beaten or starving patient need food and medicine ahead of any spiritual solace, and before any restraints upon his conduct? Society is still carrying on a pain economy, says our guide. It has been too busy licking its wounds to think of healthy enjoyments;

too preoccupied in preserving its life to have very much to do with true morals, altruism, or happiness. But to social science, these are the climaxes, the purposes and goals of human life. Positive ethics must begin where privative ethics leaves off (see *ibid.,* p. 326).

How long it will take for society to become a pleasure economy and furnish thereby the basis for a moral civilization, depends upon the social mind or will of the people. All that sociology can do is to show the way. The adoption of a program of sociocracy and a reasonable application of social telesis and collective achievement instead of rampant competition and individual aggrandizement, would soon prove the truth of the ancient principle, ever new, that negative good is of no social value. People must have conditions and circumstances which will allow them to be positively good, and that is identical with the social and moral progress which we call happiness (see *Cape,* p. 50).

The influence of the many saintly men and purely moral thinkers of all time has been practically nothing as far as the well-being of humanity is concerned. On the other hand, the achievements of votaries of science with their sleeves rolled up, of the discoverers, inventors, scientists, artists, philosophers, and teachers, doing something to explain and lighten the burdens of life have been tremendous, but few and far between. Yet the world is slowly moving forward as a result of their labors to the view that the only possible morality for civilized peoples is not that of religion but of positive ethics, although any truly religious person will recognize it as the very core of religiosity. Says Ward:

> To insure successful prosecution of man's objects (not negative objects whose nature is to tear down, which are undertaken with reluctance and soon relinquished), they must possess the elements of progress and give earnest of carrying the world forward to a more advanced position. The failure of all religious systems to accomplish this is now apparent to all capable of observing the history of the world from a wholly unbiased standpoint. The influence of imaginary advanced states beyond the present life has had no effect in securing such a state in this life. The moral systems that have been more or less mechanically mixed with religious ones have shown themselves incapable of progressing beyond a limit reached in the time of Confucius and Hillel (*D.S.,* I, 10).

Positive ethics is based upon reason and reality. It seeks to discover whether life is painful or pleasant, and what has been done to make everybody happy or miserable. It believes that men do not fall from grace because they are human, but because they are not human enough. It finds the cause of human failure in lack of knowledge and opportunity, not in any want of faith or morals. There is no truth in the copybook maxims about man rising from the ashes of his dead self. Man must rise, says this new ethics, upon the achievements of his living, dynamic self, and look untroubled into the future and away from the ghosts of the past.

What does society present instead? It is the scene of a paradoxical order, so wealthy that it cannot feed its members; so informed that error and ignorance are the rule; so cultured that great masses of the people live unhappy and brutalized lives. Why? Because society has failed to assimilate human achievement, a failure due to social inequality. A just distribution of the fruits of achievement is hardly possible in a social structure having an ignorant mass below and a small informed class at the top which owns most of the economic wealth, and still more of the intellectual wealth of the world. The solution of the single problem of education, Ward claims, would also be the solution of the moral problem. If the lower and working classes were as informed and intelligent as the upper and employing classes, exploitation and the class struggle upon the economic base would not continue very long. Men do not err when they sin, but when they do not know (see *App. S.,* pp. 314-315).

## MORALS AND PROGRESS

The neglect to distinguish between privative ethics and positive ethics has obscured the true explanation why moral progress has not kept pace with material progress. Yet Ward believed (in 1883) that there was no cause for despair. The present era, he said, has shown a greater awakening, if not an actual advance in morals than any other period in history (see *D.S.,* II, 507). One of the obvious facts in social evolution is the persistence of social problems in spite of all progress flowing from inventions and discoveries which were directly intended to solve such problems. Of course, there has been some moral improvement, but considering the amount of fervor and agitation spent upon the moral question during the historic period, moral progress has been negligible. The explanation of this paradox is not found in evil human nature, but in the lack of applied social science and the stubborn resistance of even so-called moral elements in society to any basic improvements in the condition of the mass[2] (see *Glimpses,* IV, 5-15).

The fundamental error of conventional ethics and the old sociology has been to make moral progress independent of material progress. Instead of preaching morality in the midst of an immoral social system of dog eats dog, in which the great majority are without adequate knowledge and means of subsistence, Ward argues for an entirely new concept of ethics based upon an intelligent, planned, social order in which the principle of "every man for himself and the devil take the hindmost" will no longer exist.

Up to the present, Ward adds, achievement has not been harmonized or correlated with improvement. All advance on the material side has availed little to moralize and ameliorate the condition of the people, because our grasp of the nature of human association has not kept pace with our understanding of its control and with the production of material necessary for its continuance. That is why millions upon millions of increased wealth cannot prevent or dim the sight of the relief lines. The rich simply grow richer, and the poor, poorer, and the number of people who have nothing but vanished hopes, increases (see *App. S.,* p. 20).

The only rational solution of this paradox, Ward repeats, is found in applied sociology (see *ibid.,* pp. 21-22). Material progress captured by individualism has created a system of morals all its own which philanthropic and sentimental gentlemen preach to the lower classes

[2] Morality lags woefully behind all other human achievements. Material culture remained practically the same from 4000 B.C. until the Industrial Revolution which commenced in the eighteenth century. Since then, it has leaped further ahead than in all the centuries before. But machinery and invention brought no moral order in their wake. The stalking tiger and the sudden lightning bolt are no longer to be feared, but the deadly struggle between man and man has gone on and on and become more fierce with the years. What if the average span of life has increased, or nations possess more gold than ever? Are not the poorhouses and the doles growing everywhere? What if we roll on asphalt, bathe in porcelain, draw music from the air, or read the news the day before it happened? Have we not as many tabus, prejudices, superstitions, and cruelties as of old? In the sum total of happiness, we do not relatively possess as much as our ancestors did. We know many things that they did not know, but the number of free and noble spirits who stand out as moral beings among the herd are few and far between. And in the art of life, the social art, we are like a donkey that runs after a whisp of hay held in front of its nose.

on holy days and state occasions, while science keeps on struggling bravely to displace superstition and cruelty in the physical and spiritual worlds, with knowledge and humanitarianism. As the human race grows more sapient and material civilization expands, the hope for a moral advance that will keep pace with it, increases. By giving more attention to the problem of happiness and less to that of amassing wealth or pleasing the supernatural powers, moral progress will have a chance.

## THE SELF-DESTRUCTION OF ETHICS

Instead of being the climax of human evolution and the goal of science and philosophy, as Spencer would have it, ethics, according to Ward, is only a means of bringing happiness and well-being to society. In a healthy state such as sociocracy, there will be no need of codes, any more than of medicines or doctors in a healthy community, or of economic codes in a co-operative state (see *Ps. F.,* pp. 103-115). In a normally free and happy order, there will be nothing for morals to do, and the censor will become permanently unemployed. Men will need no sympathy or altruism any more than the clouds or the mountains. The race will gradually become amoral after intellect will conquer instinct and the highest ethics will then be no ethics at all. In Ward's words:

Just as reason, even in early man, rendered instinct unnecessary, so further intellectual development and wider knowledge and wisdom will ultimately dispense with both religion and ethics as restraints to unsafe conduct, and we may conceive of the final disappearance of all restrictive laws and of government as a controlling agency. But that the world is still far from this ideal state may be realized by reflecting that all that we call vice and crime, and in general, all attacks upon the social order, constitute when we seize their true philosophical import, neither more nor less than so many deviations from the path of function in the interest of feeling (*P.S.,* p. 135).

Social evolution will not stop with sociocracy and positive ethics. The natural as well as the social forces will still function when the police duty of morals and the state will be over. Trust the universal principle of synergy to find work on higher and higher planes. Instead of wrestling with the problem of daily needs, man's struggle will continue with the more significant problems of personal development, individual intelligence, and spiritual growth. Says Ward:

The evils of society are due to the competitive system in a state of artificial inequality of intelligence, and as this state has always existed it is supposed that it always must exist. The world has scarcely begun to reflect upon the possibility of any other system. All kinds of false notions prevail on the subject, such as that the only motives to industry are the fear of want and the love of gain. . . . There are many other things to compete for besides money or wealth . . . part of it is intellectual, and consists of rivalry in achievement. On this higher plane, competition takes the form of honorable emulation (*App. S.*, pp. 320-321).

## THE NEW POSITIVE ETHICS AT WORK

In advanced countries, the new ethics has already gone to work. Legislation, at least, is being widely promoted from the "thou-shalt-not" stage into the positive and constructive stage. The Ten Commandments (eight are negative) are being illuminated in many parts of the world by movements toward positive and equal opportunities, and the private profit motive is coming to be regarded as a crime against society. The eyes of the masses are gradually being opened to the fact that individual immoral conduct is not the cause of social evil, but that the reverse is true. Ignorance and poverty are the chief sins which the community by the aid of sociology must eradicate.

The method of science under the guidance of intelligence is to attract the natural forces, not to drive them, claimed Ward; to free them, not to fetter them. Franklin did not "chain the lightning" but found the path for it where it can do incalculable good for mankind. So it will be with the social forces when they are controlled and utilized intelligently. In his words:

This is social science in its applied stage. Its purpose is to find unobstructed paths along which they may operate to their full extent. It will minimize the social friction and utilize the social energy. . . . My chief purpose has been to emphasize the fact that sociology is a science, that it is a domain of natural forces of which man may take advantage precisely as he has taken advantage of the physical forces of nature. Until this truth can be perceived and vividly brought home, not only to philosophers, but especially to men of affairs, statesmen and legislators, it is vain to speculate upon methods and details (of the character which the social machinery is likely to assume to minimize the social friction and utilize the social energy).

I have called these ethical aspects. In this I may be mistaken, but it is only a question of the meaning of words. I have never entered the field of ethics, and if the universal betterment of man's estate does not belong to ethics, it is a field into which I do not care to enter (*Glimpses*, V, 281).

The new ethics need not go into fortune telling. How impossible it would have been even for the keenest minds of the sixteenth century, for example, to predict the Industrial Revolution or the economic debacle of the present post-war era! Human nature and human character have not essentially changed or improved very much since antiquity, but the increase of knowledge and of social achievement has brought a certain measure of social progress. Yet no one can predict how far it will go in the future. The society of tomorrow will no doubt smile at our eager guesses as to how it would carry on, just as we are amused at the efforts of ancient philosophy to foresee modern trends.

Although Ward never indulged in idle prophecies of just how social ethics would function in detail in the future, there are many suggestions scattered throughout his works of what will logically follow the change from a competitive to a co-operative order. First of all will come the establishment of the necessary physical requirements for the pursuit of happiness, viz., food, shelter, and clothing. Then follows a host of other real needs, without which the exercise of human faculties would be impossible, such as leisure, liberty, art, science, and education. Society must allow their free and universal use, if achievement is to mean anything. No such utopian scheme as an equal distribution of wealth is contemplated by positive ethics, because such a step would not yield mankind enough for primary wants. Positive ethics would rather save the present waste in production and distribute the products of achievement among those who have earned it. It would rather demand the satisfaction of natural desires, in general, whether material or spiritual; the means for every person to rear a family free from the ogre of want, and to educate and to train them to the limits of taste and capacity. Accordingly, it would make possible the erection of attractive homes stocked with enlightening agencies; sufficient travel to shake off provincialism and chauvinism, and in general, insure an active participation in the immortal stream of human achievement. Since such a program would require per capita many times the means that each person is now able to acquire, the new ethics would require an enormous rise in the standard of living.

Is such a program a dream? Let no one despair, says Ward. The advance of invention and machinery is practically limitless, and everybody can have all the things he now calls luxuries, in suitable abundance. After that, given opportunity and leisure, the human organization is susceptible of being attuned to a thousand refined and ennobling sentiments to which it is practically still a stranger. When the earth will belong to the people, they will have the means of responding to ever more and higher needs. Labor will no longer be drudging toil, but an attractive function (see *App. S.*, pp. 334-339). The present odium upon labor is simply a matter of inherited caste and class feeling. There is never anything unpleasant about a task that is voluntary, and not in itself exhaustive. The exercise of the natural faculties is always agreeable, and constitutes the greatest source of happiness. Happiness is doing something, not being something, or somebody. The equalization of intelligence would soon brush away the conventional cobwebs that cover most minds, and would make all labor both moral and respectable.

To attractive labor would also be added attractive legislation, each of which is impossible without the other. Nothing worthy of the term *legislation* in the sense of scientific social invention is feasible except in a sociocracy, because only in that kind of a planned social order is positive social science, social ethics, at the helm. The representatives of society must be of sufficient intelligence to see that negative ethics expressed in prohibition laws are socially too expensive and ineffective. The only cheap and efficient way to make people do right is to offer them such inducements as will in all cases be to their advantage to accept. Such a method is not considered possible in any individualistic and competitive system (see *D.S.*, II, 156).

We leave the new ethics of dynamic sociology, firm in the belief that neither the "pure morals" of Kant nor the "absolute ethics" of Spencer will do; that where the necessities of life are absent, moral policy is also wanting; that no one can live by and for himself alone, or remain callous to human suffering unless he is a supreme egoist with an ox-thick hide; that a moral people is a happy people, and that only a system of social co-operation can usher in the moral civilization which is the aim of sociology.

We have learned that the possibilities of human achievement are without bounds, and that only a positive morality can prepare the ground for it. The spiritual heights to which man may climb are measured by the extent of his conquest over nature, the subjugation of instinct to intellect, and the elimination of the cruelties and crudities of savagery by civilization. These are things which cannot be achieved by preaching morality, but by making it possible to live it.

Whether we are evolving a moral society or moving toward a moral end, no one can say, but all can help toward making society a moral order characterized by beauty, truth, and happiness. The time is ripe for such an order, because society has arrived at a period when, in the words of Emerson, "the old and the new stand side by side, and admit of being compared; when the energies of all men are searched by fear and by hope; when the historic glories of the old can be compensated by the rich possibilities of the new era."

# EPILOGUE

THE JOURNEY THROUGH the temple of sociology is over. If our attempt not only to summarize but to point the way; not only to review the past but to look into the future, has not lit fires in the reader's mind, the fault is ours, not his. And if he has not been convinced that sociology is the synthesis of all knowledge, that it is a true science and the science of sciences, which alone can lead society out of the wilderness in which men's ignorance and stupidity have lost it, our effort has been in vain. Yet it is hard to imagine that Ward's dynamic sociology; his doctrine of education as the great panacea and the initial step toward happiness; his stress upon human effort and social control; his elevation of reason above emotion, and of science above superstition, that any of these achievements will be entirely lost upon our fellow-travelers and that they will not have grasped Ward's simple but comprehensive truth that with sociology as a guide, society may yet abolish ignorance and proverty, and fuse knowledge and experience, man and his world, into an intellectual and spiritual unity.

Our doubts are better and more bitterly expressed by Anatole France in *Penguin Island* (we can only hope that he is entirely wrong):

If you have a fresh view or an original idea you will surprise the reader. And the reader doesn't like being surprised.

He never looks into history for anything but the stupidities he knows already. If you try to instruct him, you only humiliate him and make him angry. Do not try to enlighten him. He will only cry out that you insult his beliefs. . . .

If social science is to be effective, it must go far beyond mere pessimism, protest, or propaganda. The hope grows stronger as one looks backward and forward along the road we have traveled in our adventure, that mankind will yet take control of its own estate and solve its problems through the universal spread of knowledge, the amelioration of social conditions, and the development of a truly scientific, democratic, and moral order of society.

Have we exulted too much over what mankind has achieved and passed too lightly over its obvious errors and failures? Civilization is only a day old, and culture but skin deep. What does the future hold in store for us? The answer will depend on whether we have learned anything at all from the past or understand what is happening in the present; whether knowledge, reason, and science are to be our guiding stars, or force, emotion, and intuition. Which shall it be? Are fundamentalists and totalitarians to rule the world, or socially free-minded men of science and intelligence? Shall we bind our intellects and energies to science or supernaturalism, to social science or to an autocratic competitive order of trial and error, force and terror?

The waves of fascism and obscurantism that are now sweeping around the world are not accidents. The ancient enemy of science which has so often reared its ugly head to persecute and exploit, to break machinery and banish art and culture, is back again. The wealth of modern knowledge and the cultural treasures of all the ages have not stemmed the tide of reaction, because, as Ward so often demonstrated, knowledge and culture are possessed only by a tiny minority.

Let us not fear to confess that it is not the scientists and sociologists who are leading the battle against reaction everywhere, but the abstract dreamers and idealists, the half-baked liberals and the overdone mystics, and that their leadership is as weak and futile as their opposition. Social scientists should not sit down to meditate upon human failure and ignorance and cruelty while they seek within themselves, as in a crystal ball, for clues to the abolition of human suffering. For every reformer or philosopher who believes he has done just that, there are a million hungry and despairing men waiting outside his window for bread and freedom.

We may labor for knowledge, but we live for our feelings alone. It is Ward who freed the idea of love entombed in the sex relation, and recognized its overflow into the passion for humanity and truth, an emotion by the side of which the satisfactions of the body seem trivial, indeed. The poet may forever sing that love is the dome that covers all eternity with its brilliant and beautiful rays, but his song is like a whistling through the wind, unless he becomes a social scientist and adds: "A little more attention to man's basic material and intellectual needs, my masters; a little more thought and collective action applied to the structure and the forces of society for the sake of the happiness of all of its members, and beauty, truth and morality will sooner be enjoyed by all. Achieve by the light of love, by all means, but let your achievements be, first of all, for the ameliora- tion of the human lot."

Everybody feels that there is something amiss with the social ma- chine, and many try to tinker with it in an amateurish and haphazard fashion. Few philosophers have given any real thought to the control of the social machine in a manner befitting a finely adjusted mechan- ism whose parts are not cold steel but warm-hearted, rational beings. The amazing thing about the whole problem is the absolute unin- telligence with which it has been treated, the seemingly hopeless lack of any system of marshalling knowledge or pooling forces for the common benefit.

What does sociology propose? According to Ward, not only ma- terial basic changes in the economic structure, but a scientific reor- ganization and control of society. Existing democracies as well as autocracies renounce the task of such an operation. Yet the people will begin to understand, after their liberation from metaphysical illusion, that all social progress compatible with current doctrine has been achieved only by education of the masses and that no important political institution can survive which is not based upon the new and ever old philosophy, the philosophy of happiness and security, of knowledge and intelligence for all.

Such ideas require a new system of education and that, in turn, a new social order. Ward's dynamic sociology gives us a comprehensive glance into both. Its conclusion is adamant that the society of tomor- row will not come through noble thoughts or good intentions, but only from the active will of the people led by social science which will apply those aims and ideas.

Although it is sociology and not its founder in America that we have had uppermost in mind throughout our journey, his genius is too great to be lightly passed over. A little over fifty years have passed since *Dynamic Sociology* was published. The majority of students in the field of social science have had to enter through the doors which Ward's system threw open for them, to achieve a vibrant fresh conception of society and the social forces. Nothing proves more conclusively the lifeless, unintellectual character of professional sociology in the United States than the fact that Ward's forward- looking views have not long ago stirred the stagnant or conservative pools of academic sociology while reactionary individualism, parading through Sumner's science of society, is more strongly intrenched than ever. The issue of "big business" against "little" people, the rule of those whom Alexander Hamilton named "the wise, the rich and the good" as opposed to the rule of the masses whom he called "the great beast"—that issue cannot be extricated from the issue of whether dynamic sociology or dynamic fascism, humane co-operation or inhuman competition, shall lead and engage the people.

How many educators and teachers of sociology are familiar with Ward's works? We wonder. Many social reformers and public-spirited citizens prate of liberty, extol freedom, and dedicate themselves to democracy and peace against fascism and war. Yet they move directly in the opposite direction for lack of knowledge of the fundamentals of dynamic sociology. Even a casual acquaintance with Ward's system of social philosophy would show them how with the genius of a master surgeon Ward lays bare the ills of the social body, how he uncovers the lack of unity and synthesis of the various parts and organs, the absence of the life-giving blood of science, and the presence of an anemic and stupefying flow of abstract speculation. Ward would enlighten them as to the cause of social discontent, and the imminent failure of civilization to solve the elementary problem of economic and political security. In sum, his sociology retrieves science, economics, and psychology from being feared or derided, and makes knowledge once more a coherent and thrilling instrument, instead of a mass of dull data, as he clothes social science in the brilliant robes of sympathy and practical application, to rise to its mission as the liberator and guide of society.

Aristotle found form more important than substance; Comte, method ahead of doctrine. Ward pointed out the synthesis of popular necessities and philosophical tendencies, according to which the true social point of view will gradually prevail in proportion as the active interest of the people begins to analyze and solve the grand social problem. With science at hand, men will be able for the first time in history to lay their own road into the future, and walk together, secure in the knowledge that human life through concerted action will come to mean more than a paradise for a few and an inferno for the rest.

We hope that the reader has collaborated with us in bringing sociology down from the pedestal upon which technology and pedantry have placed it, beyond the reach of the common people. Surely, he will not have failed to observe that emotion, metaphysics, romanticism, instinct, and the ideal of force—everything but science—have been tried and failed to solve the social problem. But intelligence is still to have its day. With such truths as those of dynamic sociology, the era of positive science and constructive ethics cannot be far away. Public opinion (we have called it the social will and the social mind, often enough) is waiting to be substituted for the individualistic, hit-or-miss method of competition, a method which has been proved beyond any doubt to be restricted, cruel, and blundering. Co-operation, education, and meliorism essentially grounded in sociology are here to show us the way to the promised land of a humane, moral order ruled by society and for society. For formulating that system of social science and philosophy, Ward should be forever enshrined in the hearts of humanity.

# BIBLIOGRAPHY

Ahumada, Herminio, *Los fundamentos sociológicos de la raza sintesis.* 1930.

Barnes, Harry Elmer, *Two Representative Contributions of Sociology to Political Theory: the Doctrines of William Graham Sumner and Lester F. Ward.* 1919.

Cape, Emily Palmer, *Lester F. Ward, A Personal Sketch.* 1922.

Dealey, James Q., "Lester F. Ward," *American Masters of Social Science.* 1927.

Dealey, James Q., *Sociology, Its Development and Application.* 1920.

Dewey, John, A Review of Ward's *Psychic Factors of Civilization, Psychological Review* (July, 1894).

Ellwood, Charles A., *The Story of Social Philosophy.* 1938.

Giddings, Ward, and Small, "An Interchange of Letters," ed. Bernhard J. Stern, *Social Forces* (March, 1932).

Gillette, J. M., "Critical Points in Ward's *Pure Sociology,*" *The American Journal of Sociology,* XX (1916).

Gross, Armin, *Die Soziologie L. F. Wards in ihren Hauptzügen.* 1927.

Gumplowicz, Ludwig, "Appreciation of Ward," *The American Journal of Sociology,* X (1906).

Gumplowicz, Ludwig, *Letters to Lester F. Ward* (in German), ed. Bernhard J. Stern. 1933.

Gvirtsman, A. M., *The Sociology of Ward, and his Relation to the Sociology of Marx* (in Russian). 1913.

Hankins, Frank H., "Lester F. Ward," in *The History and Prospects of the Social Sciences,* ed. Harry Elmer Barnes. 1925.

Harris, William T., Reviews, in *Educational Review,* VI (1893).

Howard, G. E., "A Review of Ward's Applied Sociology," *The American Journal of Sociology,* XII (1912).

Howerth, Ira W., "Contributions to the Sociology of Lester F. Ward," *Journal of Applied Sociology,* VIII (1924).

Kemp, Rev. George, *The Genealogy of the Descendants of Andrew Ward.* 1910.

Kimball, Elsa P., *Sociology and Education, an Analysis of the Theories of Spencer and Ward.* 1932.

Lewis, Arthur Morrow, *Introduction to Sociology.* 1925.

Lichtenberger, James P., *Development of Social Theory.* 1925.

Merbach, Paul Alfred, *L. F. Wards Philosophisches System der Soziologie in seinen Grundzügen dargestellt.* 1912.

Ross, Edward Alsworth, *Seventy Years of It, An Autobiography.* 1936.

Small, Albion W., *Letters of, to L. F. Ward,* ed. Bernhard J. Stern, *Social Forces* (Dec., 1933; March, 1935; Dec., 1936; March, 1937).

Wallace, Alfred Russel, *Letters to Lester F. Ward,* ed. Bernhard J. Stern, *The Scientific Monthly* (April, 1935-March, 1937).

Ward, Lester F., *Dynamic Sociology.* 2 vols. 1903.

    *Psychic Factors of Civilization.* 1893.

    *Pure Sociology.* 1903.

    *Applied Sociology.* 1906.

    *Outlines of Sociology.* 1897.

    *Glimpses of the Cosmos.* 6 vols. 1918.

    Appreciations of, in *The American Journal of Sociology.* 1913-1914.

Ward, Lester F., *Young Ward's Diary,* ed. Bernhard J. Stern. 1935.

Ward, Lester F., *Sociologie pure, traduit de l'anglais par Ferdinand Weil.* 1906.

Ward, Lester F. and Dealey, James Q., *Text Book of Sociology,* 1905.

"The Ward-Ross Correspondence (1891-1896)," ed. Bernhard J. Stern, *American Sociological Review,* III (June, 1938).

Wood, Clement, *Substance of the Sociology of Lester F. Ward.* 1930.

Worms, René, "Lester F. Ward," *Revue internationale de sociologie,* XXI (1913).

# INDEX OF NAMES

# GENERAL INDEX

(All references are to pages. Numbers in boldface type indicate chapter or subchapter headings.)

nature (direct method) and mind (indirect method), **453-455**
rationalism and, **221-222**
and scientific optimism, **503-505**
social and moral, **455-458**
Spencer's misconception of, **448-449**
telic, **446-448**
twofold concept of, the, 445
see Education; Environment; Ethical forces; Happiness; Inheritance and opportunity; Paradoxes; Social
*Progress and Poverty,* 210
Prohibitions of ethics, the, **524-526**
Proletariat, 288, 354; see Workingmen
Promiscuity, 389
Propaganda, 554
Property, 154, **289,** 325
concentration of, 350-351 n.
in land, 149
liberty and, **350-351**
rights, 303
see Economic forces
"Prophetic instincts," 403 n.
Propinquity, 146, 375; see Sex forces
Prosperity, 73, 291, 294, 501
Prostitution, 389; see Marriage; Woman
Protection, 163, 349, 350; see Desire; Social forces
Protective forces, 164; see Social forces
Protoplasm, 113, 114, **120,** 124, 130, 151 n.; see Life
elements of, 121
evolution of, **121-122**
Prussian, 319, 320
Psychic energy, 124, 161; see Feeling, origin of; Social forces
factor, 3, 39, 54, 100
*Psychic Factors of Civilization,* 54, 56, 93, 127, 131, 161, 162, 163, 216, 220, 232, 233, 262, 272, 294, 297, 298, 311, 315, 323, 326, 327, 332, 334, 337, 339, 340, 356, 360, 410, 447, 452, 455, 500, 501, 502, 509, 537, 542, 544, 549
phenomena, 113, 192
protoplasm, 161
Psychism, 192; see Mind
Psychobiology, 343 n.
Psychological basis of economics, **296-300;** see Economic forces
economics, **298-300**
viewpoint of society, 198
Psychology, 89, 125, 131, 192, 207, 220, 283
objective, 160
subjective, 160
and objective, 130
see Criticism of Ward's system; Feeling
Public opinion, see Social mind; Will
schools, 305, 470
service, 294
will, see Social mind

Pure ethics, 520, 537; see Ethical forces; New ethics
and applied sociology, **199-201**
sociology, 199, 200
*Pure Sociology,* 4, 50, **57-58,** 60, 83, 84, 87, 89, 90, 94, 101, 102, 104, 105, 106, 107, 108, 113, 114, 115, 121, 124, 125, 127, 129, 130, 135, 136, 138, 140, 141, 145, 146, 147, 148, 149, 151, 154, 155, 156, 159, 163, 166, 167, 185, 197, 199, 200, 201, 226, 229, 235, 248, 249, 260, 261, 263, 264, 265, 266, 267, 270, 271, 272, 273, 274, 276, 287, 288, 289, 290, 291, 292, 293, 294, 297, 298, 306, 310, 311, 324, 333, 339, 352, 361, 370, 373, 374, 375, 376, 379, 382, 385, 386, 389, 390, 401, 410, 411, 445, 446, 447, 449, 450, 452, 470, 472, 487, 502, 503, 504, 505, 507, 510, 513, 523, 524, 527, 528, 529, 542, 544, 549
Puritanism, 41, 370
Purity, see Modesty; Sex forces
Purpose, see Teleology
of sociology, **201-202;** see Ethical
Pyramid, 137

Quack, social, 13

Race, races, 83, 435 n.
assimilation of, 147-148
*Race and Civilization,* 434 n.
consciousness, 88
instinct of safety, 235, 237, 282, 525
morality, **524**
savage and civilized, 88
superiority of, **433,** 434
wars, **146**
Racial environment, **416**
see Human
Radiation, 113, 192
Radical, 73, 75
Radio-activity, 192
Radiology, 192
*Rassenkampf, Der,* 135
*Rasse und Staat,* 146
Rational civilization, 221
world, 101
subrational, 129
Rationalism, **214-222**
emotionalism, **217-218**
history of, **214-215**
opposition to, **215**
and progress, **221-222**
reason, **216-217**
Ward's hymn to, **218-220**
see Paradoxes; Progress; Religion; Science; Truth
Reality, **114,** 221; see Matter
Reason, 84, 85, 129, 130, **216-217**
life of, 230, 235, 270, 296, 361
and religion, **237-238**